Behavior modification

Behavior modification
Principles, issues, and applications

W. Edward Craighead
Alan E. Kazdin
Michael J. Mahoney
The Pennsylvania State University

Houghton Mifflin Company Boston
Atlanta Dallas Geneva, Illinois Hopewell, New Jersey
Palo Alto London

Material in Chapter 7 adapted from A. E. Kazdin, *Behavior modification in applied settings* (Homewood, Ill.: Dorsey Press, 1975), Chapter 2. Used by permission of The Dorsey Press, Homewood, Ill.

Material in Chapter 8 reprinted with permission of author and publisher from J. R. Cautela, "Covert sensitization," *Psychological Reports,* 1967, *20,* 459–468.

Printed in the U.S.A.

Library of Congress Catalog Card Number: 75-25003

ISBN: 0-395-21924-8

for

Glynn and Christine Craighead
Leon N. Kazdin
Daniel and Zita Mahoney

Contents

Preface

As its title implies, this text is intended to familiarize you with three different aspects of behavior modification—its basic principles, some of its major assumptions and issues, and the applications to which it has been put in recent years. The book begins with a section that discusses the conceptual and methodological bases of behavior modification. The second section provides an overview of the behavioral model and a discussion of the basic principles that have been derived from other experimental areas of psychology and have been utilized in behavior modification. Our initial discussion of basic issues and principles is supplemented by 15 original contributions demonstrating how behavior modification has been employed across a wide range of settings, populations, and behaviors. Because it is difficult to define many of the terms out of the context in which they are used in behavior modification, we have not included a glossary. Rather, the locations of the definitions of the important terms are provided in the subject index.

We have attempted to reach a balance between breadth and depth, giving both an overview and an expansion of each aspect. A lengthy list of references is also provided for those who would like to delve more deeply into specific areas. More than anything else, however, our goal has been stressing personal *relevance* for the reader. In the chapters that follow, a wide variety of techniques and illustrations have been employed in achieving that goal. We have written not only for the psychology student, but also for the nurse, the social worker, the teacher, the counselor, the parent, the law enforcement professional, and, in many respects, for every concerned citizen. We hope that our overview and our frequent use of illustrations and case histories will encourage an appreciation of the difficulty, the promise, and most of all the dignity of employing scientific methods to reduce human suffering.

In some ways, writing a book can be compared to going through adolescence. It is usually impossible to tell exactly when or where either process began and, in retrospect, the whole experience may seem like a confusing series of insights and frustrations. But perhaps the closest parallel is the realization that *change* is not just a single aspect of the adventure; it is the critical essence. For both adolescents and authors, a large part of the motivation to continue coping and growing is the somewhat naive assumption that there is an end to the whole process. Adolescents strive for an "adulthood" when life will be free of the continual flux of emotions and problems. In like manner, authors work toward that day when a book will be "finished," thinking that their task will then be complete. The fact of the matter in both situations is that there is no end to life's challenges and there is no completely satisfactory signal that a book has reached the pinnacle of an author's expression or adequacy.

We have grown a lot in the current undertaking. As the following chapters will attest, we abide by the primary assumption that human behavior can be studied and therapeutically enriched by a sensitive scientific approach. However, the reader will find very few pat answers in what follows. Although behavior modification research has significantly contributed to our understanding of the thoughts, feelings, and activities that characterize both adaptive and maladaptive behavior patterns, we are still a long way from any complacency about the extent of our knowledge or the power of our techniques consistently to alleviate suffering and enrich human functioning. Our approach in this text is thus one of cautious optimism: we seem to be on the right road, but our journey remains hardly begun. We see this tentative hopefulness and commitment to continued pursuit as an asset rather than a liability. Two of the most important aspects of "maturity" are the ability to endure uncertainty and the acceptance of change as inevitable. Both life and science are processes rather than outcomes and, as this text will emphasize, it may be more accurate to approach each as a journey rather than a destination. We welcome you to begin that journey in one recent and promising scientific development: behavior modification.

This text is primarily intended for use by undergraduates in courses on behavior modification in departments of psychology, education, human development, nursing, counseling, and law enforcement.

With lecture or written supplements, it can also be of use in other courses, such as psychopathology or abnormal psychology, learning, adjustment, and counseling. It may also be helpful to professionals working in applied settings where the use of behavior modification is appropriate.

Many individuals have lent their professional and personal skills to the production of this book and it would be impossible to do justice to all of them without adding an entire chapter of acknowledgments. We can, of course, retreat to the global terms of our "students" and "colleagues" without too much danger of missing anyone. Fortunately, those who have been integral in the production of this text are already aware of our gratitude and indebtedness. We are especially grateful to the Houghton Mifflin staff; to Gerald C. Davison, Frederick H. Kanfer, James T. Miller, and R. Steven Heaps for thorough reviews of the manuscript; to The Pennsylvania State University, College of Liberal Arts Central Fund for Research, for support of the manuscript's preparation; and to Mary Frank for her dedication in typing the manuscript. Last, but not least, we would like to thank all of the authors who contributed the chapters in Part III.

W. Edward Craighead
Alan E. Kazdin
Michael J. Mahoney

Part I

Conceptual foundations of behavior modification

IMAGINE for a moment that you have come home for the holidays. It has been one of those long, grueling terms, full of surprise quizzes and boring instructors. You are really looking forward to unwinding a bit and you may even be so homesick that seeing your parents actually sounds good. On your first night home you stay up until three in the morning talking with your parents and brother about the "thrill of victory and agony of defeat" in college life. Your parents finally go to bed and the conversation with your little brother continues. The excitement of the first few hours has toned down a bit now—you have already exchanged new jokes and shared the highlights of the last few months. Suddenly, your brother turns more serious and starts asking how many psychology courses you have taken. After beating around the bush for a few minutes, he confides that a "friend" of his is having dating problems and would like to know how and where to get help. This friend, it seems, has trouble getting dates and when he does get one falls all over himself trying to be "cool." He is also anxious about sexual adequacy, not to mention a weight problem and acne. As you sit there listening patiently, it gradually becomes clear that the "friend" is actually your younger brother and that, for the first time in years, he is earnestly asking for your help. You may be a psychology major and this isn't the first time family or friends have asked your advice on personal problems. But this time it is your own kid brother, and you feel a mixture of sensations. It is gratifying to know that he respects your opinion and feels close enough to you to turn to you for help. On the other hand, you are well aware of the limitations in your technical knowledge.

Although this book is not intended primarily as an introduction to clinical methods, it is designed to expand your "technical knowledge" in ways that should be relevant to your everyday life. It will familiarize you with some of the issues and evidence that bear on human dysfunction. And after having read it, you should be able to deal with situations like the one we have described with more confidence in your ability to help. You will not be a clinician, but you will have some technical information which could be valuable for troubled friends and relatives on the success rates of various techniques, sources of counseling, and basic processes of behavior change. Moreover, we have written this book in such a way that it may also help you personally.

The applied science of therapeutic behavior change is much like other sciences in the sense that it has its foundations in an extensive body of basic research. These fundamental principles are essential prerequisites for the choice and evaluation of clinical techniques. We therefore begin our presentation in this and the following part of the text with some of the more basic aspects of behavioral science—its principles, methodology, and issues. You will then be in a position to look at its products—the therapeutic applications.

Behavior modification: An overview

1

Perhaps more than any other subsection of modern psychology, behavior modification has gained prominence among both professionals and laymen as one of the most exciting and promising developments in contemporary behavioral science. This broad interest is reflected in the proliferation of behavior modification articles in both professional journals and the popular media. While its foundations were developed years ago in the experimental laboratories, its impact has been very recent. Its success rate has elicited an enormous expansion of applications and a growing list of adherents. Recent developments include the adoption of behavior modification by individual therapists, school systems, correctional facilities, industry, mental hospitals, and even middle-class homes. All in all, its versatility, recency, increasing popularity, and impressive success rate have made behavior modification an exciting, productive area for research and application.

This surge of popularity, however, has generated a number of problems. Perhaps the greatest one surrounds the definition of behavior modification. Since in a very literal sense any procedure that results in a behavior change may be labeled behavior modification, it is apparent why this is a difficult issue. For example, removal of part of the brain undoubtedly changes behavior. Is psychosurgery therefore a form of behavior modification? The injection of huge quantities of certain tranquilizing drugs into an organism undoubtedly changes that organism's behavior. Is psychopharmacology then a form of behavior modification? While popular publications have labeled such procedures as behavior modification, most contemporary behavior modifiers would reject these two clinical procedures as being unrelated to behavior modification. Thus there exists a great deal of confusion regarding the definition of behavior modification. While we do not expect to provide a final answer to that question, we do hope that as a result of reading this book you will have a clearer notion of what behavior modification is, and just as importantly, what it is not.

Definition of behavior modification

One reason for the difficulty in determining whether or not some clinical procedure should be labeled behavior modification is that no unequivocal definition of behavior modification exists. In fact, the richness of creativity demonstrated by the generation of several definitions causes one to be amazed that behavior modifiers could be criticized for their lack of creativity. The lack of a single, accepted definition not only has elicited considerable theoretical discussion, but also has had a significant impact at the practical level. For example, the Pennsylvania Offices of Mental Health and Mental Retardation recently published guidelines for the application of behavior therapy programs. One of the biggest problems in implementing those guidelines has been the effort to determine which programs incorporate behavior modification. There has been great controversy recently over whether certification should be required for the practice of behavior modification, and even if such certification is deemed desirable, who would be a bona fide behavior modifier? This controversy has resulted in renewed discussion of "What is behavior modification?"

One definitional problem has been the distinction between behavior therapy and behavior modification; in this book we will employ these terms as synonyms. Definitions of behavior modification have ranged from the application of the principles of operant conditioning (e.g., Skinner 1953, 1971) or classical conditioning (Wolpe 1958) to something called more generally principles of learning (Ullmann and Krasner 1969) to the more broadly based clinical approaches of Bandura (1969) and Lazarus (1971). Most of these definitions are characterized by an appeal to the content of the underlying principles. An alternative approach is to define behavior modification by its concern with methodology and functional behavior relationships. One problem with previous definitions is that they assume the existence of a singular theoretical model or technology of behavior modification. While such a state of affairs would solve many conceptual and practical issues, it does not exist. In this book we will use the following criteria, adopted from Mahoney, Kazdin, and Lesswing (1974), in defining behavior modification: "(1) use of a broadly defined set of clinical procedures whose description and rationale often rely on the experimental findings of psychological research (Goldstein, Heller, and Sechrest 1966); and (2) an experimental and functionally analytic approach to clinical data, relying on objective and measurable outcome (Goldfried and Pomeranz 1968)" (p. 14). The functionally analytic aspect of the definition means that the behavior modifier undertakes an experimental analysis of the problem behavior. The basic point is that behavior modification is best defined by a rationale and a methodology and not by a specified theory or set of principles. This view of behavior modification allows for the study of an extremely wide range of factors that may affect behavior and which may be employed in the modification of behavior; principles from many areas of study, including learning theory, may be utilized.

This approach to the study of behavior is called methodological behaviorism and was introduced by John B. Watson in 1913. Behavior modification does not refer to a *specified* set of clinical procedures derived from a unified learning theory nor to a *completed* collection of facts or experimental outcomes; instead, behavior modification draws from an ever-changing body of experimental findings and represents a scientific approach to the study of behavior and its modification.

Yet many people, both friend and foe, identify behavior modification as an "arrived-at," specified set of procedures based on the application of an "arrived-at" set of principles. Undoubtedly, glimpses of that view will appear in this book. But we believe that the greatest progress in understanding and modifying behavior will be made when behavior modification is seen as the application of the scientific approach of methodological behaviorism. We now turn to a brief history of the development of this approach to the study of behavior.

The history of behavior modification

To the extent that the behavioral model presented in this book represents the real world, the history of behavior modification is as old as the history of man. While humans have always modified their own, their spouses', their children's, and even their animals' behaviors, they usually have not specified that they modeled, prompted, shaped, and chained responses. Nevertheless, they have used these principles of behavior change.

The study of the systematic application of behavior modification is a comparatively new endeavor. As previously noted, the person who is usually given credit for introducing behavior modification is John B.

Watson (1878–1958). He did most of his work at the University of Chicago and Johns Hopkins University during the first quarter of this century. It was he who advocated the use of "methodological behaviorism" in the scientific study of human behavior. While he is best remembered for what is popularly labeled "radical behaviorism," or the reduction of the human organism to a bundle of responses, it was his emphasis on methodology and his scientific approach to the study of behavior that makes him truly the founder of behavior modification. Although Watson laid the groundwork and reported the well-known case study of Little Albert (Watson and Rayner 1920), behavior modification was not widely adopted for clinical application; in fact, except for a few sporadic case reports, the study of human behavior based on this approach occurred only in the laboratory until much later.

The present interest in behavior modification began in the 1950s.[1] The last twenty years have witnessed an enormous growth in both laboratory studies and applied evaluations. Although considerable discussion has occurred regarding who should be credited with beginning the current era of behavior modification, there is little doubt that the most widely known and most controversial behavior modifier is B. F. Skinner. It was he and his colleagues who, in 1953, systematically studied the use of the principles of operant conditioning with psychotic patients at the Laboratory for Behavior Research at Metropolitan State Hospital in Waltham, Massachusetts. His landmark book, *Science and Human Behavior,* was published in 1953.

Concurrently, Joseph Wolpe, later joined by Arnold Lazarus, began work in what was presented as the application of certain physiological findings and the principles of conditioning based on Hull's (1943) learning theory. Their early work, most noted for the clinical procedure of systematic desensitization, was a major force in determining the direction of behavior modification. H. J. Eysenck is usually included among the group of clinicians who claimed an alliance with the clinical applications of classical conditioning. He argued strongly against the psychoanalytic model, and his behavior therapy–oriented books of 1960 and 1964 set the tone for many behavior modifiers in their rejection of the quasi-medical (Freudian or psychoanalytic) model of abnormal behavior.

Thus, the stage was set—the psychoanalytic model was rejected and the principles of behavior modification were then synonymous with the clinical application of the principles of operant and classical conditioning. This resulted in the conceptualization of behavior modification as follows: (1) normal and abnormal behavior develop according to the

[1] This brief history is not intended to be exhaustive; therefore, the work and writings of a number of significant contributors are not included. For a more exhaustive review see Ullmann and Krasner (1969; 2nd ed. 1975).

same principles, and (2) all behavior is modified or changed according to principles of learning (meaning principles of operant and classical conditioning).[2] To the extent that the psychoanalytic model failed to be empirically verified and the application of the principles of learning could be empirically validated, this view of behavior modification was scientifically acceptable. But to maintain that behavior modification had "arrived," that the methods of change could be derived from the principles of operant and classical conditioning, and that the conceptual model was complete was not scientifically acceptable.

Empirically oriented clinicians looked for their foundations in the learning laboratories. Additionally, some psychologists in the field of learning studied the effects of clinical applications. Thus, there developed an alignment of learning theory and behavior modification, and the latter became synonymous with the application of principles of learning. However, this equation of learning theory and behavior modification was premature, and behavioral change agents, who favored an empirical approach to understanding behavior and helping their clients, began to look to other areas of research for empirical data that might enhance their understanding, prediction, and modification of behavior. These experimental findings were incorporated into a growing set of empirically validated principles of behavior change. This is clearly demonstrated in two 1969 books which, perhaps more than any others, have served as a positive force in the popularization of behavior modification. Ullmann and Krasner's *A Psychological Approach to Abnormal Behavior* incorporated extensive findings from sociology into a psychosocial model of abnormal behavior. Bandura's *Principles of Behavior Modification* went well beyond the principles of operant and classical conditioning in incorporating data on physiology and symbolic, cognitive processes into a behavioral model. This approach set the tone for the behavioral, experimental/clinical approach to the study of human problems in living (see Davison and Neale 1974).

The increased interest and broadened emphasis in behavior modification was reflected in the appearance of four behavioral journals in addition to increased publication of behavioral articles in the American Psychological Association (APA) journals. The first behavioral journal, *Behaviour Research and Therapy,* was begun in 1963 and edited by Eysenck. The second, *Journal of Applied Behavior Analysis,* emphasized the application of operant procedures and began in 1968. Two recent journals are the official journal of the Association for Advancement of Behavior Therapy entitled *Behavior Therapy* and the journal of the Behav-

[2] This view was evident in the first (and seminal) summary of the work done in behavior modification, the introduction to Ullmann and Krasner's *Case Studies in Behavior Modification* (1965).

ior Therapy and Research Society entitled *The Journal of Behavior Therapy and Experimental Psychiatry;* both these journals began in 1970. The two most recent journals are the *Mexican Journal of Applied Behavior Analysis* and the *European Journal of Behavioral Analysis and Modification.*

The behavioral, experimental/clinical approach has been employed extensively, as evidenced by the burgeoning literature in such areas as the behavioral approach to the study of self-control (traditionally called will power) and cognitive behavior modification (Mahoney 1974a). These directions, and an increasing concern with ethical issues surrounding the application of behavior modification, will be noted in several chapters in Part III, as well as in Chapter 10.

Behavior modification and "mental health" professions

Much of the application of behavior modification developed within the framework of the mental health professions. While behavior modification's foundations were laid in experimental laboratories, it has been successful clinical applications that have led to its increased utilization and present status. While many additional areas could be included today, the traditional mental health professions are social work, clinical psychology, and clinical psychiatry.

In the period 1830 to 1850 "mental health" problems were viewed simply as problems in living and were treated in a rather common sense, straightforward manner that was later labeled *moral treatment* (Bockoven 1963). However, this was gradually replaced by the assumption that people with problems in living suffered from a disease; most methods of treatment in this country have been based on this medical model.

For our purposes it is adequate to note that the medical model refers to the view that abnormal behavior has a physiological or biochemical cause. Behavioral problems develop from an underlying physical ailment. While the data supporting such a model are minimal, it was essentially *the* model for mental health professionals during the last half of the nineteenth century and the first quarter of this century, and it remains the most broadly accepted model in the field. Within this model the social worker did social histories, the psychologist gave tests and made diagnoses, and psychiatrists did therapy.

Between World War I and World War II, the medical model was partially replaced by the quasi-medical model.[3] This model has also

[3] This distinction between medical and quasi-medical models is presented in Bandura (1969), but there is no such distinction in Ullmann and Krasner (1969). The models will be discussed in more detail in Chapter 6.

been labeled the Freudian or psychoanalytic model. It is called quasi-medical because the medical model is accepted, but the underlying cause of abnormal behavior is viewed as psychological rather than physical in nature. Thus, the development of the term *mental illness.* The roles of the mental health professionals remained essentially unchanged within this model, although a few social workers sneaked in some case work and clinical psychologists did a little therapy.

A third model, represented by the nondirective therapy of Carl Rogers, developed in the late 1940s and early 1950s within the fields of educational counseling and clinical psychology. According to this model, a person developed problems because he could not admit his visceral experiences into awareness; his real self and his ideal self were not congruent. It was believed that each person had within himself a self-actualizing tendency and that nondirective therapy would enable one's "selves" to become more congruent. It was the school psychologists, counselors, and clinical psychologists who provided therapy within this model. It should also be noted that the shortage of therapists during World War II had resulted in increased clinical activities by social workers and clinical psychologists.

During the 1950s and early 1960s a new model, the behavioral one, was introduced into social work, clinical psychology, and clinical psychiatry. This model, like the others, has been characterized to some extent by its reference to a particular theory and/or a specified set of clinical procedures. The behavioral model, perhaps because of its partial derivation from and association with the experimental laboratory, has had a greater emphasis on a scientific approach to the study of human behavior. It is this characteristic that is used to define the behavioral model in this book. The next section will demonstrate this, and the model will be presented in detail in Chapter 6.

A fifth model might best be labeled the existential or phenomenological model and is represented by the work and conceptualizations of Frederick Perls and, more recently, Carl Rogers. The emphasis is on immediate subjective experience and its meaning for the client. While some authors favor an empirical evaluation of this model, typically this scientific approach is not considered appropriate. Sometimes this model is equated with humanistic psychology, but as we will see later, humanistic psychology is a much broader and more encompassing concept. It should be identified with any of the previously discussed models only to the extent that a particular model is indeed humanistic. This notion will be discussed further in Chapter 10.

While there are more conceptual models that find clinical expression, most of the clinical work done by mental health professionals can be derived from one of these five models. There are some similarities and some obvious differences among these models. One advantage of the behavioral model as defined here is that it presents no *a priori* basis for rejecting clinical procedures derived from any model, but it does demand a scientific evaluation of those procedures. The clinician may engage in activities that have not been empirically validated and the experimental clinician may develop a clinical procedure from some other area of research, but those activities and procedures should still undergo empirical validation if they are to be called behavioral. This should not thwart such clinical activities, but rather provide criteria for determining which procedures should become a part of the endeavor of behavior change. Even though such procedures may come from clinical innovation or deduction from other areas of research they should find broad application only after they have been demonstrated to be effective. Those principles and procedures that are empirically validated are incorporated into behavior modification; by the same token, principles and procedures are part of behavior modification only to the extent that they are scientifically verified.

Behavior modification at work

Perhaps the best way to provide an overview of behavior modification and its scientific emphasis is by means of a case history. The following case history is drawn from a study by Haughton and Ayllon (1965). The subject was a 54-year-old mental patient who had been hospitalized for 23 years and diagnosed as schizophrenic. One behavior that drew the attention of the researchers was broom-holding. Over the course of several days, the patient began carrying a broom with her wherever she went and even slept with it nearby. This rather bizarre behavior will constitute our point of departure for a discussion of the scientific emphasis in behavior modification. One obvious problem in this case history is the cause of the broom-holding behavior. Why did the patient begin carrying a broom around with her? We are assuming that her behavior was in some way determined or "caused," and a clarification of the latter term will be required. But first, however, our interest lies not only in the cause of her behavior but also in whatever means are necessary to modify that behavior. Excessive broom-holding is not a socially acceptable behavior (except perhaps around Halloween, and not even then by former mental patients) and therefore must be modified if the patient is to return to the community. We might also want to determine whether the patient's broom-holding behavior is one that we may observe at some future date. Perhaps some characteristic of this patient or of her history would allow us to predict future outbreaks of excessive broom-holding behavior. Notice that we have already set ourselves three goals regarding this patient's behavior: we would like to *explain* it, *control* it, and *predict* its future occurrence. Explanation, prediction, and control are the essential goals of science as a whole. Our inclusion of these goals in this example is not in any way artificial; they provide a very challenging and desirable objective. These goals characterize behavior modification and it is not a coincidence that these goals are also those of science in general. Indeed, *the most singular characteristic of behavior modification is its scientific emphasis.* This has been viewed as both a merit and a flaw in the behavior modifier's framework. However, since it is such an integral part of that framework, we will devote all of Chapter 2 to an examination of the scientific emphasis in behavior modification. There we will discuss the relevance of rigorous empirical investigation, the emphasis on scientific rationale and method, and the advantages and disadvantages of the scientific approach. There are alternatives to science; for example, in the preceding case history, one might simply speculate about the possible causes of the bizarre behavior. While such speculation might take place in the early stages of a scientific analysis, it would, by itself, not constitute a scientific approach to the problem. Such speculations often replace scientific approaches in everyday life. We may wonder why the girl next door always takes a gym bag with her when she goes on a date. Our speculations might run rampant, but unless we put them to the test (either by asking to look in the gym bag or by asking the girl for a date, or both) they remain prescientific. In the case of the broom-holding woman, simple speculation about the significance and/or cause of her bizarre behavior is no more accurate than a guess. It may turn out that the guess is correct, but the only means of determining that is a test. Enter science, stage right.

Behavior as subject matter

Speculations about the causes of the broom-holding behavior might range from conservative hypotheses to abstract and complex theories. Haughton and Ayllon (1965) asked two psychiatrists to observe and evaluate their patient. The first psychistrist expressed the following view:

> The broom represents to this patient some essential perceptual element in her field of consciousness . . . it is certainly a stereotyped form of behavior such as is commonly seen in rather regressed schizophrenics and is rather analogous to the way small children or infants refuse to be parted from some favorite toy, piece of rag, etc. (pp. 97–98)

The second psychiatrist evaluated the patient's behavior as follows:

> Her constant and compulsive pacing holding a broom in the manner she does could be seen as a ritualistic procedure, a magical action. When regression conquers the associative process, primitive and archaic forms of

> thinking control the behavior. Symbolism is a predominant mode of expression of deep seated unfulfilled desires and instinctual impulses. By magic, she controls others, cosmic powers are at her disposal and inanimate objects become living creatures.
>
> Her broom could be then:
>
> 1. a child that gives her love and she gives him in return her devotion;
> 2. a phallic symbol;
> 3. the sceptre of an omnipotent queen. (pp. 97–98)

Both evaluations attribute a symbolic significance to the excessive broom-holding; the second psychiatrist's interpretation is much more abstract. Note that neither evaluation ignores the patient's behavior. However, both go beyond that behavior and relegate it to a secondary role. The broom-holding is assumed to be an expression of more deep-seated problems, such as unfulfilled desires and instincts. Either or both hypotheses may be correct. However, unless their accuracy can be tested, we have nothing more than two professional-sounding hypotheses about a problem behavior. One problem with such intriguing speculations about behavior is that they often take the place of an attempt to modify the behavior. To label a behavior as symbolic, schizophrenic, or primitive does not explain the behavior, let alone predict or control it. Because speculations tend to get in the way of scientific investigation, behavior modifiers have chosen to restrict their dialogues and treatment strategies to definable and measurable behaviors and to limit their speculations to scientifically testable ones. For example, talk of repressed sexual needs makes for good conversation at a party, but raises all kinds of research problems. How does one verify that such repressed needs exist? By verbal responses or performance on an ambiguous psychological test? One cannot observe a repressed sexual need. One can only measure a behavior (be it on paper or in bed) that is assumed to be representative of the speculated need. The convention in behavior modification is to stick with the definable and measurable. This is not to say that behavior modifiers deny the existence of repressed sexual needs. However, since the ultimate interchange must deal with definable and measurable behaviors, behavior modifiers elect to remain parsimonious in their interpretations and explanations of behavior.

The principle of parsimony (also known as Occam's Razor) states that one should never employ a more complex explanation of an event when a less complex one will suffice. The principle, which is a convention, not a "truth," is often misinterpreted as encouraging simple-mindedness. The gist of this principle is that allegations, assertions, interpretations, and predictions should be as conservative as possible. It may, of course, turn out that a highly complicated, abstract, and unparsimonious rendition is the most accurate. However, in our blissful ignorance, we adopt the convention that keeps us closest to our evidence. Moreover, practical experience with parsimonious and unparsimonious undertakings has often found the former to be more useful.

This decision to remain parsimonious is often a difficult one since there are many instances when one is tempted to go beyond the facts and speculate about unobserved phenomena. However, in the strictly scientific sphere, one must speak in a language that enables virtually all of one's professional colleagues to agree on what has been observed. In the case mentioned, the two psychiatrists saw the patient performing what they considered to be a symbolic act—the behavior of broom-holding. However, their evaluations of the patient diverged considerably. Behavior modifiers hope to eliminate such divergence by restricting their analyses to definable and measurable behaviors.[4]

Thus we see that *behavior is the ultimate datum in behavior modification.* In order for internal or external events to be studied they must be defined as behaviors and be amenable to observation and measurement. Inference, or going from some observed behavior to some unobserved phenomenon, is discouraged because of the many problems that can arise when one gets too far from one's data. Such issues as the problems with mental states, the emphasis on behavior, and the role of inference will be discussed at greater length in Chapter 3.

Choice of methodology

Let us return to the broom-holding mental patient. We have decided that the goal is to explain, control, and predict her behavior. We have entertained some speculations about the causes of her behavior but have decided to concentrate on her observable behaviors rather than on hypothesized internal states. It is now time to choose a methodology for investigating the cause of the problem behavior. Two general classes of methodology are open to the researcher in behavior modification: (1) begin testing preconceptions and hypotheses about the behavior in question, or (2) explore and manipulate various aspects of the patient's environment to test their effect on behavior. Both methodologies contain subvarieties that allow for considerable diversity in research techniques. At times the distinction between them is far from

[4] Recent research trends have allowed for pioneering efforts in the application of behavior modification techniques to client-reported behaviors that are not measurable by anyone other than the client himself (for example, the client may record his frequency of saying to himself, "I am worthless"). Such definition and measurement of variables previously labeled internal or mental, and therefore not available for study by the behaviorist, have increased in frequency.

obvious. However, these two general classes of methodology constitute an issue in current behavior modification research. Many workers prefer one type over the other. The hypothesis-testing approach is often called hypotheticodeductive or theoretical because the researcher begins with a theory or hypothesis about behavior and deduces from it an experimental test. The second approach is often termed free research or atheoretical since it is allegedly free of a theoretical framework. In our case history, we would have to choose between testing some of our speculations about the cause of the patient's behavior and simply exploring the patient's environment for potential causes. For example, if we wanted to test the second psychiatrist's interpretation of her behavior, we might provide the patient with a doll, an artificial penis, or a queen's sceptre.[5] If the patient discontinued her broom-holding after being given any of these objects, this might lend credence to the second psychiatrist's interpretation. An alternative approach would be to observe the conditions antecedent and consequent to broom-holding. Perhaps the patient exhibits that behavior only when in the presence of a particular nurse or another patient. We could manipulate the presence of that other person to test its effect on the broom-holding behavior. Likewise, we might observe that the patient received quite a bit of attention from staff members whenever she carried the broom. We might then wish to test a hunch by withholding staff attention during broom-holding episodes. Note that hypotheses do enter into the free research approach, even though their arrival is somewhat later and less formalized than in the hypotheticodeductive method.

Let us choose the free research approach in the present situation. Next we must choose between a single-subject design or a group design. In the single-subject design (also known as *intrasubject*) only one subject is studied. Thus, we would restrict our observations and eventual conclusions to a single broom-holding woman. In the group design (also known as *intersubject*) many subjects are studied simultaneously. In our example, we could look for other broom-holding patients and submit them as a group to an experimental test. There are many relative advantages and disadvantages in both of these designs, just as there are advantages and disadvantages in hypothesis-testing and free research methodologies. We will discuss these at length in Chapters 4 and 5. For the time being, let us assume that a single-subject design is appropriate for the problem in question.

[5] Actually it is unlikely that the second psychiatrist would accept this as a test of his hypothesis. A major contention of more speculative and traditional psychotherapists is that symbolic expressions of "inner needs" are effective only because they are subtle and ambiguous. This is one reason why hypotheses regarding psychic symbolism are so hard to test.

Drawing conclusions

We have now resolved three questions: (1) we have chosen scientific goals (the explanation, prediction, and control of a behavior); (2) we have restricted our immediate attention to an observable behavior (broom-holding); and (3) we have decided upon a research methodology involving an atheoretical, single-subject design. Our immediate task is the collection and interpretation of data. The collection of data cannot be easily separated from the scientific emphasis in behavior modification. Indeed, as will be seen in Chapter 4, data reign supreme in behavioral quarters. As might be anticipated, there are several means by which data may be collected and there are different types of data. While there is some dispute over how data should be collected and what types of data are important, there is little disagreement regarding the necessity for data collection in behavior modification. If an individual can cite reliable data to support some contention, the behavior modifier will usually sit up and listen. Dataless speculations are received rather rudely.

The interpretation of data, however, often creates controversy. Several researchers may agree on the reliability of a particular set of data but may strongly disagree on the import or message in the data. The issue is one of how to weigh or evaluate the evidence. There are two popular means of data evaluation in behavior modification. The simpler method is herein called nonstatistical data analysis: data, in either numerical or graph form, are examined and it is decided whether some difference is apparent. The more complicated method is statistical data analysis and involves mathematical evaluation of data. Both methods have as their goal the interpretation of evidence. The relative advantages and disadvantages of statistical and nonstatistical data analysis will be discussed in Chapter 5.

Haughton and Ayllon used the nonstatistical approach in the case of the broom-holding woman. First, they obtained data on the original frequency of the problem behavior; then they tested the effect of removing an experimental variable from the broom-holding situation. This resulted in a decline in the frequency of the problem behavior. Continued absence of the experimental variable eventually resulted in a total cessation of broom-holding. The nature of that variable and of the research itself will be discussed next. For the moment let us review the research strategy employed by Haughton and Ayllon. They sought to explain, control, and predict the problem behavior. After choosing the broom-holding behavior as their subject matter, they proceeded to test the effect of an experimental variable in a single-subject design. They collected data and then evaluated them in a nonstatistical fashion. Their conclusions about the "cause" of the problem behavior were colored by their research strategy.

A brief digression may re-emphasize the need for parsimony in behavior modification research. Haughton and Ayllon (1965) were able to experimentally induce and later eliminate a typically bizarre psychotic behavior. Their data indicated that control over the problem behavior was obtained and that its "cause" related to a cigarette contingency. What conclusions can parsimoniously be drawn from this case study? Can we conclude that all psychotic symptoms are generated by similar learning conditions? Are all psychiatric evaluations as unhelpful as those cited in getting at the root of the behavioral problem? Can we conclude that when a learning principle is employed in the modification of a behavior then a learning principle was necessarily involved in the development of that behavior? A parsimonious response to all of the above would be a tentative "No." These issues, and some additional questions raised by this particular case study, are discussed by Davison (1969, pp. 270–275).

Unfortunately, many sweeping conclusions have been drawn from the broom-holding case study. Again, parsimony and conservatism would seem to be overlooked antidotes. The behavior modifier takes pride in his scientific bent. However, cool scientific conservatism is often overtaken by the enthusiasm generated by the progress and promise of the behavioral approach. It is just such enthusiasm that needs to be tempered if the area of behavior modification is to retain its empirical aura. It is difficult to contain one's excitement when a vegetative mental patient makes his first vocal response in 17 years as a result of the implementation of some behavior modification technique. However, such excitement should be channeled toward continued and expanding behavioral research rather than unwarranted predictions and premature theorizations. It is the intent of this book to provide a few reminders of the empirical rigor and scientific conservatism which should be the byword of researchers in behavior modification.

Ethical issues

The case history of the broom-holding woman was chosen because it is frequently cited by behavior modifiers (see Ullmann and Krasner 1965, 1969; Ayllon, Haughton, and Hughes 1965; Wenrich 1970). It is actually an illustration of an experimentally induced "symptom." By employing the behavior modification techniques of shaping and intermittent reinforcement, Haughton and Ayllon (1965) were able to create a symptom in a 54-year-old patient. That this behavior was similar to many of those exhibited by mental patients is demonstrated by the two psychiatrists' evaluations. The development of the deviant behavior was programmed by rewarding the patient with cigarettes whenever she engaged in broom-holding behavior. After the behavior had stabilized at a fairly high frequency of occurrence, two unsuspecting psychiatrists were asked to observe and evaluate the patient. Their speculative interpretations were later used as examples of the futility of nonbehavioral analyses. The broom-holding behavior was eliminated by withholding cigarettes, the experimental variable considered responsible for the maintenance of the behavior. The case history illustrates much more than the speculative penchant of many psychiatrists. It also touches upon the ethical issues that underlie any attempt at behavioral control. Is it ethically justifiable to experimentally induce symptoms? Does the fact that the researchers were aware of the conditions that generated the broom-holding behavior make their request for a psychiatric diagnosis unethical? If Haughton and Aylon had come upon an example of excessive broom-holding that they had not programmed, would there be any ethical inpediments to their modification of that behavior? These and many other issues regarding the ethics of behavior control will be discussed in Chapter 10. Suffice it to say for the moment that the control of behavior and, indeed, even the scientific investigation of behavior principles have been challenged by many contemporary psychologists on the grounds that they are unethical. We will explore some of their arguments in Chapter 10.

Another topic that will be discussed in Chapter 10 is the quasi-schism between behavioral approaches and what have come to be called humanistic approaches. For some time now there has been a mistaken assumption that some inherent incompatibility exists between humanistic concerns and scientific analyses of behavior. To be sure, some behavioral researchers have allowed their scientific coolness to generalize to their everyday interactions, so that a cold, austere prototype has been intermittently reinforced. However, most behavior modifiers are a very humane lot. They do not eye their sexual companions with a cold, objective stare, and only a handful of them carry a cumulative recorder to bed. The main contention of the final chapter is that the ultimate humanism is one based on behavioral science. Knowing how to program the most rewarding of all worlds—where individuals function in harmony with their talents, interests, values, and the needs of their community—is one goal on which both humanists and behavior modifers alike can agree.

The relevance of behavior modification

Why should you read this book or undertake a course of study in behavior modification? We would like to suggest a number of reasons in response to that question. The first is a point that was noted earlier; namely, to the extent that the behavioral model unravels the puzzle of behavior and behavior change, it will provide information regarding how we change our behavior, how we modify the behavior of others, and perhaps most importantly, how other people modify our behavior. The basic point is that the findings of behavior modification not only tell us how better to deal with clinical and social problems, but they also provide useful information relevant to all aspects of our lives. Such findings can help us improve interpersonal relationships, work habits, child-rearing practices, and methods of self-control.

Beyond the personal management sphere there are a number of reasons why the study of behavior modification is relevant to your life. If you expect to work in the area of mental health, the applicability of the behavioral approach and its emphasis on evaluation should be apparent by now. The relationship of behavior modification to the rest of psychology and related disciplines warrants its study by the serious student in psychology. This is especially true with the more recent, cognitive behavior modification approach, where there is an integration of cognitive and behavioral psychology. The rapidly expanding application of behavior modification to the prevention and alleviation of social problems at the community level is further reason to study behavior modification. These applications at the community level, such as increasing bus ridership and decreasing racial prejudice, are exciting but they raise a number of questions, especially ethical ones. You can adequately resolve these issues only by understanding what behavior modification is and is not.

Our final suggestion, which is one that will appear throughout the book, is that the more you know about yourself, your social-learning history, and the empirically validated principles of behavior change, the more choices you will have, the more self-control you will exhibit, and the more freedom and dignity you will possess.

Summary

Behavior modification, or behavior therapy, is one of the fastest growing and most promising fields of psychology. Behavior modification is tentatively defined as (1) the use of a broadly defined set of clinical procedures whose description and rationale often rely on the experimental findings of psychological research, and (2) an experimental and functionally analytic approach to clinical data, relying on objective and measurable outcome. This definition is consistent with Watson's scientific method of investigation labeled methodological behaviorism, on which behavior modification is based. The principles and procedures of behavior modification change as new research findings become available; there is no "arrived-at" set of principles or procedures.

Mental health professionals from such fields as clinical psychology, clinical psychiatry, and social work engage in behavior therapy. This, however, is a recent phenomenon and is related to the historical development of the various models for behavior change. The most singular characteristic of behavior modification is its scientific emphasis or its reliance on methodological behaviorism. Behavior modification has as its goals the explanation, prediction, and control of behavior. The example of the broom-holding mental hospital resident demonstrates the chief characteristics of behavior modification, as well as some difficulties encountered in its application.

Since behavior modification has widespread applications and is relevant to so much of one's life, it is an important area of study. With this overview of behavior therapy we are ready to launch into a discussion of the scientific method on which it is based.

Suggested readings

Davison, G. C., and Neale, J. M. *Abnormal psychology: An experimental clinical approach.* New York: Wiley, 1974. Chapter 1.

Mahoney, M. J. *Cognition and behavior modification.* Cambridge, Mass.: Ballinger, 1974. Chapters 1 and 2.

Rimm, D. C., and Masters, J. C. *Behavior therapy: Techniques and empirical findings.* New York: Academic Press, 1974. Chapter 1.

Ullmann, L. P., and Krasner, L. *A psychological approach to abnormal behavior.* Englewood Cliffs, N.J.: Prentice-Hall, 1969, 1975. Chapters 7, 8, and 11.

The scientific emphasis in behavior modification

2

A main characteristic of behavior modification is its emphasis on a scientific approach. This emphasis is expressed in such ways as rigorous definition of concepts, a heavy reliance on data, and so on. The scientific approach is not easily defined. There are several subvarieties of scientific approaches and there are many issues that may differentiate one behavior modifier's concept of science from another's. Science is not a circumscribed body of knowledge or a collection of how-to-do-it techniques. There is considerable flexibility within the scientific framework that allows for the expression of individual research biases and philosophical bents. It is the purpose of this chapter to acquaint the reader with some of the major goals and issues that characterize the nebulous entity called the scientific approach. Familiarity with the rationale and limitations of that approach is an ever-present necessity for the behavioral researcher.

The goals of a scientific approach

In simplest terms, science might be described as an empirical search for order. It seeks to discover, describe, and utilize lawful relationships among events. The events may range from the activity of a single brain cell to the actions of a large social group. It is often useful to classify events into one of two categories: *independent variables* and *dependent variables.* They are called variables because they may vary in terms of such things as quantity, quality, and type. Science seeks orderly relationships between values of these variables. In the simplest instance, the value of a variable may be its presence or absence. In more complex cases, the value may take the form of a number, such as age, or a category, such as male. Regardless of how one assigns different values to them, the independent and dependent variables constitute the subject matter of scientific investigation. The range of possible variables is, of course, infinite, thus the scope of science is virtually limitless.

The distinction between independent and dependent variables is a very important one. Basically, the *independent variable* (IV) is that variable which one manipulates in order to produce changes in the *dependent variable* (DV). The IV is independent in that it is the isolated focus of a given experiment, and the DV is dependent in that its value may or may not be affected by changes in the IV. One may roughly conceptualize their relationship as one of cause and effect [1] where changes in the independent variable cause some change in the dependent variable. A popular toothpaste advertisement offers one illustration. In evaluating the effects of two brands of toothpaste on dental cavities, the brands (A and B) are IVs and number of cavities is the DV. If fewer cavities are encountered after use of brand A than brand B, then the researcher concludes that brand A is a better product. He must be careful, however, to make sure that other IVs were not responsible for the observed difference in cavities. Suppose, for example, that more candy was eaten during the evaluation of brand B. The difference might then be due to a third unwanted or extraneous IV, namely, the difference in candy consumption. The careful isolation of IVs is an important characteristic of the scientific method.

Although the decision as to which variable is which may sometimes be arbitrary, most variable pairs can be classified easily. The search for order is pursued in hopes that if a lawful relationship exists between the two variables it will be discovered and described. For example, if some value of the independent variable is always associated with some consistent change in the dependent variable, then a lawful relationship has been discovered. The relationship is lawful in that it conforms to a regular pattern.

The goals of science, then, are the discovery and description of lawful relationships among variables. Once such relationships have been observed, they may be utilized in prediction and control. To observe that some value of variable A consistently results in some change in variable B allows one to predict and control variable B. The predic-

[1] See pp. 30–32 for discussion of some problems in cause-effect conceptualizations.

tion, of course, simply involves an "if-then" restatement of the observed lawful relationship. Control means that the predicted change in variable B can be produced or avoided simply by appropriately manipulating variable A. Closely tied with the scientific goals of prediction and control is the concept of *replication.*[2] In order to be maximally useful, a lawful relationship between two variables must be applicable to future, similar occurrences. In other words, the observed relationships must be repeatable or replicable. Ideally, future occurrences would be identical occurrences; however, such exact replication never occurs. Thus we must speak of future, similar occurrences. Replication then refers to the process of extending an observed relationship from one instance to future, similar ones. For example, if a popular reducing diet is the IV and weight change is the DV, one might wish to determine whether any observed regularity could be applied to the same person at a later time or to other people. If the relationship did hold in both situations, then it would be tentatively classified as replicable. A failure to replicate would, of course, necessitate appropriate qualifications in the description of the relationship. Note that unreplicable results are not unscientific; they are simply more circumscribed in their relevance. However, they are often looked upon unfavorably. This is because a failure to replicate may indicate that some previous finding was spurious due to poor experimental design, chance factors, or a failure to control extraneous IVs. The replicability criterion stems from an emphasis on public observability in the scientific approach.

To summarize, science might be defined as an empirical search for order. It entails the discovery and description of lawful relationships among variables (events). Such discovery and description make possible the prediction and control of future, similar occurrences of those events. Control, of course, is a utilization of the observed regularity. Replicability ensures that the observed relationship was neither unique nor accidental and that it may be usefully applied to future, similar situations.

Truth, certainty, and probable inference

It is a common assumption, especially among laymen, that science is "the royal road to truth." Perhaps because of modern emphases on scientific progress, many people look up to science as the ultimate means of obtaining certainty and indisputable facts. However, a brief look at the philosophy on which science is based will illustrate the error in

[2] Within the philosophical arena this process of prediction and control is referred to as generalization. However, in psychology generalization refers to other processes (see Chapter 7), so here we have chosen to use the concept of replication.

these conceptions. Some basic generalizations about the nature of scientific knowledge gathering may be worth noting.

1. Truth is an unattainable ideal. Science will never allow us to know the truth; it can only allow us to increase our relative confidence in the accuracy of our assumptions and theories about the world.

2. Science denies finality. Its search for order is a never-ending one.

3. Certainty and proof apply only to such abstract logical systems as mathematics and not to concrete, real-life events. Science can deal only with probabilities; it cannot claim certainty. This distinction is slightly technical but worthy of elaboration. Recall that science strives to discover and describe orderly relationships in nature. There are two broad categories of such relationships in science: (a) *analytic,* or those dealings with symbols such as words and numbers, and (b) *synthetic,* or those involving real-life experience. The "truth value" or validity of a statement depends on which kind of relationship it predicts. Generally, the terms *truth* and *proof* are used in reference to symbolic statements and *probability* and *evidence* are applied to experiential statements. One can be certain that "all bachelors are unmarried" because this statement is true by definition. Its validity is guaranteed by the respective meanings of the symbols (terms) *bachelor* and *unmarried.* On the other hand, one cannot be certain that it will snow next winter in Toronto. Although it is very probable that this event will occur (based on previous evidence), there is a very remote possibility that it won't. A good rule of thumb for distinguishing between analytic and synthetic assertions is the *principle of conceivable negation.* For any given statement, if you can conceive of its being false, then it is synthetic, or experimental (regardless of how infinitesimal is the probability of its falsehood). If the statement cannot conceivably be negated, it is analytic, or symbolic. For example, consider the proposal, "A triangle has three sides." Can you conceive of its being false? Can you conceive of a two-sided triangle? Of course not. The statement is true by definition. How about the statement, "Blondes have more fun"? Can you conceive of the possibility that they do not? The answer is "Yes," and the proposition can therefore only claim evidence, not proof, and a probability of validity, not certainty.

4. Science is a self-appraising discipline. The scientist continally re-examines both his "facts" and his methods of inquiry. Evidence is accepted regardless of its appeal or implication for popular conceptions of reality. A scientist is dependent upon his data for an evaluation of his conception of lawful relationships among events. If the data do not fit the popular conception, then the conception must be altered to fit the data.

5. All scientific facts are relative and tentative. Nothing about

science is unchangeable. It used to be a "fact" that the earth is flat. This seeming bit of truth changed, however, as contradictory evidence appeared. Contemporary "facts" are no less susceptible to change. When we use the terms *scientific fact* or *fact* later in the book, we refer to matter that is relative and tentative and not to the popular concept of fact as a proven bit of truth.

6. Science can deal only with communicable events. Truly unique or undescribable phenomena are not scientific. This does not mean that they are somehow illegitimate, but that they lie outside the framework of scientific inquiry.

7. No subject matter is inherently unscientific so long as it contains empirically testable statements. This generalization will be further explored in the next section.

8. Science assumes some degree of determinism or order in nature. If event B consistently follows event A, then their relationship is considered an orderly and determined one. Rhetorically, one might say that in future situations when event A occurs, the scientist assumes that nature is obliged to follow through with event B.

Criteria in science

Testability

The scientist's confidence in the probable validity of a statement depends upon the relevant evidence. This brings up still another characteristic of scientific inquiry; namely, its reliance on empirical tests in the evaluation of statements. A prediction or hypothesis is judged by the data encountered in its experimental assessment. Not all statements, however, are testable and philosophers of science have long debated the status of such hypotheses. Some have argued that untestable propositions are scientifically meaningless; others have imposed different criteria on hypotheses (see Weimer, in press). In everyday research, however, the contemporary scientist seldom entertains hypotheses that do not specify potential tests of their validity. A testable statement, of course, is one for which potentially confirming or disconfirming evidence is conceivable.

Without pursuing the logical arguments and philosophical issues pertaining to the testability criterion, we might consider some of its more prominent aspects and give a few examples. Originally, the testability criterion required that an empirical statement be verifiable. Thus, a scientific evaluation of the statement, "There is a God," would have required specification of the conditions that would have given support to the statement, or contributed to its verification. For reasons that the interested reader may wish to pursue (see Turner 1967; Weimer, in press), the verifiability criterion was supplemented by a falsifiability criterion, so that empirical statements had to be *verifiable or falsifiable in principle.* The qualification "in principle" stresses the fact that the statement in question need not be immediately testable, there need only be some conceivable means for testing it. For example, the statement, "There is life in other galaxies" is empirically testable because the conditions that would make it "true" or "false" can be specified. The fact that we do not now have the means to test that statement does not make it unscientific. The following is an empirically untestable statement: "There is an invisible and intangible elf who sits on the president's shoulder. It never leaves a trace of existence, but it is there all the same." Since there are no means of verifying or falsifying this statement, it would be categorized as empirically untestable. This does not necessarily categorize the statement as senseless; it simply means that the statement is beyond the jurisdiction of the scientific rationale.

Perhaps more than any other scientific discipline, behavioral science has been plagued with what would be empirically classified as untestable statements. In the field of personality and clinical psychology this shortcoming has been especially prominent. The closed system, that is, one which does not specify those data that would have bearing on it, has been all too prominent. The problems raised by such neglect of scientific criteria are not nominal. Such systems, which present themselves as empirical or scientific, are often only speculative and do not benefit from the self-appraising feedback of experimental evidence. The only way to ensure the meaningfulness of statements about behavior is to compare those statements with the behavior in question. Modern behavioral science has incorporated the testability criterion into its framework so that the speculative preoccupations of earlier times have been replaced by empirically testable assertions about behavior. This emphasis on testability and general scientific respectability is considered by some to be the most significant factor in the recent surge of progress made in behavioral research.

Objectivity and operationism

Objectivity may be defined crudely as a nonpartisan approach to subject matter. It plays an enormously significant role in all science, and its utilization is perhaps more essential in behavioral science than in any other. The reason for this is that behavioral science is particularly susceptible to *subjective* observations and descriptions. The behavioral observer often has much in common with the object of his observation, and "reading in" his own predictions and past experiences is very tempting. The best illustration of the difference between objective and subjective descriptions is given by Skinner (1963).

> In a demonstration experiment, a hungry pigeon was conditioned to turn around in a clockwise direction. A final, smoothly executed pattern of behavior was shaped by reinforcing successive approximations with food. Students who had watched the demonstration were asked to write an account of what they had seen. Their responses included the following: (i) the organism was conditioned to *expect* reinforcement for the right kind of behavior; (ii) the pigeon walked around, *hoping* that something would bring the food back again; (iii) the pigeon *observed* that a certain behavior seemed to produce a particular result; (iv) the pigeon *felt* that food would be given it because of its actions; and (v) the bird came to *associate* his action with the click of the food dispenser. The observed facts could be stated, respectively, as follows: (i) the organism was reinforced *when* its behavior was of a given kind; (ii) the pigeon walked around *until* the food container again appeared; (iii) a certain behavior *produced* a particular result; (iv) food was given to the pigeon *when* it acted in a given way; and (v) the click of the food dispenser *was temporally related* to the bird's action. . . . The events reported by the students were observed, if at all, in their own behavior. They were describing what *they* would have expected, felt, and hoped for under similar circumstances. (pp. 955–956)

The contrast between the objectively presented facts and those that were subjectively reported is very dramatic. The reference to the organism's internal states will be discussed more thoroughly in the following chapter. For the time being, however, the reader should recognize the very important distinction between these two types of accounts. In objective descriptions, the hard-core data are reported and a conscious attempt is made to avoid interpretations, inferences, or assumptions. Subjective descriptions, however, often abound with such nonobservable adornments. In a subjective account, many of the reported behavioral elements derive from the subject or observer, whereas in an objective account, the elements come from the object of observation. An illustrative exercise is to take some event and have several observers describe it. By comparing notes and discussing exactly which statements were observed and which were inferred, one can gain an appreciation of the necessity of objective accounts and the ease with which subjective statements can creep into a scientist's language.

The topic of objectivity is closely related to what has been called data language in behavioral science. As its name implies, *data language* is a type of scientific language that emphasizes objective facts. It is the cornerstone of empirical observation, since the evidence must be stated in a clear and communicable manner. Data language should be descriptive, not inferential. Because science is a search for order, it relies heavily on observation and experimentation. For the former to be useful, however, it must be as free as possible from inference and arbitrary interpretations. Inferences and interpretations are occasionally useful, but they must be closely linked to data. Data language points up the *public observability* characteristic of science. If the scientific community can agree upon the description of some event, then that description is probably an objective one.[3] However, if controversy arises, it is probably because one or more observers have garnished the data with some subjective interpretations. The use of data language is one means of ensuring some agreement as to evidence in the scientific community. For example, one might wish to say that an individual had improved after being treated for a fear of heights. Such a description, however, is very subjective, since one researcher's definition of improvement may not correspond to another's. Translating such a description into data language, one would say that after treatment the individual was capable of climbing some specific number of feet up a ladder. The observable evidence is described in a form with which all observers could agree. Whether or not improvement took place would depend on the individual's pretreatment ability to climb the ladder and on a specified criterion for improvement.

Closely related to objectivity and data language is the topic of operationism. Broadly defined, *operationism* is an attempt to objectify scientific concepts by equating them with the operations used in their measurement. When a concept is operationally defined, it is defined in such a way that one knows what procedures are necessary to observe it. For example, an operational definition of the concept of intelligence would specify the operations needed to illustrate it. Thus, Boring (1923) defined intelligence as "what the (intelligence) tests test" (p. 35). Similarly, one might operationally define anxiety as an increase in heart rate, a change in respiration, or a particular score on some paper-and-pencil test. The particular operations involved in defining a concept can be very arbitrary. One researcher might define psychotic behavior in terms of scores on a personality inventory; another may define it as the act of giving personality inventories. The point is that, regardless of how one defines a concept, if specific operations are outlined and described there is little chance of confusion over one's evidence. For example, a researcher may report that a certain drug produced drastic improvement in institutionalized psychotics. Such a statement could (and often does) lead to serious misinterpretations unless improvement is operationally defined. The researcher might operationally define improvement as a change in the reported content of the patients' dreams. Since there are many other potential behaviors which might be relevant

[3] It is important to distinguish between objectivity and validity. As mentioned in our previous discussion of "facts," public consensus does not ensure accurate knowledge.

to improvement (for example, cessation of hallucinations, delusions, and bizarre behaviors), the criterion chosen could easily vary across researchers. Thus, it is important that the researcher specify precisely what he means by his concepts so that other workers can look at his data and his criteria in defining a concept. Operational definitions and data language go hand in hand in helping to objectify scientific observations.

Scientific subject matter versus scientific methodology

A distinction frequently overlooked in behavioral science is that between scientific subject matter and scientific methodology. The former, of course, is comprised of those areas that are investigated by empirical methods. The latter is a loosely structured set of operations or procedures employed in those investigations. The distinction is an important one in that many misconceptions surround both subject matter and methodology.

With regard to scientific subject matter, it is often said that a particular topic is inherently unscientific. This is incorrect if the topic in question contains any empirically testable statements. For example, to say that the study of ESP or flying saucers is inherently unscientific is incorrect since there are many testable statements which could be generated in these two fields. If researchers do not generate such statements, then it is they who should be dubbed unscientific and not the subject matter. Keep in mind, however, that the term *unscientific* is not a pejorative label; it is a descriptive qualifier indicating phenomena or assertions which, for better or for worse, are outside the realm of contemporary science.

Misconceptions about scientific methodology often revolve around whether there exists a standardized set of techniques to be routinely employed in empirical investigations. Unless one were to define observation and experimentation as these techniques, no such storehouse exists. Scientific methodology consists of a very diverse collection of techniques. The particular techniques are often designed for a specific subject matter and may be totally irrelevant for other avenues of investigation. Thus, there is no international standard of scientific methodology. If a particular technique can reveal lawful relationships to the scientific community, it is acceptable. A sophisticated apparatus, a microscope, or even a frequency counter are not inherent to the scientific endeavor.

To summarize, there is a distinction between scientific subject matter and scientific methodology. The former is virtually any topic about which testable statements can be made. The latter is a loosely structured collection of techniques that have been found useful in observing or describing lawful relationships among variables.

Causation, correlation, and determinism

Although the reader may not immediately perceive any potential problems with the concept of causation, the fact of the matter is that it has constituted an area of philosophical debate for some time. The intricacies of "the problem of causation" would take us far afield from the present discussion, but a brief capsulization is both appropriate and beneficial. In behavior modification, as in all other scientific disciplines, the issue of causation is often a very significant one.

Perhaps the best way of summarizing the problem of causation is to describe it as an instance of inference rather than observation. Inference is a form of reasoning wherein one takes some observable bit of evidence and from it draws conclusions or makes speculations about hypothesized, unobserved phenomena. While it is sometimes unavoidable and even useful in scientific investigation, unrestricted use of inferences is discouraged because it leads to problems of disagreement and ambiguity. The gist of this digression is that one cannot *observe* causality; one must rather *infer* it. Perhaps a better way to put it is that one may observe *sequence* but not *consequence.* In searching for orderly relationships, one may observe all sorts of coordinated relations (or correlations) among variables. However, these observations can in no way imply any causal relationships. All that can be noted in the data language is that a change in the value of the IV was followed by a change in the value of the DV. Thus, for example, one may observe that shortly after sunrise there is an increase in temperature or that the flipping of a light switch is followed by highly predictable changes in illumination. However, neither of these events has illustrated causation which, as we have explained, is not demonstrable. Our stubbornness in denying causality in these examples may seem strange to the reader, but the essential distinction we are making is between actually observed data and assumed or inferred relationships. To say that variable A caused variable B is to assert that the former was in some way instrumental in the occurrence of the latter. This is going beyond the scientific data, which may indicate only a frequent co-occurrence and a temporal priority (that is, event A always precedes event B). When two variables systematically vary with respect to one another, they are said to be *correlated.* Our argument is that the scientist can observe only correlation and not causation.

Perhaps a brief example will illustrate the need for scientific conservatism in drawing causal inferences from correlational observations.

Consider the following hypothetical situation. Researchers have collected data over several years' time from a small community in an attempt to investigate the causes of drowning. After much data analysis and statistical exercise, it is reported that a very strong correlation exists between ice cream consumption and frequency of drownings. Based on these data, the researchers conclude that the drownings were in some way causally linked with ice cream consumption. Such a conclusion may seem partially justifiable. If children consume large amounts of ice cream just before swimming, it might be possible for them to develop cramps and drown. However, an alternative interpretation of the data is possible. Ice cream consumption is correlated with warm weather, which in turn is correlated with an increased frequency of swimming. Since the latter allows more opportunities for drowning, it is very possible that what our researchers have mistaken for a *causal* connection has only been a *correlational* one. That is, even though there is a systematic change in the two variables under study, such a change might be interpreted in terms of some third variable. Other examples of such unjustified jumps from correlational observation to causational inference are readily available.

The reader may well wonder how it is that science can make any progress if it is not allowed to make causal inferences. The fact of the matter is that scientists do make such inferences. Indeed, science is sometimes described as a search for causes (e.g., Mowrer 1960). The reason for this seeming discrepancy is basically a pragmatic one. The constraints of everyday observation and direct communication often lobby for the use of some conceptual shorthand. It is much simpler to say that event A caused event B than that event B has followed event A 12,645,203 times. Moreover, the finer issues of scientific philosophy generally are not delved into in everyday experimentation. Even though a researcher may agree with the foregoing analysis of problems in causal inference, he may find it convenient and practical to informally conceptualize his observations of A-B sequences in terms of causality.

The point of the foregoing has been to emphasize that (1) at a conceptual level causal descriptions always involve inference and should therefore be made conservatively, and (2) the practical demands of research and communication often encourage a loose usage of causal descriptions.

It cannot be stressed too strongly that stubborn conservatism is frequently necessary in correlation-versus-causation disputes (see Blalock 1964). Selltiz, Jahoda, Deutsch, and Cook (1959) list the following as necessary to justify functional causal inferences: (1) evidence of concomitant variation; (2) evidence that the DV did not precede the IV; and (3) evidence ruling out other causal factors. The first two of these criteria are often very easy to fulfill. The third, however, constitutes a major problem in virtually every experimental investigation in behavioral science.

Our final point relating to this topic has to do with the term *determinism.* The concepts of causality and determinism are often considered to be equivalent in both meaning and implications. Science assumes that all events are uniformly determined, in the sense that, given two identical antecedent situations, there will be two identical subsequent events. A determined relationship is one that follows some lawful order (if A, then B). Note that there is no obvious necessity for the assumption of causality. However, partly due to pragmatic considerations, defenders of the deterministic viewpoint often wave the causality banner (see Grunbaum 1952; Boring 1957). The word *defenders* may have clued the reader to the fact that the assumptions of causality and determinism are not universally held. A long-standing philosophical controversy has raged over the issue of free will versus determinism. If every event is determined or caused, then how can one assign responsibility to an individual for his actions? Don't the assumptions of determinism and causality eliminate choice and free will from human behavior? These and related questions will be discussed further in Chapter 10.

To summarize, causation is an inferred relationship. It may never be observed and always involves going beyond one's immediate data. The scientist can observe sequence or correlation but not consequence or causation. However, practical considerations often lobby for an informal use of the term *causation* in science. The concepts of causality and determinism are frequently considered equivalent. However, determinism involves an assumption of lawful relationships in nature and does not require causative influence.

The limitations of science

The scientific rationale is not a universally agreed upon avenue for the pursuit of knowledge. Other avenues include mysticism, rationalism, and personalistic science. The mystic believes that he can attain knowledge via religious experiences, meditation, rituals, and so on. The rationalist believes that some or all of reality can be investigated by means of reasoning rather than experimental test. In prosaic terms, the rationalist believes that many truths are self-evident in that they are derivable from reasoning rather than experimentation. For example, some philosophers maintain that such propositions as, "The shortest distance between two points is a straight line," can be intuitively recognized to be true. A humorous fable about the argument between rationalism and scientific empiricism goes as follows. The rationalist and empiricist were debating over which side of a buttered piece of toast would face upward if it were tossed into the air and allowed to fall. The rationalist said that it would obviously be the buttered side. The empiricist said he didn't know and that an experimental test would be required. The toast was buttered, tossed into the air, and it fell buttered side down. As the empiricist chuckled, the rationalist coolly remarked, "Obviously, the toast was buttered on the wrong side." This little story, which favors the empiricist's viewpoint, illustrates the issue of *a priori* knowledge (knowledge prior to experience) and *a posteriori* knowledge (knowledge subsequent to experience). The rationalist emphasizes the former and the empiricist, the latter. Suffice it to say that rationalism constitutes a nonscientific approach to knowledge.

The personalistic science approach is actually a quasi-scientific avenue. It employs a loose scientific framework and emphasizes intrapersonal experiences. A considerable degree of inference and subjectivity is encouraged and strict adherence to rigorous scientific criteria is absent. Many of the more humanistically oriented psychologists exemplify the personalistic science approach (e.g., Maslow 1966).

There are, of course, several other nonscientific approaches. The point to be made is that the scientist does not have a corner on the knowledge market. All too often one hears the term *unscientific* applied in a condescending and critical manner. To say that a particular investigator is unscientific is not to label him as a quack or as some misguided wretch. Rather, it is simply to state that he is not playing by the rules of that game called science (see Agnew and Pyke 1969). The choice as to which game will be played lies solely with the individual and intergame mudslinging would seem less than beneficial in our converging quest for knowledge.

At this point the reader may want to interject that there must be reasons why so many individuals choose the science game over other approaches to knowledge. Before exploring the justification of the scientific approach, let us briefly delve into some of its major shortcomings.

First, science is deficient in the sense that it does not and cannot claim certainty. As pointed out earlier, the scientist can *approach* certainty by assigning higher and higher probabilities to some event. However, he can never claim to be absolutely sure about an experimental event. This is probably not a very devastating flaw, but it is nonetheless a limitation in the scientific approach.

Second, scientific "facts," methods, and principles are tentative and relative by nature. For example, the principles of operationism and testability have undergone considerable reformulation and modification since their inclusion in the scientific framework. Because of its self-appraising nature, science is constantly changing its framework to meet the demands of new problems and new evidence. The difficulty here is that there are always at least a few scientists who are working with outmoded facts or principles. Moreover, there is often a lack of agreement among scientists as to the appropriate procedure or correct principle. Many of these controversies can be witnessed in behavior modification research. The scientist expects the most useful fact, method, or principle ultimately to win out by demonstrating its relative superiority. Meanwhile, however, there is considerable variability in the interpretation and application of the scientific approach. What is considered to be within the framework of science at one time may not be so considered at some subsequent time (see Kuhn 1962).

Third, science is restrictive. Because of its stress on observable evidence, communicability, testability, and so on, science excludes many questions and problems which might be considered significant. Moral and religious issues are often considered beyond the province of scientific evaluation.

Note that each of these shortcomings is more a limitation than a flaw. The question remains as to why so many individuals choose the scientific approach. Are there any logical arguments that favor science over other approaches? The simple answer is "No." Each approach to knowledge has as much logical justification as any other. Paradoxically, the assumption that science is the correct approach to knowledge would have to be classified by the scientist as untestable and unscientific since there are no finite tests by which to confirm or disconfirm it.

One might be tempted to conclude that science, mysticism, rationalism, and the other approaches are supported by the faith of their adherents. However, one argument that does support the scientific approach is that of pragmatism. Scientists have shown their methods and principles to be useful in the attainment of knowledge. This reliance on practicality, of course, makes some assumptions about criteria for choosing from among the various approaches. The criterion of usefulness is probably no less justified than any other. Turner's (1967) comments regarding the justification of the scientific approach are a fitting capsulization: "Empiricism itself is culpable, yet we have found no reliable substitute for a knowledge supported by the fact of its public communicability" (p. 7).

Summary

Behavior modification is characterized by an emphasis on the scientific approach to knowledge. Generally speaking, that approach may be described as an empirical search for order. It attempts to discover, describe, and utilize lawful relationships among events. For research purposes, events are often classified as independent and dependent variables. Confidence in the accuracy of a reported relationship is increased when that relationship can be replicated.

Science is a relative and approximate approach to knowledge. It denies finality and can never claim such absolute characteristics as certainty, truth, or proof. The only statements that can legitimately claim these characteristics are those dealing with the meaning and relationship among symbols. The rule of thumb for deciding whether a statement is analytic or synthetic is the principle of conceivable negation. If you can conceive of its being false, then it is synthetic.

As a continually open system of knowledge, science progresses through self-appraisal. Its facts are therefore only tentative. Among the generally conceded criteria of scientific research are those of testability and objective communicability. The relevance of science in any given area is determined by the satisfaction of these criteria.

A technical distinction can be made among the concepts of determinism, correlation, and causation. Determinism proposes that relationships among events can be described by lawful relationships. Correlation refers to an observed co-occurrence of events, while causation assigns responsibility to one or more of these events. Correlation may be observed but causation cannot be; it must be inferred. This technical distinction is sometimes overlooked in informal discussions.

Finally, science must be recognized as a fallible avenue of inquiry. It is not intrinsically superior to any other approach to knowledge. However, its demonstrated utility and self-appraising flexibility are advantages that lean heavily in its favor.

Suggested readings

Kuhn, T. S. *The structure of scientific revolutions.* Chicago: University of Chicago, 1962.

Turner, M. B. *Philosophy and the science of behavior.* New York: Appleton-Century-Crofts, 1967.

Weimer, W. B. *Psychology and the conceptual foundations of science.* Hillsdale, N.J.: Erlebaum, in press.

The role of inferred variables

3

This chapter is devoted to a controversial issue in behavior modification; namely, the usefulness and legitimacy of inferred variables in the explanation, prediction, and control of behavior. For our purposes, an inferred variable is one that has not been directly observed. For example, if one opens the refrigerator and finds that the last piece of pizza is missing, one may infer that a roommate or family member has consumed it. This conclusion is said to be inferential since the actual event was not directly observed. Note that the inferred event or variable connects or *mediates* a previous situation (the existence of the pizza) with a subsequent event (the pizza's disappearance). Like a clue in a murder mystery, the inferred variable often attempts to put things together and make sense of them. Because of this mediating function, inferred events are often called *mediational variables.* Lest the reader think that all inferred variables are alike, our discussion will begin with a brief consideration of some of the more important distinctions which have been made among inferred variables.

Intervening variables and hypothetical constructs

Perhaps the most clear-cut distinction which can be made is that offered by MacCorquodale and Meehl (1948) between intervening variables and hypothetical constructs. Although their distinction is somewhat complicated, we may abbreviate it as follows. An *intervening variable* relates two events *conceptually*. Its existence as a physical object is not proposed. For example, one might say that rewarding an organism for responses in a particular setting will increase its tendency to respond in that setting. The inferred or intervening variable (the tendency) is a conceptual probability. We are not expected to operate on the organism and locate the source of the aforementioned tendency in its spleen. Rather, our statement refers to a conceptual variable that we may or may not find useful. Another example might be the case of a young child who refuses to come to the dinner table despite repeated pleading from his mother. In attempting to explain this situation, one might say that the child has a stubborn streak. The latter, of course, is not a presumed physiological variable but is rather a convenient conceptual mediator.

The intervening variable is to be distinguished from the *hypothetical construct,* which proposes the existence of an unobserved physical object or process to relate two or more events. For example, several contemporary theories hypothesize biochemical bases for schizophrenia. Such theories speculate about the existence of some inferred variables such as hormone deficiencies, metabolic abnormalities, and so on. These hypothetical constructs are not merely conceptually useful. Rather, they are variables whose existence is hypothesized. They remain inferential only so long as they are unobserved. For example, let us return to the child who refused to come to the dinner table. We have a preceding event (the mother's pleas) and a subsequent event (the child's refusal). If these events are connected by a presumed conceptual element such as a stubborn streak, then an intervening variable has been inferred. However, if a physical mediator such as a stomach flu is presumed, then a hypothetical construct has been inferred. Hypothetical constructs should not posit the existence of entities or the occurrence of processes that prior scientific facts would render unbelievable.

Intervening variables have been more common in psychology than have hypothetical constructs. Common examples may be found in the popular use of such terms as *self-concept, ego,* and *internal conflicts.* Indeed, the fields of personality theory and assessment are thoroughly imbued with such variables (see Mischel 1968, 1971). Theoreticians and researchers use these inferential concepts as a means of relating environmental situations to behavioral events. They do not usually contend that these variables are potentially observable.

As pointed out earlier, both intervening variables and hypothetical constructs are mediating variables. However, this does not mean that all mediating variables, such as hypothetical constructs, must remain inferred. For example, Hilgard and Bower (1966) cite the hormone adrenaline as a variable which was originally hypothetical (unobserved). After being observed and described it ceased being inferred, but it remains a mediating variable in the sense of our previous definition. Observed or inferred, a mediating variable occupies a position between input (stimulus) and output (response).

To summarize, an intervening variable is one that fills a conceptual role in relating behavioral events. A hypothetical construct, in contrast, proposes the existence of a physical object or process to relate such events. Both of these are inferred variables in the sense that they are unobserved mediating variables. The interested reader should consult the readings in Marx (1951) for a more complete discussion.

The foregoing is a brief introduction to some of the distinctions made among inferred variables in behavioral science. We are now ready to explore some of the arguments for and against specific types of inferred variables. Then we will consider the utility of such variables in behavior modification.

Mentalism versus behaviorism

Psychology has always been filled with inferred variables. There are several reasons for this, not the least of which are the remnants of psychology's early preoccupation with "mental" states and processes. All mental events such as love or hate must be inferred from preceding situations and observed behaviors. One cannot see joy and anguish; these private experiences are inferred from a person's observable actions.

Mentalism

The earliest students of behavior were behavioral philosophers rather than behavioral scientists. Their interests were in the mind and its functions. Speculative views on the nature of the mind, soul, and life were very widespread. Consciousness was a frequent topic and its contents, form, and governing relationships became the subjects of early debates in behavioral philosophy. There were other debates on whether such a thing as mind exists and on the possibility of a relationship between mind and body. In general, those who argued in favor of the existence of the mind or made reference to mental states were called mentalists. For many years, mentalism was the convention in psychology. Indeed, its remnants can be observed in the everyday use of such mentalistic terms as *remind, slip one's mind, mental illness, mind over matter,* and so on. However, some very serious shortcomings in the mentalistic approach have become apparent during the last few decades. Although mentalism still predominates in some sub-areas of psychology, increasing attention is now given to behaviorism, which constitutes the foundation of concepts and research methods comprising behavior modification. Before discussing behaviorism, we will explore some of the shortcomings that have characterized the mentalistic approach to behavior.

One of the earliest objections to mentalistic hypotheses related to what has been called the mind-body problem; namely, how can a nonmaterial entity affect a material one, and vice versa? At first glance this may not appear especially devastating, particularly in a culture where a mind-body dichotomy is cultivated. However, upon further examination, the difficulty becomes more apparent. For the mind to be nonmaterial, it must, by definition, have no mass and occupy no space. However, the mind is typically posited as occupying the skull. Likewise, it is spoken of in terms of psychic energies and mental forces. In physics, a force is defined as an accelerated *mass,* and according to Einsteinian theory, mass and energy are interchangeable; thus, talk of psychic energy entails talk of potential mass. In sum, then, positing any sort of mind-body interaction is a weighty affair. It goes against the conservation of mass-energy principle of modern physics and raises some auxiliary problems such as spatial location and site of interaction.

A second problem associated with mentalistic formulations relates to their highly inferential nature. A mentalist typically chooses some behavior such as eating and from that *infers* a mental state such as hunger. While such an inference may seem justified, it introduces difficulties of interpretation. There are many behaviors for which very different inferences might be made. The frequent disagreements of psychiatrists and psychologists regarding alleged mental events attest to the extremely subjective nature of many inferences. One psychiatrist or psychologist may attribute smoking to repressed sexual impulses while another may see it as expressive of strong aggressive urges. As we saw in Chapter 2, once a scientist leaves his or her data (for example, observed behaviors), there is wide room for personal speculation and subjectivity. In addition to their use of subjective and often untestable inferences, mentalistic formulations frequently violate the principle of parsimony. The reader will recall that this principle recommends that one use as few assumptions as possible. It is not uncommon, however, for theories of mental functioning to employ extensive assumptions and inferences. These complicate attempts to directly apply and evaluate the theory.

A third problem with mentalistic formulations lies in their linguistic circularity. An explanation is circular or tautologous when it fails to go beyond the definition of the event to be explained. For instance, one might wish to explain eating behavior by reference to an internal state of hunger. If, however, hunger is defined in terms of eating ("Hunger is a tendency to eat"), then a circularity results. The alleged explanation is a translation of "He eats because he is hungry," to "He eats because he has a tendency to eat." The circuitous journey began with a behavior, visited a mental way station, and ended up with the original behavior. The distinction between *describing* and *explaining* an event may be helpful here. It is easy to describe an event and thereafter assume that it has been explained. Such an assumption not only is logically unjustified but also discourages further inquiry into the actual explanation. For example, one often hears or reads statements like, "He shot her *because* he hated her." If one were to ask, "How do you know that he hated her?" the typical answer would be, "Well, he shot her, didn't he?" The problem here, of course, is that the observed behavior (shooting) has been attributed to an inferred mental state (hate) which has in turn been deduced from the observed behavior (shooting). In this example, a behavioral description has illegitimately passed for a causal explanation. Since shooting is often classified as a hateful behavior, the situation has been described twice but not explained. Another example of such linguistic circularity is evident in the case of such inferred predispositions as hunger and thirst. To say, "He drinks *because* he is thirsty" is circular and meaningless if one uses drinking behavior as part of the definition of thirst. Further illustrations of this tautologous trend in mentalistic hypotheses could be provided, but the central point is that the assumption of a mental event or state is both meaningless and unnecessary unless that event or state can be differentiated from observable behaviors. Otherwise, one may as well stick to the observable behaviors.

One final objection to mentalistic formulations—and perhaps the most important to contemporary psychologists—is that they are often considered empirically untestable. Since mental events are, by definition, unobservable except to the person experiencing them, there is no way for an external observer to test hypotheses about them.[1] One may wish to make inferences about them, but the ultimate scientific data in such cases must be an observable response, whether it be a verbalization, a psychological measurement, or whatever. There is no direct external means for getting at mental phenomena. Science can deal only with events that are *assumed* to be somehow related to mental events. Until recently, the scientific emphasis on public observability relegated most intrapersonal behaviors (thoughts, images, and so on) to an unscientific limbo. For some psychologists and philosophers, the fact that mentalistic propositions are often considered scientifically unrespect-

[1] The problem of testability is further complicated when the mental events in question are allegedly unobservable to the person experiencing them (for example, "unconscious" events; see Mahoney 1970).

able indicates the shortcomings of science rather than the undesirability of mentalism.

Behaviorism

Having explored some of the major objections to mentalistic views of behavior, we may now proceed to a discussion of the behavioristic alternative. John B. Watson was the most outspoken critic of the mentalistic emphases of early psychology.

Watsonian behaviorism. Watson sought to establish a purely objective psychology grounded in natural science and based upon the logical and evidential support of contemporary empiricism. He called that objectified psychology "behaviorism" since its basic data involved observable behaviors. Because Watson's approach was so radical and because he demanded abrupt changes of emphasis in psychology, his earliest formulations have come to be known as *radical behaviorism.* Among its propositions was the metaphysical contention that the mind did not exist. As noted in Chapter 1, a less radical and much more enduring contribution of Watson has been his influence on techniques and methodology in psychology, which has come to be known as *methodological behaviorism.* The difference might be conceptualized as one of subject matter versus methodology. In radical behaviorism, Watson was philosophizing about the nonexistence of the mind and the meaninglessness of mentalistic propositions. In methodological behaviorism, Watson was invoking an objectification of psychological research. The former has raised a lot of dust in both philosophical and psychological circles. The latter, however, has probably been one of the most significant contributions toward making psychology a productive and respectable science. Watson's emphasis on *behavior*—objective, observable, and quantifiable data—gave a new twist to the psychologist's task. While radical behaviorism has remained a somewhat controversial issue in philosophy of mind, methodological behaviorism has become a widely adopted approach among behavioral scientists. Before we explore some of the more contemporary offshoots of behaviorism, it might be worthwhile to examine Watson's radical and methodological behaviorisms.

Watson maintained that the mind-body problem was a dead issue for the science of psychology. However, because he treated it at length in his early writings, he succeeded in focusing attention on the very issue that he considered dead. His main objection was that mental propositions were not scientifically legitimate. Watson (1924) considered consciousness "neither a definite nor a usable concept" (p. 2). He analyzed all behaviors in terms of muscular and glandular responses. Thus, thinking became an "implicit" verbal response. Early support for

Watson's contention that thinking was implicit speech came from some early experiments by Jacobson (1932) and Max (1935b, 1937). Jacobson found that minute muscular responses could be detected in the vocal cords when individuals were instructed to think or imagine various tasks. Max followed these findings with some corroborative research on deaf-mutes. He found that these individuals showed some minute finger and arm movements during "abstract thinking" tasks. Since deaf-mutes communicate via hand signals, Max's findings accorded well with those of Jacobson. Finally, Shaw (1940) found that when individuals were instructed to imagine lifting various small weights there were corresponding differences in the amount of recorded muscular activity.

These early findings, along with Watson's radical claims, raised no small amount of controversy. One reaction to the contention that thinking is implicit speech was to show that individuals whose vocal cords had been removed were still capable of thought. This implied an understandable misinterpretation of Watson's contention. He explicitly denied that laryngeal movement was equivalent to or necessary for thought (see Watson 1924, p. 238). Nevertheless, his reduction of all behaviors to glandular and muscular responses would certainly lead one to believe that if thinking is indeed a behavior, it must be either glandular or muscular in nature. The misunderstanding arose from the assumed association between laryngeal movement and thought; as noted, while Watson had indicated that thinking may be muscular or glandular, he did not define it as laryngeal movement. This contention has fallen by the wayside in modern behaviorism.

A second characteristic of early, and especially radical, behaviorism was its almost exclusive emphasis on *learned behavior*. Watson was very critical of statements implying inborn or innate behaviors. He did acknowledge the existence of a group of *unlearned behaviors,* but beyond that he believed all behaviors, and especially complex ones, to be learned through conditioning. Indeed, much to the ire of ethologists and instinct psychologists, Watson (1924) advocated the total abandonment of the concept of instinct in psychology.

> There are then for us no instincts—we no longer need the term in psychology. Everything we have been in the habit of calling an "instinct" today is a result largely of training—belongs to man's *learned behavior.*
>
> As a corollary from this we draw the conclusion that there is no such thing as an inheritance of *capacity, talent, temperament, mental constitution* and *characteristics.* These things again depend on training that goes on mainly in the cradle. (p. 94)

Perhaps the most famous Watsonian quotation, and one of the most controversial, dealt with the role of learning or environmental conditioning in the development of individual behavior patterns.

> I should like to go one step further now and say, "Give me a dozen healthy infants, well-formed, and my own specified world to bring them up in and I'll guarantee to take any one at random and train him to become any type of specialist I might select—doctor, lawyer, artist, merchant-chief and, yes, even beggar-man and thief, regardless of his talents, penchants, tendencies, abilities, vocations, and race of his ancestors." (1924, p. 104)

Watson readily admitted that such an ambitious statement went well beyond his data. However, such statements enlivened the controversy over the domain and dialogue of behavioral science. Watson incited a revolution in psychology. His radical statements about prevailing research topics and the techniques employed to study them set psychology to reassessing its subject matter and methodology.

Without doubt, Watson's most significant and lasting contribution to psychology was his emphasis on objectifying the methodology of behavioral research. In stating the behavioristic platform, Watson (1924) stressed the need for empirical data: "Let us limit ourselves to things that can be observed, and formulate laws concerning only these things" (p. 6). His goal was to make psychology a natural science. His metaphysical statements on the nonexistence of mind and the meaninglessness of mentalistic propositions constituted an attempt to rid psychology of the many philosophical influences that had persisted since its inception as a discipline. However, his most valuable legacy was his strong emphasis on *behavior* as the subject matter of psychology and on *the scientific method* as the means for studying that subject. Watson's conception of behavior was a very broad one and included thinking, feeling, talking, and imagining. All of these were to come under the purview of scientific investigation. Watson sought to put an end to armchair philosophizing about man's behavior. While he is probably better known for some of his more radical statements regarding the mind, conscious processes, and environmental influences, Watson's views on the subject matter and methodology of psychology laid the groundwork for modern behaviorism.

Watsonian behaviorism and contemporary behaviorism. The behavioristic movement has branched out in many directions since the era of John B. Watson. However, it continues to emphasize observable data, behavior as subject matter, and scientific methodology. Contemporary behaviorism is variously referred to as stimulus-response (S-R) psychology, neo-behaviorism, and learning theory. Behavior modification represents a contemporary application of methodological behaviorism. Although taking several paths, the behavioristic movement is a growing and productive influence in modern psychology. Its effects on the tenor of behavioral science are almost inestimable. However, several modifications have been made in the behaviorist's outlook which justify the distinction between Watsonian behaviorism and contemporary or neo-behaviorism. We will take the time at this point to explore these modifications.

In the first place, the mind-body problem has all but disappeared as an issue in behavioral science. There are several reasons for this. First, although writings in the philosophy of mind have continued, they have not reached most modern behaviorists. The mind-body problem can quickly become tiresome, and many contemporary behavioral scientists seem to have tired of its blind alleys. This may be an unjustifiable reason for ignoring an issue, but it does seem to be what has actually happened. Second, the area of linguistic analysis in philosophy has suggested that many mind-body dilemmas may be purely a matter of semantics (see Ryle 1949). Finally, the fact that mentalistic propositions and mind-body assertions are often considered scientifically untestable has led many modern workers to classify them as meaningless and to ignore them. This has probably been the most significant factor in deterring behavioral scientists from pursuing the issue.

Early behaviorism also differs from contemporary behaviorism in its definition of behavior. While there is no universally agreed upon definition for the terms *behavior* or *response,* the modern connotation of these terms is somewhat broader than that of the Watsonian era. Recall that Watson categorized all behaviors as muscular or glandular. The modern behaviorist would not be so restrictive. Indeed, the electrochemical firing of a single cell in the nervous system is now considered a discrete behavior.

Early behaviorism is distinguished from modern behaviorism in its emphasis on animal research and its views on the role of heredity. Although Watson's research dealt with humans, many of his immediate followers concentrated their research efforts in the animal laboratories. Since that time, the findings gathered in the animal laboratories have been applied to humans with remarkable success. However, the infrahuman emphases of early behavioristic research have led many to categorize all behaviorists as rat psychologists. The incongruity of such a generalization is readily apparent to any who familiarize themselves with the behavior therapy journals. As for heredity, contemporary behaviorism sees it in a much less negative light than did Watson. Although talk of instincts and inborn tendencies is still infrequent in behavioristic writings, it is not excluded. The current stance would seem to be that such concepts are admissible if they are useful.

Another distinction between early and contemporary behaviorism relates to the previously discussed dichotomy between subject matter and methodology. That behavior is and has been the subject matter of behavioral psychology since Watson's time can scarcely be denied. However, the emphasis on methodology which Watson initiated has become so extensive that some, including ourselves, equate contemporary behaviorism with methodological behaviorism. Karl Lashley, one of Watson's students, made some of the earliest attempts at specifying the requirements of methodological behaviorism. His efforts, and those of later behaviorists, have culminated in contemporary behavioral methodology. The modern standard places no restraints on the subject matter of behavioral science so long as it meets with the minimal criteria for empirical investigation.

One final characteristic distinguishing the old from the new behaviorism relates to the role of cognitive behaviors. Recall that Watson readily admitted the reality of such behaviors as thinking, feeling, and so on. However, his contention that only observable behaviors were amenable to scientific study placed such behaviors as thinking and feeling in a sort of empirical limbo. Unless such private events could be defined in terms of publicly observable physical responses, Watson and his immediate followers considered them beyond the scope of behavioral science. That view has been modified drastically by modern behaviorists, and this probably constitutes the most significant single characteristic distinguishing Watsonian from contemporary behaviorism. Partly because of developments in methodological behaviorism and partly because of the great need for research on cognitive behaviors, this area has received increasing attention from behavioral researchers (see Bandura 1969; Meichenbaum 1973; Mahoney 1974a).

In cognitive behaviorism, research is done according to the following standard: "operationism and observable anchors." This means that any talk of cognitive processes must be defined in terms of the operations used to measure them (see Chapter 2 in this volume) and that all cognitive behaviors must be anchored to publicly observable behaviors. For example, the cognitive behaviorist can deal with imagery by means of operationalizing the concept and anchoring it to observable data. Thus, imagery might be defined as that behavior in which an individual engages and later reports when asked to imagine something. The observable anchors in this instance are the experimenter's instructions and the subject's verbal report. An even more recent development in cognitive behaviorism is the possibility of using participant observation to make private events an area amenable to scientific inquiry. Homme (1965) had noted that even though private events such as thoughts, feelings, images, and sensations are not publicly observable, they are not beyond the reach of scientific research. The individual who is experiencing those publicly unobserved behaviors is certainly in a position to observe them and report on his observations. Thus, although we must add some precautions in relying on the accuracy and honesty of our participant observer, private events are within the boundaries of an empirical analysis of behavior (see Mahoney 1974a).

Despite the aforementioned modifications, contemporary behaviorism still carries with it many of the essential characteristics of early behaviorism; namely, the strong emphasis on *behavior* and on *scientific methodology*. To review and explore the many facets of contemporary behaviorism would be a monumental task. Suffice it to say that of all the schools and movements that have come and gone in psychology, behaviorism appears to be one that is here to stay. Its productive applications and its rapidly expanding approach to complex behaviors have made it one of the most popular and promising developments in behavioral science.

A final note

The foregoing account of the mentalism-behaviorism controversy has necessarily been superficial. There are many subissues and arguments whose discussion would take us far from our path. The relatively positive account of behaviorism given here would not be universally accepted. Numerous critiques of behavioristic philosophies are available (see Mahoney et al. 1974). Lest the reader think that antibehavioral critiques are extinct or that the behavioral approach is universally accepted, the following statement from Matson (1971) is provided.

> Plainly, the differences between us must be very deep—not just technical or strategic or methodological but philosophical and perhaps moral. For my part, I believe that Skinner and his gentle friends state the case against their own philosophy so openly and candidly that one need only cry "Hark! See there? They are exposing themselves (the Grand Conditioner has no clothes)!" (p. 2)

Inferred variables in behavior modification

Thus far in this chapter we have examined the nature of inferred variables, some distinctions among them, and a few of the more common examples. We may now turn our attention to a discussion of their usefulness in the explanation, prediction, and control of behavior.

As we have pointed out, the role of inference has been a controversial one in behavior modification. Because of Watson's emphasis on observable behavior, early behavioral researchers were hesitant to engage in any inferential speculations.[2] Dealing with the observed be-

[2] Exceptions to this were the early learning theorists (see Hilgard and Bower 1966).

havior was deemed both necessary and sufficient. However, more recent trends in behavior modification have seen some cautious steps taken in the direction of controlled inference. Such inference is "controlled" in the sense that many sources of evidence are employed and observable anchors are required.

We might take a moment here to discuss the role of inference in everyday life so that the reader can discriminate between justified and unjustified inference. For example, one might see a newspaper on a doorstep and from that infer that the newspaper boy had deposited it there. Such an inference would seem justified, for one frequently observes newsboys depositing papers on doorsteps. Another example would be the motorist who looks at his fuel gauge and from the position of its needle infers the presence or absence of a certain quantity of gasoline in his tank. He does not observe the actual fuel level, but only a needle designed to reflect that level. Such inference is fairly well justified. Nevertheless, most of us probably have had the experience of making a faulty inference from a fuel gauge reading—and may also have suffered the inconvenience resulting from such a faulty inference. If the needle on such a gauge behaved erratically or never moved, then inferring fuel capacity from its position would be unjustified. The point is that an inference is justified only when it is based on sufficient evidence to make it useful in predicting or understanding events. If an inference helps establish or clarify a testable relationship, then it is justified. In science, just as in everyday life, an inference that does not "pay off" in the sense of aiding scientific goals is unjustified. Many of the more popular inferences in psychology have had dubious utility.

B. F. Skinner is probably the best-known critic of unjustified inferences and mediational accounts in the analysis of behavior. Many of his observations regarding the difficulties involved in inferential variables have already been previewed in our discussion of the shortcomings of mentalism. For example, the problem of circularity is invoked. To say that an individual behaves strangely because of some inferred mental abnormality and then to justify one's inference of that abnormality by reference to the behavior is totally meaningless. John bites his nails because he is nervous. How do you know he is nervous? Well, he bites his nails. Such reasoning as this, although in much subtler form, pervades many theories of personality. It is circular and it is often unnecessary. If to say that John bites his nails is equivalent to saying that John is nervous, one might just as well make only one of these statements. Another problem with inferred variables is that they often lead to premature conclusions. By allegedly explaining John's nail biting through reference to nervousness, one may come away thinking that the observed behavior has actually been explained rather than merely described in different terms. Such a premature conclusion may be dangerous if it discourages further analysis of the behavior.

Perhaps one of the most serious problems with inferential accounts of behavior is that of reification. Reification is a process whereby some concept gradually attains the status of an existing entity. For example, we have noted that many contemporary personality theorists make reference to various inferred variables. These are employed conceptually in explaining, predicting, and controlling behavior. However, these conceptual aids often become reified in the sense that they are talked about as if they were real-life entities (for example, hypothetical constructs). Terms such as *id, ego,* and *superego* were originally offered as conceptual variables by Freud. However, many researchers have fallen into the habit of considering such terms as names for real entities. Such reification might be conceptualized as an inadvertent shift from adjective to noun. One begins by saying, "George is exhibiting schizophrenic behavior." Later one may say, "George has schizophrenia." The change is obvious. We start by describing what George *does* and end by talking about what George *has.* Schizophrenia becomes a mystical demon or hypothetical illness within the individual rather than a descriptive label for bizarre behavior patterns.

It is problems like these that buttress Skinner's argument against the use of inferential and also mediational accounts of behavior. His contention is that lawful behavioral relationships can be described and utilized without reference to various intermediaries. One may roughly conceptualize an organism as being in an input-output relationship with the environment. So long as one can describe that relationship accurately without reference to "internal" variables, there would seem to be little use for them. Where other behavioral researchers might wish to posit a three-variable sequence (stimulus—mediating variable—response), Skinner emphasizes a two-variable one (stimulus—response). Note that he does not deny the existence or importance of mediating variables. He simply maintains that they may be unnecessary. Skinner's argument applies to noninferred mediating variables (for example, physiological processes, hormone levels, and so on) as well as inferred ones. Although the former are less susceptible to some of the difficulties outlined previously, Skinner asserts that they rarely aid and often impede the experimental analysis of behavior. His basic objection to mediational accounts of behavior—whether they involve hypothetical constructs, intervening variables, or observable intra-organismic processes—is that they often result in incomplete causal analyses. Skinner argues that the explanation of behavior by reference to some mediating variable is both useless and incomplete unless the latter can, in turn, be accounted for by some preceding external situation. Thus, to "explain" a child's aggressive behaviors by reference to an internal state of hostility is meaningless unless the conditions that give rise to that hostility are specified. Again, the input-output analogy is stressed. Given that certain variables feed into the organism and certain behaviors are emitted by that organism, it matters little what happens in between if one can lawfully predict the input-output relationship. The usefulness of the mediating variable in discovering, describing, and predicting that relationship is considered much more important than the nature of the variable itself. Indeed, Skinner (1963, p. 958) states that "no entity or process which has any useful explanatory force is to be rejected on the ground that it is subjective or mental." His rejection of inferred variables thus stems from their inutility rather then from the nature of such variables.

The role of inference in behavior modification might be compared to its parallel role in the physical sciences. While the latter make use of inferential variables such as "atom" or "electron," they do so in a very conservative manner. The nonmediational argument, which criticizes both inferential and noninferential mediating variables, likewise emphasizes the utility or inutility of mediational variables in behavioral research. Thus, the role one assigns to inferred variables depends on one's opinion of their *utility* in research.

If it can be capsulized, the gist of Skinner's position is that mediational accounts of behavior are often troublesome and useless. The early history of psychology shows what a preoccupation with inferred variables can do. The issue, of course, has two sides. Just as Skinner has criticized mediational, and especially inferential, accounts of behavior, so have other workers criticized nonmediational accounts (e.g., Breger and McGaugh 1965; Dulany 1968). Their main contention is that nonmediational accounts of behavior omit too much. As some have put it, "There is a lot going on in the dash between S and R." Critics of the nonmediational stance have accused it of oversimplifying behavior, especially at the human level. Although an input-output model might simplify our understanding of behavior, such a model is often sorely inadequate. Human beings do not passively register stimuli and then reflexively respond. Their actions are dramatically affected by intrapersonal variables—beliefs, perceptions, and self-statements—that are no less deserving of experimental scrutiny (see Homme 1965; Meichenbaum 1973; Mahoney 1974a).

To summarize, the role of inferred variables in behavior modification has been a controversial one. Early behavioral researchers cautiously avoided inferential speculations. However, recent trends such as cognitive behaviorism have witnessed the introduction of controlled inferences in research. The majority of behavior modifiers continue to avoid inferential variables. However, noninferred mediational variables have received increasing attention from behavioral researchers so that "intra-organismic" behaviors have returned to the arena. Their comeback has been enhanced by methodological innovations which show the promise of establishing empirical bases for an experimental analysis of mediating behaviors. Likewise, the criterion of *utility* in evaluating mediating variables has allowed the behavior modifier to consider them as potential aids in the explanation, prediction, and control of behavior. But the byword in any scientific use of inferential variables is *caution.* Their potential usefulness in behavioral science must be qualified by the realization that inference is a conceptual step away from the data.

Summary

An inferred variable is one that has not been observed. It is often used to mediate or connect observable input and output. Intervening variables and hypothetical constructs are two major categories of mediators in psychology. In general, the former perform conceptual functions while the latter are more empirical or physical in function.

The legitimate role for inferred mediators in the analysis of behavior has caused extensive debate. Nonmediational theorists like Skinner have pointed out the problems that often accompany the use of inferred variables: mind-body problems, tautologies, explanatory fictions, and so on.

The avoidance of inferred variables was stressed in John B. Watson's radical behaviorism. However, Watson's methodological behaviorism, which outlines the process rather than the content of scientific inquiry, is his enduring contribution to contemporary psychology. Although the essence of methodological behaviorism is still apparent in current behavior modification research, the same cannot be said of radical behaviorism.

Inferred variables such as thoughts, feelings, and memories have become increasingly popular in present-day efforts to understand human behavior. Mediating variables are admissible if they are operationally defined and observable. Even then, they are employed only if they are useful in the explanation, prediction, or control of behavior.

Suggested readings

Mahoney, M. J. *Cognition and behavior modification.* Cambridge, Mass.: Ballinger, 1974.

Skinner, B. F. Behaviorism at fifty. *Science,* 1963, *140,* 951–958.

Watson, J. B. *Behaviorism.* Chicago: University of Chicago, 1924.

Data collection and research design

4

The cornerstone of any science is its data, obtained through objective assessment procedures. As Bachrach (1965) has indicated, the basic step in the scientific method is the collection of data. It would be difficult to overemphasize the need for objective data collection and data analysis in behavioral science. Until the advent of methodological behaviorism, the lack of objective data in psychology was abysmal. To avoid data collection is to refuse the invaluable services of the scientific method.

In its search for orderly relationships, science requires an endless array of comparisons—comparing values of the dependent variable associated with different values of the independent variable. However, such comparisons are virtually meaningless unless we can agree upon an objective standard of comparison. The datum and the data language provide such a standard. Granted, one's choice of a datum may be arbitrary (for example, a lever press rather than a somersault); however, the fact that a community of researchers can agree upon some publicly observable and replicable datum provides a means whereby objective comparisons can be made. It is by means of such comparisons that a scientific discipline can progress.

Data collection

Data collection, as a form of scientific observation, may range from the simple acknowledgment of an event to the precise recording of minute changes in a variable. The byword in data collection is *objectivity*. Without it, data become ambiguous, unreplicable, and virtually meaningless. There are several ways by which researchers can enhance the objectivity of data collection. They may utilize instruments that automatically record the behavior of interest. They may film the situation so that repeated checks for objectivity may be carried out by themselves or other researchers. They may employ two or more independent observers, who are unaware of one another's data collection, to record the behavior in question. A subsequent comparison of the records of each of these observers should allow a determination of the objectivity of the data.

Before exploring some of the types of data and methods of data collection that are popular in the field of behavior modification, we should make one very emphatic point: *the data are always right.* One may argue about hypotheses, theories, methods of data collection, data interpretation, the generality of the data, or what have you, but one cannot sensibly argue about data.[1] This point is clearly expressed by Skinner in *Science and Human Behavior* (1953).

> Scientists have simply found that being honest—with oneself as much as with others—is essential to progress. Experiments do not always come out as one expects, but the facts stand and the expectations fall. The subject matter, not the scientist, knows best. (p. 13)

As Bachrach (1965) puts it, "*Data prevail, not men*" (p. 28). This complete reliance on empirical evidence is a necessary and significant aspect of any scientific discipline. Its role in behavioral science is crucial.

Having thus noted the tremendous significance of objective data in the field of behavior modification, we may now turn to some of the different types of data utilized. Although there are several ways of classifying data, the categorization offered here will provide a general familiarity with popular data classes in behavior modification.

Classes of behavioral data

All behavioral data belong to one of four classes: (1) magnitude data, (2) temporal data, (3) frequency data, and (4) categorical data. *Magnitude data* include any measures that involve the strength or intensity of a response. For example, if one were to record the pressure exerted on

[1] Unless one is asserting that the data in question are nonexistent or that the data are not objective.

the lever in a Skinner box, one would obtain a magnitude datum. Weight and height are also magnitude data. *Temporal data,* as the name suggests, involve measurement of time. The elapsed time between two events is an example of a temporal datum. Such measures as speed (distance divided by time) are here classified as temporal data; such measures include response latency, maze-running speed, and response duration. *Frequency data* involve discrete responses whose occurrences can be counted and used to make objective comparisons. Thus, such responses as the number of times a child hits himself on the head or bites his little brother, or the number of bar presses a laboratory animal makes, may be classified as frequency data. Note that frequency data often are temporally bound. For example, one may wish to report the number of occurrences of a particular behavior during some specified time period. For our purposes, the data would still qualify as frequency data. Thus, response rate, which is one of the most popular dependent variables in behavior modification, would be classified as a frequency measure even though it involves frequency divided by time. *Categorical data* involve measurements differentiating one response from another. In the simplest instance, such categorization may involve recording the presence or absence of a particular response. Likewise, recording whether response A or B occurred constitutes the accumulation of categorical data. Thus, for example, a right instead of a left turn in a maze would be a categorical datum. The presence of a bar press in situation A and its absence in situation B is another categorical datum.

The four data classes are not employed in a mutually exclusive manner. One may record whether a right or left turn occurred in a maze (categorical data), the number of right and left turns that were made (frequency data), and the running speed associated with each (temporal data). The foregoing data classification system is not intended as an ideal schema, but rather as a means of familiarizing the reader with the wide range of data types employed in the field of behavior modification.

Methods of data collection

An investigator must decide if he will collect data for the entire time period in which a target behavior may occur, or if he will collect data only for some portion of the time. This decision leads to the use of one of the two methods of data collection: continuous and sampling. In the *continuous* method, data are collected continuously over a period of time. In the *sampling* method (also known as *time sampling*), data are collected only for a portion of the total time. For example, one might want to know how many cars cross a particular intersection in one year's time. If the continuous method of data collection were used, the number of cars crossing the intersection would be recorded twenty-four hours a day for an entire year. Such an undertaking would, of course, be expensive, but it would provide complete data. A less expensive approach would be the sampling method. In the sampling method, one would choose a number of representative days or weeks and the number of cars crossing the intersection would be recorded only at those times. From the data obtained, one could generalize to the entire year by multiplying appropriately. Note that in the sampling method one gathers data only for some fraction of the total time during which the variable of interest is potentially recordable. Thus, one measures a sample of the total time in question.

Each of these methods of data collection has received extensive application in behavior modification. The continuous method is most often utilized when the time period in question is relatively short. The sampling method, on the other hand, is used in situations where the behavior of interest is evaluated over a relatively long time period. For example, one might wish to measure the amount of tantrum behavior emitted by a child in a month. The sampling method would be most useful, because the behavior of interest is to be measured over a long time period. It would be very expensive, if not impossible, to station an observer in the home for 720 consecutive hours.

There are several varieties of the sampling method. One can employ either *fixed* or *randomized* time samples. For example, one might sample the behavior in a classroom every day from noon until one o'clock. This would be a fixed time sample. A randomized time sample would entail sampling during randomly selected one-hour periods throughout the school day. The relative advantages of the latter method should be obvious. Unless one is interested in the behaviors that occur during some fixed time, the randomized method usually provides a more representative sample of the behavior in question. In the above example, it may well be that classroom behaviors between eight and nine o'clock are quite different from those between noon and one o'clock.

Both the continuous and the sampling methods have their relative advantages and disadvantages. The continuous method is more accurate since it entails full coverage of the behavior in question. The sampling method can be very misleading if one's choice of time samples is not representative. For example, if one were to monitor the traffic at an intersection only on weekdays and from that generalize to the entire year, such a projection would probably be grossly inaccurate. Likewise, if one were to sample a student's studying behaviors only on weekends, an inaccurate representation might result. The advantage of the sampling method is that it is much less expensive than the continuous method. It is also very helpful in the measurement of nondiscrete behaviors. In general, the continuous method of data collection is to be preferred when it is practical. However, when correctly applied, the sampling method is also a very reliable means of data collection.

Data collection formats

Within both the continuous and sampling methods a data collection format must be chosen. Two of the most frequently used data collection formats are *actual counts* of the behavior or an *all-or-none classification.* To measure the frequency of crying, for example, the all-or-none classification might be more appropriate; any crying that occurs during the observation time is recorded as a unit. This means of data collection is sometimes labeled interval recording and is particularly valuable with a behavior such as crying or tantrums. In this situation if the behavior occurs at all during the time period in which it is observed, then that time period is scored as an "occurrence." Over some particular time, one can compare the relative percentages (for instance, on a daily basis) of time samples in which a particular behavior occurred.

Summary

In sum, the process of data collection is perhaps the most significant single undertaking in behavioral research. It is only with objective data that meaningful scientific comparisons can be made. There are four basic classes of data in behavioral science: (1) magnitude data, (2) temporal data, (3) frequency data, and (4) categorical data. These classes often are used in conjunction with one another and testify to the variety of useful measures in behavioral research. Methods of data collection are generally of two types: continuous and sampling. There are several formats for data collection; two frequently used ones are actual counts and all-or-none classification.

Research design

In behavior modification, the collection of data allows one to determine whether behavior has changed. For example, treatment might be given to clients who have an intense fear of heights. Usually, data are collected before and after treatment to determine whether the fear has changed. In some behavioral interventions, data are collected while the treatment program is in effect as well as before and after treatment. For example, parents of a child with temper tantrums might observe the frequency of tantrums over several days prior to implementing a behavior-change program. Eventually a program might be implemented to eliminate tantrums. Data on frequency of tantrums would be collected while the program was in effect to see if there was a change. Assessment of behavior while a program is in effect allows one to alter the program if behavior is not changing. The collection of data is needed to evaluate behavior change. Objective measures of behavior change are the most convincing demonstration of therapeutic improvement. Objective measures represent a distinct improvement over subjective judgment and anecdotal information, which are sometimes relied upon exclusively in clinical work. Sometimes subjective judgments reflect improvement although objective behavioral data do not. For example, judgments of parents or teachers about behavior change in their children or students often do not correspond to actual behavioral data (Kazdin 1973a; Schnelle 1974). It has been found that even behavioral observers' subjective evaluations of data they have collected may not correspond with the actual data (Kent, O'Leary, Diament, and Dietz 1974).

The experimental design

Data collection is a necessary but not sufficient means of treatment evaluation. Although data can determine whether behavior has changed, it can never explain *why* it has changed. Clients may improve in their performance on the dependent measures after receiving treatment or while treatment is in effect. Yet this does not mean that the treatment *caused* the behavior change.[2] To determine the cause of behavior change requires more than merely gathering data. The scientist must arrange a situation so that a causal relation can be demonstrated between certain conditions, such as treatment intervention, and behavior. The manner in which the situation is arranged in order to evaluate the effect of treatment intervention or some independent variable is referred to as the *experimental design.* The purpose of the experimental design is to structure the situation in such a fashion that the cause of behavior change can be unambiguously demonstrated. The importance and the essential features of the experimental design can be seen by examining a case study. A case study is not an experimental design but illustrates very clearly the need for experimental design.

The case study

In everyday experience, the case study is perhaps the most commonly relied upon source of information; many of our beliefs are based upon practical notions derived from case material. The case study is a report of the events in an individual's life which supposedly account for given behaviors.

People often make unwarranted conclusions about causal relations

[2] In this chapter, causal relationships will refer to causation as described in Chapter 2.

on the basis of events that happen to one or a few individuals in their experience. The problem is not so much with the number of individuals serving as a basis for information, but rather with the fact that the observations are made in an uncontrolled fashion whereby unambiguous conclusions cannot be drawn. For example, octogenarians often attribute their longevity to one or several factors such as hard work, "clean living," piety, or good eating habits. Certainly, specific factors do cause longevity; yet the precise factors cannot be pinpointed on the basis of one individual's statements about what he *believes* those factors to be. These statements are unsubstantiated inferences based upon uncontrolled observations. They cannot provide evidence for unambiguous relationships between events and consequences.

In psychology, case studies frequently are cited to posit that a given psychotherapeutic intervention is responsible for behavior change. An example of a case study can be seen in an interesting report of treatment for an eleven-year-old girl who suffered from insomnia (Weil and Goldfried 1973). The girl took approximately two hours to fall asleep each night. To ameliorate insomnia, an attempt was made to train the girl to relax while lying in bed. A therapist visited the child at home and attempted to relax her while she was trying to go to sleep. The therapist had the girl alternately tense and relax her muscles to develop deep muscle relaxation. The girl responded favorably and fell asleep within one hour rather than the usual amount of time. The therapist then made a thirty-minute tape recording of the relaxation instructions. The girl used the tape by herself for two weeks, typically falling asleep during the tape or immediately after its completion. Relaxation tapes of shorter duration were gradually introduced until a tape of only five minutes was used. Eventually, all tapes were eliminated and the girl was told to concentrate on self-relaxation (that is, giving herself instructions to relax). The parents indicated that insomnia continued not to be a problem 6 months after treatment had terminated.

This case study is interesting because it indicates that a person with a difficult problem was successfully treated. In the absence of objective data such as the actual records of the onset of sleep, we cannot be certain of the precise extent of improvement. However, we can assume that there was some change. Certainly the implication from such a case study is that treatment was responsible for behavior change. Yet there is no way to determine whether treatment caused the change. A number of influences may have been responsible for change. Life events other than the therapy may have altered the significance of the problem or may have eliminated the sources of stress. Improvement may have resulted merely from meeting with a therapist, receiving reassurance, or from other factors. In short, in a case study there is no way to determine whether change resulted from a specific treatment or whether it would have occurred in time without treatment.

In behavior modification, a variety of experimental designs are used to determine whether a given intervention is responsible for behavior change. Basically, two major design categories are used: *intrasubject* and *intersubject* designs. In an *intrasubject design* the performance of an individual or group of individuals is compared across different conditions over time. Behavior of the individual or group is assessed under two or more conditions. For example, the effect of parental praise on the amount of time a child practices a musical instrument might be examined. The amount of time the child practices when the parents are providing praise would be assessed. The results would be compared with the amount of practice time when the parents are not providing praise. During alternating weeks the parents might offer praise for practice and then withdraw praise for practice. The difference in the amount of practice time across these alternating conditions would reveal the effect of praise.

In an *intersubject design,* the performance of two or more groups, each of which is exposed to a different intervention, is compared. For example, the effect of praise upon child behavior might be evaluated by giving praise to one group of subjects for a particular response but not to another group of subjects. The effect would be evaluated by comparing the average performance of the two groups.

The two design categories do not represent uncompromising extremes; it is possible to combine these designs. The present discussion will focus on major versions of intrasubject and intersubject designs.[3] We will present various issues and will evaluate the several designs, but this does not imply that one design is inherently better and should always be used. An experimental design is a research tool and the experimenter should utilize the one which best helps to answer the posed experimental question.

Intrasubject experimental designs

Reversal or ABAB design. In a number of programs, the effects of different procedures are evaluated by comparing the performance of an individual or several individuals under different experimental conditions. Specifically, data are collected on the frequency (or some other measure) of a certain behavior, such as tantrums, in a single individual or group. Observations are usually made for several days prior to any treatment intervention. The rate of behavior prior to treatment or in-

[3] Additional versions of these designs and design combinations may be obtained from the Suggested Readings.

tervention is referred to as the *baseline* or *operant rate.* The period during which the baseline rate of behavior is assessed is referred to as the *baseline* or *A phase.* After a pattern of behavior emerges and performance is relatively stable, a particular program is implemented to alter behavior. The phase during which a program or treatment intervention is being implemented is referred to as the *treatment* or *B phase.* Data are gathered throughout baseline and treatment phases to determine whether behavior changes. If behavior changes after the program is implemented, this does not necessarily mean that the program was responsible for the change. Additional phases are required to determine what caused the change. After the program is in effect for some time and a consistent pattern is evident, the program may be withdrawn temporarily. This third phase is referred to as a *reversal phase* and is usually a re-introduction of the conditions which were in effect during the initial baseline phase. If behavior reverts to baseline levels when the program is withdrawn, this strongly suggests that the program was responsible for change. To increase the plausibility of this conclusion, the program is reinstated in the final phase of the experiment. If behavior again changes when the intervention is implemented, this is a clear demonstration that the intervention was responsible for the change. Of course, in an applied setting where one is attempting to modify an undesirable behavior it is always essential to undertake this final phase.

To illustrate the reversal design, let us consider a psychiatric patient in a hospital ward who engages in frequent complaining about fellow patients and staff. We will assume that the complaints have no basis, in fact, but have continued for a long time. The staff may wish to eliminate the complaints and may employ a reversal design to demonstrate the effect of the treatment procedure used to achieve this goal. To establish a baseline, they may record the daily frequency of complaints. After a stable rate of complaints emerges and the extent of the problem is clear, the staff may begin specific procedures to reduce complaints. For example, the staff may ignore the patient whenever he or she complains. This may represent a change from the usual routine in which staff is likely to listen to the complaints. During the program, staff may simply walk away from the patient when complaining begins. Also, the staff may provide copious attention to the patient when he or she is not complaining. Under this procedure, the frequency of complaints may decline. To evaluate whether ignoring complaints and providing attention for noncomplaints is responsible for change, a reversal phase may be implemented. During this phase, the baseline conditions would be reinstated, with the staff again providing attention for complaints. In the final phase, the program to reduce

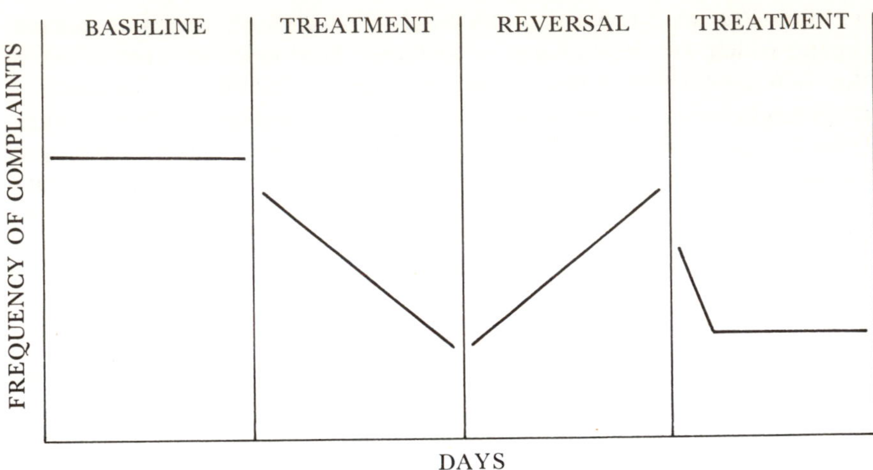

Figure 4-1 Hypothetical data from a program designed to reduce complaints

complaints would be implemented again. Figure 4-1 presents hypothetical data indicating that the program was effective. Was the treatment responsible for the change? A decrease in complaints when the program was in effect and the increase in complaints when the program was temporarily withdrawn strongly suggest that treatment was the crucial ingredient.

Such a design is referred to as a reversal design because the phases are alternated or reversed; after baseline the program is first implemented, then withdrawn or altered in some fashion, and then implemented again. Behavior usually reverses as the phases are altered. The design is also referred to as an ABAB design because baseline (A) and treatment (B) phases are alternated to demonstrate that treatment was responsible for the observed change.

Evaluation of the reversal design. The reversal design has been used extensively with single subjects and with groups, such as children in a classroom or patients in a psychiatric ward. Although the design can determine a causal relationship between behavior and an experimental intervention, there are some limitations in its use. First, changed behaviors sometimes do not reverse when the program is temporarily withdrawn (Kazdin 1975b). Behavior may remain at the level achieved during treatment. Thus, in the foregoing example, the patient might not have increased complaints when the program was temporarily withdrawn. If the behavior does not reverse or approach baseline when treatment is withdrawn or altered, it suggests that the program may not be responsible for the change. Behavior change may be a function of some event occurring simultaneously with the program.

Behavior may not reverse during withdrawal of treatment for another reason. Often, changes in behavior alter the environment in a way that supports and maintains the behavior change. For example, a child might be trained to interact socially with peers by receiving praise from a teacher or parent. When praise is withdrawn, this behavior may not reverse because the favorable consequences associated with peer interaction now maintain the behavior. Although teacher or parent praise may have been responsible for the initial behavior change, the behavior may now be maintained by consequences provided by peers. Because of failure of the behavior to reverse, a reversal design would not show what caused the behavior change.[4]

A second problem with the reversal design is that it is often undesirable or even unethical to show a reversal in a behavior even if a reversal can be achieved. For example, a program might be effective in altering extremely aggressive behavior in a child. However, few people would be willing to withdraw the program temporarily and permit an increase in aggressive behavior. There may be no clear justification for making the individual "worse" and possibly endangering others by purposefully encouraging an increase in aggressive behavior.

Reversal designs have been used extensively in situations where a temporary reversal in behavior is not harmful to the individual. The reversal phase need not be long. Sometimes the program needs only to be altered or withdrawn for a few days. Once the behavior reverts toward baseline, treatment can be reinstated immediately. It should be emphasized that the purpose of the reversal design is to obtain causal knowledge about behavior change. This knowledge is essential for scientific validation of treatments. In many instances, temporary worsening of behavior must be avoided. Fortunately, there are a number of other designs that can be used when one of the aforementioned limitations causes an investigator to have reservations about employing a reversal design.

Multiple-baseline designs. In multiple-baseline designs, a causal relationship between treatment and behavior is demonstrated by showing that behavior changes when treatment is introduced at several different points in time (Baer, Wolf, and Risley 1968; Kazdin 1973b). However, this is accomplished without a reversal procedure.

There are several types of multiple-baseline designs, one of which is a *multiple-baseline design across behaviors.* Baseline data are gathered across two or more behaviors in a given individual or group. After the behaviors have stabilized, a treatment may be introduced for the first

[4] Procedures that increase the likelihood that a behavior will reverse have been outlined elsewhere (Hersen and Barlow 1976; Kazdin 1975a, 1976b).

behavior while baseline data continue to be gathered for the other behaviors. The first behavior should change while the other behaviors should not. If this is the case, the experimental intervention is introduced for the second behavior. Treatment for other behaviors is introduced at different points in time. Throughout the program, data are gathered on all behaviors. The treatment effect is demonstrated if each behavior changes only when the treatment intervention is introduced and not before then.

A multiple-baseline design might be used to evaluate a classroom program directed toward improving the accuracy of academic performance across three areas such as arithmetic, spelling, and reading comprehension. In each area, students complete daily assignments. The percentage of correct answers can serve as the measure of performance. The teacher records accuracy in each area to obtain baseline data. After several days, the teacher begins a program designed to improve accuracy. The teacher tells the class that students who improve by a given percentage (for example, 10 percent higher than their baseline average or over 90 percent accuracy in arithmetic) can have an extra 10 minutes of afternoon recess. The extra recess time depends upon arithmetic performance and not upon spelling or reading accuracy. However, data are continuously gathered on all three behaviors. Accuracy in arithmetic should change while accuracy in the other areas should not. After a while, the program is extended to include a second behavior, accuracy in spelling. The class is told that to earn extra recess time a student must show improvement in *both* arithmetic and spelling for that day. After a few more days the last behavior, reading comprehension, is added to the requirement so that an extra 10 minutes of recess is earned only if improvement is shown in all three areas.

Was the program effective? Figure 4-2 shows that accuracy improved in a given area only when the recess privilege was provided for that behavior and suggests that the program caused an increase in accuracy.

Another version of the multiple-baseline design is the *multiple-baseline design across individuals,* in which baseline data are gathered for a single behavior across two or more individuals. After data are gathered separately for each individual, treatment is applied to the behavior of one individual. Baseline observations are continued for the other individuals. After the behavior of each individual shows a clear pattern, treatment is applied to another individual. The contingency is introduced to all other individuals at different points in time until everyone has been included in the program. For example, the multiple-baseline design across individuals might be used to alter the academic

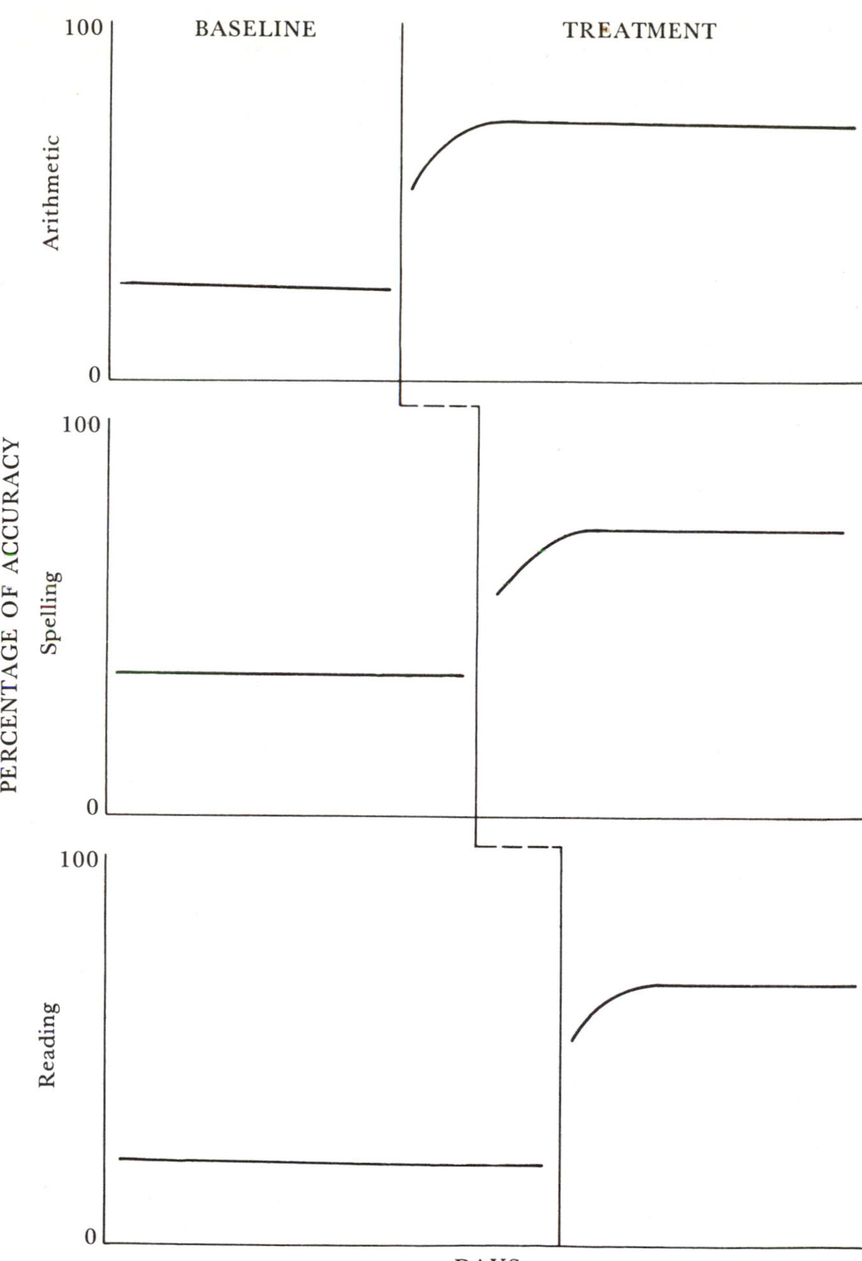

Figure 4-2 Hypothetical data from a program designed to increase academic performance across three areas

performance of three students. The recess privilege, mentioned earlier, might be given to one student for high levels of academic performance while baseline conditions (no privilege) are continued for the other students. Eventually, each student could earn the privilege contingent upon academic performance. The contingency would be introduced to each individual at a different point in time.

Another version of the design is a *multiple-baseline across situations.* In this version, baseline data are gathered across a given behavior for one individual or a group of individuals across two or more situations. After baseline data are obtained across all situations, treatment is introduced to alter behavior in the first situation. The program is introduced at different points in time for the remaining situations. For example, the recess privilege might be used to change academic behavior across two different class periods, namely, morning and afternoon class sessions. Baseline data would be gathered on academic performance during the morning and afternoon each day. Then the students would be informed that 10 extra minutes of recess could be earned by a predetermined amount of improvement in academic performance during the morning. The privilege would initially be withheld from the afternoon session. Eventually it would be extended to the afternoon session. Behavior should change when and only when the recess privilege is introduced for each session.

Evaluation of multiple-baseline designs. In the multiple-baseline design across different behaviors, individuals, or situations, a baseline phase is followed by a treatment phase. No reversal is required. A causal relationship is demonstrated if behavior changes when and only when treatment is introduced. Under some circumstances, the design may not demonstrate a causal relationship between treatment and behavior. This occurs when the introduction of the treatment has widespread effects and one behavior change in an individual alters other behaviors as well. For example, in one study a preschool child was praised for using play equipment. Not only did this behavior increase, but social interaction with peers increased as well (Buell, Stoddard, Harris, and Baer 1968). In such a situation, a multiple-baseline design across behaviors would not show clearly that the treatment caused the change.

Similarly, in a multiple-baseline design across individuals, altering the behavior of one individual may change the behavior of others. For example, it has been shown that providing attention to a child for appropriate classroom behavior sometimes increases the appropriate behavior of other students as well (Broden, Bruce, Mitchell, Carter, and Hall 1970; Kazdin 1973c). In such situations, the multiple-baseline design across individuals would not show that the contingency resulted in the change in behavior.

Finally, in a multiple-baseline design across situations, behavior change in one situation sometimes carries over to other situations. For example, in a program with psychiatric patients, talking was increased in a restricted laboratory room. Even though the attempt to modify this behavior occurred only in a restricted setting, talking increased on the ward (Bennett and Maley 1973). Use of a multiple-baseline design across settings would not have yielded clear results in this situation. Such problems with demonstrating a clear causal relationship between treatment and behavior in multiple-baseline designs do not occur often. Thus, the designs generally are quite useful, particularly in situations where a reversal phase could present problems or where behavior change is desired across different behaviors, different individuals, or different situations.

Changing-criterion design. Another intrasubject design to demonstrate the effect of treatment is the changing-criterion design (Axelrod, Hall, Weis, and Rohrer 1974). No reversal is required, nor are multiple-baseline data gathered across different behaviors. The design begins with a baseline phase at which time data are gathered for a single behavior. After the baseline rate is established, treatment is introduced. The treatment may consist of rewarding a particular behavior. Early in the program the criterion for receiving the reward may be relatively undemanding. As behavior changes, the criterion for earning the reward is changed. As further progress is shown, the criterion is continually changed. If behavior changes as the criterion for the reward is altered, one may conclude that the program is responsible for the change.

A changing-criterion design might be useful in demonstrating the effect of a particular program to alter the caloric intake of someone who is trying to lose weight. Baseline data might consist of daily number of calories consumed. After a stable or consistent pattern of calorie consumption emerges, the spouse or roommate of the client may decide to provide a monetary incentive (two dollars daily) for showing a reduction in caloric intake. Baseline may have revealed an average daily consumption of 3,000 calories—more than are needed to maintain the ideal weight of most individuals. At the beginning of the incentive program, the daily requirement to earn the reward may be relatively undemanding. For the first few days two dollars may be earned if 2,800 or fewer calories per day are consumed. As the criterion is met over a few days, it may be altered to 2,700 or 2,600 until the desired caloric intake is set as the criterion. The criterion is changed gradually as behavior matches the level that has been set. Figure 4-3 presents data from a weight control program based upon monetary incentives for calorie consumption. Was the program responsible for

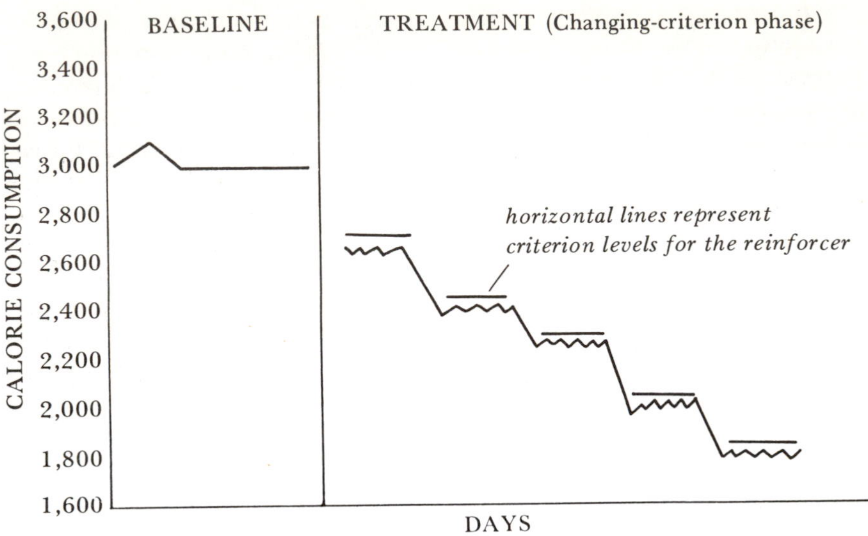

Figure 4-3 Hypothetical data from a program designed to decrease calorie consumption

the change? It appears that the program did cause the change, since calorie consumption closely followed changes in the criterion.

Evaluation of the changing-criterion design. The changing-criterion design provides a fairly clear demonstration of a causal relationship if a behavior change correlates closely with changes in criterion as the latter is altered throughout treatment. The design is suited to those situations in which performance can be changed gradually and the final goal is reached in a series of steps. So that the performance criterion can be repeatedly altered, attainment of the goal must be gradual. Certainly, there would be a problem in the design if the performance criterion required a moderate change, such as reduction in the number of cigarettes smoked or alcoholic beverages consumed, but the behavior change was dramatic, such as elimination of smoking or drinking. In cases where the behavior does not closely follow the criterion, it is possible that something other than treatment accounted for the behavior change. Even when the criterion is followed by the change in behavior, it is possible that some concurrent event is responsible for the change. If behavior changes in the desired direction during the program for reasons other than the program, it may appear to be following changes in the criterion. Thus, the changing-criterion design does not give the clearest demonstration of a causal relationship between the behavior and the program.

Intersubject experimental designs

An alternative to intrasubject experimentation is evaluation and comparison of groups. With *intersubject* designs, the effect of a given independent variable or treatment is evaluated primarily between groups rather than within subjects or groups over time (see Underwood 1957). Usually, two or more groups receive different treatments. As with the intrasubject design, the goal is to arrive at a conclusion about the effects of treatment. However, the conclusion is reached by comparing a group that receives the treatment intervention with another group that does not. Of course, in order to conclude that any differences between groups are due to their differential treatment, the groups should be similar prior to treatment. To reduce the likelihood that groups differ prior to treatment, individuals are assigned *randomly* to groups. Assignment to groups must be unbiased. This may be accomplished by using numbers drawn from a random numbers table, selecting numbers from a hat, and so on. If bias enters into the assignment of subjects to groups then performance on the dependent measure might be due to the initial differences rather than to the effects of treatment.

Control group experimental design. The control group experimental design includes at least two groups whose subjects have been randomly assigned. One group receives treatment; the other does not. Both groups are usually assessed before and after treatment on the dependent measure. The differences between groups at the end of treatment can then be evaluated to determine the effect of treatment.

If only a single group is used, any changes in its performance over time cannot be attributed to treatment. For example, a group of depressive clients may complete psychological measures of depression, undergo treatment for several weeks, and then undergo reassessment on the dependent measures. Posttreatment performance may reveal a substantial decrease in depression. Was treatment responsible for the change? The question cannot be answered in the situation described here. With the same amount of time between initial and final assessment, an untreated group might experience a similar reduction in depression. Having the group retake the test may have resulted in improved performance whether or not treatment was provided. A reduction in depression may occur for other reasons as well. Some individuals may be less depressed because they are no longer preoccupied with events that were once viewed with despair. Furthermore, events other than therapy, such as new social acquaintances, changes in employment, world or local events, may influence performance. There are a number of other interpretations of such changes over time (see Campbell and Stanley 1963; Underwood 1957). The point remains that without a no-treatment control group, a single group measured before and after treatment is equivalent to the case study. The use of an equivalent control group excludes a variety of alternative interpretations of the results.

To show the effects of treatment for depression, clients can be assigned randomly to the treatment or no-treatment control group. When the treatment subjects complete therapy, both groups are reassessed on the dependent measures. If there are differences in the reassessment data, it is likely that treatment accounted for the change. Hypothetical data comparing treatment and no-treatment groups are presented in Figure 4-4. Was treatment responsible for the change? The results suggest that extraneous factors such as repeated testing on the dependent measure or a progressive reduction in depression over time were not responsible. If these factors were responsible for the improvement, both treated and control groups should have improved equally. The differences appear to be the result of treatment.

Evaluation of the control group design. The basic control group design can determine a causal relationship between treatment and behavior change. However, it provides limited information. Additional groups are required to pose finer questions for investigation. Let us consider a therapy technique, nude group marathons, which is said to provide a wide range of therapeutic benefits (Bindrim 1969). In nude group marathons individuals discuss emotionally significant material

Figure 4-4 Hypothetical data comparing treatment and no-treatment groups participating in a study on reducing depression

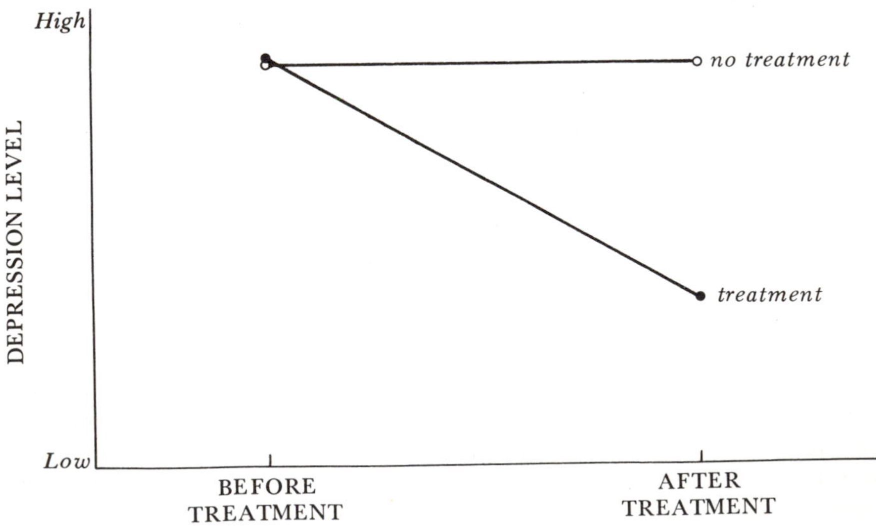

(personal problems and sources of anxiety) and meet for an extended period of time (an entire weekend). During some portion of the marathon, individuals conduct their discussion while undressed.

An important question for investigation is whether nude marathons are effective in reducing anxiety in social situations, one of the supposed therapeutic effects. This question might be answered by use of the basic control group design with two groups, a treatment group and a no-treatment control group. Prior to the investigation all individuals are assessed on interpersonal anxiety, the dependent measure. Assessment might take place during an interview in which various behaviors of the client such as number of stutters or eye contact with the interviewer could be measured. All individuals would be randomly assigned to one of the two groups. (To satisfy the requirements of the experimental design, the control group may not receive treatment initially, although they may receive treatment after the experiment is completed.)

At the end of treatment, let us suppose that clients in the nude marathon group demonstrate less interpersonal anxiety than clients in the no-treatment group. This demonstrates that treatment was more effective than no treatment. While this knowledge is important, it is limited. Was participation in nude marathon therapy important or would *any* therapy have shown such a difference? When individuals *expect* to improve in therapy, they may improve independently of the actual technique to which they are exposed. Also, merely visiting with other individuals (not even under the guise of treatment) may have some therapeutic effect. Although treatment was better than no treatment, it is unclear whether (1) a specific ingredient in the nude marathon session, (2) participation in treatment per se, or (3) the expectation of the therapist was responsible for the change. To answer more analytic questions such as these, the basic control group design must be expanded.

The basic design can be expanded by adding groups to answer different questions. The major purpose of adding groups is to control for various events that may account for behavior change and to exclude rival interpretations of the results (Campbell and Stanley 1963). Different groups can be used to determine which components of treatment are the crucial ingredients in altering behavior.

For example, nude marathons consist of three important ingredients: (1) discussion of emotionally valenced material; (2) participation in an extended session, perhaps for a few days; and (3) undressing during the session. Merely demonstrating that treatment is better than no treatment does not reveal whether anything peculiar to nude marathons is therapeutic or what specific ingredients might be therapeutic.

It would be useful to add various groups to the basic design of treatment and no-treatment groups. Perhaps in one control group clients would be exposed to a procedure that excludes the crucial features of marathon therapy. Clients might merely come to therapy, discuss mundane events rather than personally significant problems, have a short session or sessions rather than a marathon, and stay clothed rather than undress. According to the rationale underlying nude marathon therapy this treatment should not be very effective. This control group is not provided with any of the supposedly essential treatment components. If this group improves, it probably would be due in part to changes that could be attributed simply to coming to therapy per se. In another control group, clients might receive ingredients 1 and 2 but not ingredient 3. This group would discuss emotionally valenced material for an extended period of time but would not undress. The progress made by this group would reveal the contribution of nudity in changing behavior. Another control group might receive ingredients 1 and 3 but not ingredient 2. These clients would discuss emotionally valenced material and undress but would have short sessions rather than an extended meeting. This group would control for the influence of the marathon feature of nude marathon therapy. A final group might include ingredients 2 and 3 while omitting ingredient 1. These clients would meet for an extended period of time and undress, but would be permitted to discuss only mundane events rather than emotionally valenced material. At this point we have added four groups to the basic control group design. The groups include:

1. Nude marathon therapy (ingredients 1, 2, and 3).
2. Therapy sessions alone (none of the three ingredients).
3. Nude marathon without nudity (ingredients 1 and 2 only).
4. Nude marathon without extended meeting (ingredients 1 and 3 only).
5. Nude marathon without discussing emotional material (ingredients 2 and 3 only).
6. No treatment (none of the ingredients, and no sessions of any kind).

Other groups could be added which provide only one of the ingredients at a time. At the end of the marathon, when all subjects are reassessed, it is important to compare the different groups. It may be that all groups that receive some form of treatment improved equally in reducing interpersonal anxiety and only the no-treatment group experienced no improvement. Such a result would suggest that nude marathons have no uniquely successful features. Merely spending time in a session discussing any material and expecting therapeutic change could account for the results.

Variations in control group design are unlimited depending upon the questions the investigator wishes to ask. All possible control groups are not used; only those that help answer the questions that provided the impetus for the study are included.

Factorial designs. In many instances, merely elaborating the basic control group design will not answer all the questions of interest. Factorial designs are control group designs in which two or more variables are examined simultaneously, permitting evaluation of separate and combined effects of each variable. To continue the above example, the investigator may wish to evaluate the combined and separate effects of two independent variables such as the length of time of the session (a few hours versus a few days) and material discussed in the session (emotionally significant material versus mundane topics). This would require four groups (see Figure 4-5). At the end of treatment it will be possible to determine the effect of length of the marathon session alone by comparing groups 1 and 2 with groups 3 and 4. It will also be possible to examine the effect of the material discussed during the session by comparing groups 1 and 3 with groups 2 and 4. Finally, it will be possible to examine whether the effect of duration of the session depended upon the kind of material discussed (that is, the combined or interactive effects). It may be that discussing emotionally significant material is helpful only when the session is long and individuals can resolve some of the problems and anxieties that are aroused. Thus, discussion of emotionally significant material might be helpful in group 1 but not in group 3. The groups must be compared to determine this.

MATERIAL DISCUSSED	LENGTH OF SESSION: Few hours	LENGTH OF SESSION: Few days
Emotional topics	1	3
Mundane topics	2	4

Figure 4-5 Factorial design with four groups examining the effect on treatment outcome of the topic discussed in therapy and the length of session

Evaluation of factorial designs. Factorial designs are useful for two major reasons. First, they can determine the manner in which independent variables combine or interact to affect behavior. A variable that may seem important alone may depend for its effect upon other variables that are also operative. Second, the effects of several variables can be examined simultaneously in a single experiment. The experiment can answer a number of questions that would otherwise require separate experiments. In terms of utilization of clients, personnel, and time, a single study with several variables is more efficient than several individual studies. Because of these advantages, factorial designs are commonly used in psychological research.

Summary

Data collection is a prerequisite to scientific research. In behavior modification, data collection can be accomplished in a variety of ways. Four classes of data are magnitude, temporal, frequency, and categorical data. Continuous data collection and sampling procedures are two methods of data collection. The format of data collection may vary; two frequently employed formats are actual counts and all-or-none classification. Data collected in behavior modification programs tell the therapist whether behavior is changing. Because the goal of treatment is to alter behavior, careful assessment of change is essential. However, objective evidence of behavior change does not explain *why* behavior changes.

To assess the reasons for behavior change, an experimental design is necessary. Experimental designs are classified according to whether intrasubject or intersubject comparisons are made to infer a relationship between treatment and behavior change. Intrasubject designs include reversal, multiple-baseline, and changing-criterion designs. Intersubject designs include control group and factorial designs. The purpose of these designs is to rule out factors other than the treatment intervention which could account for changes in behavior.

Suggested readings

DATA COLLECTION

Bijou, S. W.; Peterson, R. F.; Harris, F. R.; Allen, K. E.; and Johnston, M. S. Methodology for experimental studies of young children in natural settings. *Psychological Record,* 1969, *19,* 177–210.

Kazdin, A. E. *Behavior modification in applied settings.* Homewood, Ill.: Dorsey Press, 1975. Chapter 4.

Peterson, D. R. *The clinical study of social behavior.* New York: Appleton-Century-Crofts, 1968.

RESEARCH DESIGN

Baer, D. M.; Wolf, M. M.; and Risley, T. R. Some current dimensions of applied behavior analysis. *Journal of Applied Behavior Analysis,* 1968, *1,* 91–97.

Campbell, D. T., and Stanley, J. C. *Experimental and quasi-experimental designs for research.* Chicago: Rand McNally, 1966.

Crano, W. D., and Brewer, M. B. *Principles of research in social psychology.* New York: McGraw-Hill, 1973.

Hersen, M., and Barlow, D. H. *Strategies for studying behavior change.* New York: Pergamon, 1976.

Kazdin, A. E. Methodological and assessment considerations in evaluating reinforcement programs in applied settings. *Journal of Applied Behavior Analysis,* 1973, *6,* 517–531.

Underwood, B. J. *Psychological research.* New York: Appleton-Century-Crofts, 1957.

Data analysis and interpretation

5

As we saw in the last chapter, the collection of objective data is a prerequisite for scientific comparisons. But the collection of data alone does not ensure that the data can be unambiguously interpreted. One must be able to evaluate the meaningfulness of observational or experimental evidence. Evaluation of the data derives from comparisons of the data obtained. These comparisons constitute data analysis. Comparisons on the dependent variable usually are among performances at different points in time for an individual or group (intrasubject designs) or between different groups (intersubject designs). Once the comparisons have been made, or the data analyzed, the results must be interpreted.

There are two basic approaches to data analysis; namely, nonstatistical data analysis and statistical data analysis. *Nonstatistical data analysis* is most often applied to intrasubject experimental designs. Conversely, *statistical data analysis* is regularly applied to intersubject designs. There are exceptions, of course, and statistical analysis can be used in the evaluation of results from intrasubject designs (Gottman and Lieblum 1974; Kazdin 1976b). However, investigators who employ intrasubject designs tend either to avoid or to minimize the use of statistical tests (Michael 1974).

Nonstatistical data analysis

A basic characteristic of nonstatistical data analysis is that it involves simple visual inspection of the data. Sidman (1960) refers to this evaluation procedure as "criterion-by-inspection." The inspection usually involves comparison of graphic data in the form of lines (slopes) or the height of data columns under different conditions such as baseline and treatment phases. As indicated earlier, investigators employing intrasubject designs tend to use the nonstatistical method of data analysis. The reasons for this are best understood by elaborating the criteria for nonstatistical data analysis.

Criteria for nonstatistical method

The nonstatistical evaluation of data includes two criteria; namely, the *experimental* evaluation of change and the *therapeutic* evaluation of change (Risley 1970). The *experimental criterion* refers to a comparison between what behavior is (as revealed in baseline) and what behavior would have been had the experimental procedures *not* been introduced (Risley 1970). (The experimental criterion applies to both statistical and nonstatistical evaluation procedures.) Studies employing nonstatistical evaluation make this comparison by establishing baseline performance, which serves as a basis for determining the present level of behavior and for predicting what behavior would be like without the intervention. The data collected during the treatment phase of the program may then reveal a change from the projected or predicted performance. Within a reversal design the reliability of a finding is achieved by replicating the baseline level of performance and the different level of performance achieved during the intervention. Other intrasubject designs make different comparisons to project what performance would be if treatment were not implemented; for example, a baseline can be made across several behaviors as in the multiple-baseline design across behaviors.

In practice, there are few ways in which the results may clearly meet the experimental criterion for nonstatistical evaluation. First, performance during the treatment intervention, when plotted graphically, may not overlap with performance during baseline. For example, a treatment program may be introduced for a hospitalized psychiatric patient who makes frequent bizarre verbalizations. After baseline rates of bizarre verbalizations on the ward are assessed, some intervention may be introduced to decrease or eliminate them. Hypothetical data are plotted across the initial baseline and treatment phases in Figure 5-1(*a*). Note that the values of the data points in baseline do not approach any of the values of the data points during treatment. If these results were replicated over time with the same subject (reversal design) or across other subjects (multiple-baseline design), there would be little question that the treatment resulted in a behavior change.

A more typical, but less stringent, procedure for experimental evaluation is related to nonoverlapping slopes in baseline and treatment phases. This criterion emphasizes the trends in each phase. Usually, the baseline phase is not terminated if there is a trend toward improvement in the behavior that is to be changed. Since experimental evaluation depends upon extrapolating how performance would be if no intervention were made, it is important to have a stable rate of behavior during baseline. If there is a trend, it should be opposite from the direction that is to be achieved with the intervention. In any case, baseline usually shows a relatively stable performance rate with no particular trend. If we are to conclude that treatment had an effect, a definite trend should be evident indicating that behavior is changing from baseline. Figure 5-1(*b*) shows hypothetical data for the patient mentioned earlier. When treatment was introduced the data began to show a trend that differed from the baseline trend. The data points during treatment overlap with those of baseline, although the trend during treatment reveals a marked change. Ordinarily, the intervention is continued until the trend is stable, indicating that continued intervention would bring behavior that is vastly different from baseline behavior. If baseline conditions are re-implemented for a reversal phase, the trend is likely to be in the opposite direction from that in the treatment phase. By alternating baseline and treatment phases, one can be convinced of the effect of the intervention even though the data points across phases may overlap.

The second criterion employed for nonstatistical data analysis—the therapeutic criterion—is unique and distinguishes nonstatistical from statistical data evaluation. The *therapeutic criterion* for nonstatistical evaluation measures whether behavior has changed in a manner that is of applied or clinical importance. Behavior must change enough to enhance an individual's functioning in a given context. Therapeutic evaluation of a program is achieved by comparing the behavior change required for a given individual to function adequately in society or in a particular setting and the level achieved as a result of the program (Risley 1970). For example, a behavior modification program may be implemented to alter delusional statements in a psychiatric patient. Sampling behavior over several days of baseline may reveal that a patient engages in a daily average of 50 delusional statements in a 3-hour period. A procedure may be implemented to reduce or eliminate the statements. The results might indicate that delusional statements decreased to a daily average of 30 statements in a 3-hour period—a clear difference from baseline. But is this change of applied significance?

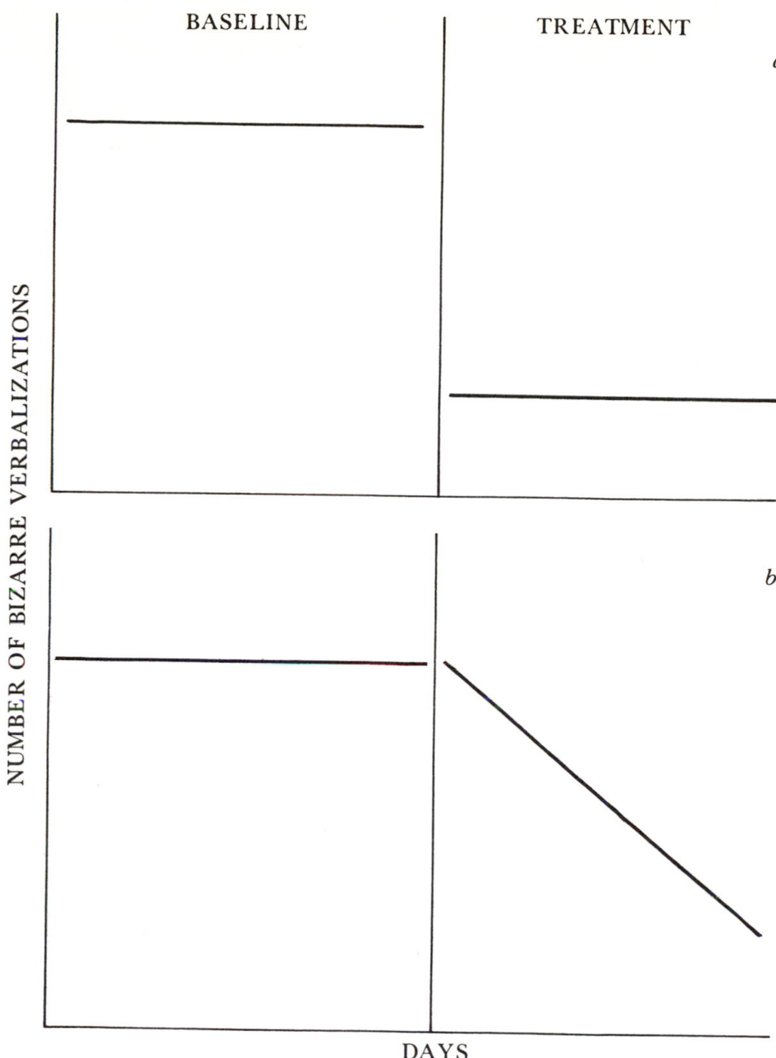

Figure 5-1 Hypothetical data showing nonoverlapping distributions (*a*) and changes in trend (*b*) across baseline and treatment phases

Investigators who rely on nonstatistical evaluation, as well as individuals in contact with the patient, probably would not be pleased with such a change. Although the change might be highly reliable and clearly due to the treatment intervention, its applied significance is dubious. Even with the intervention, delusional statements are not eliminated or reduced to a negligible level. It is unlikely that there is a significant change in the patient's life. Because of the frequency of bizarre statements, the patient still could not function in a community without censure of peers, or work on a job without being conspicuous. A change of applied significance would require a much greater reduction of delusional statements.

The precise criterion by which a given change is determined to be of therapeutic or applied significance is difficult to specify because individuals in everyday life (parents, teachers, peers, colleagues, spouse, friends) determine what behaviors are deviant, obnoxious, intolerable, desirable, or acceptable. When a behavior is altered as evidenced by objective data *and* when individuals in contact with the client indicate that behavior is no longer problematic or that the original behavioral goal has been achieved, the program has clearly attained a change of applied significance.

Because of the concern with applied significance, investigators who employ nonstatistical data evaluation focus on independent variables that produce dramatic changes. Variables having only a subtle influence on behavior, at least at present, are given lower priority. The reason for this, of course, is that significant therapeutic results require gross rather than subtle changes in behavior. While subtle independent variables might be interesting in their effects, they would not solve the immediate problem of making a change of therapeutic significance.

Possible shortcomings

There are some possible shortcomings to the nonstatistical approach to data analysis. First, the changes that are referred to as reliable must be very obvious and dramatic. While many regard this as an advantage of the nonstatistical approach, others consider the neglect of subtle variables which effect nondramatic but reliable changes as a disadvantage. Nondramatic but reliable changes represent variables that are relevant for a complete understanding of behavior. Also, variables that by themselves appear to have subtle effects may combine with other variables to produce marked changes in behavior (Kazdin 1975b).

A second potential problem is the lack of clear rules to establish when a finding is not reliable. In some cases, it is not clear whether there is a change over baseline or whether the change is sufficiently dramatic to conclude that the intervention was important (Jones, Weinrott, and Vaught 1975). In cases of doubt, a finding is usually judged unreliable by the scientific community. Of course, a given finding can almost always be subjected to statistical evaluation to determine whether it meets conventional statistical criteria. However, to individuals employing intrasubject designs statistical proof generally is not regarded as relevant. The changes required to obtain a finding of applied significance make statistical proof a relatively weak test.

A final point worth noting is that the method of nonstatistical data analysis is often defended not so much because of its own merits, but rather because of the numerous shortcomings of its only competitor, statistical data analysis. This last point will be explored in the discussion of statistical analysis.

To summarize, data analysis involves an objective comparison of dependent measure values. In the nonstatistical approach, these comparisons usually involve visual inspection of the data. Whether or not a particular intervention effected a change in behavior is evaluated by experimental and therapeutic criteria. The experimental criterion refers to the extent to which behavior during the intervention phase diverges from a projection of what behavior would have been had no intervention occurred. The criterion requires stable baseline rates of behavior so that projections of future behavior without intervention can be made with confidence. The criterion requires replication of the effect of different treatments across an individual or group (as in a reversal design) or across behaviors, individuals, or situations (as in multiple-baseline design). The therapeutic criterion refers to the extent of behavioral change achieved relative to the change required for improved functioning in a given social context. This criterion cannot be evaluated independently of the opinions of those who are in contact with the client.

Ordinarily, the criteria for evaluating change in the nonstatistical approach are stringent. Indeed, statistical evaluation is looked upon by many investigators as a much less stringent technique. Typically, less behavior change is required to achieve statistical confidence than to demonstrate a change of applied significance. A disadvantage of the nonstatistical evaluation of data is that variables that reliably affect behavior but do not show dramatic effects are neglected.

Statistical data analysis

The statistical approach to data analysis employs mathematical procedures in comparing dependent variable values. Although this approach is used predominantly with intersubject investigations, it is also applicable to intrasubject designs (Gottman and Lieblum 1974; Kazdin 1976b). Because of the complexity of the subject matter, our discussion of statistical data analysis will be very rudimentary. The interested reader is urged to consult the Suggested Readings for reference to more comprehensive and detailed accounts.

Basic statistical method

Statistical data analysis involves probability. There are many real-life events that can be assigned a theoretical likelihood or *probability.* For example, when flipping a coin, the probability of obtaining heads is 1/2 or .50. This means that in the long run the coin will come up heads half the time. Now then, imagine a situation in which a friend comes to you with a coin and offers to bet you $10 per coin toss that the coin will come up heads. You might reason that if your friend always chooses heads and you always choose tails you would both come out even in the long run. However, the fact that your friend is so anxious to begin the betting makes you suspect that the coin may not be "fair." You inspect it and see that it has heads and tails. However, the possibility remains that the coin is loaded, or unevenly weighted. You might conceive the following hypothesis: "The coin is loaded in such a way that heads and tails do not come up equally often." The competing hypothesis would be that the coin is fair. Based on your knowledge of statistical data analysis, you might ask your friend to allow some experimentation on the fairness of the coin. You flip the coin 100 times and record the outcome (heads or tails) on each trial. If the coin is indeed fair, the theoretical value of the dependent variable (outcomes) is 50 heads and 50 tails.

As it turns out, the coin comes up heads 82 times and tails 18 times. You might conclude that the coin probably is loaded. If the ratio of heads to tails were 55/45 instead of 82/18 determining its fairness would be much more difficult. However, there are some statistical conventions that might help you in making such a decision. It is possible to assign a probability to the event of 82 percent heads. As you might expect, the probability of a fair coin coming up heads 82 percent of the time is very low.

As a matter of convention, psychologists often choose some standard level of improbability by which to guide their decisions. These levels, called critical significance or simply significance levels, may vary depending on researcher, subject matter, and so on. However, the most common level employed in psychology is 5 percent or .05. *Critical significance level* provides a standardized and objective criterion to evaluate comparisons. It is a means of ensuring that the data probably reflect some *real* difference in dependent variable values rather than some chance variation. In the coin tossing example, the occurrence of 82 percent heads with a fair coin is very improbable. Note that it is not impossible, but only improbable. Indeed, the computed probability of such an occurrence is well below the critical significance level of .05. You are thus fairly well justified in concluding that the coin was not fair. There is a possibility that you are wrong and that the 82 percent heads was just a chance occurrence with a fair coin. However, you must choose some arbitrary cutoff point to guide your decision. If your reservations are strong enough, you can impose a more stringent critical significance level. Thus, you might require that the observed data (82 percent heads) be extremely improbable (for example, less than .01 or

.001) before concluding that the coin is not fair. This would make you less open to the error of rejecting the fair coin hypothesis when it is actually true.

The general paradigm in statistical data analysis may be conceptualized in terms of four stages.

1. A hypothesis is stated.
2. A critical significance level is chosen.
3. Relevant data are collected.
4. The data are analyzed (compared) and interpreted as being supportive, neutral, or nonsupportive of the hypothesis.

Each of these stages was illustrated in the coin tossing example.

It should be noted at this point that statistical data analysis places considerable emphasis on variability in data. As we saw in the foregoing example, some variability in the 50/50 ratio was expected. A ratio of 52/48 or 55/45 is possible. Perhaps a more meaningful illustration of the concept of variability would be helpful. Let us suppose that you are taking a daily record of your weight. You weigh in every evening at approximately the same time. However, you have noticed on past occasions that your bathroom scale does not always give consistent readings. You step on it and it registers 155 pounds. You step off, bite your lip in disbelief, and step back on the scale again. This time it might register 153.5! Bolstered by the apparently instantaneous weight loss, you step off and then back on again. Now it reads 156.5! This variation might be explained by a number of factors, such as weak springs or different foot placements. The important point is that there is an apparent variability in your data. The source might be called chance or uncontrolled variables. In either case, the variability persists and must be taken into account when conclusions about weight loss are entertained. Pursuing the example, you might weigh yourself the following evening and obtain recordings of 152, 153.5, and 151.5. Note that the previous night's data seemed to vary around a central point of 155 pounds. Can we conclude that this central point, your "real" weight, has changed on the second night? Well, the data from the second night also show variability, but their central point does seem to be lower (about 152 pounds). Thus, even taking chance variation into account, there does seem to be a decrease in weight from one night to the next.[1]

[1] This illustration of variability ties in well with the concept of critical significance levels. It is possible that your real weight on the second night was identical to that on the first night. However, if you were allowed to make certain important assumptions (see Hays 1963), you could assign a probability to the event of a registered average weight of 152 when your actual weight was 155. If that probability were less than the chosen critical significance level, then you could reject the hypothesis that the weights were the same on the two evenings.

The concept of *statistical significance* deserves mention at this point. When a given outcome satisfies the critical significance level of improbability, then it is said to have achieved statistical significance at that level. For example, one might statistically analyze the weight data and find that the probability of a chance variation accounting for the divergent readings is less than .05. One could then state that a weight loss which was statistically significant at the .05 level had been observed. In essence, one would be asserting that the probability of such an observation being obtained as a function of "chance" was less than .05. In other words, the probability of obtaining two weight measurements that differ that much, if in fact you really weighed the same on both occasions, is less than .05. In our terms, the comparison of dependent variable values has revealed a statistically significant difference. A difference is statistically significant when it is greater than that which might be expected due to uncontrolled variables and/or random variation.

The statistical approach to data analysis, then, relies heavily on mathematical probabilities, basic assumptions, variability, and critical significance levels. These combine in a way that gives the data analyst a numerical basis for data interpretation. Note that the process of *comparison* is still paramount. Whether the data analysis is statistical or nonstatistical, the core of the analysis involves comparison of specific dependent variable values. In one case, the comparison is made visually; in the other, the comparison is mathematical.

Possible shortcomings

The use of statistical data analysis has been a controversial issue in behavior modification. Many researchers have criticized the statistical approach on several points. Let us explore a few of their arguments and rejoinders offered by statistically oriented behavior modifiers.

The first criticism relates to the obscuring of individual performance. Statistical data analysis is employed predominantly with groups. The argument against statistical measures is that they often summarize group performance without accurately representing any single individual's performance. A popular example is the census report. When the statistics of the Census Bureau indicate that the average family has 2.9 children, there can be little doubt that the statistical representation fails to coincide with any individual instance. Nine-tenths of a child is a rare occurrence! Although it is justified in some instances, this criticism usually meets the rejoinder that there are many situations in which a statistical measure may be representative of the individual performance. Moreover, statistical analyses may correct for the very deviant score of an atypical subject.

A second criticism of statistical data analysis is that it obscures "transition states" (see Sidman 1960). Gradual changes or trends in behavior are often overlooked when traditional before-and-after (pretest to posttest) statistical analyses are made. Nonstatistical analyses often allow one to monitor moment-by-moment changes in behavior. The argument here is that a simple before-and-after comparison of dependent variable values is a very crude method of data analysis. Many relevant behavior changes occur between the pretest and the posttest. The statistician's rejoinder here might be that there are statistical measures that are sensitive to changes over time (Glass, Willson, and Gottmann 1973). The fact that such measures are infrequently employed casts a reflection on the statistical analyst rather than on statistics per se.

A third criticism deals with the distinction between statistical and clinical or practical significance. It is possible and, indeed, common for a statistically significant result to be irrelevant for applied purposes (Hersen and Barlow 1976). A reliable finding may not be of applied significance. This is especially true when extremely large numbers of subjects are employed. The larger the number of individuals used in an intersubject design, the smaller the actual differences required between the groups to achieve statistical significance. For example, we might wish to find out whether individuals in the United States who live east or west of the Mississippi River are the same height. If we measure an extremely large number of individuals in both locations, it is possible for a trivial difference in height, such as .001 inch, to be highly significant statistically. Although the results are statistically significant, they would not be useful in selecting an Olympic basketball team to compete against other countries. The failure of statistical significance to be necessarily of applied or practical significance is conceded by statisticians. Yet often, investigations employing statistical significance are testing predictions based on different theories. Although a particular statistically significant finding may not have applied significance, the ultimate consequences of supporting a given theory may be great.

A fourth criticism relates to the hallowed status of statistical techniques and statistical significance. You are probably aware of the great extent to which statistics are used and perhaps abused in modern advertising. The lay public frequently respects statistics as indisputable evidence. This glorification of statistics is also prevalent in some areas of behavioral science. Many journals will not publish experiments that fail to test for or demonstrate statistical significance. This bias prevents the publication of numerous experiments that may contain extremely important findings. Remember, the data never lie. Failure to obtain a statistically significant difference among dependent variable values may be a very important finding. Unfortunately, the professional emphasis on significance forces many researchers to "persevere until significance." That is, they may try dozens of statistical tests on the same set of data until something of statistical significance is found (Barber 1975). Likewise, the researcher may repeat an experiment over and over until significance is obtained. Recall that the use of a 5 percent or .05 critical significance level of improbability allows for 5 percent of one's "significant" results to occur by chance. Thus, it is possible that one out of every twenty articles in the statistically biased journals is actually reporting on a spurious or chance finding.[2] This criticism has been conceded by statistically oriented researchers (see Neher 1967). A journal publishing negative results, or results that are not statistically significant, has been suggested to alleviate some of the foregoing problems.

These, then, are some of the objections that have been raised regarding statistical data analysis.[3] A more complete understanding of these objections would entail elaboration of statistical methods. The interested reader is urged to consult the Suggested Readings for reference to some of the more comprehensive accounts of statistical data analysis.

To summarize, the statistical approach employs mathematical procedures in comparing dependent variable values. Basic assumptions, variability, probability, and critical significance levels play important roles in statistical data analysis. The role of statistics in behavioral research has been a controversial one (Kazdin 1976b). Some workers have emphasized the advantages of statistics in data analysis; these include objectivity, ability to use formalized mathematical systems, and ability to detect meaningful but nonobvious differences in comparisons. Other researchers have enumerated the disadvantages of statistics, such as obscuration of the individual performance, obscuration of transition states, failure of assumptions, the contrast between statistical and applied or practical significance, and the disproportionate emphasis placed on statistical results. Whether one uses the statistical or nonstatistical approach, however, data analysis always involves a comparison of dependent variable values.

[2] This assumes exact replication of each of those twenty studies. It does not mean that one of twenty *independent* studies should be so evaluated.

[3] A fifth criticism, somewhat more complex than the others, relates to the important assumptions involved in the statistical approach. These are assumptions about the nature of the subject matter under study. When these assumptions are inaccurate, then the application of certain statistical measures is inappropriate. There are many examples of inappropriate statistical applications and failure of assumptions. The rejoinder to this argument is that there are many situations in which such assumptions are of considerably less importance. For example, when dealing with extremely large groups, a failure of assumptions is much less devastating. Furthermore, there are many statistical techniques that require few, if any, assumptions.

The approaches compared

The different approaches to data analysis have been dichotomized purposely to stress extreme views. Although it is true that intrasubject designs are usually analyzed on the basis of nonstatistical criteria and intersubject designs are almost always analyzed statistically, there is an overlap that was not discussed. Statistical evaluation is sometimes used with intrasubject designs. Also, it is possible to combine the features of intrasubject with intersubject designs in one experiment and subject the results to both nonstatistical and statistical evaluation. Ordinarily, individuals who adhere to either a nonstatistical or a statistical approach are emphasizing and evaluating different effects. Nonstatistical evaluation is concerned more with large changes of therapeutic significance and repeated demonstration of the effects with an individual or group. Statistical evaluation is concerned more with comparing differentially treated groups to show reliable changes across groups. Experimentation can benefit tremendously by applying both approaches to a given experiment and then judging the results both statistically and nonstatistically.

Interpretation of data

Once the data have been analyzed, they must be interpreted in terms of their implications for the topic under study. When the experiment has derived from a formal hypothesis, then the data must be evaluated in light of that hypothesis. When experimentation has been of a purely exploratory nature, the data must be interpreted in terms of their meaning for behavioral research. Note, however, that data interpretation is sometimes less objective when hypothesis testing is involved. This may be because a researcher with a vested interest or a pet hypothesis is often biased toward viewing the data as being favorable to that interest. In a sense, he or she may be bending the data to fit a hypothesis. This is especially apparent when the data do not present a clear-cut directionality. To avoid personal biases in such instances, the researcher should either adopt very stringent criteria or allow an independent worker to analyze the data.

One might conceptualize the purposes of data interpretation as being twofold: (1) to evaluate the implications of the data for the particular situation from which they were drawn; and (2) to evaluate their implications for future and similar situations. These purposes correspond roughly to what has been termed internal and external validity (Campbell and Stanley 1963). The first purpose is internal in that it deals with relationships within the experiment performed. The latter, in contrast, pertains to the generality of such relationships.

The interpretation of data is a somewhat nebulous area. Except for the organizational outlines and decision procedures of statistical methods, no standard formula for data interpretation exists. This lack of an agreed upon standard often results in differing interpretations of the same data. Surprising as it may seem, it is not unusual to find researchers citing the same experiment in support of contradictory hypotheses. For example, many of the early studies on the effectiveness of psychotherapy were interpreted in opposite manners by researchers. Although the data are incontestable, their interpretation is certainly open to dispute.

Perhaps the most important point to be stressed in data interpretation is the option of abstention. When the data are insufficient or ambiguous, the researcher should refrain from drawing conclusions. This emphasizes the importance of conservatism in the evaluation of evidence. The researcher should always be inclined to doubt the implications of data. Interpretations must be considered only in a tentative and cautious manner. This stubborn reluctance to concede the implications of one's evidence ensures that scientific conclusions will be reached only in a gradual and cautious manner. The advantages of such a conservatism should be very obvious: incorrect conclusions are thereby avoided. The expense, of course, is one of time and effort. Numerous replications of the evidence are required. However, the result will be a more accurate and reliable basis for scientific conclusions.

In summary, then, data interpretation involves the evaluation of evidence in light of a particular hypothesis or a particular subject matter. Interpretative biases are often encountered due to vested interests in the research. Thus, stringent criteria, objectivity, and conservatism should be emphasized, as they help eliminate ambiguities and contradictory interpretations. The scientific researcher should abstain from directional conclusions when data are either insufficient or ambiguous. Stubborn reluctance to accept premature conclusions is a scientific prerequisite in the interpretation of data.

Summary

Data analysis requires making comparisons on the dependent measures to determine the effect of an independent variable. The two basic approaches to data analysis are nonstatistical and statistical.

Nonstatistical data analysis is usually associated with intrasubject designs. The criteria for evaluating an effect are establishing the replicability of the results (experimental criterion) and the extent to which clinical change has been achieved (therapeutic criterion). Nonstatistical data analysis frequently is employed for interventions that produce dramatic effects readily evident through graphic display and visual inspection of the results.

Statistical data analysis is usually associated with intersubject designs. The analysis relies upon comparisons between groups and upon estimates of the probability that differences can be attributed to chance. Rules regarding probability levels help determine whether a particular difference between groups meets the criterion for statistical significance. A statistical criterion refers to the reliability of a finding rather than its applied or practical importance.

Once the data are analyzed, they must be interpreted. Interpretation serves to evaluate the implications of the data with respect to the particular experiment and the generality of the findings to situations not included in the experiment.

Suggested readings

Gottman, J. M., and Lieblum, S. *How to do psychotherapy and how to evaluate it.* New York: Holt, Rinehart and Winston, 1974.

Hays, W. L. *Statistics for psychologists.* New York: Holt, Rinehart and Winston, 1963.

Kazdin, A. E. Statistical analysis for single-case experimental designs. In M. Hersen and D. Barlow, eds., *Strategies for studying behavior change.* New York: Pergamon, 1976.

Michael, J. Statistical inference for individual organism research: Mixed blessing or curse? *Journal of Applied Behavior Analysis,* 1974, *7,* 647–653.

Part II

Empirical foundations of behavior modification

UNDOUBTEDLY many people will be tempted to begin reading this book with Part II or even Part III, so why should we place Part I first or even include Part I at all? If you have been a good reader and have completed Part I, that becomes a rhetorical question. Within the model of this book, the scientific approach to the study of human behavior—including its assumptions as set forth in Chapters 1 through 5—reigns supreme. It is via this model of methodological behaviorism that we can most expediently and efficiently come to an understanding of behavior. As indicated earlier, this model and its resulting empirical data have been derived from the experimental laboratory. The real contribution of behavior modification has been in the application of that model or approach to clinical and social problems. Part I has come first so that you will have a grasp of the rationale, assumptions, and methodology of behavior modification, as well as an understanding that behavior modification does not represent an arrived-at body of knowledge or procedures. On that basis we can begin discussion, in Parts II and III, of what we do know at this point, without worrying that the reader will assume that is all there is to know about human behavior.

Let us review briefly what we have said thus far. In the opening sentences of this book it was stated that behavior modification is "one of the most exciting and promising developments in contemporary behavioral science." The paragraph goes on to laud the versatility, popularity, expansiveness, and success rate of behavior modification applications. To any but the most avid supporters, statements like these probably sound more like television commercials or drug advertisements than objective descriptions of some development in behavioral science. Ironically, there is some truth to both the opening statements and the television commercial analogy. The behavior modification approach has received increasing attention and application during the last decade. Its success rate, while far from perfect, has been very rewarding, especially when compared with those for prevailing models of clinical intervention. Converts to behavior modification have ranged from traditionally oriented psychotherapists to grandmothers. There have, of course, been a few defectors. Thus, while there is some deserving praise to be accorded behavior modification, an unfortunate "school" aura has developed around it. It is often spoken of as if it were a miracle cure, the ultimate in man's search for behavioral therapeutics, and with the same awe and reverence that the peddler used in selling brain pills and bust developers. To be sure, the success rates have often encouraged enthusiastic predictions and exaggerated inferences; Skinner remarks (in Evans 1969) that one of the characteristic features of the behavior modifier is his enthusiasm. However, many behavior modifiers have fallen into the unfortunate habit of considering learning theory–based behavior modification to be both centrally and exclusively true. The rest of psychology is often talked of as if it were a deranged psychotic whose only glimpses of reality are provided by the behavioral model. In some instances behavioral science is talked of as if it were equivalent to behavior modification, and disciplines like sociology, anthropology, and political science are relegated to questionable positions, in an unscientific limbo. A particular set of principles and procedures is often stretched far beyond its limits—not to mention its data—in an attempt to explain virtually every aspect of behavior. Although this tendency to scientifically deify and consecrate the area of behavior modification is fortunately not as widespread as it once was, its continued presence is still an impediment to the field because it encourages premature smugness in the face of behavioral ignorance. It likewise creates both inter- and intradisciplinary animosities which discourage the free interchange of ideas and information.

The foregoing may have left the reader somewhat puzzled as to our intent. This is supposed to be a book that presents the rationale and methodology of research in behavior modification. It presumes an interest in or acceptance of the behavioral frame of reference. Now, however, we have presented several criticisms of behavior modification. This potentially puzzling act actually stems from our concern for and support of behavior modification. We hope that this book will provide the reader with an appreciation for conservative modesty and *parsimony* in the execution and interpretation of behavior modification research.

The purpose of research—as well as of science in general—is to discover functional relationships among events. The unparsimonious glorification of behavior modification or any other area discourages continuing and expanding research. The mark of a good scientist lies not solely in his ability to speculate or explain, but also in his ability to modestly admit the limitations of his field's knowledge. Finality is one thing that science denies. However, when one describes a field in such glowing terms that it appears to be the ultimate answer, then finality is implied. Such close-mindedness impedes progress in any field of research. If assumptions are erroneously accepted and remain unresearched, they may misguide and retard the delineation of behavioral principles and methods of behavior change. Similarly, if data are squeezed into a specified behavior modification framework (rather than the latter being modified to fit the former), knowledge will again be eluded. If an effective technique is avoided or de-emphasized because it does not fit comfortably into the present behavioral view of things, then behavioral science has been cheated.

It is our intent, then, to point out the ever-present need for objective research. The evaluation and re-evaluation of various techniques, the modification of these techniques according to experimental findings, and the generation of new research ideas are all integral parts of that "exciting and promising" development called behavior modification. An understanding of the rationale behind research, the various methods available to researchers, and the limited but meaningful interpretations obtainable from such research provides the reader with a valuable anchor in the evaluation and appreciation of behavior modification.

This approach to the study of behavior change allows us to evaluate what we do in attempting to solve clinical and social problems. One does not appeal to a theory as justification for actions; one appeals to data, which will allow for corrective feedback. This approach should be the hallmark of the behavior modifier, underscoring the necessity of understanding the scientific method and how to utilize it in applied settings. If one is to understand, employ, or be the recipient of behavior modification, then it is imperative that its scientific underpinnings be understood.

Models of behavior change

6

Utilization of any set of procedures such as psychotherapy or behavior modification to alter personality or behavior assumes some model or conceptualization of the nature of man. The model includes assumptions about motivational forces, the processes that contribute to and shape attitudes and behavior, the degree to which various events influence an individual's life, and the degree to which the influence of such events can be modified. In addition, the model dictates the way in which behavior is viewed, the causes to which behaviors are ascribed, and the procedures considered appropriate to modify behavior.

Many models have been posed to explain behavior (see Hall and Lindzey 1970). It is beyond the scope of this chapter to review the entire range of approaches. For our purposes, it is important to note the models that have had a major impact on the conceptualization of deviant behavior and psychological treatment procedures. Three models will be discussed; these include the medical, intrapsychic, and behavioral models.

The medical model

The medical model of abnormal behavior is patterned after views adhered to in medicine. The medical model assumes that deviant behavior is the result of a disease. As in any disease, there is a specific group of symptoms (deviant behaviors) that go together and each group of symptoms is the result of a specific disease, which has a specific etiology or course of development. Such a cluster or group of behaviors is referred to as a *syndrome*. To explain the implications of such a position and the current form of the medical model, which is a source of controversy, we must discuss briefly the forms of disease in medicine. In medicine, at least three types of disease can be distinguished (Buss 1966). First, there are *infectious diseases,* which are attributed to some pathogen such as a bacteria or virus (as in the common cold). Second, there are *systemic diseases,* which result from a failure or malfunction of a physiological system or organ. A particular organ may fail to function and cause a severe medical problem (for example, appendicitis). Third, there are *traumatic diseases,* which result from some external event such as a physical blow or ingestion of a toxic substance. An example would be lead poisoning.

The conceptualization of the three types of diseases has been extended to the study of deviant behavior. The infectious disease model advanced considerably with the discovery of the etiology of general paresis. Neural degeneration resulting from the syphilitic spirochete was found to be the cause of general paresis (Buss 1966; Ullmann and Krasner 1969). Since some of the behaviors associated with general paresis resembled forms of mental illness (that is, psychoses), it was thought that other infectious causes might account for other deviant behavior. Generally, infectious diseases are not presently considered to be responsible for deviant behavior, although various infectious diseases do have behavioral concomitants. Rather, it is the systemic disease model that is used in research on deviant behavior. For example, some investigators are examining whether various forms of abnormal behavior, such as schizophrenia, represent a breakdown in bodily functions, such as a failure to metabolize certain substances, lack of specific enzymes, or a malfunction of neurochemical processes. The traumatic disease model also has been extended to abnormal behavior. Some deviant behaviors clearly result from externally induced trauma, including birth defects and severe head injury.

Within the realm of medicine and physiology, each of these approaches is useful and not a major source of contention. Investigating the physiological causes (infection, systemic defect, exogenous trauma) of correlates of abnormal behavior has led to important discoveries. However, for many behaviors considered deviant, there is no known organic cause, and in order to account for many of these behaviors, aspects of the medical model have been extrapolated and altered. Specifically, the model has been extended beyond the search for biological causes of deviant behavior. The current controversy focuses on the questionable utility of such a model in explaining deviant behavior that has not been shown to have a clear physiological basis. The medical model suggests that there must be some underlying disease to which the symptoms can be attributed. Thus, the model that posits that physical symptoms are due to underlying physical disorders has been extended to psychology where "psychological symptoms" are seen as resulting from "psychological disorders." In these cases, the supposed causal agent underlying "abnormal" or deviant behaviors is a set of "diseased" personality attributes (Buss 1966; Hutt and Gibby 1957). This extrapolation of the medical model, which utilizes the model but not its content, has been labeled the intrapsychic model or the quasi-medical model (Bandura 1969).

Intrapsychic or quasi-medical models

The quasi-medical model of abnormal behavior relies on personality and intrapsychic processes and includes assumptions that have been useful in physical medicine. First, it is assumed that there are "symptoms" (deviant behaviors) which result from some underlying "disease" process. The "psychological diseases," while not considered to be real entities, except as a result of reification, function analogously to the systemic or traumatic disorders in the medical model. Second, to arrive at the root of the problem, treatment must focus on the underlying psychic state. To understand the extrapolation of the medical model to the realm of behavior disorders requires explanation of the intrapsychic or quasi-medical model in general and of psychoanalytic theory in particular.

The intrapsychic model focuses on psychological forces that are assumed to exist within the individual. A number of personality theorists have posited an assortment of psychic forces inside the individual including drives, needs, impulses, motives, personality traits, and other attributes. The forces are assumed to propel behavior. There are many versions of the intrapsychic view; they differ on the precise forces and motives to which behavior is ascribed.

Psychoanalytic theory

Sigmund Freud (1856–1939) provided an elaborate theory to explain the supposed motivational underpinnings of behavior. Freud emphasized those causes to which abnormal behaviors might be traced. Regarding psychological disorders, Freud accepted the structure of the medical model itself, but not its content. Psychological disorders were viewed as analogous to physical disorders; thus failure of the personality to function appropriately would be analogous to systemic disease, while psychological trauma would correspond to traumatic disease.

Freud traced behaviors to psychological impulses, drives, forces, and unconscious processes occurring within the individual. According to psychoanalytic theory, all behavior can be traced to some underlying psychological process. The processes described by Freud are referred to as *psychodynamic processes* and the theory sometimes is referred to as a psychodynamic theory.[1] Freud's psychodynamic view of personality describes behavior in terms of psychological energies, or motivating forces, drives, and impulses and their expression at various stages early in the individual's development.

Freud posed three structures of personality, the id, ego, and superego. The id is the reservoir of all instincts and is the source of psychic energy (libido) for all psychological processes and behavior. The ego interacts with the demands of reality and the need to fulfill instinctual wishes. Finally, the superego represents the internalization of social and parental standards and ideals of behavior. These personality structures are in constant conflict, which usually occurs at an unconscious level. Each structure contributes to determining whether an impulse will be expressed, and precisely when and in what form it will be expressed. The expression of psychic energy can be traced to different focuses for instinctual gratification as the child develops.

Freud delineated stages of psychosexual development through which everyone supposedly passes. At each stage, the focus or source of pleasure or instinctual gratification is associated with different areas and functions of the body. As the child develops, the expression of psychic energy invariably leads to conflicts with reality and within the structures of personality. Anxiety reactions, defense mechanisms, and alternate modes of behaving result from instincts not obtaining direct and immediate expression. Impulses, such as attraction toward the opposite-sexed parent, may not be resolved and may result in a breakdown of normal personality development. Normal behavior develops from the expression of impulses, wishes, and desires in socially appropriate ways. Deviant behavior, according to the psychoanalytic view, is due to an internal unconscious conflict resulting from the disruption of the normal development and expression of drives and needs, and their gratification. Psychological drives can fail to find expression in socially appropriate ways. Drives and unresolved conflicts may find symbolic expression in aberrant behaviors, which are considered symptoms of the real underlying problem. According to Freud's theory, normal everyday behaviors, as well as abnormal behaviors, can be traced to particular personality processes and the expression of psychic impulses. For example, cigarette smoking is not merely an unwanted or bother-

[1] Dynamics refers to a branch of mechanics in which phenomena are explained by referring to energy forces and their relation to motion, growth, and change in physical matter.

some habit but also a reflection of an individual's need for oral gratification; it might result from insufficient or overindulgent oral stimulation early in life.

The intrapsychic model, and primarily the psychoanalytic approach, has had a tremendous impact on clinical psychology and psychiatry, and indeed, has dominated the field of mental health. This is evident in a variety of ways, such as the language associated with the development, occurrence, and amelioration of deviant behavior. Terms such as *etiology, treatment, mental hospital, patient, clinic, psychopathology,* and *mental illness* all reflect the carryover from the medical model.

Other intrapsychic approaches

Psychoanalytic theory has been referred to as an intrapsychic position because it posits that psychological forces within the organism account for behavior. There are a number of other intrapsychic views of personality and behavior. These views also explain behavior by looking to underlying psychological processes. Many of these models were designed to account for all of human behavior, normal and abnormal; much less emphasis, therefore, has been given to the development and alleviation of abnormal behavior.

In some theories, traits are posited as the psychological features that account for behavior. Behaviors are attributed to differential amounts of a given trait, such as kindness, or to different traits across individuals. In trait theories, an individual's behavior is explained by the dispositions or traits he possesses (see Allport 1961). In other intrapsychic positions, the self-concept or notion of the self is believed to be an important basis for behavior (see Rogers 1959). One's perception of oneself in relation to others and of various experiences in the world is assumed to dictate one's behavior. In yet another intrapsychic position, a taxonomy of needs is posited to account for behavior (see Maslow 1966). The needs are internal psychological processes that give rise to overt behavior. Behavior can be traced to a diverse series of needs. Knowledge of the specific needs and the ways in which they are expressed is necessary in order to understand behavior. While various forms of intrapsychic theories could be elaborated, their unique features are not required to examine implications of the general approach.[2]

Implications of intrapsychic models

Adoption of the medical model and the intrapsychic models has significant implications not only for conceptualizing personality but also for

[2] See the Suggested Readings for information regarding intrapsychic theories.

psychological assessment and the labeling of behavioral problems (diagnosis) and for altering behavior (treatment).

The intrapsychic model has strongly influenced psychological assessment and diagnosis of behavioral disorders. Assessment focuses upon underlying processes that explain behavior, and thus a client's overt behavior is not of direct interest. For example, an individual may seek therapy to overcome anxiety that arises in social situations. The focus is not upon specific situations that appear to precipitate anxiety. Assessment focuses on the client's psychodynamics or personality attributes, to which the anxiety is assumed to be traceable. Through psychodynamic assessment, the psychologist attempts to provide global descriptions of personality; to reconstruct the individual's psychological development; to determine how the person reacted to important psychological impulses such as sex and aggression in the past; to determine what defense mechanisms have developed; and to determine what basic characteristic traits or psychological defects account for behavior. Assessment searches for the psychological processes that are considered to be the sources of behavioral problems.

Projective tests are examples of the diagnostic tools of traditional personality assessment. These tests attempt to assess personality indirectly through reactions to ink blots, stories created in response to ambiguous stimuli, free associations, or other unstructured tasks. Projective tests provide the client with ambiguous stimuli onto which he must impose meaning and structure. The responses are considered as *signs* that reveal personality structure, psychodynamics, and unconscious motivation. Conclusions are reached by interpreting the meaning of the behavioral signs and inferring underlying processes. Interpretation of projective tests requires clinical judgment to extract meaning from responses. There has been serious criticism of the reliability and validity of these interpretations in predicting behavior. Individuals often disagree on the interpretation of test responses and the psychological processes to which the responses are attributed (Chambers and Hamlin 1957; Wanderer 1966). In fact, a number of authors have questioned the utility of projective tests (Mischel 1968, 1971; Lanyon and Goodstein 1971; Peterson 1968; Sechrest 1963).

There are many other psychological tests and inventories designed to assess aspects of the client's personality, character traits, and psychological needs, deficits, or defects (for example, tests of anxiety, paranoid tendencies, extroversion, impulsiveness, brain damage, intelligence). Psychological assessment with various inventories attempts to provide a profile of traits and to identify problem areas in personality or psychological development. In clinical use, the purpose of such tests is to help the clinician understand behavior and describe or diagnose personality.

A major task of diagnosis is to assign an individual a label that implies the underlying condition or defect responsible for the behavioral problem. Such labels include "schizophrenia," "neurosis," "mental retardation," "learning disability," "hyperactivity," "emotional disturbance," and numerous others which depict the motivational problem, inherent deficit, or "disease." Traditionally, the focus has been on identifying disorders and "symptom" patterns that go together, along the lines practiced in medicine (Phillips and Draguns 1971). Once the disorders are clearly described, it is assumed that their etiology will be apparent.

Diagnosis attempts to describe the presenting problem, to isolate the conditions related to its occurrence, to proffer a therapeutic plan, and to predict the outcome of treatment (Stuart 1970). While these purposes have been fulfilled with many physical disorders in medicine, the traditional diagnostic approach to behavior problems has not fared well (Kanfer and Saslow 1969; Zigler and Phillips 1961a). For example, professionals who independently assign patients to diagnostic categories often disagree over the precise diagnosis (Ash 1949; Hunt, Wittson, and Hunt 1953; Sandifer, Hordern, Timbury, and Green 1969; Schmidt and Fonda 1956). Moreover, there are great differences in the behavior of persons ascribed the same diagnosis (Freudenberg and Robertson 1956; Wittenborn, Holtzberg, and Simon 1953) as well as similar behaviors in individuals assigned diverse diagnoses (Phillips and Rabinovitch 1958). Psychological or psychiatric diagnosis seems to provide little information about behavior beyond that which was known when the diagnosis was made. Specifically, little information is given about the etiology, treatment of choice, and prognosis (Kanfer and Saslow 1969; Zigler and Phillips 1961c).

There is relatively little to recommend the general approach of the quasi-medical model in the way of treatment for individuals whose behavior is labeled abnormal. Psychological treatments based upon the approach have not advanced as well as have medical treatments for physical disorders. Yet the promise of effective treatment is implicit in the development of psychiatric hospitals, outpatient clinics, and other facilities modeled after medical treatment. The efficacy of treatment for people labeled as psychotics, neurotics, sociopaths, retardates, delinquents, emotionally disturbed children, and others has been severely questioned (Dunn 1971; Eysenck 1966; Fairweather and Simon 1963; Hoch 1966; Levitt 1957, 1971; Paul 1969b; Sanders, Smith, and Weinman 1967). There is little treatment of demonstrated efficacy. Individual or group psychotherapy or counseling, which are conducted in outpatient and inpatient settings, are the general treatment strategies regardless of diagnosis or supposed personality problems (London 1964; Stuart 1970). Depending upon the orientation of the therapist, a client receiving psychotherapy is usually required to relate aspects of experiences to the therapist to uncover the underlying personality. It is assumed that therapy can progress only when intrapsychic processes are revealed and altered.

Unfortunately, for many individuals treatment may even be associated with deleterious effects. For example, psychotherapy with different types of patients (Bergin 1966, 1971) and institutional care for psychiatric patients (Goffman 1961; Scheff 1966) and the retarded (Schlanger 1954; Kaufman 1967) sometimes are associated with decrements in adaptive behaviors. When individuals are hospitalized for psychiatric treatment, they often must give up many of their responsibilities and rights as citizens. Thus, "treatment" sometimes further weakens the tie with society. The institution fosters dependency and lack of self-sufficiency, which may detract from the individual's subsequent adjustment to the community (Paul 1969b). The stigma resulting from institutionalization ensures that posthospitalization adjustment will be difficult.

The medical and intrapsychic models assume that problematic behaviors are symptomatic of some underlying disorder. In medicine, of course, internal conditions such as infection or organ dysfunction, which are responsible for symptoms such as fever or discomfort, are treated. But treatment of symptoms alone is insufficient if the underlying condition is not altered as well. In medicine, symptomatic treatment is employed and a disease is allowed to run its course only in cases where there is no acceptable cure for the underlying disorder, as with the common cold or a terminal illness. In these cases, symptoms may be ameliorated with decongestants or pain killers. However, in cases where a cure for the underlying physiological problem is known (for example, rabies, gall stones, ruptured appendix), symptomatic treatment alone is obviously inappropriate.

Within the medical and quasi-medical models, then, treatment focuses on underlying processes. It is believed that if treatment were focused upon the actual problematic behavior, the individual might not be cured. The notion of *symptom substitution* has been suggested as a possible consequence of symptomatic treatment. This notion suggests that if a maladaptive behavior is altered without treatment of the underlying disorder, another symptom might substitute for the problematic behavior. Symptom substitution is expected from a psychodynamic position because, according to this view, impulses, drives, and psychological forces not resolved through normal channels of behavior seek release through the formation of symptoms such as anxieties, obsessions, tics, and so on. Alteration of the symptom through which release of a psychological impulse was sought will not alter the underlying impulse. So the impulse may seek re-expression in another form, or another symptom. Cure can result only from the removal or reduction of the impulse, drive, or conflict that led to the maladaptive behavior.

There has been considerable dispute about symptom substitution. Disagreement has centered around these points: whether symptom substitution occurs, whether it can be assessed empirically, whether substitute symptoms can be predicted in advance, and whether its occurrence necessarily supports a psychodynamic position (Bandura 1969; Cahoon 1968; Mahoney et al. 1974; Stuart 1970; Ullmann and Krasner 1965, 1969). At present there is little evidence indicating deleterious effects following treatment of specific behavior problems (see Baker 1967; Nolan, Mattis, and Holliday 1970; Yates 1958). Indeed, as discussed later, beneficial side effects frequently are associated with the alteration of specific behaviors.

Criticisms of the intrapsychic model

One major historical benefit has accrued from the popularity of the quasi-medical models of deviant behavior. Prior to their presentation, deviant behavior was attributed to possession by demons, evil spirits, and supernatural forces. Ancient and medieval conceptualizations were based on the assumption that individuals were inhabited by evil spirits as retribution for their wickedness and sins. Exorcism was required to treat abnormal behaviors. Often, harsh and inhumane procedures such as flogging and starvation were used to make the body uninhabitable for the spirits. Recasting the deviant individual as "mentally ill" or "diseased" probably has contributed to increased sympathy and humane treatment (Ausubel 1961). Although the public still rejects and negatively evaluates individuals labeled mentally ill or associated with psychiatric treatment (Cumming and Cumming 1957; Nunnally 1961; Sarbin and Mancuso 1970), current attitudes are more favorable and treatment is more humane than previously.

However, the quasi-medical or intrapsychic model has been faulted on several grounds. Some authors have noted that pessimism results from diagnosis and traditional formulation of the deviant behavior (Stuart 1970). The problems clients express are reformulated in terms of personality or characterological defects, deficits, inabilities, or deeply rooted causes. The labels imply a permanent complex psychological state that is not readily alterable. Behavioral problems are attributed to defects in personality or psychological development. The defects are considered to be deeply rooted, making treatment an extremely elaborate endeavor. Of course, behavior change may never be a simple matter. Yet, attributing behavior to reified and complex inferred states makes behavior change even less straightforward than might otherwise be the case. Indeed, psychodynamic formulations of behavior probably have discouraged the direct alteration of behavior because of the inability to alter supposedly underlying causes in the individual.

The greatest and most frequent criticisms of the intrapsychic model have been leveled against Freud's psychodynamic position. Several authors have noted the difficulty in scientifically establishing several of its propositions; the inconsistencies within the theory itself and the therapeutic procedures derived from the theory and the lack of empirical support in many areas (for example, some features of child development) in which relevant research has been conducted (Bandura 1969; London 1964; Mischel 1971; Sears 1943; Stuart 1970; Ullmann and Krasner 1965).

The behavioral approach

The behavioral approach departs from the medical model and the intrapsychic views of behavior in a number of ways. As noted in previous chapters, some unique features of the behavioral approach are methodological, in terms of emphasis on assessment of behavior, objectification of concepts, evaluation of treatment interventions, and minimization of inferred variables. The behavioral approach tries to avoid unverifiable, unobservable inner states. However, it would be inaccurate to state that internal states are avoided altogether. Within the behavioral approach various viewpoints differ on the extent to which inferred variables and inner states are utilized. For example, among operant conditioners inferred variables are usually totally rejected. The focus is entirely on overt or publicly observable behavior. On the other hand, some behavior modifiers posit inferred or mediating variables to account for some overt behaviors. It is exceedingly important to distinguish the inferred variables posited by some behaviorists from intrapsychic notions. As noted in Chapter 3, inferred variables posited by behaviorists are amenable to objective assessment or have empirical ramifications. Anxiety, posited by some behavior theorists (e.g., Wolpe 1958), can be assessed objectively, for example, through physiological means. Some behaviorists stress covert events such as thoughts, self-verbalizations, and imagery which mediate overt behavior. Yet the internal or private events are amenable to assessment, at least by the individual experiencing them. Moreover, overt procedures that alter private events can be observed publicly.

Despite differences among behaviorists, it is generally correct to state that the focus is on behavior rather than on underlying states. The inferred variables posited by behavior modifiers generally are more accessible both to the client who comes for treatment and to the therapist who undertakes a program of behavior change (Rimm and

Masters 1974) than are psychodynamic states. For example, a client may wish to eliminate obsessive thoughts or undesirable urges. Although these are not overt behaviors, the behavioral focus would be on the occurrence of these thoughts or urges. Indeed, the client can observe the frequency of these thoughts to provide data for the therapist. The private event focused upon here is accessible, at least to the client. Moreover, behavioral treatment will focus on the thoughts and urges themselves rather than on supposed sources of these covert events. In contrast, a psychodynamic view of the obsessional thoughts would hold that they reflect underlying dynamic processes; the thoughts would be considered signs of something else. They would not be taken as the problem itself.

The behavioral approach is concerned with the development, maintenance, and alteration of behavior. Abnormal behavior is not regarded as distinct from normal behavior in terms of how it develops or is maintained. Abnormal behavior does not represent a dysfunction or a disease process that has overtaken normal personality development. Rather, certain learning experiences or a failure to receive or profit from various learning experiences can account for behavior. Behavior develops according to the same principles, whether it is labeled normal or abnormal.[3]

Labeling behavior as abnormal is frequently based upon subjective judgments rather than objective criteria (Bandura 1969; Becker 1963; Ferster 1965; Sarbin 1967; Szasz 1966; Ullmann and Krasner 1965). A given behavior may be viewed by different people as abnormal or normal. For example, fighting among male children may be regarded as an expression of masculinity by peers and parents, but regarded as a sign of emotional disturbance by teachers and school counselors. Thus, the values of the individual who evaluates behavior play a major role in determining whether it is normal or deviant.

The social context is also important in determining whether a given behavior is regarded as deviant. Abnormal behavior is inferred

[3] This assumption, which is present in most variations of the behavioral model, has been much debated. Several alternative views have been suggested. The combining of the systemic medical model and a behavioral model is one example. Within such a model, schizophrenia may be viewed as a function of the interaction of a genetic predisposition with a particular type of environment. If supportive empirical data were forthcoming, the findings should be incorporated into an appropriate conceptual model. Unfortunately, with the vast majority of behavior disorders, research findings supporting such an approach are meager or nonexistent. Another point worth noting is that many psychologists successfully utilize behavior modification without making the assumption that the behavioral problem developed according to the same principles that are being used to change the behavior. Because reinforcement of a particular behavior leads to change in that behavior, one cannot argue that the behavior must have developed because it was reinforced; on the other hand, such a finding does not rule out the possibility that such a behavior developed because it was reinforced. This issue was raised in the example of the broom-holding woman in Chapter 1.

from the degree to which behavior deviates from social norms (Scheff 1966). Because social norms vary across cultures and across groups and settings within a given culture, it is difficult to posit objective criteria for abnormal behavior. For example, behaviors labeled by some as antisocial reflect patterns of behavior that are socially condoned and strongly supported in many peer groups where street fighting and theft are accepted activities. Labeling the behavior as antisocial and indicative of psychological disturbance is based on value judgments rather than on evidence of "diseased" psychological processes. There is no objective or value-free basis for claiming the behavior is "sick." Obviously, there are differences in behaviors across individuals. However, the differences probably reflect differences on a continuum rather than in terms of illness versus health (Becker 1963; Scheff 1966).

The behavioral model and learning

Behavior modification assumes that behavior, whether labeled abnormal or normal, depends to a great extent on environmental factors. The processes through which adaptive behaviors usually develop can explain the development of maladaptive or deviant behaviors as well. Moreover, therapeutic interventions involve training clients to engage in certain behaviors and not to engage in others, that is, to learn new modes of behaving. A goal of behavior modification is to provide learning experiences that promote adaptive and prosocial behavior.

To demonstrate how behavior is learned and how new behaviors can be taught, we will outline three types of learning. These types of learning have played a major role in conceptualizing behavior and generating treatment techniques. The present discussion will merely outline types of learning. In subsequent chapters, various aspects of learning will be elaborated and additional processes that influence behavior will be discussed. As will be seen in Chapter 8, those factors and principles that affect the development and modification of behavior have been extended beyond the learning laboratory. While behavior modifiers have historically drawn heavily from the learning area of psychology, current views are much broader, and it would be incorrect to assume that behavior modification is merely the application of principles of learning. However, for historical reasons and due to to their broad-scale effective applications we have incorporated basic learning principles in this chapter. A more comprehensive presentation of operant principles will be found in Chapter 7; a thorough understanding of all these principles will be necessary for the applications discussed in Part III.

Three types of learning have been considered important in explaining and altering behavior: classical or respondent conditioning, operant conditioning, and observational learning.

Classical conditioning. Classical conditioning, extensively investigated by Pavlov (1848–1936), is concerned with stimuli that automatically evoke reflex responses. Some stimuli in the environment, such as noise, light, shock, and taste of food (referred to as unconditioned stimuli), *elicit* reflex responses (referred to as respondents). Respondents frequently are considered involuntary or autonomic responses that are not under control of the individual; this has recently become a much-debated point. Examples of respondents include pupil constriction in response to bright light, flexion of a muscle in response to pain, or a startle reaction in response to loud noise. The relationship between the unconditioned stimulus and the response is automatic or unlearned. A neutral stimulus, referred to as a conditioned stimulus, may be associated with the unconditioned stimulus that elicits the response. If a conditioned stimulus is paired with an unconditioned stimulus, the conditioned stimulus alone eventually elicits the response. *Classical conditioning refers to the process whereby new stimuli gain the power to elicit respondent behavior.* In classical conditioning, events or stimuli that *precede* behavior control a reflex response.

An example based upon classical conditioning has been provided by Watson and Rayner (1920), who demonstrated that fears could be learned. An 11-month-old-boy named Albert served as a subject. Albert freely played with a white rat without any adverse reaction. Prior to the actual conditioning, the investigators noted that a loud noise (unconditioned stimulus) produced a startle and fear reaction (unconditioned response) in Albert. To condition the startle reaction in response to the rat, the presence of the rat (neutral or conditioned stimulus) was immediately followed by the noise. When Albert reached out and touched the rat, the noise sounded and Albert was startled. Within a relatively short time, the presence of the rat alone elicited a startle reaction. The conditioned stimulus elicited the fear response (conditioned response). Interestingly, the fear generalized so that objects Albert had not feared previously, including a rabbit, a dog, a Santa Claus mask, a sealskin coat, cotton, and wool, also produced the fear reaction. This demonstrated that fears can be acquired through classical conditioning. (Of course, whether fears evident in everyday experience are in fact acquired through classical conditioning is difficult to say, because one rarely observes an individual at the time fears develop.)

Operant conditioning. Much of human behavior is not involuntary or *elicited* by stimuli in the sense of reflexive reactions. Rather, behavior is *emitted* and is controlled primarily by the consequences that follow. Behaviors amenable to control by a change in the consequences that follow them are referred to as *operants,* because they are responses that operate on or have some influence on the environment and generate consequences (Skinner 1953). Operants are strengthened or weakened as a function of the events that follow them. Most behaviors performed in everyday life are operants. They are not reflex responses elicited by stimuli. Operant behaviors include talking, reading, walking, working, smiling, or any response freely emitted. As will be apparent from reading the next two chapters, many complex human behaviors involve more than just emitting a response that has a consequence applied to it. Even from an operant standpoint a more complex explanation is required; operant conditioning will be discussed in greater detail in Chapter 7.

Distinguishing classical and operant conditioning. The distinction between classical and operant conditioning is obscure in many situations (Kimble 1961). It has been thought that classical conditioning is restricted to involuntary behaviors while operant conditioning is restricted to voluntary behaviors. Yet a great deal of research has shown that such supposedly involuntary responses as heart rate, blood pressure, galvanic skin responses, intestinal contractions, and vasomotor reflexes can be altered through operant conditioning (Kimmel 1967, 1974).

In everyday experience, the difficulty in distinguishing respondent and operant behaviors is evident. A response may be elicited (classical conditioning); it may also be controlled by the consequences that follow it (operant conditioning). For example, a child may cry in response to a painful fall. This crying is a respondent, or a reflexive response to pain. Once the crying begins, it may be sustained by its consequences, such as cuddling and effusive sympathy, and become an operant. It is sometimes difficult to separate operant from respondent crying.

The distinction between classical and operant conditioning seems vague also because operant behaviors can be controlled by preceding stimuli. Operant behaviors are performed in certain situations with various cues present. When the consequences that follow behavior consistently occur in the presence of a particular set of cues, such as a certain person or place, the cues alone increase the probability that the behavior will be emitted. The stimuli that precede the response set the *occasion* for the response, or increase the likelihood that the response will occur. For example, the sound of music on the radio may serve as a stimulus for singing or dancing. This is not an example of classical conditioning because the preceding stimulus (music) does not *force* (elicit) the response (singing) to occur. In operant conditioning, the stimulus does not elicit or produce a response; it only increases the probability that the response will occur (Reynolds 1968). The following major difference between classical and operant conditioning should be kept in mind. In classical conditioning, the primary result is a change in the power of a stimulus to *elicit* a reflex response. In operant conditioning, the primary result is a change in an *emitted* response.

Observational learning. Observational or vicarious learning, or modeling (Bandura and Walters 1963), includes both types of responses, respondents and operants. In observational learning, an individual observes a model's behavior but need not engage in overt responses or receive direct consequences. By observing a model, the observer may learn a response without actually performing it. Modeling can develop new responses and can alter the frequency of previously learned responses as well (Bandura 1969).

To understand the effects of modeling, it is useful to distinguish *learning* from *performance.* The requirement for learning through modeling is the observation of a model. The modeled response is assumed to be acquired by the observer through a cognitive or covert coding of the observed events (Bandura 1970, 1971). However, whether a learned response is *performed* may depend upon response consequences or incentives associated with that response. The role of response consequences in dictating performance has been demonstrated by Bandura (1965). Children observed a film where an adult modeled aggressive responses (hitting and kicking a large doll). For some children, the model's aggression was rewarded; for others, aggression was punished; and for others, no consequences followed the model's behavior. When children had the opportunity to perform the aggressive responses, those who had observed the model being punished displayed less aggression than those who observed aggression being rewarded or ignored. To determine whether all children had *learned* the responses, an attractive incentive was subsequently given to children for performing aggressive responses. There were no differences in aggressive responses among the three groups. Apparently all groups learned the aggressive responses, but consequences to the model and observer determined whether they would be performed.

The effect of modeling on performance depends upon other variables in addition to the consequences that follow the model's performance (Bandura 1971a; Flanders 1968; Rachman 1972). Observers imitate models who are similar to themselves more than models who are less similar. Certain model characteristics also facilitate imitation. For example, greater imitation usually results from models who are high in prestige, status, or expertise. Imitation is also greater after observation of several models than after observation of a single model.

A classic example of modeling for purposes of treatment was reported by Jones (1924). A young boy, Peter, was afraid of a rabbit and several other furry objects (rat, fur coat, feather, cotton, wool). Peter was placed with three other children in a play situation in which a rabbit was present. The other children, who were unafraid of rabbits, freely interacted with the animal. Peter touched the rabbit immediately after observing others touching it. The example suggests the importance of modeling. However, other procedures were employed with Peter, such as associating the rabbit with the presence of food, so the precise contribution of modeling in reducing his fear is unclear.

The behavioral approach considers the majority of behaviors to be learned or alterable through the learning procedures outlined here. Attempts are made to alter behaviors that have been learned or to develop new behaviors rather than to alter psychological processes that traditionally have been assumed to underlie behavior. The behavioral view, like the medical model, has far-reaching implications for assessment and treatment of behavior problems.

Implications of the behavioral view

The behavioral approach to assessment of behaviors departs from traditional diagnostic assessment (Arthur 1969; Goldfried and Pomeranz 1968; Mischel 1968; Peterson 1968), although they have some problems in common, such as reliability (Goldfried and Spraflin 1974). The behavioral approach focuses directly on the behaviors that are to be altered rather than on the underlying personality. Although a problem may be described in vague or general terms (for example, hyperactivity), the behavior modifier seeks to observe the behavior that requires change and the events that prompted the diagnosis, the frequency of these behaviors, and the antecedent and consequent events associated with any outbursts. In short, assessment focuses on the behavior of the client as well as on environmental events. Assessment of the behavior to be changed (referred to as the *target behavior*) is essential to ascertain the extent of change that is required or the extent of the problem. Behaviors are not considered to reflect underlying psychological problems but are of direct interest in their own right. Sometimes the factors that precede and follow behavior are assessed. These factors may be useful in altering the target behavior. Events that precede behavior may include the presence of a particular person, instructions, and other cues in the environment that affect the response. This will be discussed in more detail in Chapter 9.

Behavior modifiers emphasize external events in the environment which can be used to alter behavior. This is not to say that events within the individual do not influence behavior. Indeed, internal events and covert behaviors, such as thoughts, feelings, and perceptions, can directly influence behavior. Behavior modifiers, however, disagree on the extent to which internal events are to be regarded as determinants of behavior.

It is important to distinguish the internal events sometimes focused upon in behavior modification and the seemingly similar processes relied upon by psychodynamic theorists. Psychodynamic theorists make inferences about underlying states that represent complex abstractions far removed from behavior. It is difficult and frequently impossible to verify that the internal state is or could be related to overt behavior. Few predictions can be made that could be subjected to scientific scrutiny. In contrast, behavior modifiers attempt to relate covert or underlying events closely to observable phenomena. In addition, predictions are made about the relationship between covert events and overt behavior. For example, some behavior modifiers believe that things people say to themselves privately ("I can't do that," or "I am incompetent") dictate performance. The influence of self-statements can be examined empirically by altering what people say to themselves and seeing whether this affects overt behavior (Meichenbaum 1973). The role of such covert, cognitive, and mediational factors in behavior is discussed in Chapter 8.

It is considered unlikely that altering a problematic behavior will result in its replacement by another problem behavior, as in symptom substitution. Behaviorists do not consider problematic behavior a reflection of supposed psychic impulses that seek expression. In fact, behaviorists predict that once a particular problem behavior is altered for an individual, other aspects of his life and behaviors may improve as well. The beneficial effects of treating one behavior may *generalize* to other behaviors. If a stutterer is trained to speak more fluently, it can be expected that additional positive changes will result. He may become more confident and extroverted, and less shy. Resolution of one problem may begin a series of favorable changes in a person's life. The notion of symptom substitution has little support. In contrast, several studies with diverse behavioral techniques confirm the generalization of beneficial effects to behaviors not originally included in treatment (Kazdin 1973b; Mahoney et al. 1974). Of course, it is possible that a person who has one behavior altered will still have additional problems. However, this is far removed from the notion of symptom substitution. New problematic behaviors are not necessarily re-expressions of psychic conflicts. Treatment, whether medical or psychological in nature, is no guarantee against the development of further problems. For example, repairing a broken limb does not guarantee the absence of future injuries of a similar nature. Problematic behaviors may appear as a result of psychological treatment. It is possible, for example, that once deviant behavior is reduced, the person may have no appropriate response in his repertoire to take its place (Cahoon 1968). The deficit may be evident in continued inappropriate social behaviors. If this occurs it is frequently the result of poor assessment whereby all the problem areas are not evaluated, and thus the treatment program employed is inappropriate and too limited. This deficit can be corrected by a treatment program that develops appropriate behaviors while eliminating inappropriate ones.

Summary

This chapter provides an outline of different models of behavior. The medical model can be broken down into three types: infectious, systemic, and traumatic. The quasi-medical or intrapsychic model is based on the systemic and traumatic medical models; however, it is only the structure of the medical model and not its content that is utilized. Thus, just as physical symptoms are considered to have underlying physical causes, the intrapsychic model assumes that deviant behavior has underlying psychological causes. The most popular intrapsychic model has been the psychoanalytic model proposed by Freud. In both assessment and treatment the emphasis has been upon the underlying psychological causes rather than upon the deviant behavior.

The typical behavioral model assumes that all behaviors (those labeled normal as well as abnormal) develop according to the same principles. In both assessment and treatment the emphasis is upon the problem behavior and the internal and external events associated with it. The importance of learning is stressed in the behavioral model. Learning is emphasized because it has in fact played a major role in behavior modification. However, as a general approach behavior modification is not restricted to particular theories or orientations. The characteristic feature of behavior modification is the application of empirical findings for the purpose of behavior change. The content of behavior modification cannot be definitively specified because empirical findings and the science of behavior are constantly expanding. Nevertheless, subsequent chapters will detail the findings and principles currently included in the realm of behavior modification.

Suggested readings

Hall, C. S., and Lindzey, G. *Theories of personality.* 2nd ed. New York: Wiley, 1970.

Krasner, L., and Ullmann, L. P. *Behavior influence and personality: The social matrix of human action.* New York: Holt, Rinehart and Winston, 1973. Chapters 1–6.

Sarason, I. G. *Personality: An objective approach.* 2nd ed. New York: Wiley, 1972.

Principles of operant conditioning

7

Behavior modification relies upon a body of established findings from psychology, many of which derive from the psychology of learning. In the previous chapter, types of learning were discussed. The present chapter describes the principles of operant conditioning in greater detail because several techniques of behavior modification have been based on these principles. In the next chapter, empirical findings from cognitive and other areas of psychology will be discussed.

The principles of operant conditioning describe the relationship between behavior and various environmental events (antecedents and consequences) that influence behavior. Although both antecedents and consequences can alter behavior, most applications of operant conditioning principles emphasize the *consequences* that follow behavior. Behavior change occurs when certain consequences are *contingent* upon performance. A consequence is contingent when it is delivered *only* after the target behavior is performed.

In everyday life, many consequences are contingent upon behavior. For example, wages are contingent upon working and grades are contingent upon studying for exams. *A contingency refers to the relationship between a behavior and the events that follow the behavior.* The notion of contingency is important because behavior modification techniques often alter behavior by altering the contingencies that control or fail to control a particular behavior.

Before we take a detailed look at the principles of operant conditioning, it may be helpful to clarify some common misuses by presenting a brief overview of the principles. In order to avoid confusion of terms it is essential to distinguish between the label for an event or stimulus and the label for the principle that describes what occurs when an event or stimulus is used in a contingent manner. For example, the confusion surrounding the principle of negative reinforcement has largely resulted from the failure to distinguish between a negative reinforcer—that is, a stimulus or event—and negative reinforcement. Events or stimuli traditionally have been classified as positive reinforcers and negative reinforcers (aversive stimuli). Each class of stimuli or events may have different effects on the frequency of a behavior; the effect is determined by whether a stimulus or event is applied or removed following the occurrence of a behavior.

As can be seen in Figure 7-1, *positive reinforcement,* an increase in the frequency of a behavior, occurs when a positive reinforcer is contingently applied or presented. *Negative reinforcement,* also an increase in the frequency of a behavior, occurs when a negative reinforcer is contingently removed. Thus, the *principle of reinforcement* always refers to an *increase* in the frequency of a response when it is followed by a contingent stimulus or event. Likewise, the *principle of punishment* always refers to a *decrease* in the frequency of a response when it is followed by

Figure 7-1 Principles of operant conditioning based upon whether positive or negative reinforcers are applied or removed after a response is performed

	APPLIED	REMOVED
POSITIVE REINFORCER	POSITIVE REINFORCEMENT	PUNISHMENT BY REMOVAL
NEGATIVE REINFORCER	PUNISHMENT BY APPLICATION	NEGATIVE REINFORCEMENT

a contingent stimulus or event. Again, as shown in Figure 7-1, there are two types of punishment.[1] Several labels have been suggested for the two types of punishment; we prefer the following ones because they seem most clearly related to the procedures employed. *Punishment by removal,* a *decrease* in the frequency of a response, occurs when a positive reinforcer is contingently removed. *Punishment by application,* also a *decrease* in the frequency of a response, occurs when a negative reinforcer is contingently applied.

Reinforcement

Reinforcement refers to the presentation of a positive reinforcer or the removal of a negative reinforcer after a response; it increases the frequency of that response. The event that follows behavior must be contingent upon behavior. Again, we have noted there are two types of reinforcement: positive reinforcement and negative reinforcement.

Positive reinforcement

Positive reinforcement refers to an increase in the frequency of a response that is followed by a positive reinforcer. It is important to distinguish the term *positive reinforcer* from *reward.* A positive reinforcer is defined by its effect on behavior. If an event follows behavior and the frequency of behavior increases, the event is a positive reinforcer. Any event that does not increase the behavior it follows is not a positive reinforcer. An increase in the frequency of the preceding behavior is *the* defining characteristic of a positive reinforcer. In contrast, rewards are defined as something given or received in return for service, merit, or achievement. Although rewards are subjectively highly valued, they do not necessarily increase the frequency of the behavior they follow. Many events that a person evaluates favorably may serve as reinforcers, yet this cannot be known on the basis of verbal statements alone. Moreover, there may be many reinforcers available for an individual of which he is unaware or which he does not consider as rewards. For example, in some situations verbal reprimands inadvertently serve as positive reinforcers because they provide attention for a response. Behaviors followed by reprimands may increase (Madsen, Becker, and Thomas 1968). Even though reprimands may sometimes serve as positive reinforcers, most people would not refer to them as rewards. Thus, a reward is not synonymous with a positive reinforcer. Whether an

[1] These distinctions regarding punishment and questions regarding whether punishment by removal is in fact punishment have been much argued. Because of the practical advantages and because much of the research has been based on the distinctions presented in Figure 7-1, we have chosen to present the material in this fashion.

event is a positive reinforcer is empirically determined. Only if the frequency of a particular behavior increases when the event immediately follows the behavior is the event a positive reinforcer.

There are many examples of positive reinforcement in everyday life. (Of course, rarely does anyone systematically measure whether a favorable event that followed behavior increased the frequency of that behavior.) A student who studies for an examination and receives an A is probably reinforced, and studying is likely to increase in the future because it was reinforced by an excellent grade. Winning money at a slot machine usually increases the frequency of putting money into the machine and pulling the lever. Money is a powerful reinforcer that increases performance of a variety of behaviors.

Positive reinforcers include any event that increases the frequency of the behavior it follows. There are two categories of positive reinforcers, namely, primary or unconditioned and secondary or conditioned reinforcers. Stimuli that do not require an individual to learn their reinforcing value are *primary reinforcers*. For example, food and water serve as primary reinforcers to hungry and thirsty people. Primary reinforcers may not be reinforcing all of the time. For example, food will not reinforce someone who has just finished a large meal. However, when food does serve as a reinforcer, its value is automatic or unlearned and does not depend upon previous association with any other reinforcers.

Some events that control behavior, such as praise, grades, money, and completion of a goal, become reinforcers through learning. *Secondary reinforcers* are not automatically reinforcing. Events that once were neutral in value may acquire reinforcing properties as a result of being paired with events that are already reinforcing (either primary or other conditioned reinforcers). If a neutral stimulus is repeatedly presented prior to or along with a reinforcing stimulus, the neutral stimulus becomes a reinforcer. Operant and classical conditioning may occur simultaneously. For example, praise may not be reinforcing for some individuals. It is a neutral stimulus for them, rather than a positive reinforcer. If praise is to be established as a reinforcer, it must be paired with an event that is reinforcing, such as food or money. After several pairings of the delivery of food with praise, the praise alone serves as a reinforcer and can be used to increase the frequency of other responses.

Some conditioned reinforcers are paired with several other reinforcers and are referred to as *generalized conditioned reinforcers*. Generalized conditioned reinforcers are extremely effective in altering behaviors because they are paired with a variety of events rather than just one. Money is a good example of a generalized conditioned reinforcer.

It is a *conditioned* or *secondary* reinforcer because its reinforcing value is acquired through learning. It is a *generalized* reinforcer because a variety of reinforcing events contributes to its value. Additional examples of generalized conditioned reinforcers include attention, approval, and affection from others (Skinner 1953). These are generalized reinforcers because their occurrence is often associated with a variety of other events which are themselves reinforcing. For example, attention from someone may be followed by physical contact, praise, smiles, affection, or delivery of tangible rewards such as food.

In behavior modification programs, generalized reinforcers in the form of *tokens* are used frequently. The tokens may consist of poker chips, coins, tickets, stars, points, or check marks. Tokens serve as generalized reinforcers because they can be exchanged for other things or events which are reinforcing. For example, in a psychiatric institution, residents receive tokens for attending group activities, socializing with others, grooming, and bathing. The tokens may be exchanged for snacks, cigarettes, and privileges such as watching television and attending social events. The strength of tokens derives from these reinforcers which back up their value. The events or stimuli that tokens can purchase are referred to as *back-up reinforcers.* Generalized conditioned reinforcers such as money or tokens are more powerful than any single reinforcer because they can purchase a variety of back-up reinforcers.

Reinforcing events include *stimuli* such as praise, smiles, food, or money, which are presented to an individual after a response. However, reinforcers are not limited to stimuli. Allowing an individual to engage in certain *responses* also can serve as a reinforcer. Certain responses can be used to reinforce other responses. Premack (1959, 1965) demonstrated that behaviors which have a high probability of occurring can reinforce behaviors with a relatively low probability of occurring. If the opportunity to perform a high probability response is made contingent upon performance of a low probability response, the frequency of the lower probability response will increase. It is important to note that Premack was speaking of high and low probability of behaviors and not high and low frequency of behaviors. The probability of a behavior is measured in a situation that is relatively free of extraneous contingencies. For example, if your choice of pizza over sirloin is not influenced by such factors as their availability, your budget, or a friend's insistence, then your choice is contingency-free. Behaviors can be high in frequency without accurately reflecting your preferences; paying taxes, attending nonbehavioral lectures, and cleaning house are examples.

In ingenious laboratory experiments, Premack (1962) altered the probability of rats' drinking and running behaviors by depriving them of access to water or to an activity wheel. When rats were deprived of water (which made drinking a high probability behavior), drinking would reinforce running (a low probability response). When the animals were deprived of activity (which made running a high probability behavior), running would reinforce drinking. In each case, a lower probability behavior was increased or reinforced by following it with a high probability behavior. At different times, drinking was the higher probability response and running the lower probability response and vice versa.

On the basis of the foregoing laboratory work, the *Premack principle* was formulated as follows: *Of any pair of responses or activities in which an individual engages, the more probable one will reinforce the less probable one.* For example, for most children, playing with friends is more probable than completing homework. If the higher probability behavior (playing with friends) is made contingent upon the lower probability behavior (completing homework), the lower probability behavior will increase.

Homme, de Baca, Devine, Steinhorst, and Rickert (1963) applied the Premack principle in a nursery school classroom, where three children spent a great deal of time running around the room, screaming, pushing chairs, or playing games. The disruptive behaviors were considered more highly probable than sitting quietly. When the children were instructed to sit in their chairs, they would continue to engage in the undesirable high probability behaviors. To increase sitting quietly, the higher probability behaviors were made to follow the lower probability behavior. After sitting quietly for a short period of time (lower probability behaviors), they were told they could "run and scream" (higher probability behaviors). On several occasions, the opportunity to run and scream was made contingent upon sitting quietly. Within a few days, the children sat quietly for longer periods of time when instructed than they had before. Sitting quietly increased in frequency, which suggested that access to the high probability behavior, running and screaming, was a positive reinforcer. This example was chosen to demonstrate how the Premack principle functions, not to argue that one should use it to train "quiet sitting" in the classroom. This question of what behaviors should be changed will be discussed in Chapter 10.

A variety of behaviors, such as engaging in recreational activities, hobbies, going on trips, or being with friends, are relatively more probable responses and usually can serve as reinforcers for other behaviors. To employ the Premack principle, the target response must be of a lower probability than the behavior used to reinforce that response.

Antecedent as well as consequent events affect the occurrence of behaviors. Antecedent stimuli serve as cues signaling that the reinforcer will follow a behavior. Such a stimulus, which marks or indicates the time and place that a response will be reinforced, is called a discriminative stimulus or an S^D (Reynolds 1968). Such stimuli affect our lives every day. One needs only to visualize the grocery market to see how buying behavior is affected by the stimuli that precede it; for example, think of the cookie shelf or the check-out counter. Both contain stimuli that are likely to stimulate buying responses. Such stimulus control will be discussed in detail later in this chapter.

Negative reinforcement

Negative reinforcement refers to an increase in the frequency of a response following removal of a negative reinforcer (aversive event or stimulus) immediately after the response occurs. An event is a *negative reinforcer* only if its removal after a response increases performance of that response. Events that appear to be annoying, undesirable, or unpleasant are not necessarily negative reinforcers. A negative reinforcer is defined solely by its effect on behavior.

It is important to note that reinforcement, whether positive or negative, always *increases* a behavior. Negative reinforcement requires an ongoing aversive event which can be removed or terminated after a specific response occurs. A familiar example of negative reinforcement is putting on a coat while standing outside on a cold day. Putting on a coat (the behavior) usually terminates an aversive condition, namely, being cold (negative reinforcer). The probability of wearing a coat in cold weather is increased. Similarly, taking medicine to relieve a headache may be negatively reinforced by the termination of pain. Of course, whether negative reinforcement occurs in the foregoing examples depends upon whether or not the behavior that terminates the undesirable condition increases.

An interesting example of negative reinforcement was reported in a study with psychotic patients (Heckel, Wiggins, and Salzberg 1962). The purpose of the study was to increase conversation in group therapy sessions. The group of patients tended to be silent for long periods. To demonstrate the effect of negative reinforcement, the investigators used a loud noise as an aversive event. The noise sounded from a speaker hidden in an air-conditioning vent in the therapy room. When the group was silent for more than one minute, the noise sounded. The noise continued until one patient broke the silence. Thus, a response (talking) eliminated the aversive event (loud noise). The procedure was effective in increasing patient conversation.

Negative reinforcement requires some aversive event, such as shock, noise, or isolation, which is presented to the individual *before* he responds. The event is removed or reduced immediately after a response. As with positive reinforcers, there are two types of negative reinforcers: primary and secondary. Intense stimuli, such as shock or loud noise, which impinge on the sensory receptors of an organism serve as *primary negative reinforcers.* The aversive response to them is unlearned. Secondary negative reinforcers or *conditioned aversive events* become aversive by being paired with events which already are aversive. For example, disapproving facial expressions or saying the word *no* can serve as aversive events after being paired with events that are already aversive (Lovaas, Schaeffer, and Simmons 1965).

One type of negative reinforcement occurs when an individual *escapes* from an aversive situation. Both classical and operant conditioning may be involved. An aversive stimulus or event may elicit an escape response (classical conditioning) that serves to terminate the aversive stimulus or event (operant conditioning). Escape behaviors gradually occur earlier and earlier as the individual approaches the aversive stimuli, and eventually the individual avoids the aversive situation. This avoidance response is maintained and the individual stays out of the aversive situation. Escape and avoidance responses may be learned by a combination of a number of the factors we have summarized to this point. In everyday life, various secondary negative reinforcers may gain the power to elicit escape responses and therefore lead to avoidance responses. These factors interact in simple ways at some times and in complex ways at other times.

As with positive reinforcement, antecedent or discriminative stimuli may affect behavior. Such stimuli signal the individual that negative reinforcement will follow a response; that is, if the response occurs a negative reinforcer will be terminated. Thus, a camper who hears a bear growl may make an avoidance response, or a new mailman who sees your "Beware of Dog" sign may not deliver your mail. Several other examples from everyday experience show that avoidance behavior is under the control of antecedent stimuli such as air raid sirens, screeching car tires, threats, and traffic signals.

Punishment

Punishment refers to the presentation of an aversive stimulus or event or the removal of a positive event after a response that decreases the probability of that response. This definition diverges from the everyday use of the term, when punishment refers merely to a penalty imposed for performing a particular act. For an event to meet the technical definition of punishment, the frequency of the response must decrease (Azrin and Holz 1966). Because of the negative connotations frequently associated with punishment, it is important to dispel some stereotypic notions that do not apply to the technical definition of punishment. Punishment does not necessarily entail pain or physical coercion. Punishment is neither a means of retribution nor a retaliation for misbehaving. Sometimes in everyday life "punishment" is employed independently of its effects on subsequent behavior. For example, children are "taught a lesson" for misbehaving by undergoing a sacrifice of some kind. Similarly, criminals may receive penalties that do not necessarily decrease the frequency of their criminal acts. In the technical sense punishment is defined solely by its effect on behavior. Punishment is operative only if the frequency of a response is reduced.

There are two types of punishment. First, an aversive stimulus can be applied after a response; this is *punishment by application.* Familiar examples include being reprimanded or spanked after engaging in some behavior, or being burned after touching a hot stove. Whether these examples from everyday life qualify as punishment depends upon whether they decrease the frequency of the antecedent response. Second, a positive reinforcer can be removed after a response; this is *punishment by removal.* Examples include losing privileges after staying out late, losing money for misbehaving, and having one's driver's license revoked.

There are a variety of conditions that may influence the effectiveness of punishment. As you will see, the satisfaction of these conditions in nonlaboratory applications of punishment is often quite difficult. Generally, each of the following enhances the suppressive effects of punishment:

1. *Immediate* application or removal of the contingent stimulus after the undesired response.
2. Punishment of each and every occurrence of the response.
3. Introduction of the contingent punishing stimulus at maximal intensity, rather than with gradual increases in severity.
4. Removal of motivation for the undesired response.
5. Training of an alternative, acceptable response, especially when the motivation for the undesired response cannot be eliminated.
6. Reinforcement of responses that are incompatible with the punished response.
7. In humans, a description of the punishment contingency.

Aside from the question of its effectiveness, there are a number of side effects from punishment that have caused its use in applied settings to be questioned. Some of these side effects are (1) increased emotional responding, (2) avoidance of the punishing agent, and (3) imitation of the use of punishment. (In many instances, positive side effects have also been reported, however.) It is frequently argued that, whenever possible, positive reinforcement of a behavior incompatible with the one to be decreased should be employed. Another alternative to punishment is the use of extinction. However, there are some situations whose exigencies require the use of punishment. For example, head-banging behavior must be decreased quickly and punishment is frequently employed. Even then, positive reinforcement programs for alternative behaviors should be used concurrently with punishment procedures. Other examples will be presented in Part III.

To summarize, behaviors are affected by contingent consequences. Reinforcement refers to procedures that increase the frequency of a response, whereas punishment refers to procedures that decrease a response. There are two kinds of reinforcement: positive and negative. There are two kinds of punishment: punishment by application and punishment by removal. It is important to note the distinction between negative reinforcement and punishment. The Premack principle demonstrates that a high probability response may be used to reinforce a low probability response. Behaviors may also increase as a function of their antecedents, i.e. stimulus control.

Operant extinction

Operant extinction refers to a reduction in response frequency following the cessation of reinforcement. A previously reinforced behavior will decrease when it ceases to produce positive reinforcers or to terminate negative reinforcers.[2] Technically speaking, extinction is the process of "disconnecting" the prior relationship between a response and its consequences. It is common, however, for people to use the term in reference to its effects. When this occurs, the term *extinction* may be inappropriately used as a synonym for *reduction.* For example, a parent might say that he "extinguished" his child's swearing behavior. This usage is misleading for two reasons. First, it overlooks the fact that other procedures, such as punishment, also reduce behavior, but would hardly be called extinguishing. Bear in mind that in punishment a response is followed by the presentation or removal of a stimulus. In extinction, no such change occurs—the response is not followed by any contingent environmental change.

Extinction should also be kept distinct from recovery. Recovery refers to the increase in behavior that may occur with a cessation of

[2] The situation described here is one in which a response has previously terminated an ongoing negative reinforcer. In extinction, the negative reinforcer would be ongoing, but the previously learned response would no longer terminate it. This should not be confused with the situation wherein the organism, by totally avoiding the negative reinforcer, precludes the opportunity for extinction to occur.

punishment. A previously punished response may increase when it ceases to produce negative stimuli or to cause the removal of positive stimuli. In the absence of any other changes, the suspension of fines for speeding may increase the frequency of that behavior. Recovery undoubtedly occurs in applied behavior modification, but usually there is an attempt to minimize its effect. On the other hand, extinction is a widely used principle, upon which several clinical procedures are based.

In everyday life, the most common use of extinction is ignoring a behavior that may have been reinforced previously with attention. A parent may ignore a whining child. A physician may ignore the complaints of a hypochondriac. A teacher may ignore children who talk without raising their hands. A therapist or counselor may ignore certain self-defeating statements made by the client. In each of these examples, the prior reinforcer (attention, approval, or sympathy) for the response is no longer presented. The following are additional examples of extinction: putting money into vending machines (the behavior) will cease if gum, food, or drink (the reinforcer) is not forthcoming; turning on a radio will cease if the radio no longer functions; and attempting to start a car will extinguish if the car will not start. In these examples, the consequences that maintain the behavior are no longer forthcoming. The absence of reinforcing consequences reduces the behavior. In clinical applications, the stimuli or events that previously reinforced the behavior must be identified so that their occurrence can be controlled. It is important to note that extinction frequently results in a temporary increase in the behavior and a subsequent decrease. However, such an extinction burst, or temporarily increased response rate, does not always occur when extinction is employed.

Reinforcement schedules

Reinforcement schedules are the rules describing the manner in which consequences follow behavior. Reinforcement is always administered according to some schedule. In the simplest schedule the response is reinforced each time it occurs. When each instance of a response is reinforced the schedule is called *continuous reinforcement.* If reinforcement is provided only after some instances of a response but not after each response, the schedule is called *intermittent reinforcement.*

Continuous and intermittent reinforcement schedules produce important differences in performance. These differences are most apparent at three stages in learning. First, during the initial development of a response, continuous reinforcement is preferable because it accelerates this early performance and produces higher rates of response. At the second stage, however, when response maintenance is an important consideration, intermittent schedules of reinforcement result in dramatically higher performance rates. Although continuous reinforcement is more efficient during response acquisition, intermittent reinforcement is generally preferable for response maintenance. Another advantage of intermittent reinforcement becomes apparent in the third stage (extinction). When a previous response-reinforcer relationship is terminated, extinction will occur fairly rapidly if the response was on a continuous reinforcement schedule. If the response was maintained by intermittent reinforcement, however, the rate of extinction will be much slower. That is, the individual will respond more frequently and for a longer period of time. This phenomenon is often expressed by saying that intermittent reinforcement schedules increase resistance to extinction. The advantages of that resistance will become more apparent as we discuss clinical applications.

The different effects of continuous and intermittent reinforcement are apparent in everyday experience. Examples of relatively continuous reinforcement might be opening the refrigerator (assuming that it always contains goodies), or placing a favorite album on a stereo turntable. Examples of intermittent reinforcement include casting a fishing line into the water (which does not always result in a fish) or entering a lottery (which seldom results in winning a prize). The different effects of continuous and intermittent reinforcement are well illustrated by looking at responses made in the presence of vending and slot machines. Vending machines require a response (placing coins into a slot and pulling a lever) that is reinforced with a stimulus (cigarettes or candy) virtually every time. Thus, there is continuous reinforcement. When a reinforcer is no longer provided for putting in coins and pulling a lever, rapid extinction follows. As soon as the reinforcer, or the product, is no longer delivered, performance most likely stops immediately. Few individuals would place more coins into the machine. Behaviors associated with slot machines reveal a very different pattern. The response (putting money into a machine and pulling a lever) is only intermittently reinforced with "jackpot" money. If money were never delivered the response would eventually extinguish. With an intermittent schedule, and especially one where the reinforcer is delivered very infrequently, responding may continue for a long time. The more intermittent the schedule, the closer it approaches an extinction procedure.

Although the major emphasis in schedules research has been on reinforcement, it is worth mentioning that punishment can also be scheduled in the same ways as reinforcement. There are some differences in the resulting performances, but in general what we have written about reinforcement schedules can be inverted and applied to punishment schedules. Most relevant, perhaps, is the generality that intermittent punishment tends to increase resistance to recovery; that is, it suppresses the undesired response for longer periods than does continuous punishment. Since our current understanding and application of schedules is considerably more extensive for reinforcement than for punishment, we will restrict our focus to that area.

Intermittent reinforcement can be scheduled in a variety of ways. First, reinforcers can be delivered after the emission of a certain *number of responses.* This type of delivery is referred to as a *ratio schedule* because the schedule specifies the number of responses required for each reinforcement. Second, reinforcers can be delivered on the basis of the *time interval* that separates available reinforcers. This is referred to as an *interval schedule,* meaning that the response will be reinforced after a specified time interval.

The delivery of reinforcers on either ratio or interval schedules can be *fixed* (unvarying) or *variable* (constantly changing). Thus, four simple schedules of reinforcement can be distinguished, namely, fixed ratio, variable ratio, fixed interval, and variable interval. Each of these schedules leads to a different pattern of performance.

A *fixed ratio schedule* requires that a certain number of responses occur prior to delivery of the reinforcer. For example, a fixed ratio 2 schedule (FR:2) denotes that every second response is reinforced. A *variable ratio schedule* also requires that a certain number of responses occur prior to delivery of the reinforcer. However, the number varies around an *average* from one reinforcement to the next. On the average, a specific number of responses are required for reinforcement. For example, a variable ratio 5 schedule (VR:5) means that on the average every fifth response is reinforced. Over ten trials, the required number of responses for reinforcement might be as follows: 2, 4, 7, 5, 3, 3, 9, 8, 5, 4. If you calculate the average of these numbers, it will be 5. On any given trial, however, the organism does not know how many responses are required.

Performance differs under fixed and variable ratio reinforcement schedules. On fixed schedules, typically there is a temporary pause in response after reinforcement occurs and then a rapid rise in response rate until the number of responses required for reinforcement is reached. The length of the pause after reinforcement is a function of the ratio specified by the schedule. Larger ratios produce longer pauses. In contrast, variable ratio schedules lead to fairly consistent performance and relatively constant response rates. Because of the unpredictable schedule, performance rates tend to be relatively high.

Interval schedules can be either fixed or variable. A *fixed interval schedule* requires that an unvarying time interval must pass before the reinforcer is available. The first response to occur after this interval is reinforced. For example, in a fixed interval 1 schedule (FI:1), where the number refers to minutes, reinforcement is produced by the first response occurring after 1 minute has elapsed. An interval schedule requires that only one response occur after the interval elapses. Any responses occurring before the interval elapses are not reinforced. With a *variable interval schedule,* the length of the interval varies around an average. For example, in a variable interval 4 schedule (VI:4), reinforcers might become available after the following number of minutes: 6, 4, 4, 2, 7, 5, 4, 1, 3, 4. Notice that the average is 4 minutes. The interval units may vary from seconds to weeks, depending on the organism and the response. The first response after the interval elapses is reinforced.

Performance differs under fixed and variable interval schedules. Fixed interval schedules tend to lead to marked pauses after the reinforcer is delivered. Unlike the pattern in fixed ratio schedules, responding after the pause is only gradually resumed—the organism often learns to wait until the interval is almost over. After extensive training, fixed ratio and fixed interval performances may look very similar. With variable ratio schedules, pauses are usually absent and performance is more consistent. In general, the rate of response is higher for variable than for fixed interval schedules.

Across the four simple schedules discussed, it is worth noting that higher rates of response usually are achieved with ratio rather than interval schedules. This is understandable because high response rates do not necessarily speed up the delivery of reinforcement in an interval schedule as they do with ratio schedules. Moreover, variable schedules tend to produce more consistent response patterns, that is, they are not marked by the all-or-none pauses and response bursts of fixed schedules.

The various intermittent schedules are important for developing resistance to extinction. Variable schedules are particularly effective in prolonging extinction. As performance is achieved under a particular schedule, the schedule can be made "leaner" by gradually requiring more responses (ratio) or longer periods of time (interval) prior to reinforcement. With very lean schedules few reinforcers need to be delivered to maintain a high level of performance. The shift from a "dense" or more generous schedule to a leaner one, however, must be made gradually to avoid extinction.

Examples of reinforcement schedules are not difficult to find in everyday experience. Individuals who fish, hunt, gamble, enter lotteries, or work for commissions, are familiar with variable ratio schedules.

Each response is not reinforced. These behaviors are under ratio reinforcement schedules because the reinforcer—if it follows at all—will come only after numerous responses. A number of situations demonstrate interval scheduling. For example, television programs, buses, and wages frequently occur at particular intervals that are relatively fixed. Performance under fixed interval schedules is often marked by all-or-none patterns such as last-minute cramming for exams and post-examination pauses. For a more detailed discussion of reinforcement schedules, the reader is referred to the Suggested Readings.

Shaping

New behavior cannot always be developed by reinforcing a response. In many cases, the desired response may never occur. The behavior may be so complex that its component elements are not in the repertoire of the individual. For example, developing appropriate eating behaviors requires, among other things, selecting and using appropriate utensils, which may not be in the repertoire of very young children. *Shaping* refers to reinforcing small steps or approximations toward a terminal response rather than reinforcing the terminal response itself. Responses which resemble the final response or which include components of that response are reinforced. Through reinforcement of *successive approximations* of the terminal response, the final response is gradually achieved. Responses that are increasingly similar to the final response (goal) are reinforced and they increase, while those responses dissimilar to the final response are not reinforced and they extinguish.

One of the most familiar examples of shaping is training animals to perform various tricks. If the animal trainer waited until the tricks were performed to administer a reinforcer, the reinforcer might never be delivered. However, by shaping the response, the trainer can achieve the terminal goal. Initially, food may be delivered for running toward the trainer. As that response becomes stable, the trainer may reinforce running up to the trainer when he is holding the hoop. Other steps closer to the final goal would be reinforced in sequence such as walking through the hoop on the ground, jumping through the hoop when it is slightly off the ground, and jumping through the hoop when it is high off the ground. Eventually, the terminal response will be performed with a high frequency, whereas the unnecessary responses or steps developed along the way will have extinguished.

Shaping requires reinforcing behaviors that resemble the terminal response or approximate the goal. As the initial approximation is performed consistently, the criterion for reinforcement is altered slightly so that the next response resembles the final goal more closely than did the previous response. This procedure is continued until the terminal response is developed.

Chaining

Behaviors can be divided into a sequence of responses referred to as a chain. The components of a chain represent individual responses which may already be in the behavioral repertoire of the individual. The unique feature of a chain is that individual responses are ordered in a particular sequence. The behavior of attending a party illustrates the ordering of component responses in a chain. Going to a party may be initiated by a call from someone or by a written invitation. Once the behavior is initiated, several responses follow in sequence including getting dressed for the party, leaving the house, entering a car, traveling to the party, parking the car, entering the house, and eating, drinking, and socializing. The response sequence unfolds in a relatively fixed order until the chain is completed and the last response is reinforced (eating, drinking, and socializing may serve as the reinforcers). Later responses in the chain (entering the house where the party is) are preceded by a series of responses (traveling in the car and so on). The order is fixed so that early responses must precede later ones. Each response in the chain does not appear to be reinforced. Only the last response (the response immediately preceding eating, drinking, and socializing) is followed by the reinforcers. Because a reinforcer alters or sustains only the behavior that immediately precedes it, it is unclear what maintains the entire chain of behaviors leading to the final response. However, there are many chains of responses that are maintained in everyday experience. For example, mastering a musical instrument or preparing for athletic competition both require a series of intermediate responses before the final reinforcing event is achieved. The major question is what maintains all the intermediate responses that precede achievement of the final goal. The answer requires explanation of the factors that link the response components of a chain.

An important concept which is basic to understanding chains is that an event or stimulus which immediately precedes reinforcement becomes a cue or signal for reinforcement. As noted earlier, an event that signals reinforcement for a particular response is referred to as a discriminative stimulus (S^D). An S^D sets the *occasion* for behavior; that is, it increases the probability that a previously reinforced behavior will occur. Yet, an S^D serves another function as well. An S^D not only signals reinforcement but eventually becomes a reinforcer itself. With frequent pairing of an S^D and a reinforcer, the S^D gradually develops reinforcing properties of its own. This procedure was mentioned in the discussion of conditioned reinforcement. The discriminative stimulus properties of events which precede reinforcement and the reinforcing properties of these events, when they are frequently presented prior to or paired with reinforcers, are important in explaining how chains of response are maintained.

Consider the chain of responses involved in going to a party, described previously.[3] A phone call may have signaled the first response to go to the party. All the behaviors in the chain of reponses are then performed, ending in positive reinforcement (eating, drinking, and socializing). The final response in the chain before reinforcement was entering the house. This response is directly reinforced with food and drink. Yet, any event that precedes reinforcement becomes an S^D for reinforcement. In the chain, the last response (entering the house) becomes an S^D for reinforcement, because this response signals that reinforcement will follow. The constant pairing of an S^D with a reinforcer (food and drink) eventually results in the S^D becoming a reinforcer as well as a discriminative stimulus. Hence, the response that preceded direct reinforcement has become an S^D for subsequent reinforcement and a reinforcer in its own right. The response serves as a reinforcer for the previous link in the chain of responses. The response (entering the house) becomes a reinforcer for the previous behavior (parking the car). Since parking the car now precedes reinforcement, it too becomes an S^D. As with other responses, the pairing of the S^D with reinforcement results in the S^D becoming a reinforcer. The process continues in a *backward* direction so that each response in the chain becomes an S^D and a reinforcer. Each component response is both an S^D for the next response in the chain and a reinforcer for the previous response in the chain. Even the very first response becomes an S^D, but it does not reinforce a prior response. Although the sequence appears to be maintained by the reinforcers at the end of the chain of responses, the links in the chain are assumed to take on conditioned reinforcement value. The building of response chains requires training from the last response in the sequence, which precedes direct reinforcement, back to the first response. Since the last response in the sequence is followed immediately and directly by the reinforcer, it is most easily established as a conditioned reinforcer that can maintain other responses.

The differences between shaping and chaining may appear unclear. Generally, shaping is used to develop new behaviors. Cues such as instructions and gestures may be used as discriminative stimuli com-

[3] Of course, the chain could be further divided into several components smaller than those mentioned.

bined with direct reinforcement, such as praise, for responses that approach the terminal goal. In contrast, chaining is usually employed to develop a sequence of behaviors, using responses that are already present in the individual's repertoire. To obtain a chain of responses consisting of discrete behaviors, shaping may be used first to develop component behaviors. The clearest difference between the procedures is that chaining proceeds in a backward direction beginning with the last response and linking together prior behaviors, whereas shaping works in a forward direction. Furthermore, shaping focuses upon developing a particular terminal response; the behaviors performed during training for the terminal response may not be evident when shaping is completed. In chaining, behaviors developed early in training are still evident when training is completed.

Prompts

Antecedent events such as cues, instructions, gestures, directions, examples, and models can facilitate development of a behavior. Events that help initiate a response are referred to as *prompts.* Prompts precede a response. When the prompt results in the response, the response can be reinforced. When a prompt initiates behaviors that are reinforced, the prompt becomes an S^D for reinforcement. For example, if a parent tells a child to return from school early and the child is reinforced for doing so, the instruction or prompt becomes an S^D. Instructions signal that reinforcement is likely when certain behaviors are performed. Eventually, instructions alone are likely to be followed by the behavior. As a general rule, when a prompt consistently precedes reinforcement of a response, the prompt becomes an S^D and can effectively control behavior.

Developing behavior can be facilitated in different ways using various kinds of prompts, such as physically *guiding* the behavior, *instructing* the child to do something, *gesturing* to the child, and *observing* another person (a model) performing a behavior (such as watching someone play a game). Prompts play a major role in shaping and chaining. Developing a terminal response using reinforcement alone may be tedious and time-consuming. If the person is prompted to begin the response, more rapid approximations to the final response can be made.

Although prompts may be required early in training, they can be withdrawn gradually or faded as training progresses. If a prompt is abruptly removed early in training, the response may no longer occur. But if the response is performed consistently with a prompt, the prompt can be progressively reduced and finally omitted. Gradually removing a prompt is referred to as *fading*. To achieve behavior without continued dependence on prompts requires fading of prompts and reinforcement of responses in the absence of cues or signals. For example, prompts may be used to train a child to feed himself. Initially, a trainer may guide the child's arm to help the child place a spoon into the food and bring the food to his mouth. At the beginning of training, prompts may be essential to initiate performance of the appropriate behavior. The completion of the behavior, even though accompanied by prompts, is reinforced. Gradually, guidance by the trainer is reduced. Perhaps the trainer will exert less physical strength in initiating movement of the spoon to the food. Eventually, the trainer may fade all touching of the child and merely point or say to the child, "Eat." Ultimately, the trainer may eliminate prompts and merely reinforce the child for completing the eating sequence. Thus, although prompts may figure heavily in the development of the behavior, at the end of training they may be omitted. It is not always essential to remove all prompts or cues because much of ordinary behavior is controlled by such cues. For example, it is important to train individuals to respond to the presence of certain prompts such as instructions that exert control over a variety of behaviors in everyday life.

Discrimination and stimulus control

The discussion of prompts and discriminative stimuli reveals the importance of antecedent events in controlling behavior. It is important to elaborate the role of antecedent events and explain how they acquire control over behavior.

In some situations or in the presence of certain stimuli, a particular response may be reinforced, while in other situations or in the presence of other stimuli it is not. When a response is consistently reinforced in the presence of a particular stimulus and consistently not reinforced in the presence of another stimulus, each stimulus signals the consequences that are likely to follow. The stimulus present when the response is reinforced signals that performance is likely to be reinforced. Conversely, the stimulus present during nonreinforcement signals that the response is not likely to be reinforced. As mentioned earlier, a stimulus whose presence has been associated with reinforcement is referred to as an S^D. A stimulus whose presence has been associated with nonreinforcement is referred to as an S^Δ (S delta). The effect of differentially reinforcing behavior in different stimulus conditions is that eventually the reinforced response is likely to occur in the presence of the S^D but unlikely to occur in the presence of the S^Δ. The probability of a response can be increased or decreased by presenting or removing the

S^D. The S^D occasions the previously reinforced response or increases the likelihood that the response will occur. When the individual responds differently in the presence of different stimuli, he has made a *discrimination.* When responses are differentially controlled by antecedent stimuli behavior is considered to be under *stimulus control.*

Instances of stimulus control pervade everyday life. For example, the ring of a telephone signals that a certain behavior (answering the phone) is likely to be reinforced (by hearing someone's voice). Specifically, the ring of the phone is associated with the voice of someone on the phone (the reinforcer). The ring of the phone (S^D) increases the likelihood that the receiver will be picked up. In the absence of the ring (S^Δ), the probability of answering the phone to hear someone's voice is very low. The rings of a door bell, telephone, alarm, and kitchen timer all serve as discriminative stimuli and increase the likelihood that certain responses will be reinforced. In social interaction, stimulus control also is important. For example, a greeting or gesture from someone is likely to occasion a social response such as initiation of conversation. Whereas a greeting serves as an S^D, or signals that reinforcement is likely to follow a social response, a frown serves as an S^Δ, or signals that reinforcement is not likely to follow a social response.

The notion of stimulus control is exceedingly important in behavior modification. In many behavior modification programs, the goal is to alter the relationship between behavior and the stimulus conditions in which the behavior occurs. Some behavior problems stem from a failure to certain stimuli such as instructions to control behavior although such control would be desirable. Other behavioral problems occur when certain behaviors such as overeating or smoking *are* under control of antecedent stimuli when such control is undesirable.

Generalization

The effect of the contingencies on behavior may generalize across either the stimulus conditions beyond which training has taken place or across the responses that were included in the contingency. These two types of generalization are referred to as stimulus generalization and response generalization, respectively.

Stimulus generalization

A response that is repeatedly reinforced in a particular situation is likely to be repeated in that situation. Situations and stimuli often share common properties. Control of behavior exerted by a given stimulus is shared by other stimuli that are similar or which share common properties (Skinner 1953). Thus, a behavior may be performed in new situations similar to the original situation in which reinforcement occurred. If a response reinforced in one setting also increases in other settings, even though it is not reinforced in these other settings, this is referred to as *stimulus generalization.* Stimulus generalization refers to the transfer of a response to situations other than those in which training has taken place.

Numerous examples of stimulus generalization can be seen in everyday life. For example, a child may develop fear in response to a physician because of an association of the physician with pain from an injection. The avoidance and fear responses that occur in the presence of the physician may also occur in the presence of dentists, nurses, and milkmen. To the child, the fear may generalize to any individual wearing a white uniform. Until the child has different contingencies associated with different uniforms across different settings, the fear response may remain across diverse types of uniforms. The example entails generalization because the fear was acquired in a specific stimulus context but generalized to other similar contexts.

Stimulus generalization is the opposite of discrimination. When an individual discriminates in performing responses, the response fails to generalize. Conversely, when a response generalizes across situations, the individual fails to discriminate in performing the response. The degree of stimulus generalization is a function of the similarity of a new stimulus or situation to the stimulus under which the response was trained (Kimble 1961). Over a long period of time, a response may not generalize across situations because the individual discriminates that the response is reinforced in one situation but not in others.

Stimulus generalization represents an important area in behavior modification. Although training takes place in a restricted setting, such as an institution, special classroom, hospital, day-care center, or home, it may be desirable that the behaviors developed in these settings generalize or transfer to other settings.

Response generalization

An additional type of generalization involves responses rather than stimulus conditions. Alteration of one response can inadvertently influence other responses; this is referred to as *response generalization.* For example, if a person is reinforced for smiling, the frequency of laughing and talking might also increase. The reinforcement of a response increases the probability of other responses which are similar (Skinner 1953). To the extent that a nonreinforced response is similar to a reinforced one, the probability of the similar response is also increased.

Alteration of one behavior is sometimes associated with alteration of related behaviors. For example, one study reported response generalization in a preschool child (Buell et al. 1968). Teacher attention reinforced the child's use of outdoor play equipment. Not only did the reinforced response increase, but related behaviors such as touching and talking with other children increased as well. Alteration of one behavior is frequently associated with changes in behaviors that are not directly reinforced (Kazdin 1975b). For example, decreasing the disruptive behavior of a 6-year-old boy was associated with increases in punctuality, although the latter behavior was not included in the contingencies (Kubany, Weiss, and Sloggett 1971). In some cases it is unclear precisely how the change in one behavior affects other behaviors. For example, with one child reduction of uncooperative behavior was associated with a reduction of stuttering even though stuttering was not focused upon directly (Wahler, Sperling, Thomas, Teeter, and Luper 1970). In any case, alternation of one behavior with the direct application of contingencies is often associated with changes in a variety of other behaviors.

Summary

Although behavior modification has borrowed extensively from a number of other areas of psychology, it has relied most heavily on the psychology of learning, including classical conditioning, operant conditioning, and observational learning (modeling). Classical conditioning and modeling were presented briefly in the last chapter and modeling will be discussed again in Chapter 9. The present chapter outlines the principles of operant conditioning, which have served as the basis for several behavior modification techniques.

Contingent consequences affect behavior. There are two reinforcement procedures that increase the frequency of a response: the application of a positive reinforcer (positive reinforcement) and the removal of a negative reinforcer (negative reinforcement). There are two punishment procedures that decrease the frequency of a response: the application of a negative reinforcer (punishment by application) and the removal of a positive reinforcer (punishment by removal). Extinction refers to a reduction in response frequency following the cessation of reinforcement. Reinforcement may follow a continuous or intermittent schedule. Four types of intermittent schedules were discussed: fixed ratio, variable ratio, fixed interval, and variable interval.

Shaping refers to reinforcing small steps or approximations toward a terminal response. Chaining refers to the linking together of responses within an individual's repertoire; this is done in a backward direction. Prompts are events that precede a response and help to initiate it; prompts may gradually be faded.

Antecedent stimuli or events may also affect behavior. When this occurs a response is under stimulus control.

There are two types of generalization: stimulus and response. Stimulus generalization refers to the transfer of a response to situations other than those in which training has taken place. Response generalization refers to the altering of other responses in addition to the response which has been trained. Discrimination is the opposite of generalization.

Suggested readings

PRINCIPLES OF OPERANT CONDITIONING

Holland, J. G., and Skinner, B. F. *The analysis of behavior.* New York: McGraw-Hill, 1961.

Kazdin, A. E. *Behavior modification in applied settings.* Homewood, Ill.: Dorsey Press, 1975.

Rachlin, H. *Introduction to modern behaviorism.* San Francisco: W. H. Freeman, 1970.

Williams, J. L. *Operant learning: Procedures for changing behavior.* Belmont, Calif.: Brooks/Cole, 1973.

REINFORCEMENT SCHEDULES

Logan, F. A. *Fundamentals of learning and motivation.* Dubuque, Iowa: William C. Brown, 1969.

Reynolds, G. S. *A primer of operant conditioning.* Glenview, Ill.: Scott, Foresman, 1968.

Cognitive influences in behavior modification

8

As noted in the previous chapter, behavior modification attempts to rely on research from general psychology. Thus, findings culled from diverse areas may be relevant to achieving behavior change. It is difficult to specify all the available findings that might be employed to alter behavior for clinical purposes. In the main, findings from the psychology of learning have generated the largest number of ideas and techniques.

Recently, however, cognitive psychology has been utilized in behavior modification. Several investigators have emphasized the role of cognitions (perceptions, thoughts, beliefs) on behavior (Bandura 1969; Meichenbaum 1974; Ellis 1962; Kanfer and Phillips 1970; Mahoney 1974a). The cognitive position emphasizes the role of mediation in learning, or the cognitive and symbolic processes that influence behavior. The effects of variables in these areas have been evaluated according to the demands of scientific investigation as discussed in Part I. The processes include perception and interpretation of environmental events, belief systems, verbal and imaginal coding systems, thinking, planning, problem solving, and others. These processes are crucial to understanding the interrelationship between the individual and environmental events. Understanding either cognitive processes of the individual or the environmental events alone without understanding their interaction provides an insufficient account of many behaviors. The importance of environmental consequences of behavior was emphasized in the previous chapter. In the present chapter, the importance of an individual's interpretation and cognitive organization of environmental events assumes greater importance. An individual's perception of environmental events rather than the events themselves often accounts for behavior. Two individuals exposed to an identical situation respond differently, depending in part upon the interpretations and meaning that they place upon the situation.

Cognitive processes and environmental events

Bandura (1969) and Mahoney (1974a) have discussed four cognitive processes and environmental events that influence behavior. These include attention, mediation, component behaviors, and incentive or motivational conditions. These will be outlined briefly.

Attention refers to those conditions that enhance an individual's awareness of specific environmental events. Because a person is confronted with many events, attention is selective. The events to which individuals attend determine behavior. In a given situation, different individuals attend to diverse stimuli. Attentiveness to different events accounts in part for differences in behavior. For example, individuals taking an ocean cruise may attend to different stimuli associated with the cruise. One individual may be struck by the peaceful nature of the surroundings. Another might attend to the extreme isolation and lack of touch with the mainland. Yet another may attend to the hazards, real and imagined, of ocean travel. The behaviors in which these individuals engage, such as relaxing on the deck, letter writing, or remaining in the cabin, respectively, may in part be determined by the events to which they attend. In everyday life, as well as in therapy, knowledge of the stimuli to which individuals attend is important in explaining behavior. In the treatment of clinical problems such as sexual deviance and obesity a great deal of emphasis often is placed on the stimuli to which the individuals attend.

Mediation refers to those processes that account for coding or cognitive representation of events upon which attention has been focused. Material to which we attend is stored in memory and subsequently influences behavior. To effect enduring behavior change, it may be important to ensure that observed or learned material has been coded in some fashion. Various procedures such as symbolic coding operations in the form of verbal or imaginal rehearsal can influence retention of learned material (Bandura 1971). For example, observational learning is facilitated by having the observer code the model's behavior. Individuals who observe a model and symbolically code the observed material through either imaginal or verbal representation (that is, describe verbally to themselves what the model did) are better able to reproduce the material than individuals who have not engaged in the coding processes (e.g., Gerst 1971).

The manner in which events are mediated or coded is relevant to the understanding of diverse forms of maladaptive behavior. Mediational phenomena such as anticipation of outcomes of courses of action, superstitions, expectations, and misperceptions, may be related to maladaptive behavior (see Rotter 1954). For example, an individual's expectation of failure may lead him continually to avoid various situations.

Component behaviors or response repertoires of an individual must also be considered in explaining behavior. Attention to environmental events and symbolic coding of these events do not ensure performance of a given behavior (Bandura 1969). Attentiveness to and perception of environmental events are preconditions for certain kinds of performance but they are not sufficient in themselves; a person must also possess the specific skills required to behave in a particular fashion. Exposure to environmental events may not result in behavior change if an individual has severe response deficits. For example, a socially inept individual may not show behavioral improvement merely by watching others perform in an adept fashion. Being socially adept requires a number of skills and responsiveness to a variety of nuances which are not quickly learned. For someone who has very few or none of the initial response components in his or her repertoire, behavior change may require building of individual responses. In such cases, shaping procedures may have to be employed to teach the final, target behavior.

Motivational or incentive conditions also dictate performance. The control that external consequences exert over behavior was detailed in the discussion of operant conditioning principles in Chapter 7. For understanding and altering behavior, one should know the consequences associated with a particular behavior in a given environment and what consequences can be used to influence behavior.

Aside from focusing on the actual consequences of behavior, the cognitive position focuses upon an individual's thoughts about and perceptions of the consequences. Anticipation of consequences occurs in many situations and plays a role in a variety of behaviors, such as entering lotteries, carrying an umbrella, and leaving a sinking ship. Indeed, the anticipation of consequences probably plays a major role in behaviors assumed to be indicative of self-control, such as following the law, refusing a final drink when offered the proverbial "one for the road," refusing an extra dessert, and maintaining a rigorous exercise regimen. Anticipation refers to imaginally bringing delayed consequences closer in proximity to the behavior which will eventually produce the consequences. Anticipation is the symbolic (verbal or imaginal) representation of the consequences that might result from the behavior. Cognitive representation of consequences determines many of the behaviors that we undertake, complete, or terminate.

The foregoing discussion outlines the importance of perceptions and cognitions (attention, mediation, anticipation of consequences), the behavior of the individual (component responses), and environmental events (incentive conditions) in explaining and changing behavior. These factors provide an expanded account and different points of emphasis from those outlined in the previous chapter.

Contributions of cognitive psychology

A number of areas in behavior modification pertain to an individual's perceptions of or cognitions about events. A number of covert events mediate behavior change. In the following discussion, significant areas of research that are drawn upon in behavior modification will be sampled. The discussion provides an overview of various cognitive influences. In some ways this information expands upon the discussion of cognitive factors or processes examined in the previous section.

Attribution

One area of research that appears relevant for behavior modification is the area of attribution. *Attribution* refers to explanations of and perceptions about the cause of particular events. The causal agents to which events are attributed account for many behaviors. The role of attribution in behavior modification is particularly interesting because it points out the importance of cognitions or thoughts regarding observed events. The importance of cognitions is readily apparent when an environmental event receives differing interpretations from different people. For example, a simple sound such as the ticking of a clock may be interpreted by one person as a harmless clock and by another person as a time bomb. Such attributions placed upon events may dictate different behaviors.

A classic experiment in the area of attribution was performed by Schachter and Singer (1962). These authors demonstrated that an individual's emotional state depends upon physiological arousal plus cues in the environment to which this arousal might be attributed. In their experiment, some subjects received an injection of epinephrine (adrenalin), which results in physiological arousal, and others received placebo injections of salt water. One-third of the subjects in each group received correct information regarding the effects of epinephrine (for example, the heart rate increases), one-third received incorrect information (about irrelevant effects such as itchy feet), and one-third received no information. After the injection, subjects were exposed to someone who was behaving in either a euphoric or an angry manner. The individuals who acted euphoric or angry were confederates actually working for the experimenter. The euphoric confederate appeared elated and played games such as throwing crumpled paper into the wastebasket, singing, and so on. The angry confederate made nasty remarks and appeared generally upset. The main issue was the reactions of subjects exposed to the euphoric or angry confederates. The results indicated that those who received the injection of epinephrine and had no clear explanation for their arousal described their feelings in terms of the cues available to them, that is, in terms of the actions of the confederate. Thus, the attributions made about their own feelings were dictated not only by a physiological state but by interpretations of the environment.

The research on attribution has been extended along several lines (see Hastorf, Schneider, and Polefka 1970). An interesting study by Valins (1966) investigated the extent to which perceptions of internal feelings are used to label feelings. Males looked at *Playboy* centerfold nudes while listening to a background noise. They were told the noise was their own heartbeat. Actually the noise was preprogrammed and did not reflect any subject's heartbeat. During the experiment, the "heartbeat" remained constant for all subjects while viewing half of the pictures. While they were viewing the other half of the pictures, the "heartbeat" increased for some subjects and decreased for others. Subsequently, subjects rated the attractiveness of the pictures. Interestingly, subjects rated as more attractive those pictures associated with a change in their heartbeat (either an increase or a decrease) compared with the pictures associated with a constant heartbeat. It appears as if subjects attributed significance to their own apparent change in heartbeat. Further, the subjects interpreted this change as indicating positive evaluation of the pictures.

The clinical relevance of attribution may be potentially great although it has not been completely evaluated. One study (Davison and Valins 1969) explored the role of attribution in maintaining behavior change after drugs are withdrawn. Individuals whose behavior is altered with the use of drugs may show behavior change only while the drugs are administered. Once the drugs are withdrawn, the gains may no longer be maintained. Quite possibly, individuals attribute changes in their own behavior to the drugs rather than to themselves. Such attribution may account for whether or not behavior is maintained once the drugs are withdrawn. An important question in understanding behavior change is the effect of having individuals attribute behavior change to themselves rather than to extraneous events.

Davison and Valins gave subjects a series of shocks and then administered a placebo drug. Subjects were then given a series of milder shocks and led to believe that they were now able to tolerate more pain. The implication, of course, was that the drug helped the individuals tolerate greater pain. After this, some subjects were told that the drug actually was a placebo. Those who were led to believe in the power of the drug were told that the real effects of the drug were wearing off. During the final series of shocks, these two groups differed in their pain tolerance. Those subjects who attributed their increased tolerance to the drug did not tolerate as much pain as did those who had attributed their increased tolerance to themselves. In short, the putative increased tolerance of some subjects could not be attributed to the drug, for they were told that it was only a placebo. These individuals, in fact, were able to tolerate more pain subsequently because of the self-attribution.

In clinical practice, attribution may play a major role in behavior change. As part of therapy, individuals may learn to alter the attributions that they impose upon themselves, others, and the events in the environment. Individuals may learn to attribute to themselves greater control over their own behavior and view themselves as agents who can affect the world rather than as passive objects victimized by environmental fiat.

Placebo reaction and demand characteristics

A phenomenon related to attribution is the placebo reaction. Within medical circles *placebo reaction* refers to a psychological, physiological, or psychophysiological effect of a drug which is independent of its specific pharmacological effect (Shapiro 1960, 1971). The placebo reaction is a general response to a procedure per se rather than a reaction to any specific chemical. For example, patients may show improvements in a particular physiological symptom as a result of taking medicine per se (that is, any medicine) whether or not the medicine is pharmacologically active. The term *placebo* has been employed in psychology with much the same meaning; usually the reaction is to some psychological procedure rather than to a drug.

Historically, several concoctions under the guise of medical treatment have succeeded as curative agents (Shapiro 1971; Ullmann and Krasner 1969). Often, it has subsequently been established that the curative procedures were placebos because the agents or drugs themselves did not possess sufficient pharmacological powers to alter the disorder. The importance of placebo reactions is widely recognized.

Research has shown the effectiveness of placebos in treating pain, migraine headaches, anxiety, colds, and a host of other disorders (see Haas, Fink, and Hartfeldter 1963; Shapiro 1971). In the area of psychotherapy and behavior modification the importance of placebo effects is well recognized (Frank 1973). Individuals participating in psychotherapy often show some improvement independently of the specific treatment that is provided. Indeed, as noted in Chapter 5, it is important to separate placebo reactions from specific treatment effects when evaluating therapy. To evaluate therapy, it is not sufficient to compare clients who receive treatment with those who do not receive treatment. Any changes in behavior as a result of treatment may be due to the actual therapeutic effect of a specific treatment, to placebo effects, or to their combination. Research often employs placebo control groups to control for the *nonspecific* effects due to participation in treatment per se. For example, clients in a placebo control group may receive a procedure that seems effective from the client's standpoint. That is, the rationale for the procedure is reasonable and the client is likely to expect therapeutic change; however, the placebo treatment is designed so that it does not have a specific ingredient that should result in behavior change (Paul 1969a).

Clinically, placebo effects play a major role in treatment. Indeed, for the benefit of the client it may be wise to maximize placebo effects when a veridical treatment is provided. If treatment is one that is likely to work, it still may be useful to maximize the client's belief in its curative powers. This is not deception in the sense that a useless or inert treatment is portrayed as effective. Rather, an effective procedure may be enhanced by increasing a client's expectations for improvement. For example, in the area of systematic desensitization, various studies have shown that increasing subjects' expectation of improvement enhances treatment effects (e.g., McGlynn, Mealiea, and Nawas 1969), although there are conflicting data (e.g., Lomont and Brock 1971; Miller 1972).

Because placebo effects have been shown to be important in altering behavior, they must be considered as an important means of behavior change. Indeed, placebo effects are so well established that the burden of proof is placed upon any new therapy technique to demonstrate that something other than placebo effects is operative.

Placebo reactions are referred to when nonspecific effects occur in a therapeutic context. An analogous effect in an experimental setting is referred to as the *demand characteristics* of the situation (Orne 1962). Demand characteristics refer to an individual's responsiveness to cues in an experimental setting. Cues in the setting convey to the individual how he or she is to behave and thus affect performance in the experimental situation (see Weber and Cook 1972). A number of investigations have shown that in psychological experiments, individuals can be induced to perform in a particular way depending upon the manipulation of extraneous cues. For example, Orne and Schiebe (1964) conducted an experiment on meaning deprivation in which individuals were to be isolated and deprived of stimulation in a manner similar to that used in sensory deprivation investigations. Experimental subjects were treated in an elaborate fashion to provide cues suggesting that certain kinds of behaviors were expected of them. These subjects were given an initial interview in a hospital setting by someone wearing a white coat, had their medical histories taken, and viewed drugs and equipment displayed conspicuously on an "Emergency Tray." Experimental subjects were instructed to note any unusual or hallucinatory experiences (which have been reported in sensory deprivation experiments). Finally, subjects were shown an "Emergency Alarm" they could press to escape from the situation. In contrast to the elaborate treatment provided for experimental subjects, control subjects were merely told they were a control group for a sensory deprivation study. They were not led to believe that anything unusual would happen. All subjects were then placed in an isolation room for a few hours. At the end of the task, experimental subjects demonstrated greater impairment on cognitive and perceptual tasks (behaviors associated with sensory deprivation) than did control subjects. Moreover, the experimental group reported a greater number of bizarre experiences. These results were interpreted to reflect the effect of the cues to which subjects were exposed rather than of the isolation itself.

Placebo reactions and demand characteristics reveal the importance of suggesting to individuals in a *subtle* fashion that their behavior is going to change in a particular direction. Situations in treatment and experimentation often lead to behavior change because of the meaning subjects place upon various events rather than because of the events themselves.

Problem solving

Traditionally, behavior modification has focused upon discrete responses for therapeutic change in a given client. Yet, many of the problems individuals encounter are not discrete or easily specifiable in advance. In everyday life, individuals meet a number of situations ranging from minor sources of frustration to major traumas. Experience suggests that some individuals usually handle diverse situations rather effectively while others, for whatever reason, experience difficulty in coping with a variety of situations. Individuals sometimes seek therapy and counseling in unmanageable situations, such as death of a relative, marital discord, extreme anxiety, or hopelessness.

Frequently, individuals in therapy are trained to resolve a particularly difficult situation. However, it is not uncommon that a person so trained is not able to use that particular skill to deal with additional problems. Recently, then, some attempts have been made to teach individuals problem-solving skills so that they not only can manage the reported problem situation but also can apply the learned problem-solving skills to many other situations (D'Zurilla and Goldfried 1971).

Problem solving has been defined as "a behavioral process, whether overt or cognitive in nature, which (a) makes available a variety of potentially effective response alternatives for dealing with the problematic situation, and (b) increases the probability of selecting the most effective response among these various alternatives" (D'Zurilla and Goldfried 1971, p. 108). The goal in developing problem-solving skills is to train an individual in how to resolve new problems as they arise rather than merely to solve a single problem. Through training, it is assumed that the client will develop a strategy to manage or cope with virtually all problems encountered. This does not mean that a client will effectively solve all the problems, but only that he will have the skills to develop and select solutions.

D'Zurilla and Goldfried (1971) divide problem solving into five stages or components. To resolve a problem, an individual must:

1. Develop a general orientation or set to recognize the problem.
2. Define the specifics of the problem and determine what needs to be accomplished.
3. Generate alternative courses of action that might be used to resolve the problem and achieve the desired goals.
4. Decide among the alternatives by evaluating their consequences and relative gains and losses.
5. Verify the results of the decision process and determine whether the alternative selected is achieving the desired outcome.

Problems may arise in everyday life if any of these steps is not utilized. A person may not recognize that there is a problem and may even deny its presence; may not recognize specific features of the problem which, if noted, might be more manageable; may not generate viable solutions to the problem; or may pursue unsuccessful courses of action without recognizing their futility. For example, a student may have deficits in social skills in relation to the opposite sex. Rather than recognizing the real problem (failure to interact at all), the individual may think of it as simply undue shyness. Even if the individual recognizes the problem, it might well be that he or she does not know which specific encounters are problematic or how to formulate alternative courses of action to remedy the problem.

Individuals who show response deficits or inhibitions that transcend a single situation might be trained in problem-solving skills. Training is accomplished by progressively shaping problem-solving skills in the client. Simulated and actual problems can be introduced to the client in therapy and the requisite component skills outlined above can be gradually developed. Initially, minor problems can be introduced for practice while the problem-solving approach is being developed. The final goal is to train the individual to approach all problematic situations with the problem-solving strategy. Training proceeds by developing each of the five components. The client focuses on recognizing problems and on controlling impulsive reactions that short-circuit the entire problem-solving sequence. After the general problem is formulated, specific aspects of the problem are focused upon. By identifying specific features of the overall problem—that is, external events that account for the problem and internal reactions that contribute to its status as a problem—the client finds solutions more readily available. An explicit definition of the problem also helps to clarify goals. Once the goals are clear, the alternatives for specific action may be posed. Then the individual, in conjunction with the therapist, weighs the consequences associated with each alternative. The long- and short-term advantages and disadvantages of each alternative are evaluated. Next, one alternative is selected in light of its likely consequences. Once a specific plan is decided upon, the client tries to develop concrete procedures for implementing the plan. When the plan is finally implemented, the client must evaluate whether the intended effect is achieved and whether he or she is satisfied within the constraints of the available alternatives.

The problem-solving strategy is demonstrated in the following example. A female college senior may be in conflict about two aspects of her future. Specifically, she may be indecisive about an impending marriage because of the possibility that it will interfere with her graduate work and career plans. The general problem must be specified as carefully as possible. The abstract problem of conflict and indecisiveness must be clarified by an expression of the goals the client wishes to accomplish and their relative value. Of course, selecting alternative goals that are desirable but potentially incompatible is difficult. However, the student may decide she wishes both to marry and to continue her education. Once deciding upon the specific goals, the student can generate alternative plans to attain them. One might be to marry and temporarily leave her husband (who might already be committed to a job) to attend graduate school. Another plan might be to postpone marriage until graduate work is completed. A third plan might be to marry her fiancé only if he agrees to accompany her to graduate school. Assume for the sake of the example that the last alternative is selected as the most viable solution. The final step of the problem-solving approach is determining whether the course of action selected satisfies the original goals. It might well be that once the student enters graduate school accompanied by her spouse, graduate school and a dissatisfied spouse make living conditions deplorable. The goals of completing graduate work and having a reasonably happy marriage might not be compatible. Thus, an alternative plan is selected and implemented. The procedure of selecting alternative plans and evaluating their utility continues until the problematic situation is resolved.

It should be clear from this example that the stages of problem solving outlined earlier are not discrete steps that one follows in an unvarying sequence. In everyday situations, the conflict of goals makes selecting alternative plans difficult. Sometimes decisions must be made before there is a clear, unequivocal commitment to a goal or before the consequences of alternative sources of action can be predicted. Nevertheless, the problem-solving strategy helps specify the different features of a problem that must be approached to reach a solution.

The therapeutic strategy emphasizes the client's cognitive abilities for handling problems. The therapist serves to develop individual component skills and to help the client use the processes which will lead to resolution of problems. Thus, the therapist is likely to help the client weigh the alternative plans for action, enumerate the range of consequences associated with alternative plans, and later verify or assess the effect of a particular course of action.

An interesting feature of the problem-solving approach, consistent with various behavior therapy techniques, is that it encourages experimentation with oneself. When alternative courses of action are selected, their efficacy in achieving the anticipated outcome is evaluated. If the course of action is not achieving its purpose or is inefficient in reaching a goal, it can be altered. Part of problem-solving training is to give the individual experience in trying out new courses of action.

Clinical research on the efficacy of problem-solving training, at least as outlined, has not been completed. Laboratory research has provided evidence for the specific steps of problem solving. For example, in the context of laboratory tasks, the importance of carefully defining the task requirements and of generating a variety of alternative solutions has been demonstrated (see D'Zurilla and Goldfried 1971). In applied contexts such as education, various components of the problem-solving skills also have been shown to change behavior.[1] Some components of problem solving and their role in behavior

[1] For example, performance on measures of creativity and concept skills (see Mahoney 1974a).

change have been studied in a therapeutic context. In self-instructional training, individuals are trained to ascertain the requirements for performance in particular situations and plan their responses or course of action. Such training has effected therapeutic change in behavior.

Verbal mediators of behavior

The role of language in controlling behavior has long been recognized in psychology. Obviously, individuals respond to language in the form of instructions, commands, and rules that govern behavior. However, there are more subtle means, such as in self-verbalizations, through which language influences behavior. It is important to outline some forms of verbalization that may control behavior.

Instructions. One area of interest pertains to the influence of instructions in controlling behavior. As noted earlier, an individual's perceptions of various environmental events dictate reactions to the events. One way to alter a person's perception is to provide instructions. In this context, *instructions* refers to statements describing the relationship between events. Several investigations have shown that instructions can alter an individual's responsiveness to external events in a conditioning situation. For example, the development and extinction of classically conditioned responses are enhanced by informing subjects about the events that are to occur (Bridger and Mandel 1964, 1965; Grings and Lockhart 1963; Notterman, Schoenfeld, and Bersh 1962). Similarly, in laboratory investigations of operant conditioning, instructions about the contingencies markedly affect the level and pattern of acquisition (e.g., Dulany 1968; Kaufman, Baron, and Kopp 1966; Merbaum and Lukens 1968). Related research, mostly in the area of verbal conditioning, has emphasized the importance of awareness in learning. Individuals who are aware of reinforcement contingencies, or of the relationship between the target response and consequences, perform at a higher rate than those who are unaware (see Bandura 1969; Kanfer 1965).

The importance of instructions about the reinforcement contingencies has been demonstrated in applied settings. In one investigation (Kazdin 1973a), the role of instructions and reinforcement was examined with elementary school children. Some children were told that they could earn tokens exchangeable for a variety of rewards for appropriate classroom behavior such as paying attention to the lesson, sitting in their seats, and so on. Thus, individuals were led to *believe* that they were reinforced for appropriate behavior. However, tokens were delivered noncontingently on a predetermined random schedule. Students received tokens on the basis of their eye color, sex, and place of the first initial of their name in the alphabet. Instructions and the noncontingent delivery of reinforcement improved the behavior of a number of children in the three-week period that tokens were administered. Thus, tokens did not have to be delivered contingently to improve behavior as long as individuals were led to believe that reinforcement was delivered contingently. The procedure did not alter the behavior of students who were particularly disruptive. Yet evidence was provided that the students' perceptions of the contingency partially dictated performance.

Other studies have shown that reinforcement can be enhanced by the use of instructions. Ayllon and Azrin (1968) trained psychotic clients to use utensils instead of their hands when eating meals. Providing a reinforcer (extra dessert) for the use of utensils was not very effective in improving their behavior. However, providing instructions stating the relationship between the desired behavior and the consequences enhanced performance tremendously. Instructions or rules about behavior in a given situation by themselves, on the other hand, do not always control behavior. This, of course, is obvious from the violation of laws in everyday life. Several studies in applied settings have demonstrated that instructions alone, when not backed by consequences for behavior, do not lead to consistent behavior change (Herman and Tramontana 1971; Kazdin 1973c; O'Leary, Becker, Evans, and Saudargas 1969; Packard 1970). Yet, much behavior is controlled by instructions in both verbal and written form. Warnings like weather reports of impending disasters or signs that note "Beware of Dog" demonstrate the importance of instructions in controlling what individuals believe and how they behave in various situations. Instructions can be used similarly to enhance behavior change in therapeutic contexts. For example, placebo effects and expectations for improvement can be altered by verbal suggestions about the efficacy of various procedures.

Self-verbal mediators. Individuals frequently make comments to themselves that may influence their own behavior. For example, young children can be seen to speak out loud to describe what they are doing while playing. Similarly, adults may covertly make comments to themselves. For example, in preparing to ask an employer for a raise, individuals may verbally rehearse and direct themselves in how to make the request. Of course, saying something to oneself prior to or while performing a particular behavior does not necessarily mean that the self-verbalizations cause the behavior. *Self-verbalizations* refer to concomitants of behavior or to actual guides of behavior.

Various therapy techniques are based on the assumption that self-instructions guide or control one's behavior. For example, Albert Ellis's

(1957) *rational emotive therapy* assumes that psychological disorders derive from irrational patterns of thinking. The irrational patterns of thinking are represented in what individuals say to themselves in explicit or implicit self-verbalization. Ellis maintains that a variety of specific irrational ideas may cause and maintain maladaptive behavior. One irrational idea is the notion that because some past event has strongly influenced one's life, it should indefinitely affect it (instead of the notion that one can learn from one's past experience but not be a victim of it). Another irrational idea is that it is essential for an adult to be loved by everyone for every action (instead of focusing on self-respect and on loving rather than being loved). There are several additional irrational beliefs that have been detailed elsewhere (Ellis 1962, 1970; Ellis and Harper 1961).[2] The main point of Ellis's position is that thought patterns are responsible for most problems in everyday experience. The actual events that one encounters, such as rejection by a loved one, are not themselves traumatic except insofar as one's assumptions, ideas, and interpretations of them make them catastrophic. Even inevitable events that one might argue are traumatic (for example, death) affect individuals differently depending upon the interpretations placed upon such events.

From the standpoint of effecting behavior change, rational emotive therapy attempts to make explicit those cognitions and self-verbalizations that account for one's feelings and actions. Essentially, therapy focuses on restructuring the cognitions that have led to problems. The therapist points out the illogic of the premises and self-verbalizations that are implicit in the client's actions. Therapy provides the client with insight into the source of the problems and trains the client to examine the belief system under which he operates. The premises under which an individual acts are shown to relate directly to various negative emotions such as feelings of failure, rejection, and self-denigration. The therapist emphasizes that certain events, such as being rejected by a lover, do not necessarily entail irrational conclusions, such as that one is worthless. As a function of rational emotive therapy, the individual supposedly eliminates self-defeating thoughts and verbalizations and develops constructive verbalizations in their place. Rational emotive therapy has been increasingly employed in recent years. Despite a number of successful case reports, unequivocal evidence for its efficacy remains to be provided. As noted in a review of the relevant research (Mahoney 1974a), too little rigorous research has been done to support definitively the efficacy of the procedures.

[2] For an elaboration of the place of rational emotive therapy in behavior modification, see Mahoney (1974a).

Ellis's therapy includes a number of components, although self-instructions and self-verbalizations are most strongly emphasized. The role of self-verbalizations has received a great deal of attention in its own right. Laboratory investigations, for example, have evaluated the impact of saying things to oneself to control various behaviors. For example, in one investigation, elementary school boys earned prizes by working on a task (O'Leary 1968). The likelihood of earning a prize could be enhanced by "cheating," or at the inappropriate time taking tokens exchangeable for prizes. All children were made aware of the "right" and "wrong" behaviors. Some children were told to tell themselves whether they *should* make a response before actually doing so. Other children were not told to instruct themselves in this fashion. The children who self-instructed made fewer transgressions, or "wrong" responses, than those who did not self-instruct; thus, self-instruction controlled behavior. A variety of investigations have shown that self-instruction enhances performance across diverse tasks (S. Bem 1967; Hartig and Kanfer 1973; Monahan and O'Leary 1971; Palkes, Stewart, and Kahana 1968).

Self-instructional training recently has been systematically investigated as a behavior modification strategy for therapeutic purposes. Meichenbaum (1973) has trained individuals to engage in self-instruction to control their own behavior. For example, in one project (Meichenbaum and Goodman 1971), impulsive and hyperactive children were trained to administer self-instructions. Prior to training, the children made frequent errors on various tasks because of their rapid and careless performance. During self-instructional training, the experimenter modeled how to perform various tasks such as coloring figures and copying lines. While performing each task, the experimenter described its performance. By talking, the experimenter modeled thinking out loud and verbally reinforced himself for working carefully. An example of the verbalizations modeled by the experimenter for the line-drawing task was:

> Okay, what is it I have to do? You want me to copy the picture with the different lines. I have to go slow and be careful. Okay, draw the line down, down, good; then to the right, that's it; now down some more and to the left. Good, I'm doing fine so far. Remember go slow. Now back up again. No, I was supposed to go down. That's okay. Just erase the line carefully. . . . Good. Even if I make an error I can go slowly and carefully. Okay, I have to go down now. Finished. I did it. (Meichenbaum and Goodman 1971, p. 117)

The children were trained to instruct themselves out loud while performing the task. Eventually, they were trained to instruct themselves covertly without talking but only by moving their lips, and finally without lip movements. Individuals who were trained to instruct themselves on how to perform were more methodical in their work than individuals who practiced the experimental task but did not receive self-instructional training.

Self-instructional training has been successful with a number of behaviors and populations. In analogue studies, which focus on behaviors considered to resemble clinical problems, self-instructional training has decreased test anxiety and fear of snakes. Individuals who are trained to verbalize statements that facilitate adaptation to anxiety-provoking situations can substantially reduce their anxiety (Meichenbaum 1971a, 1972). A recent demonstration of self-instructional training was completed by Meichenbaum and Cameron (1973) with clients diagnosed as schizophrenic. In two experiments these authors demonstrated the effect of training the schizophrenic clients to "talk to themselves" in improving performance on perceptual and cognitive tasks.

Another interesting research finding is that changes effected with self-instructional training seem to generalize. For example, training individuals to cope with one anxiety-provoking situation or to perform on one task results in beneficial effects in other situations (Meichenbaum 1973). Moreover, effects achieved with self-instructional training appear to be maintained over time. These two features of self-instructional training, if borne out by future research, will provide further support for the notion that self-instructional training makes alterations in general cognitive strategy rather than effecting isolated changes in specific target behaviors.

Imaginal mediators of behavior

Increasingly, the role of imagery has been recognized as an important influence on behavior. Indeed, in everyday life imagery is frequently relied upon to direct one's behavior; examples are envisioning the outcome of a task or vividly recalling a pleasant event or experience. Research has shown that imagined stimuli appear to elicit reactions similar to those elicited by actual events (Barber and Hahn 1964; Clark 1963). Of course, this is known to anyone who has awakened frightened from a nightmare.

A number of behavior therapy techniques depend upon the similarity of responses evoked by imagined and by real-life cues. For example, *systematic desensitization* relies upon imagery to alleviate anxiety. Typically, individuals imagine a graded hierarchy of anxiety-provoking stimuli. If relaxation is associated with the images of anxiety-provoking situations, anxiety in the actual situations abates. Therapeutically, anxiety is alleviated in the presence of imagined stimuli only, rather than in the situations themselves. Thus, behavior change is achieved by engaging a person's imagination.[3]

Aside from desensitization, a series of techniques referred to as *covert conditioning* (Cautela 1972) rely extensively upon imagery. Covert conditioning techniques are characterized by having individuals imagine themselves performing behaviors that they wish to change or develop and then imagine certain consequences directly following from the behaviors. One technique, referred to as *covert sensitization,* is used in attempts to decrease maladaptive approach behaviors such as overeating, excessive alcohol consumption, drug abuse, and sexual deviance. Individuals imagine themselves engaging in the behaviors they wish to decrease or eliminate. When the behavior is clearly imagined, the individuals are instructed to imagine highly aversive events. The aversive events are designed to suppress the behaviors. As treatment progresses, individuals are told to imagine themselves resisting performance of the deviant behavior and feeling relieved as a result. For example, in treating overeating, a scene used to suppress eating desserts might be:

> I want you to imagine you've just had your main meal and you are about to eat your dessert, which is apple pie. As you are about to reach for the fork, you get a funny feeling in the pit of your stomach. You start to feel queasy, nauseous, and sick all over. As you touch the fork, you can feel food particles inching up your throat. You're just about to vomit. As you put the fork into the pie, the food comes up into your mouth. You try to keep your mouth closed because you are afraid that you'll spit the food out all over the place. You bring the piece of pie to your mouth. As you're about to open your mouth, you puke; you vomit all over your hands, the fork, over the pie. It goes all over the table, over the other people's food. Your eyes are watering. Snot and mucus are all over your mouth and nose. Your hands feel sticky. There is an awful smell. As you look at this mess you just can't help but vomit again and again until just watery stuff is coming out. Everybody is looking at you with shocked expressions. You run out of the room, and as you run out, you feel better and better. You wash and clean yourself up, and it feels wonderful. (Cautela 1967, p. 462)

As treatment progresses, the scenes become less dramatic and focus on individuals' successful resistance to temptation. For example, later in therapy the following scene might be imagined in the session.

> You've just finished eating your meal and you decide to have dessert. As soon as you make the decision, you start to get that funny feeling in the pit

[3] On occasion, systematic desensitization is conducted in the actual situations rather than with imagery; this is known as *in vivo* desensitization.

> of your stomach. You say, "Oh, oh; oh, no; I won't eat that dessert." Then you immediately feel calm and comfortable. (Cautela 1967, p. 463)

Across several sessions clients imagine a variety of situations until they are no longer attracted to the previously desired stimuli. Clients are asked to employ the scenes outside of treatment so that control over behavior can be achieved in the actual situations as well as in the therapy session (Cautela 1967, 1969).

Recently, a number of covert techniques have been derived from operant conditioning principles. For example, one technique referred to as *covert reinforcement* requires an individual to imagine engaging in some response he or she wishes to increase, such as speaking up in a group. After the response is imagined, the individual imagines some reinforcing event taking place, such as skiing down a mountain. The procedure is designed to increase the probability that the client will engage in the imagined target behaviors. There are additional covert techniques such as *covert extinction, covert punishment,* and *covert modeling,* which are conducted entirely in imagination. With each technique the imagery of the client is guided by instructions from the therapist.

Covert techniques have been applied in a number of clinical cases to alter alcohol consumption, sexual deviance, drug abuse, social skills, overeating, and diverse fears, to name a few major applications. Unequivocal evidence for the efficacy of given techniques has been sparse, in part because of the recency of the procedures. Since most of the techniques have been proposed only since 1970, too few investigations have been completed to provide conclusive statements (Cautela 1972a). Also, some of the research that has been completed in support of various covert techniques has been criticized on methodological grounds (Mahoney 1974a).

Summary

This chapter outlines several areas relevant to behavior change which reflect research in the cognitive tradition. The processes posed to account for behavior (attention, mediation, component behavior, and incentive conditions) and the specific areas of research included (attribution, placebo reactions, demand characteristics, problem solving, and verbal and imaginal mediators of behavior) broaden the areas from which behavior modification can draw principles. Cognitive influences go beyond external environmental events. To account for behavior, both cognitive and environmental influences should be considered. However, these influences should not be considered as exhausting those factors that control behavior, because they exclude other obvious factors, such as sociological and genetic influences. Nevertheless, for the purpose of achieving behavior change in therapeutic contexts, findings from general psychology, particularly in the areas of learning and cognition, have proven heuristically valuable.

It is important to reiterate that the domain of behavior modification cannot be described definitively by its current content. Indeed, it may not be meaningful to refer to a specific domain since the field is defined by applying experimental findings to behavior change. Not all of the experimental findings that might be relevant for altering behavior are known. Thus, the domain of behavior modification is always expanding. For example, social and physical features of the environment are known to affect behavior and are included in the realm of findings that might be relevant for changing behavior in a clinical context. In this book, those findings pertaining to human learning and cognition are stressed because of the role they currently play in many behavior modification techniques. However, it is important to keep in mind that the general area of behavior change is much broader (Krasner and Ullmann 1973).

Suggested readings

Ellis, A., and Harper, R. A. *A guide to rational living.* Hollywood, Calif.: Wilshire, 1961.

Mahoney, M. J. *Cognition and behavior modification.* Cambridge, Mass.: Ballinger, 1974.

Meichenbaum, D. *Cognitive behavior modification.* Morristown, N.J.: General Learning Press, 1974.

Rimm, D. C., and Masters, J. C. *Behavior therapy: Techniques and empirical findings.* New York: Academic Press, 1974. Chapter 10.

Assessment and treatment strategies

9

Behavior modification has broad applications, ranging from the home to the mental hospital; however, it has received its most extensive utilization in individual clinical work. In this chapter we will discuss general guidelines for the application of behavior modification, and we have chosen as our example the individual therapy setting. These guidelines are equally applicable in other clinical settings involving the application of behavior modification and even extend to broader community problems (Meyers, Craighead, and Meyers 1974), although specific practical details may vary from setting to setting. This chapter is not intended as a how-to-do-it cookbook, but as a general model for experimental/clincial invervention.

Issues regarding assessment procedures have received increasing attention from behaviorally oriented clinicians and researchers. The focus has largely been on traditional issues of personality assessment, such as reliability and validity of the assessment procedures (Wiggins 1973; Goldfried and Sprafkin 1974). Many of these issues will be discussed and empirical findings will be presented in Part III. This chapter will focus on the clinical situation.

In the typical clinical situation, a person comes to a therapist with a problem. Ullmann and Krasner (1969) have described that situation as follows.

> An individual may do something (e.g., verbalize hallucinations, hit a person, collect rolls of toilet paper, refuse to eat, stutter, stare into space, or dress sloppily) under a set of circumstances (e.g., during a school class, while working at his desk, during a church service) which upsets, annoys, angers, or strongly disturbs somebody (e.g., employer, teacher, parent, or the individual himself) sufficiently that some action results (e.g., a policeman is called, seeing a psychiatrist is recommended, commitment proceedings are started) so that society's professional labelers (e.g., physicians, psychiatrists, psychologists, judges, social workers) come into contact with the individual and determine which of the current set of labels (e.g., schizophrenic reaction, sociopathic personality, anxiety reaction) is most appropriate. Finally, there follow attempts to change the emission of the offending behavior (e.g., institutionalization, psychotherapy, medication). (p. 21)

All the behaviors in this sequence of events may be analyzed from an experimental standpoint. Each person and his or her behavior plays a functional role in this sequence, and each behavior may be analyzed and modified. For example, we might focus on the role of the therapist. The traditional role of the therapist in this sequence has been making a diagnosis. However, because of the relative lack of reliability and validity of traditional diagnostic categories and because of data indicating that the treatment which follows may be unrelated to the differential diagnosis, most experimentally oriented clinicians have discontinued such diagnoses. This change in the therapist's role was reflected in the models presented in Chapter 6. Our experimental clinician will not utilize traditional assessment devices to look for underlying problems but rather will attempt to discover what the client has done, thought, or said to upset someone. The therapist's job is to change that behavior and alleviate its accompanying distress by means of some clinical intervention.

As the behavior modifier, where would you look for a model to serve as your guideline for clinical intervention? At first glance, you might feel a good starting place would be the behavioral model and the empirical findings from psychology that were summarized in Chapters 6 through 8. At the present time, that might be a reasonable choice. However, after extended consideration, you might realize that a more appropriate guide would be the more general scientific or experimental model. The material in Chapters 6 through 8 represents a compilation of current findings derived from experimental applications of the model of methodological behaviorism presented in Chapters 1 through 5. The scientific method is important even in clinical work.

Experimental/clinical model

The scientific model provides both the general objectives and the methodology for the experimental/clinical model of therapeutic intervention. As explained in earlier chapters, the objectives of the scientific approach of methodological behaviorism are the explanation, prediction, and control of behavior. These objectives find their counterparts in the clinical activities of assessment (explanation), development of a treatment strategy (prediction), and implementation of a treatment program (control). Thus, the overall objectives of the scientific endeavor are identical with the overall objectives of the therapeutic endeavor. The means of accomplishing those therapeutic objectives also may be derived from the scientific model. Just as the experimenter at times engages in activities that are difficult to fit within the conceptual model that specifies what he or she is supposed to do, so will the clinician at times engage in behaviors that are difficult to fit within this model. However, it is maintained that therapeutic effectiveness will most readily be obtained by the therapist who submits his or her endeavors to this experimental/clinical model.

The experimental/clinical model suggests that the methodology applied in the laboratory experiment should also be employed in the clinical setting. The ingredients of the experimental methodology outlined in earlier chapters become the ingredients of the clinical methodology proposed here. There are, of course, many empirically verified procedures that the clinician may employ, but we are speaking here of general guidelines for clinical intervention and not of specific behaviors to be employed in the therapy session.

As we have seen, the ingredients of the experimental methodology are the identification or definition of independent and dependent variables, the collection of data within an experimental design, the analysis of data, and data interpretation. Within the experimental/clinical model the therapist's first job is defining the problem behavior (dependent variable) and the factors maintaining that behavior (independent variables). This is referred to as the *functional analysis of behavior*, although sometimes the more traditional label of *assessment* is used. Next, the therapist must develop a treatment strategy; essentially he or she must design an experiment, deciding what the dependent variable will be. The dependent variable may be the one noted in the assessment or it may be some new variable. For example, it might be a new behavior that is incompatible with the prior dependent variable; if this new variable were to be increased in frequency, then the old one would automatically decrease. The therapist must define what variable or treatment strategy will be employed in an effort to affect the dependent variable. The experimental clinician will want to utilize all the other steps of the scientific method in order to assess the treatment's effectiveness. The clinician will choose a research design, a method of data collection and analysis, and a means of data interpretation. While the clinical situation may make such an ideal difficult to achieve, it is an ideal toward which the clinician should constantly strive. It is posited that the more closely a clinician comes to this ideal, the more effective he or she will be.

From the foregoing it can be seen that the clinical endeavor is comparable to the experimental endeavor—hence the label *experimental/clinical model.* With these guidelines, we can now look at some of the specific activities in which a contemporary behavior modifier might engage while doing clinical work.

Clinical assessment

When an individual asks for professional help, that individual has said, thought, or done something upsetting and is seeking this means of alleviating the distress associated with the behavior. The first job of the behavioral change agent is to identify the upsetting behavior (the dependent variable) and what is causing and maintaining that behavior (the independent variable). This means that the clinician must conduct a functional behavior analysis of the client's present life situation, specifically in regard to the behavior the client reports as a problem. By functional analysis we mean that the therapist identifies dependent and independent variables that have led the client to see therapy.

Model for assessment

Many behavior modifiers, especially those with an operant bent, have described the assessment process in terms of an A→B→C model. The change agent first identifies the problem behaviors (B), or responses that are to be changed. These are sometimes labeled the target behaviors. The change agent proceeds to identify those events or stimuli that immediately precede the target behavior (antecedent stimuli, A) and those events that immediately follow the target behavior (consequences, C). Within the operant framework these variables are viewed as being outside the body. They are called environmental variables and thus, in the very strict operant sense, are external to the human body. While there may be a few internal variables, such as physiological ones, which may be measured directly, even these internal responses have frequently been excluded from consideration. This model for assessment serves some valuable functions. Occasionally, the problem is rather simple and straightforward, and this type of assessment is adequate. This is most likely to be true with cases involving small children and severely retarded residential populations for whom cognitive activity seems to be of less significance. However, even where this model is inadequate to account for human behavior, it frequently serves to teach the client the language that will be employed in the therapy situation.

This model has been expanded; variables inside the organism are considered important and should be included in the assessment process. These internal variables may be difficult to measure, but if they are important in understanding, predicting, and modifying human behavior they must be assessed. At the most basic level, this is a measurement rather than a conceptual problem. At the present time, except for some physiological measures, the client is dependent upon self-report as a measure of internal variables. However, refinements are presently being made in the means of assessment and modification of these internal variables. As will be seen in Part III, there is considerable promise in the clinical data derived from studies that have attempted to modify behavior via the modification of internal cognitive processes. While the A→B→C assessment model may still serve a practical purpose in the functional analysis of behavior, its primary utility lies in the sequencing and the correlation (in a literal sense of the word) of events. Any of the As, Bs, or Cs may be inside or outside the organism. Variables may range from simple, external reinforcers to reasonably far-removed variables of nutritional deficiencies, to a sequence of internal self-reinforcing statements. The internal biofeedback self-reinforcement sequence following an autistic child's self-stimulatory behavior may far exceed the strength of punishment from an external source. Thus, assessment should be as broad and exhaustive as possible. *Every variable that the experimental psychology literature has delineated as being important in this problem area should be assessed via the best available procedures. An experimental clinician should not just learn operant conditioning, but should also know the experimental psychology literature.* Other factors being equal, the more the clinician knows or the broader the experimental base, the more effective clinical interventions are likely to be.

Areas of assessment

There are three general areas of assessment that the experimental clinician should consider. First, there is the area for which behavior modifiers have been best known: the *somatic-motor responses.* These are most often referred to as "behaviors"—they are the actual physical responses of the organism. Second, there is the area of *physiological responses;* they have received some consideration by behaviorists, especially with problems traditionally labeled as anxiety and mental retardation. However, these variables need to be assessed with as much expertise as the behavioral change agent can develop. Where necessary and appropriate, professional consultation or collaboration should be employed (for example, gynecological examination in orgasmic dysfunction, or nutritional consultation in obesity). Third, there is the area of *cognitive responses,* which until recently was largely ignored by behavior modifiers. What is going on in the client's head? What does the client feel in certain situations? How are these cognitive variables related to external behavior? These are legitimate questions for the behavior modifier. These variables may be difficult to measure and quantify, but if they are important and essential in the explanation, prediction, and control of behavior, they must be considered.

Like most clinicians, a behavioral change agent does not begin assessment sessions by simply asking straightforward questions regarding the above areas of consideration. The interview begins with an attempt to establish rapport and a good working relationship with the client. The therapist emits behaviors that would be described as warm, friendly, empathetic, reassuring, and kind. The therapist is aware that such attention and behaviors will affect client output. The behavioral change agent expects to obtain the information necessary for an adequate assessment by covering many areas of life and yet maintaining awareness of the client's three response classes (somatic-motor, cognitive, and physiological) in a broad spectrum of situations. The therapist is attuned to both verbal and nonverbal cues from the client during the interview process. The therapist may follow an outline of potential problem situations in the client's life. Outlines that we have found useful in clinical practice and in training graduate students in assessment are included in Figures 9-1 and 9-2.[1] Figure 9-1 is for an initial interview only, while Figure 9-2 covers the entire assessment process. These serve as general guidelines and are used with great flexibility. They are not intended to serve as a model for interview behavior, but only as an example of how assessment might be conducted. More extensive examples are presented by Peterson (1968), Lazarus (1972), and Gottman and Lieblum (1974).

The information garnered from the assessment process must be synthesized and ordered so that the change agent may identify the dependent variables (client's problem behaviors) and independent variables (causing and maintaining factors). Once this assessment is completed it is presented to the client, and then the clinical experiment (treatment program or behavior modification program) is explained to the client and subsequently is implemented. In clinical practice this

[1] These outlines reflect the impact of a number of our professional mentors. It is not possible to recall who added what to the outline, but undoubtedly each will recognize his or her contribution and should be blamed accordingly.

Initial Interview Outline

I. Objectives
   1. Establish good relationship with the client.
   2. Obtain adequate information to identify dependent and independent variables of client's problem.

II. Assessment session
   1. Opening question: "Why are you here?"
      a. Begin by introducing self, confidentiality, and clinic policies.
      b. Invite client to tell about problem as client sees it, by asking the opening question.
      c. Find out how and why the decision to come in was made.
      d. Use of "reflection and clarification" to keep client talking about how he sees his problem.

   (Depending on what is said in response to the opening question, go on to either 2 or 3 below.)

   2. Inquiry into assets and liabilities.
      a. Socioeconomic situation. (How is the situation financially?)
      b. Job situation. (Does he or she have a job? What?)
      c. Work situation. (What is the relation to others on the job?)
      d. Educational background.
      e. Religious background.
      f. Peer relations. (What are relations to the same and the opposite sex?)
      g. Relationship with spouse.
      h. Relationship with in-laws.
      i. Relationship with children (each specific child).

   (Gaining information in these areas will allow you to: (1) develop a better understanding of the client; (2) determine strengths and weaknesses; and (3) determine if and how problems in these areas may be related to the problem presented in Section I.)

   3. Set clear definition and specification of problem areas (dependent variables) and the associated independent variables.
      a. Identify and define each distressing problem.
      b. Presence and absence of positive and negative eliciting and discriminative stimuli (internal and external).
      c. Presence and absence of reinforcement and punishment (internal and external).
      d. To whom it is distressing.
      e. Timing and frequency.
      f. Circumstances under which behavior occurs (focus on specific situations).
      g. What happens afterward.
      h. What client says to himself before the behavior.
      i. What client says to himself after the behavior.
      j. What is currently being done about problem.
      k. Availability of reinforcement.
   4. Objectives of therapy.
      a. What do you want to be different at end of therapy?
      b. Just a beginning in formulating objectives.

III. Closing first interview

Give a nebulous statement with regard to helpfulness of the information and your feelings of being able to help the client with his problem. Inform the client that you need more information to complete the assessment (if such is, in fact, the case) and that you need to look at the information already gained. TELL THE TRUTH, BUT BE AS POSITIVE AS POSSIBLE.

Figure 9-1 Initial interview outline

Behavior Assessment Form

Date ______

Therapist ______

Name ______ Address ______

Phone ______ Age ______ Occupation ______

Marital Status ______ Children ______

Previous Therapy ______

Outcome ______ Orientation ______

Current expectancies ______

Known Medical Problems ______

Most recent exam ______ Current drugs ______

Atypical Background or Experiences ______

Average Hours of Sleep per Night ______ Regular? ______

Eating Patterns ______

Physical Description ______

Social & Interview Behaviors ______

Self-Description: (Aver.)

1. Physical condition	(V. Poor)	0	1	2	3	4	5	6	7	8	9	10	(Athletic)
2. Intelligence	(Stupid)	0	1	2	3	4	5	6	7	8	9	10	(Bright)
3. Physical looks	(Ugly)	0	1	2	3	4	5	6	7	8	9	10	(Attractive)
4. Assertiveness	(Shy)	0	1	2	3	4	5	6	7	8	9	10	(Aggressive)
5. Likeability	(Disliked)	0	1	2	3	4	5	6	7	8	9	10	(Well liked)
6. Self-confidence	(Inferior)	0	1	2	3	4	5	6	7	8	9	10	(Confident)
7. Coping style	(Anxious)	0	1	2	3	4	5	6	7	8	9	10	(Relaxed)
8. Personal worth	(Bad)	0	1	2	3	4	5	6	7	8	9	10	(Good)

Sum = ______ Mean = ______

9. Name some of the particularly good things about yourself (assets, talents, etc.): (space is provided for answer)

10. Name some of the particularly bad things about yourself (faults, deficiencies, etc.): (space provided)

Figure 9-2 Behavior assessment form

2

Presenting Problem(s):

1. Definition & description: (space provided)
2. Historical development (recency, etc.): (space provided)
3. Current state & correlates:
   a. Frequency/intensity
   b. Situationality
   c. Temporal distribution
   d. Antecedents (environmental & cognitive)
   e. Consequences (social & self-presented)
4. Atypical or complicating factors: (space provided)
5. Comments: (space provided)

Tentative Treatment Program:

1. Modification targets: (space provided)
2. Assessment methods: (space provided)
3. Probable determinants: (space provided)
4. Tentative treatment strategies: (space provided)
5. Auxiliary topics or comments: (space provided)

Figure 9-2 (*cont.*)

summary presentation of the assessment is often referred to as a summary interview.

This same assessment model may be utilized in working with children at home or in a residential treatment center. The specific outline followed or procedures employed may vary from situation to situation, but the experimental/clinical *model* of assessment remains the same.

Treatment strategies

Following presentation of the summary clinical assessment to the client, the therapist explains the proposed treatment strategy. This treatment strategy is again based upon the experimental/clinical model. The therapist and/or the client is going to conduct an experiment.

The objectives of the clinical experiment have been developed from the assessment process. The client has informed the therapist why he or she has sought professional help and what he or she expects to gain from the treatment sessions. These objectives provide the basis for the development of the experimental/clinical hypothesis. These objectives serve the same function as in the development of an experimental hypothesis in the laboratory setting. The objectives allow the clinician to determine what directions the treatment strategies will take, and they provide the basis from which the criteria of success can be drawn. When it seems likely that the therapy process will be lengthy or difficult, or if client motivation is low, intermediate objectives may be formulated and utilized. These are especially helpful in providing feedback to the client regarding progress. (Such feedback may not hurt the therapist's motivation either.)

How does a behavior modification therapist decide what treatment strategy to employ? We return to the experimental/clinical paradigm for the initial answer to this question. Given the assessment of the ongoing situation in the client's life and the formulation of therapeutic objectives, the therapist must design an appropriate clinical intervention project. First, the dependent variable must be identified. In many cases this will be the one identified as the problem behavior during the assessment process, and the one that will be directly modified in the treatment program. Many times there is more than one dependent variable. In some cases, additional dependent variables may be identified and focused upon during the treatment program; for example, the therapist may decide to decrease one dependent variable by increasing the frequency of another, incompatible dependent variable.

Once the behavior (dependent variable) to be changed has been clearly identified, the therapist must decide what treatment procedures will be employed in the effort to change that dependent variable. This treatment constitutes the independent variable. As will be seen in Part III, several procedures are often combined in one treatment package. While the therapist may be able to evaluate the overall effectiveness of such a treatment program, he or she cannot identify which components of the treatment package are responsible for the package's effectiveness. Although sometimes the components of a treatment package may be systematically evaluated (for example, within a specific single subject design), sometimes this is not possible. Nevertheless it is hoped that this experimental/clinical approach will eventually identify the active ingredients of various treatment strategies, so that they may be employed more efficiently.

Thus, we have seen that the therapist's task in developing the treatment strategy is to identify dependent and independent variables. The dependent variables have been derived in one way or another from the assessment sessions, but where does the therapist derive independent variables? Ideally, they originate from the presently available experimental literature. The procedures derived from that literature are continually being expanded and improved upon by new findings. The present findings in the clinically relevant literature were presented in summary form in Chapters 6 through 8. It is from these findings and from empirical evaluations of their effectiveness in clinical situations (as presented in Part III) that the therapist decides what procedures or treatment strategies will be employed in a given clinical situation. Fortunately, the experimental/clinical literature is a burgeoning one, and the clinician increasingly can look to that literature for direction. However, at our current level of knowledge, the experimental clinician must frequently rely on past experience and clinical hunches, since there may not be a directly applicable experimental literature. As a result, the clinician, either from practical necessity or experimental creativity, must often decide upon a new independent variable. As always, however, the effects of such a variable must be evaluated. One advantage of this approach to clinical intervention is that the experimental clinician not only can draw upon the experimental/clinical literature, but also may contribute to it through systematic evaluation of intervention procedures.

Once the dependent and independent variables are selected, the therapist must decide what data to collect and what research design to employ in evaluating the clinical experiment. These would be determined by referring to the guidelines presented in Chapters 4 and 5. The client's objectives will allow the therapist to decide these issues in accordance with the suggestions for research design, data collection, and data analysis.

The foregoing description refers to an individual therapy program, but the general treatment model is applicable in all treatment situations. As with assessment procedures, the specifics may vary widely across different situations in which an experimental approach to clinical intervention is used.

Examples of experimental/clinical approaches

The following case study demonstrates the utilization of the experimental/clinical method of clinical assessment and treatment. In some cases, such as this one, the exigencies of clinical intervention make it impossible to specify which particular treatment procedure is responsible for the treatment's effectiveness. Several treatment procedures that have been shown to have clinical promise are included in an overall treatment package. Furthermore, the design does not permit any clear causal statements to be made. However, it does demonstrate the value of defining independent and dependent variables and evaluating the effect of the independent variables (clinical procedures) upon the dependent variable. Of course, with the limited design other factors may be responsible for the behavior change.

The following example was chosen because frequently in a clinical setting a client will report a specific problem that precludes utilization of an intrasubject design. While it might have been possible to employ an ABAB design, clinical exigencies precluded the use of a reversal procedure. The method of evaluation in this case study is an improvement over reliance on clinical intuition. At least the therapists would have known if the program had not had an effect.

The client (Mrs. W.) was a 41-year-old woman with a history of asthma since the age of 7. Her breathing difficulties had become quite severe during the preceding 3 years. Medical treatments ranging from desensitization shots to cortisone therapy had resulted in only minor improvement, and the client's performance of routine daily activities was seriously jeopardized. Prior to behavior therapy, the client was consuming medically contraindicated amounts of prescription drugs, including ephedrine-based bronchodilators, corticosteroids, and phenobarbital, in order to maintain marginal respiratory functioning. A portable nebulizer, or "Bronkometer," prescribed only for the alleviation of severe attacks, was being used extensively. Since chronic heavy dosages of medication can result in serious pulmonary impairment, reduced consumption became a major focus of therapy. The client was therefore instructed to self-record the daily frequency of her Bronkometer use (Sirota and Mahoney 1974).

The foregoing information was gained from an interview based on one of the assessment formats presented earlier. Additionally, it was determined that the client's breathing difficulties not only were caused by diagnosed reactions to typical allergies, but also occurred in anxiety-eliciting situations. For example, being physically separated from the Bronkometer would elicit a near panic reaction followed by an asthma attack. Such upsets as a family squabble or noisy children would also precipitate the onset of an asthma attack. The dependent variable thus was the frequency of Bronkometer use. Since the client always used this when an attack occurred and since this level of usage is contraindicated, it was chosen as the target behavior to be changed. The series of events leading to the utilization of the Bronkometer was broken down into a sequence of small steps. Treatment was then introduced as early as possible in each behavioral sequence in order to break the chain and prevent a full-blown attack.

The client was trained in the use of deep muscle relaxation as a coping response for stress and anxiety. This procedure includes sitting quietly and alternately tensing and relaxing 16 different muscle groups covering the entire body (Bernstein and Borkovec 1973). She was instructed to practice relaxation at home twice daily for one week with the aid of a cassette tape. After a brief (3-day) baseline study of self-monitored Bronkometer use, an immediate treatment intervention was deemed advisable. The client was given a portable timer that she was to carry at all times. For the first 5 days of treatment, she was instructed to set the timer for semirandom intervals averaging 30 minutes in length. When the timer buzzed, the client was to perform a brief muscle inventory, noting her anxiety level and relaxing away any incipient tension. This technique was intended to help interrupt anxiety chains and to encourage spontaneous and natural self-monitoring of performance. The timer interval was subsequently lengthened to 1 hour.

An additional treatment strategy (begun on day 9) involved brief postponement of Bronkometer use. Any time the client experienced breathing difficulty and wanted to use her inhalant, she was told to set the timer for 3–4 minutes, practice abbreviated relaxation, and then employ the Bronkometer if it was still necessary. Systematic desensitization and the systematic pairing of visualizations of stressful situations with deep muscle relaxation was begun along two hierarchies (Bronkometer separation and domestic situations), but it was terminated before completion due to dramatic decreases in the use of the Bronkometer. A total of nine therapy sessions were conducted.

The results of the study are presented in Figure 9-3. As can be seen, the client was using the Bronkometer an average of nine times per day during baseline. During the course of treatment the use of the Bronkometer gradually decreased and by day 14 of treatment it was not being used at all. It was not used through the rest of the treatment period. Data were not taken during the time between termination and followup, but at the 5-day followup 6 months later the client still was not using the Bronkometer. Additionally, during treatment the client had terminated cortisone therapy, reduced ephedrine-based broncodilators by 80 percent, and reduced or eliminated all remaining asthmatic medications.

The utilization of several clinical procedures does not allow us to determine which factors may have resulted in the behavior change, and the design does not allow us to draw any causative conclusions regarding the entire treatment package, although treatment does seem to be

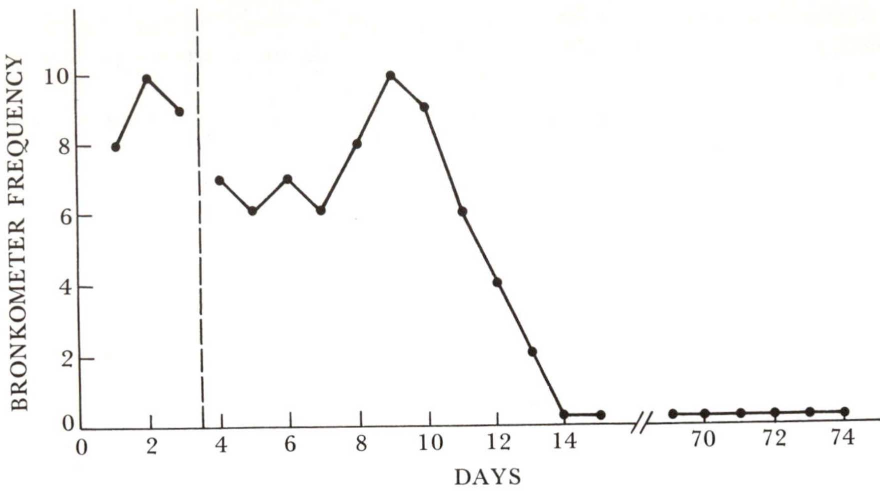

Figure 9-3 Frequency of Bronkometer use before and during behavioral treatment (SOURCE: A. D. Sirota and M. J. Mahoney, "Relaxing on cue: The self-regulation of asthma," *Journal of Behavior Therapy and Experimental Psychiatry*, 1974, *5*, 65–66. Reprinted by permission of Pergamon Press Ltd.)

the cause of the change. More definitive conclusions and the isolation of the effective treatment components might occur in additional research. Mrs. W. felt that the early identification of tension and the ability "to relax it away" had been very important in the alleviation of her asthma attacks. She also reported that the ticking of the timer eventually became a cue that helped her to remain calm.

The reader should be cautioned that not all clients present problems that can be dealt with in only nine sessions. In fact, many clients have more complex problems requiring more complex interventions over much longer periods of time. It is also important to note that not every intervention is so effective. But if the experimental clinician evaluates what is done, at least he or she will know whether or not it is effective even if, as in this study, one cannot specify exactly why.

The following example from Morganstern (1974) demonstrates the utilization of the multiple-baseline design in clinical intervention. A search of the behavior therapy journals will reveal that there are very few examples of such an evaluation of clinical procedures; however, as we have noted, such systematic evaluation must remain the ideal.

Morganstern's client was a 24-year-old obese female graduate student. She reported that she ate not only three meals daily but also consumed candy and "junk" all day. A number of treatment procedures were considered, but since the client disliked cigarette smoke, it was finally decided that inhaled cigarette smoke would be used as an aversive stimulus to affect her rate of consumption of junk foods (candy, cookies, and doughnuts). The intervention procedure was described as follows.

> A cigarette was lit and Miss C was asked to hold it in her hand as she took a bite of candy (the food which showed the highest consumption rate during baseline) and chewed it for a few seconds. Before swallowing the candy she was told to take one long "drag" on the cigarette and then to immediately spit out the food, exclaiming at the same time, "Eating this junk makes me sick." The procedure was repeated 10 times in each session and the client was also asked to practice it on her own twice each day. (Morganstern 1974, pp. 256–257)

The client was seen for 18 weeks and data were reported for a 3-week (week 21) and a 6-week (week 24) followup. The data evaluating the treatment procedure are presented in Figure 9-4. Baseline data were taken across all behaviors for 4 weeks, and then the treatment procedure was applied to candy consumption at week 5, cookie consumption at week 11, and doughnut consumption at week 15. The data reveal that the procedure resulted in a decrease in food consumption for each type of food when, and only when, the treatment procedure was applied to that type of food. The treatment effectiveness was maintained at followup. It is interesting to note that the client did not habituate to the aversiveness of the cigarette smoke. Given the reported deleterious effects of smoking, future applications of such a procedure might employ a different aversive stimulus.

Figure 9-4 also shows the amount of weight lost during the clinical intervention procedure. Whether the weight loss was a function of the treatment program or of other variables cannot be stated conclusively. It does seem likely that the decreased caloric intake resulting from the treatment program was partially responsible for the weight loss. Morganstern does point out that at week 15 the client began a low-calorie diet and at week 18 she was maintaining the diet and chose to terminate the aversive procedure. Morganstern hypothesized that the successful adoption of the diet, after many previous unsuccessful attempts, was a function of the client's learning from the program that she could control her own behavior.

The significant aspect of this study is that the therapist used the principle of aversive conditioning to decrease certain food consumption

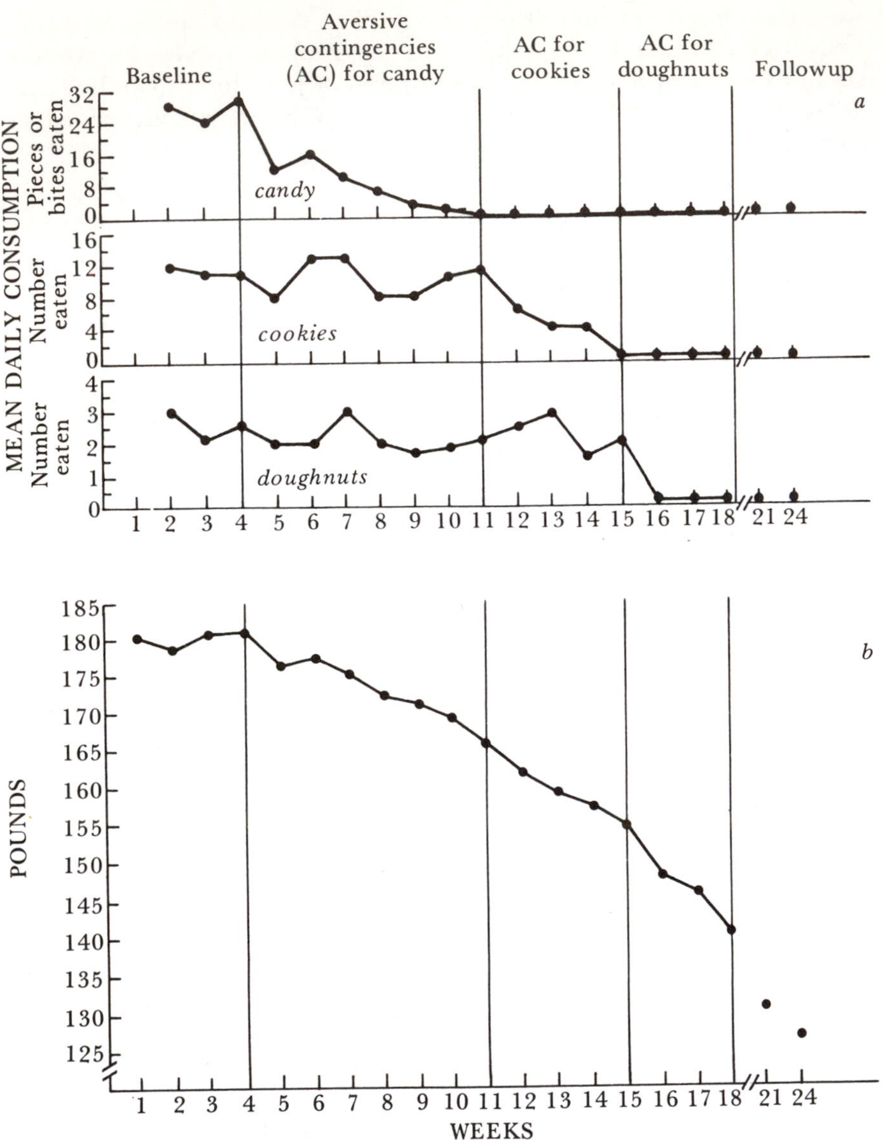

Figure 9-4 Graphs of (a) average weekly consumption of candy, cookies, and doughnuts as a function of the application of the aversive contingency and (b) weight loss occurring concurrently with the aversive contingency (SOURCE: K. P. Morganstern, "Cigarette smoke as a noxious stimulus in self-managed aversion therapy for compulsive eating: Technique and case illustration," *Behavior Therapy,* 1974, *5,* 255–260. Reprinted by permission of Academic Press and the author.)

behaviors. The effectiveness of the intervention procedure was systematically evaluated; it was clear that the procedure was responsible for the reduction of "junk" food consumption.

A final note

Up until this point we have seen the behavior modifier as a person who designs a clinical experiment to allow for the modification of a behavior (as broadly defined in this book) which is upsetting or annoying someone. The overall objective of that modification is to make the upset or annoyed person feel better and thus in a small way contribute to making this a better world. As will be seen later in the book, these same methodologies and procedures may have broad social applications and implications. This broad application and the evaluative statement regarding "making the world a better place" direct our thoughts to ethical questions. Better for whom? Better for what? Who will modify whose behavior? These issues have become of such significant importance that they are discussed in detail in the next chapter and will appear intermittently throughout the chapters in Part III.

Summary

This chapter presents the experimental/clinical approach to the assessment and treatment of behavioral problems. The experimental/clinical model represents the use of methodological behaviorism in applied settings. Our example is the individual therapy setting, but the model is equally appropriate for all areas of behavior modification.

Experimental/clinical assessment is frequently done within an operant paradigm in which the clinician identifies the behavioral problem (B) and its antecedent (A) and consequent (C) stimuli. Even when the therapist goes beyond the operant model, it may be advisable to conceptualize the assessment in operant language. In assessment the clinician needs to evaluate somatic-motor, physiological, and cognitive behaviors.

Experimental/clinical intervention or the use of treatment strategies is also seen within the model of methodological behaviorism. The clinician and the client conduct an experiment. The target behavior is seen as the dependent variable and the treatment program becomes an independent variable. Ideally, the program's effectiveness is evaluated within an intrasubject design, though in clinical settings this may be difficult. The cases of the asthmatic and obese clients illustrate the practical utilization of the experimental/clinical model.

Suggested readings

Goldfried, M. R., and Sprafkin, J. N. *Behavioral personality assessment.* Morristown, N.J.: General Learning Press, 1974.

Gottman, J. M., and Lieblum, S. R. *How to do psychotherapy and how to evaluate it.* New York: Holt, Rinehart and Winston, 1974.

Mischel, W. *Personality and assessment.* New York: Wiley, 1968.

Peterson, D. R. *The clinical study of social behavior.* New York: Appleton-Century-Crofts, 1968.

Ethical issues

10

As was pointed out in Chapter 2, the prediction and control of behavior are basic goals in the science of psychology. These goals, of course, are based on the assumption that human behavior is systematic, that it obeys functional relationships. There is now a substantial amount of research evidence supporting the notion that some very complex human actions can be accurately predicted and controlled. Psychologists are far from being capable of such prediction and control with all or even most behaviors, but their progress over the last decade has been quite impressive. Patterson and Hops (1969) have even previewed the possibility of a "six-second theory of personality": given an organism's learning history, the present situation, and events which have occurred during the last six seconds, one can often predict accurately what the organism will do during the next six seconds. This small but ambitious beginning points to the possibilities that may arise during the next decade. Some therapists/researchers have already attained more than 90 percent prediction and control for a few limited behaviors. What are the ethical implications of this mushrooming technology of behavior control? If human performances can be reliably modified, who gets to choose "desired" behavior? Who controls whom?

Free will, determinism, and responsibility

Scientific prediction and control require the assumption of determinism. Recall from Chapter 2 that the principle of determinism states that all events must have a cause. Phenomena are said to be determined in the sense that they obey a lawful functional relationship; they consistently follow a preceding set of circumstances. For example, when one billiard ball strikes a second one, the latter's reaction is determined: it will move in a predictable direction at a predictable speed for a predictable distance. This consistency is necessary for accurate prediction. If the reactions of the second billiard ball were not determined, then it would show no consistent relationship to preceding events and its movements would be said to occur by chance rather than in response to specific forces acting upon it.

An alternative explanation of order and consistency is contained in the assumption of free will. Philosophically, free will is one's alleged ability to initiate or alter a causal chain. Although individuals frequently may be influenced by learning history or environmental events, the free will doctrine asserts that they can moderate and alter their actions in various ways through "will power." This capacity for free will is usually reserved for humans (one seldom observes a self-determined rat or turtle). Usually its mechanism is very vaguely described: individuals somehow step in and override the influences that are impinging on them. For centuries, philosophical debate has centered around the issue of free will versus determinism. Religious philosophers have been particularly interested in demonstrating that humans are free to determine their own destiny. However, the overwhelming consensus among philosophers, logicians, and scientists has been in favor of determinism. Several attempts have been made to salvage some artifacts of freedom, unpredictability, or randomness in physical events (for example, the principle of "indeterminacy" in physics). Many of these arguments have been based on inadequacies inherent in our measurement systems (see Mahoney et al. 1974). In the last few decades psychological research has amply demonstrated that the assumption of determinism is both justified and essential in dealing with human behavior. Although only a small minority of the cause-effect relationships in human performance have been identified to date, these modest beginnings have indicated that we are on the right track. Complex human performances are a function of complex variables, and it is the task of the behavioral scientist to identify and describe those functional relations.

Before we discuss the implications of determinism for human behavior, an important distinction should be made. There is a critical difference between the assumption of determinism and notions of *predeterminism.* The latter term refers to a fatalistic predestination of cause-effect chains. Let us consider any two related events, A and B. Determinism states that event B is caused or determined by event A; this relationship allows one to predict with some probability that whenever event A is encountered, event B will soon follow. Predeterminism, on the other hand, states not only that event A causes event B but also that event A is going to happen no matter what. This is a more sweeping and ambitious prediction. While the determinist is stating, "If event A occurs, I predict that event B will follow," the predeterminist says, "Event A must occur and will be followed by event B." Most scientists adopt only the assumption of determinism.

If human performance is composed of many complex behavioral events, the assumption of determinism states that those events are determined and therefore predictable, at least in principle. The fact that we cannot now accurately predict 100 percent of a person's actions is assumed to be a result of our ignorance rather than the capriciousness or randomness of the behavior. We have not yet identified the elements that comprise event A.

Most individuals will admit that to some extent their current performances are influenced by preceding events such as childhood experiences, praise for previous performance, and so on. However, at a gut level many people feel that they are not walking billiard balls, predictably pushed and pulled by environmental forces. Most of us feel that we play some role in determining our future—that our actions are influenced by our hopes, aspirations, and expectations. The determinist would agree and add, however, that one's hopes, aspirations, and expectations are themselves determined by previous events. You are pursuing a college degree because you "want" to. Yes, but your "want" has been caused by a complex learning history of modeling from others, praise and/or pressure from family, stimulating instructors, and so on. One cannot override the causal chain—if a person rebels against the predictions of the determinist, in principle that rebellion is predictable from previous experience. The Russian novelist Dostoevsky once stated that man would go to great extremes to avoid being predictable. As a last resort, he stated that an individual would go mad just to maintain independence from determinism. Skinner has pointed out that Dostoevsky's prediction closed all possible routes of escape from deterministic predictability; by stating that man would go mad to avoid being predictable, Dostoevsky himself had made a prediction!

If our actions are totally determined by preceding events, then they are in a sense out of our hands, aren't they? This question raises the issue of responsibility. If environment or learning history is the cause of a criminal behavior, is it not both futile and unethical to hold a person responsible for it? Many determinists have adopted this view. According to Skinner (1971), an individual should not be held responsible for either positive or negative accomplishments; the environment has been the cause of both. What is overlooked in this contention is that the act of holding people responsible or making them accountable for their behavior is in itself a very important environmental event. To neglect to thank a person for a kindness because it was only the environment that caused it is to dramatically alter that environment. Praise and blame are environmental events. If holding someone responsible for behavior means that a systematic relationship will be enforced (for example, behavior A will be rewarded; behavior B will not), then the behavioral scientist is both justified in assigning and obliged to assign responsibility to the person. In this sense, the term *responsibility* does not try to isolate a cause. Instead, it predicts a consequence. We are not responsible in that we cause or will ourselves to do something. In determinism there can be no single or first cause: event B was determined by event A which, in turn, was determined by a preceding event and so on into infinity. However, we are responsible in the sense that we usually have at least two alternative response options to choose from and frequently we know what the consequences of those various responses are. If those consequences are removed, a significant element of our controlling environment is eliminated. One is reminded here of a utopian community that was patterned after Skinner's *Walden II* (1948). The inhabitants of this community decided that an individual would neither be thanked nor criticized for performance since it was the environment rather than the person which was responsible. This arrangement led to a great deal of personal stress because most of the community residents were accustomed to receiving evaluative feedback on their actions. When this feedback was eliminated, a critical element in their environment had been removed.

Despite the rather overwhelming logical and scientific support for the assumption of determinism, the fact remains that most individuals *believe* that they are free, self-determining beings. Thus, efforts to demonstrate and convince them otherwise may be ill aimed. As Kanfer and Karoly (1972) point out, the important issue is not whether free will or determinism is in fact valid, for the fact of the matter is that most individuals function under the assumptions of freedom and personal responsibility. These beliefs become important variables in the prediction and control of behavior.

Behavior control and countercontrol

Most discussions of behavioral determinism highlight the fact that human performance is controlled by environmental forces. The individual is portrayed as a mindless robot, passively responding in a reflexive fashion to surrounding environmental forces. This rather unsavory portrayal has unfortunately been encouraged by some behavioral scientists. However, just as there is no first cause of a specific response, *the influence process between environment and behavior is not a one-way street.* The existing psychological evidence does strongly support the notion that environmental events exert control over behavior. However, there is equally strong evidence illustrating that *behaviors exert control over environments* (Bandura 1969). For example, one might argue that rewarding a rat with food pellets for pressing a lever has exerted an influence: the environment (the food dispenser) has determined the rat's behavior. On the other hand, one is equally justified in pointing out that the environment, or at least the rate of food pellet delivery, is being determined by the rat's behavior. The influence process is reciprocal in that it works both ways. Environments influence behavior; behaviors influence environments. Which comes first? The question is, of course, unanswerable. The relationship between environment and behavior is an interdependent one; that is, each influences the other in such a complex manner that it is both meaningless and inaccurate to assign one the primary role in the relationship. It should be noted that the term *environment* as used here includes those significant private events (thoughts, feelings, images) that play such an important role in complex human performance. Phenomena in this "internal environment" can exert a tremendous influence on behavior (Mahoney 1974a). They thus become significant elements in the endless reciprocity.

This *reciprocal determinism* between behavior and environment has tremendous significance for human performance and the issues of personal freedom, responsibility, and choice. Since environments are a function of behavior, the individual can take an active role in self-determination. That is, one can arrange one's environment to produce or eliminate specified behaviors. Does this re-introduce the concept of free will? No; the act of taking an active role in engineering one's personal environment is determined by previous environmental influences (which may, in turn, have been determined by previous behaviors). However, the interdependence of behavior and environment points up the fact that we are not passive recipients of environmental influence; our performance is a critical determinant of that environment.

One of the popular issues that arises in a discussion of behavior control is a political one. Given that human performance can be reliably predicted and controlled, *who will control whom?* Who will be the controllers? Who will be the controlled? A frequent assumption here is that one individual or a small group of sophisticated behavioral engineers will condition the masses. Visions of a mad scientist manipulating herds of humans are implied. There are three basic misconceptions here. To begin with, even if behavior control were a one-way street, there is little reason to believe that it would entail a totalitarian system.

One could envision a democracy in which citizens elected persons to engineer their environments. Indeed, this is the underlying assumption in contemporary Western democracy. We select representatives who we think will implement contingencies like laws, taxes, and response opportunities that are to our liking. Congressmen, law enforcement officers, and the like are paid by us to control us. We, of course, attempt to control them, which brings us to the second major misunderstanding in the issue of behavior control.

The question is not just one of who shall control whom, because the influence process is reciprocal. A does not simply control B; B also controls A. As many a parent or teacher will attest, adults do not have a monopoly on behavior influence processes. The controller is also a controllee, producing changes in others' behavior which may, in turn, have a dramatic influence on his own actions. In some instances, this reciprocal system is highlighted by the phenomenon of countercontrol. If individuals object to the behavior change efforts directed toward them by others, they may respond in a negative or opposite-to-prediction manner. For example, the rebellious adolescent frequently bucks the system and performs contrary to prevailing expectations or contingencies. In so doing, he or she is countercontrolling, that is, exerting an influence on the person or persons who are attempting to control his or her behavior. Research on the phenomenon of countercontrol has suggested that it may be influenced by such variables as the magnitude of incentives, the subtlety of the behavior change influences, and the availability of choice (alternate responses) to the individual (Davison 1973; Mahoney 1974a).

The phenomenon of countercontrol points up still a third aspect of the behavior control issue. In a classic debate Rogers and Skinner (1956) discussed the desirability of investigating and refining behavior modification techniques. According to Rogers, the dangerous and dehumanizing menace of those techniques warrants their avoidance. He contends that we should not research techniques of behavior change because of their potential use for unethical purposes. Skinner, on the other hand, points out that we have an obligation to study and identify the principles and processes involved in human behavior. The issue is not whether we should control behavior; behavior is always controlled. Your actions at this very moment are being influenced by a variety of factors. The point is that much of the environmental control that currently prevails is haphazard and detrimental. Investigating the principles of behavior will not produce behavior control; it will refine and improve the control that now exists. It is not as if psychological research is introducing an element of determinism that did not previously exist. One's behaviors are always determined. However, until its determinants are identified, one's performance and perhaps happiness may be left to haphazard influences rather than to systematically planned and managed ones. Skinner points out that part of Rogers's objections to the development of a behavior technology may stem from the assumption that to engineer a culture or performance is bad. Man's development and his culture are best left to "natural evolution," according to this view. However, the dangers of such passivity are readily apparent in the contemporary dilemmas of overpopulation, aggression, and obesity. Sexual productivity, physical aggressiveness, and high calorie consumption are patterns that persist in part because of their survival value during the dawn of the species. However, we are currently facing an early demise of the species unless these naturally evolved behavior patterns are modified through extensive systematic planning and management. The gross trial-and-error aspect of "natural" developments often makes them expensive and time-consuming. By taking an active part in one's own behavioral and cultural evolution, it is possible to enhance and refine its course. Indeed, recent limited efforts employing this approach to social change have been promising (Meyers et al., 1974).

Another objection to Rogers's argument that we terminate research on applied behavior principles relates to the previously discussed phenomenon of countercontrol. If we are to take an active part in our own development, we must be familiar with the behavior change techniques that others may be directing toward us. To remain ignorant of the laws governing behavior is to encourage a one-way influence process; it effectively reduces our own chances of having an impact on the environmental events that influence us. Evidence on consumer and voting behavior illustrates that extensive behavior change efforts are being continually directed at the public. Many of these efforts are both sophisticated and effective. An informed public—one familiar with the principles and techniques of behavior change—would be better equipped to identify and influence these efforts.

Behavioral freedom and humanistic issues

Another frequently encountered objection to behavioral approaches to human performance is that they are simplistic and stultifying. A complex and intricate being is analyzed down into discrete responses. Man is funneled into a composite of stimuli and responses; the human essence is sacrificed and creativity is abandoned.

This funnel effect, if it does exist, is a reflection of specific applications of behavior technology rather than any deficiencies in the technology itself. That is, behavior principles and the technology that has developed around them are neither good nor bad in and of themselves. Atomic energy is similarly amoral. However, any technology can be put to appropriate or inappropriate uses. If a teacher uses behavior change principles to elicit docile and uncreative responses from students, the error lies in the application of those principles and not in the principles themselves.[1] In one sense, we may be near the Los Alamos stage of behavioral research. Some very powerful techniques have been developed for the prediction and control of performance. How those techniques are applied will be partially determined by the extent to which they are understood and influenced by the public. The same principles that may be inappropriately used by one teacher to produce docility may be applied by another to encourage creativity and personal growth in students. As a matter of fact, Skinner (1971) has recommended the programming of innovative and diverse responses because of their beneficial role in the accelerated evolution of improved performance and cultures. By designing a learning environment that encourages creative problem solving, the teacher can increase the likelihood of those responses that often become landmarks in the progress of civilization—new conceptual systems, inventions, and so on.

One final issue relates to the question of behavioral freedom. Earlier we discussed the concept of free will and self-determination in human performance. Behavioral freedom refers to the number of response options available to us at any given time. To the extent that we have a wide range of behaviors to draw upon, we are free to react with diversity to environmental influences. This behavioral freedom plays a significant role in personal adjustment and growth. Mahoney and Thoresen (1974) discuss the relevance of behavioral technology as a means for attaining humanistic ends. If individuals are trained to become their own behavioral engineers, they can take an active part in the direction and development of their own lives. This behavioral humanism represents a new and exciting avenue of psychological research. Familiarity with the processes and principles of human performance allows individuals to enter into their own behavioral equation. Instead of being mere recipients of environmental influence, they become significant factors in the form and direction of that influence. The pursuit and refinement of behavioral research may thus become a uniquely humane endeavor.

Summary

The assumptions and applications of behavior modification have stimulated increasing concern in the last few years. Apprehensions about the abuse of behavioral principles have been particularly apparent. Many

[1] The scientific method does not presently seem applicable to the question of the determination of goals or objectives. To what *ends* the findings of scientific investigation will be directed is not a question to which the scientific method itself has been addressed.

of these ethical objections, however, seem to be based on inaccurate views and invalid inferences regarding the behavioral perspective. The assumption of determinism, for example, does not strip man of choice or responsibility. Likewise, fears that a small group of individuals may gain totalitarian behavioral control are unwarranted. Reciprocal determinism, or the interdependence of behavior and environment, discourages a one-way influence process. The phenomenon of countercontrol is an apt illustration of this reciprocity. To the extent that individuals remain ignorant of the behavior change principles applied to them, they will be more susceptible to inequitable control.

Behavior modification does not legislate that we "should" control behavior—behavior is always controlled. The issue is whether or not we should take an active part in creating and directing the variables that control us. Like any other technology, the principles of behavior modification can be abused and applied in destructive or unethical ways. This potential abuse, however, can be averted only by a sensitive and conscientious dedication to the continued exploration of humane applications. In this respect, rather than forcing the human being into a passive and rigid mold, behavior modification may offer an exciting means for attaining humanistic ends. By providing us with an understanding of our own behavior, it may afford us the invaluable freedom and responsibility to take an active part in our own becoming.

Suggested readings

Mahoney, M. J. The sensitive scientist in empirical humanism. *American Psychologist,* in press.

Mahoney, M. J.; Kazdin, A. E.; and Lesswing, W. J. Behavior modification: Delusion or deliverance? In C. M. Franks and G. T. Wilson, eds., *Annual review of behavior therapy: Theory and practice.* Volume 2. New York: Brunner/Mazel, 1974. Pages 11–40.

Matson, F. W. *Without/within: Behaviorism and humanism.* Belmont, Calif.: Brooks/Cole, 1973.

Part III

Applications of behavior modification

SO FAR we have talked primarily about conceptual and ethical issues and the laboratory research from which the principles of behavior change have been developed. It has been repeatedly emphasized that a familiarity with these conceptual and experimental foundations is essential for an adequate understanding of therapeutic applications. We are now ready to explore some of those applications. The chapters that follow represent a sample of contemporary uses of behavioral principles. The topics and authors were selected to provide a broad overview of both well-established and relatively recent applications. These chapters presume an understanding of the fundamental principles covered in the preceding sections.

Perhaps the question most frequently asked regarding any clinical approach or technique is "Does it work?" As you know by now, the behavioral researcher attempts to answer that question by relying on the principles of methodological behaviorism; the experimental clinician asks for an empirical evaluation of procedures. While this may not always be achieved, it is the ideal toward which researchers aspire. Because of our commitment to this ideal we requested the authors of the following chapters to present data-based material. By that we did not mean that all the numbers and statistical probabilities for each reported study should be cited, but rather that the authors review the evidence bearing on each area of application. In addition, the authors were invited to present the issues and findings with freedom of style and opinion. Some authors have presented an overall evaluation of treatment procedures, others have focused on conceptual and treatment issues, and still others have examined specific treatment or clinical research programs. It is hoped that these different styles and emphases will provide the reader with a working knowledge of the current "state of the science" in applied behavior modification. As the final chapter by Kanfer and Grimm indicates, this area of applied research is continuing to grow rapidly in both volume and perspective. A textbook on the topic of applied behavior change will probably look very different a decade from now. This commitment to continual growth and refinement is a critical element in clinical science and an exciting aspect of the helping professions.

Anxiety management [1]

Douglas A. Bernstein
University of Illinois at Urbana-Champaign

11

Anxiety has been posited as the central problem in what have traditionally been labeled as neurotic disorders. Within this traditional framework, anxiety has been viewed as a unitary construct. However, as Bernstein points out, behaviorists employ the term anxiety *as a shorthand label for a complex pattern of responses which may be self-report, physiological, or somatic-motor in nature. Bernstein presents a succinct statement of the most widely accepted behavioral account of the development of anxiety, emphasizing the role of classical conditioning, modeling, and cognitive factors. In addition to problems in which anxiety is the central focus, the role of anxiety is observed in a number of other problem behaviors, such as sexual dysfunction and bizarre behaviors of the hospitalized patient.*

The treatment of anxiety has been one of the most extensively studied areas of behavior modification. Bernstein reviews and summarizes the research on three treatment procedures: (1) systematic desensitization, (2) modeling, and (3) flooding and implosion. The therapeutic effectiveness of systematic desensitization and modeling procedures has been demonstrated across a variety of problems in which anxiety is a factor; the results with flooding and implosion are less promising at this stage. Perhaps the most effective approach to anxiety management is Meichenbaum's recent work (1974), which combines systematic desensitization, modeling, and self-instructional training.

[1] Preparation of this manuscript was facilitated by support from the Department of Psychology at Western Washington State College, while the author was on leave from the University of Illinois at Urbana-Champaign.

The bulk of this chapter deals with behavioral or social learning approaches to the reduction or elimination of anxiety, but before specific techniques are discussed, it is necessary to clarify what it is that one attempts to reduce or eliminate. Dealing with the concept of anxiety is a lot like dealing with the idea of "class." Many people feel that having class is good, but everyone has a slightly different idea of what it is and there is considerable disagreement on how to tell when someone has it.

Similarly, most people would probably agree that "having anxiety" or "being anxious" is bad, unpleasant, and to be avoided if possible, but no universally accepted definition of anxiety is available. This lack of consensus is reflected in the fact that there are at least 120 specific procedures available that purport to measure anxiety (Cattell and Scheier 1961). The main problem with trying to define anxiety is that it is not a single entity like an arm or leg which a person does or does not have. Rather, it is a shorthand term that originally referred only to a painful, choking sensation in the throat (Sarbin 1964), but which, primarily because of the influence of Freud's emphasis upon *Angst* (translated as "anxiety") in the development of behavior and behavior disorders, has come to have much broader meaning.

Definition and measurement of anxiety

Today, the word *anxiety* refers to a complex and variable pattern of behavior which occurs in response to internally (cognitively) or externally (environmentally) produced stimuli and which can show up in three dimensions or response channels. The first of these is the subjective or *self-report* channel, in which an individual may indicate informally as in "I was scared to death!" or formally through psychological test scores the degree of anxiety he or she experiences, either as a rule (trait anxiety) or in response to specific situations (state anxiety). Various general purpose and specialized paper-and-pencil tests are available to measure this aspect of anxiety (Levitt 1967; Spielberger 1972), but their results must be interpreted cautiously since individuals' responses to self-report measures may be subject to intentional or unintentional bias of many types (Azrin, Holz, and Goldiamond 1961; Mischel 1968; Sundberg and Tyler 1962). Some individuals may report lower levels of anxiety than they actually experience in order to please a therapist or to appear "mentally healthy"; others may spuriously inflate their reports in an effort to give responses they think are desired by an experimenter or as a means of gaining attention.

The second response channel is that of *physiological arousal*, primarily involving activity of the sympathetic branch of the autonomic nervous system. Persons showing anxiety in this channel display changes in one or more indices of arousal including galvanic skin response (GSR), heart rate, blood pressure, blood volume, respiration, muscle tension, pupillary response, and the like. Many technical problems make accurate, unbiased measurement of the physiological component of anxiety difficult. Temperature, movement, body weight, diet, cognitive activity, and the presence of drugs are just a few of the factors which may affect physiological responses. It is not enough to measure anxiety through only one index of physiological activity, such as heart rate; each individual's arousal may appear in a slightly different way (Lacey 1967; Lacey and Lacey 1968), thus necessitating the use of multiple response measures.

The third anxiety response channel involves overt *somatic-motor behavior,* such as trembling or stuttering, which occurs either as an observable consequence of physiological arousal or as a means of escape from or avoidance of certain stimuli. Assessment of anxiety through this channel usually consists of direct observation of an individual's avoidance and/or performance during what is, for that person, some kind of stress, such as giving a speech, taking an exam, climbing a ladder, touching a snake, or whatever. Observations are quantified through the use of an approach scale or other rating system (e.g., Paul 1966) that allows each subject's overt behavioral responses to be compared in standard fashion with those of any other subject; however, this approach to anxiety measurement is also vulnerable to a certain amount of bias, mainly through social/situational factors. For example, subjects who are not strongly encouraged to perform a stressful task may display more overt behavioral anxiety than they would if the test situation clearly demanded fearlessness (e.g., Bernstein 1973; Bernstein and Nietzel 1973; Blom and Craighead 1974; Smith, Diener, and Beaman 1974).

The problem of defining anxiety is further complicated by the fact that the three channels of anxiety response often do not correlate well with one another (Lacey 1959; Lang 1968). A person who is anxious in relation to a particular stimulus situation may display strong reactions in only one channel; for example, in self-report but not in overt behavior or physiological activity. Such discrepancies are due mainly to the fact that the appearance of anxiety in each channel is a function not only of the target stimulus situation, such as a dentist's office, but also of other variables as well. For example, a male college student may show strong physiological arousal and a great deal of overt avoidance behavior in relation to large dogs, but because he does not wish to appear foolish or unmasculine, he may vigorously deny any discomfort. A person who is learning to sky dive may display clear physiological arousal, and some avoidance behavior before a jump, but that arousal may be interpreted by the individual as excitement (Schachter 1964; Schachter and Singer 1962) and thus no anxiety is reported. Finally, an individual who reports strong anxiety in relation to dentistry and displays clear autonomic arousal in the dentist's chair may show no overt avoidance behavior because of the anticipated positive consequences of receiving treatment.

Obviously, whether or not a person is labeled as anxious, fearful, phobic, or the like depends to a great extent upon (1) which anxiety channel is assessed and (2) what social/situational, cognitive, consequential, or other factors are operative. Many researchers in the field now recognize this problem and seek to base statements about anxiety upon measures that reflect all three channels and that minimize the influence of artifacts. In fact, because of the complexity, multidimensionality, and elusiveness of the anxiety construct, some social learning theorists and practitioners (e.g., Bandura 1969; Krasner and Ullmann 1973; Ullmann 1967; Ullmann and Krasner 1969) hardly use the term *anxiety*, referring instead either to the external or internal stimulus conditions that result in behaviors labeled as anxiety or to some specific components of anxiety, such as emotional arousal or avoidance behavior. This approach is based upon the notion that the theoretical construct called *anxiety* provides little in the way of specific information about behavior, and that it has become reified and used as an explanation of maladaptive, irrational, or unusual behavior when, in fact, it provides only a description. Krasner and Ullmann (1973) put it succinctly.

> We have to deal not with . . . anxiety, but with the conditions giving rise to anxiety. . . . The concept of anxiety is superfluous in dealing directly with people rather than with theories. In a clinical interaction we deal with what is being avoided, with what a person needs to learn or unlearn or relearn. . . . [The concept of anxiety] makes us think we know something when we do not and should be looking harder. (pp. 98–99)

Consistent with this kind of thinking, the behavioral or social learning approach to anxiety and anxiety measurement focuses upon clear specification of stimulus conditions and upon objectively quantified responses to those stimuli rather than upon use of psychological tests designed to measure the presence of or changes in a generalized trait or construct. This has resulted in the development of anxiety management techniques that are designed not to eliminate anxiety, but to alter individuals' maladaptive response patterns to specific classes of stressful stimuli. The success of these treatment procedures is evaluated in terms of the magnitude of desirable changes in specified target behaviors (often in all three anxiety channels), which are assessed before and after treatment.

Nature and development of anxiety as a clinical problem

Everyone experiences negative emotional arousal and/or displays behavioral avoidance in relation to stressful stimulus situations. In fact, a certain degree of arousal or activation is a prerequisite to adequate everyday functioning; a totally nonaroused person would be in a coma twenty-four hours a day. However, too much activation can also be debilitating (Hunt 1961); when response patterns referred to collectively as anxiety reach high levels of intensity, frequency, duration, and generality, the individual and those around her or him experience severe discomfort, and disruption of adaptive behavior occurs. For example, an individual whose arousal is too high before and during an academic examination or a date may experience physical discomfort and "draw a blank" when attempting to answer test questions or think of conversation topics. Such experiences may make future tests or dates even more stressful, thus adding to the discomfort and further disrupting performance.

In addition, overaroused individuals may engage in behaviors that seem irrational or bizarre to others but which are merely attempts to escape or avoid stimuli that they find strongly aversive. Thus, a salesman who is upset by driving might refuse to deal with customers except on the telephone or in his office. If he refused to explain the basis for this behavior, and especially if he were hostile and defensive about it, his actions might ultimately result in loss of employment. If intense arousal continues for extended periods of time, other results such as depression, exhaustion, and even actual tissue damage (ulcers, for example) may appear (e.g., Selye 1956, 1969).

Thus, when anxiety becomes a clinical problem, the client's presenting complaints may involve clearly defined and recognized maladaptive responses in one or more of the three anxiety channels discussed earlier, or they may reflect the consequences of those responses. The clinician must always be alert to the possibility that anxiety responses may be involved in cases which at first glance appear to be of a totally unrelated nature.[2]

In developing intervention procedures applicable to anxiety, the behavioral or social learning approach begins with the assumption that

[2] We shall refer to this point again later, but see Paul and Bernstein (1973) for a fuller discussion of the issues.

maladaptive response patterns that produce client discomfort are learned on the basis of the same principles as is most other behavior, adaptive or maladaptive (e.g., Ullmann and Krasner 1969; see also Chapters 6, 7, and 8 in this volume). This assumption is based upon and supported by a great deal of research, the results of which can only be summarized and illustrated here (see Bandura 1969, for details).

Suppose that you are holding a 4-year-old child on your lap while two other 4-year-olds play on separate areas of your living room floor and that, as child A gently pets your English sheepdog, child B inserts a butter knife into an electrical outlet. Everyone would learn something from this incident. Because it was directly associated with severe, unexpected pain and accompanying autonomic arousal, child B would learn to avoid using wall sockets as knife holders, and possibly, to stay away from electrical outlets altogether. Child A might learn, or at least begin to learn, to avoid the sheepdog, or dogs in general. When child B suddenly screamed and cried, it startled child A, and since the occurrence of any strong, sudden, unexpected, and novel stimulus produces autonomic arousal, the harmless dog was associated with a strong, unconditioned response to a stressful stimulus.[3] Depending upon the focus of his or her attention at the time, the child on your lap might later display avoidance of wall sockets (if he/she was watching child B), of dogs (if he/she was watching child A), or of you. Incidentally, since many of the principles of learning apply to both humans and animals, it is also possible that this sheepdog may subsequently try to avoid children.

This somewhat oversimplified example illustrates several important points. First, strong arousal in relation to specific stimuli or classes of stimuli can be learned. Second, learned arousal can be attached to harmless stimuli in the same way as it can to those that are objectively dangerous. Third, an individual may acquire anxiety responses on the basis of observation of another person's behavior and its consequences, thus underscoring the role of cognitive anxiety in the development and maintenance of such responses. Finally, learned anxiety responses may be adaptive ("rational") or maladaptive ("irrational"), a distinction that is very important in making clinical treatment decisions.

Obviously, when anxiety responses are appropriate and adaptive, as when an individual faces a clearly hazardous situation (for example, walking across the Grand Canyon on a greased clothesline), the clinician is unlikely to suggest or implement treatment; but, when such responses are inappropriate or maladaptive, intervention is both rea-

[3] Watson and Rayner (1920) produced the same effect over several trials by suddenly producing a loud noise while a small child played with a tame white rat.

sonable and beneficial. As we will see below, most of the anxiety-related problems dealt with by clinicians involve inappropriate reactions to or attempts to avoid or escape stimuli which are, by and large, harmless.

Targets of anxiety management

Clinical interventions that employ the social learning approach are aimed at two broad categories of anxiety-related target problems. The first of these involves situations in which an individual's overarousal occurs as an appropriate reaction to actual stress conditions which themselves occur partly as a function of the person's own behavior. As an example of this target category, called *reactive anxiety*, consider the person who reports strong arousal related to parties and other social gatherings as a result of having been ignored or insulted by others in those situations in the past. If the individual actually elicits these consequences by obnoxious social behavior, we have an instance of reactive anxiety. In these cases, treatment focuses first upon alteration of the behaviors that bring about negative consequences from others, not upon elimination of anxiety responses to those consequences. When skill deficits and/or behavioral excesses are eliminated, the likelihood of pleasant social interactions is increased, thus reducing reactive anxiety (see Chapter 20 in this volume, for a discussion of some of the techniques involved).

If after successful social skills training, the person continues to respond to social situations *as if* they were threatening, we have an example of the second category of target problems: *conditioned, inappropriate anxiety responses.* Such responses may develop in other ways than from a prior deficit in skills. Four subtypes of such problems and the intervention tactics available to deal with them will be discussed.

1. *"Simple" conditioned anxiety.* In these cases, the client responds with strong arousal to stimulus classes that are not objectively threatening. Usually, the client clearly reports anxiety as the main problem and pinpoints the stimulus or class of stimuli, such as public speaking, air travel, or elevators, that results in discomfort. Sometimes, however, overarousal may have generalized to the point that discomfort occurs in relation to such complex stimulus patterns, or in extreme cases, to so many stimulus conditions (both external and cognitive) that the client is unable to specify the nature of the problem. Depending upon severity, this situation has been called free-floating anxiety, nervous breakdown, or even acute psychotic episode.

2. *Psychosomatic or psychophysiological disorders.* Anxiety responses that occur in the physiological channel, especially if they are of long duration and are focused in specific response systems, can result in

actual tissue damage such as ulcerative colitis or peptic ulcer. When this occurs, the intervention tactics described in this chapter are often effective in reducing and preventing learned, inappropriate arousal, but the physical disorders themselves must be dealt with medically. In other cases, physiologically expressed anxiety may take the form of physical symptoms which do not necessarily involve obvious damage, but which are nonetheless uncomfortable or potentially dangerous. Migraine headache, high blood pressure, asthma, and chronic fatigue are examples of physical problems which may be based upon conditioned, inappropriate anxiety responses and which may disappear when those responses are reduced.

3. *Breakdown of complex behavior.* When too much arousal occurs, disruption of performance, especially of the type that involves complex tasks, may result. When this happens, the client may not complain of anxiety but rather of inability to concentrate, poor memory, confusion, cognitive "flooding," breakdown of physical skills such as typing or other motor behaviors, or lack of fluency in speech. Sexual functioning, a complex combination of physiological, cognitive, and motor responses, may also be disrupted, resulting in reports of impotence, frigidity, ejaculatory incompetence, orgasmic dysfunction, vaginismus, or other problems (Masters and Johnson 1970).

4. *Development of appropriate or inappropriate escape or avoidance behaviors.* It is rare that an individual has no opportunity to escape or avoid stressful stimuli, and most escape or avoidance behaviors do not qualify as clinical intervention targets. However, when a person seeks to avoid or escape stimuli that result in anxiety responses by engaging in behaviors that are either socially appropriate but restricting or socially inappropriate and thus problematic in themselves, clinical intervention may be helpful. Examples of the former include avoidance of air travel, public places, elevators, escalators, and other stimulus situations that can be circumvented but only by causing considerable inconvenience for the client or others. If escape or avoidance is successful, clients' complaints usually do not include reports of strong, everyday discomfort (because they do not allow themselves to be exposed to feared stimuli), but they focus instead upon dissatisfaction with or depression over the lengths to which they must go to remain at ease. Often, clients fail to display or report the problem until some change in their life situation necessitates contact with stressful stimuli, as when a high school student who avoids unfamiliar surroundings must leave home to attend college. In other cases, clients' escape or avoidance strategies take forms that are not only inconvenient but also very obviously maladaptive, inappropriate, and even bizarre. Examples may include various classical "neurotic" or even "psychotic" behaviors such as amnesia, ob-

sessions and compulsions, delusions, "hysterical" paralyses or other "conversion reactions." In addition, many cases of alcoholism, drug abuse, homosexuality, and criminal behavior can be related to attempts to avoid stressful stimulus situations.

Behavioral approaches to anxiety management

There is insufficient space in a brief chapter to present in detail every one of the many intervention strategies that have been developed within the behavioral or social learning framework for dealing with the broad array of anxiety-related problems brought to the clinician. What follows, therefore, is a general description of two of the most important and frequently employed treatment packages, each of which is altered and adapted somewhat in clinical practice to meet the specific needs of each client (for more detailed coverage, see Bandura 1969; Kanfer and Phillips 1970; Rimm and Masters 1974). It should be understood that each of the procedures to be discussed is not employed in a single, ritualized fashion as if all clients were identical, but rather is implemented within the context of a positive and trusting therapeutic relationship. The client is viewed as an important and active participant in a cooperative educative process designed to bring about not only unlearning of maladaptive behaviors but also acquisition or reacquisition of more appropriate and adaptive behaviors. The clinician is thus a sort of teacher and assistant who acts not as an all-knowing judge or manipulator of behavior, but as a consultant whose expertise lies in analysis of human behavior problems and in planning and implementing strategies for change.

The most influential of these strategies are systematic desensitization and modeling. Both share the assumption that maladaptive anxiety responses are based upon learning, but each approaches the task of producing unlearning and/or relearning with a slightly different emphasis.

Systematic desensitization – Wolpe

The set of anxiety reduction techniques known as *systematic desensitization* has been employed informally for many years (e.g., Jones 1924) but did not achieve the status of a clearly recognizable treatment package until publication of Wolpe's volume, *Psychotherapy by Reciprocal Inhibition*, in 1958. As the title indicates, the approach is based upon what Wolpe called the reciprocal inhibition principle, which was derived from laboratory research by Wolpe and others upon the nature of the autonomic nervous system and upon mechanisms involved in the learning and unlearning of anxiety responses by animals and humans.

Wolpe (1958) states, "If a response antagonistic to anxiety can be made to occur in the presence of anxiety-evoking stimuli so that it is accompanied by a complete or partial suppression of the anxiety responses, the bond between these stimuli and the anxiety responses will be weakened" (p. 71). In simplest terms, this means that since a person cannot be anxious and nonaroused at the same time, one can break the learned link between a particular stimulus and the anxiety response it evokes by seeing to it that the stimulus occurs while the anxiety response is prevented from occurring.

Wolpe identified several behaviors that are incompatible with anxiety responses. Some of these, such as sexual arousal, eating, or assertion (that is, standing up for one's rights and/or expressing feelings) are somewhat specialized in that they are employed therapeutically only when anxiety-eliciting stimuli are directly related to them. However, the most generally applicable and commonly employed anxiety-inhibiting response or state is deep muscle relaxation, which Wolpe induced first by hypnosis and later by means of waking-state procedures called progressive relaxation (Jacobson 1938). At first glance systematic desensitization procedures appear to be relatively simple, but actually they are quite complex and require a great deal of technical skill. As dictated by the reciprocal inhibition principle, the clinician's task is to expose the client to anxiety-provoking stimuli without producing an anxiety response. Three steps are required. First, a behavior incompatible with anxiety responses must be established. When muscle relaxation is chosen, this requires several weeks of specific training and at-home practice (Bernstein and Borkovec 1973; Paul and Bernstein 1973).

Second, care must be taken that the stressful stimuli presented to the client are weak enough that relaxation can effectively prevent discomfort. This is done by breaking up feared stimulus classes into graded hierarchies, ordered from least to most distressing. As an example, the hierarchy for a person who expresses fear of closed spaces (claustrophobia) might begin with easy items like sitting in a comfortable chair in a large, well-lit living room and progress in many small steps to much more threatening items such as standing in a crowded elevator. Some hierarchies are thematic in the sense that their items progress along an increasingly distressful theme (for example, being in a room with one small dog; being in a room with three small dogs; being in a room with five large dogs) while others are spatial-temporal in the sense that they vary along space and/or time dimensions (for example, buying an airline ticket; checking your baggage; boarding the plane). In many cases, thematic and spatial-temporal hierarchies are combined to form a mixed hierarchy.

Third, hierarchy items must be presented to the client in some way while anxiety responses are inhibited. The most commonly employed means of doing this is to ask the client to visualize each hierarchy item, beginning with the least threatening, while deeply relaxed. Because only weak versions of stressful stimuli are presented at first, anxiety responses to them will easily be prevented by relaxation, thus diluting their ability to provoke discomfort.[4] As each item is desensitized, the item above it in the hierarchy becomes a little less threatening and can be dealt with in the same way. Ideally, the client never experiences anxiety in relation to any hierarchy item because (1) each represents only a small and easily tolerated increase in threat value over the one prior to it, and (2) no new item is visualized until the one below it no longer causes discomfort. If arousal is encountered, the item causing it is either diluted (for example, by presenting it again for a shorter time or by changing it slightly to make it less threatening) or a new one is inserted which requires a smaller step up from the last successfully completed stimulus.

Since each visualized hierarchy item provides a symbolic representation of actual stressful stimuli, the client's ability to imagine these items without discomfort transfers to real life. Thus, when the client actually encounters previously feared stimuli, the weakening of the learned link between those stimuli and anxiety responses which took place in treatment results in a greatly if not completely reduced level of arousal. If transfer does not occur as desensitization progresses, the clinician seeks out and corrects any procedural or other problems which may be evident and makes other necessary changes in the intervention program. Sometimes these alterations take the form of new or revised hierarchy items, additional relaxation training, or practice at item visualization. Whatever the specifics, the goal is to adjust and readjust the treatment program until it becomes effective in eliminating the clients' maladaptive anxiety responses.

The standard systematic desensitization package has been subjected to increasingly intense research since about 1960, and for the most part, it has received high marks (see reviews by Borkovec 1970; Lang 1969a; Paul 1969c, 1969d; Rachman 1967). Paul (1969d) summarized his review by noting, "For the first time in the history of psychological treatments, a specific therapeutic package reliably produced

[4] Whether this reduction in potential for anxiety elicitation occurs because a new response such as relaxation actually replaces anxiety (the counterconditioning hypothesis) or because the client simply learns that no adverse consequences follow imagination of feared stimuli (the extinction hypothesis) is not entirely clear. The question has resulted in much research and debate (e.g., Benjamin, Marks, and Huson 1972; Cooke 1968; Davison 1968; Lader and Mathews 1968; Wilson and Davison 1971), but resolution of the issue is of academic rather than practical importance (Craighead 1973).

measurable benefits for clients across a broad range of distressing problems in which anxiety was of fundamental importance" (p. 159). Although some doubt and considerable controversy exists regarding the mechanisms through which desensitization produces its effects (e.g., Borkovec 1972; Brown 1973; Davison and Wilson 1972, 1973; Goldfried 1971; Morgan 1973; Wilkins 1971, 1972, 1973), it is agreed that the effects themselves are strong.

In some cases, the use of systematic desensitization alone and in its standard form constitutes an incomplete approach to maladaptive conditioned anxiety responses. In addition to helping clients unlearn inappropriate behaviors, the clinician must also assure that adaptive alternative behaviors are available.[5] If clients are unskilled at or unfamiliar with behaviors appropriate to previously avoided stimulus situations, unsupplemented systematic desensitization may only temporarily weaken conditioned arousal, which is subsequently relearned. For example, a child's unrealistic fear of dogs may easily return following successful desensitization unless steps are taken to assure that the child has the knowledge and skills necessary to maintain friendly relations with dogs, to control their behavior, and to recognize potential danger. As Bandura (1971a) has noted, "No psychological methods exist that can render an organism insensitive to the consequences of its actions" (p. 693).

So that the development of appropriate and adaptive behaviors following desensitization is not left to chance, behavioral theorists and therapists have added variations, supplements, and alternatives to the basic and well-established package. An important example is called *in vivo desensitization* (Wolpe 1969). The procedures involved parallel those of imaginal desensitization with several important exceptions. First, the hierarchy stimuli are not imagined but presented "live," although in some cases slides, films, audio-tapes, and videotapes are employed. Second, while progressive relaxation or variations on it such as conditioned or differential relaxation (Paul and Bernstein 1973) may be enlisted as an anxiety-inhibiting influence, the calm and reassuring presence of the therapist (along with careful hierarchy gradations) is often used to serve the same function. Third, and perhaps most important, the client is allowed to actually deal with (rather than merely be exposed to) feared stimuli, and thereby to develop or reacquire requisite skills while unlearning maladaptive responses.

Thus, a person who is overaroused while speaking to a group may first present a short, simple talk to an audience of one (perhaps the

[5] Because humans and animals are constantly behaving, when one response pattern changes, another always replaces it. The question is simply whether the new pattern is desirable or undesirable.

therapist), then to two, three, and so on until no disruptive discomfort is experienced while addressing relatively large groups. Later, the length and spontaneity of the talk may be varied to assure generalization to a wide variety of situations. Some research (e.g., Garfield, Darwin, Singer, and McBrearty 1967; Goldstein 1969; Hamilton and Schroeder 1973; Sherman 1972) and many case reports (e.g., Gurman 1973; Kohlenberg 1974; Weidner 1970) confirm the utility of this approach. It is obviously the treatment of choice when unassertiveness or sexual dysfunction are treatment targets, but it is also applicable whenever stressful stimuli can be graded and presented live in a controlled fashion.

In a recent variation Meichenbaum (1974) has combined systematic desensitization with training in corrective self-statements, similar to those utilized in Ellis's rational emotive therapy (see Chapter 8 in this volume). With the early items in the hierarchy the client visualizes the scenes as in systematic desensitization, but if in the latter part of the hierarchy the client experiences anxiety, rather than having the scene altered to weaken it, the client visualizes himself making adaptive and coping self-statements until the experienced anxiety is successfully handled. These self-statements then not only may facilitate the person's approach to a previously feared situation, but may also be used as coping responses in that and other situations.

Modeling

Some of the basic ideas behind systematic desensitization are employed by behavioral therapists in *modeling*, a related intervention approach that capitalizes on the fact that human beings can learn by observation as well as by direct participation. Our behavior is thus strongly influenced by what we observe and/or hear about other individuals' behavior and its consequences.[6] Modeling techniques seek to reduce anxiety responses by providing a programmed learning experience which emphasizes such vicarious processes. In simplest form, the clinician who uses modeling arranges for the client to observe other people, usually of the client's age and sex, as they fearlessly and successfully deal with increasingly threatening versions of the stimuli that frighten the client. The graduated nature of the stimuli and the use of relaxation or other anxiety-inhibiting factors, such as physical distance or

[6] This can be very fortunate since it spares us the necessity of actually experiencing disastrous consequences (for example, being hit by a truck) in the process of learning to avoid danger, but it can also result in the acquisition of emotional arousal and avoidance behaviors in response to stimuli that are not dangerous. (For example, because of what they have heard, some women respond to all men as if they were sex maniacs, when this is not always true.)

the presence of a reassuring therapist, during the demonstration act to suppress the client's anxiety responses and thus increase attention to the model's behavior. In some situations someone other than the therapist may serve as the calm and reassuring person, such as a parent with a child or a cooperative sexual partner in sexual dysfunction (Meyers, Farr, and Craighead, in press).

The modeling display may be live or symbolic (that is, filmed, videotaped, or even imagined) and contains at least two beneficial elements. First, it provides the client with information. For example, by watching a film depicting others playing with a dog, a person who fears dogs can learn much about both the animal's behavior and the human skills needed to deal with it. Second, it demonstrates that an encounter with feared stimuli can have a positive outcome. The filmed models experience no discomfort; they smile, laugh, enjoy themselves, and of course, are not harmed or threatened by the dog in any way. These elements combine to reduce both maladaptive cognitions relating to the feared stimulus and in turn, the emotional arousal stemming from such thoughts. This reduction in self-produced arousal increases the likelihood that the client will be able to approach the feared stimulus and practice the adaptive behaviors displayed by the models.

The effectiveness of modeling for anxiety response reduction is well supported (e.g., Bandura, Grusec, and Menlove 1967; Bandura and Menlove 1968; Bandura, Blanchard, and Ritter 1969; Geer and Turtletaub 1967; Meichenbaum 1971b), but as with desensitization, the original modeling package did not include procedures that allowed clients actually to deal with feared stimuli under controlled circumstances, and thus it was incomplete. When this feature was added (e.g., Bandura, Jeffery, and Wright 1974; Ritter 1969), it substantially enhanced the effectiveness of the intervention (Bandura, Blanchard, and Ritter 1969; Blanchard 1970). For instance, instead of simply giving snake-fearful clients a demonstration of other people's interaction with snakes, the elaborated modeling approach goes on to invite the client to emulate each gradual step of the model. The model thus acts as a teacher who not only shows what to do but how to do it, and in addition, provides physical assistance, reassurance, encouragement, and praise while the client unlearns anxiety responses and acquires adaptive alternative behaviors.

Especially when anxiety responses are related to relatively concrete physical or social stimuli that can be presented in a controlled and graduated manner, treatments that combine the principles of *in vivo* desensitization with those of vicarious learning and then add specific training in and practice at adaptive alternative behaviors are more effective than approaches employing any one of these components in isolation (e.g., Bandura, Blanchard, and Ritter 1969; Blanchard 1970; Bandura, Jeffery, and Gajdos 1975; Hersen, Eisler, Miller, Johnson, and Pinkston 1973; McFall and Twentyman 1973; Ritter 1969).

Flooding and implosion

So far, we have been considering anxiety management techniques that involve graded presentation of stressful stimuli under conditions designed to produce little or no discomfort. Two alternative approaches, both based upon the principle of extinction (see Chapter 7 in this volume), are also available. Though not used or researched as extensively as desensitization or modeling, they have nevertheless generated enough interest to be briefly mentioned here. These techniques are called flooding and implosion and, though they differ in procedural details, each stems from the notion that responses which are not reinforced will ultimately disappear, or extinguish (Masserman 1943; Solomon, Kamin, and Wynne 1953; Solomon and Wynne 1954). It is assumed that an individual's continued overarousal to stimuli that are not objectively dangerous, such as domestic cats, is maintained in part by the fact that they escape or avoid such stimuli (Mowrer 1939). In other words, the escape or avoidance behavior of a person who never stays around them long enough to discover that cats are harmless is continually rewarded by thoughts and feelings of relief and relaxation at having prevented what he or she assumes would be disastrous consequences.[7]

Flooding and *implosion* both seek to disrupt this maladaptive learning by preventing escape or avoidance, and by keeping the client in contact with strong versions of stressful stimuli until the arousal they cause finally disappears. Flooding simply involves repeated presentation, usually in imagination, but sometimes *in vivo,* of highly distressing stimuli (for example, "You are in a telephone booth with 22 cats."), while implosion, an approach that was developed by Stampfl (e.g., Stampfl and Levis 1967), goes several steps further. Clients receiving implosive therapy are asked not only to visualize strongly arousing stimuli, but also, because maximum arousal is desired, to imagine the most terrifying consequences. The therapist provides a more or less continuously running monologue designed to describe and intensify the horrors of each scene (for example, "You are in a small room with no doors or windows, when suddenly, hundreds of cats emerge from

[7] An old joke is relevant here. A woman sits on a park bench in New York City watching a man sticking small pieces of toilet paper on his nose and then blowing them away. After some time, she asks the man for an explanation of his strange behavior and is told, "It protects me from attack by rogue elephants." When the woman points out that there are no rogue elephants in New York City, the man says, "It works great, doesn't it?"

the walls and begin attacking you. You scream as they tear at your flesh, and your blood begins to cover the floor." [8]).

The nature of these interventions, especially implosion, has forced behavioral theorists and practitioners to question whether clients actually benefit from the approach, and if so, whether equivalent improvement can be brought about through less stressful means. In a recent review of literature on the effects of flooding and implosion, Morganstern (1973) concluded that there is at present "no convincing evidence of the effectiveness of implosion or flooding with human subjects nor is there any evidence that the techniques are superior to systematic desensitization" (p. 318). Others (e.g., Bandura 1969; Wolpe 1969) have expressed concern over possible detrimental consequences of implosion, but its proponents (e.g., Levis 1974) feel that this concern is unfounded. Only additional, well-controlled research will resolve the controversy.

Unfortunately, implosion and flooding focus almost entirely upon extinction of anxiety responses and not at all upon fostering development of adaptive alternative behaviors. In this sense, these approaches appear incomplete and certainly less useful clinically than other, less stressful and more comprehensive treatment packages that are available.

Some concluding comments

As indicated earlier, the development of behavioral procedures for anxiety management such as systematic desensitization, modeling, and the dozens of variations on each of them (see Bandura 1969; Kanfer and Phillips 1970; Lazarus 1971, 1972; Meichenbaum 1974; Paul and Bernstein 1973; Rimm and Masters 1974; Wolpe 1969; Yates 1970) has stimulated a great deal of research activity aimed both at evaluation of these techniques and at their refinement into more streamlined packages. On the basis of this research as well as a mountain of case reports, it can now be stated with considerable confidence that in most cases the social learning or behavioral approach to the problem of maladaptive anxiety responses provides an effective solution which not only brings about initial changes in behavior, but also promotes the generalization and durability of those changes. At the risk of sounding like a television commercial, it can be said that today no one need endure the discomforts of strong, disruptive, maladaptive anxiety responses.

Yet behavioral theorists and practitioners are far from having all the answers about the development, maintenance, and elimination of

[8] Sorry about that, but reading this example may give some idea of the feelings produced during implosion.

these problems. Their most notable initial achievements came in dealing with a fairly restricted set of anxiety-related difficulties, such as specific phobias and performance disruptions, and the knowledge gained from the research and practice of the last 15 years is constantly being applied to new and diverse targets. In addition, innovations such as self-administered treatment, automated treatment, and anxiety prevention procedures are receiving attention. The role of cognitive factors in the development and modification of anxiety responses has become an increasingly popular topic of discussion and research. Much more needs to be learned about those combinations of client, therapist, and treatment characteristics that result in the greatest and most rapid reductions in various presenting problems.

In short, it is not enough to know that social learning approaches to anxiety management are effective; rather we must deal with what Paul (1969c) called the "ultimate question": "What treatment, by whom, is most effective for this individual with what specific problem, under which set of circumstances, and how does it come about?" (p. 44). Working on the answer to this question and those that follow from it will keep researchers and clinicians very busy for many years to come.

Behavioral formulations of depression

Linda A. Wilcoxon, Susan L. Schrader, and R. Eric Nelson
The Pennsylvania State University

12

Although we all have some general idea of what a person means when he says, "I'm depressed," no clear-cut definition of the term depression *exists. As Wilcoxon, Schrader, and Nelson indicate, this lack of a definition has hindered progress in depression research, but the extent of the problem and the frequency of client-reported depression demand that research efforts be continued. In exploring the problem, the authors provide an excellent overview of four of the experimental/clinical models of depression: (1) socio-environmental (primarily operant); (2) learned helplessness; (3) cognitive; and (4) self-reinforcement. Within their discussion of each model the authors present an evaluative review of the development of depression and its treatment, concluding that while each model has made a significant contribution, none presents an explanation adequate to account for all the data. The authors therefore propose an integrative model that incorporates findings from the various approaches; its empirical validation awaits investigation.*

Some of the more important issues touched upon in this chapter derive from the basic questions: Is depression merely a label for an extended "down" mood, or is it entirely different in its etiology? Can the findings of the case studies be replicated with intrasubject and intersubject designs? Are cognitive factors essential or necessary for an adequate explanation of depression?

Depression is one of the many psychological problems that have plagued mankind throughout recorded history. The Biblical patriarch

Job suffered from severe depression and feelings of guilt; in the first century Plutarch graphically described behaviors characteristic of the disorder; in 1621, Sir Robert Burton devoted an entire treatise to "The Anatomy of Melancholy"; and in the twentieth century, depression has become so widespread that it has been called "the common cold of mental illness" (Miller and Seligman 1973, p. 62). Some writers have indicted the pressures of technological society for its prevalence; others have been more cautious in their search for explanations. But whatever its ultimate cause, one thing is clear: depression ranks second only to schizophrenia in accounting for first and second admissions to psychiatric hospitals, and it has been estimated that its prevalence among the nonhospitalized population is five times greater than that of schizophrenia (Dunlop 1965). Indeed, studies have indicated that anywhere from 4 to 24 percent of the population may experience episodes of depression severe enough to warrant clinical intervention (Schwab, Brown, Holzer, and Sokolof 1968).

Definitions of depression

The prevalence of the disorder, coupled with its association with suicide, has made depression the target of extensive research efforts into its causes, treatment, and possible prevention. However, this research has been complicated by the lack of a clear definition of depression. Everyone feels "down" at times, but is clinically severe depression merely an intensification of these feelings or is it something entirely different? Does clinical depression represent a psychological reaction to stress or is it a disease? Are low mood and crying spells the primary hallmarks of depression or are other behaviors the chief characteristics of the disorder? In his excellent book on the subject, Beck (1967) points out that the term *depression* has been used to describe many things: ". . . a particular feeling or symptom, a symptom-complex or syndrome, and a well-defined disease entity" (p. 6). Communication among researchers has been hampered because of this lack of consistency of definition.

Most experimental clinicians currently regard depression as a group of related behaviors, which may have either an organic or a psychological basis. In an exhaustive study, Grinker, Miller, Sabshin, Nunn, and Nunnaly (1961) found these "depressive behaviors" to include verbal statements of dysphoria, self-depreciation, guilt, material burden, and fatigue; a low rate of motor behavior; and somatic complaints such as sleeplessness, loss of appetite, and headaches. Unfortunately, these behaviors can occur in a large number of combinations, and to further complicate matters, they often occur in conjunction with other psychological problems such as generalized anxiety or hostility.

Thus, it is impossible to present a "typical" clinical picture of depression. Given the problems in definition, it is quite likely that the statement, "The person is depressed," is one of the least informative communications in clinical practice (Derogatis, Klerman, and Lipman 1972, p. 395).

In developing the *Diagnostic and Statistical Manual of Mental Disorders* (DSM-II), the American Psychiatric Association (1968) attempted to clarify the definition of depression. The manual lists 10 major categories of mental disorders, and depression may be diagnosed under two of these: neuroses or psychoses. "Neurotic depression" is the less severe form of the disorder and is assumed to be caused by some specific environmental event. Although he may be acutely unhappy, a depressed person labeled neurotic is usually able to function adequately in his environment. There are two types of depressive psychoses: "psychotic depression" and the "major affective disorders." Psychotic depression is presumed to be associated with a significant event in the person's life (although physiological factors may be involved), but the presence of delusions and other extremely disordered behaviors makes psychotic depression a far more serious disorder than a neurotic depressive reaction. A psychotic depressive often "loses touch with reality," cannot function in his environment, and usually is hospitalized. Depressive behaviors that cannot be readily associated with an environmental event are often placed under "major affective disorders." The two primary subtypes of major affective disorders are "involutional melancholia," or depression occurring near middle age, and "manic-depression," or behaviors alternating between depression and agitation.

Patterns of depressive behaviors vary so greatly from person to person, however, that they cannot be identified and clarified as easily as the DSM-II categories might suggest. Consequently, clinicians using this system often disagree on the category to which a particular depressed person should be assigned (Blinder 1966). Furthermore, the use of almost any discrete classification system tends to encourage reification of the labels used in classification; that is, it permits one to assume that a person acts in a particular way as a result of "having," say, involutional melancholia, as if this were some kind of viral infection. Such labels often seem to acquire a life of their own, even though they were originally devised only to describe a certain pattern of behavior. This problem with labels was discussed at length in Chapter 6, "Models of behavior change."

One of the greatest advantages of the recent experimental/clinical approaches to psychopathology is their attempt to circumvent traditional diagnostic labels in favor of a closer examination of the *specific be-*

haviors which are distressing to the particular individual (see Bandura 1969; Kanfer and Saslow 1969). Indeed, it has been argued that the term *depression* might profitably be dropped from the clinician's vocabulary. The term is practically undefinable anyway, and it infers a hypothetical internal state that can be conceptualized only in terms of the behaviors it is supposed to explain. Although we tend to agree with the crux of this argument, we also agree with Lazarus's (1968b) comment that "the temptation to deny depression as a subject matter for scientific inquiry must be resisted—if for no other reason than the fact that clinicians daily are consulted by thousands of people who say they feel depressed" (p. 84).

When consulted by an individual labeling himself depressed, the behavioral clinician must effectively redefine depression in terms of the specific behaviors that are distressing to the client or others in his environment. Specifically, four categories of behavior must be examined (Beck 1967): (1) emotional difficulties (Is the person unhappy? Does he/she feel guilty?); (2) cognitive difficulties (Does the client have an unrealistically low self-image? Is he/she delusional?); (3) motivational and behavioral difficulties (Does the person engage in few pleasurable activities? Does he/she lack appropriate social behaviors?); and (4) physical problems (Does the client complain of headaches, sleeplessness, loss of interest in sex?). When a list of these behaviors has been compiled, the clinician must examine the most serious difficulties in an attempt to determine the contingencies that may be maintaining the behaviors. For example, he may assess the timing and frequency of the behaviors, the stimuli that may elicit them, what happens after they occur, and what the client says to himself about them. When this information has been gathered, the clinician has a far more accurate definition of what the client is labeling depression than could be gained from an assessment ending in a diagnosis of neurotic depression or involutional melancholia. Furthermore, the behavioral "definition" can be used to guide the clinician in choosing the treatment strategy most likely to be effective with that particular individual.

Measurement of depression

Several questionnaires and other measurement devices have been developed to aid the clinician in assessing the severity of depression. Both Hamilton (1960) and Grinker et al. (1961) devised structured interviews by which the client's depressive behaviors can be evaluated and objectively quantified in terms of his or her responses to a standard set of questions. Williams, Barlow, and Agras (1972) recently developed a "behavioral check list" which paraprofessionals such as ward attendants at a psychiatric hospital can use to rate the timing, frequency, and intensity of a person's overt depressive behaviors. This check list avoids the necessity of questioning a depressed client about these behaviors in a detailed interview, and it provides a fairly reliable index of the extent of a person's depression.

There are also available a number of pencil-and-paper, self-report measures, and these are used more frequently than the foregoing instruments. The Multiple Affective Adjective Check List (Zuckerman and Lubin 1965) and the Depression Adjective Check List (Lubin 1965) include a number of words that are unflattering or connote dissatisfaction, unhappiness, or apathy; the client is asked to check those adjectives that describe his feelings and behaviors, and the number of "depressive" adjectives checked is presumed to provide a quantitative measure of his depression. The Beck Depression Inventory (Beck, Ward, Mendelson, Mock, and Erbaugh 1961) and the Zung Self-Rating Depression Scale (Zung 1965) are both short questionnaires in which the client can indicate the frequency and intensity of many depressive behaviors (including emotional, cognitive, and physical difficulties) which he may be experiencing. The D-Scale of the Minnesota Multiphasic Personality Inventory (Hathaway and McKinley 1942)[1] is longer, more complex in format, and contains more oblique questions than either the Beck Depression Inventory or the Zung Scale, but like the other instruments, it is designed to yield a single score which can be interpreted as a measure of depression.

Unfortunately, the value of all these measures is limited by several serious problems. On a practical level, a person's score on any one of the scales gives no clue to the nature of the particular problems he is experiencing, nor does it suggest what type of therapeutic intervention might be effective. With the possible exception of the Beck Inventory, all the self-report measures have been shown to be fairly unreliable in discriminating depression from other psychological disorders (see Beck 1967), and it has been demonstrated that a person's score can be strongly influenced by such factors as anxiety, social desirability, and the individual's "response set." Thus, it would appear that these scales are valuable primarily as an adjunct to, rather than as a replacement for, a more thorough assessment procedure.

The experimental/clinical approach to depression

The goals of the experimental/clinical approach are the explanation, prediction, and control of the behaviors under investigation. In the next few pages we will examine the several conceptual formulations

[1] The D-Scale is also included in the Repression-Sensitization Scale (Byrne 1961).

and clinical interventions for depression that have evolved within the experimental/clinical approach. Unlike the behavioral analyses of anxiety and some other behavior disorders, these formulations of depression have been developed only within the last ten years, and not enough research evidence has yet been accumulated to indicate which model possesses the greatest amount of conceptual and/or clinical utility. However, the data have generally supported the experimental/clinical approach, and it is likely that each of them will make a significant contribution to whatever comprehensive theory of depression finally evolves. Some of these theories have focused primarily upon the depressed person's overt behaviors and social interaction patterns, while others have been more concerned with the cognitive manifestations of the disorder. Despite their differences, however, all these models have been formulated in terms of definable *behaviors* (either overt or covert), and they have shared the common assumption that these depressive behaviors are learned, can be unlearned, and can be replaced by more adaptive behaviors.

Before we review the experimental/clinical formulations of depression, we should point out that some depressive behaviors may have a discernible physiological basis, for example, some metabolic, enzymatic, genetic, or other biological dysfunction (see Aillon 1971; Dorfman 1969). In fact, Akiskal and McKinney (1973) suggest that depression is an interaction among biological, psychological, and sociological factors. They speculate further that a common neurological pathway may underlie all types of depression, that the neurological mechanisms of reward and punishment are in some way temporarily impaired. Although no consistent pattern of physiological abnormality in depression has yet been found,[2] it seems premature to reject completely the systemic medical model of depression. Obviously, physiological factors must be included in any thorough clinical assessment of the depressed individual's problem behaviors.

Socio-environmental model

Researchers working within the socio-environmental model of depression have searched for a key to the development and maintenance of depressive behaviors in terms of the patterns by which a depressed person interacts with his environment. They have attempted to link many depressive behaviors to maladaptive patterns of reinforcement

[2] Though it does not necessarily invalidate the model, it should be noted that drug therapy and electroconvulsive therapy, which have been based on the systemic medical model, have had distressingly inconsistent results from person to person (Beck 1967; Mendels 1970; Morrison and Beck 1974; Raskin 1972).

(Ferster 1965; Lewinsohn, Weinstein, and Shaw 1969; Liberman and Raskin 1971), and have extrapolated from experimental studies of animal behavior to explain some aspects of human depression (Ferster 1966). The cognitive manifestations of depression are assumed to be a product of maladaptive overt behavior patterns, and the socio-environmental theorists maintain that these cognitive behaviors will improve as overt behavior patterns and schedules of reinforcement are modified.

Development of depression

Ferster (1965, 1966, 1973) was among the first to analyze depressive behaviors within an experimental/clinical framework, and his hypotheses have strongly influenced later research. Ferster defined the essential characteristic of depression as a reduction in the frequency of behaviors that are positively reinforced, and drawing upon analogue research from the animal laboratory, he specified three factors that might contribute, alone or in combination, to the development of a depressive reaction. First, the frequency of positively reinforced behaviors will decrease if the schedule of reinforcement becomes too lean, that is, if the person is reinforced on a very infrequent basis. In this sense, the person might be considered to be on a "prolonged extinction schedule" (Lewinsohn, Weinstein, and Shaw 1969). Second, the presence of anxiety can depress the rate of behavior. Third, behavioral frequency can decrease as a function of sudden changes in the environment, especially if discriminative stimuli for ongoing behaviors are removed, for example, through the loss of a loved one.

Lewinsohn and his associates at the University of Oregon have refined and elaborated many of Ferster's hypotheses, although they have focused on the relationship between a loss of reinforcement and the development of depression. Lewinsohn (1974) maintains that a *low rate of response-contingent positive reinforcement* is a sufficient explanation for the depressed person's low rate of behavior and also elicits many of the cognitive and somatic manifestions of the disorder (including feelings of dysphoria and guilt, fatigue, loss of appetite, and so on). Furthermore, Lewinsohn maintains that the total amount of response-contingent positive reinforcement received by an individual is a complex function of three factors: the number of activities and events that are potentially reinforcing for him, the number of reinforcers that can be provided by the environment, and the extent to which he possesses the skills necessary to elicit reinforcement for himself from the environment. Deficits in any of these three areas are considered likely targets for therapeutic intervention.

The experience of many clinicians who have dealt with depressed clients lends a certain amount of support to the hypothesis that depressive behaviors are often triggered by a loss of positive reinforcement. Because it is pragmatically impossible to identify and compare the amount of reinforcement that a person receives both before and after the onset of depression, the major hypothesis of the socio-environmental model of depression is difficult to investigate. Paykel, Myers, Dienelt, Klerman, Lindenthal, and Pepper (1969) matched 185 depressed subjects with 185 normal control subjects on several socio-demographic variables and surveyed the life events of the preceding 6 months for each subject. They found that, in general, the depressed subjects had experienced more stressful events during that time period, more events generally regarded as undesirable, and more of those "involving losses or exits from the social field." In short, the depressed subjects had experienced more events that might be associated with an overall loss of positive reinforcement. Studies reported by Lewinsohn and Libet (1972) and Lewinsohn and Graf (1973) lend further support to this hypothesis. By asking depressed and normal subjects to complete forms each evening indicating their mood level and the amount of positive reinforcement they had received that day (operationally defined as the number of predetermined "pleasant events" in which each subject had engaged), these researchers found that depressed mood was significantly correlated with a low level of enjoyable activity. Although these data do not reveal a causal relationship between a loss of reinforcement and the development of depression, they are at least consistent with the hypothesis that depressed people receive less reinforcement from their environments than do people who are not depressed.

While the socio-environmental model of depression offers a plausible explanation of the variables that may affect the onset of depressive behaviors, it does leave several questions unanswered. First, why do some people fail to become depressed following a loss of reinforcement? Second, how are depressive behaviors themselves maintained? Third, if depressive behaviors are maintained by reinforcement, can the person still be considered depressed?

A clue to the answer to the first question may be provided by Lewinsohn's argument that the total amount of positive reinforcement received by an individual is partially dependent upon his or her skill in eliciting reinforcement from the environment. Indeed, the concept of social skill is an important component of Lewinsohn's general formulation of depression, and several studies of the interpersonal behavior of depressed and nondepressed subjects have indicated that, in general, depressed individuals are less effective than nondepressed individuals in eliciting social reinforcement from others in their environments (Lewinsohn and Atwood 1969; Libet and Lewinsohn 1973; Patterson and Rosenberry 1969; Rosenberry, Weiss, and Lewinsohn 1968). These findings suggest that an individual possessing poor social skills would be likely to enjoy less positive reinforcement from fewer sources than would a person with more adequate social skills.

Costello (1972) speculates that reinforcement and social skills are likely to be mutually interdependent in the following way. A person with inadequate social skills might be particularly prone to depression because even a minor loss of reinforcement would be quite significant. Conversely, a person is unlikely to become depressed if he exercises social skills adequate to obtain reinforcement from a wide variety of sources—a loss of one source of reinforcement would not be "the end of the world." These hypotheses also suggest that, following a real or potential loss of positive reinforcement, a person may remain depressed simply because he lacks the skills necessary to generate alternative sources of reinforcement.

However, other factors can also influence the maintenance of depressive behaviors. A depressed person rarely sits at home all day doing nothing; rather, he may tell others of his problems, complain about fatigue or other somatic symptoms, cry for help, or threaten suicide. In this way, he seeks reinforcement for his depressive behavior. Burgess (1969b) differentiated between performing (or adaptive) behaviors and depressive behaviors, and suggested that depressive behaviors might not be an *unconditioned response* to a loss of reinforcement, as Lewinsohn's hypothesis suggests. Instead, she argued that depressive behaviors may be acquired and reinforced.

> Concurrent with the extinction of performing behaviors [from a loss of reinforcement] may be the *conditioned acquisition* of depressive behaviors. If this is the case, the client may not, in fact, be suffering from reinforcement deficiencies at the time he seeks treatment, for he obtains frequent reinforcements as a consequence to the emission of depressive behaviors. Individuals in the environment invite lengthy reiteration of his troubles, pay attention to his moods, attempt to "help" by performing tasks for him, and generally organize their behavior to accommodate his depressed state. (Burgess 1969b, p. 193; italics added)

Liberman and Raskin (1971) have argued that this concept of "secondary gain" may be sufficient to explain the maintenance of depressive behaviors. It may also explain why clinically depressed individuals are often refractory to advice to "pull yourself together and get with it": why expend the effort necessary to develop new behavior patterns for which the reinforcement contingencies are uncertain, and concomitantly risk the loss of reinforcement that is now contingent upon depressive behaviors?

Secondary gain does, however, generate something of a paradox for the socio-environmental formulations of depression: if a person is being reinforced for emitting depressive behaviors, how can she or he still be depressed? After all, Lewinsohn's model is predicated on the assumption of an overall *reduction* in the rate of positive reinforcement received by the individual. Many investigators have commented that the depressed person's complaints and other verbal behaviors often become noxious stimuli for others in his or her environment (Burgess 1969b; Lewinsohn and Atwood 1969; Robinson and Lewinsohn, 1973). As a result, many people avoid interaction with the depressed person, whose "interpersonal range" then becomes limited to those who are willing to listen and sympathize. This is hardly conducive to an increase in positively reinforced behaviors.

Ferster (1973) elaborated on the operant nature of depressive behaviors and noted that many such behaviors permit the person to avoid aversive stimuli or unpleasant situations in which he or she might expect a further loss of positive reinforcement. Thus, while most nondepressive (or adaptive) behaviors are maintained by positive reinforcement, many depressive behaviors may be maintained by negative reinforcement. Ferster (1973) further states, "Were more effective methods of avoiding aversive situations available to the depressed person, they would be prepotent over the less effective, simpler, and more primitive ones" (p. 858). In many respects, Ferster's analysis recalls the social skills hypothesis discussed previously: depressed individuals may lack the skills necessary to generate much positive reinforcement from their environments. They do attempt to maximize environmental reinforcement, but their strategy for doing so may be to "minimize their losses"; their response repertoire is depleted and they must rely upon these "simpler and more primitive" responses to obtain reinforcement. Indeed, it has been suggested that attempted suicide may be a "last ditch" effort to generate reinforcement. In the long run, of course, this is a self-defeating strategy; other people are seldom positively reinforced for attending to a person's depressive behaviors by seeing him become happy and active. Eventually they will stop attending to him, and the depressed person will move farther and farther away from the social world, cutting himself off from possibilities for reinforcement for more adaptive behaviors. Therapeutic intervention may be needed at this point to help reorient the depressed person to his social world and to train him in alternative, adaptive strategies to recoup his losses.

Treatment strategies

The socio-environmental model offers a reasonably well supported explanation of the development and maintenance of many depressive behaviors. However, such a theoretical formulation should be evaluated primarily in terms of utility, that is, its potential to generate treatments to relieve the distress experienced by depressed human beings. A number of strategies have already been developed by researchers in the area, although evaluation of their effectiveness remains at a preliminary stage. Several case reports and a handful of controlled experiments have revealed, almost without exception, strikingly favorable results. Conclusions drawn from the data must be made with some reservations pending replications with more adequate control procedures. Although each treatment strategy reflects the theoretical emphasis of the individual researcher, they share the common goal of increasing adaptive, nondepressive behaviors and decreasing depressive behaviors. Each treatment package incorporates as its primary therapeutic elements one or more of the specific techniques discussed below.

Overt behavior focus. The first subset of these treatment strategies focuses directly on the individual client's overt behaviors in order to alter the probability that he will perform certain target behaviors. The objective is to reinstate previous adaptive behaviors or teach new ones and ensure that they will be reinforced. Use of contingent therapist attention plays an important role in all these treatments. After establishing a supportive relationship during the first few sessions, the therapist consistently ignores the client's complaints or other depressive verbalizations while attending carefully to reports of adequate coping with problematic situations. Liberman and Raskin (1971) reported on two cases in which contingent therapist attention and approval were sufficient to initially elicit previously reinforced behaviors or to establish new adaptive, coping behaviors.

Burgess (1969) presented a treatment that was successful with several clients whose depression was related to an inability to perform in a variety of situations. A "graded tasks" approach was used in which events were ordered to maximize the client's success experiences relative to his failure experiences. A hierarchy of tasks relevant to the client's problematic situation was constructed. The initial tasks required minimal effort and the therapist saw the client every day the first week in order to reinforce these first approximations. Required tasks were gradually increased in frequency and difficulty until the desired target behaviors were performed.

Lewinsohn (1974) has reported the development of a technique to identify activities that seem especially important to the way a particular individual feels. In a study with 10 depressed college students, Lewinsohn and Graf (1972) tested the effectiveness of increasing the subject's participation in pleasant activities as a means of relieving depressed mood. For each subject, the 10 activities that correlated most highly with nondepressed mood over a 30-day period were selected as target behaviors. Subjects were reinforced with therapy time (nondirective, reflective listening) for increasing the frequency of these activities. The target behaviors increased significantly more than did 10 "control" behaviors, and positive change in mood paralleled increases in these pleasant activities.

Shipley and Fazio (1973) conducted a controlled analogue study in which subjects were trained in problem-solving skills to supply alternatives for the depressive behaviors with which the subject ordinarily approached a problematic situation. Mutually agreed upon, "recommended" assignments were established for each session and the therapist gave feedback regarding the client's attempts to complete them. The client was instructed to limit depressive verbalizations to designated isolation periods when others would not be responsive to them. Compared to an "interest-supportive" control group, the experimental treatment group showed greater decreases in MMPI D-scale (depression) scores.

Emotional response focus. The second subset of treatment strategies has focused more specifically upon the depressed client's emotional responses in order to reinstate previous adaptive behaviors. The potential utility of systematic desensitization, at least when anxiety may be inhibiting a response that would otherwise be rewarding, has been pointed out in several case reports (Wanderer 1972; Wolpe 1970). In a case report of a severely depressed inpatient with a history of frequent hospitalizations, Sammons (1974) presented a procedure, "systematic resensitization," which combines aspects of desensitization with a graded tasks approach. The first phase of the treatment program is designed to overcome the general lack of reinforcer effectiveness often found in severe depression in which the patient cannot identify anything that is currently reinforcing. The procedure used is similar to desensitization, with the hierarchy constructed around previously reinforcing activities; it attempts to replace the current negative associations to these activities with pleasant, positive associations. The second phase, a behavioral reorientation, introduces graded, *in vivo* exposure and ensures that the client's contact with the activity continues to be positive. The client engages in the activity as long as he continues to feel good, or at least neutral; as soon as he feels uncomfortable he must leave the situation for a specified length of time. Sammons reported the behavioral reorientation procedure alone was effective with five, less severely depressed outpatients.

Several techniques have attempted to induce affect incompatible with depression as a means of overcoming the client's initial apathy and inability to respond. "Time projection with positive reinforcement"

(Lazarus 1968b, 1971) elicits positive affect. While deeply relaxed, the client imaginally projects himself into the future and concentrates on pleasant activities. He projects himself to a point in time at which he can no longer imagine being upset over his present losses. The client is then instructed to gradually come back through time to the present and is given direct suggestions that he will retain the pleasant feelings associated with those activities. Lazarus reports that this procedure succeeded in inducing seven of twelve clients initially to perform previously reinforcing activities. Another technique, "affective expression," (Lazarus 1971) is designed to elicit any strong emotion, such as anger, to force the client initially to respond in some fashion. The anti-depressive program reported by Taulbee and Wright (1971) provides suggestive evidence regarding the possible effectiveness of such a technique. A depressed institutionalized patient is required to perform a monotonous and nongratifying task, such as sanding a block of wood, until he or she finally becomes angry and refuses to continue; the patient is then praised and moved to the more pleasant, regular ward. It may be that expressing anger is an alternative response that is incompatible with feelings of depression and helplessness. Lazarus (1971) also speculates that a sensory deprivation procedure might enhance a depressed person's responsiveness to previously reinforcing stimuli; he cites Morita sleep therapy (Kora 1965) as a possible example of such a treatment.

Environmental focus. A third subset of treatment strategies focuses upon the client's environment as a means of modifying his behavior. The therapist actively intervenes to set up contingencies that will reinforce adaptive behaviors and extinguish or punish depressive behaviors. These techniques try to alter the way an individual's family or associates react to his behavior, thereby increasing the probability that he will perform adaptive behaviors. Home intervention in terms of contingency management has not been explored extensively, although Burgess (1969b) reported training the client's spouse to give contingent attention for nondepressive behaviors. Additional clinical evidence supporting the use of such a technique is found in Liberman and Raskin's (1971) case study employing a reversal intrasubject design. The entire family was taught to pay attention to the client's attempts to carry out tasks and to begin ignoring her depressive behaviors. After the client had demonstrated considerable improvement, the family was asked to resume their old habits for a short time. The client returned to her previous condition but quickly improved when the treatment procedure was reinstated. Effective functioning had been maintained at followup a year later.

A more rigorous demonstration of the effect of contingency management was documented in a case study of a mentally retarded resident (Reisinger 1972). Since the resident lived on a token economy ward setting up the contingency was relatively straightforward. The patient was given a token each time she smiled and was fined a token each time she cried; a modified ABAB design indicated that the tokens exerted control over these responses. Social reinforcement was then paired with the tokens and tokens were gradually faded from the program. The resident was discharged shortly thereafter and had not been rehospitalized at followup 14 months later.

Within an experimental case study (ABA) design, Hersen, Eisler, Alford, and Agras (1973a) showed that a typical token economy program decreased observable depression with three neurotically depressed inpatients. Their program reinforced target behaviors in several areas: work assignments, occupational therapy, responsibility, and personal hygiene. A behavior rating scale used by the nursing staff on a time-sampling basis assessed depression in three major categories: talking, smiling, and motor activity. During baseline conditions, receiving tokens was contingent upon performance of the target behaviors but the tokens had no value (privileges were noncontingent); both the number of tokens earned and the behavioral ratings were low. With the introduction of treatment, privileges became contingent upon tokens, and there was a substantial increase in number of tokens earned and a corresponding increase in behavioral ratings (more smiling and so on). When baseline conditions were reinstated, a sharp drop in tokens earned and behavior ratings was noted. The authors suggest that the token economy increased the patient's activity level, which increased his range of social contacts; in these social situations, adaptive target behaviors such as smiling were more likely to be elicited and reinforced.

Client-environment interaction focus. The interaction of the individual client with his social environment is the focus of the fourth subset of treatment strategies. More effective social skills are developed to remedy the client's interpersonal deficits so that he will be able to elicit more positive responses from others. Socially undesirable behaviors which might make the client aversive to others are decreased. However, since the focus of treatment is the interaction patterns, it is crucial to treat the client within his social environment. The cooperation and participation of significant others forms part of the treatment strategy.

Lewinsohn and his colleagues (Lewinsohn and Atwood 1969; Lewinsohn and Shaw 1969; Lewinsohn, Weinstein, and Shaw 1969; Patterson and Rosenberry 1969) have presented six case reports that specify details of a home intervention treatment program and provide data that demonstrate the therapeutic results obtained. Initial home observations are made, with trained observers coding the interpersonal behaviors of all present. These data form the basis for the treatment program and reveal that depressed clients typically emit few responses and their responses are seldom reinforced. The clients are usually ignored by other members of the family or receive negative responses from them. A behavioral diagnosis is made which identifies the faulty interaction patterns, and these conclusions are presented to the client and spouse. A mutually acceptable contract specifying goals and procedures is agreed upon. Target behaviors that have been selected by their clients include: increases in affectionate responses; increases in particular topics of conversation of interest to the parents or the spouse; increases in initiating conversation; increases in participation in new or previously pleasant activities (going to movies, skiing); and decreases in statements regarding problems. Home observations during the treatment period and at termination reveal that therapeutic intervention effects significant changes in the interaction patterns and a concomitant decrease in client-reported depression.

A group treatment program (Lewinsohn, Weinstein, and Alper 1970) has shown initially positive results, and may be particularly useful for those cases in which home intervention is not appropriate. The group creates a social environment in which the client's social skills can be assessed. At each session, trained observers compute for each client an Interpersonal Efficiency Ratio, defined as the number of responses emitted to others compared to the number of responses directed to the client. These data are used to define individual behavioral goals such as initiating more responses, reducing critical statements, and directing comments toward group members rather than the therapist. Successive approximations to the goals are reinforced both by the therapist and by other group members.

McLean, Ogston, and Grauer (1973) offered empirical evidence to support the efficacy of treatment strategies designed to change a client's social interaction patterns. This program focused on a coercive communication pattern (a high rate of negative interchanges between the client and a significant other) that disrupted efforts to solve problems constructively. Clients referred by physicians were randomly assigned to an experimental and a comparison group. Couples in the experimental treatment were trained in social learning principles, which focused on methods of changing interpersonal behaviors. Specifically, verbal interaction styles were modified through daily home practice sessions providing immediate feedback. Using cue boxes (green light for positive and red light for negative), each person signaled how he or she perceived each of the spouse's verbal statements during a discussion period. To modify interpersonal behavior patterns, partners were trained in the construction and use of reciprocal behavioral contracts. Clients in the comparison group were referred to their physician and received a variety of traditional treatments for depression (group therapy, individual psychotherapy, or antidepressant medication). Their progress was monitored during the treatment period. In relation to them, the experimental group showed significant changes in target behaviors, mood ratings, and verbal communication style.

Learned helplessness model

Martin Seligman (1972, 1973, 1975; Miller and Seligman 1973) has proposed a model of depression in which the concept of a loss of reinforcement is an auxiliary rather than a central component. His formulation acknowledges the extent to which cognitive factors may interact with specific environmental variables in the development of depressive behaviors.

In earlier research, Seligman and his associates found that after dogs had been exposed to several trials of inescapable shock by being restrained in a harness, they would not learn to escape shock when the escape response was then allowed (Seligman and Maier 1967; Seligman and Groves 1970). Indeed, they found that the animals would learn an appropriate escape response only after they had been physically dragged to the safe side of the shuttlebox on a number of consecutive trials. Seligman hypothesized that the dogs' escape response had been extinguished in the inescapable shock situation, and he coined the term *learned helplessness* to describe this phenomenon.

In his more recent work, Seligman has argued that there may be a close parallel between learned helplessness and the development of depressive behaviors. The critical element in this formulation is the depressed person's *perceived* inability to control environmental events, and it has been hypothesized that this perceived loss of control may be a product of either of two types of previous experiences. First, a history of failure in dealing with stress-inducing situations may generate a "negative expectancy" of success in coping with any new stressors. When faced with a stressful situation, such as a loss of reinforcement or even a potential loss, individuals prone to depression are likely to give up even though appropriate coping strategies may be available. Second, a person who has been continuously reinforced, *but on a noncontingent basis,* may never have learned the complex skills necessary to elicit reinforcement from the environment and may not have learned the contingencies under which any skills he does have are likely to be reinforced. Should this be the case, the person may believe that he is actually unable to control the amount of reinforcement he receives, and even the slightest change in the environment is likely to trigger a depressive reaction. Miller and Seligman (1973) provide data that lend some support to this hypothesis. They found that depressed subjects, working on a task in which the amount of reinforcement received was directly response-contingent, perceived that they had less control over the amount of reinforcement they received than did non-depressed subjects working on the same task. Thus, Seligman's model suggests that the depression prone person does not have an adequate set of coping responses readily available to handle sudden changes in the environment. In a sense, then, the depressed person has learned to be helpless.

Of the formulations discussed in the present chapter, the learned helplessness model of depression is the most recent, and consequently it has received the least amount of research attention. Seligman has proposed no specific treatment strategies on the basis of the learned helplessness model; however, some of the socio-environmental treatments discussed in the previous section may be useful. For example, a depressed person could be taught the coping and problem-solving skills necessary to deal effectively with stressful situations. Alternatively, Burgess's (1969) graded tasks approach could be used to show a depressed person that he does have the ability to control the amount of reinforcement he receives. Other intervention strategies may be developed as the implications of the learned helplessness model of depression become better understood.

Cognitive model

A cognitive formulation of depression differs from the socio-environmental model in two important respects. First, the cognitive model focuses on covert behaviors, such as self-statements, attitudes, and beliefs, as opposed to overt behaviors. Second, maladaptive or irrational cognitions are considered the cause of depression; negative affect, lack of motivation, and other depressive behaviors are regarded as secondary manifestations resulting from maladaptive cognitions.

Development of depression

While there have been a few limited attempts by other cognitive theorists (e.g., Hauck 1971; Trexler 1972) to formulate a cognitive model of depression, Beck's model remains the best articulated and most comprehensive. According to Beck (1967, 1973) depression results from the activation and ascendancy of three interrelated patterns of thought which distort the depressed person's perception of reality.

This "primary triad" (Beck 1967, p. 255) consists of negative views of self, of present experiences, and of the future. The depressed individual commits four logical errors in the process of distorting environmental input regarding himself, the world, and the future. The first error, *arbitrary inference,* is defined as drawing a conclusion from a situation or experience that is not supported by the evidence. The second, *selective abstraction,* is the process whereby the depressed individual focuses on only one detail while ignoring other details of a multifaceted situation. The depressed person commits the logical error of *overgeneralization* when he draws a conclusion about his ability, performance, or worth on the basis of only one incident. *Magnification* (or alternatively, *minimization*) constitutes the fourth faulty logical process whereby the person makes gross inaccuracies in judging the significance of events and/or his performance. How does the depressed person acquire such maladaptive, illogical thought processes? Beck (1967) hypothesizes that the depression prone individual acquires these negative patterns of thought during the childhood and adolescent developmental periods from interactions with the environment, others' opinions of him, and by identification with significant figures such as parents. The specific depressive "constellation," or thought patterns, that the person learns consists of a network of negative attitudes. One cluster of attitudes centers around supposed personal deficiencies (for example, "It is awful to be dumb."). Another set revolves around self-blame, whereby the individual holds himself responsible for his deficiencies. A third set, negative expectations, reflects the person's pessimism about things getting any better. An individual who possesses this constellation of attitudes is predisposed to depression. Depression is precipitated either by exposure to generally stressful environmental events or to idiosyncratic stressors. Vulnerability to these specific stressors is determined by the individual's past learning history. It is interesting to note that the situations that Beck offers as examples of stressors—the thwarting of goals, the loss of a job, and so on—can all be interpreted in terms of a loss of reinforcement.

Although it is difficult if not impossible to test Beck's assumptions about the development of depression, some clinical and experimental data are available to support his thesis that the depressed individual's cognitive behavior can be conceptualized in terms of the "primary triad," that is, a negative view of the self (low self-esteem), of experience, and of the future. Beck's own notes, based upon numerous interviews with depressed patients, provide limited evidence that the content of a depressed person's cognitions are indeed characterized by ideas of deprivation, self-blame, low self-esteem, escapist or suicidal wishes, overwhelming problems, and rigid self-commands. In addition, several investigators (Beck, Feshbach, and Legg 1972; Freidman 1964; Granick 1963; Loeb, Beck, Diggory, and Tuthill 1967; Nutter, Gruise, Spreng, Weckowicz, and Yonge 1973) have demonstrated that in spite of their complaints of impaired cognitive abilities, depressed individuals do not perform more poorly than do nondepressed persons on batteries of perceptual, psychomotor, and cognitive (abstract intelligence) tests. These data suggest that some distortion process must occur which causes the depressed person to regard himself as being so inadequate.

Other investigators (Flippo and Lewinsohn 1971; Loeb, Feshbach, Beck, and Wolf 1964) have examined the effect that success and failure experiences have on the self-esteem of depressed and nondepressed individuals. Failure experiences lowered self-esteem in both depressed and nondepressed subjects; however, only nondepressed persons manifested any positive changes in self-esteem as a function of success. These results suggest that the depressed person may tend to take only negative experiences into account when he evaluates himself; positive experiences are ignored. Failure experiences have been found to have a more adverse effect on a depressed person's expectations of future success than on those of a nondepressed person (Loeb et al. 1967; Wener and Rehm 1975). Working within the framework of learned helplessness, Miller and Seligman (1973) demonstrated that a depressed person's negative expectations about achieving success were not global in nature but were limited to situations in which skill, not chance, were involved.

Treatment strategies

Beck (1967, 1970, 1973) has developed a cognitive therapy for depression and other disorders which is derived from his theoretical orientation toward depression. Beck allies his approach with Ellis's rational emotive therapy (RET), a therapeutic strategy designed to restructure illogical thinking patterns (see Chapter 8 in this volume).[3]

The therapeutic strategy outlined by Beck (1967, 1973) is directed toward breaking down the existing negative cognitive patterns and replacing them with more realistic, positive ones. This process entails three major steps. First, the therapist identifies major patterns and sequences of difficulties in a depressed person's life history in order to demonstrate to the client that he has learned to respond selectively to certain kinds of situations in a negative, stereotyped manner. Hence,

[3] Although there have been a few outcome studies assessing the therapeutic effectiveness of RET with disorders other than depression (see Mahoney 1974; Meichenbaum 1973; Rimm and Masters 1974), research on the effectiveness of RET with depression consists of a single case study (Geis 1971).

the client gains understanding of the development of his depression and the pervasive influence of the primary triad. Next, the depressed person is taught to detect his depression-generating self-statements and to distance himself from these cognitions so that they may be examined more objectively. By considering alternative explanations and rehearsing counterarguments to these negative cognitions, the client is taught to correct his distorted perceptions resulting from arbitrary inference, selective abstraction, overgeneralization, and magnification. Finally, the therapist focuses on modifying the depressed person's basic attitudes and assumptions about himself and the world. It is assumed that once these higher order thought patterns are modified, individual negative cognitions that are derived from them also will change.

Before any conclusive statements can be made regarding the effectiveness of cognitive therapy in the treatment of depression, considerably more research must be conducted. In addition, researchers and clinicians should explore the applicability of more recent cognitive therapies such as self-instruction (see Mahoney 1974; Meichenbaum 1973) to the treatment of depression.

Self-reinforcement model

A self-reinforcement model of depression incorporates features from both the socio-environmental and cognitive models of the disorder. Like the cognitive model, it acknowledges the importance of cognitions in contributing to and alleviating depression. On the other hand, the self-reinforcement model concurs with the socio-environmental model in assuming that positive reinforcement is vital for the maintenance of nondepressed behaviors. However, the two theories differ in that the socio-environmental position contends that reinforcement provided by the external environment determines depression, while the self-reinforcement model focuses on the reinforcers and punishers that the individual dispenses to himself.

Development of depression

The self-reinforcement model of depression states that depressive behaviors result from faulty self-reinforcement systems (Marston 1964; Bandura 1971a). It is hypothesized that depressed persons dispense low rates of positive reinforcement to themselves while meting out high rates of self-punishment.

Bandura (1971a) and Kanfer (1970, 1971) propose that a self-reinforcement sequence be divided into three components: self-monitoring, self-evaluation, and self-reinforcement. One reason a person may self-reinforce infrequently and subsequently become depressed is that he possesses excessively high performance standards. Since it is extremely difficult for his behavior to match his stringent standards, failure to equal or exceed his standards results in a negative self-evaluation of his performance. Hence, it is proposed that austere criteria for self-reinforcement can give rise to feelings of worthlessness, a decline in motivation, and depression in general. Additional reasons why a depressed person may not self-reinforce for a particular behavior may be that he does not consider the task difficult, he does not value the task, or he expects himself already to be competent at the task (Bandura 1971a). There is a wealth of research delineating the processes by which performance standards are adopted (see Bandura 1969; Thoresen and Mahoney 1974). Briefly, both direct training in self-reinforcement, with an external agent as the instructor, and observation of modeled self-reinforcement have been found to be effective in the transmission and modification of standards.

Bandura (1971a) discusses several mechanisms that maintain established patterns of self-reinforcement and self-punishment. Presumably, self-reinforcement is maintained by periodic social reinforcement. The performance of punishable behavior is hypothesized to generate anxiety or guilt. Self-punishment terminates these distressing thoughts and forestalls possible social condemnation. In addition, self-punishment may elicit social approval from others who are pleased with a person's efforts to control his own misbehavior.

Treatment strategies

Therapeutic strategies have been directed toward retraining depressed individuals in self-reinforcement. The strategy that has been employed most frequently has been coverant control therapy (Homme 1965; Mahoney 1970). Theoretically, coverant control therapy (CCT) is an application of Premack's differential probability principle, in which the emission of a high probability behavior is made contingent upon the emission of a desired low probability behavior (Premack 1965, 1971). In theory, the low probability behavior is reinforced by the high probability behavior and hence should increase in frequency. Mahoney (1972, 1974a) questions whether CCT as it has been applied in the clinical setting is truly an application of the Premack principle, since researchers have confused *high probability behaviors* with *high frequency behaviors.* Furthermore, Mahoney suggests that in instances where a high frequency behavior is used instead of a high probability behavior, the behavior serves as a cue for emitting the low probability behavior and not as a reinforcer for it. In the treatment of depression, CCT has been used to increase the frequency of positive self-thoughts; these thoughts may themselves become secondary reinforcers which the person can use to reinforce particular thoughts or behaviors. Changes in self-thoughts are hypothesized to effect changes in a depressed person's self-evaluation.

Johnson (1971) described a case in which CCT was used to increase the rate of spontaneous positive self-thoughts in a 17-year-old college freshman who reported episodes of severe depression. Initially, positive self-statements occurred at a very low rate. Positive self-thoughts, consisting of descriptions of therapeutic gains the client had already achieved, were written on index cards. The client was then instructed to recite one of the positive self-statements each time before he urinated. Hence urination, the high probability behavior, was made contingent upon the emission of a positive self-statement, the low probability behavior. After two weeks of CCT the client reported no depressive episodes, a high frequency of spontaneous positive self-statements, and increased social interactions.

Mahoney (1971) employed CCT with a 22-year-old depressed client to increase the rate of positive self-statements. Cigarette smoking was made contingent upon self-verbalization of a positive self-thought. In addition, Mahoney instituted a self-punishment procedure (tactile aversion) to decrease the frequency of negative self-thoughts. Mahoney reported that after 6 weeks the client was generating positive self-thoughts without the use of the high probability behavior and had improved in mood and self-confidence. Behavioral improvements had been maintained at a 4-month followup.

Todd (1972) reported a case involving a 49-year-old woman who experienced a high frequency of self-denigrating thoughts and a low frequency of positive self-statements. Todd utilized the CCT index card procedure, with cigarette smoking as the high probability behavior used to increase the frequency of positive self-statements. Although the negative self-thoughts were not attacked directly, they decreased in frequency as the frequency of the positive self-statements increased.

Although not working with clinically depressed persons, Hannum, Thoresen, and Hubbard (1974) reported an attempt to increase self-esteem in three school teachers. Self-esteem was operationalized as an increase in positive self-evaluations. CCT was used to increase the rate of positive self-evaluations while thought-stopping (Wolpe and Lazarus 1966) was employed to decelerate negative self-evaluations. Intervention was effective in increasing the rate of positive self-thoughts, but the effect of thought-stopping on the frequency of negative self-thoughts was not conclusively demonstrated.

Tharp, Watson, and Kaya (1974) presented a brief report on the effects of the self-change projects instituted by four depressed college students. Positive thoughts or positive self-evaluations were used to decrease feelings of depression. For example, one student who felt alienated from her thoughts and feelings began reinforcing "honest" statements of her feelings made either aloud or to herself. The frequency of such statements increased and was accompanied by a therapeutic change in her MMPI score.

All the aforementioned studies were characterized by their choice of covert behaviors or self-statements as the target behaviors to be modified. In contrast, Jackson (1972) sought to directly manipulate the self-reinforcement pattern of a 22-year-old client who was plagued by feelings of worthlessness, thoughts of self-denigration, and inactivity. Examination revealed that she held exceedingly stringent standards for self-reinforcing her behavior. The first therapeutic step was to modify her standards and to set a goal she could reasonably expect to accomplish. Next, she was instructed to overtly reinforce herself with poker chips when her performance equalled or surpassed her set goal. Initially, she was taught to self-reinforce only one class of behaviors. Gradually, self-reinforcement was extended to other behavior classes; the overt reinforcement was faded out and replaced by self-praise. Intervention resulted in an increase in the rate of self-reinforcement and a decrease in self-reported depression.

An integrative model

Throughout this chapter it has been emphasized that the term *depression,* although useful as a general concept, does not specify any single pattern of behavior. Instead, idiosyncratic depressive behaviors in any of four different categories (emotional, cognitive, motivational, and physical) may cause a person to label himself depressed. We have attempted to describe four basic formulations of depression that have evolved within an experimental/clinical approach. Each of these models offers a reasonably plausible, perhaps even intuitively appealing, explanation of the development and maintenance of depressive behaviors. Although a large amount of data has been accumulated to support each model's basic assumptions, a more critical look reveals that no one model is able to account for all the available data. Each model is predicated upon quite different assumptions regarding the nature of depression; these in turn generate hypotheses for further investigation. Findings that cannot be readily explained within a particular theoretical model tend to be ignored, and no theory is sufficiently broad to explain the multitude of problematic behaviors that constitute depression. Each model has its own strengths, yet each still leaves many questions unanswered.

Researchers working within the socio-environmental model argue that depression results primarily from a loss of environmentally supplied positive reinforcement and is maintained because the depressed person lacks the skills to generate alternative sources of reinforcement. Although this formulation can undoubtedly explain many cases of depression, it does not account for an "existentialist" type of depression characterized primarily by depressive thoughts and mood that may not be accompanied either by inadequate social skills or by obvious, external losses. By objective standards, the person seems to be living a relatively good life. The learned helplessness model offers an explanation of this type of depression in terms of a perceived loss of control over the environment. If the person begins to believe he does not control events (either positive or negative) that occur in his life, he is no longer motivated to continue his efforts. However, this formulation does not account for some evidence that indicates that depressed people are indeed trying to obtain reinforcement but are not choosing effective strategies.

The strength of the cognitive model lies in its focus on a domain of behaviors that are all too often ignored in other models. The theory is based on the assumption that illogical thought patterns elicit the depressive behaviors; however, a causal relationship between thoughts and behaviors has not yet been demonstrated. The explanation of how these patterns develop during childhood and adolescence remains speculative. The theory suggests that certain people may be depression prone but offers no method of predicting who they may be.

Within the self-reinforcement model a depressed individual is viewed as emitting a high rate of negative self-thoughts; this could account for cases of depression in which external loss of reinforcement is not apparent. In addition, the self-reinforcement model could explain why not all people become depressed following external losses. These people may generate sufficient self-reinforcement to keep themselves "above board" in times of stress. However, in some cases, the high rate of negative self-thoughts may be in response to accurate negative feedback from the environment. In such cases, it is the individual's performance, not his self-reinforcement patterns, that needs to be modified.

Each model has made a substantial contribution to our overall understanding of depression, and while each focuses on a particular aspect of depression, they are not mutually exclusive. An integrative approach can be taken in an attempt to provide a more complete explanation. All behavior can be analyzed in terms of long, fairly complex behavioral chains. These chains can be broken down into five major stages: (1) standard setting, (2) performance of the behavior, (3) self-evaluation, (4) self-presented consequences, and (5) external consequences. Each of the variables emphasized previously (environmental influences, social skills, cognition or thought patterns, and self-reinforcement or self-punishment) exerts a strong influence at one or more of these stages. Each of the four models that were presented may be looking at depression from different points in the behavioral chain. This framework, however, may provide a way to integrate them and show their interdependence. Each variable influences the others and is, in turn, influenced by them. People remain nondepressed as long as they maintain the minimal level of external or self-reinforcement needed to sustain adaptive functioning. Inappropriate standard setting, inability to perform, or inaccurate self-evaluation may lead to low levels of external and self-reinforcement. Large losses of external reinforcement may be sufficient in themselves to disrupt the chain. Alternatively, external factors may interact with the internal factors to suggest why some individuals respond to losses with depressive reactions rather than with adaptive, coping strategies. In any event, if the total amount of reinforcement received either from the environment or the self is not sufficient, depression results. Therapeutic intervention at any point in the chain is also likely to affect the entire chain.

Assessment of a depressed person's standards may reveal that they are unattainable. His goals may be unreasonable in relation to his abilities. Alternatively, his goals may not be out of reach in the long run, but if they are not broken down into subgoals, they may not be appropriate at a given point in time. Hence, therapy would be directed toward making the client's standards more realistic.

Many variables affect the individual's ability to perform the behaviors that would lead him to his goals. Specific deficits in requisite skills (for example, social, physical or intellectual skills) may preclude him from behaving as he would like to behave. Anxiety elicited by a stressful situation may interfere with responding. A history of failure experiences, which may or may not be due to his incompetence, may influence his present performance, as suggested within the model of learned helplessness. The person may not be motivated to respond due to his expectation of failure. The literature on problem solving (Spivack and Shure 1974) suggests that the ability to generate alternatives and anticipate their consequences facilitates choosing a response that is likely to be effective or positively reinforced. Therefore, therapy might be directed toward learning general problem-solving strategies (see Chapter 8 in this volume).

After performing (or not performing) the behavior, the person self-evaluates to see if his behavior measures up to his standards. Cognitive factors may intervene here, since the person's perception of reality may be distorted; at this point, the individual's perception of failure or loss of positive consequences is more important than the actual (or therapist-perceived) reality. His judgment of success is determined by several factors. In a situation that is ambiguous or in which he does not have well-defined standards, the person may rely upon the evaluation of others. He may compare his performance with that of others, and this feedback must be taken into consideration.

In conjunction with his evaluation, the person follows through with self-presented consequences at a covert level (positive and negative self-thoughts). At an overt level, he may self-reinforce, fail to self-reinforce, or self-punish. If a person attributes his success to luck or to other external factors rather than to his own competence, he may not self-reinforce. Hence, therapy might be directed toward modifying the faulty cognitive patterns involved in self-reinforcement.

Even appropriate self-reinforcement patterns are not sufficient to maintain the long, complex chains of adaptive behaviors required for independent functioning. Self-reinforcement patterns must themselves be positively reinforced periodically to be maintained; or, on the other hand, these self-reinforcement patterns may be continued because they help the person avoid negative external consequences (i.e., they are negatively reinforced). Thus, both positive and negative environmental events indirectly affect the entire chain by telling the person whether his self-reinforcement patterns are appropriate.

In light of this integrative approach the goal of treatment would be to determine at which point these chains have been disrupted, and therapeutic strategies would be instituted to reestablish adaptive, nondepressive functioning. First, the client's depressive behaviors would be assessed. This would include an analysis of depressive verbalizations (cognitive patterns), performance deficits (anxiety, lack of skills, level of motivation), self-reinforcement patterns (negative and positive self-thoughts), and external events (stressful situations, loss of reinforcement).

Second, a therapeutic strategy would be chosen to modify the client's depressive behaviors. Even at this preliminary stage of research in the area, there is evidence that several techniques alter both overt and covert depressive behaviors. Cognitive therapy may be effective in dealing with unreasonable standards. Deficits in performance could be approached from several angles: graded tasks or assignments, social skills training, or problem solving. Lack of motivation could indicate a loss of reinforcement for particular behaviors; the therapist could supply contingent attention initially to elicit more adaptive behaviors which would then be maintained by their natural consequences, or he might intervene in the environment to set up contingencies that would provide such contingent reinforcement. Problems that are related to self-evaluation and self-presentation of consequences suggest using cognitive therapy, increasing the frequency of positive self-thoughts, and programming appropriate self-reinforcement contingencies.

Other attempts have been made to integrate the varied approaches to the treatment of depression. For example, Lazarus (1974) recently outlined a multi-modal behavioral treatment of depression. Seven interactive modalities are assessed and incorporated within the treatment program: overt behavior, affective processes, sensory reactions, emotive imagery, cognitive components, interpersonal relationships, and medication. He reported that 22 of 26 clients with chronic depression made significant gains with an average of 3 months of this multimodal therapy.

The data now available do not provide a unitary explanation for the phenomenon of depression. The data suggest that several important factors are involved in both the development and maintenance of depressive behaviors. Even though the cause or causes of depression have not been determined, several techniques have been tentatively demonstrated to be effective in altering particular depressive behaviors. Additional research on therapeutic results is necessary to substantiate these therapeutic strategies, and more rigorous experimental procedures would improve the validity of the results obtained. Specifically, well-controlled research should be conducted so that experimental treatments may be compared with each other, with no treatment, and with attention-placebo procedures. Both single-subject and controlled group designs could provide the data necessary for treatment evaluation. Research must also be extended to investigate client variables that may interact with treatment. The final goal is to establish which technique or treatment package is most effective in modifying a particular client's depressive behaviors.

Behavior modification in the classroom

Ronald S. Drabman
University of Mississippi Medical Center

13

One of the most extensively evaluated areas of behavior modification has been classroom management. In the schools the focus has largely been on the use of operant procedures. This chapter provides an overview of several of the basic procedures used to change classroom behavior. Drabman describes the systematic use of teacher attention through praising and ignoring, token economies, and punishment procedures. He goes on to discuss current areas of research including: (1) peer reinforcement; (2) self-control; (3) sociometric changes; and (4) generalization of treatment effects.

A number of additional issues have recently received the attention of researchers working in this area. The importance of adequate teacher training has recently been demonstrated (Ringer 1973; Kazdin and Moyer, in press). The emphasis of behavioral procedures has shifted toward such target behaviors as creative writing (Houten, Morrison, Jarvis, and MacDonald 1974) and academic performance (Ayllon and Roberts 1974; Kazdin 1975a). It has also recently been demonstrated that students in the classroom not only affect their peers' behaviors, but also effectively modify their teachers' behavior (Sherman and Cormier 1974). Additionally, behavior modification procedures have been used to facilitate social interaction (Strain and Timm 1974) and racial integration (Hauserman, Walen, and Behling 1973).

The broad outline of the behavioral approach to classroom management seems like common sense. But whereas common sense is not always consistent, the hallmark of the behavioral approach is consistency. The behavioral approach is also differentiated from the common sense approach in that the former requires the use of procedures that have been scientifically validated. For example, data collection by teachers using the procedures, rather than reliance on impressions, is essential. In fact, it is the use of behavioral techniques in combination with the collection of data that constitutes the behavioral approach to classroom management. In this chapter a variety of behavioral techniques for increasing or decreasing classroom behaviors will be examined and new areas of research will be discussed.

Before *any* behavioral technique is initiated, a baseline study must be done on the behavior of interest. The baseline data permit assessment of the severity of the problem, force the teacher to construe the problem in behavioral terms, and are essential for evaluation of the program. Occasionally the act of taking a baseline can by itself be a modification procedure, improving the children's behavior and eliminating the need for more powerful programs.

Praise and ignore technique

With individual children

The early use of behavior modification procedures in the classroom occurred at the University of Washington Laboratory Preschool (Bijou and Baer 1963). These researchers noticed that the probability of adult attention to a child after that child's emission of inappropriate behavior was disproportionately high. They hypothesized that adult attention may have been acting as a reinforcer to maintain the child's inappropriate behavior. To test this hypothesis, it was decided to systematically vary the contingencies under which adult attention would be dispensed.

A typical study used the ABAB design. Ann, for example, was four years old at the beginning of one of these studies; she had a better than average family background and IQ. Despite a varied and competent repertoire of physical and mental skills, Ann carried out most of her activities independently of other children. She rarely initiated conversation or cooperative play with an adjacent child or responded in any way to overtures directed toward her. Moreover, she was so diffident and passive that she seldom cried or defended herself even when another child hit her, pushed her, or took her possessions. Behavioral assessment indicated that only 10 percent of her time was spent in social interaction with children. The majority of her time was spent either alone or interacting with adults. Close scrutiny revealed that most of the adult attention she received was contingent upon behaviors incompatible with social play.

Within the ABAB design, the 10 percent peer social interaction served as a baseline (A). Next, adult attention was made contingent upon Ann's social interaction with other children (B). During this phase, Ann spent better than 60 percent of her time interacting with children. To determine whether it was the experimental procedure or simply time in preschool that was responsible for the improved behavior, the contingencies were reversed (A) and Ann received adult attention only when she was not interacting with children. Soon after the reversal began, Ann began spending less than 20 percent of her time in interaction with children. Finally, the experimental contingencies were resumed (B) and frequency of interaction with peers again increased. A followup check was made several weeks later. At that time Ann's peer interaction was still higher than baseline although the explicit contingencies had been removed. Apparently she had found peer interaction reinforcing in its own right (Allen, Hart, Buell, Harris, and Wolf 1964).

Procedures in which adult praise and attention are made contingent upon appropriate behavior, while inappropriate behavior is ignored, have proven very successful, especially with young children. Other school behaviors that have been controlled or improved by this method include: restricting playmate choice (Bijou and Baer 1967), hyperactivity (Allen, Henke, Harris, Baer, and Reynolds 1967), motor skills (Johnston, Kelley, Harris and Wolf 1966), climbing (Hall and Broden 1967; Wolf and Risley 1967), cooperative behavior (Hart, Reynolds, Baer, Brawley, and Harris 1968), operant crying (Harris, Wolf, and Baer 1964; Hart, Allen, Buell, Harris, and Wolf 1965), regressed crawling (Harris, Johnston, Kelley, and Wolf 1964), excessive fantasy play (Bijou and Baer 1967), attending school (Copeland, Brown, and Hall 1974), and, finally, paying attention in class (Hawkins, McArthur, Rinaldi, Gray, and Schaftenaur 1967). Taken together, these studies indicate that teachers are undoubtedly contributing to the maintenance, and perhaps the acquisition, of classroom problem behavior. This is emphasized by a research project we are currently conducting in which we are finding that individual children rarely get attention for appropriate behavior. Indeed, the majority of teacher interactions with individual children are of a pejorative nature. Very often young children engaging in problem behavior are simply performing for the only teacher attention, or reinforcement, available.

With entire class

In 1967 Becker and his colleagues at the University of Illinois began to use the methodology and techniques that had proved so successful at the Washington Preschool, now applying them to entire classes of elementary school students. They reasoned that if misdirected teacher reinforcement was responsible for maintaining problem behavior in preschool children, then training elementary school teachers to contingently praise desirable behavior while ignoring undesirable behavior would be an important contribution to classroom management. In a series of studies Becker and his colleagues demonstrated that teachers' use or misuse of contingent praise and ignore techniques could predictably create and reduce problem behavior (Becker, Madsen, Arnold, and Thomas 1967; Madsen, Becker, and Thomas 1968; Thomas, Becker, and Armstrong 1968).

As an example of this work, a study by Madsen, Becker, and Thomas (1968) will be presented. This study uses a variation of the ABAB design that might be summarized as ABCDAD. Two students in one middle primary class and one student in another class were selected as target children because they displayed a high frequency of problem behaviors. It was felt that a major reduction of their disruptive behaviors would be a convincing demonstration of the experimental effect.

Baseline measurement was taken on the following inappropriate behaviors: gross motor, object noise, disturbance of other's property, contact, verbalization, turning around, mouthing objects, and isolated play. These behaviors had been identified both by the teacher and by preliminary observation as hindering the learning of the target children and their classmates.

After baseline rates of problem behavior had been established (A), the teacher was asked to write a set of class rules on the board (B). The children repeated these rules until they knew them. In the third phase, the rules were left visible, and the teacher was instructed to ignore inappropriate behavior (C). Next, praise for appropriate behavior was added to the already present rules and ignoring (D). To assess the effect of the treatment package, baseline procedures were reintroduced and rules, praise, and ignoring were removed for a short time (A). Finally, the study terminated with a return to the treatment package of rules, ignoring inappropriate behavior, and praise for appropriate behavior (D).

Results indicated that the combination of rules, ignoring, and praise was differentially effective in reducing problem behavior. Similar procedures have been used to increase study behavior (Hall, Lund, and Jackson 1968), and decrease aggressive behavior (Brown and Elliot 1965). Taken together, these studies on preschool and elementary school children demonstrate the importance of what the teacher says to what the pupil does.

Contingent praising and ignoring are very powerful techniques and should be part of every teacher's repertoire of instructional procedures. However, they are not without potential problems, and in using them care should be taken to avoid two pitfalls. First, a teacher must not forget that he or she is but one of several possible reinforcers available in the classroom. Peer reinforcement is a competing reinforcer which grows more powerful as children get older. Sometimes peer reinforcement in the classroom is so powerful that a teacher's ignoring technique leads to greater levels of disruptive behavior (O'Leary et al. 1969). In such situations, ignoring is not an extinction procedure; it simply makes it easier for alternate reinforcers to create problem behaviors. Second, a teacher may fail to note the importance of descriptive praise. While saying "Good" to a child is often an effective reinforcer, it is not as effective as describing what he did that earned him the praise (Drabman and Tucker 1974; Madsen and Madsen 1974). The statement, "That was very good the way you raised your hand and waited to be recognized," is preferable to simply saying "Good," because it restates the contingencies and prompts the child to engage in the appropriate behavior again.

Teachers can avoid falling into either of these traps by taking continuous data on any behavior modification procedure they attempt. Monitoring the data will help teachers discover if they are ignoring too much or not using enough descriptive praise. The data will indicate when changes need to be made. Using behavioral techniques without taking data is not behavior modification; it is simply capricious use of behavioral technology.

Back-up reinforcers: The token economy

Unfortunately, systematic manipulation of social reinforcement will not always bring behavior to acceptable levels. In some cases the classroom data, which can be taken by the teacher, teacher's aide, room-mother, or the pupils themselves, will indicate that a more powerful procedure is needed to bring problem behaviors under control. In other cases, the occurrence of appropriate behavior is too infrequent for the effective use of social reinforcement. In such cases it may be necessary to use a stronger back-up reinforcer.

In a token system, the child is periodically rated on the behaviors in which the teacher is interested and is given some symbol of this rating, called a token. These tokens are exchangeable for back-up reinforcers. At its best, a token reinforcement program teaches a child to work for symbolic rewards, to delay gratification, and to work on an intermittent schedule. The development of such behaviors is crucial if the child is to be returned to normal classroom procedures.

Although some classroom token programs cost as much as $250 per student (Wolf, Giles, and Hall 1968), most are practical enough for the normal schoolroom (O'Leary and Drabman 1971; Lipe and Jung 1971), and some cost virtually nothing (Osborne 1969; Drabman, Spitalnik, and Spitalnik 1974).

What can be used as a token? A token should have several properties: (1) it should be easy to dispense; (2) it should be readily portable; (3) its value should be easily understandable; (4) it should not require extensive outside work by teachers or other personnel; and (5) it should be easily identifiable as the property of the recipient (O'Leary and Drabman 1971). Most token programs have used check marks or points given out by the teacher, although stamps (Wolf, Giles, and Hall 1968), stars (Birnbrauer, Bijou, Wolf, and Kidder 1965), cumulated light flashes (Patterson 1965), and poker chips (Bushell, Wrobel, and Michaelis 1968) have also been used successfully.

Choosing a token is more a practical than theoretical decision. Check mark or point systems usually involve fewer administrative problems, but they may not be as interesting or effective as physical tokens. With retarded children, points or check marks probably have very little intrinsic value and a teacher may have to use physical tokens. The teacher can hand one physical token to the child and then immediately exchange it for a back-up reinforcer. Repeating this procedure while gradually increasing the delay in exchange will teach the child to value the tokens. It is essential that the child learn the value of tokens.

Since physical tokens are like money, they can be used to teach practical mathematics to older children. They also allow children a display of wealth, thus increasing their value as reinforcers. The problem with tangible reinforcers is that because they are tangible they can be thrown, chewed upon, played with, lent, stolen, or used to buy favors (Bushell, Wrobel, and Michaelis 1968). A teacher who decides to use physical tokens has decided to risk potentially disruptive byproducts in favor of the interest and excitement generated by a tangible reinforcement system. As a compromise, a teacher might want to begin the program with points or check marks, and as classroom behavior improves, gradually switch to tangible tokens.

Should children be allowed to accumulate their tokens? If pupils are able to save their tokens, they can "take a holiday" from good work or behavior and use their past earnings. The teacher must decide whether he wants to accept this behavior in his class. If he does not want "holidays" in his class, yet still wants to encourage savings, he can provide the students with high priced reinforcers and allow them to make nonrefundable deposits.

A question often asked by teachers or school psychologists who are initiating a classroom token program is, "What should the tokens buy?" In other words, what should be used as a back-up reinforcer? The answer is simple: "Anything that works." The teacher may judge how well particular reinforcers are working by checking the data. Many studies have used candy, small toys, or trinkets as back-up reinforcers; however, money (Martin, Burkholder, Rosenthal, Tharp, and Thorne 1968a), a class party (Valett 1966), a story (Ulrich, Wolfe, and Bluhm 1968) and special events (Bushell, Wrobel, and Michaelis 1968) have also shown excellent results. Research just completed has demonstrated that the opportunity to be tutored in reading by an older schoolmate or a college student can also serve as a reinforcer in a classroom token program (Robertson, DeReus, and Drabman 1975). For young children, activities like painting, clay, and tumbling mats have proven very effective. Young children also respond well to "grown up" activities like running errands, cleaning the room, or being a teaching assistant. Even retarded children will work for these "grown up" activities (Whalen and Henker 1970; Drabman and Spitalnik 1973). For older children, activities like playing records, dancing, checkers, games, pool, and ping-pong are very effective (Rollins, McCandless, Thompson, and Brassell 1974).

In selecting reinforcers, teachers should be aware of the Premack principle and realize that any high probability activity can serve as a reinforcer. Several studies (e.g., Homme et al. 1963; Nolen, Kunzelmann, and Haring 1967; Wasik 1970) have made explicit use of the Premack principle in selecting back-up reinforcers. For example, Homme et al. (1963) noticed that running around the room, pushing chairs, screaming, throwing things, and other behaviors usually labeled disruptive were of high probability in a free environment. Consequently, they improved preschool children's behavior by allowing participation in those activities contingent upon more socially approved activities such as looking at the blackboard. Of course, using disruptive activities as reinforcers is not generally recommended. But the notion that high probability behaviors can serve as reinforcers for lower probability behaviors is something the successful classroom manager may use to advantage.

Classroom token programs have been used successfully with a wide variety of children. However, most behavior modification practitioners eschew the traditional diagnostic labels. Instead, they concentrate their efforts on increasing those behaviors in which children have a deficit and/or decreasing those behaviors that occur too frequently. The goal is to allow the child to maximize the reinforcing and minimize the punishing aspects of his environment. In terms of the traditional diagnostic labels, classroom token problems have been used effectively with children who might have been labeled retarded (Birnbrauer, Wolf, Kidder, and Tague 1965; Sulzbacher and Houser, 1968; Zimmerman,

Zimmerman and Russell 1969), autistic (Martin, England, Kaprowy, Kilgour, and Pilek 1968b; Craighead and Myers 1973), hyperactive (Quay, Sprague, Werry, and McQueen 1967), childhood schizophrenic (Drabman 1973), emotionally disturbed (O'Leary and Becker 1967; Hewett, Taylor, and Artuso 1969), and delinquent (Martin et al. 1968a; Meichenbaum, Bowers, and Ross 1968).

Program with individual contingencies

Instead of presenting a formal study, we will describe a token program that was recently established (Drabman 1973). The 24 worst behaving children (ages 11 to 15 years) in a children's psychiatric hospital were assigned to four classes of six children each. The procedure followed in two of these classes will be described here.

Trained observers monitored the children and recorded instances of aggressive behaviors, noise making, disturbing another's property, inappropriate vocalizations, playing with their own property during lessons, and turning around. During the 3-week baseline period, the teachers were asked to handle disruptive behavior in whatever way they felt appropriate. Additionally, the teachers were asked to display the following institutional rules.

1. Come to class on time.
2. Sit in your own seat.
3. Do not leave seat without permission.
4. Keep quiet.
5. Do your own work.
6. Do not distract your neighbor.
7. Do not touch things that do not belong to you.
8. Do not sleep in class.

Presentation of rules was not a separate phase because it has been shown that simple presentation of rules has little effect upon the behavior of disruptive children (Madsen et al. 1968; O'Leary et al. 1969). Teachers were asked to remind the pupils of the rules occasionally and to try to limit their reprimands to individual children. Additionally, they were asked to establish permanent seating arrangements, and except in emergencies, not to use any punishment that would involve the child's removal from class.

During baseline, three meetings were held with the experimental teachers and the assistant principal to explain the workings and paraphernalia of the token program. On the last day of baseline the assistant principal entered the classroom and explained the workings of the token program. The children helped choose the reinforcers during the discussion conducted by the assistant principal. They were priced at a ratio of one point for every three cents of object retail value. The reinforcer's "psychological value" (Drabman and Tucker 1974) was also considered, so that some objects such as pencils were priced below their monetary value and other objects such as combs sold for more. Posters containing pictures or facsimiles of the reinforcers, as well as their cost, were displayed in front of the class. The posters served the dual purpose of providing a constant reminder of the token program while allowing the actual prizes to be protected from destruction or theft.

Opaque canisters marked with the name of each child were placed on the teacher's desk along with a dated record sheet and poker chip tokens. Every 20 minutes a timer would ring. When the timer rang, the teacher reset it to prevent a "free time" period during token administration. Next, he would decide upon a rating (0–10) for each child, based upon the child's performance during the preceding 20 minutes. The teacher would then mark the amount of tokens awarded on the record sheet and deposit a corresponding number of chips into each canister. Next, the teacher informed each child of the amount of points he or she had earned. The children were informed only after the teacher had recorded the marks so that they would not attempt to cajole or coerce the teacher.

The poker chip tokens were exchangeable for trinkets or edibles at the end of each class. All tokens not spent could be saved until Fridays. On Fridays they had to be spent or used as a nonrefundable down payment on a larger prize. After a down payment was received, a child had to complete payment in an agreed upon time limit or the deposit would be lost. The child who had scored the most points for that day was allowed to select a reinforcer first.

Program with group contingencies

The preceding program stressed individual reinforcement for individual behavior; an alternative is group reinforcement for individual behavior. As an example, a classroom token economy known as The Good Behavior Game will be presented (Barrish, Saunders, and Wolf 1969).

A fourth-grade classroom of 24 students was divided into two teams. Classroom rules were re-emphasized and the game was introduced. The teacher explained that whenever she saw anyone on either team breaking a class rule that team would receive a mark. The winning team (or both teams if neither team had more than five marks) would receive privileges and free time at the end of the day. This procedure was very successful in decreasing out-of-seat and talking-out behavior for the entire class.

Teachers often find group procedures more practical with large classes where individual token administration consumes too much class time. Because of this, several studies have compared the effectiveness of group and individual classroom token economies (Herman and Tramontana 1971; Drabman, Spitalnik, and Spitalnik 1974; Greenwood, Hops, Delquadri, and Guild 1974), and they indicate that both kinds of contingencies are effective in controlling disruptive behavior. However, a group program may not be appropriate when the class is too heterogeneous. In this case, the class might be divided into homogeneous groups with each group on its own token program.

When choosing between group and individual token economy programs teachers often ask, "What will happen to the rest of the class if I initiate a behavioral program for just one child?" While the data are not complete, it seems that the answer may be very positive. Kazdin (1973) and Drabman and Lahey (1974) monitored the behavior of untreated classmates while initiating a program involving target children. Both studies reported improved behavior in the untreated classmates. The Drabman and Lahey (1974) study also found that the target child received both more sociometric votes and more positive comments from her peers. It appears, therefore, that teachers who prefer to use behavioral procedures for only some of their pupils will receive dual benefits: both the problem children and their classmates will improve.

Punishment in the classroom

When disruptive behavior is maintained either wholly or substantially by peer reinforcement, it can be expected to increase if ignored by the teacher. Since peer reinforcement is more immediate, it may be even more powerful than the reinforcers available in a token program. When this is the case, a teacher needs another tool if classroom stability is to be maintained. Some form of punishment is the likely candidate. But what form shall this punishment take?

Most behavioral psychologists feel that punishment should not be used unless other more positive alternatives have been unsuccessful. But since classroom punishment procedures may be necessary, they should be explored scientifically so that teachers can apply them as effectively as possible.

Three procedures, which may be subsumed under the rubric of classroom punishment techniques, have been investigated: response cost, time out from positive reinforcement, and verbal reprimands.

Response cost

Response cost may be defined as removal of previously acquired reinforcers contingent upon a response. In the classroom token economy, response cost is usually accomplished by removal of tokens contingent upon inappropriate behavior (Birnbrauer et al. 1965a; Broden, Hall, Dunlop, and Clark 1970; McLaughlin and Malaby 1972; Kaufman and O'Leary 1972; Iwata and Bailey 1974). For example, Iwata and Bailey (1974) took 15 special classroom elementary school children and divided them into two groups. After baseline measurements, one group was given 10 free tokens and told that they would *lose* them if they did not follow the class rules (response cost). The other group was not given any tokens but was told that they could *earn* 10 if they followed class rules (positive reinforcement). Both groups had to pay 6 tokens for an afternoon snack reinforcer. After a brief return to baseline for both groups, the systems were switched so that the group that had previously been earning tokens was shifted to a response cost program and the group that had been losing tokens began a positive reinforcement program.

Results indicated that the procedures were equally effective in reducing rule violations and off-task behavior. The pupils did not express a preference for one program over the other. Although the two procedures were equally effective, we suggest that teachers use the positive reinforcement approach since this may encourage them to use more verbal reinforcement (Iwata and Bailey 1974).

Time out from positive reinforcement

Time out from positive reinforcement has been the classroom punishment procedure used most often by behavioral teachers and clinicians. Time out can be defined as contingent removal of the opportunity to earn positive reinforcement. Because of the way time out has been used in classroom studies, the procedure might better be labeled contingent social isolation (Drabman and Spitalnik 1973). A child is placed in a restricted environment following disruptive behavior. The child remains in isolation for a minimum time period, usually about 10 minutes. Return to the classroom is contingent upon the passage of a fixed period of time or the passage of that time period plus appropriate behavior in the last minutes of the isolation period.

Several classroom studies have used a social isolation procedure, usually in conjunction with other behavior programs (Whelan and Haring 1966; Walker, Mattson, and Buckley 1968; Sibley, Abbott, and Cooper 1969; Wasik, Senn, Welch, and Cooper 1969; Drabman and Spitalnik 1973). Although the use of multiple procedures is important for a successful clinical effort, it is not possible to ascertain the contributions of the individual procedures when more than one is used. In the development of a scientifically based classroom technology it is important that the contribution of each procedure be assessed so that practitioners do not waste time and effort implementing procedures that are of little value.

A study that looked at the effects of social isolation as an independent procedure rather than as a segment of a larger classroom program was reported by Drabman and Spitalnik (1973). In this study, three residents of a children's psychiatric hospital were selected because of their high levels of disruptive classroom behavior. A baseline was taken on three types of disruptive behavior—inappropriate vocalizations, aggression, and out-of-seat without permission. Two of these behaviors, out-of-seat and aggression, were selected for the social isolation punishment procedure. When a student violated previously determined criteria, the teacher told him that because of his misbehavior he must leave the room. A teaching assistant escorted him to a small room where the child spent the next 10 minutes. After this time, the child could return to the classroom.

Results indicated that out-of-seat disruption, which was occurring 34 percent of the time during baseline, decreased to 11 percent of the time with the use of social isolation. Aggression occurred 2.8 percent of the time during baseline, but only .37 percent of the time during the social isolation phase. On the other hand, vocalization, the unpunished behavior, occurred 32 percent of the time during baseline and continued at about the same rate (28 percent during the isolation phase). Interestingly, when the punishment was removed, the occurrence of the previously punished behaviors increased only slightly (out-of-seat, 15 percent; vocalization, .40 percent).

This study indicated that social isolation is an effective although relatively specific punisher that can be an important part of a behavioral program. A note of caution is necessary here. Some teachers have viewed behavioral procedures as being used only for punishment. This gives them a faulty perspective. Punishment procedures should *never* be used unless they are used in conjunction with a reinforcement procedure for an alternative appropriate response. Remember, punishment does not teach a child to *do* anything, only what not to do. It also deprives him of some reinforcers that he has received in the past for performing the undesired acts. A successful behavioral practitioner will therefore always provide reinforcement to the child for performing a new appropriate behavior.

Verbal reprimands

Several studies have related teacher's verbal reprimands to pupils' behavior. O'Leary and Becker (1968) and O'Leary, Kaufman, Kass, and Drabman (1970) showed that quiet reprimands are more effective than loud reprimands. Thomas, Becker, and Armstrong (1968) had demonstrated that systematically increasing a teacher's disapproving behavior led to parallel increases in disruptive behavior among the pupils.

One of the most interesting studies in this area was conducted by

Madsen, Becker, Thomas, Koser, and Plager (1970). A team-taught first-grade classroom of 48 children was monitored for inappropriate out-of-seat behavior. Observers also monitored how often the teachers reprimanded children for being out of their seats or told anyone to sit down. They also recorded the number of times that either teacher praised a child for sitting.

After baseline (A), the experimenters asked the teachers to triple their frequency of "sit down" commands (B). Next, they returned to baseline levels of "sit down" commands (A). Then they returned to the high level of commands of the first treatment phase (B). Finally, teachers were asked to praise behaviors incompatible with standing (C).

Results indicated that standing up was functionally related to amount of "sit down" commands in that the more "sit down" commands the teachers gave, the more the children stood up! In fact, tripling the amount of "sit down" commands led to a 33 percent increase in out-of-seat behavior. Praising behavior incompatible with standing up led to a 33 percent decrease in standing up behavior.

When using "punishment," teachers should recall this study and remember that what they believe to be punishment might be acting as reinforcement. Since the opposite could also be true, the classroom data must be consulted in order to determine what role a particular teacher behavior is playing.

Current topics of research

There is currently a great deal of research taking place in the area of classroom behavior modification. Four areas receiving increased attention are: peers as behavior modifiers, self-control, sociometric behavior, and generalization.

Peers as behavior modifiers

Some of the early classroom token studies (Patterson 1965; O'Leary and Becker 1967) reported anecdotally that children in the class had aided the teacher in making the token program effective. More recently, other researchers (Evans and Oswalt 1968; Surratt, Ulrich, and Hawkins 1969; Starlin 1971; Drabman 1973; Drabman and Spitalnik 1973; Johnson and Bailey 1974) have designed peer-administered classroom programs which demonstrated increases in both academic and social behavor. These programs made explicit use of elementary school students as captains, tutors, teaching assistants, or behavior engineers working to improve their schoolmates' performance. Even retarded children have served as behavioral teaching assistants (Drabman and Spitalnik 1973; cf. Craighead and Mercatoris 1973).

In the experiment by Drabman (1973) described previously in this chapter ("The token economy" section) two other classes of institutionalized children underwent the same token economy. The only difference was that in these classes an elected captain rated each child and distributed the tokens. Results indicated that children selected for their high level of classroom disruption showed significant increases in appropriate behavior when the captain system was operating. In fact, there were no differences in effectiveness between the captain-administered system and teacher-administered systems. Of course, this does not mean that the captain systems would have been effective without the teacher's presence, but only that teachers can turn some responsibility for classroom management over to their pupils.

Self-control

Very recently, behavioral researchers have asked to what extent the control of classroom token economies could be turned over to the pupils themselves. Several investigators (Lovitt and Curtiss 1969; Glynn 1970; Broden, Hall, and Mitts 1971; Bolstad and Johnson 1972; Glynn, Thomas, and Shee 1973; Glynn and Thomas 1974) have demonstrated that normal children can accurately assign themselves redeemable points. Furthermore, children in these studies showed improved social and academic behavior as a result of the self-assigned contingent reinforcement. Two studies (Kaufman and O'Leary 1972; Drabman, Spitalnik, and O'Leary 1973) have demonstrated that a self-reinforcement program can also be successful with severely disruptive children.

While normal children can be put directly on a self-control token system (Glynn 1970), disruptive children probably have to be shaped. One way of shaping has been to first teach the children to match their teachers' ratings (Drabman, Spitalnik, and O'Leary 1973). In one study, pupils' self-ratings were negotiable only if they matched or nearly matched their teachers'. Through a series of steps the number of children checked for matching was reduced from 100 percent to 50 percent to 25 percent to 12 percent, then to zero. Children not checked for matching received the amount of points they awarded themselves. Children who matched the teacher exactly were given a bonus point. By this procedure, children who had averaged .86 disruptive behaviors per 20-second interval during baseline averaged only .19 disruptions during self-evaluation.

It is expected that self-control will be a prominent part of classroom behavior modification programs of the future.

Sociometric behavior

Most of the behavioral programs that have been discussed up to now have dealt with either academic or social behavior in the classroom. In the last 2 years we have been looking at another kind of behavior, the sociometric ratings of pupils in classroom behavioral programs. Sociometric ratings are ratings in terms of votes for a target child on questions such as: "If you were going on a long trip, who would you want to take along?" or "If you needed to pick a very responsible person with whom to do a difficult job, who would you pick?" Sociometric ratings are very important since behavioral procedures may affect how children rate their classmates.

Our data indicate that a successful behavior modification program on a target child in a classroom can increase the amount of votes that child receives (Drabman and Lahey 1974). In addition, formerly disruptive children were rated as more responsible when they were placed in token economies in which group reinforcement was dependent upon the behavior of the most disruptive child in the group. These children were rated more responsible in group procedures in which they had potential control than in other kinds of group or individual token programs (Drabman, Spitalnik, and Spitalnik 1974).

Although this research is new, it has as its goal the development of procedures through which behavioral engineers can alter a child's sociometric ratings. These procedures could be used when lack of popularity is causing a problem in a child's life.

Generalization

Although there are many forms of generalization, the one that most concerns behavioral researchers is maintenance. That is, what will happen when a program, especially a token program, is removed? Behavior modifiers have lost their early optimism and now realize that maintenance is not to be expected but must be programmed (Baer, Wolf, and Risley 1968; Kazdin and Bootzin 1972). The goal is to somehow change the reinforcement network for disruptive pupils so that they can function on the same reinforcers as do the majority of their classmates. Unfortunately, this is not easy. In fact, as this review has pointed out, by simply looking at classroom reinforcement contingencies it is often easier to explain why children misbehave than why they behave.

Little is known regarding the most successful ways to program maintenance. O'Leary and Drabman (1971) suggested a variety of techniques that might achieve generalization, including the following:

1. Providing a good academic program.
2. Giving children the expectation that they are doing well.
3. Involving the children in the program.
4. Teaching the children the ways in which academic achievement will be important later.
5. Involving the parents.
6. Teaching the teachers behavioral principles.

Recently, classroom studies that have used these suggestions as well as other methods to obtain generalization have appeared in the literature (Drabman 1973; O'Leary, Drabman, and Kass 1973). Even these studies give no conclusive information on how to effectively program generalization; they should be seen more as accounts of preliminary success from which further research should stem.

It is known that abrupt withdrawal of a behavioral program does not usually lead to successful generalization. Therefore, some form of gradual withdrawal is probably the key. With token economies, perhaps gradual increases in the length of time necessary to hold the tokens before exchange with concurrent decreases in their purchasing power will lead to generalization. An alternative might be to gradually change the program from contingent and redeemable tokens to contingent but nonredeemable tokens (feedback), and then gradually decrease the occasions of feedback.

Concluding comments

Considerable progress has been made in the use of behavior modification in the classroom. In this chapter we have looked at the contingent use of teacher attention, token economies, and punishment procedures. Data should always be collected to permit assessment of these procedures. Significant areas of research include use of peers as behavior modifiers and self-control programs, as well as programs that evaluate sociometric behavior and generalization or maintenance of program effectiveness.

Treating the hospitalized person

John M. Atthowe, Jr.
Rutgers Medical School

14

Throughout recorded history there have been individuals who have acted in ways deviating markedly from their culture's norms. In contemporary times, many such people are placed in mental hospitals. Until recently such hospitalized individuals were treated as if they had a medical problem; that is, they were assumed to be suffering from a mental illness. Atthowe presents information indicating that such an approach has been unsuccessful, and that the emphasis in treatment has shifted away from "cure" and toward effective functioning, at first in the hospital and then in the community.

After enumerating some of the problems associated with hospitalization and discussing the limited effectiveness of traditional therapies, Atthowe describes the development of behavioral treatment programs. Behavioral intervention initially was used for specific problems of specific clients; then it was used in ward-wide programs (usually token economies); finally, comprehensive behavioral rehabilitation programs began to be developed. This historical perspective is apparent from Atthowe's pioneering work with token economies and in his more recent comprehensive program, which is explained in this chapter.

Recent research has focused on comprehensive behavioral treatment programs and the development of better assessment procedures. Robert Liberman and his colleagues in California and Gordon Paul and his colleagues in Illinois have reported substantial improvements in various measures used to assess the level of psychological and social functioning of clients. They also have developed comprehensive treatment programs, but have not yet provided outcome data, though the preliminary findings are promising.

Society has been both fascinated and repelled by individuals whose behaviors deviate markedly from what is considered normal or adequate. It has been estimated that 50 million or more Americans, or about one in every four or five people, suffer from some type of mental or behavioral disorder (Glidewell and Swallow 1968; Gurin, Veroff, and Feld 1960; Strange 1965).[1] Each year about 2.5 million people are hospitalized for what has been labeled mental illness or emotional disorders (NIMH 1970). It is further estimated that 1 in every 10 Americans will be hospitalized for an emotional disturbance at least once in his or her lifetime.

Questions about mental hospitals

Who goes there?

Those individuals who end up in mental hospitals are generally suffering from a serious disturbance which demands both supervision and care. These people are most frequently classified or labeled as psychotic (schizophrenia, manic-depressive illnesses, psychotic depression, and paranoid states), and chronic schizophrenia is an especially common diagnostic category. The remainder of the mental hospital population consists of patients having a disorder of the brain (organic brain syndromes) such as senile and presenile dementia, disturbances in brain metabolism, intracranial infection, and so on; certain personality disorders such as the antisocial personality; sexual deviation; alcoholism and other drug dependence; and a few severe neurotic reactions such as anxiety and depressive neurosis.

About one-half of those hospitalized will be labeled schizophrenic. Alcoholics and those with other drug-related disorders, the brain-damaged, and persons with severe depression constitute most of the remaining clients. In recent years, an increasing number of persons over 65 years of age have come to occupy public mental hospital beds.[2] Except for those in mental retardation training institutions, children and adolescents constitute a small percentage of the hospital population. Most hospitalized children and adolescents are classified as having childhood types of schizophrenia.

There are a number of ways in which hospitalized persons are classified or labeled. The classifications just noted represent the traditional clinical nomenclature (see Chapter 6 in this volume). Another classification divides such persons into two distinct groups: (1) *acute patients,* who are labeled primarily paranoid and depressive and constitute a short-term treatment population; and (2) *chronic patients,* repre-

[1] This does not take into account the 5 to 10 million persons who will end up in jail or prison each year.
[2] Approximately 30 percent in 1970 (NIMH 1970).

senting most of those labeled schizophrenic, those over 65 years of age, and the brain damaged, and constituting a custodial and long-term treatment population. It is this chronic population that currently fills two-thirds of the mental hospital beds (Paul 1969b). This group of chronic, hospitalized persons has not been affected by the current upsurge in discharge rates; consequently, chronic disorders constitute the major problem facing mental institutions today.

Are admissions rates decreasing?
Formerly, mental hospitals were the only places of refuge and the only treatment centers for severely disturbed individuals (that is, those individuals whose behavior was such that society would not tolerate their independent existence). However, from 1955 to 1970 the number of persons in public mental hospitals decreased by 39 percent while the overall population of the United States increased by 24 percent (Kanno 1971). But this does not mean that at last we know how to cure severe mental disorders. What seems to be happening is that the concept of cure has been superceded by the concept of more effective functioning. The question asked in treating the hospitalized patient has been rephrased as follows: Can the client function effectively outside the protective walls of the institution and, if so, how and for what length of time? The search for "cures" has not been abandoned, but now practitioners and researchers are focusing upon how to modify disturbed reactions as well as upon why such people act and think the way they do.

Instead of being institutionalized in mental hospitals, most clients are now entering short-term treatment programs in general hospitals. Other individuals who in the past might have entered mental hospitals are now being seen in community mental health centers as outpatients or are undergoing some form of partial hospitalization (day, evening, or night care). When problems become too pressing, the outpatient or partial-hospital client is briefly hospitalized, usually no longer than 20 or 30 days. In addition, residential treatment centers (NIMH 1971) and psychosocial centers or social rehabilitation clubs (Glasscote 1971) have emerged and have helped minimize hospitalization. The net effect of this new approach to hospitalization has been a reduction in dependency and a marked savings in the dollars spent and the effort expended by society. Some mental health experts have concluded, however, that the true effect of minimizing hospital stay has been to transfer the problem of care and supervision from the hospital to the community (e.g., Freeman and Simmons 1963). This point of view questions the efficacy of this form of treatment for the client and further argues that the community suffers markedly from the vast number of "mental patients" in its midst.

Despite the decline in the number of hospitalized persons, the rate of admissions continues to climb; this is largely a function of repeated admissions. In a special report from the National Institute of Mental Health's Center for Studies of Schizophrenia, Mosher and Feinsilver (1971) conclude:

> The rising admission rate seems to be, in part, a result of multiple hospital stays of individual patients. Thus, there has developed, over the last decade and a half, a "revolving door" phenomenon; patients are being hospitalized for shorter periods than previously, but they are also being more frequently readmitted. The probability of readmission within two years of discharge from an initial episode of schizophrenia, for example, varies between 40 and 60 percent, depending on the study. . . . Furthermore, and perhaps more distressing, is the fact that only 15 to 40 percent of schizophrenics living in the community achieve what might be termed an average level of adjustment. (p. 1)

In "revolving door" patients mental hospitals face a problem almost as significant as the chronic mental patient problem. In both cases serious questions are raised regarding the effectiveness of typical hospital treatment programs. We will return to this issue of treatment effectiveness later in the chapter.

What are the costs?

The cost to society of keeping one person in a public mental institution in New Jersey in 1970 was approximately $14,200 per year. The cost of hospital treatment was approximately $9,500 and the productivity loss from keeping someone out of the labor market was designated at $4,700. In a 2-year followup study of a group of 92 patients admitted to the receiving ward of a New Jersey state hospital, it was found that 25 patients remained in the hospital, 34 were discharged and remained out of the hospital, and 33 were repeatedly in and out of the hospital (Johnson and Pollack 1973). For the 34 who stayed out of the hospital after discharge, the actual savings to society was approximately $12,000 per person per year. But of equal interest was the great savings with the persons who were in and out of the hospital (revolving door patients) during the 2-year followup period. For this group, the savings to society was approximately $10,500 per person per year.

In terms of personal costs everyone will agree that long-term hospitalization should be avoided if at all possible. The longer an individual remains in the hospital the less likely that person will ever have the desire to leave the protection and security of the institution. As Paul (1969) reports, the likelihood of discharge after two years of continuous hospitalization is approximately 6 percent. Prolonged hospitalization produces an individual who comes to accept the status of a chronic mental patient, having little if any expectation of recovery (Scheff 1966), and with desires and wants that are minimal and almost nonexistent by extrahospital standards.

There seems little doubt that keeping individuals in a large mental institution is very expensive as well as detrimental to the client's chances of recovery. Releasing individuals can markedly reduce this expense if we can assume that other social expenses, such as police, public assistance, social security, and various public and/or voluntary agencies' expenses do not markedly increase. This latter assumption is probably not valid in most cases. The issue, however, is not merely one of discharging mental patients or developing outpatient or partial hospital programs to handle "would-be patients," but rather finding an effective way of treating individuals and of maintaining the effects of treatment so that both the individual and society can benefit.

Treatment in the hospital setting

With hospitalized persons the ultimate goals of treatment are (1) a reduction in the length of stay within the hospital and an increase in the length of stay outside the hospital, and (2) an increase in posthospital employment and social and community functioning. Ratings of improvement by the patient, the therapist, or significant others in the patient's life are important in determining the overall success of treatment. However, these ratings are subjective and often are unrelated to the ultimate criteria of posthospital performance. The following sections discuss various treatment strategies that have been employed within the mental hospital setting.

Psychotherapy and drugs

Studies of the outcome of psychotherapy with hospitalized persons indicate that psychotherapy alone is not as effective as the administration of drugs in improving hospital and posthospital adjustment (Feinsilver and Gunderson 1972). But drugs per se have not been shown to be effective in reducing recidivism or in helping patients attain and keep posthospital employment. Studies suggest that the major tranquilizers are effective in curbing delusions and hallucinations and that they positively effect performance in situations where brief or simple rehabilitation is attempted, but in more structured programs requiring the learning of complex skills and demanding a higher level of performance, drugs may actually hinder rehabilitation (Paul, Tobias, and Holly 1972; Tobias and MacDonald 1974).

None of the traditional methods of treating hospitalized mental patients has demonstrated specific effects on posthospital performance.

In their recent review of hospital treatment, Anthony, Buell, Sharratt, and Althoff (1972) concluded, "Individual therapy, group therapy, work therapy and drug therapy, do not affect differentially the discharged patients' community functioning as measured by recidivism and post-hospital employment" (p. 454). The advent of residential treatment centers and the community mental health movement have failed to remedy this situation, largely due to the continuance of traditional methods of treatment in these nontraditional settings (Meyers et al. 1974).

Family therapy

The results of family therapy or multiple family therapy, though difficult to assess, suggest that acutely disturbed adolescents and young adults stay out of the hospital longer and their rate of recidivism is lower than the average base rates (Massie and Beels 1972). It seems that working with the main reference group or within the social environment where the patient will reside can help to maintain people in the community and to develop more effective social performance. The people who provide the most reinforcement or punishment for the younger ex-patient are members of his family. As Patterson (1971) points out, "These 'dispensers' (the dispensers of reinforcers) are people who constitute the social environment for the deviant child [or young adult]. Presumably, it is they who shape and maintain his deviant behavior" (p. 752).

Individually tailored behavioral programs

Instead of or in addition to the traditional forms of therapy, individually tailored treatment programs have been developed to deal with specific problems or behavior. For example, delusional speech has been decreased by linking realistic talk to a desired activity, such as a 40-minute informal chat with a favorite staff member over snacks. As rational talk increased, delusional talk decreased (Liberman 1972). Compulsive hoarding was arrested and eventually eliminated by providing a patient with more and more of the hoarded object (in this case towels). After 625 towels were given to the patient by the nursing staff, the reinforcing effect of towels became aversive and the patient stopped hoarding (Ayllon and Azrin 1968). These individually tailored programs involving the use of positive reinforcement and the satiation of a particular reinforcer have helped reduce the bizarre responses and aberrant behavior of many patients. However, the goal of rehabilitation is not simply to reduce aberrant reactions but rather to increase the patient's overall effectiveness within the hospital and eventually within the community. Thus, the trend has been toward more comprehensive rehabilitation programs within the hospital setting, rather than focusing upon a specific problem in a specific situation.

Token economy programs

One of the most effective means of improving the hospital patient's motivation, sense of responsibility, and self-reliance, and of reducing maladaptive behavior, overdependence, and feelings of helplessness has been the introduction of broad contingent reinforcement programs such as the token economy program (see Atthowe 1973b; Kazdin and Bootzin 1972).

Description of a token program. The token economy is a highly complex program involving the behavior of all the persons on a unit or in a ward or hospital setting, including the staff and even the patient's family as well as the patient. It is not a mechanical program but rather a humanistic one that focuses on the individual patient as a human being who can determine his own fate. It involves training the staff to enable them to react to patients in a manner that maximizes the likelihood that each patient will behave more effectively (within his competence).

A token program involves at least five procedural steps: (1) systematic observation of the patient's behavior, its antecedents, and its consequences to determine what elicits the behavior in question and what maintains it; (2) designation of a specific activity as therapeutic and hence reinforceable; (3) determination of what stimuli or events may serve as reinforcers (that is, learning what a person is willing to work for); (4) use of a medium of exchange—the token—which is given for carrying out some therapeutic course of action and which can be exchanged for any number of back-up reinforcers (goods or privileges); and (5) a system for balancing the cost of items with income received (supply and demand). Thus, the token economy can be seen as clearly analogous to what occurs in everyday life. The patient comes to realize that he determines his own fate within the limits of the social and political system of which he is a part, and he further learns ways of modifying the political system.

Example of a token economy. A token program was used with a number of chronic patients who had been hospitalized for over 20 years and who were so apathetic that they did nothing but sit or sleep in large overstuffed chairs on the hospital ward (Atthowe and Krasner 1968). They moved only at mealtimes and then only after much prodding and coercion, and in some cases they would not even leave their chairs to go to the bathroom. The hospital staff was constantly "on their backs" to carry out the normal routines of hospital existence. Initially the introduction of a token program had little effect on this group of 10 to 12 patients. However, when sitting in the chairs was made a reinforcer rather than a "routine right," and this privilege was made contingent upon the performance of certain therapeutic activities, these patients soon assumed much more responsibility and began to take more interest in themselves and in the world around them. After a few months, sitting in the chairs markedly diminished as the main goal in life for these patients; their new activity and motivation provided them with the opportunity for a richer life. In other words, the initial reinforcing event which triggered the action sequence soon became obsolete as increased activity and renewed self-reliance opened up a wider variety of options and potential interests for each patient. This is a common occurrence in most contingent reinforcement programs and is a by-product of the essential learning or retraining procedure in contingency management. In a broad sense, this may be viewed as a shaping procedure.

Shaping involves rewarding closer and closer approximations to the short-term or long-term goals of the treatment program. Shaping usually involves verbal instructions and prompting in order to get some activity initiated, which is then reinforced. As shaping proceeds, the initial reinforcer (in the above example, sitting on the ward) would be associated with the more common reinforcements found in the setting, such as food or praise, and the initial one would be faded out gradually. As the individual receives more and more reinforcement, he becomes more motivated and interested in the world around him. At the same time, the likelihood of discovering new reinforcing events and more effective ways of attaining them rapidly increases. In essence, success breeds further success. The ultimate goal of shaping is that of complete rehabilitation. The use of "constructed" reinforcers is lessened and use of those natural reinforcers found in the world outside the hospital is increased. Tokens can be effectively faded into money. Social reinforcement, such as praise and consideration, and self-generated reinforcement ("I did well," "I achieved my objective") are additionally developed in order to help maintain the person's post-hospital adjustment in the outside community.

Every patient has the right to receive treatment, whether he is a chronic, back-ward schizophrenic or is suffering from an acute reaction. Yet the development of a treatment plan that includes eventual discharge from the hospital as a long-term goal may not be satisfactory to the patient. The patient may not like that goal. An ethical dilemma arises. Should you carry out a treatment plan with which the patient does not agree even if you are convinced he will benefit? This was a concern in the foregoing example of patients sitting on the ward. By making sitting in special chairs a "contingent right" that had to be earned, the therapist was denying the patient the right to choose a custodial form of existence. Yet creating the special contingencies eventually led to more self-determination and increased the patients' options for living. Still, we must be on guard to minimize the possibility of interfering with the rights of hospitalized patients; some form of a peer or advocate review should be part of any treatment plan.

Results of token economies. A token economy is one of the more successful rehabilitation programs for hospitalized patients. It can provide a simulated version of all of the major facets of the natural environment. Inappropriate and appropriate reactions can be observed within the context of an ongoing social-community system and dealt with accordingly. Token economies have been quite successful in changing specific problem behavior and in motivating patients (Atthowe 1973b; Kazdin and Bootzin 1972). A few programs have demonstrated a low recidivism rate. After 2 years, 32 of 44 patients on one token economy program had left the hospital and remained in the community (Ellsworth 1969). When compared with a control (traditional ward) group, a token economy program imposed on an active milieu treatment ward reduced recidivism from 50 to 17 percent in the first 6 months of treatment (Cochran 1969). After 35 months of operation, another token program's recidivism rate was 14 percent compared to 50 percent for the rest of the hospital (Heap, Boblitt, Moore, and Hord 1970). However, the token program is but one phase of a contingent reinforcement program, which has as its goals not only to shorten the patient's stay in the hospital but also to return him to the community and maintain him outside the hospital and to maximize his social effectiveness and productivity.

In their review of psychiatric rehabilitation, Anthony et al. (1972) concluded that aftercare programs produced a significant drop in recidivism for those who attend; however, social effectiveness and productivity were not effected. However, programs that created transitional living and work arrangements (that is, successive approximations to independent living and self-sufficiency) provided an even greater drop in recidivism and markedly increased employment. In other words, an active treatment program designed to train patients to live in a sheltered environment outside the hospital and to work in a sheltered workshop atmosphere allowed the patient to learn to behave as a non-patient.

One group of investigators (Fairweather, Sanders, Maynard, and Cressler 1969) found that ex-patients who created their own living and working facilities in the community and lived and worked together under minimal guidance remained in the community almost 3 times longer and worked almost 17 times as much as a comparable control group from a traditional ward. At the end of 40 months, the median percentage of time spent in the community was approximately 75 percent and the median amount of time spent working was 40 percent for the experimental group as compared to 15 and 1 percent, respectively, for the control group. In this program, patients were assigned to groups of six or more and worked their way by steps through the ward program in which the contingencies were based on group performance (group pressure) rather than on individual achievement. The patients were transferred, usually in groups, to a reconverted motel in the community where a staff member directed the work program and oversaw the living program. Fairweather and his colleagues demonstrated that the most effective way to achieve a certain end result is to create the occasion for that behavior to be performed and then to reinforce the behavior. For example, the big difficulty in changing a person's feelings of worthlessness is to get the person to genuinely feel worthy. It is likely that a feeling of worth stems from doing things well and receiving sufficient reinforcement to expect that reinforcement will recur and that, when it does not, a person can reinforce himself. Irrespective of their particular problems, most mental patients have a long history of being treated aversively by others or of not measuring up to society's standards. The effectiveness of token economy programs and the importance of a job skill and support within the community in reducing recidivism have led to the development of more comprehensive behavioral rehabilitation programs.

Comprehensive behavioral or psychiatric rehabilitation

Behavioral or psychiatric rehabilitation involves more than hospital care and treatment. Rehabilitation, as the name implies, involves a systematic plan of in-hospital and posthospital treatment. The effects of hospital treatment do not persist in most instances. Therefore, steps must be taken to maintain the effects of the treatment the patient has received and to continue treating the individual.

Why a comprehensive program?

The person's natural environment creates and will continue to create the stresses and strains that bring him to the hospital. When a patient leaves the hospital, he generally returns from whence he came. His family, friends, and former associates will generally act in the same old ways that helped bring him to the institution in the first place. But now these community figures have an added expectation or "demand characteristic." That is, the ex-patient is "crazy" and should be watched carefully. He is more often expected to fail than to succeed, and more often than not these expectations are fulfilled. In other instances the ex-patient may try to live alone; this is especially true for the chronic patient who has no family or whose family has renounced him or vice versa. The ex-patient may report periodically to a drug maintenance clinic or to a social worker, but the greater part of his life takes place within a depersonalized and often hostile community. Consequently, many ex-patients who live alone become lonely, drink excessively, and isolate themselves from those around them. Frequently the hospital has failed to provide the returnee with realistic expectations of what he will meet, or with appropriate behaviors and skills and ways of maintaining these appropriate actions. Above all, hospitals have failed to provide society with the necessary attitudes and skills to help maintain the ex-patient and to prevent the occurrence of aberrant behavior.

For the older patient, the one with the more severe problem and the one who has been institutionalized for many years, readjustment to the world outside the hospital is a long and extensive process. Many professionals feel that some type of aftercare or maintenance will always be necessary for a large number of chronic patients if they are to remain out of the hospital and live productive lives. It is evident that merely discharging patients into halfway houses or drug maintenance programs is not enough. In such instances little is done to effect the maintaining milieu in which the ex-patient resides. Essentially we have transferred the problem of chronic care from the hospital to the community, and neither the person nor society benefits. Recently, one New York City suburb passed a law forbidding discharged mental patients to live within its limits (the law was later amended). This residential community was said to look like the grounds of a typical state mental hospital, with apathetic and heavily drugged patients wandering the streets.

A person is sent to a mental hospital because of what he does or fails to do. His behavior is either too excessive or too deficient or too inappropriate according to the standards of the power structure controlling the social system in which he lives. Whether the person is able to stay out of the hospital depends not only on his behavior but also on what the social system, or his relevant environment, accepts.

It has been demonstrated over and over that the consequences of our actions play a very important role in determining what we will do in the future. Our actions are maintained, enhanced, or extinguished by the reactions of others to our behavior. Inaction is just as aversive to most of us as punishment, but to the chronic patient who expects and receives a great deal of aversive consequences, inaction is often a positive reinforcer which in turn maintains his chronicity. To a great extent, human problems are determined by the way people act upon and are reacted to within their relevant environments, that is, within their major reference groups. One of the major reference groups for the former mental patient is all those who have never been hospitalized. As Skinner (1971) suggests, it is the environment that must be changed if the goals of freedom and human dignity are to be reached.

Areas for rehabilitation

In this more comprehensive approach to treatment, Paul (1969b) has suggested the following areas as targets for rehabilitation:

> (a) *resocialization*, including the development of self-maintenance, interpersonal interaction, and communication skills;
>
> (b) *instrumental role performance*, including the provision of "salable" vocational skills, and "housekeeping" skills;
>
> (c) *reduction or elimination of extreme bizarre behavior*, including appropriate changes in frequency, intensity, or timing of individual acts or mannerisms consensually identified as distressing;
>
> (d) *provisions of at least one supportive "roommate" in the community*, including either a spouse, relative, parent, or friend. (p. 84)

Behavioral rehabilitation involves a number of successive steps in which the ultimate goal is self-sufficiency and effective functioning. It is possible that some individuals may never reach the latter goal; however, this should not deter us. Behavioral rehabilitation that is both comprehensive and effective would normally consist of seven steps or conceptual phases.

Phase 1: Preparation and training. Prepare and train the staff and develop community acceptance and participation in creating the in-hospital treatment and posthospital rehabilitation programs.

Phase 2: A behavioral analysis. Determine the patient's current level of functioning (both his appropriate and inappropriate behaviors). What are the typical consequences of his actions (what are the reinforcers and punishing events?); what maintains and elicits them?

Determine what the relevant social systems (the ward, the staff, community groups) expect of patients, how the staff and community behave toward mental patients, and what reinforcers and punishing events affect these agents of change.

Phase 3: State the goals of rehabilitation. Define precisely both the short-term and long-term goals of treatment for each patient. Goals should be stated in terms of the behavior that a person should be displaying when he reaches that goal (Houts and Scott 1972).

Phase 4: State the positive treatment plan. Specify as precisely as possible those behaviors that would be instrumental in reaching both the short-term and long-term goals. Specify the sequential relationships between the desired behaviors and the conditions that elicit and the consequences that maintain them, and the role of the treatment team in this program. Specify the shaping sequence, in other words, determine what instrumental acts set the occasion for the succeeding ones as the goals are approached.

Phase 5: State the problem treatment plan. Specify in behavioral terms those problem behaviors that should be arrested or extinguished in order to reach the defined goals; describe how these problems are to be treated. State the specific therapeutic techniques to be used and what staff members will do.

Phase 6: Program evaluation. Measure the frequency of the desired and problem behaviors and the progress toward the program's goals. Determine how much progress the patients and staff perceive and which parts of the treatment have or have not been carried out.

Phase 7: Self-correction. Those activities associated with progress should be maintained and enhanced, while those associated with a lack of progress should be re-evaluated and if necessary dropped. A continuous account of the program's effectiveness (progress) should be made available to all concerned—the patient, staff, and significant community members. The key question in the nonattainment of a goal is, "Where did things break down?"

These seven phases state in abstract language the steps one takes in planning and carrying out a comprehensive rehabilitation program. The main agents in such a program are the patient or patients, the treatment staff, and significant community figures (patient's family or employer, social agencies, community leaders). A rehabilitation program is essentially a training program. The most effective training methods stem from the application of behavioral principles to social systems. The key learning concepts are reinforcement and shaping. Patients are taught skills that will help them have a more satisfying hospital existence while they are being trained in social and daily living skills and relevant work habits and skills. The posthospital environment should be simulated as much as possible within the hospital. Hospital reinforcing events (tokens, sitting on ward, going to meals early) are faded out gradually and social and posthospital reinforcers (money, approval, attendance at social events) increased. Patients are prepared to live together and with others and to support one another while efforts are made to coordinate the resources in the community to maximize the likelihood of self-sufficiency and productive living.

Example of a comprehensive program

One rehabilitation program utilizing these principles started on a chronic ward in a Veterans Administration hospital in California (Atthowe and McDonough 1969; Atthowe 1975). A token economy was developed on a number of wards. The performance of some patients was very apathetic and required constant supervision; other patients were more active and motivated and could go off the ward unescorted, while a few patients were socially quite responsive and had made a fairly self-sufficient adjustment to hospital living. It soon became apparent that a token economy would have to function at different levels to motivate each of these patient groups. Consequently, three levels of performance were developed. At each level more socially relevant activities were reinforced. Thus, at each succeeding level the kind of performance required was socially more relevant, and the individual became more productive and self-sufficient. In the process, greater status and a more rewarding existence were attained.

As patients progressed through the token program to the status of Group I patients, they not only earned their way out of the token system but also went to work in a sheltered workshop on the hospital grounds. The workshop, a nonprofit corporporation (see Atthowe and McDonough 1969), provided patients with a number of meaningful jobs, which were designed to approximate the performance level of a patient at any given time. A few patients merely bundled newspapers, while others nailed crates or polished telephones and cleaned telephone cords or painted. In addition, a number of off-the-grounds work programs were instituted such as house renovation, gardening, and operating gas stations. These latter jobs provided training in the activities that patients were expected to be performing when discharged. We found that those patients who worked were less likely to return to the hospital. At first, patients were paid quite nominal or therapeutic wages. As patients progressed within the program, their wages increased. In some of the work programs, patients were earning (in 1971) more than $4 per hour. Money, status, comradeship, social reinforcement, self-reinforcement, and self-reliance increased at each step.

As a patient advanced through the program, token reinforcements were increased, thinned out, and eventually replaced by natural reinforcers. The natural reinforcers in turn increased in value as the patient assumed more responsibility. At the same time, patient living arrangements were noticeably improved. At first, patients lived in large dormitories. As they earned more tokens they could buy their way into more private quarters and eventually into Group I. Group I, the elite group, was quartered in a separate area of the ward open only to those patients. They had their own day room and television, and they arranged their living and sleeping areas according to their own desires. Recidivism was found to decrease if Group I patients were moved to a special self-help ward before discharge instead of being discharged directly. Living on the self-help ward was more like living in a halfway house than in a regular ward. Patients assumed more responsiblity for their own lives. They worked in the sheltered workshop programs both on and off the grounds. They took their own medication (occasionally, the taking of medication was checked by chemical tests). No staff people were allowed on the ward, with the exception of one therapist who ran group therapy sessions. Therapy consisted of a review of progress, information, job and posthospital orientation, and everyday problems encountered at work and in getting along with others.

A survey of discharged patients at this and other Veterans Administration hospitals found that loneliness was the major factor causing people to return to the hospital. Movement out of the hospital in groups seems to be one answer to this problem. Consequently, patients were assigned to groups of four to six on the self-help ward. These groups became the basis for therapy and movement into the community. It was suggested that these small groups move into a small house set up on the grounds, where they would encounter the problems of everyday living before moving off the grounds. However, this plan was not implemented; rather, a number of three-bedroom houses near the hospital were rented and patients moved into the community in groups of five. Later, apartments were rented in the same housing complex and two patients were assigned to each apartment.

Thus, a series of steps were developed—from traditional ward activities to special privileges and greater responsibility within the ward, to a more independent self-help ward. The step off the grounds was facilitated by the creation of group cohesion and group pressure. Small groups of patients lived together, first on a self-help ward (quarter-way house), and then in a rented home in the outside community (three-quarter-way house). The use of a halfway house, a small house on the grounds, was conceptualized but never materialized; however, in the ideal step system it would be a necessary step. At each step, the behaviors necessary to self-maintenance at that step and at the next step were taught. In order to overcome some of the resistance to living in the community, ex-patients who were living outside the hospital worked side by side with patients in workshop jobs. These ex-patients volunteered to act as group leaders or cotherapists in the therapy groups. We found the peer therapist to be more effective than a staff member in helping patients overcome the fear of leaving the hospital. The use of peers as therapists not only helped orient patients to getting out, but also helped ex-patients in staying out.

Each step in the program is viewed as a move toward the ultimate goal of self-sufficiency and effective functioning. Progress can be measured in terms of nearness to the ultimate goal, with time in the community, time working, and the quality of work performed used as indicators. Behavioral definitions of each step or subgoal permit one to scale the degree of attainment and to assess whether or not progress is being made.

Our recidivism rate over 1 year was less than 12 percent (Atthowe 1973a), and compares very favorably to the typical base rate of 40 to 50 percent in general (Anthony et al. 1972) and to the higher one (60 to 70 percent) for Veterans Administration hospital patients. All of our ex-patients worked 40 hours per week. It seems that as long as ex-patients can be desensitized to moving into the community through experience, training, and observation of others who have succeeded; as long as they advance in small, manageable steps; and as long as they live and work together in small groups in a supportive community, the likelihood of their remaining out of the institution and becoming productive is greatly increased. As patients gain confidence and new skills they can venture more and more on their own with the knowledge that peers are not too far away. The shaping of the newly asked for behaviors and mastery goes hand-in-hand with a lessening of hospital control and "constructed" contingencies.

The broader the range of contingencies within the program and the greater the frequency of natural reinforcers, the greater the chances for persistence. If we make persistence itself a goal, then we need to create the environment or maintaining milieu that we desire and to reinforce it. We cannot lessen our support too soon nor maintain it too long. The final step to self-sufficiency must be a small one for the chronic patient. If any step along the way is too large, the patient will withdraw; a lack of progress is usually associated with steps that are too far apart.

Recent and future directions

The development of halfway houses, aftercare clinics, day treatment centers, and other transitional facilities has reduced the rate of recidivism (Anthony et al. 1972), but there is little evidence that such programs increase productivity or community participation. The offering of a sheltered workshop without community placement produces little or no noticeable effect on later vocational adjustment (McDonald and Miles 1969). A few programs, such as the Fountain House Foundation in New York City (Schmidt, Nessel, and Malamud 1969), have partially succeeded in increasing the likelihood of a patient being placed in a productive position by stressing personal adjustment training, transitional employment, and job placement while creating a social-recreational center and an apartment program. Fountain House is one of several new psychosocial centers that have been developed to maintain and to integrate ex-patients within the community. Such centers are a necessary step on the route to self-sufficiency. At Rutgers Community

Mental Health Center a similar program is attached to a Comprehensive Community Mental Health Center to help patients achieve the transition from inpatient status to self-sufficient living. One of the more innovative aspects of this program is its stress on clients being members of a "social club," rather than on their patient status (Julius Lanoil, personal communication). One of the areas of greatest neglect has been the lack of social skills and social confidence found in mental patients. Socialization skills must be developed and used along with drug therapy. But whereas drugs should be faded out or their use made much more intermittent, reinforced social experiences should be faded in both at work and at play. Contingency contracts guaranteeing that a person will always be on the job are being made with a number of local employers, especially those whose employee turnover is high. In this way the community is positively reinforced as the ex-patients return.

Comprehensive behavioral or psychiatric rehabilitation is being developed in various places to help patients make a more lasting and effective transition from hospital care to living and participating in society as self-sufficient individuals. However, such programs demand a great deal of follow-through and community action. Community action requires some influence upon the social, political, and economic systems within the community. Effective rehabilitation awaits changes in the way society views its outsiders, its growing number of "mentally ill" citizens.

Behavior management in medical and nursing practice

Terry J. Knapp and Linda Whitney Peterson
University of Nevada at Reno

15

Perhaps because of the polemic nature of the controversy surrounding the rejection of the medical model, behavioral research relating to medical problems was slow to develop. However, there has been a recent mushrooming of such endeavors. Many of the examples cited in this chapter point to the essential and much-needed collaboration across different professions, an approach that might be emulated in other problem areas.

Knapp and Peterson have organized their presentation of experimental findings around the various bodily systems. Their suggestions regarding patient self-management represent a radical departure from traditional procedures, as do their ideas regarding self-evaluation by health professionals. Many of the findings reported in this chapter are both dramatic and exciting, but as the authors warn several times, many of the results are based on case histories. These findings need to be replicated in more adequately controlled studies; if they are, then behavioral science should become a more integral part of medical practice.

At admission to the rehabilitation unit of a large northwestern hospital, Carolyn experienced virtually constant pain in her lower back. She had lived with this pain for the last 20 years. The home that Carolyn shared with her school administrator husband, Brent, and teenage son, Troy, had become too much for her to manage. During the past several months Carolyn's daily activities had decreased to a few 20-minute periods in which she would attempt to carry out household chores but then require a rest period. Her days now consisted of a total of 2 hours of activity, with the remaining time devoted to reading, watching television, or sleeping. When severe pain attacks occurred, all activities were suspended and Carolyn would typically take several analgesic tablets, recline on the couch or bed, and cry until the pain ceased. Brent and Troy did what anyone would do in the presence of such persistent pain behavior; Carolyn was consoled and comforted. Her pain brought her much attention and affection.

On four occasions during the past 20 years physicians had surgically intervened, and while surgery had alleviated some of the discomfort, the pain behavior persisted. At the time of admission, a thorough physical and radiologic examination detected no underlying neurologic pathology. Since surgery and pharmacology had not eliminated the pain behavior, a treatment team of psychologists, doctors, and nurses from the Operant Pain Program (Fordyce, Fowler, and DeLateur 1968) decided to attempt a behavioral intervention program to reduce the pain behavior.

A program was designed to decrease the rate of pain behavior and simultaneously to increase Carolyn's activity level. The treatment team focused on three areas: medication, attention, and rest. These appeared to be the major sources of reinforcement in Carolyn's life, since a great deal of her time and talk concerned "meds," resting in front of the television, and complaining to Brent and Troy about her back. A behavioral contract was negotiated with Carolyn and her family. She would work to change her own behavior.

Carolyn took analgesic tablets whenever she felt the onset of pain; that is, the medication was on a PRN schedule (*pro re nata,* "as occasion arises"). In negotiations with Carolyn, the therapy team changed the delivery of medication to a fixed interval (FI) schedule, so that it became available only at the end of fixed periods of time instead of whenever she felt the need. In the beginning, the fixed intervals were shorter than those Carolyn originally had used in taking the medication; but the intervals of medication delivery were gradually lengthened. In addition, the analgesic tablets were placed in a color- and taste-masking vehicle so that Carolyn did not know the exact dosage. During the ensuing weeks, the narcotic component was gradually reduced; after a 40-day period Carolyn received no medication other than the masking vehicle. Later, the masking vehicle itself was faded out.

A second line of behavioral intervention involved instructing the staff to be socially neutral to Carolyn's talk of pain and discomfort, and at the same time to respond readily to any social or physical activity. To further increase Carolyn's activity level, she agreed to walk a required distance around the ward dayroom. Carolyn kept her own record of her walking and could then directly observe the progress on a graph, as well as show it to Brent and Troy. Initially, the distance required fell well within the range she could walk without complaining of any fatigue and pain. Gradually, the lap quota was increased. After each lap she received immediate praise and attention from the ward personnel. By the end of 7 weeks, Carolyn could walk 25 laps around the ward room in the time it had taken her to do just 10 when she began. This speed was about twice that of a normal walk. Social praise and attention, together with her own self-recording, helped to maintain the increased level of activity.

A final potential source of reinforcement was rest. The occupational therapist negotiated a program of weaving with Carolyn which involved a great deal of arm and leg movement while she remained in a seated position. Carolyn described this as one of her most painful positions. The occupational therapist said, "Don't try to be a hero; see how many threads you can weave *before* you feel pain." The first day Carolyn completed 25 threads within her 20-minute work period before she returned to the ward to rest. Each day she added 10 more threads to her task before she allowed herself to rest. Carolyn's rate of weaving increased dramatically. At the end of 30 days she worked for the full 2 hours allotted to occupational therapy and did not complain of fatigue or pain. Carolyn kept her own record of increased activity and showed it to the staff members, who responded attentively.

Remember that prior to the behavioral intervention Carolyn had devoted only about 2 hours per day to activity of any sort. Figure 15-1 presents weekly data on the increase in activity level that followed introduction of the Operant Pain Program. Upon her release from the rehabilitation unit, Carolyn's number of active hours had increased to about 40 per week. As we might expect, a slight decrease in the amount of activity and a slight increase in complaints of pain occurred when she returned to her old home environment. However, as part of the behavioral contract, her family had received training in behavior change principles. As the outpatient program continued, with activity reinforced and talk of discomfort ignored, the level of activity quickly recovered and increased. Eight weeks of in-patient behavioral intervention had resulted in a sharp increase in activity and a virtual disappearance of pain behavior of 20 years' duration.

The success of the Operant Pain Program in getting Carolyn and many others like her (Fordyce 1970; Fordyce, Fowler, Lehman, and DeLateur 1968; Gannon and Sternbach 1971; Sternbach 1974; Toomey 1974; Weiss 1974) to resume normal levels of activity in their home environments with their family and friends demonstrates the effectiveness of applied behavior analysis in health care. The fact that the patient suffered from chronic pain, frequently viewed as solely a physi-

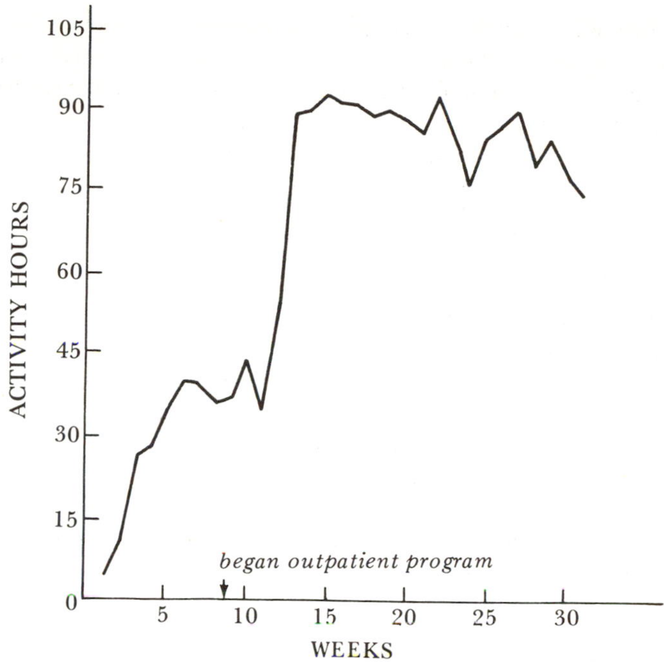

Figure 15-1 Hours of nonreclining activity per week (SOURCE: W. E. Fordyce, R. S. Fowler, and B. DeLateur, "An application of behavior modification technique to a problem of chronic pain," *Behaviour Research and Therapy,* 1968, *6,* 105–107. Reprinted by permission of Pergamon Press and the authors.)

cal problem, makes this case especially suitable to exemplify the manner in which behavioral intervention can *complement* traditional medical procedures.

The joint efforts of behavior management and traditional medical intervention techniques are discussed in this chapter as they apply to three major areas of health concern: (1) the patients who suffer from specific diseases and illnesses associated with one of the organ systems of the body; (2) the technological advances that allow patients to self-manage their own behavior; and (3) the professionals who provide medical and health care. Before we turn to the first of these concerns, a brief discussion of the relationship between medical and behavioral intervention is in order.

Relationship of medical and behavioral treatments

Most often somatic complaints, including pain, are viewed as straightforward biological phenomena. A person is in pain because his or her pain receptors are stimulated either by an external or internal stimulus.

Thus, a biological problem requires a biological intervention procedure, which in the medical sciences could be surgery to remove the affected tissue, a pharmacological agent to deaden pain receptors, or perhaps a modern innovation such as radiologic treatment to destroy selected organ sites. Whichever means is employed, the tendency in each case is to view pain as physical, and hence requiring physical treatment by a physician.

The bio-behavioral model

Physical medicine has long recognized the bio-behavioral nature of pain and of somatic disorders in general. The bedside manner of Marcus Welby and the entire specialty of psychosomatic medicine testify to the interface between physical illness and the behavioral milieu in which it occurs. For example, pain is always a matter of pain behavior. The patient may groan and grimace. A portion of the body may be held. Medication is often requested. Physical activity remains at a low rate. There is an interaction between the patient's biological and behavioral environments.

> There is always a compounding of factors which influences the character and intensity of the pain and which determines whether the pain is felt and/or reported at all, even with injury. By the time a consultation is requested the picture usually is complicated by the chronic nature of the pain, the many diagnostic and therapeutic interventions, and by the reactions of family, friends and frequently a number of physicians from whom the patient has sought advice. The picture becomes even more complex when the pain has a traumatic setting for its beginning and possible financial compensation for injury or work lost. (Hill 1970, p. 16)

The complexity of the interaction between the biological and behavioral components of pain has been experimentally demonstrated by several researchers. In a study entitled "Cognitive Manipulation of Pain," Nisbett and Schacter (1966) found that the amount of pain reported and tolerated was a function of stimulus conditions other than the actual intensity of the aversive event. By training experimental subjects in deep muscle relaxation, Bobey and Davidson (1970) were able to increase the subjects' tolerance for painful electric shock stimuli. A three-year cultural study of pain has shown that the manner in which a person expresses pain is in large part culturally determined (Zborowski 1969).

Thus, pain behavior is sometimes clearly under the control of stimulation of internal pain receptors and at other times entirely under the control of external environmental stimuli. Most often, however, and especially in chronic cases, pain behavior is simultaneously controlled by both sources. Environmental "pathology" may take the form of antecedent and consequential stimuli which maintain pain behavior, such as social and physical attention (Sank and Biglan 1974). Such a conceptualization might be referred to as the operant analysis of pain behavior (Fordyce 1973). What is true of pain behavior is true of sick behavior in general (Kirkpatrick 1972). The operant model of pain behavior and sick behavior leads one to the conclusion that *in selected instances surgical, pharmacological, and behavioral intervention can combine to reduce and eliminate a somatic ailment.*

Behavioral intervention

What is a behavioral intervention procedure? In medical nursing practice behavior management simply refers to the employment within health care settings of the principles and procedures outlined in Parts I and II of this book. In health care management, the techniques of behavior analysis are either applied directly to various organ systems of the body or to behaviors such as physical activity, verbal complaints, or preventive health practices. Time out of bed, verbal statements ("I'm hurting, Doc"), 24-hour fluid intake, the pulse and heart rate, or the amount of glucose in urine—all are examples of frequently measured biological and behavioral responses. The bio-behavioral model views the control of such behaviors not simply as a function of a physiological organ system, but as functionally related to the social and cognitive environment as well.

It is important to understand that when we refer to the bio-behavioral nature of pain and sick behavior in general, we do not mean that "faith healing" is in order, or that some vague psychology of sympathy and empathy will remediate disorders; instead we are referring to the systematic application of specific principles, under the rubric of applied behavior analysis, in medical and nursing practice.

There are certain prerequisites to the employment of behavioral intervention in medical and nursing practice. It is important to rule out patients whose presenting complaint is clearly of physiologic origin. Obviously, an appendectomy is a more appropriate intervention for a patient with a temperature of 104°, vomiting, and umbilical or right flank pain, than a behavior modification program directed toward decreasing pain behavior and increasing patient activity. Thus, a complete history, physical evaluation, and laboratory data are always prerequisite to the development of a behavior change program. A behavior analysis (Goldiamond 1974; Kanfer and Saslow 1969) is appropriate when there is no physiological reason for a symptom or if there are questionable or minimal physiological antecedents. In some instances, however, the etiology of a disorder may be insidious. For example, many brain tumors and lesions are diagnosed only with great difficulty; the presenting symptoms (behaviors) could be under environmental control. Patients who have experienced failure of surgical or pharmacological intervention, or for whom there is no alternative medical intervention, may be appropriate candidates for behavioral analysis.

Once a thorough patient examination is completed, a behavioral contract must be developed. This should be negotiated with the patient, specifying treatment objectives and techniques. For example, the patient is made aware that there may be a removal of professional attention for somatic complaints, with attention contingent upon incompatible behavior and improvement. The patient contract often requires that the family or significant others participate in training sessions to learn how to implement and assist in treatment.

Behavior management may require that the patient record his own behavior, keep his records with him, and show them to staff, family, and friends. This stands in stark contrast to the typical hospital policy of guarding patient records, even from the patient himself. Many of the studies discussed later utilize patient self-recording, not only as a data collection system, but as a means of behavior change as well.

Behavior management and the somatic systems

Cardiovascular system

Cardiovascular disease constitutes the nation's number one health care problem. Psychologists and other scientists, particularly those employing biofeedback technology, are conducting an ever-increasing number of investigations aimed at providing new procedures with which to combat coronary and peripheral vascular disease. As of this writing, few significant clinical procedures have evolved. The greatest successes are reported in connection with self-control of essential hypertension. However, recent research by Lynch and his associates (Lynch, Thomas, Mills, Malinow, and Katcher 1974; Thomas, Lynch, and Mills 1975) gives a clear indication of the interdependency between cardiac function and environmental variables.

Imagine a cardiac care unit. A circular nursing station allows for ready observation and continuous monitoring of the 12 surrounding patient stations. Wayne occupies bed number 8. He was admitted several days ago complaining of "shooting pains" in the chest. From their station the nurses can watch the beat of Wayne's heart on an oscilloscope. A nearby electrocardiogram (EKG) records the beats on paper. Arrhythmias can easily be spotted. Wayne has had repeated 2:1 AV blocking (the atria beat twice to each ventricular beat) during the past several days. This morning psychologists are present to observe the effects of human contact on Wayne's arrhythmia. Three minutes of baseline recording show him continuing to have 2:1 AV blocks. The nurse enters Wayne's cubicle and begins to take his pulse. The electrocardiogram pen jumps, indicating a changing in arrhythmia. Wayne now has first degree AV blocking (the atria beats one time to each ventricular beat, but there is a slight delay in conduction at the AV node). The nurse finishes in less than a minute. As she leaves, Wayne's heart returns to 2:1 AV blocking and remains there. The brief interaction appeared to control the changes in arrhythmias. Other reactions with the patient are observed and recorded throughout the day and night. They reveal similar effects.

Lynch and his associates have clearly shown that heart rate and arrhythmia in cardiac care patients are in part controlled by such setting events as entry of nurses, doctors, and aides. They reported "heart rate changes over 30 beats/minute, a doubling of the frequency of abnormal heart beats, and major changes in the conduction of electrical impulses in the heart" (Lynch et al. 1974, p. 88). The implications of such research results are clear: the bio-behavioral environment, especially in critical illness, may be crucial to the patient's recovery. Even disease and illness with clear underlying pathology may be exacerbated by such subtle environmental factors as pulse taking, ward rounds, and comforting tasks. Other research has concerned patients with arrhythmia, essential hypertension, and Raynaud's disease.

Heart rate, variability, and arrhythmias. A number of studies have shown the possibility of altering various heart functions through feedback to the patient of the relevant information. Publications have acclaimed enthusiastically the benefits and potential of biofeedback in cardiac disorders (Karlins and Andrews 1973). However, in recent exhaustive reviews, Blanchard and Young (1973, 1974a, 1974b) conclude that on the basis of current research findings pharmacology rather than psychology will remain the principal form of intervention with cardiac care patients, at least with respect to heart rate, variability, and arrhythmia.

Hypertension. Elevated systolic and diastolic blood pressure of unknown etiology, that is, essential hypertension, represents the largest single category of hypertensive patients. Numerous researchers (see the reviews by Blanchard and Young 1973; Schwartz and Shapiro 1973) have demonstrated that subjects can learn to control blood pressure level. A few clinical hypertensive patients, as opposed to normotensive experimental subjects, were able to bring their pressure to within normal limits. Biofeedback can apparently produce beneficial results,

results that are better supported than those connected with arrhythmia. However, most investigations of biofeedback procedures are confounded with relaxation procedures. But the biggest problem is that no studies have demonstrated generalization from the laboratory to the natural environment. Some reviewers (Blanchard and Young 1973; Schwartz and Shapiro 1973) have suggested that teaching patients deep muscle relaxation (see Chapter 11 in this volume) to reduce anxiety and assertive training to reduce aggressive responses may be a more effective procedure than biofeedback per se.

Raynaud's disease. This disorder, occurring most often in young and middle-aged women, involves no observable organic pathology, at least not in the initial stages. The symptoms manifested are vasospasms of the digital arteries, often producing coldness and numbness of the hands and feet. Behaviorists have treated the disease with feedback of hand-skin temperature and large toe photoplethysmograph (see the review by Surwit 1973). While feedback was effective in eliminating the symptoms in a number of patients, no appropriate control study has yet been conducted. However, since pharmacological remedies are relatively ineffective in alleviating the symptoms of Raynaud's disease, the biofeedback procedure should perhaps be tried before the less conservative surgical intervention.

Future directions. While few applications of behavioral intervention with cardiovascular patients have proved clinically significant, the future may hold great promise based on these early attempts. Some researchers (Friedman 1969; Freidman and Rosenman 1974) present evidence, for example, that a particular behavior pattern, termed Type A, is associated with the propensity to develop coronary heart disease. Friedman (1969) described the behavior pattern as:

> a characteristic action-emotion complex which is exhibited by those individuals who are engaged in a relatively chronic struggle to obtain an unlimited number of poorly defined things from their environment in the shortest period of time and, if necessary, against the opposing efforts of other things or persons in this environment. This struggle has been encouraged by the contemporary western environment because, unlike any previously known milieu, it appears to offer special rewards and opportunities to those who can think, perform, communicate, move, live and even play, more rapidly and aggressively than their fellow men. (pp. 84–85)

Preliminary reports indicate that this pattern might be altered through behavior modification procedures (Suinn 1974a, 1974b). Others have suggested the possibility of teaching children behaviors incompatible with those associated with coronary heart disease (Boyer 1974). Clearly, cardiology is an area of health care to which behaviorists must give more attention. Behavioral techniques and procedures, especially those of a preventive nature, such as environmental programming rather than the narrow application of biofeedback, may actually hold the greatest promise.

Respiratory system

Diseases of the respiratory system may include disorders of the nose, mouth, pharynx, larynx, trachea, or bronchial tree. The focus of behavior analysis interventions has primarily been on patients with asthmatic conditions, although preliminary work is reported in the areas of tracheostomy dependency and chronic cough.

Asthma. This is a condition associated with difficulty in breathing, a constriction of the chest, mucoid secretions, and a characteristic wheezing. A behavioral analysis of asthma was presented by Turnbull (1972) and by Wohl (1971). Psychologists have employed several procedures in treating asthma. Walton (1960a) used assertive training to reduce stressful situations that elicited asthmatic responding. Systematic desensitization served a similar purpose in cases reported by Cooper (1964) and others (Sergeant and Yorkston 1969; Yorkston, McHugh, Brady, Serber, and Sergeant 1974); while Rathus (1973) had success employing just the deep muscle relaxation component of desensitization. Counterconditioning has also been utilized (Khan, Staerk, and Bonk 1973). An innovation is to use electromyogram (EMG) feedback as an assist to relaxation techniques. Davis, Saunders, Creer, and Chai (1973) found this useful, and Kinsman (1972) currently has a research program underway to assess further the effects of EMG feedback with asthmatic patients. Hypnosis has also been used in conjunction with behavioral procedures (Moorefield 1971).

That environmental factors may play a role in producing asthmatic responding is evident in a case described by Neisworth and Moore (1972). The patient was a 7-year-old boy who had been seen almost monthly by various medical professionals, who had tried a variety of intervention techniques. None of them produced significant reductions in asthmatic responses. A behavioral analysis was performed, indicating that parental attention might be maintaining the behavior. The parents were taught to ignore the asthmatic responding, and additionally, the boy was told he could earn money by decreasing the time he spent coughing at bedtime. Figure 15-2 presents the experimental conditions and shows the effect of the treatment procedure. This study serves to illustrate the manner in which parents and significant others can serve

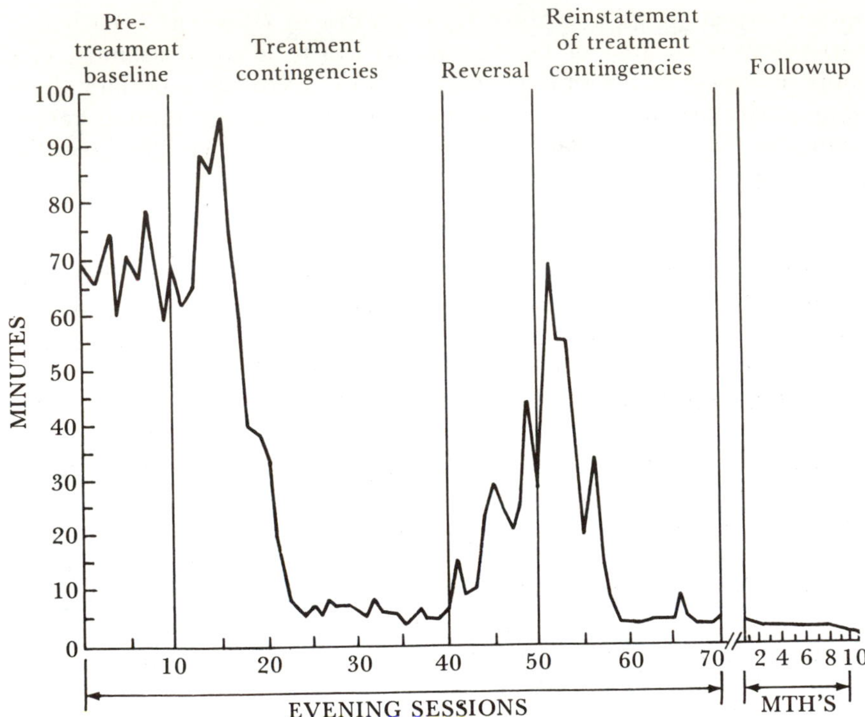

Figure 15-2 Duration of bedtime asthmatic responding as a function of contingency changes (SOURCE: J. T. Neisworth and F. Moore, "Operant treatment of asthmatic responding with the parent as therapist," *Behavior Therapy,* 1972, *3,* 95–99. Reprinted by permission of Academic Press and the authors.)

to maintain "sick" behavior, but it also shows how they can be therapists in arresting the behavior.

When parents or significant others are unavailable, patients can be taught self-monitoring and self-control. Sirota and Mahoney (1974) were able to teach a 41-year-old female who had had asthma for 7 years to inhibit her attacks through relaxation. She carried a timer which would buzz at various intervals, and she relaxed on that cue. Additionally, whenever she felt an urge to use her Bronkometer (nebulized bronchodilator medication) she set the timer, practiced relaxation for 3 or 4 minutes, and usually the urge went away. While these cases seem clearly to support the efficacy of behavioral intervention with asthmatic patients, the literature contains only two controlled investigations. Moore (1965) tested 12 patients in conditions of relaxation through systematic desensitization, relaxation and suggestion, and relaxation alone. All three groups reported subjective improvement, but only relaxation and systematic desensitization produced significant change in physiological measures of the respiratory system. Alexander, Miklich, and Hershkoff (1972) compared two matched groups of asthmatic children, giving one relaxation training and the other no treatment. The relaxation group had significant increases in their mean peak expiratory flow compared to the control group.

Without doubt, behavioral intervention in the form of relaxation training and control of environmental consequences has proved itself a clinically significant and effective technique with *some* asthmatic patients.

Tracheostomy dependency. When the upper respiratory passage becomes occluded, an opening is made into the trachea and breathing takes place through a cannula. Upon disappearance of the obstruction, the cannula is removed and the opening closed; but occasionally, dependency on the cannula develops. Wright, Nunnery, Eichel, and Scott (1969) applied operant principles to two 8-month-old infants who had developed dependency to breathing through the cannula. Attempts to remove the cannula and to restore normal breathing resulted in cyanosis, deep retractions, and labored breathing. A shaping procedure was undertaken, using social reinforcers. During normal breathing, initially only a few minutes in length, the social reinforcers of touch and talk were given. During breathing through the cannula, the infants were placed in social isolation. Gradually, the normal breathing interval was lengthened. In 3 weeks the cannulae were removed and normal breathing restored. No further difficulties developed during the 9-month followup period.

Chronic cough. A variety of respiratory ailments can produce coughing. In some cases a person may cough chronically although no underlying physical pathology can be discerned. Munford, Reardon, Liberman, and Allen (1974) have shown that the cough rate (40 to 50 per minute) of a patient was directly related to environmental conditions. The cough rate varied with the task performed, the social situation, and the structural nature of the interaction. In another study, the chronic cough of a 15-year-old male was treated with an avoidance procedure (Alexander, Chai, Creer, Miklich, Renne, and Cardoso 1973). The cough had persisted for 14 months, requiring hospitalization on 25 occasions. This teenager had missed 113 school days and yet no organic pathology was found. In behavioral treatment, the patient avoided a slight shock by postponing a cough, elicited by known stimuli such as shampoo or beef oil, for increasing longer intervals of time. At completion of treatment, the coughing had been eliminated and it did not reappear during the 18-month followup period. Intractable sneezing has been treated in a manner similar to chronic cough (Kushner 1968). The respiratory system and its disorders is an area where behavioral intervention has been especially fruitful.

Dermatological system

The skin provides a protective cover for the other somatic systems. It is itself susceptible to a variety of disorders. Illnesses treated with behavior therapy have included neurodermatitis, burns, and urticaria. Bar and Kuypers (1973) provide a review of the relevant behavioral literature.

Neurodermatitis. This is a condition in which some portion of the skin is inflamed due to emotional or nervous influences. The disorder is frequently exacerbated by self-scratching. Walton (1960b) treated a 20-year-old female who had been undergoing medical therapy for two years with no improvement. The parents and fiancé were instructed not to attend to the inflamed areas, to refuse discussion of the condition, and to no longer assist in applying ointment. The skin cleared in 2 months, and the patient remained clear throughout a 4-month followup period. In addition to an extinction procedure, Allen and Harris (1966) added a token system and immediate tangible reinforcers to reduce excessive scratching in a 5-year-old girl. Ratliff and Stein (1968) paired contingent electric shock with a shout of "Don't scratch," but no reduction in the response occurred outside of the training sessions until deep muscle relaxation was substituted for the aversive procedure. The patient relaxed each time he desired to scratch. The scratching response abated in 5 weeks, and the skin stayed clear throughout the 6-month followup. Bar and Kuypers (1973) also found that the procedures of extinction and contingent electric shock, combined with relaxation training, were effective with a variety of patients having neurodermatitis. Finally, Watson, Tharp, and Krisberg (1972) described a patient who managed her own treatment of neurodermatitis. She first substituted a stroking response for the scratching, and later patting for stroking. She also placed herself on a token system. By the end of 20 days, all scratching, stroking, and patting were eliminated. The entire treatment required only brief nonprofessional consultation, and serves to demonstrate the extent to which patients can come to manage their own behavior.

Burns. Patients with burns present some of the most difficult physiological as well as behavioral problems. Physiologically, the protective skin covering has been broken and is open to infection and there is loss of fluid and electrolyte balance. Typically, these patients are isolated, subjected to painful *débridement* (removal of burned skin), and stinging antiseptic medications. These conditions frequently lead to patient behavior problems, such as screaming and abusive language, or withdrawal and regressive bed wetting.

Shorkey and Taylor (1973) provided one of the most innovative approaches to this multiphasic problem. Lynn was only 17 months old when admitted to the trauma care unit. Deep second and third degree burns covered 37 percent of her body. She would cry and agitate her limbs when the nurses sprayed silver-nitrate medication over the bandages. Her agitation increased as the weeks passed, and by the fourth week she refused food, screamed, and became agitated whenever a staff member approached. Her physical condition deteriorated to such a degree that her skin would slough skin grafting applied to the burn areas.

The nurses tried several tactics to change Lynn's behavior. They interrupted treatment procedures to talk, sing, or play with her, but her crying and agitation continued. The nurses visited between the treatment sessions. At those visitation times, Lynn still became agitated; she would cry loudly, fling her limbs about, and look away from the nurses.

The hospital social worker, trained in behavior modification, was called as this infant's condition worsened. After the interaction between the staff and Lynn was observed, a treatment program was designed in which Lynn might learn to discriminate between the aversive conditions of treatment and the nonaversive nature of social visits. During the silver-nitrate treatment, nurses wore green isolation gowns. They did not talk to, handle, or play with Lynn or her toys. Under this condition, the staff spent as little time as possible in the room. However, during the social visitation time, large red sterilized bags with armholes were worn. At these times the staff talked to Lynn, played with her, and massaged her neck and shoulder to reduce tension. Differentiating green lights were turned on during treatment time, and red lights during social visitations. Lynn's mother at first refused to participate in the planned program, because she thought Lynn would recognize her whether she wore a red gown or not. Unfortunately, Lynn was highly agitated when her mother visited; after the mother agreed to wear a red apron, Lynn calmed.

By the second day of the differentiating conditions, Lynn began to decrease her rate of crying during the social visits. She would watch silently as staff members entered her room. Several days later, Lynn smiled during the social visit period. The staff began to reinforce smiling with a peek-a-boo game. The agitation and crying continued during the treatment sessions, but Lynn's physical condition was improving. When skin grafts were applied, they adhered. By the end of hospitalization, Lynn showed little fear of hospital personnel.

The fear and anxiety experienced by Lynn are reactions repeatedly encountered by health care professionals who must inflict intramuscular and intravenous medications, as well as painful treatments. The program developed by Shorkey and Taylor illustrated a method whereby systematic attention to timing and social interaction can minimize patient discomfort.

Urticaria. Hives is a vascular reaction of the skin. Protruding reddish or whitish patches are accompanied by itching sensations. Daniels (1973) successfully treated a 23-year-old female who reported an acute onset of facial swelling, with itching over her entire body. The condition seemed associated with anxiety resulting from interactions with her husband and his family. After she was desensitized to hierarchies containing items concerning her husband and father-in-law, within 2 weeks the hives ceased during the daytime and within 12 weeks they completely disappeared. They did not reappear during the entire 23-month followup.

Gastrointestinal system

The system of organs and tissues which constitute the gastrointestinal tract include the mouth, esophagus, stomach, small and large intestines, and anus. Although usually not regarded as disorders of the gastrointestinal system per se, obesity (see the reviews by Abramson 1973; Hall and Hall 1974), anorexia nervosa (see the review by Stunkard 1972; criticism by Burch 1974; also Stunkard and Mahoney, in press), and enuresis/encopresis (see the review by Yates 1970) have been treated behaviorally with considerable success.

Emesis and rumination. Repetitive vomiting and later consumption of the vomit is a disorder frequently seen in mental retardates and occasionally in normal children of the 1- to 5-year-old range. Treatment procedures of extinction and contingent electric shock have been used with such patients. Wolf, Birnbrauer, Lawler, and Williams (1970) found the vomiting behavior of a 9-year-old mentally retarded girl to be a direct function of her being allowed to leave the classroom immediately after vomiting. When she was required to stay in class without attention for vomiting, the vomiting ceased. Similarly, Smeets (1970) and Alford, Blanchard, and Buckley (1972) found withdrawal of social attention effective in reducing the rate of vomiting.

Contradictory results are associated with the use of contingent electric shock techniques. Kohlenberg (1970) applied contingent shock to a 21-year-old severely retarded girl who was in medical danger from weight loss due to excessive vomiting. The shock procedure proved effective initially, and the girl gained 10 pounds; however, during the followup period, there were repeated periods of vomiting requiring additional shock sessions. Luckey, Waston, and Musick (1968) report that contingent electric shock significantly reduced vomiting and rumination, and no remission occurred during followup. Gailbraith, Byrick, and Rutledge (1970) had similar results, but noted side effects of hyperactivity, self-mutilation, and other behaviors. White and Taylor (1967) found contingent electric shock to be successful and observed no side effects. Counterconditioning, through pairing the vomiting response with its physiological opposite (sipping ginger ale), was successful in a case reported by Morgan and O'Brien (1972). None of these applications, however, represent carefully controlled studies.

The most notable case of emesis is that of a 9-month-old infant who was treated with contingent electric shock by Lang and Melamed (1969). The infant would vomit within 10 to 15 minutes of eating. He had undergone three hospitalizations, repeated testing, and medical procedures designed to eliminate the vomiting. No organic basis could be found for the disorder, nor were any of the many medical intervention techniques helpful in its elimination. At the time the psychologists intervened, the infant was in critical condition, weighing only 9 pounds, and being fed via a nasogastric pump.

The psychologists observed the infant to determine the first sign indicating vomiting. Muscle tension was monitored by electromyogram as part of the assessment procedure. Electric shock was made contingent upon the first indication (judged by a nurse and muscle recordings) of reverse peristalsis. After the second of such 1-hour sessions, shock was rarely required; a tone which had been paired with the shock was sufficient. The vomiting soon ceased; the infant was discharged after the fifth day and quickly gained weight. A 1-year followup showed no significant alteration in his eating behavior, nor was there a return of the vomiting. Without the contingent electric shock intervention, it is likely the infant would have soon died. When used under proper care and supervision, it would appear that shock contingent on emesis is an effective clinical procedure for selected patients.

Electrolyte imbalance. In some cases, for example, with burn victims and spinal cord injury patients, careful management of fluid intake is required. Operant principles have proved effective in increasing the fluid intake of patients (Fowler, Fordyce, and Berni 1969; Sand, Trieschman, Fordyce, and Fowler 1970; Sand, Fordyce, and Fowler 1973). The procedure involves several steps. First, the patient is made aware of the importance of increased fluid intake. However, studies have revealed that providing only educational information, in the form of oral and written instructions, is not sufficient to increase fluid intake appreciably (Sand, Fordyce, and Fowler 1973). Second, the patient is taught self-recording procedures to measure the amount of daily fluid intake, with the record being posted by the bedside. Self-recording has proved effective in some cases (Fowler, Fordyce, and Berni 1969). Third, if self-recording does not increase the consumption of fluids, consequences are added. Attention from physicians, nurses, and psychologists, contingent upon increased fluid intake, will usually result in more fluid consumption (Sand, Fordyce, and Fowler 1973).

Diarrhea. Excessive and loose bowels may be the result of a wide variety of disorders. When no underlying physical pathology can be discovered, the condition is termed functional diarrhea. Cohen and Reed (1968) found systematic desensitization effective in treating functional diarrhea of 4 years' duration in a 20-year-old male, and in a 30-year-old male who had suffered from the same disorder for 7 years. The desensitization hierarchies concerned the situations in which the response was likely to occur, as well as the response itself. A 6-month followup showed continued maintenance of the new behavior. A woman who had begun restricting her movement to within 15 seconds of a bathroom was treated by Hedberg (1973) with a similar procedure, and she is now free to go wherever she chooses. An alternative to systematic desensitization is audio feedback of bowel sounds (borborygmi). Furman (1973) treated functional diarrhea in five patients. All were able to gain control of peristaltic activity through such audio feedback. Patients remained asymptomatic during the followup period.

Constipation. The retention of fecal matter is frequently a problem in the young and the elderly, and occasionally it becomes a chronic condition. Quarti and Renaud (1964) have provided a behavioral analysis of the manner in which chronic constipation may develop. Lal and Lindsley (1968) reported on a 3-year-old male who could defecate only when medicated. Playing in the bathtub was used as a reinforcer following the first bowel movement, which was elicited by a suppository. The play time in the tub and appropriate parental attention produced reliable bowel movements following the first elicited one. In a similar patient, Tomlinson (1970) used bubble gum as a reinforcer for defecation, while others have employed popsicles (Perzan, Boulanger, and Fischer 1972).

Sphincter pressure. On some occasions fecal incontinence is produced by insufficient anal sphincter pressure. Kohlenberg (1973) provided a 13-year-old male with visual feedback (in the form of a column of water) and monetary rewards for increased sphincter pressure. While training did not result in complete continence, it did lengthen the period between bowel movements to 8 hours compared with the previous constant movement, and it did postpone a colostomy. A similar feedback of sphincter pressure improved the continence of five patients who had chronic incontinence problems (Engel, Nikoomanesh, and Schuster 1974).

Gynecological system

Few studies report behavior modification techniques employed in diseases and illness unique to the female. Although a variety of procedures which in part resemble behavior analysis techniques have found application in sexual disorders (Masters and Johnson 1966, 1970; Murphy and Mikulas 1974), a literature search revealed only a few studies that could be classified as gynecological. Mullen (1968) treated a patient with dysmenorrhea (excessive pain during menstruation) by systemetic desensitization. The client, a 31-year-old married school teacher, was taught deep muscle relaxation, and then desensitized to a hierarchy of both menstruation and pregnancy items. She also practiced relaxation at home in the presence of objects associated with the menstruation period. Following 16 sessions, over several months' time, she reported that she no longer experienced pain during her periods, nor did she remain in bed during any of the menstrual days. A 6-month followup showed no change in the improved conditions. Student therapists have utilized this same technique (Mullen 1971), and Tasto and Chesney (1974) have extended the procedure to group-administered desensitization.

Neurological systems

Neurological disorders may occur in either the central or peripheral nervous systems. Behavioral intervention associated with neurological impairment has concentrated on several areas: spasmodic torticollis, cerebral palsy, seizures and associated spasms, tension and migraine headaches, sleep disorders, and epilepsy. In addition to these areas, behavior therapists have for some time devoted their attention to tics, or spasmodic muscular contractions of nonorganic origin. Hersen and Eisler (1973) and Yates (1970) recently did a thorough review of the literature on tics, and a promising new technique, habit reversal, has received some support (Azrin and Nunn 1973).

Spasmodic torticollis. This is a condition in which the patient suffers from intermittent spasms in the cervical and sternocleidomastoid muscles of the head and neck, producing a rotation or lifting of the head. While some evidence implicates disease in the basal ganglia, patients are more frequently referred to a psychiatrist for treatment of the "underlying psychological disturbance." A number of procedures have been employed in attempts to lessen the spasms. Negative practice, or engaging the muscle in a direction opposite the spasm, was successful in one patient treated by Agras and Marshall (1965), but it failed in a second. The results of a similar procedure, massed practice (voluntarily engaging in the spasm repeatedly) are contradictory. Meares (1973) had no success with eight patients, while Turner, Hersen, and Alford (1974) found the technique effective in reducing spasms during the experimental sessions. A third procedure, contingent electric shock, has proved effective when used alone (Brierley 1967), and when used in conjunction with EMG feedback (Cleeland 1973). Finally, systematic desensitization (Meares 1973) and video feedback (Bernhardt, Hersen, and Barlow 1972) also are reported as successful techniques.

All of the foregoing procedures have been successful with at least one patient, and all show symptom-free followup periods of a year or two. A consistently effective clinical procedure for treating spasmodic torticollis is yet to emerge, however.

Cerebral palsy. With this condition central nervous system damage has been produced *in utero,* at birth, or in early life. A typical behavior problem of children with cerebral palsy is drooling. Garber (1971) eliminated drooling behavior in a 14-year-old male by prompting him to swallow his saliva, then faded out the prompts. The boy was also reinforced with pennies for nondrooling periods. The nondrooling behavior remained low throughout the several months of followup. The spasms of a 20-year-old male were decreased during experimental sessions by Sachs and Mayhall (1971), who employed contingent electric shock. No tests for generalization were conducted, however, nor were followup data collected. Finally, Halpern and Kottke (1968) have reported some success in teaching head posture in cerebral palsy children through repeated practice procedures and a mechanical supportive device. Since many of the problems associated with cerebral palsy are muscular in nature, the techniques described in the section on the musculoskeletal system are equally applicable.

Seizures. A variety of neurological disorders produce seizure behavior. Frequently an underlying pathology is easily identified and medication prescribed. On some occasions, however, the seizure behavior may be influenced by environmental factors. Gardner (1967) treated a 10-year-old female who had many somatic complaints and was brought to a hospital following a seizure in her home. No organic basis could be found for the seizure; her electroencephalogram (EEG) was normal. Gardner instructed the parents to ignore seizure-like behavior and to attend to appropriate behavior. No more seizures occurred until a reversal phase was initiated, with the parents once again attending to her somatic complaints and seizure-like behavior. A return to the treatment conditions resulted in no further seizures. In a patient originally diagnosed as having Jakob Creutzfeldt syndrome (a neurological disorder producing gross muscular movements), Parrino (1971) produced a systematic reduction in seizures through desensitization to anxiety-provoking stimuli.

Tension and migraine headaches. Tension headaches usually involve a severe contraction of the frontalis muscle. Blanchard and Young (1973) concluded that providing patients with EMG feedback of muscle potential, in addition to training in deep muscle relaxation, was most effective in reducing and eliminating tension headaches.

The etiology of migraine headache is not known, although disturbance of cranial circulation is most often implicated. Behavioral treatment has involved differential temperature feedback between the hands and the frontalis area. By warming the former with respect to the latter, some researchers (Sargent, Walters, and Green 1973) have reported success in training patients to control migraine headache; however, no control comparisons were made (Miller 1974). Other behavior therapists have treated migraine headache with relaxation training (Lutker 1971) or a treatment package combining assertive training, relaxation instruction, and systematic desensitization (Mitchell 1969; Mitchell and Mitchell 1971). Since headache is a symptom associated with a variety of acute neurological disorders, a differential diagnosis is extremely important to eliminate the possibility of an underlying pathology.

Sleep disorders. When a person has difficulty getting to sleep and remaining asleep, the condition is termed *insomnia.* In cases where the person gets to sleep but develops periods of semiawakeness during which he carries out activities for which he later has amnesia, the condition is termed *somnambulism.* Insomnia is typically managed by teaching the person deep muscle relaxation (Baker and Kahn 1972; Borkovec and Fowles 1973; Borkovec, Kaloupek, and Slama, in press; Eisenman 1970; Evans and Bond 1969; Geer and Katkin 1966; Haynes, Woodward, Moran, and Alexander 1974; Haynes, Follingstad, and McGowan 1974; Hinkle and Lutker 1972; Kahn, Baker, and Weiss 1968; Nicassio and Bootzin 1974). It is assumed that a major component of insomnia is the inability to produce a reduction in muscle tone. Weil and Goldfried (1973) have based treatment on this assumption. They utilized a tape recording to provide *in vivo* relaxation instructions to an 11-year-old female who had not slept well for many months. The taped instructions were played each night and within a few days the girl was asleep before the conclusion of the tape. The length of the tape was systematically reduced from 30 to 15 to 5 minutes. A 6-month followup showed continued improvement in her sleep pattern.

While relaxation procedures appear the most obvious behavioral technique for insomnia and are supported by controlled investigations, the need to break the nonsleep chain should not be neglected. If a patient remains in bed without sleep for longer than 30 minutes, he might, for example, be instructed to arise, change clothes, go into a different room, sit in a particular chair and read a book, or make a list of his worries until tired, then make another try at sleep. Thus, the bed should remain a setting for sleep, and not for worry or working, tossing or turning. Bootzin (1972) and others (Tokarz and Lawrence 1974; Price, Simmons, and Haynes 1974) have employed such a procedure in treating patients.

Somnambulism was treated by Walton (1961) with one session of assertive training (see Chapter 20 in this volume), producing an immediate reduction in the attacks and comfortable sleep patterns during the next 6 months. Edmonds (1967) found contingent electric shock ineffective in reducing sleep talking and walking in a patient who had a 7-year history of somnambulism. Sleep disorders may be secondary to an underlying pathology, and hence a thorough physical assessment, including EEG recordings in a sleep laboratory may be in order (Dement 1972).

Epilepsy. This condition is actually a group of central nervous system disorders which usually, though not always, results in convulsive behaviors. Several techniques have been applied to arrest the seizures induced by epilepsy. Sterman and Friar (1972) report a suppression in the number of seizures in a 23-year-old female when she was provided with feedback of activity (12 to 14 Hz) in the sensory-motor cortex. In a very early study, Efron (1956, 1957) employed a classical conditioning paradigm with a woman diagnosed as having temporal lobe epilepsy. An unpleasant odor was found to arrest the seizure if presented during the aura prior to seizure onset. Later Efron paired the odor with a bracelet which came to act as a conditioned stimulus. Staring at the bracelet, and on some occasions, just thinking of the bracelet was a stimulus sufficient to arrest the seizures. No seizure activity was reported during the 8-month followup period.

Musculoskeletal system

Many of the behavioral interventions described in the section on the neurological system could be applied as well to the musculoskeletal system. For example, MacPherson (1967) treated a 60-year-old female with a long history of involuntary muscle movements of the mouth and jaw. He employed a procedure that closely resembles those used with spasmodic torticollis. The patient was taught deep muscle relaxation, and instructed to induce relaxation at the first indication of muscle spasm. At the end of a 1-year followup, the patient's involuntary movements were "barely" noticeable.

Numerous publications have described the manner in which similar behavioral techniques can assist in physical rehabilitation (Fordyce, Sand, Trieschmann, and Fowler 1971; Meyerson, Kerr, and Michael 1967; Michael 1970). Other studies have demonstrated specific applications of behavioral principles to rehabilitative problems, such as fluid intake in a paraplegic (Sand et al. 1970), fear of falling in a semiambulatory patient (DiScipo and Feldman 1971), increasing the rate of exercise (Fordyce et al. 1971), and refusal to push a wheelchair (Goodkin 1966). Couch and Allen (1973) provide a comprehensive review of behavior modification applications in physical rehabilitative facilities.

Two procedures are worthy of extended discussion. The first of these is EMG feedback from muscles which are currently weak. Such feedback has proved effective in restoring the use of various muscles in patients with neuromuscular disorders (Blanchard and Young 1974a). Improvement from biofeedback of muscle activity has allowed some patients to discard braces that they had relied upon for over a year.

The second procedure involves the use of shaping, fading, and reinforcement. This procedure was used in the case of Nancy, a 5-year-old girl with cerebral palsy. Although Nancy's physician had told her mother that the child would never walk, O'Neil (1972) decided to try to change Nancy's scooting behavior, her only form of locomotion, to walking with the assistance of a single crutch. The behavioral principles of shaping, fading, and positive reinforcement were used. The first step of treatment involved teaching Nancy to pull up to a kneeling position, move to a standing position, and with the support of a nearby cabinet, walk. These behaviors were shaped with social and edible reinforcers. Next, Nancy needed to free herself from holding onto the cabinet and instead use the crutch. This was accomplished in several steps. Initially, a special harness was introduced, allowing a person to stand behind Nancy and support her as she walked. During this stage Nancy was provided with hand support. Then she went through a sequence of harness support only, hand support using a stick and spring, support of a weighted crutch, and finally she reached the terminal behavior, walking with a single weighted crutch.

The procedures employed in this study are, of course, not new, but their application is significant. Nancy, a child who was diagnosed as being incapable of ambulation, is now walking. She joins a large number of other children who are currently doing things they "physically" are not "capable of."

Genitourinary system

A few illnesses associated with the genital and urinary systems have come under scrutiny from the behavior analyst. The work on sexual dysfunction has been cited previously (Masters and Johnson 1966, 1970; Murphy and Mikulas 1974). In addition, behavioral techniques have been used with urinary retention, excessive micturition, and hemodialysis.

Urinary retention. Some patients develop the habit of retaining urine in the bladder for extended periods of time. Barnard, Flesher, and Steinbook (1966) treated a 27-year-old female who had suffered from psychogenic urinary retention for 15 years. She had undergone repeated surgery, medication, electroconvulsive therapy, catheterization, and psychotherapy. None of these treatments had significantly altered the retention. She was provided with a mild electric shock stimulator which, upon the creation of stress, seemed to elicit urination. The patient was taught to self-administer the treatment, and concurrently underwent assertive training. Within 1 month she was free of the symptom, and remained so during the 18-month followup.

Fazio (1974) assisted a 22-year-old college student with partial paralysis who could not completely empty his bladder. The program involved self-observation of discriminative stimuli (a tugging sensation in the bladder) associated with full emptying of the bladder. While this case study does not allow a clear specification of the precise procedures that led to full emptying of the bladder, the functional analysis seems to have directed the patient's attention to the relevant proprioceptive stimuli.

Occasionally the problem is one of stimulus control. Lamontagne and Marks (1973) describe the case of a person who could urinate only in his own home. The therapists asked him to remain in a distressing situation (for example, a public toilet) until he passed urine. Replications of this procedure were successful with other patients.

Excessive micturition. Some patients suffer from a condition opposite to urinary retention, that is, excessive frequency of urination. Normative data on rate of urination are provided by Yates and Poole (1972). Cohen and Reed (1968) describe a patient with a 6-year history of frequent micturition which had reached the point that she severely restricted her social life. Prior applications of medication and psychotherapy had been to no avail. A combination of systematic desensitization and practice in relaxation with a full bladder was successful with this patient. Taylor (1972) presented a case study in which desensitization also proved effective. In contrast, a classical conditioning procedure was utilized by Jones (1956) in modifying excessive micturition in a 23-year-old female who had given up a promising career as a dancer because of her difficulty. False feedback of bladder pressure was presented concurrently with increased amounts of fluid in the bladder. She soon learned to tolerate increased levels, and the frequent urge abated. No difficulty was reported during the 15-month followup.

Hemodialysis. Patients suffering from renal failure require a "cleansing" of the blood. This is accomplished by a hemodialyzer (artificial kidney), and the process is called *hemodialysis.* Katz (1974) describes the treatment of a patient requiring hemodialysis who became phobic to the procedure during the first administration. One lengthy session of systematic desensitization caused remission of the phobia. To assure that it would not return, additional operant procedures were employed. In this case the phobic response developed because hemodialysis was administered by a student technician who caused irregularities to occur. When dialysis was begun again, initially only experienced personnel administered the treatment, while later, an inexperienced technician was paired with an experienced one. Other technicians who would eventually participate in the treatment were faded in during the early sessions. In addition, the patient was given a detailed explanation of hemodialysis, along with praise and attention for calm behavior. Other medical phobias (Freeman, Roy, and Hemmick 1974; Nash 1971; Nimmer and Kapp 1974; Rachman 1959; Turnage and Logan 1974) have been treated in a similar manner.

A final note

The behavioral studies discussed in this section represent the majority of those in the psychological and medical literature. Other reviews of behavior modification in medical practice are available (Chesser and Meyer 1970; Katz and Zlutnick 1974; Price 1974) and offer a slightly different perspective.

Patient self-management through behavioral technology

Many of the studies described in this chapter give the patient a larger role in the management of his own health care. The impetus for self-control procedures has come from the patients' rights movement, the increased availability of behavioral technology allowing for self-monitoring and measuring, and the recognition that the patient can play a significant role in the health care mix. Work on patient self-control (Goldiamond 1973) is reported in several areas.

Self-medication

Pharmacology has made great gains in the past several years. A wide variety of patients suffering from chronic illnesses can now live normal lives through regulatory medications. Unfortunately, one continuing difficulty is the failure of patients to take prescribed drugs. To help alleviate this problem, Azrin and Powell (1969) constructed a pill delivery device which is small enough to be carried in a pocket or purse. It sounds an alarm whenever a pill is to be taken. Turning the alarm off causes the device to automatically deliver a pill into the patient's hand. In tests on nonpatients using inert pills, the subjects more regularly took their "medication" with this device than when using a mere alarm, or simply having a container of pills. Others (Parrino, George, and Daniels 1971) have described procedures for decreasing pill-taking behavior when patients become unnecessarily dependent on medication.

Self-prevention

Patients with paraplegia (paralysis of the lower limbs) develop decubitus ulcers if they sit in the wheelchair for too long without doing push-ups. In order to prevent these sores from developing on the buttocks, Fordyce (1968) produced an ingenious electromechanical device that sounds an alarm and turns on a warning light if the patient does not arise from the wheelchair for at least 6 seconds during a 20-minute period. During testing, the device increased push-ups by one patient from 2.5 per hour to 5 or 6 per hour. Malament, Dunn, and Davis (in press) have eleborated on this technique.

Other mechanical devices worn beneath the clothing and providing either audio (Azrin, Rubin, O'Brien, Aylion, and Roll 1968) or vibrotactile (O'Brien and Azrin 1970) feedback have been designed to correct rounding of the back and slouching. Tests with experimental patients show that the devices are effective in promoting correct posture. These devices hold promise for helping patients prevent health problems, or for modifying the course of rehabilitation.

Behavioral self-examination for health professionals

The health sciences are currently undergoing vast changes in locus of control, as more responsibilities are diversified from single practitioners to multiphasic treatment teams. Innovative techniques are being integrated into the traditional sets of procedures and policies. Among the innovations is behavior modification as it applies to the behavior of health practitioners.

Despite the volume of applications of behavior management to the somatic systems, behavioral principles are taught in few medical schools and then typically in elective courses (Brady 1973). Few physicians have employed behavioral interventions. The core of studies reviewed in this chapter represent the efforts of psychologists, nurses, and physical therapists. Physicians have yet to look at their own behavior from an environmental contingency perspective, whereas other health professionals have engaged in such analysis.

Measurement and monitoring

Alterations in health care interventions are based upon clinical judgment, patient self-reports, and a variety of physiological and somatic measurements. As Goldstein (1974) has noted, except with hospitalized patients, such measurements are made on an intermittent basis, usually in the physician's office, an environment vastly different from the one in which the patient lives his life. Goldstein and his coworkers (Goldstein, Stein, and Smolen 1974) have devised and tested a system that attempts to provide daily feedback of medical measurements from the natural environment. Patients are provided with written forms and instructions to allow daily recording of physical activities, medical indicators such as heart and pulse rate, social behaviors, and diet. The patients contact the hospital once every 2 weeks and the data are fed directly into a computer, allowing the physician to receive a readout of his patient's daily behavior profile. Feedback to the patient is then given in the form of instructions to increase, decrease, or maintain the current rate of these behaviors. In the preliminary test of the system, most patients moved their behaviors in the recommended and healthful direction.

Automated health care for ambulatory patients seems prudent when we hear Goldstein (in Hilts 1974) describe the contemporary delivery system.

> There are 1,440 minutes in a day, times thirty days. That's 43,200 minutes. The doc sees him for twenty of those minutes, and has to make an estimate about the rest. The doc gives him advice when he leaves, about five to eight seconds of advice for each visit. That's supposed to last for a month. We've determined that the advice lasts about twenty minutes. No effect after that. (p. 161)

The professional duties and responsibilities of nursing personnel have increased considerably during the last several decades. The use of behavioral principles has grown with the increase in independence of nurses. The *Index to Nursing Literature* provides an extensive bibliography of publications in which nursing personnel have employed behavior modification procedures. The initial studies described the basic principles and methods of operant techniques as they might apply to nursing tasks (Aiken 1970; Ayllon and Michael 1959; Peterson 1967; Whitney 1966b). Later, book-length publications (Berni and Fordyce 1973; LeBow 1973) extended the range of principles discussed, while recent papers provide the rationale for the use of behavior management in health care settings (O'Neil 1974a). Detailed specialized applications are accumulating in mental retardation nursing (Whitney 1966a; Whitney and Barnard 1966), public health nursing (Barnes, Wootten, and Wood 1972), psychiatric nursing (Darden 1965; Layton 1966), and pediatric nursing (Berni, Dressler, and Baxter 1971; Coyne, Peterson, and Peterson 1968; O'Neil 1974b).

Nurses have not only taught their patients behavioral control, they have applied these techniques to themselves. Mikulic (1971) conducted an observation of nursing behavior in an extended care facility to determine whether nurses reinforced dependent patient behaviors (patients asking others to do things for them) or independent patient behaviors (doing things for themselves). She found that nursing personnel more consistently provided attention and praise for dependent behaviors. Although the staff unintentionally reinforced dependent behaviors, their own behavior could easily be altered through a behavior management program.

A study at the University of North Carolina (Melton 1973) found that student nurses who received assertive and sensitivity training were more likely to report, question, and refuse a doctor's order prescribing an overdose than were nursing students who had received no such training or had received training emphasizing communication skills.

Emerging themes in behavioral health care

The studies and applications reviewed in this chapter suggest a number of emerging themes as health personnel make use of behavior modification principles and as health care systems and problems are further analyzed. First, there is a strong tendency to teach the techniques of behavior management to patients rather than to apply the procedures *on* patients. Self-control and management through behavior analysis could easily serve among the key terms with which to index many of the articles reviewed in this chapter. Certainly the work of Goldiamond, and that of Fordyce and Fowler, as well as the biofeedback literature illustrate this theme more clearly than most applications. Continued development of patient self-control in health care seems a worthy goal.

Second, a team approach emerges as a theme in behavior management in health care. When behavioral, surgical, and pharmacological intervention combine to heal patients, people from various professional and scientific fields are called upon. Psychologist, nursing personnel, physician, physical therapist, occupational specialist, and social worker provide a joint effort at modifying the patient's internal as well as external environment. The patient himself, to the extent that self-recording and control techniques are taught and implemented, becomes part of the health care team, while remaining its focus of attention.

Third, as O'Neil (1972) has emphasized, there is obviously a need for increased quantification and systematic evaluation of behavioral procedures as they apply to medical and health problems. Most of the studies cited are in fact merely case reports, lacking the methodology appropriate for direct assessment of the experimental treatment effects. True, in most instances the patients improved, but the specific contingencies that led to improvement cannot be clearly determined. The work of Fordyce and Fowler in pain, O'Neil in nursing, and Lang and Melamed on emesis, as well as Blanchard and Young's review of biofeedback illustrate the direction in which the field should move.

A fourth important theme concerns the health system itself. The examples of behavior management in health care contained in this chapter are for the most part reports of presenting problems of individual patients who had not responded to earlier kinds of medical intervention. This indicates the manner in which behavior analysis has evolved historically: first being used with clients for whom other kinds of procedures had not proved effective, later applied to the management of a wider range of patients, and finally to the delivery system itself. Only in the work of Goldiamond (1974) and Goldstein, Stein, and Smolen (1974) do we find a concern for the complexity of current health care systems. Hospitals, rehabilitative facilities, physicians and nurses, families and friends, drug companies, federal and state governments, psychologists and social workers, administrators and boards of trustees, and of course patients, are only a partial list of the persons and structures that comprise the health care system in the United States. Behavior analysts need to devote some attention to the complex contingencies operating in this system as a whole.

A final theme worthy of discussion is preventive medicine and health care. The instances of behavioral intervention described in the preceding pages have related primarily to patients with chronic disorders or acute illnesses. Behavioral principles could be applied to promote health or prevent disease. One could intervene with patients who have selected disorders to prevent development of the chronic aspects of the disease. Acute asthmatic patients can come under environmental contingencies in rapid order and acquire a chronic condition. By preventing environmental reinforcement, one might alleviate chronic conditions before they can escalate into serious disabilities. In addition, as Boyer (1974) has suggested, in cases where clear behavior patterns are associated with the development of illness (for example, cardiovascular disease in adults), behavioral technology might be used in health education to teach children behaviors incompatible with the disease process (exercise, rational dietary habits, relaxation and satisfaction with a moderate rate of output). Prevention might also take the form of preparation. For example, women might be desensitized to reduce the pain and anxiety associated with childbirth (Kondas and Scetnicka 1972).

The future

The application of behavior analysis to the problems of health care is a neophyte endeavor. Ten years ago there were no examples. While the future will certainly hold near-miraculous advances in surgery, pharmacology, and medical procedures, it is not equally clear to what degree behavior modification will assist in health care. The principles exemplified in this chapter have thousands of hours of experimental and clinical support. Their use in health care and in specific medical disorders represents only a few hundred hours of application, most of them in nonreplicated case studies. However, few other areas of applied behavior analysis offer both the need and the excitement often associated with the medical and nursing sciences. Can behavioral procedures keep a diabetic on his diet? How might patients be taught self-management of medication? Will hypertension ever be controlled by biofeedback in the natural environment?

What the future holds is uncertain. What it requires is clear. "What we need are procedures that individuals can learn and adapt for themselves, so as to analyze and control the contingencies governing their own behavior" (Goldiamond 1973, p. 102).

Behavioral principles and experimental communities

L. Keith Miller
University of Kansas

16

In Walden II, *B. F. Skinner describes a fictional community, organized on the basis of principles of operant conditioning. At the University of Kansas, L. Keith Miller has made such a community a reality. While the details differ substantially from* Walden II, *the University of Kansas Experimental Living Project is a community based on operant principles, and one which has taken an empirical approach to self-evaluation. In this chapter Miller outlines how the community operates to solve three basic problems of group living: worksharing, leadership, and self-government. He describes how the University of Kansas students use a systematic and scientific approach to problems in these areas. The major focus of community psychology has been on the prevention of behavior disorders; the program Miller describes represents an alternative approach to this goal.*
The principles of behavior change have been employed in other community settings. Systematic evaluation of community intervention has occurred in such diverse areas as ecology, industry, bus ridership, noise reduction, and race relations (see Kazdin 1975a; Meyers, Craighead, and Meyers, 1974). These community intervention programs have been both preventive and rehabilitative in nature. The empirical approach of methodological behaviorism appears well suited to assess the utility of community intervention programs.

The story of experimental living arrangements goes back to the dawn of written history. Many city-states in the ancient world were based on constitutions drawn up by philosophers (Morgan 1957). Since that time such diverse proposals for experimental living arrangements as Sir Thomas More's *Utopia* and Skinner's *Walden II* (1948) have appeared. Records exist for at least 150 utopian community experiments in nineteenth-century America (Kanter 1972).

The commune movement in the United States provides a more recent example of experimental living arrangements. Estimates suggest that there may have been as many as 10,000 communal experiments in the period 1964 to 1974 (Haughey 1971; Jones 1973; Otto 1971; Walker 1971). A recent Yankelovich poll found that 40 percent of all college students would like to live in a commune (Velie 1973). Although middle-class families are not actively experimenting with group living arrangements, it is clear that experimentation with living arrangements is a mass phenomenon in contemporary America, at least among the young.

Evidence suggests that most such experiments with communal living end in the dissolution of the group (e.g., Gardner 1973; Hedgepeth 1971), often within as short a time as 2 to 4 months (Speck 1972). There are undoubtedly many reasons for the failure of such groups. It has been argued that the failure to share the common work, particularly household chores, may be the single most critical factor (Feallock and Miller 1974). However, problems with leadership, problem solving, and interpersonal interaction are also of prime importance. Any experimental living arrangement will undoubtedly have to solve these four problems in order to survive, let alone succeed.

Can a science of behavior help solve the problems of experimental communities?

B. F. Skinner has frequently written about the possibility that the behavioral principles discovered by operant psychology could be used to produce a successful experimental community. In 1948, Skinner published *Walden II,* a novel describing what a small community based on behavioral engineering might be like. As he described it, people would lead "the good life." The social environment would be arranged so that discord between people would be eliminated, so that work would be reduced to 4 hours a day, and so that marital problems would not occur. Such a community would teach its young by using behavioral principles with the result that they would have superior intellectual abilities, more manual skills, and an ability to control anxiety and other disabling psychological problems. Such a community would be devoted to the arts and to a wide variety of pleasant social interactions among its members. All of these outcomes would be achieved through the use of positive reinforcement. People would be consistently reinforced for desirable behaviors. By the proper use of reinforcement, punishment would be rendered unnecessary. In short, Skinner's message was that the use of behavioral principles would produce a far better and more positive world in which to live.

Since the publication of *Walden II,* Skinner has broadened his assertion. In *Beyond Freedom and Dignity* (1971), he states that behavioral principles could be used to determine values. Thus, he is asserting that behavioral principles can be used not only to engineer social outcomes that the members of a group value but also to determine which are the best values. To oversimplify, he suggests that a value is nothing more than a verbal statement that contains a prediction about what will be reinforcing. If a person believes that it is good to live by the golden rule, this can be translated into a prediction that living according to the golden rule will be reinforcing. This value could be studied scientifically by observing the person as he lives according to the golden rule. The person, or an outside observer, could determine whether living in that way was actually reinforcing. If so, then living according to the golden rule would be a functional value. If not, it would be a dysfunctional value. By means of the same approach, the values of a community or society could also be examined. Are they values that lead to sufficient reinforcement for the members so that the society or community survives? If so, they are functional values; if not, they are dysfunctional values. Thus Skinner demonstrates that values are an aspect of human behavior that is amenable to scientific analysis.

Skinner's view might be summarized in the following way. Everything that human beings do is behavior. All behavior is subject to natural laws. Operant psychology has discovered many basic laws of behavior. Therefore, these laws of behavior can be used to produce "the good life" within a rational society based on these laws.

Skinner's views have produced violent reactions from his critics. An early reaction was that *Walden II* was nothing more than "the skin on baloney!" Other reactions have been more thoughtful. Reactions to *Beyond Freedom and Dignity* have suggested that a society based on Skinner's behavioral principles would be similar to a Nazi concentration camp (Chomsky 1973). Some reactions have included visions of Orwell's *1984.* It has been feared that a planned society in which behavioral control would be used to condition people into acceptance of the *status quo* would arise. These are fears and reactions that any socially conscious person could legitimately have in the face of proposals for a new society based on behavioral control.

It is my conclusion that both Skinner and his critics may be engaging in the wrong behavior. Broad philosophical speculations of the sort in which both sides have engaged tend to generate a great deal of heat but little light. Such dialogues are only loosely based on fact. They are guesses as to what would happen if such a society were, indeed, created. But the guesses are really wild guesses; no one knows what such a society would be like. Therefore, if such dialogues continue, they are likely to end up in a childish shouting match: "Yes, it does!" "No, it doesn't!!" "Yes, it does!!!"

An alternative approach would be to establish a small community of consenting individuals that is based on behavioral principles. If this community were run completely in terms of behavioral principles and their appropriate application, then behaviorists and critics alike could examine the outcome and evaluate it. The need for polemics could disappear under the "cool wind" of scientific analysis.

Several attempts have been made to do just that. In 1966, a group of behaviorists from across the country met in Waldenwood, Michigan, to discuss the establishment of an experimental community based on behavioral principles (Veysey 1973). At least six such communities were established (Roberts 1971). One of them consisted of four to eight people in an urban setting; this experiment failed rather quickly (Israel 1971). But perhaps the most extensive test is a small community in Virginia named Twin Oaks. This community has existed since 1967. Hence, it is one of the most long-lived experimental communities in the country. A recent description of it makes it sound quite human and positive—not at all like the manipulative, totalitarian community that many critics have imagined (Kincaid 1973).

Unfortunately, the Twin Oaks community may be regarded by many as less than a definitive exploration of the implications of behaviorism for the design of an ideal community. It was not founded, and is not run, by operant psychologists. It has not been in the mainstream of the development of behavior modification procedures, that is, applying behavioral principles to the solution of practical problems. And it has not been subjected to the type of scientific experimentation that has come to be considered an essential part of behaviorism. Thus, the critic might, with considerable justification, assert that Twin Oaks is behavioral only superficially, not definitively. Thus, it may not be a valid test of the use of behavioral principles to organize an ideal community.

Fortunately, there is now an experimental community that is definitively behavioral, namely, the University of Kansas Experimental Living Project, which has been in existence since January 1972. It is a 30-member group-living project at the University of Kansas. It is located in a large frame house in Lawrence, Kansas, and its membership consists of male and female students. It was initiated by an operant psychologist and it has been designed in terms of basic behavioral principles. Furthermore, most members of the group have been taught the use of the basic principles of behaviorism. Thus, it is clearly a behaviorally designed community.

This community is designed to solve three basic problems of group living. These problems were identified by reading descriptions of communes, by numerous interviews with people who have lived in communes, and by interpreting our experience in our own community. The information gained was then analyzed from a behavioral point of view, in an attempt to understand the significance of the basic problems and to deduce behavioral solutions to the problems. These three basic problems involve worksharing, leadership, and self-government.

First, the community must be able to provide certain basic necessities of life in order to survive. The exact list of necessities will vary from group to group, but they would ordinarily include shelter, food, and cleanliness. I will argue that equal sharing of the work is an important value because otherwise there would be interpersonal discord, particularly between the workers and the nonworkers.

Second, the community must develop leadership capable of organizing the work and maintaining the community. I will argue that an egalitarian sharing of leadership is important because otherwise leaders would gradually exercise their differential power for their own advantage, thereby creating a corrupt system that would no longer be reinforcing to many of its members.

Third, the community must develop a stable system of self-government by means of which decisions are made democratically. The decisions must solve the problems of the group realistically. I will argue that teaching community members to make governing decisions on the basis of behavioral principles will permit an evaluation of whether decisions based on behavioral principles produce a community that is effectively run, and also one that people will voluntarily choose to live in.

The University of Kansas Experimental Living Project

The Experimental Living Project was founded in the summer of 1969. Since January 1972 it has operated as a strictly behavioral research project on experimental living. The Project owns a large frame house in Lawrence, Kansas; a small community of 30 University of Kansas students occupy the house. A private bedroom-study is provided for each student. In addition to these private areas, there are a variety of shared areas including a lounge, an institutional kitchen in which a common evening meal is prepared, a small kitchen for other meals and snacks, a shop, a game room, and a dining room–meeting room. Costs of running the facility (such as taxes, utilities, food, and mortgage payments) are paid entirely out of rental payments made by each member. Thus, the community is financially self-supporting.

The student members of the community are selected on a first come, first served basis. They are required to read a description of how the community is organized before they are permitted to join. However, anyone who wishes to join after reading the description, and who signs a contract and pays the initial fees, is permitted to join if there is a private room available. There is no selection process. This is reflected in the broad diversity of majors, including Chinese, design, education, sociology, engineering, and psychology. There is no apparent "personality type" choosing to live there. The members of the community seem to represent a cross-section of the student population.

The organization of the community will be described in the following three sections. Each section contains two parts. The first part provides a theoretical behavioral analysis of a basic problem. The second part describes a system based on behavior modification principles which solves that problem.

The first section deals with the problem of getting community members to share the common work so that everyone contributes a portion. The second section deals with the problem of ensuring that the group generates sufficient leadership to organize the community while maintaining an equality of power and influence among all members. The third section deals with the problem of creating a completely democratic system of self-government based on the principles of behaviorism. A fourth section provides an overview of the system and indicates future directions.

The worksharing system

Conceptual analysis

The most fundamental problem of group living is probably that of getting group members to share equitably in the common work. All group living creates the need for such jobs as sweeping, washing dishes, cooking, cleaning toilets, and making physical repairs to the house. However, the orientation of many commune enthusiasts, which emphasizes lack of structure, anarchistic ideology, and "freedom," suggests that the tendency to do such work may break down rather rapidly. Accounts of communal living make frequent reference to the breakdown in the sharing of work (e.g., Lanes 1971).

An analysis of worksharing from the point of view of operant psychology suggests a number of possible reasons for the importance of household worksharing. It seems likely that the services delivered by such work are reinforcing to most members of communes, even though they might not admit it. The reinforcing nature of such services is suggested by the fact that commune members are generally from middle-class families where such services, and more, are taken for granted. It is more strongly suggested by the fact that some communes fail even when there is little evidence of other problems. It may be supposed that members find group living less reinforcing if such crucial services are not available.

At least three behavioral principles point to negative consequences when group members fail to share the basic work. These are the principles of aggression, escape, and counterpunishment. All of these principles indicate that a gradual reduction in household work done would lead to a great increase in negative interpersonal behaviors among group members.

It is well known that aggressive responses increase when the delivery of a reinforcer is terminated (Azrin, Hutchinson, and Hake 1966; Kelly and Hake 1970). Thus, when such reinforcers as food, cleanliness, and comfort are reduced because people are no longer doing their share of the work, operant psychology would predict an increase in interpersonal aggression—quite likely in the form of negative verbal behavior.

It is well known that when aversive stimulation is directed at a person who is not doing his or her share of the work, the person will tend to escape from it by doing that task. Thus, if members of the group complain, gripe, and nag at someone who is not doing his or her share of the work, this may lead to an increase in that member's work behaviors. Since such an increase in work is likely to reinforce the nagging, complaining, and griping, these negative behaviors would increase, thus producing another source of increased negative verbal behavior.

It is well known that when aversive stimulation is directed at someone who is "hassling" another person, it will tend to punish the hassling behavior. Thus, if a worker starts to hassle a nonworker by nagging about doing a job, the nonworker (instead of doing the work as in the previous situation) may be able to punish that nagging effectively enough to stop it. Clearly, if the punishment works and the nagging decreases, this would reinforce the nonworker to use more punishment in the future. The use of such punishment will probably involve negative verbal behavior.

The dynamics of the worksharing situation suggest, then, that the rate of negative interpersonal behaviors will probably increase as a result of a decrease in the amount of household work. The resulting decrease in reinforcing services will probably lead directly to aggressive behaviors and indirectly to the perpetuation of both escape and punishment situations that may greatly increase the amount of negative behaviors.

Behavioral solution

The importance of worksharing is easily seen. What can be done to promote cooperative worksharing behavior? The typical behavior analysis approach to such a question is: define the desired behavior, decide how to observe it, and provide consequences capable of maintaining it. This is exactly what was done in the Experimental Living Project.

The desired behavior was defined by listing the basic jobs that were desired and needed by the group. Approximately 100 jobs were decided upon in this way. Each job was then defined in terms of the desired outcomes expected from the job. This involved listing between 4 and 100 outcomes for each job.

These outcomes were then observed by training members of the house to conduct a thorough inspection of the house once a day between 8:00 and 9:00 in the evening. An observer checks between 500 and 700 separate outcomes throughout the house on each inspection. This procedure is a simple way to find out if the desired jobs were done.

Finally, a consequences system was developed. This system was based on the observation that if the members of the group did the basic household chores, it would not be necessary to hire a maid, a cook, a janitor, or a handyman. Savings created by eliminating the need to hire such outsiders could be passed on to the group members. The idea involved setting a rent figure sufficiently high to permit the group to hire such outsiders, and then giving each member who did his or her share of the work a rent reduction. The total size of the rent reduction for the entire group was equal to the cost of hiring outside help. The remaining rent that was collected was set at an amount sufficient to pay all basic expenses of the house.

In practice, the average monthly room and board payment before rent reduction is about $105. Each member who has done his or her share of the work for the month is granted a $40 rent reduction so that the actual rent after reduction is $65.

A credit system is utilized to provide immediate consequences for each person's worksharing behavior and to provide a basis for determining whether each has done his or her share of the work. Each job is assigned a credit value based on a rate of 15 credits per hour. Full credit is given if a member does the job correctly; if not, only partial credit is given. Each member must earn 100 credits per week in order to be awarded the full rent reduction. For every credit less than that, 10 cents is eliminated from the rent reduction. The credit system provides an easily understood link between work performance and the rent reduction that is earned.

The system works in the following way: On Thursday night, a member of the house, the credit recorder, posts a list of all 100 jobs. People sign up for the jobs that they want to do for the next week. Another person, the inspector, checks the outcomes of all jobs each day during the week to determine how well the jobs have been done. At the end of the week, the credit recorder checks the sign-up sheet and the inspection results and determines how many credits each member earned during the week. This list is then posted so that everyone will know how he or she stands. At the end of the month, the posted credit earnings are delivered to the treasurer, who determines each member's rent for the coming month.

Does it work? The answer is an unqualified "Yes." An average of about 95 percent of all desired outcomes are produced each day. Thus, the house is clean and comfortably repaired, and members are well fed.

A number of experiments have been conducted to determine whether the various features of the system are really required to keep it working. During Experiment 1 it was found that when inspections were eliminated, work decreased to below 60 percent of the desired outcomes (see Figure 16-1). During Experiment 2, when credits were not

Figure 16-1 Average percentage of cleaning done during the credits-noncontingent-upon-inspection and the credits-contingent-upon-inspection conditions in Experiment 1

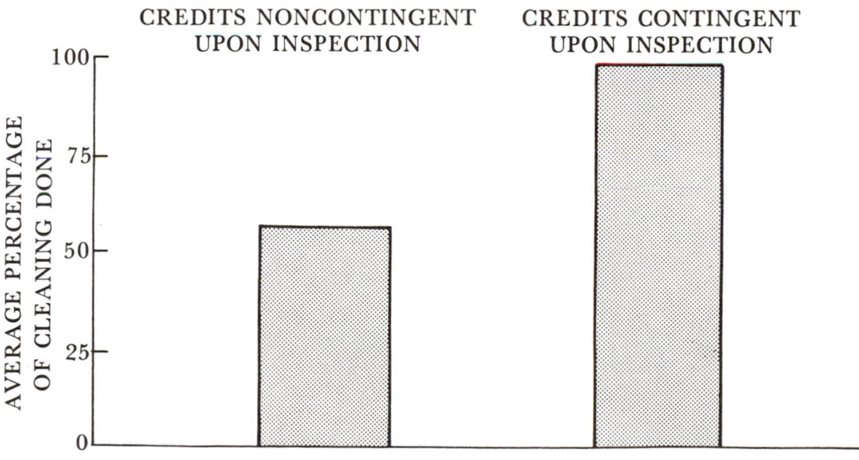

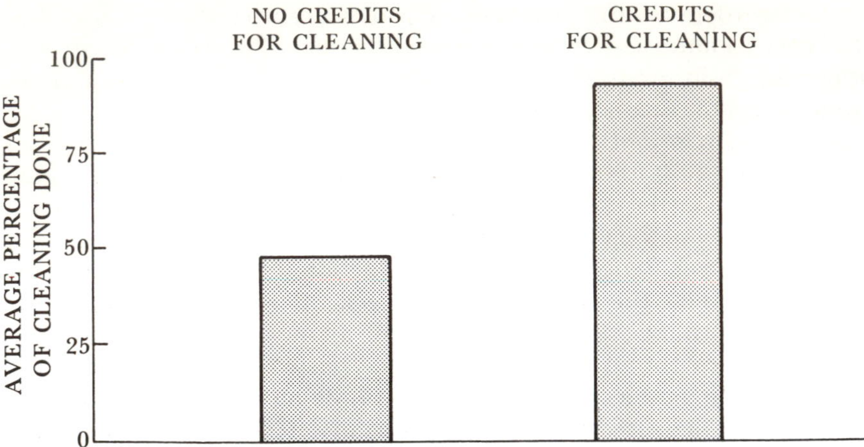

Figure 16-2 Average percentage of cleaning done during the no-credits-for-cleaning and the credits-for-cleaning conditions in Experiment 2

awarded for work, work decreased to less than 50 percent of the desired outcomes (see Figure 16-2). During Experiment 3, when rent reductions were eliminated, work decreased to less than 80 percent of the desired outcomes (see Figure 16-3). Thus, there is strong evidence that all of the basic features of the system are necessary to keep it functioning properly (Miller, Lies, Paterson, and Feallock, in press).

Figure 16-3 Average percentage of cleaning done during noncontingent rent reduction and contingent rent reduction in Experiment 3

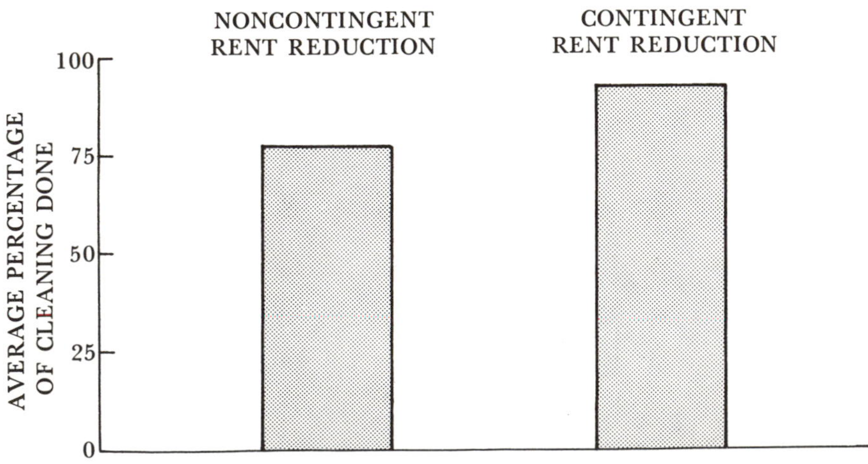

The coordinating system

Conceptual analysis

The coordinating system is concerned with providing the community with reasonable leadership by its members. It involves roles that are necessary for the smooth functioning of the community. This includes handling and recording financial transactions, managing the credit system, inspecting the work of others, and coordinating the work of others. These are the jobs that someone must do if the more routine day-to-day jobs of the worksharing system are to run smoothly.

Coordinating jobs are those that frequently would be handled by an emergent group leader. In fact, it might be speculated that those communes that have survived are ones in which group leaders emerged and helped organize some form of a worksharing system. Many observers of the commune scene have suggested that the days of the unorganized "anarchistic" or "hip" communes are through and that they have been replaced by a variety of communal styles, all of which are organized around a leader (Gardner 1973). The price of success for experimental communities seems to be the acceptance of some form of leadership (Roberts 1971). Thus, it seems that developing leadership is one of the most important tasks for any experimental community.

Unfortunately, leadership may well be abused so that an experimental community becomes simply another kind of dictatorial society. Since a major attraction of experimental communities is the opportunity to develop a fully democratic, leaderless group (Mellville 1972), any such abuses would be self-defeating. At least three features of leadership jobs create a tendency for the leader to accumulate too much power.

First, since such jobs are not routine it is difficult to hold a leader strictly accountable for doing the job in the prescribed way. In fact, the nature of the job is often left undefined. Inspection similar to that used in the worksharing system could not be adapted to this job. As a result, abuses of the job frequently will not be observed for a long period and thus corrective procedures are not likely to be introduced.

Second, a leadership job usually involves responsibility for valued objects such as money or food, or it involves responsibility for the behavior of other individuals. The person holding the job can, therefore, use these items to do "favors" for other group members. The treasurer, for example, can permit an individual member to pay rent late with very little chance of being detected. Or the inspector can record that a person has done a job correctly when he or she did not do it at all. These favors can, of course, be used as reinforcers. The leader can use them to reinforce other group members when they engage in behavior that is desired. Such behavior can involve voting for the person on important issues, doing favors for the person in return, and even helping that person corrupt the system. One can easily construct a hypothetical situation in which a leader begins by using power to reinforce another member for a relatively simple and innocuous task. If that is reinforcing to the leader, then one would expect him or her to reinforce more and more important tasks, perhaps eventually involving a total corruption of the system to the leader's own ends. The Watergate scandal is a powerful reminder of this possibility. In any event, a leader's responsibility over valued objects and the behavior of others makes corruption a real danger for any system of leadership.

Third, leadership jobs usually involve the use of rare skills not possessed by many in the community. Keeping books involves a combination of bookkeeping skills, precision, and punctuality that are not widespread. An important implication of this is that there may not be any other members of the community who are willing and able to fill any specific leadership position. This gives the occupant of such a position a great deal of bargaining power. For if he or she resigns the job (or is kicked out), the group may not have anyone else to do the job. Threats such as "Well, if you don't like how I'm doing the job, I'll resign" often permit such a person to blackmail the group into accepting his or her decisions or overlooking corruption of the office.

Taken together, these three features of leadership jobs make corruption of the office quite likely. First, the power inherent in such positions to do favors for other individuals means that the occupant can reinforce behavior that is compliant with his or her desires. Second, the fact that persons in such jobs are not easily held accountable means that any serious subversion of the office will not be quickly discovered. Third, the lack of other individuals with the necessary skills for the job means that even if subversion of the office is discovered, the group may not easily be able to do anything about it. All three of these features suggest that a situation must become quite desperate before a group would be willing to invest the time and energy necessary to correct the situation. And it may be too late at that point.

Behavioral solution

A coordinating system has been designed using behavioral technology to solve these problems. This system has at least six important characteristics, including: (1) specific job definitions, (2) auditing of job performance, (3) consequences, (4) training programs for each job, (5) limited term, and (6) a limit on the number of credits that can be earned as a coordinator. An explanation of each of these characteristics follows.

1. The coordinating jobs are defined in terms of the desired outcomes for each job. Thus, the treasurer's job includes balancing the

books by the end of the month, making rent collection postings at three critical dates during the month, forwarding all proof of financial transactions to the comptroller within 24 hours, and the like. This job definition permits every member to understand exactly the duties of any position in the community and the correct and incorrect way of doing the job.

2. An auditor is charged with observing the desired outcomes of the coordinator's performance at specific times and dates. This permits a determination of whether a coordinator is accomplishing those outcomes with which he or she is charged in the way specified by the rest of the community. It thus permits rapid detection of any deviations from the desired conduct of the job.

3. Each coordinator is paid a salary that can amount to as much as 50 credits per week (or half of what is required for a rent reduction). Credits are deducted for any outcomes that are not accomplished satisfactorily. Monetary fines are given to office holders who do not correctly achieve certain critical outcomes. Thus, coordinators are reinforced for doing their job correctly and penalized for doing it incorrectly.

4. Carefully designed training programs have been developed for all of the coordinating positions. The community can train many individuals for each job so that there is always a pool of skilled persons ready to assume any of the jobs. In fact, community members are paid simply to undertake the training. This means that any particular person holding the job cannot blackmail the rest of the community into condoning undesirable actions by threatening to resign; there are always others ready to take on the job. It also means that there are many other members of the community who understand the job well enough to evaluate the performance of the job holder; they can give support when the job holder is right and point out errors when he or she is wrong. The development of detailed training programs is a crucial element in creating a leadership system that is responsive to the needs and desires of the community.

5. A contract is signed by the job holder specifying that this term is limited to 5 months. At the end of that time another member must assume the job. This constant rotation of personnel in the leadership positions means that a person cannot gradually learn subtle and unanticipated ways to subvert the office. By the time that any one member could understand the job that well, that member is long gone. This constant rotation reduces the probability of subtle manipulations of the leadership jobs.

6. The rules of the group prohibit a member from holding more than one leadership position or from earning more than half of his or her credits from such a position. This means that every leader in the

community also must do a major share of the routine jobs of the house. Thus, a leader is kept in constant contact with the effect of decisions made as a leader. Furthermore, a leader is thus restricted from gradually accumulating the power of several leadership positions. In the Experimental Living Project the 10 leadership positions are distributed among 10 of the 30 community members.

A key component in the coordinating system has been the development of an effective training procedure for such complex jobs. The job is broken down into *subtasks* and then several widely used behavioral procedures are applied. The training procedure involves three parts: a behavioral specification, programmed situational examples, and behavioral rehearsal.

The subtasks are selected so that they represent a specifiable part of the overall job that can be taught as a unit. For the treasurer's job, for example, one subtask might involve teaching people how to close the books at the end of the month. An instructional package is developed for that one aspect of the job. That package, along with perhaps 15 other packages for other aspects of the job, make up the training manual for the treasurer's job.

The first part of each package involves specifying the steps that the person must undertake to do that subtask. These steps are sufficiently detailed for the trainee to know exactly what is required. A short quiz is given to ensure that the trainee recalls all the steps.

The second part of each package involves presenting the trainee with a series of problems similar to what would be encountered on the job, but in which many hints are programmed to help him or her do the job correctly. By dealing with many problems, the trainee learns how to apply the steps described in the first part of the package. Since hints are provided (many for the first problems and fewer for the later problems), the trainee is assisted in gradually learning the skill with a minimum of setbacks along the way.

The third part of each package involves presenting the trainee with a simulated real-life situation. A person training for the treasurer's job might be given a set of pages similar to those that he or she would have at the end of the month. The person is then asked to go through the steps required to close the books. This part of the program presents the trainee with a total problem and no hints. He or she can practice the steps learned in the second part. If the programming in the first and second parts is correct, the trainee should emerge from this rehearsal with the skills necessary for the job of treasurer.

If these training packages are carefully designed, many people with a wide variety of skill levels can effectively be taught quite complex skills. Thus, this method opens up and democratizes many of the skills associated with leadership in a group living situation. Data are now being gathered to evaluate the coordinating system.

The governance system

Conceptual analysis

Decision making is a major problem in any group setting. Frequently group leaders are most active in making decisions. However, with a diffused system of leadership designed along the lines of the coordinating system, there are no individual leaders within the community. Furthermore, within the goal of an egalitarian community, it is necessary that everyone in the group share equally in the decision-making process. For this reason we have attempted to design an egalitarian system of self-governance.

A behavioral analysis of self-government would reveal that governing behavior involves members of the group talking to one another about group problems. Most of the talking occurs in formal governmental meetings. In such meetings problems are raised. These problems might involve a job not getting done properly as a result of some small, incorrectly designed aspect of the worksharing system. They might involve a coordinator who is making decisions with which others disagree. Or they might involve a more personal problem, such as a fellow member making too much noise to permit sleeping or studying. Most problems brought up and discussed in a self-government meeting are problems with someone's behavior. Either an undesirable behavior is occurring or a desirable behavior is not occurring. Self-government involves discussing such behavioral problems and deciding what to do about them.

Self-government is also greatly influenced by informal discussions of problems outside of self-government meetings. These discussions raise the same kind of issues and frequently involve specifying possible solutions to them. In any formal meeting it is often true that many members have already discussed a problem and arrived at a decision that will strongly influence the formal governmental decision. Both the informal and the formal discussion of behavioral problems should be regarded as a part of the self-government process.

A behavioral analysis of self-government as it works in nonbehavioral living arrangements reveals that the talking behavior of group members involved in decision-making is influenced by the behavioral principles of reinforcement and punishment. If a person brings up something regarded as a problem, the others may agree that it is a valid problem, thereby reinforcing the person for mentioning it, or they may disagree and contend that it is not a valid problem, thereby likely punishing the person and making it less likely that he or she will mention it again. A person may suggest a solution to a problem. Again, other members of the group may reinforce or punish the suggested solution. Much of the reinforcement or punishment that occurs in this type of interaction is "valid." That is, when someone suggests a solution to a problem, others may punish him or her by making a clear argument that shows how the solution will not work. The ultimate solution is likely to be the one that at least a majority of the members of the group reinforced. Thus, the governmental process may be understood as a behavioral process.

This behavioral analysis of the governmental process suggests an immediate problem for any attempt to design a behaviorally oriented system. The past experience and learning of the members will determine what statements of others they are likely to reinforce. Since most individuals are not behaviorists, they will tend to punish, or at least ignore, suggestions that provide behavioral solutions to problems. And likewise they will tend to reinforce nonbehavioral suggestions. In fact, this tendency could easily extend to abolishing any behavioral systems, such as the worksharing or the coordinating system, that already exist. Clearly, such a tendency could quickly eliminate the behavioral aspects of the commune. In short, the conditioning of members within the broader society will cause them to favor nonbehavioral solutions to problems at the expense of behavioral solutions.

Behavioral solution

Three procedures have been developed to increase the probability that behavioral solutions will be reinforced by members of the group. At heart, the strategy is an educational one. We seek only to teach members of the community how behavioral solutions are supposed to work so that they will be better able to evaluate them fairly.

First, we provide the group with a 65-page handbook. This handbook provides a set of behaviorally based rules that define a starting point for the group. These behaviorally based rules govern the group until they decide to change them. There are chapters on the worksharing system, norms relating to such behavior as use of illegal drugs (they are banned!), and how the finances are to be handled. Every rule is explained and the reasons for it are stated clearly. Furthermore, every member is required to read the handbook prior to entering the group. As a result, the member understands exactly what he or she is joining. The approach is similar to Rousseau's "social contract." It provides all members and potential members with an understanding of how the group members are to relate to one another.

It was our assumption that if group members determined their own initial set of rules, they would most likely select nonbehavioral rules. Assuming that all experimental living groups select some set of rules for governing themselves, even if they are implicit rules, one might conjecture that the high failure rate among communes is the result of a bad set of rules. For example, our data suggest that by selecting rules that do not involve an effective worksharing system, such groups may be condemning themselves to interpersonal strife and rapid dissolution. Our goal in providing the group with a behaviorally based handbook was simply to permit the group members to *start* with a behavioral system so that they could determine whether or not they liked it.

Second, we provide a formal procedure by means of which the group can change the rules formulated in the handbook. This procedure is designed to make sure that everyone has equal access to the decision-making process. A group meeting occurs every Monday and that is the only meeting during which rule changes can be made. Most of the self-governance rules are similar to those that you would find in any democratic group. There are rules about quorums to ensure that a small group does not make rules for everyone else. There are rules about what constitutes a voting majority, and so on.

What does not appear in the formal rules are the implications of the coordinating system on the self-governance process. By setting up a system that eliminates the need for emergent leaders and severely restricts the access to power of coordinators, we reduce the probability that the democratic process within the group can be subverted by individuals with too much power. Thus, it is rare that someone would be influenced to vote by the possibility of a favor from a coordinator. This greatly enhances the equality of group members within the formally democratic system.

Third, we teach group members basic behavioral concepts and how they apply to everyday situations. Our assumption was that most members do not understand these concepts, but if they did understand them they would reinforce proposed behavioral solutions to problems that arise in the house. If such an understanding would produce such reinforcement in both formal and informal discussions of house problems, then our analysis of self-government would suggest not only that behavioral solutions would be maintained in the house to the extent that they worked, but also that they would be modified according to behavioral principles. The strategy was to provide an understanding of behavioral procedures so that members could act on them if they were convinced. It must be pointed out that there is no coercion involved. Our only goal was to provide members with an understanding of the principles so that they could freely choose to act on them. We took a strictly educational approach to the problem.

It was our assumption that in the long run members would decide to use or to discard behavioral principles according to whether they produced the effect that they wanted. Thus, if behavioral principles led to a system that did not work, was unpleasant, or was too costly, it was our assumption that this would punish the use of behavioral principles and lead to an abandonment of them. On the other hand, if such principles produced a system that did work, that was pleasant, and that was not too costly, it was our assumption that this would reinforce the use of behavioral principles and increase their use over time. The educational program is in no way a program of "brainwashing," because members can evaluate the usefulness of the program directly in terms of their everyday lives.

The overall strategy in the area of self-government involves a three-step procedure. First, the group is required to start with a behavioral system. This permits the members to directly evaluate such a system in their own living environment. Second, they are given democratic control of the system so that they can change it in any way that they wish. Third, they are provided with a thorough understanding of behavioral principles. This permits them to change the system in ways that are consistent with a behavioral approach if they freely choose to do so. Clearly, the success of such changes will determine whether they continue to use them in the long run.

The educational system by which members learn about behavioral principles is itself behavioral. The material is presented in a course taught in the community; the course uses a specially programmed textbook entitled *Principles of Everyday Behavior Analysis* (Miller 1974). The goal is to provide students with short fictional examples of everyday situations that they have never directly learned about and to have them identify correctly the basic principles illustrated by the examples. It was our assumption that if they could do that, then they could identify the behavioral principles at work in their own lives in the community. This would, of course, permit them to undertake a behavioral analysis of such situations and even to act on them in the decision-making process. A detailed explanation of the programming procedure (called concept programming) is available elsewhere (Miller and Weaver 1974). The course is taught by means of behavioral procedures. It is taught within the house, and other house members are the only teachers. It is taught within what is called a "personalized system of instruction" (Keller 1968). What this means is: all learning is done from the book; a private tutor is assigned to each student to help him or her master the material; frequent quizzes are given so that the student can evaluate his or her performance; detailed assistance in the form of written study guides is provided so that the student knows what to study; and quizzes are taken whenever the student wants to (as long as a minimum rate is maintained). Other research has shown that such a personalized system not only produces superior learning but also is liked better (McMichael and Corey 1969).

It is interesting to note that the educational system is completely a part of the overall system. Not only is it designed according to behavioral principles, but it is run by members of the community and it can be changed or eliminated by democratic vote of the full membership. While small changes have been introduced to improve the educational system, it still functions in accordance with behavioral principles to teach the membership principles of behavior.

In an effort to find out to what extent community members view the system of self-government as democratic, we asked them, "How much influence do you have in determining important aspects of the Project compared to a dormitory?" The community members rated their influence as being much more (5.8 on a scale of 7), which suggests that they view the community as being much more democratic than a dormitory.

An overview

This chapter has described three major problems confronting any group living arrangement. Each problem has been analyzed from a behavioral point of view and then a behavior modification system designed to solve that problem was described.

It was argued that creating a system in which community members share equally in the work is an important goal. If work is not shared equally, then basic needs of the group such as food, shelter, and cleanliness will not be provided for. On the assumption that food, shelter, and cleanliness are reinforcers, it was argued that their gradual elimination would lead members to aggression against one another, setting up escape contingencies through griping and reminding of nonworkers, and using punishment to stop such escape contingencies. These behavioral mechanisms will, it was argued, lead to increased strife between members until the house is no longer a pleasant place in which to live. The final outcome would be a group that does not provide for its members' basic physical needs and which does not provide a pleasant social environment. These problems have been solved through a worksharing system in which jobs are specified and inspected, and in which work completion produces a rent reduction through a credit system procedure. The evidence suggests that this system does solve the problem.

Second, it was argued that an important goal of the community is to develop a system of egalitarian leadership in which members are roughly equal in power. A leader with the usual overabundance of power is reinforced for power abuses by obtaining compliant behavior from other members. This can happen quite accidentally when a leader does a person an unauthorized favor and later realizes that the person is hence more likely to engage in behavior desired by the leader. If this is permitted, the leader will accumulate far more power than other group members and may then change the system in ways that are not reinforcing to other members. This problem has been solved through the creation of a coordinating system in which leadership jobs are carefully specified and audited, and in which the leader is reinforced for doing the job according to the wishes of the rest of the group. By creating training programs, the group is assured that many other individuals will be able to do the jobs involved in the coordinating system. The evidence suggests that this system does solve the problem.

Third, it was argued that it is an important goal of the group to develop a system of completely democratic self-government in which behaviorally oriented solutions are used. Normally, a self-government system would lead to the abandonment of behavioral systems. Our analysis suggested that self-government consists of talking among members about common problems, and that proposed solutions will be reinforced or punished by the listeners. Clearly, if behavioral solutions are consistently punished, they will be offered much less often. It is likely that the training of most people will not be behavioral prior to entering the community because the broader society has not been trained in the use of behavioral principles. The solution to this problem has been to provide a behavioral starting point for the group so that they could directly experience a behavioral system. Additionally, an educational program designed to teach behavioral concepts is run by the members of the community. The evidence suggests that this system does solve the problem.

At this point, many readers will wonder if this description of the Experimental Living Project provides *all* of the relevant information about the community. Perhaps the reader feels that if he or she could visit the community and talk with the members, he or she would find that most of the members really do not like the system, in spite of how reasonable it sounds. This suspicion is fostered by the widespread idea that behavioral engineering is by its very nature cold and mechanical —even antihumanistic. Sometimes it is, just as any other approach can sometimes be cold and mechanical.

Since the reader cannot visit the Project, our research staff has asked the members of the community the crucial question: "Overall, how much do you enjoy living here, compared to a dormitory?" The members reported enjoying living in the community considerably more, rating it an average of 5.8 on a 7-point scale. It is reasonable to conclude that the reader who could visit and talk with community members would find it to be a well-liked, warm, and supportive environment in which people share equally in the work and the power.

A peek at the future

The project that you have just read about is a self-governing community based on behavioral principles for about 30 unmarried university students. Would this same approach make sense for families? In fact, would it make sense for small communities of families? My own answer is that, with some additional procedures, it would. My guess is that such a community would represent a reversal of the trend toward isolation and alienation that is evident in our society (Miller and Lies 1974; Miller et al., in press). The additional procedures involve creation of warmer and closer relationships among members. At present we have eliminated the causes of negative interpersonal behavior through equalizing work and power. This has resulted in a much more positive community. But we have been taught most of our lives to be negative, cold, and cynical. Just living in a community for a few months cannot be expected to reverse a lifetime of experience. Thus, we are now developing a training program to teach people how to be closer to one another and how to be more positive and supportive.

In addition to this training program, it will be necessary for the Project to develop procedures to ensure that marriages are positive and supportive. Otherwise, the close proximity of a multifamily living arrangement will surely tear many marriages apart and bring jealousy and discord to the community (Miller et al., in press). Thus, some procedure to assist marriages in being mutually reinforcing must be developed. Since the methods of child care differ so much from family to family, some system governing how an adult is supposed to treat someone else's child will be necessary. The child's benefits from contact with many adults will be a major positive outcome of such a community, but only if the contacts do not end up confusing the child and making him or her feel insecure.

The development of these procedures will permit the grand experiment: Can behavioral principles be used to design communities that will permit individuals to live together in productive harmony in a warm and supportive social environment, one that treats every man, woman, and child as equal? Perhaps we will soon know the answer to that question.

The teaching-family model of group home treatment [1]

Dean L. Fixsen, Elery L. Phillips, Elaine A. Phillips, and Montrose M. Wolf
University of Kansas

17

Delinquency has presented one of the most difficult challenges to both theoretical and therapeutic efforts. Among the factors thought to contribute to delinquent behavior patterns are the following: shaping and reinforcement of aggression, inadequate problem-solving skills, the use of inconsistent and severe physical punishment by parents, inaccurate beliefs about contingencies, effects of the diagnostic label, and extensive modeling of aggression by parents, peers, and individuals in the mass media. With a phenomenon as broadly influenced as this, it may come as no surprise that treatments have varied considerably.

Early institutional programs used a variety of traditional psychotherapeutic techniques in the treatment of delinquency. Their success rates were consistently disappointing. Rates of recidivism were very high and there is some evidence that delinquent inmates actually improved *their criminal skills during their stay in the institutions. One study showed that the reward system within these institutions may favor maintenance and intensification of delinquent behavior patterns. Buehler, Patterson, and Furniss (1966) reported that the delinquent inmates were much more consistent in encouraging antisocial behavior than were the hospital staff in shaping prosocial skills. In terms of learning principles, it*

[1] This report was presented at the American Psychological Association Convention, Honolulu, Hawaii, September 1972. This research was supported by Grant #MH 20030 from the National Institute of Mental Health (Center for Studies of Crime and Delinquency) to the Bureau of Child Research and Department of Human Development, University of Kansas, Lawrence, Kansas, 66045.

appears that the delinquents within the institution were "better" behavior modifiers than the staff! With the advent of token economies, a few institutions began to develop structured contingency programs for delinquents. Burchard (1967) reported several successful applications with individual delinquents, and Cohen and his colleagues described some impressive success in improving the academic performance of delinquents (Cohen, Filipczak, Bis, Cohen, Goldiamond, and Larkin 1968). The Robert F. Kennedy Youth Center in Morgantown, West Virginia, established an elaborate system of graduated contingencies and has likewise reported some impressive success in several areas of delinquent rehabilitation. Institutional programs employing behavior modification principles have become very popular in the last half-decade, although there has been some concern about the ethical boundaries of these efforts (Schwitzgebel 1970; Kennedy in this volume).

One of the most exciting recent developments in the treatment of delinquency is the trend toward family-style homes located in the community. Although they bear some resemblance to the halfway houses used in some other areas of therapy, these homes are typically more structured and usually involve a professionally trained live-in staff. "Teaching-parents," who often have advanced training in behavior modification, help to structure the delinquent's relearning of prosocial skills. This may involve a graduated series of performances much like the "step system" described earlier in token economies. The delinquent is informed about the contingencies of the home and gradually earns more flexible and mature arrangements. This system highlights response-consequence relationships, a factor whose absence may have contributed to the youth's problem. As he demonstrates increasing responsibility, the delinquent earns more privileges and trust. He is given the freedom to play an active part in his own rehabilitation. Through graduated experiences, he learns to cope with academic, social, and personal problems in a mature and adaptive manner. The underlying philosophy in these homes, of course, emphasizes education rather than confinement. Shipping the delinquent off to a large institution may keep him off the streets—for a while—but it seldom has a significant impact on reducing his subsequent antisocial patterns. By keeping him in the community in a quasi-family environment, the family-style homes give him structured opportunities for the development of coping skills where they are needed most—in the real world.

The grandparent of behavioral "family-style" programs is Achievement Place in Lawrence, Kansas. It was established in 1967 by Elery and Elaine Phillips as an experimental project (Phillips 1968). Judging from its data, its expansion, and its imitation by subsequent workers, we must conclude that the experiment was a big success. There are now several dozen such homes in the United States and Canada, and their popularity seems to be increasing. Their success, of course, has not been unqualified, but their consistent superiority over alternative treatments suggest that Achievement Place may have charted a very promising route to follow in future research. The following chapter gives a brief description of the organization and outcome of the Achievement Place program.

Achievement Place is a community-based, family-style, behavior modification group home treatment program for delinquent youths in Lawrence, Kansas. The goals of Achievement Place are to teach the youths: (1) appropriate social skills, such as manners and introductions; (2) academic skills, such as study and homework behaviors; (3) self-help skills, such as meal preparation and personal hygiene; and (4) prevocational skills, which are thought to be necessary for them to be successful in the community. The youths who come to Achievement Place have been in legal trouble and have been court adjudicated. They are typically 12 to 16 years old, in junior high school, and about 3 to 4 years below grade level on academic achievement tests.

Description of the program

When a youth enters Achievement Place he meets the other youths in the program and is given a tour of the house. Then he is introduced to the point system that is used to help motivate the youths to learn new, appropriate behavior. Each youth uses a point card to record his behavior and the number of points he earns and loses. When a youth first enters the program his points are exchanged for privileges each day. After the youth learns the connection between earning points and earning privileges this daily point system is extended to a weekly point system in which he exchanges points for privileges only once each week. Eventually, the point system is faded to a merit system where no points are given or taken away and all privileges are free. The merit system is the last system through which a youth must progress before returning to his natural home. Most youths are on the weekly point system for most of their 9- to 12-month stay at Achievement Place. Because there are extensive opportunities to earn points, most youths earn all the privileges most of the time. Occasionally one or two youths fail to earn enough points to buy all of their privileges, and once in a while a youth earns so many points that he becomes the new "point champion."

The privileges that are available to the youths are: *Basics,* which include the use of the telephone, tools, and the yard; *Snacks* after school and before bedtime; *Television* watching; and *Hometime,* which permits youths to return to their natural homes for the weekend or to go downtown. These privileges are naturally available in Achievement Place and add nothing to the cost of the treatment program. Other privileges that can be earned are $1 to $3 of *Allowance* each week, and *Bonds,* which can be accumulated to purchase clothing or other needed items.

A typical day at Achievement Place begins when the manager wakens the boys at about half-past six. The boys wash their faces, brush their teeth, and clean their bathroom and bedrooms. The manager, who is elected by his peers (see Phillips, Wolf, and Fixsen 1973), supervises these morning chores by assigning specific cleaning tasks to his peers, monitoring the completion of these tasks, and providing point consequences for their performance. While some of the boys are cleaning their rooms and bathrooms, other boys are helping prepare breakfast.

After breakfast the boys check their appearance and pick up a daily school note (see Bailey, Wolf, and Phillips 1970) before leaving Achievement Place to attend the local public schools. Since Achievement Place is a community-based facility, the boys continue to attend the same schools they had problems with before entering the facility, and the teaching-parents work closely with the teachers and school administrators to remediate each youth's problems in school. The feedback that teachers provide is systematized by having each teacher fill out a report card for each youth each day. A teacher can quickly answer a series of questions about the youth's behavior by checking "yes" or "no" on the card. Some youths do not require daily feedback, and they carry a weekly school note to class each Monday. In either case the youths return their completed report cards to the teaching-parents, and they earn or lose points depending upon the teachers' judgment of their in-class performance.

When the boys return to Achievement Place they have their afterschool snacks before starting their homework or other point-earning activities. In the late afternoon one or two boys usually volunteer to help prepare dinner. During the meal, or just after the meal, the teaching-parents and youths hold a family conference (Fixsen, Phillips, and Wolf 1973). During the family conference the teaching-parents and the youths discuss the events of the day, evaluate the manager's performance, establish or modify rules, and decide on consequences for any rule violations that were reported to the teaching-parents. These self-government behaviors are specifically taught to the youths and they are encouraged to participate in discussions about any aspect of the program.

After the family conference the boys usually listen to records or watch television before "figuring up" their point cards for the day and going to bed at about half-past ten. This brief description of a day at Achievement Place should give you an idea of the treatment program and how it operates. A complete description can be found in *The Teach-*

ing-Family Handbook (Phillips, Phillips, Fixsen, and Wolf 1975) and *The Achievement Place Novel* (Allen, Phillips, Phillips, Fixsen, and Wolf 1972).

The main emphasis of the program is on *teaching* the youths the appropriate behaviors needed for successful participation in the community. We have found that a community-based group home that keeps the youths in daily contact with their community offers many opportunities to observe and modify deviant behaviors and to teach the youths alternative ways to deal with their parents, teachers, and friends. These behaviors are taught by the professional teaching-parents who direct and operate the treatment program. The teaching-parents live at Achievement Place with their "family" of six to eight delinquent youths and provide them with 24-hour care and guidance. The teaching-parents also work with the youth's parents and teachers to help solve problems that occur at home and at school.

Evaluation of the program [2]

Although we have evaluated many of the specific procedures the teaching-parents have developed to teach appropriate behaviors (Bailey, Wolf, and Phillips 1970; Bailey, Timbers, Phillips, and Wolf 1971; Braukmann, Maloney, Fixsen, Phillips, and Wolf 1974; Fixsen, Phillips, and Wolf 1972; Fixsen, Phillips, and Wolf 1973; Kirigin, Phillips, Fixsen, and Wolf 1971; Phillips 1968; Phillips, Phillips, Fixsen, and Wolf 1973; Phillips, Wolf, and Fixsen 1973; Timber, Phillips, Fixsen, and Wolf 1971; Wolf, Phillips, and Fixsen 1972) we have only recently begun to evaluate the overall effectiveness of the Achievement Place program. Our preliminary data include measures of recidivism, police and court contacts, grades and attendance at school, and school dropouts. We have taken these measures for 16 youths who were committed to Achievement Place, for 15 youths who were committed to the Kansas Boys School (an institution for about 250 delinquent boys), and for 13 youths placed on formal probation. All 44 youths had been released from treatment for at least 1 year at the time we collected these data and all had been originally adjudicated by the Douglas County Juvenile Court, Lawrence, Kansas. In the opinion of the probation department all of the youths were potential candidates for Achievement Place when they were adjudicated.

The boys were *not* randomly assigned to each group. Rather, they were committed to each treatment by the local juvenile court for rea-

[2] Recent followup data (Wolf, Phillips, and Fixsen 1975) which became available after this chapter was completed show that the initial differences in police and court contacts and school behavior indicated here have not been totally maintained over time; however, the results for the recidivism measure have remained virtually the same as those reported here.

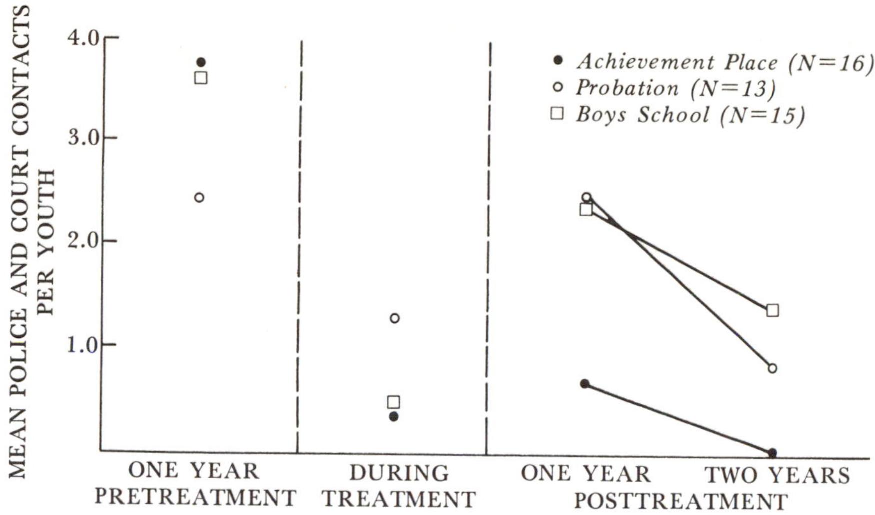

Figure 17-1 Average number of police and court contacts

sons that we cannot specify. Therefore, any differences among the three groups could be attributed to initial differences among the boys committed to each group or to the effects of each treatment. That is, the differences among the groups may be due to a "population effect" or to a "treatment effect." However, in the past year we have begun randomly selecting youths for admission to Achievement Place. We plan to collect data on these youths to provide an experimental evaluation of the long-term effects of the Achievement Place treatment program.

Figure 17-1 shows the average number of police and court contacts for the youths before, during, and after the respective treatments. As shown in this figure, the Achievement Place youths and Boys School youths each had about 4 contacts with the police and court during the year preceding their formal adjudication, while the Probation youths averaged about 2.5 contacts each. During treatment, the Probation youths averaged over 1 police and court contact apiece, while the Achievement Place youths and Boys School youths averaged about 0.5 contact during treatment. During the first year after treatment, the Probation youths and Boys School youths averaged about 2.5 contacts with the police and court; this decreased to about 1 and 1.5 contacts during the second year after treatment ended. The Achievement Place youths averaged about 0.5 contact with the police and court during their first year after treatment, and this decreased to no contacts during the second year.

These data indicate that the Achievement Place youths and Boys School youths were similar before and during treatment but were very

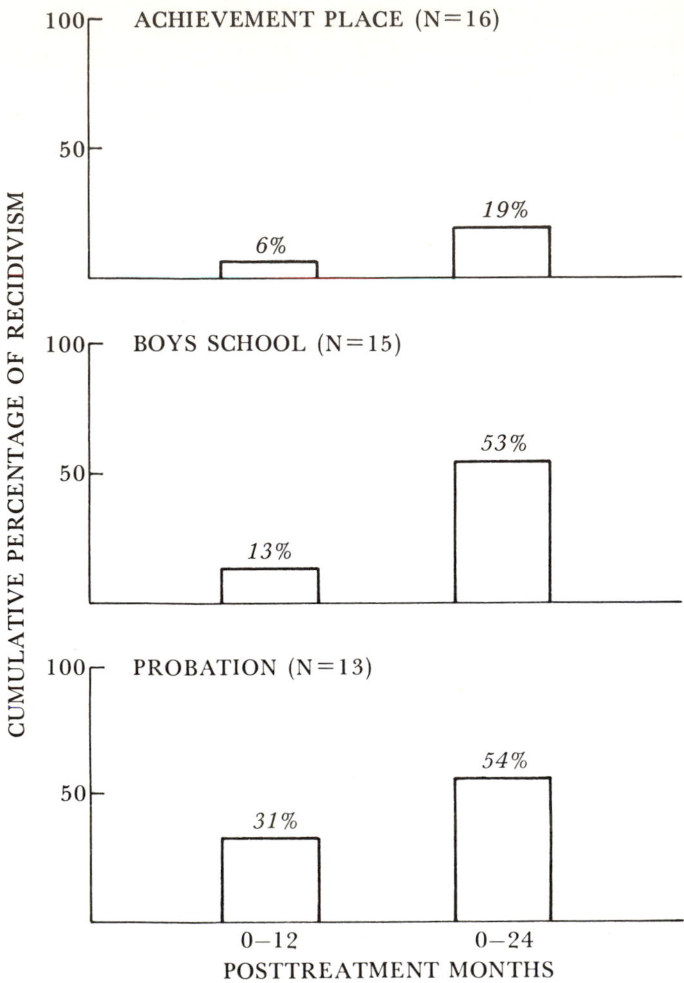

Figure 17-2 Recidivism rates after treatment

dissimilar after treatment. The Boys School youths returned to a fairly high number of police and court contacts while the Achievement Place youths maintained a low number of contacts with the police and court.

Figure 17-2 shows the percentage of boys in each group who, after treatment, committed some delinquent act which resulted in their being readjudicated by the court and placed in the Boys School, in a state mental hospital, in jail, or sent to adult court for prosecution. As shown in this graph, 6 percent of the Achievement Place youths, 13 percent of the Boys School youths, and 31 percent of the Probation youths were readjudicated during the first 12 months after their release. By the end of 24 months after their release, a cumulative total of 19 percent of the Achievement Place youths, 53 percent of the Boys School youths, and 54 percent of the Probation youths had been readjudicated. The large number of police and court contacts experienced by the Boys School and Probation youths indicates a larger recidivism percentage for these two groups. The Achievement Place youths had a smaller number of police and court contacts and a smaller recidivism percentage.

Although these police and court data reveal substantial differences among the groups, they are measures of failure, not success. It is difficult to argue that lack of failure means success since there are many factors unrelated to a youth's behavior that may influence whether he is readjudicated or not. For this reason we also took three measures of school behavior. Figure 17-3 shows the percentage of nonadjudicated youths in school before, during, and after treatment for each group. For two semesters before treatment about 75 percent of the youths in each group attended public school at least 45 days during each 90-day semester. During treatment 100 percent of the Achievement Place youths, 100 percent of the Boys School youths, and 84 percent of the Probation youths attended school each semester. During treatment the Achievement Place youths and the Probation youths attended the public schools in Lawrence while the Boys School youths attended the school provided in the institution. During the first semester after their release, 84 percent of the Achievement Place youths, 58 percent of the Boys School youths, and 69 percent of the Probation youths attended public school. By the third semester after treatment, 90 percent of the Achievement Place youths still attended public school, while only 9 percent of the Boys School youths and 37 percent of the Probation youths were still in school.

Figure 17-4 shows the average number of days absent and the average grades each semester for those youths in each group who attended school. The Boys School youths averaged about 20 days absent during each 90-day semester for two semesters prior to treatment and again averaged about 20 days absent for each semester after treatment. The Boys School did not supply us with information regarding attendance at their school but we would guess that the youths had fewer than 20 days absent each semester during treatment. The Probation youths averaged about 15 days absent each semester prior to treatment, about 8 to 10 days absent during treatment, and about 7 to 10 days absent each semester after treatment. Data for only two semesters after treatment are shown for the Boys School and Probation groups because, as we saw in Figure 17-3, only a few boys in these two groups were still in school by the third semester. The Achievement Place

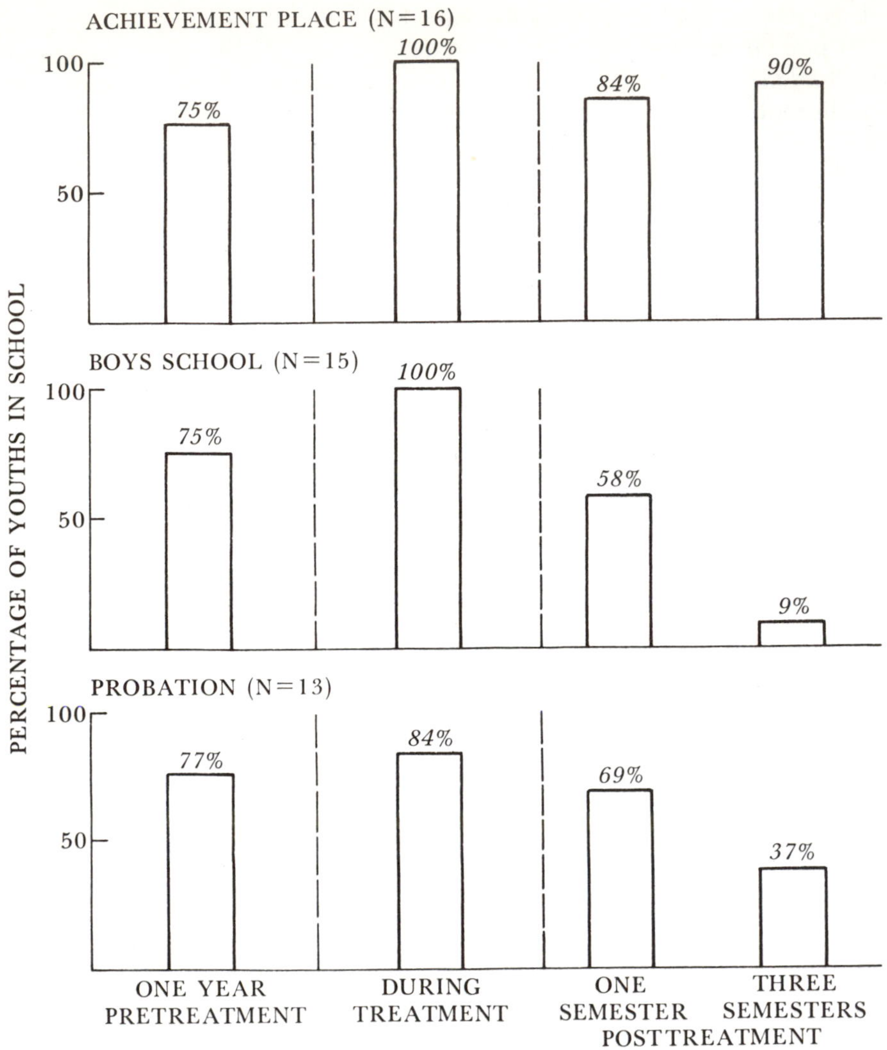

Figure 17-3 Percentage of youths in school before, during, and after treatment

youths averaged about 12 days absent each semester prior to treatment, about 3 to 5 days absent during treatment, and about 3 to 8 days absent each semester after treatment.

The average grades earned by the youths are shown in the bottom graph in Figure 17-4. The grades for the Boys School youths averaged D – to D prior to treatment, increased to a little over a C average while they attended the school in the institution during treatment, then de-

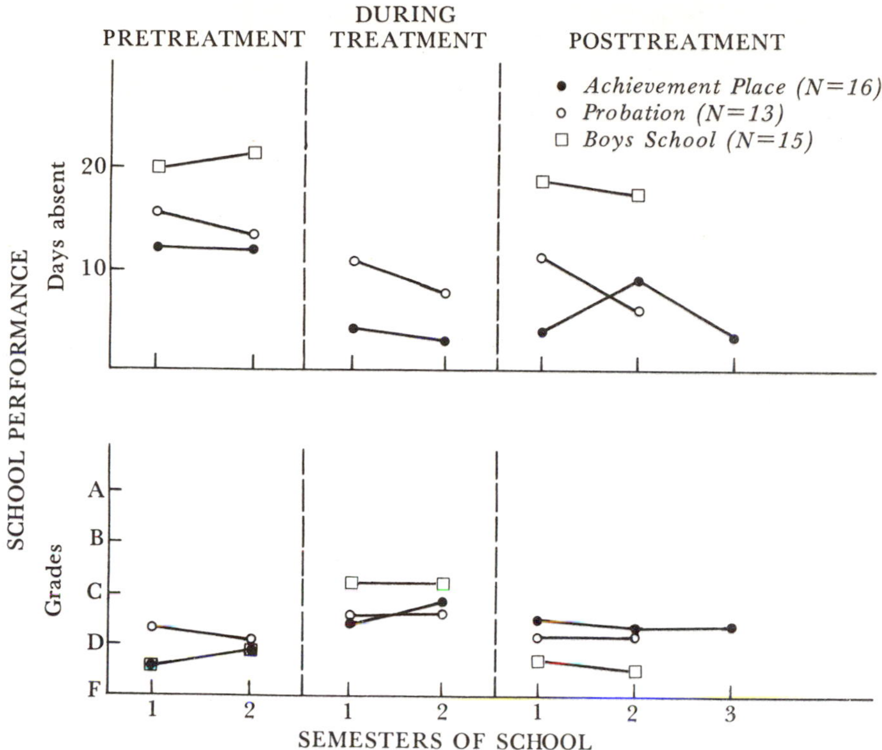

Figure 17-4 Average number of days absent and average grades per semester

creased to about a D− average after treatment. The grades for the Probation youths averaged a little over a D each semester before, during, and after treatment. The grades for the Achievement Place youths averaged D− to D before treatment, increased to C− and C during treatment, and were maintained at about C− after treatment.

These school data indicate that the Achievement Place youths were similar to the youths in the other two groups prior to treatment but after treatment were more successful than the Boys School youths or Probation youths in terms of staying in school, days absent, and grades. Although the C− average maintained by the Achievement Place youths after treatment is probably not sufficient to arouse the admiration of most middle-class parents, it does indicate that the youths are passing their classes and progressing toward the graduation requirements for junior high and high school.

The police, court, and school data indicate that the Achievement Place youths are progressing much better than their peers who were sent to the Boys School or placed on Probation. As indicated earlier,

Table 17-1 Comparative costs (1971)

	Achievement Place	*Institution*
Capital investment per youth	$6,000	$20,000 to $30,000
Yearly operating cost per youth	$4,100	$ 6,000 to $12,000

these data may reflect a "treatment effect" or a "population effect" attributable to the initial differences among the youths because the youths were *not* randomly assigned to the groups. However, we plan to collect similar data on a sample of randomly selected youths to provide an experimental evaluation of the long-term effects of the Achievement Place treatment program.

However, even if the results of this random selection procedure show that the Achievement Place youths do no better than youths who were sent to an institution, we would continue to advocate replacing most institutions with group home treatment programs. We would do this for two reasons. First, group home programs are more humane than institutional programs because the youths receive more individual care; they remain in close contact with their community and parents and friends; and programs can be provided to teach them important social, family, and community-living skills. Second, group homes are less expensive to operate. Table 17-1 shows that the cost per bed of purchasing, renovating, and furnishing Achievement Place was about one-fourth the cost of building an institution. The operating costs per youth for Achievement Place are less than one-half the operating costs for the Boys School in Kansas. To build a Boys School for 250 youths and operate it for 1 year would cost about $8 million. To purchase, renovate, and furnish group homes for 250 youths and operate them for 1 year would cost about $2.5 million, a savings to the taxpayer of $5.5 million. If the followup data collected at Achievement Place and at other group homes eventually provide evidence that systematic group home treatment programs are also more effective than institutional programs, we can expect a major shift away from institutions and toward community-based programs.

Behavior modification in prisons

Robert E. Kennedy
The Pennsylvania State University

18

The utilization of behavior modification in prison settings has generated greater controversy than its application in any other area. The controversy has focused primarily on ethical concerns, and Kennedy provides an overview of the issues and their development.

Kennedy describes the better known prison programs–Patuxent, START, Rehabilitation Research Foundation (RRF)—and provides a summary of the results and an evaluation of each of the programs. He bases his chapter on the outcome data from the programs, legal decisions, and court testimony of "expert" behavior modifiers. It is his conclusion that the programs, with the possible exception of RRF's, have been largely unsuccessful. Kennedy does not just present a critical review, but rather suggests some alternative behavioral strategies to deal with problems specific to prison rehabilitation. He maintains that many of the problems in prison programs have arisen from the conflicting roles of the prison as a rehabilitator and a punisher. The position taken in this chapter is that the emphases of prison programs should be on rehabilitation, and that participation in rehabilitation programs should be on a voluntary basis. One of Kennedy's criticisms of some of the prison programs is their frequent appeal to the scientific justification, when the data on which they presumably are based do not, in fact, support the programs. This invalid use of the imprimatur of science may also apply to programs in other social and personal problem areas.

No application of behavioral principles has been beset by so much opposition as their use in the control and rehabilitation of prison inmates.

Prisoners' widely publicized opposition to some behavioral programs has gained the support of civil rights groups, led to a host of lawsuits, and brought about congressional hearings. Rising judicial and political pressure, in fact, led the Federal Bureau of Prisons in February 1974, to discontinue its widely criticized Project START. A week later, the Law Enforcement Assistance Agency [1] (LEAA) announced that it was discontinuing its funding of prison programs involving behavior modification, although LEAA officials could not identify what specific procedures or programs constituted "behavior modification" (Trotter and Warren 1974).[2]

Development of the controversy

Some of the first adverse publicity given behavior modification in prisons came in 1970 when the *Medical World News* (cited by Mitford 1973) published an account of an aversion therapy program at the prison hospital at Vacaville, California. Researchers there were reported to be administering Anectine, a derivative of curare, to men who were guilty of frequent fights, verbal threatening, deviant sexual behavior, stealing, and unresponsiveness to group therapy. The most noticeable effect of the drug was cessation of respiration for 1 to 2 minutes, inducing feelings of suffocation and, frequently, extreme fright. According to an unpublished account by two staff researchers (Mattocks and Jew, undated), a therapist would tell the suffocating convict that, when he next had an impulse to transgress, he should stop and remember the sensations created by the drug.[3] It was expected that a prisoner would thereby develop a strong association between the problem behaviors and the aversive effects of the drug.

Although the bulk of the inmates in this project had signed an "informed consent" form, five reportedly had refused to sign the form but had had their consent given for them by an institutional review board (Weiner 1972). Actually, with any prison treatment program it is open to question whether those who sign consent forms do so feeling free from coercion. Implicit coercion in the present case stemmed from Cal-

[1] The division of the U.S. Department of Justice created by the Omnibus Crime and Safe Streets Act of 1968 to channel federal monies to state and local law enforcement agencies and to provide the agencies with technical assistance.

[2] Four months later the LEAA announced that they were banning "medical" behavior modification and would continue to fund programs involving only social or environmental changes (Saunders 1974).

[3] This is similar to the procedure described in *A Clockwork Orange* (Burgess 1963), leading critics to use the title of this novel as a derogatory epithet for behavior modification in prisons.

ifornia's "indeterminate" sentence law, under which an offender is given a sentence with a maximum (frequently "life") highly disparate from its minimum. The actual length of the sentence and the time of parole is determined by parole boards, who frequently emphasize convicts' participation in treatment programs as evidence of their rehabilitation. According to one survey of California inmates (California Assembly 1968), 77 percent of those participating in treatment report that they do so solely to impress the boards. Since involuntary aversion treatments tend to have relatively high failure rates (e.g., Freund 1960), it is not surprising that of 64 Vacaville prisoners administered Anectine, 9 actually increased their rate of infractions (Mattocks and Jew, undated). The program was discontinued soon after one of the involuntary participants sued to have it stopped (*Mackey* v. *Procunier* 1973).

Publicity of the Vacaville program was followed by reports that sexual offenders at the state prison mental hospital at Atascadero, California, were being subjected to electric shock to their genitals while they watched films of sexual activity (Weiner 1972). The reported title of this unusual program was "Errorless Extinction of Penile Responses." Other aversion therapy programs that came to public attention included: (1) the controversial use of apomorphine, a nausea-producing drug, in an Iowa program similar to Vacaville's; and (2) the application of electric shock to sensitive body areas (but not to the genitals) of sexual offenders in Wisconsin and Connecticut ("Behavior Mod" 1974). These programs also became the objects of prisoners' lawsuits (e.g., *Knecht* v. *Gillman* 1973).

At about the same time that the aversion therapy programs were first publicized, prisoners' rights groups discovered and made public the plans of the California Corrections Department for treating aggressive inmates with brain surgery and sex offenders with chemically "castrating" hormones (Mitford 1973; Trotter 1974). As a result, the aversion programs, and by extension all behavior modification, came to be associated in the minds of prisoners, lawyers, and journalists with psychosurgery and chemotherapy (e.g., Mitford 1973; U.S. modifies 1974). Although almost any procedure that is intended to alter a person's behavior could be designated behavior modification, such a designation is usually restricted to procedures derived from psychological studies of human and animal learning, thus excluding psychosurgery, chemotherapy, and similar treatments (Bandura 1969). Such a distinction has in fact been made official by the director of the federal prison system (Carlson 1974). Unfortunately, this pronouncement and the LEAA's clarification of its guidelines came too late to prevent the journalistic damage to behavior modification's reputation.

Three examples of behavioral prison programs[4]

Patuxent Institution

Another behavioral program that has been called a "clockwork orange" is that of Maryland's Patuxent Institution. Under a 1951 Maryland law, convicted criminals suspected of being "defective delinquents"[5] are sent by the courts or by other prisons to Patuxent for examination. If such an examination results in a diagnosis of "defective delinquency," a semijudicial hearing is held to determine whether or not the convict will be permanently assigned to Patuxent. A convict assigned to Patuxent by such a hearing is given an indeterminate sentence (that is, one with no upper limit) no matter how long his original sentence was or how much of it he had already served. Once committed, an inmate may be released only by the decision of a new judicial hearing or by the Institutional Board of Review.[6] A prisoner can request an initial rehearing after his first 2 years at Patuxent or after two-thirds of his original sentence, whichever is longer, and once every 3 years thereafter. The institutional review board must review each prisoner's status at least once a year.

Program. After a program of individual and group psychotherapy proved insufficient to produce significant behavioral change, Patuxent added a four-level "Graded Tier System," purportedly "taken from psychological learning theory" (Patuxent Institution 1973, p. 18). On Patuxent's first tier, the prisoner has an ordinary cell, exercises in a bleak recreation yard, works on a sanitation crew, and has little access to the "luxuries" of prison life—television, canteen, freedom of movement within the institution, and so on. As the prisoner moves up through the second and third tiers, he acquires more and more privileges: later lock-in times, more time to use the dayroom, greater freedom of movement. At the third tier he becomes eligible for vocational training and parole. On the fourth tier individual cells are not locked and can be extensively decorated by the inmate himself. Family visiting privileges are greatly expanded beyond those allowed in most prisons and the tier is self-governing in some aspects.

[4] The description and results of an important program, directed by a pioneer in behavior modification, Dr. Teodoro Ayllon, were received too late to be included in this chapter. The interested reader should see Ayllon and Roberts (1973) and Roberts (1974).

[5] That is, repeated offenders "who were defective emotionally and/or intellectually" and "physically dangerous to society" (Patuxent Institution 1973, p. 1).

[6] The 1951 statute and recent legal arguments by the State of Maryland attempt to justify this psychiatric form of preventive detention by citing the necessity of protecting the public from extremely dangerous criminals. However, there is little evidence that either medical or social scientists can predict with any accuracy whether an individual convict will commit a serious crime if released (Rubin 1972; Steadman and Cocozza 1975).

Although there are some specified behavioral criteria for promotion within this system, the final decision is made by the "classification committee" of the inmate's treatment unit. The criteria are apparently vague enough to allow frequent disagreements among committee members and many closely divided votes (Goldfarb and Singer 1970). For example, demotions can be given not only for serious disciplinary infractions but also for "failure to show sufficient motivation" (Goldfarb and Singer 1970, p. 231). In fact, the judge in an inmate's lawsuit against the institution severely criticized Patuxent for its lack of specified rules (*McCray* v. *Maryland* 1971).

Despite the official emphasis on positive reinforcement through promotion, demotion within the system was not the only punishment used by the staff. In *McCray* v. *Maryland* (1971), the court found that noncooperative prisoners were placed in solitary confinement cells for up to 30 days without adequate light, ventilation, exercise, or sanitation. Other punishments, according to prisoner witnesses, included beatings, hosings, and Macings.

Prisoners released from Patuxent by judicial rehearing (68 percent of all men released from 1955 to 1972) are sent to other prisons, put on conventional parole, or—if their sentences have expired—freed from all legal bondage rather than paroled. However, men released by the institutional review board are usually placed in Patuxent's own parole program, which includes employment counseling, counseling by noninstitutional social workers, continued contact with the prisoners' institutional counselors, and housing for prisoners with no families, friends, or resources.

Results. Despite Patuxent's ambition to establish a total therapeutic environment, the findings of *McCray* v. *Maryland* (1971) suggest that the guards' treatment of the prisoners differed little from that found in conventional prisons. In return, according to a recent visitor to Patuxent, "The prisoners curse the guards, spit at them, throw feces at them. . . . The guards and inmates . . . seem to be victims of the same mutual abuse that characterizes such relationships in other prisons" (Goldberg 1973, pp. 24–25). Disturbances such as sit-ins and strikes have become so frequent in recent years (Stanford 1972) that a prison reform writer formerly sympathetic to Patuxent (Goldfarb and Singer 1970) has described it as "besieged by riots" (Goldfarb 1974, p. 18).

A more objective measure of Patuxent's effectiveness is its recidivism rate, that is, the percentage of releasees who are convicted of new crimes within a certain period of time after release. Recidivism rates are sometimes difficult to evaluate because different institutions frequently use different criteria for defining recidivism. For example,

Patuxent's overall rate of 31 percent includes releasees convicted of a new crime during the first *three* years after release (Patuxent 1973), while the most recent figure for the federal prisons—33 percent—includes those convicted during the first *two* years out (Recidivism 1974). If we assume that the federal rate would rise substantially during a third year, Patuxent's rate does seem superior. However, Patuxent, unlike the federal system, does not include in its figures those convicted of a new crime while on parole, but only those reconvicted after complete release from custody. An earlier study of Patuxent releasees (Hodges 1971), which did include criminal parole violators, showed a 51 percent 3-year recidivism rate for Patuxent. In addition, Patuxent's releasees were older than the national sample. Since recidivism decreases with age (Glaser 1964), Patuxent's lower rate may be partly a result of this difference.

While no conclusive evidence exists for the relative superiority of Patuxent's prison programs, the combination of the institutional treatment programs with Patuxent's extended, supportive, and intensely supervised form of parole seems to have had impressive results: a 7 percent recidivism rate for those who had completed 3 years of parole and had then been released from custody. However, these data cannot be considered unequivocal evidence for the relative superiority of Patuxent's entire treatment package. First, the treatment was confounded with a selection factor: only those released by the institutional review board (rather than by the courts at rehearing) received the intensive parole treatment. Second, it may be that the parole alone was responsible for the impressive results. Only if the Patuxent releasee group had been compared with a group of releasees from a different prison who had also received the Patuxent parole treatment could the effect of Patuxent's institutional program be evaluated. Another problem with the data is that, like Patuxent's other recidivism figures, this one does not include those men who had committed new crimes while on parole and were either back in prison or out on parole again. Finally, the average age of the men in this group was relatively high: 34.1 years old when released from custody, after having spent an average of 3.6 years *longer* in prison and on parole than had been called for by their original sentences (Patuxent 1973).

Patuxent's program then offers only a very rough approximation of applied behavioral principles. Whatever success it may have achieved in reducing recidivism may be as much a result of its sophisticated form of preventive detention [7] as of its actual treatment.

[7] In 1972, for example, 38 percent of Patuxent's inmates were reportedly serving beyond their original sentences, including 75 percent of those originally given terms of five years or less (Stanford 1972).

START

The Federal Bureau of Prisons' START (Special Treatment and Rehabilitative Training) program in Springfield, Missouri, was similar to Patuxent in that it attempted to deal with a particularly problematic segment of the inmate population. In START's case this was the "1 percent of the Federal offender population" who are not only frequently placed in "segregation" or solitary confinement for continually violating institutional rules but who "continue to be assaultive, abusive, and generally recalcitrant even while in the segregation unit" (Federal Bureau of Prisons 1972, p. 2). The purpose of the program was admittedly not to prepare such prisoners for release from penal custody but rather to serve as a type of "prerehabilitation," the object of which was to train the inmate to be cooperative enough to exist in the regular or "open" prison environment without being a constant source of trouble.

Program. An inmate was transferred involuntarily to START from any institution within the federal system on the basis of his warden's recommendation and a review by the central office of the Bureau.

The three basic parts of the START program were a *progressive level system,* a *point system,* and an *individualized contract system.* The *level system* began on an "orientation" level which was similar to the segregation blocks from which the prisoners had just come. Inmates were locked in their cells almost continuously, were not allowed any reading material except a hometown newspaper and a Bible, and were denied use of a radio, the commissary, and most personal property. As the inmate moved up through the levels, he gradually moved into a schedule similar to that in normal prisons and acquired most of the privileges denied him on the orientation level. However, since the purpose of the program was to return the inmates to conventional prisons, they could not earn privileges beyond those available to normal prisoners, except the return of previously forfeited statutory "good time" (time taken off sentence for good behavior).

Promotions in the level system were made on the basis of "good days," the number required for promotion increasing as the inmate moved up through the various levels. The criteria for a good day involved daily measures of 12 target behaviors that incorporated the program's three subgoals: maintenance of personal care and hygiene, adequacy of interactions with others, and learning productive work habits. As with the number of good days required for promotion, the number of successfully performed behaviors required for earning a good day was a function of the level.

In the *point system,* certain behaviors earned the inmate points which he could use for buying commissary items; renting radios, musical instruments, or recreational equipment; ordering books or periodicals; and so on. The reinforced behaviors were again those relating to personal care, relations with others, and work habits.

Points could also be earned in the *contract system.* Contracts between the inmate and his treatment team called for the prisoner to earn a certain number of points by completing a certain task in an individualized treatment program, developed cooperatively by staff and inmate. (Above the third stage of the level system, the points were eliminated and contracts were written directly in terms of the desired items.)

A fourth part of the START program which was not designated as treatment but which played a large part in the lives of the inmates was "discipline." Rule infractions were punished by a "time out," which consisted of the inmate's being confined to his room for a period of time set by the staff. During that time he could not earn, lose, or spend points, could not earn a good day, and suffered all the deprivations common to "segregation" in normal prisons. This segregation could be continued as long as the inmate refused to cooperate and continued to be disruptive.

Results. Of the 21 men transferred to START since September 1972, only six remained there as of January 7, 1974. Three others were in the segregation unit in the psychiatric hospital which contained the project; and five had been released to the hospital itself, although all START prisoners had been certified as nonpsychotic when transferred to the program. Four prisoners had been transferred out of the program because they had failed to progress beyond the orientation level, while one was transferred back to his home institution without completing the program. One prisoner was released upon expiration of his sentence and one completed all phases of the program and was transferred to a conventional prison (Saunders, Milstein, and Rosen 1974). Seven prisoners had staged a 65-day hunger strike to protest their treatment and then sued to have the program closed, charging the staff with multiple violations of their constitutional rights (Steinman 1973). In February 1974, the Bureau of Prisons, facing the possibility that a federal judge was about to order the project stopped, announced that it was closing START for economic reasons (Warren 1974). Despite the government's argument that the closure of START made the case moot, the judge subsequently ruled that START's program had been a form of punishment and that the prisoners' involuntary transfer to START without a due process hearing had been unlawful (*Clonce* v. *Richardson* 1974).

Evaluation. The essentially negative results of START were attributed by expert witnesses in the inmates' suit to a number of basic flaws in the project's design and to deficiencies in its implementation (Cohen 1974; DeRisi 1974). One major flaw in the program was that it was highly coercive. Behavioral programs like START are less likely to succeed if they are involuntary or do not allow for some form of subject participation in program planning and administration (Kazdin 1973). Transfer into START was involuntary and hence was perceived as punishment by many prisoners (Saunders, Milstein, and Rosen 1974). Furthermore, there was almost no opportunity for prisoner input into START's design or operation. Besides denying prisoner representatives a share in the administrative power, the staff tended to react to prisoner complaints during group meetings by threatening loss of privileges or demotion in status (Cohen 1974).

One method of increasing the probable effectiveness of a token program is to provide a wide variety of back-up reinforcers, especially ones that have been found effective for each individual (Cohen 1974; Kazdin 1973a). In START the reinforcers available were restricted to those that had already proved ineffective in controlling the prisoners' behavior in their "home" prisons; and little effort was made to determine individually effective reinforcers (Cohen 1974; DeRisi 1974). This paucity of reinforcers was, of course, especially pronounced on the lower levels.

One problem with START may have been its apparent goal: the production of *submissive* inmates. For example, some of the behavioral criteria for a prisoner's "good day" were the following:

> Accepted a "no" . . . when making requests.
> Made requests in a non-abusive manner.
> Accepted or performed assignments, duties, or tasks without needing persuasion.
> Followed directions and instructions in a willing manner without bickering.
> Followed rules, regulations, and policies. (Federal Bureau of Prisons 1972, p. 8)

Behaviors reinforced in the point system included:

> Accept designated area(s) to be cleaned without bickering.
> Accept industry assignment(s) without controversy.
> Accept special assignment without becoming abusive. (Federal Bureau 1972, p. 17)

Some rule infractions punishable by "time out," demotion, and so on were:

> Excessive use of abusive language after first warning.
> Agitation of others without stopping after first warning.
> Excessive arguing with another participant or staff member after first warning.
> Disobeying a staff member after first warning. (Federal Bureau 1972, p. 11)

According to Cohen (1974), the general attitude of the staff was "wait until the subject submits and then reinforce him" (p. 9).

The program's obvious emphasis on submissiveness seems to have had three results. First, it seems to have increased the inmates' perception of START as aversive (Saunders, Milstein, and Roseman 1974). Second, it apparently led to an increasing emphasis on punishment of undesired behavior rather than positive reinforcement of cooperation (Cohen 1974; DeRisi 1974). Court testimony and evidence (Saunders, Milstein, and Roseman 1974) and an eyewitness account (Steinman 1973) indicate that physical abuse of prisoners may not have been infrequent. Of course, this punitiveness may have been partly a result of the guards' previous training in standard prison procedures and their inadequate understanding of behavioral principles (Cohen 1974).

A third possible result of the emphasis on submission was that START generally ignored antecedent conditions of inmate aggression and overlooked their deficits in the nonaggressive social skills necessary to handle conflict situations. Perhaps the most important antecedent condition ignored in START was the prisoners' previously aggressive responses to punitive discipline. The probability was low that the same punitive procedures used in conventional prisons would produce different responses when coupled with only the weak and sparse reinforcers awarded in START.

Because of its emphasis on submission, START offered the inmates few opportunities for even semiindependent decision making and problem solving. The individualized contracting system was supposed to have provided opportunities for exercising responsibility; but expert evaluators of the program (Azrin 1974; Cohen 1974; DeRisi 1974) found little evidence that the contract system or other program individualization had been put into effect. Also generally unavailable were vocational training and educational opportunities, which might have made the program both more valuable and more attractive to the inmates.

A final shortcoming in START's design was that it did not include the ongoing data analysis and evaluation that are integral parts of behavioral programs. This component might have aided in the early detection and effective alteration of the program's deficiencies.

The Rehabilitation Research Foundation

The Rehabilitation Research Foundation (RRF) at Draper Correctional Center in Elmore, Alabama, has attempted to apply behavioral principles to prison problems in a more tentative, experimental manner than was apparent in either Patuxent or START.

Individualized programmed instruction. On the assumption that a great many inmates, through frequent failure, have developed an aversion to traditional classroom methods of instruction, the RRF began in 1961 to adapt programmed instruction for use in prisons' academic and vocational programs. RRF director John McKee and his colleagues developed an instructional system that includes an initial diagnosis of an individual's academic or vocational deficiencies and a prescription of specific materials to correct these. Daily contingency contracts specify work that is to be accomplished in a 3- to 4-hour period and provide reinforcements such as money, free time, or other privileges for passing the frequent tests. Also utilized is a procedure, based on Homme's (1966) application of the Premack principle, in which the learner, upon completing a specified segment of work (for example, a number of frames in a program), is allowed a 15-minute period of a reinforcing activity chosen from a list of such activities, or a "reinforcing event (RE) menu," originally generated by the inmate. Throughout the program there is an emphasis on involving the student in developing his own goals and in managing as much of his own work as possible (McKee 1970).

In an evaluation of this system (McKee 1971), it was found that 16 subjects not only increased the number of frames completed per day 78 percent over baseline productivity, but simultaneously increased work speed and percentage of tests passed. Perhaps more importantly, during a followup "self-management" phase, the inmates maintained a significantly higher output and efficiency than during baseline.

Correctional officer training at RRF. Since the prison personnel who have most contact with the inmates are not treatment professionals but the custodial staff, RRF researchers attempted to train the guards at Draper Correctional Center as behavioral "technicians" (McKee, Smith, Wood, and Milan, in press). During both classroom instruction and a supervised practicum, the guards were taught the full repertoire of behavioral techniques, with emphasis on positive reinforcement and related procedures. A requirement of the practicum was an individual project in which the guard identified a specific inmate behavior that he wanted to change, took baseline data, devised a behavioral strategy, implemented it, continued to collect data, and observed the results.

This training project was designed less as an attempt to change the functioning of the institution than as a feasibility study to assess the guards' potential for becoming change agents. The training did increase the frequency of the guards' personal interactions with inmates and their use of positive reinforcement during these interactions. A less encouraging result, however, was that almost all the target behaviors chosen by the guards for their projects were matters of institutional control. Procedures invented by the guards to deal with these problems were generally less severe than the usual punishments outlined in the institutional rule book. But almost all guards used either negative reinforcement, punishment, or time out, while few utilized positive contingencies. The authors attributed this trend to the guards' training in the typical prison management system—noncontingent awarding of most available reinforcers followed by behavior control through their removal, that is, through punishment.

Evaluation of the "punishment model." In an experiment to determine the effects of this typical system, a "laissez faire" baseline, during which guards merely reminded the inmates of their self-management tasks, was followed by an intervention in which the guards (not behaviorally trained) used whatever control methods they thought would ensure performance of the tasks (Milan and McKee 1974). Although punitive procedures used by the guards doubled the task performance rate, they also generated about four times as high a rate of aggression on the experimental cell block as had been present during baseline. A return to the "laissez faire" procedure led to a return to baseline levels for both aggression and task performance.

Token economy. Hypothesizing that response-contingent positive reinforcement would be less costly than the "punishment model" in terms of counteraggression and hostility, RRF workers instituted a token economy system in an experimental cell block (Milan, Wood, Williams, Rogers, Hampton, and McKee 1974). For the first 420 days target behaviors were limited to those that could be controlled on the cell block itself: self-management tasks and participation and performance in a voluntary remedial education program. During a second 340-day phase, the project also covered the inmates' performances in their institutional work assignments and educational programs. Reinforcers included canteen items; access to television, pool tables, lounges, and so on; time off for recreation; and choices from an RE menu of legitimate but difficult to obtain privileges or objects such as 2 hours of fishing, a television rental, a visit to a woman's prison, and an interview with a parole board member. In contrast to START, the Draper system did not begin with severe deprivation, did make some rather unusual and attractive reinforcers available from the beginning, and stressed independent performance skills rather than mere submissiveness to the prison staff.

After the system's introduction, the level of aggression did not rise above that observed during a "laissez faire" baseline; but daily percentage of self-management tasks performed did rise from a baseline rate of 60 percent to over 90 percent. Percentage of volunteered-for maintenance tasks also increased from 40 to 90 percent; and participation in the leisure-time education program rose from almost zero to a daily rate of 50 percent, with 80 percent of all inmates spending over 10 free-time hours per week on it (Milan and McKee 1974).

Unfortunately, even such a relatively successful program as RRF's token system may not by itself be able to produce a significant difference in prisoners' ability to "make it" after release. In an 18-month followup comparing the postrelease performances of token-system releasees, a control group, and two groups who had received two different types of vocational training, the token group had the lowest recidivism level and reached that level more slowly than the other groups (who had more arrests during the first few months after release) (Jenkins, Witherspoon, DeVine, deValera, Muller, Barton, and McKee 1974). However, on neither of these variables did the token group differ significantly from the control group. Milan et al. (1974) noted that *the beneficial effects of token programs within a prison may be short-lived unless they are sustained by transitional and community-based followup programs.*

Implementing the behavioral model in prisons

Problems stemming from conflicting roles of a prison

The relative ineffectiveness of behavioral programs in reducing recidivism stems in part from the conflict between the role of the prison as a rehabilitator and its other major role, that of a punisher. The prison cannot effectively fulfill its conventional purposes—punishing its inmates, protecting society from them, and serving as a threat to potential lawbreakers (National Advisory Commission on Criminal Justice 1973)—unless it has enough control over its convicts to prevent their escape. Consequently, control is often considered the first order of business in prisons. Although this emphasis on punishment and control might well undermine any type of "treatment" (see Cressey 1973; Mitford 1973), it is especially damaging to behavioral approaches because of its effects in the following areas.

Allocation of resources. Less than 10 percent of the national prison budget goes for personnel, equipment, and materials devoted to rehabilitation (National Advisory Commission 1973). Substantially less than

10 percent of the budget, then, is spent on preparing the convict to hold down a noncriminal job when he leaves the prison, despite the fact that continuous employment after release is the best single predictor of nonrecidivism (Glaser 1964).

That employment is such a good predictor of nonrecidivism suggests that a great deal of crime may be committed mainly for the financial gain involved. This is especially true of the crimes that Glaser (1964) found to have the highest recidivism rates: car theft, burglary, larceny, forgery, and so on. Social learning theory (Bandura 1969, 1973) predicts that punishment of such *instrumental* acts will be ineffective unless the convict learns the skills necessary for legitimately obtaining what his illegal behavior has netted him in the past. But the prison system has provided relatively little money for the training of such skills.

Graduated release. Like token programs in mental hospitals (see Kazdin and Bootzin 1972), behavioral programs in prisons should include some method of weaning the inmate from the artificial support of the program by helping him apply skills learned in the institution to the completely different environment of the outside world. In mental hospitals, this problem of *generalization* is frequently handled by a system of graduated release, which allows the patient to spend a progressively larger part of his day or week at home or at a job outside the hospital. Also included in some of these programs are various types of halfway houses and intensive outpatient care (Paul 1969b).

Unfortunately, the emphasis on control and punishment in the criminal justice system has limited the opportunity for such graduated release procedures as work furlough, educational leave, and home leave (Mitford 1973; Smith and Milan 1971). Instead, a two-step system is most common: the releasee goes abruptly from the total institution of prison to complete independence or to the minimal supervision and assistance of the typical parole program (Goldfarb and Singer 1973).

Powerlessness of inmates. Being a prison inmate means being stripped of most of the rights that accrue to a normal citizen. Until the agitation of the Black Muslims in the early 1960s led to the first major judicial interventions in the internal affairs of prisons, almost all judges maintained that it was not the function of the judiciary to interfere with the administration of prisons, no matter how flagrant the abuses brought to their attention. Courts in many areas still seem to hold to this hands-off doctrine despite the many victories that have been won by the prisoners' rights movement in the last decade (Atkins and Glick 1972; Rothman 1974).

Probably the worst effect of granting arbitrary power to prison guards and administrators is that it greatly increases the likelihood that they will use punishment as the major method of control and that they will abuse this power to punish. Aggression is much more probable when the potential aggressor can be sure that his victim will not retaliate (Bandura 1973). When guards physically and verbally abuse inmates, as they reportedly did in Patuxent and START, they provide models for aggressive and sometimes lawless methods of conflict resolution, and reinforce the inmates' belief that society in general is lawless (Irwin 1970).

With inmates stripped of their rights, authorities are more likely to be arbitrary in their actions. In fact, arbitrary decision-making procedures based on poorly defined criteria were part of the Patuxent program despite the emphasis of behavior modification on the *specification* of behaviors to be reinforced and punished. Such arbitrariness, most infuriating to prisoners when practiced by parole boards (see Jackson 1970; Mitford 1973), does little to increase prisoners' acceptance of the legitimacy of social authority or to further their rehabilitation.

Finally, experimental evidence indicates that persons who feel that they have little control over their own fates are less likely to initiate attempts at problem solving, are less likely to remember response-relevant information such as instructions, and have less accurate conceptions of environmental contingencies than do individuals who do not feel externally controlled (Lefcourt 1973; Phares 1973). These effects of feeling controlled by others and by the environment in general are similar to the effects of long-term confinement described by Goffman (1962) in his sociological study of total institutions such as prisons and mental hospitals.

Steps for implementing a behavioral model [8]

Although the following suggestions are presented as means of dealing with those presently imprisoned, the system proposed would also deal with future offenders. For example, a convicted criminal could be "sentenced" to a halfway house, a sheltered workshop, or to any of a variety of community-based programs rather than to prison. Allowing the person to maintain a large part of his life in his community would help prevent the impoverishment of behavioral repertoires that seems to result from long-term incarceration (Goffman 1962).

Decarceration of most prisoners. Decarcerating most prisoners would eliminate punishment as a basic societal response to crime. This would

[8] Many of the following suggestions are similar or identical to those made by the National Advisory Commission on Criminal Justice Standards and Goals in *Corrections* (1973).

not be as drastic a step as it appears since well over half of first offenders and many multiple offenders are now placed on probation rather than imprisoned (President's Commission 1967). Furthermore, many of those actually imprisoned are guilty of "victimless" crimes, the decriminalization of which has been recommended by numerous commissions and authorities. Even many prison wardens agree that 80 to 90 percent of all prisoners presently confined could be safely released outright or to improved parole programs (Goldfarb and Singer 1973).

The other major rationale for punishment—deterrence of potential criminals—is undercut considerably by statistics on crime and imprisonment. The statistics of the Presidential Crime Commission of 1967 indicate that only in approximately 1 of every 100 serious crimes committed is the criminal imprisoned. Although many of those imprisoned may have been responsible for a significant portion of the 99 unaccounted for crimes, there can be little doubt that the "hit rate" of punishment by imprisonment is extremely low and that, consequently, its deterrence value is relatively small. Even those who have been imprisoned come back for more in large numbers.

Graduated-release programs. Decarcerating most prisoners does not necessarily mean releasing them outright. Small, community-based facilities, allowing varying degrees of freedom and independence, could provide the transition from total imprisonment to total freedom (see Goldfarb and Singer 1973, for examples). An intensive and supportive parole program would also be important in a graduated-release system. Money for such programs could come from the savings accrued by the eventual abandonment of most conventional prisons.

Inmate self-government. The failure of initially successful experiments in inmate self-government in the early 1900s may have been due to the enormous size of the prisons in which they were attempted (Glaser 1964). More recently, inmate governments have been tried in smaller facilities with delinquents (Fixsen, Phillips, and Wolf 1973) and with adult criminals (Murten 1972) and have resulted in fewer serious discipline problems and more inmate cooperation with the administration and among the inmates themselves. Self-government combined with a token program would be most feasible in small, graduated-release facilities and would enable the residents to gain experience in making responsible decisions within a somewhat structured environment. As mentioned previously, allowing inmates to contribute to program design and administration increases program effectiveness (Kazdin 1973a). It also might reduce the prisoners' feelings of being externally controlled and alleviate the effects of those feelings.

Specification of required behaviors. As a basic principle of behavior modification, specification of required behaviors should be extended to every possible aspect of rehabilitation programs. Even the requirements for earning parole could be specified in a contract drawn up co-operatively by the prisoner and parole board (with external arbitration when serious disputes arise). Since the emphasis in such a contract should be on the development of legitimate adaptive skills, the behaviors to be reinforced in the rehabilitation program should be similar to those reinforced in the Draper token system rather than to those emphasized in START.

Emphasis on skills training. Since intensive vocational training alone is not sufficient to increase the probability of an ex-convict's retaining a job after release (Rehabilitation Research Foundation 1973), a behavioral program should also provide training in many social skills necessary for successful employment: steady work habits, cooperation with other personnel, positive methods of coping with conflict, financial management skills, and so on. Most prison industries do not presently offer inmates opportunities to practice vocational skills in a realistic setting (National Advisory Commission 1973). What is needed, again, is a graduated system of programs and facilities in which inmates would be slowly exposed to demands of a conventional work environment.

Voluntary behavior therapy. Effective behavioral techniques have been developed to deal with problems affecting many convicts, for example, alcoholism (Sobell and Sobell 1973) and sexual deviance (Annon 1973; Barlow 1973). However, some of these procedures involve the use of electric shock and are less likely to work with involuntary subjects (Davison 1973; Freund 1960). Others explicitly require the subject's co-operation. Consequently, it is both ethically and practically imperative that prisoners not be coerced into such treatments.

Contingency systems for correctional personnel. A system of accountability based on the number of successful releasees should be instituted for prison administrators and personnel. California, for example, recently began a system in which counties were differentially rewarded with funds depending upon their probation success rates. New offenses by those on probation subsequently decreased (Smith 1972).

Ethical issues

Lack of restraints on prison administrators and guards, as noted previously, increases the probability that they will abuse their power. There is no reason to assume that this tendency should change because prisons adopt behavior modification as a method of control and treatment. In fact, physical and psychological abuse of inmates in behavioral programs has often been justified by reference to "behavioral principles": Vacaville's use of drug-induced suffocation was called "aversion therapy," Atascadero's reported application of electric shock to prisoners' genitals was termed "errorless extinction," and START's extended periods of segregation and isolation were described as "time out." Such attempts to obscure the punitiveness or painfulness of procedures by applying neutral-technical titles to them has made the programs (and by erroneous implication, behavior modification in general) easy targets for criticism and ridicule (see Figure 18-1).

Several prominent behavior modifiers have suggested that misapplications of behavior modification in prisons can be averted by periodic inspection and evaluation of the programs by boards of outside professionals, including experienced behavior modifiers (Trotter and Warren 1974). While this procedure might eliminate the more obvious abuses, its adoption would not necessarily solve a more basic ethical problem, that is, the use of coercion.

In an article widely quoted by critics of behavior modification, McConnell (1970) suggested that anyone convicted of a crime should be considered to have forfeited his rights as a citizen and thus could legitimately be subjected to coercive modification of his behavior and personality. McConnell's main point was an ethical and political one, but suggestions like his ignore data indicating that behavioral programs in which the subjects' participation is involuntary frequently have poor results. The Vacaville and START programs bear out this generalization. In contrast, the most successful behavioral programs with delinquents have provided a wide range of behavioral options and reinforcers and allowed the subjects a substantial role in the design and operation of the program (e.g., Cohen and Filipczak 1971; Phillips et al. 1973). The relative success of the RRF programs may have been a function of their including some of these procedures.

McConnell's contention that convicted criminals should be stripped of all rights of self-determination and be "brainwashed" [9] into becoming law abiding citizens is also politically naive and dangerous. Goodell's (1973) review of political imprisonment in the United States presents evidence that in times of political unrest both federal and state

[9] McConnell apparently went about "brainwashing" prisoners by having volunteer undergraduates tutor prisoners in academic work (McConnell 1974a, 1974b). What reinforcement do behavior modifiers derive from incensing the public by advocating that we "brainwash" prisoners or that we move "beyond freedom and dignity" when what they really mean is that we should help inmates learn skills and should enhance people's real freedom by increasing their behavioral options?

Figure 18-1 One critic's view of behavior modification in prisons (SOURCE: Robyn Johnson-Ross, *The Civil Liberties Review,* 1973, *1,* 23. Copyright © 1973 by the American Civil Liberties Union. Reprinted by permission of the copyright holder and the publisher, John Wiley & Sons, Inc.)

authorities frequently attempt to use the criminal justice system to harrass, or if possible, silence their more radical opponents. The legitimization of coercive behavior modification and "brainwashing" of political prisoners would greatly increase the threat to and undermining of democratic processes that occur at such times.

A simplistic solution to this problem would be to exempt "political" prisoners from compulsory behavior modification. The difficulty with such a policy would be in defining "political prisoners." Would only prisoners who had committed a specifically "political" crime such as draft refusal or political conspiracy be exempted? Or would exemption include those inmates who had been convicted of a nonpolitical crime but who during their imprisonment had become outspoken critics of the political and social status quo? Prison authorities often see such politically oriented inmates as those *most* in need of changes in "attitude" (see Jackson 1970; Mitford 1973).

Even if such politically oriented prisoners were excluded when a coercive treatment program was begun, the program would still have serious political consequences in that it could be used to prevent the emergence of a similar political consciousness in future prisoners. Consequently, effective "rehabilitation" of criminals by coercive behavior modification may represent a politically attractive alternative for those who oppose attempts to eliminate such societal causes of crime as inequitable distribution of income, racism, and inadequate social services. In fact, even a voluntary and humane behavioral program could serve this function, since it could, in effect, "buy off" the troublemakers (criminals) among the poor. The Nixon administration, for example, strongly advocated prison reform (Chaneles 1973) while simultaneously dismantling the federal antipoverty effort.

This is not to say that behavior modifiers should abandon attempts to provide *voluntary* [10] programs in which prison inmates or parolees can learn skills for coping with society as it is. Nor should they refrain from developing management systems that offer prisoners positive incentives for cooperation without first depriving them of rights and amenities common even in many conventional prisons. However, if behavior modifiers wish to refute the widely voiced charge that their work supports inequities and injustices in the status quo, they must do more than just promote these and other progressive changes in the criminal justice system. They must also begin to explore ways in which their "science of human behavior" can aid efforts to improve the material and political lot of the deprived, as with community organizing (Alinsky 1971) or socio-political education of the poor (Freire 1971; Meyers et al. 1974). It seems unlikely that such explorations would be as generously funded by the powerful as are programs to change the illegally aggressive poor into law abiding, uncontentious citizens. Such differential support would make plain what I believe to be the naiveté of behavior modifiers who claim that theirs is a neutral technology. Like any technology of control, it will be bought, adapted, and monopolized by the powerful for their own not always benevolent purposes—unless the technologists themselves assume responsibility for disseminating it to the powerless.

[10] On the complicated issue of voluntary, informed consent in total institutions, see Davison and Stuart (1975), Friedman (1975), Goldiamond (1974, 1975), and Wexler (1975).

Sexual deviation

David H. Barlow
Section of Psychiatry and Human Behavior, Brown University and Butler Hospital

Gene G. Abel
Department of Psychiatry, University of Tennessee Medical School

19

Changing attitudes toward sexual functioning (or at least a change in the verbal expression of those attitudes) has resulted in a proliferation of sexual research. The past few years have witnessed the deletion of homosexuality as a diagnostic category from the American Psychiatric Association classification, increases in the frequency of transsexual surgery, publication of the work of Masters and Johnson, and behavior modification of sexual functioning.

In this chapter, Barlow and Abel discuss the development of accurate assessment devices, which allow them to evaluate treatment of sexual deviation. They report primarily on their own work, which has been mostly with males. They delineate four problem areas: (1) deviant sexual arousal; (2) deficiencies in heterosexual arousal; (3) deficiencies in heterosocial skills; and (4) gender role deviation. They then describe the changes that occurred in these areas as a result of their treatment program with a young, adult male who was labeled transsexual. The program demonstrates well the ongoing assessment which occurs in conjunction with the treatment program.

There are two significant points that deserve mention. First, as Barlow and Abel maintain, the therapist should not attempt to decrease any sexual response until some alternative one has been learned by the client. Thus, aversion therapy, if used at all, should occur only when the client has available a repertoire of alternative sexual responses. Second, considerable research on sexual functioning has been reported, the most notable of which is the work of Masters and Johnson. They and other experimenters in this area report success with a broad range of sexual functioning. The data indicate that problems labeled as orgasmic dysfunction and vaginismus in females and impotence and premature ejaculation in males are amenable to short-term sexual therapy on an outpatient basis (see Masters and Johnson 1970; Kaplan 1974).

The discussion and treatment of sexual functioning raises a number of ethical questions. For example, there has been considerable recent controversy over the legal and cultural issue of "sexual deviance." In some states, such practices as masturbation, oral sex, and premarital intercourse are categorized as unlawful. The recent growth of sexual liberation movements has likewise been influential. Does society have the right to prohibit certain behaviors among consenting adults? Are there any legitimate grounds for endorsing some sexual behaviors and condemning others? What are the psychological implications of labeling individuals as "deviant" if they prefer less conventional modes of sexual expression? Is the psychologist supporting the "establishment" or the status quo by offering therapy for culturally prohibited sexual patterns? As Davison (1973) and others have pointed out, offering therapy for a particular behavior pattern could be interpreted as an index of the therapist's values—i.e., that he considers the pattern deviant or maladaptive. These are only a few of the questions that demand thoughtful appraisal by both the therapist and the public. As has been noted at several points in this book, ethical issues extend far beyond sexual behavior and apply to nonbehavioral as well as behavioral therapies. In addition to their experimental research, Barlow and Abel have been active contributors to the analysis of these ethical issues.

Until we have reached some consensus on an appropriate terminology for various sexual patterns, effective communication demands that we use the prevailing vocabulary. In the chapter that follows, the use of such terms as sexual deviance *should therefore be viewed as descriptive and not necessarily evaluative.*

The early treatment of sexual deviation by behavioral techniques was related to the rising interest in behavior therapy during the 1960s. This focus on behavioral approaches to sexual deviation was due in large part to the unpromising results derived from traditional therapies and the radically different nature of the most popular behavioral approach, aversion therapy.

Development of behavioral approaches

Aversion therapy

Aversion therapy actually encompasses many different procedures. Several types of aversive stimuli have been used. The most frequently used are emetic drugs, peripheral electric shock, and covert sensitization (Cautela 1967) in which the stimulus is a description of an aversive scene which the client visualizes. These aversive stimuli have presumably been drawn from several learning paradigms such as classical fear conditioning, avoidance, escape, and punishment. (See Barlow 1973, for a review of aversive procedures.)

When applied to sexual behavior, the purpose of aversion therapy is to suppress deviant sexual arousal and behavior; early case histories based on anecdotal reports from patients indicated that this occurred (e.g., Max 1935a; Barker 1963). While a variety of aversive stimuli were used with other behavior disorders, the most popular stimulus for treatment of sexual deviation was electric shock applied in either a classical fear conditioning or an avoidance paradigm. The wave of enthusiasm generated by these case studies, and the focus on aversion therapy as treatment of choice, led to the premature conclusion that this treatment was the definitive procedure for sexual deviation and that failures were due only to improper application.

A more important consequence was the preclusion of careful assessment of the multiple behavioral excesses and deficits that comprise sexual deviation and which reveal the complexity of the problem. In fact, reducing excesses in deviant arousal, which is the major goal of aversion therapy, comprises only a small part in treatment as it has evolved, and sometimes no part at all (Barlow 1973).

The enthusiasm toward and commitment to aversion therapy during the 1960s, however, is understandable in view of the prevailing tendency to apply one treatment to all problems, in this case all sexual problems. In fact, this was the strategy behind the application of psychotherapy to all "neurotic" disorders (Bergin and Strupp 1972), and early behaviorists, like their traditional dynamic forebears, attended more to the technique than to the problem at hand.

The successful case studies generated further case reports as well as group comparison studies on the effects of aversion therapy. One of the best known studies was reported by Feldman and MacCulloch (1971). In this controlled experiment, three groups of 10 homosexuals each were treated. The first group received electrical aversion therapy in an avoidance paradigm. The second group also received electrical aversion therapy but in a straight classical fear conditioning paradigm. A third group received traditional psychotherapy. Interviews and a rating scale measure of homosexual responsiveness after treatment demonstrated that the aversive procedure was significantly more effective than psychotherapy. However, there were no differences in results between the two aversion techniques, each of which produced significant decreases in homosexual responsiveness in 60 percent of the clients, as opposed to a 20 percent decrease rate for the psychotherapy group. These results were maintained at a 1-year followup. The 60 percent success rate was similar to that in an earlier series reported by these authors (Feldman and MacCulloch 1966) and was quite impressive when compared to the results from traditional psychotherapy, where only between 10 and 30 percent of homosexuals show substantial therapeutic benefit (Woodward 1958; Curran and Parr 1957; Bieber, Bieber, Dain, Dince, Drellich, Grand, Grundlach, Kremer, Wilber, and Bieber 1963).

Results from other studies testing aversion therapy, however, were not so impressive. In controlled studies on homosexuality, Bancroft reported a 30 percent success rate, and Birk, Huddleston, Miller, and Cohler (1971) reported that only two out of eight homosexuals (25 percent) were heterosexual at a 2-year followup. These studies indicate that aversion therapy is statistically more effective than psychotherapy or no treatment, but the results are far from impressive clinically. With the exception of the 60 percent success rate in Feldman and MacCulloch's study, the success rate, even if success is narrowly defined as diminution of the deviant arousal and/or behavior, is quite low.

Expanding the approach

It is a hallmark of behavior therapy that faith in individual procedures gives way in the face of accumulating empirical evidence indicating failure or little success. As behavior therapy matured and new facts were brought to light, it became clear that aversion therapy alone was at best inadequate as treatment of sexual deviation. The key to this discovery was a more thorough and detailed behavioral assessment of the various problems found in sexual deviation. The major finding was that sexual deviation, whatever its object, was far more complex than heretofore assumed. While the emphasis found in textbooks and diagnostic schema is on the deviant arousal or behavior (for example, homosexuality, pedophilia), it is very seldom indeed that a client who complains of deviant sexual arousal does not present associated behavioral excesses or deficits. Often these associated problems are the major concern of the client. For example, a homosexual male may not be concerned about occasional homosexual relations, but rather complains of inability to become aroused with females. There are at least three associated problems that may accompany deviant arousal.

1. *Deficiencies in heterosexual arousal.* Deviant arousal may or may not be associated with absence or minimal levels of heterosexual arousal. Occasionally a client may have frequent heterosexual arousal and behavior with a wife or girlfriend and still engage in deviant sexual behavior. Such behavior marks the "true" bisexual as well as some fetishistic clients. Often, however, deviant sexual arousal is accompanied by diminished heterosexual arousal.

2. *Deficiencies in heterosocial skills.* Deviant arousal may or may not

be accompanied by deficiencies in heterosocial skills necessary for meeting, dating, and relating to persons of the opposite sex. Some clients who complain of deviant arousal also have adequate heterosexual arousal but may be unable to act on this arousal due to inadequate heterosocial skills. On the other hand, a client with deviant arousal may have adequate heterosocial skills but may experience no sexual arousal to the opposite sex.

3. *Gender role deviation.* Finally, a client with deviant arousal may have some degree of gender role deviation in which opposite sex role behaviors are present and some preference for the opposite sex role is verbalized. This is most common in some homosexuals and transvestites. When opposite sex role behavior is completely adopted and the client consistently thinks, feels, and behaves in the opposite sex role, this "mistaken gender identity" is called transsexualism (Green and Money 1969). These clients usually request sex reassignment surgery.

Recent findings from our laboratory (e.g., Abel, Blanchard, Barlow, and Mavissakalian, in press) indicate that patterns of deviant arousal cannot be glibly categorized under our traditional headings of homosexuality, pedophilia, and so on, since the type of stimuli or behavior that arouses one pedophiliac may be entirely different from the stimuli or behavior that arouses a second client, also called a pedophiliac.

The increased precision in assessment of the various problems associated with sexual deviation has also modified our treatment strategies. As Bergin and Strupp (1972) note, more accurate assessment of the various problems comprising any diagnostic category will lead to the construction of specific treatments aimed at specific components of a problem. In sexual deviation no two clients are the same; each has some combination of behavioral excesses and deficits and requires individual assessment and construction of a specific treatment package suited to his or her own goals. For this reason, any chapter on behavior therapy for sexual deviation (or any behavior disorder) cannot retain the typical division between diagnostic categories on the one hand, and treatment considerations on the other. In behavior therapy, where assessment and treatment are often one process, a meaningful description of these procedures must intermesh the two (see Chapter 9 in this volume). Thus, this chapter will dispense for the most part with a description of the various labels given to deviant sexual behaviors, such as pedophilia, and concentrate on problems that cut across the various categories, such as deficiencies in heterosexual arousal. In the remainder of the chapter the issue of assessment of patterns of sexual arousal will be examined in some detail, followed by a discussion of assessment and treatment of various components of sexual deviation, with one particularly complex case presented as an example.

Assessment of patterns of sexual arousal

Since behavioral techniques rely heavily on valid, objective measures of the course of treatment, it is not surprising that rapid advancements in the area of assessment techniques have been made with the advent of behavior therapy. This is of critical importance, for as we shall see, better assessment permits development of further behavioral treatments. Prior to the use of behavioral treatment techniques, clinicians and researchers relied heavily on assessment by either verbal report or attitudinal measures.

Verbal report

Verbal report is information provided by the client or members of his environment regarding his clinical course: for example, does he still expose himself, or is the homosexual patient interacting with adult women and what is the nature of that interaction? Such global information is rather easily obtainable and has been one of the major evaluative tools of other therapeutic approaches such as dynamically oriented therapy. Unfortunately, verbal report is easily invalidated by the client, and many times it is difficult for the client to assess adequately his own course since his own perception of his behavior may be unintentionally distorted for various reasons. Recent evidence demonstrates that under certain conditions clients will say they are sexually aroused when they are not (Barlow, Agras, Leitenberg, Callahan, and Moore 1972) or will report that they are aroused by one stimulus when, in fact, another is responsible for the arousal (Abel et al., in press). In these cases the client attempts to report accurately but fails. To complicate matters further, some sexual deviates such as voyeurs or exhibitionists carry out behaviors that are contrary to prevailing legal standards, and which may lead to their arrest. In such cases, in order to avoid legal contingencies, they are likely to give a verbal report that is at variance with behavior. These factors make verbal report a poor means of assessing patterns of sexual arousal.

Attitudinal measures

Attitudinal measures, the second major type of assessment techniques, attempt to quantify patients' sexual attitudes and beliefs concerning their arousal patterns. This usually involves scaling written statements along a continuum. Repeated scaling of the same statements allows a quantitative comparison of a client's attitudes with his prior ratings or ratings made by other groups. Older global measures of sexual orientation or arousal such as the masculine-feminine scale of the Minnesota Multiphasic Personality Inventory or the Rorschach tests have been cast aside as too vague. More recent attitudinal measures have attempted to pinpoint the specific attitude the therapist is attempting to alter. The measure of male or female preference devised by Feldman, MacCulloch, Mellor, and Pinschof (1966) or card sort techniques constructed specifically for each individual client (Barlow, Leitenberg, and Agras 1969) are examples of such recent attitudinal measures. In the SOM scale of Feldman et al., a homosexual rates a sentence such as "Men are attractive to me," on a 5-point scale ranging from "not at all" to "very." Similar statements concerning women are rated and a measure of homo- versus heterosexual interest is obtained. The scale can be modified for clients other than homosexuals.

In sexual assessment, all such attitudinal measures have two limitations. Since it is the client who does the rating, attitudinal measures, like verbal reports, are easily distorted by the client. Furthermore, behavioral programs do not primarily attempt to alter inner attitudes, although such changes enhance the validity of client improvement. The primary goal of treatment is behavior change; that is, the client's deviate behavior stops and nondeviate behavior begins or increases. Often, attitudinal changes *follow* behavioral changes and these measures can provide valuable information when used in conjunction with more objective measures.

Physiological measures of sexual arousal

Since an objective measure of sexual arousal is so necessary for the assessment of any behavioral treatment, it should not be surprising that the greatest advancements in recent years have been made in this area. Masters and Johnson (1966) have pioneered physiological measures of sexual arousal during the sexual act. Vaginal lubrication, elevation of blood pressure, tachycardia, and muscular contraction are but a few of the objective physiological changes that occur during orgasm.

Most sexual deviates, however, have problems of sexual arousal that precede the act of sexual intercourse. A male homosexual, for example, may be able to have sexual intercourse with an adult female, reaching orgasm without difficulty. He may accomplish this feat, however, by fantasizing that he is having anal intercourse with a male. In reality, the antecedents of intercourse with a female, such as attraction to the woman's personal characteristics and sexual features, the social interactions that precede intercourse, and fantasies of social and sexual interaction with the woman, are very alien and nonarousing to the client. In other words, most of the homosexual's problems occur very early in the chain of events leading to sexual intercourse. Thus, the necessary measurement must be a measurement of *early* sexual arousal. Many deviates lack a sexual partner, that is, they do not have a wife or a girlfriend. Since their very problem includes avoidance of women, measures that require the client to interact sexually with an adult female cannot always be used with these clients.

Types of measures. Zuckerman (1971) has reviewed the available literature regarding physiological measures of early sexual arousal, such as galvanic skin response, cardiac rate, respiration, and so on. Many of these physiological measures change considerably during sexual arousal, but other emotional states such as fear, anger, and pain can cause similar changes, so that these measures are not specific to sexual arousal. Penile erections appear to be the one objective physiological measure specifically correlated with sexual arousal in males,[1] and consequently several devices have been developed to calibrate changes in penile size. Because penile measurement has become such an integral part of the assessment technique for behavioral treatments and since penile measurement itself has given us considerable new insights into the nature of sexual arousal, these methods will be reviewed in some detail. Two penile measurement devices are currently available.

Circumference measurement. A number of authors describe the use of mercury-filled tubing (Bancroft, Jones, and Pullan 1966) or a strain gauge (Barlow, Becker, Leitenberg, and Agras 1970) that encircles the penis. As penile size increases, the electrical properties of these gauges change. Such changes, when compared with those of a full erection, enable the client's erection to be expressed as a percentage of full erection. Sexual arousal thus becomes quantifiable. The advantages of circumferential devices are that they are relatively small and lightweight, and their use does not cause major stimulation of the penis during the measurement process. More importantly, these devices measure within a functional and thus clinically relevant range of sexual arousal, for example, 25 to 100 percent full erection.

Volumetric measurement. Freund, Sedlarcek, and Knob (1965) pioneered the use of the penile plethysmograph, a volumetric device that encloses a significant portion of the penis, measuring even minute changes in penile volume, which are frequently so small that they are beyond the client's awareness. The advantage of this apparatus is its marked sensitivity to even minute changes. Disadvantages include its bulky size, causing considerable penile stimulation during its application,

[1] Exceptions are apparent in certain pathological conditions where erections may be present without the client being sexually aroused (priapism) or sexual arousal present without concomitant erections (impotence, or following spinal cord transsections).

its expense, and the fact that most studies using the apparatus deal with erection values less than 10 percent of a full erection, which are obviously outside a functional range for the patient. Each apparatus, however, appears to have advantages for specific types of studies.

Uses of penile measures. Freund (1963, 1965, 1967), using a plethysmograph, presented diagnostic groups of male sexual deviates with still pictures of men, women, and children. Relying on small subliminal changes, measurable by the volumetric device, he successfully categorized these subjects as homosexuals, heterosexuals, and pedophiliacs on the basis of their erection responses alone. Such results illustrate our current ability to objectify sexual preferences by means of this physiological measure.

Further understanding of the concept of deviation has resulted from investigations of subliminal arousal patterns with the volumetric device. Freund, McKnight, Langevin, and Cibiri (1972) isolated specific body parts of females of various ages (5 to 26 years old) and recorded normal heterosexual males' erection responses during such stimulus presentation. Results indicated that nondeviates responded to such female stimuli along an age continuum, with greatest erection responses to the adult women and smaller but still significant erection responses to very young, prepubertal girls. These findings suggest that the distinction between adult heterosexuals and pedophiliacs on the basis of erection responses to adult versus female children may be more of a quantitative difference than a qualitative one, since even normal males responded to stimuli depicting young girls. Such results from improved instrumentation are contributing considerably to ever-expanding appreciation of patterns of sexual arousal.

To determine patterns of sexual arousal in our laboratories, we most often use audio-taped descriptions of erotic scenes (Abel, Levis, and Clancy 1970; Abel et al., in press), since with this method we can pinpoint idiosyncratic patterns of arousal. Typically, during a 2-minute description of an erotic scene certain portions of the auditory description will produce erection blips (see Figure 19-1, B and C), while other content will not be correlated with erections. Often, subjects will admit that the content during some blips was highly erotic, but occasionally they will deny arousal at these points. The content under each of the erection blips is discussed with the subject and elaborated in a second description; content not correlated with erection responses during the first description is dropped when the tape is replayed (D). The second description usually generates even larger erection responses (E and F) when the tape is played back to the subject. The content under these larger blips is discussed further with the subject and is

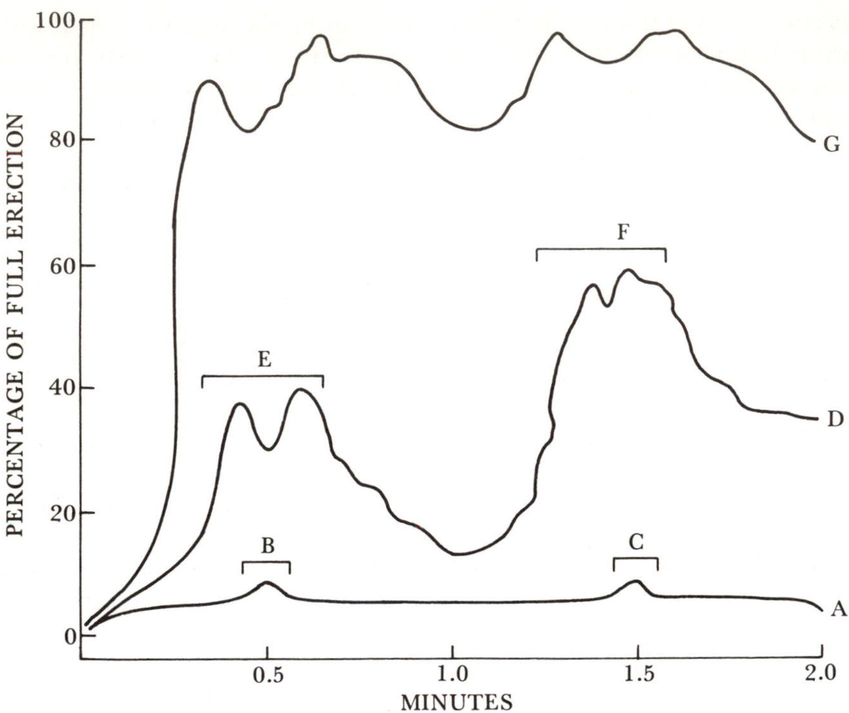

Figure 19-1 Patterns of arousal to 2 minutes of audio-taped erotic scenes

elaborated in greater detail in the final replay of the tape (G); the content in the second description (D) not correlated with erections is excluded. The final taped description (G) will elicit marked erections, sometimes when depicting sexual material that the subject had denied to be sexually arousing (see Abel et al., in press, for examples). These studies demonstrate the importance of obtaining behavioral as well as self-report data.

A major advantage of the audio-tape method is the capacity to control stimulus content presented to the client during penile measurement. This would be important, for example, in determining transsexual arousal patterns. A transsexual, unlike a homosexual, is one who entirely identifies with the opposite sex, that is, a transsexual male will think, feel, and act as a female. Like a homosexual, the transsexual will be attracted to males, but only if he fantasizes himself in the role of a female—an important distinction between the two. An attempt to measure what is erotic to a transsexual client might include, for example, measuring his erection while he views a heterosexual videotape depicting a couple engaged in sexual intercourse. The client's marked erection to such a scene may lead the therapist to conclude that the client has marked arousal to female cues. Questioning the client may reveal that he is imagining himself as the woman in the scene, and his arousal actually reflects his arousal to the male, from the vantage point of his identification with the female.

To illustrate this procedure, actual descriptions used with a client who presented mixed transsexual and homosexual features will be presented. To determine the specific erotic cues, we constructed a 4-minute audiotaped description that alternated every minute between descriptions of transsexual scenes and homosexual scenes. The first two 1-minute segments of the audio description were as follows:

> It's in the evening time and you're with George. You're a woman, you're a woman and you're in bed with him and you're having intercourse. He really loves you and he's right on top of you there. You can feel the weight of his body. George is right on top of you. You see his face, beard. He's right on top of you and he's got a stiff erection. You can feel his erection, it's right in your vagina. He's moving up and down on top of you. He's whispering that he loves you, whispering that he loves you and you can feel his penis right in you. Deep in you, he's got his penis deep into your vagina, he's really excited and just losing control of his sexual arousal. He's really stimulated. You can feel his penis right in your vagina. [End of first minute of audio description with patient as a woman.]
>
> Now you're a man, he's having intercourse with you, you're a man and he's having anal intercourse with you. He has his arms around you. He really loves you and cares for you and is really excited by your body. You're a man and he's having anal intercourse with you. You can feel his penis in you. You can feel his penis in you, deep in you, and he's really penetrated you deep. You're a man and he's holding on to you, he has his arms around you. You can feel his arms around you. He's holding you very closely, he really cares about you. He's a man. He's really attracted by your body. He says he loves you, you can hear him, he says he loves you. His arms around you, he has penetrated you deep, deep into your rectum. He's having intercourse with you. He's really enjoying you, he's really excited. [End of second minute of description with patient as a homosexual.]

The client's erection response (see Figure 19-2) to the successive minutes of transsexual followed by homosexual scenes demonstrates tumescence to the transsexual cues and detumescence to homosexual cues, suggesting that the diagnosis is transsexualism, not homosexuality. This case reflects the necessity of precisely controlling the stimuli presented and not leaving to chance the client's interpretation of the stimuli he's experiencing.

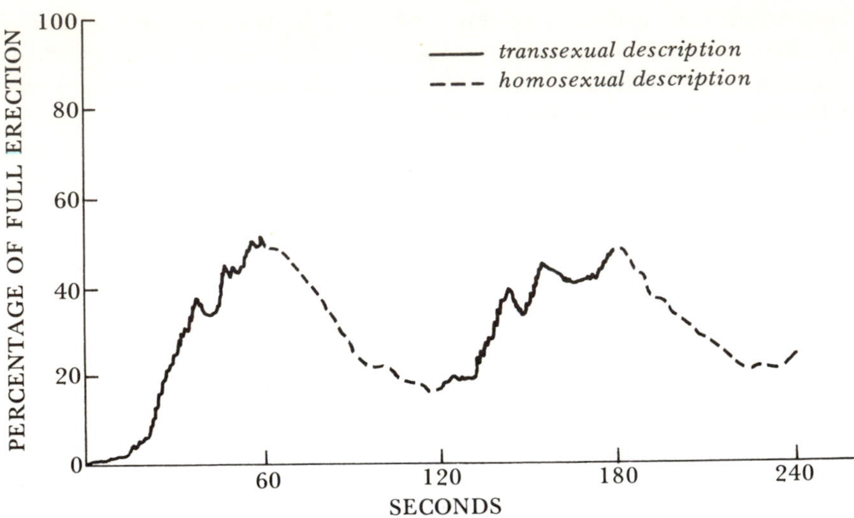

Figure 19-2 Erections to transsexual and homosexual audio descriptions

Once patterns of arousal are determined, erection measures are used in two ways. First, the client's erections to sexual cues can be used as an integral part of treatment. For instance, some techniques to accelerate heterosexual responsiveness (Barlow and Agras 1973) involve contingencies applied to erection responses while clients view erotic stimuli involving adult females. Similarly, erections to deviant stimuli may be used in constructing an aversive procedure. Second, the most common use of erection responses is to assess patterns of arousal as treatment proceeds. This allows the therapist continually to sample the client's sexual responses to determine the effectiveness of any treatment procedure.

New developments in treatment of sexual deviation

Development of alternative treatments

While assessment of heterosexual and deviant patterns of arousal is essential before construction of a treatment package suited to a particular client, equally important is proper assessment of social skills in heterosexual situations and assessment of deviation in gender role. In the beginning of the chapter, we noted that problems in these areas may or may not accompany deviation in patterns of sexual arousal, since the problems appear to be relatively independent of one another. Although it is not common to find all four major components of sexual deviation present in a single case, there is one clinical entity where this does occur with some consistency. This behavior disorder is called transsexualism or the gender dysphoric syndrome and is the most severe problem among the sexual deviations. As noted previously, transsexualism occurs when a biologically and genetically normal male or female thinks, feels, and behaves as a member of the opposite sex. Many such clients will say something like, "I am a woman trapped in a man's body" (Green and Money 1969).

The most usual treatment for this condition to date has been sex reassignment surgery. The purpose of this surgical procedure is to modify a patient's primary sexual characteristics to those of the opposite sex. For a male to female transsexual, castration is followed by creation of an artificial vagina. To qualify for surgery, the patient must live in the opposite sex role for at least 1 year. During this period, administration of hormones facilitates development of secondary sexual characteristics, as well as breast development in men. This radical procedure has been relatively successful in synchronizing the patient's body with gender identity, which in turn enables him or her to lead a more normal life.

Recently, we approached this problem from the psychological rather than the surgical point of view (Barlow, Agras, and Reynolds 1972). Employing newly developed behavior therapy procedures with a young, adult male transsexual, we modified the four basic components of sexual deviation one by one, with a resulting change in the client's gender identity. Since transsexualism does involve all four components of sexual deviation, examples of newly developed behavior therapy procedures for each component will be presented in description of our treatment of this transsexual. From this description, one may extrapolate a typical treatment program for other sexual deviates with fewer components of the problem. For instance, a pedophiliac may demonstrate marked pedophilic arousal, deficits in heterosexual arousal, and inadequate heterosocial skills on assessment, but evidence no signs of gender role deviation. In this case, treatments used with the transsexual would be administered to the pedophiliac in the first three areas only; of course, the treatments would be modified to adapt them to the individual patient.

Example of behavioral treatment

The client was a 17-year-old male and the last of five children. The boy was a keen disappointment to his mother, since she desired a girl. Nevertheless, he became her favorite child. His father worked long hours and had little contact with the boy. For as long as the client could remember, he had thought of himself as a girl. Spontaneous cross-dressing, as reported by the client and as confirmed by his parents, began before the age of 5 years and continued into the junior high school years. During this period his mother reported that he developed an interest in cooking, knitting, crocheting, and embroidering, skills which he acquired by reading an encyclopedia. His older brother often scorned him for his distaste of "masculine" activities such as hunting. The client reported associating mostly with girls during this period, although he remembered being strongly attracted to a "boyfriend" in the first grade. In his sexual fantasies, which developed when he was about 12 years of age, he pictured himself as a female having intercourse with a male.

Upon referral he was moderately depressed, withdrawn, and attending secretarial school, where he was the only boy in the class. He reported a strong desire to change his sex. Since surgery was not possible at his age, he agreed to enter a treatment program designed to change his gender identity, on the premise that it might at least make him more comfortable and that surgery was always possible at a later date.

The first step, as in any behavioral treatment, was a thorough assessment of the behavioral excesses and deficits comprising the four major components of sexual deviation. This assessment revealed that the client had severe gender role deviation, the most obvious manifestation being extremely effeminate behavior; demonstrated grossly inadequate social skills; had no heterosexual arousal; and was strongly aroused by transsexual fantasies.

Changing gender role. Experience with this case, as well as other evidence (Barlow 1974), indicated that inappropriate gender role behavior had to be modified before other components were treated. Thus the client's effeminate behavior, which was eliciting much scorn and ridicule from his peers, was chosen as the first target for treatment. To this end, a behavioral check list of gender-specific motor behaviors was developed. Males and females were observed over a period of time in the natural environment, and characteristic ways of sitting, standing, and walking were chosen on the basis of uniqueness to sex. Four male characteristics and four female characteristics of sitting, walking, and standing were chosen to form the scale. For example, one of the behavioral components characteristic of sitting in males is crossing the legs with one ankle resting on the opposite knee. One of the female behaviors is legs crossed, closely together, with one knee on top of the other.

Direct modification of sitting, standing, and walking was then attempted by modeling and videotape feedback. The effect of modeling and videotape feedback was experimentally analyzed in a multiple-baseline design in which the modification of only one category of behavior was attempted while measures of all three categories were collected. After completion of work on the first category, modification of the second category was attempted, and so on.

In the experimental treatment phase, daily measures of masculine and feminine components of sitting, standing, and walking were taken (by a rater who was not aware of changes in the treatment program) as the client came into the waiting room before his session. A 30-minute session was held daily. After 5 days of baseline procedures in which no treatment was given, modification of sitting behavior was begun. In each session the constellation of appropriate behavior was broken down and taught piece by piece. Each behavior was modeled by a male therapist and then attempted by the client. Praise for success and verbal feedback of errors was administered. The last trial of the day was videotaped and shown at the beginning of the following session. When the client was sitting appropriately in the session and reported feeling comfortable, treatment was begun on walking.

Pretreatment measurement showed that this client's motor behavior was almost exclusively feminine with only an occasional instance of masculine behavior. During treatment, he learned to behave in a more masculine manner while sitting, standing, and walking. Furthermore, the experimental design demonstrated that the treatment was responsible for these changes since female sitting and walking behaviors did not change appreciably until treated. That is, treatment of sitting produced changes in that category, but not in walking behavior; the latter, in turn, improved when treatment was administered directly to walking.

Few clients will demonstrate such a predominance of feminine behavior. The extent of gender role deviation observed in this client is most often found only in the transsexual. Nevertheless, some degree of gender role deviation and effeminate behavior is present in many clients. Recently, Freund, Nagler, Langevin, Zajac, and Steiner (1974) discovered that gender role deviation for homosexuals is on a continuum from masculine to feminine. Many homosexuals are entirely masculine in their gender identity and behavior. Other homosexuals, however, may be found at any point along the continuum from entirely masculine to entirely feminine. While data are not available, clinical evidence indicates that the same may be said for transvestites who dress in clothing of the opposite sex for sexual pleasure only. In all of these clients, the available evidence (Barlow, 1974) indicates that modification of deviant gender role behavior must be the first stage in any treatment approach.

When this treatment phase was completed, the client reported that he enjoyed his masculine behavior since people did not stare at him so much and since the severe ridicule experienced from his peers had decreased substantially. No changes were noted, however, in his patterns of sexual arousal, which remained strongly transsexual with little or no heterosexual arousal. In addition, the client remained withdrawn and socially inadequate.

Increasing heterosocial skills. Accordingly, the next component requiring therapeutic attention was social skills appropriate to a heterosexual orientation. Treating sexual deviation by teaching new heterosocial skills is not a new idea. Case reports indicate that this approach often constitutes a major part of the psychoanalytic-oriented psychotherapeutic treatment of sexual deviation with individuals or groups. Although procedures are seldom specified, several case reports illustrate the process.

Approaching homosexuality from the analytic viewpoint of heterosexual phobia, Ovesey, Gaylin, and Hendin (1963) state, "Psychotherapy of homosexuality is essentially that of any phobia. Sooner or later the homosexual patient must make the necessary attempts and he must make them again and again" (p. 22). Insight in the approach is "a means to an end." They then describe successful treatment of three homosexuals, each of whom seemed gradually to learn more effective heterosexual approach behavior. These clinicians also state, "The patient must become more masculine by learning appropriate patterns of assertion and increasing his self-sufficiency. In some cases merely an increase in non-sexual assertion may prove sufficient to initiate and maintain heterosexual behavior" (p. 22).

It is interesting to note that this is precisely the approach advocated by Wolpe (1969) working within a behavioral framework. Several cases of sexual deviation have been successfully treated by assertive training (Stevenson and Wolpe 1960; Edwards 1972). Clients were taught nonsexual assertion that presumably enabled them to be more successful in heterosocial situations, which, in turn, led to heterosexual relations. In many of these cases it seems that deviant responsiveness dropped out once heterosexual behavior was established.

In a group psychotherapy approach, Birk, Miller, and Cohler (1970) report that a female cotherapist was most useful during therapy in that homosexuals had opportunities to learn to relate to the female in a heterosocial way. Their newly learned feelings and behaviors then generalized to other heterosocial situations, according to reports of the clients. A similar procedure within a behavioral framework is reported by Cautela and Wisocki (1969). Their homosexual clients actually rehearsed such heterosocial behaviors as asking for a date with a young female therapist before being sent out to attempt these steps.

Treatment for our client followed a similar pattern, although the first step in behavior rehearsal involved learning to relate to the males in his environment since his skills were also quite deficient in this area. Behavior rehearsal enabled the client to acquire the social skills necessary to interact with males and females in his environment. Such behavior as eye contact, appropriate affect in social situations, content of conversation (how to make small talk, and so on) were taught in a painstaking step-by-step process. An additional procedure for this client was voice retraining, since like many transsexuals, he had affected a high-pitched, effeminate voice. Practice in lowering his voice was successful after he was instructed to place his finger on his thyroid cartilage (Adam's apple) while speaking. As the thyroid cartilage lowers, so does pitch. When this phase was completed, the client reported he was quite capable socially and was getting on well with his peers. A subsequent fantasy retraining phase (Barlow, Agras, and Reynolds 1972) removed the last vestige of mistaken gender identity, so that he now acted like a male and believed he was a male. Continuing assessment of patterns of sexual arousal, however, revealed that he was still strongly attracted to males and demonstrated no heterosexual arousal. In other words, he could now be called a homosexual. At this point his homosexual arousal contained no signs of transsexual fantasies in which he would imagine himself as a female making love to a male. His arousal, measured by penile circumference measures, was now typically homosexual.

Increasing heterosexual arousal. With treatment of gender role deviation and heterosocial deficits complete, intervention in a third component, deficits in heterosexual arousal, was instituted. Several procedures have been devised to increase heterosexual responsiveness. However, due to the emphasis on aversion during the 1960s, most techniques are still in a preliminary stage of development (Barlow 1973). This is surprising when one examines the prevailing theories on the etiology of homosexuality, and to some extent, deviant sexual behavior in general. Both psychoanalytic and behavioral theories emphasize the importance of avoidance of heterosexuality in the genesis and maintenance of deviant behavior (e.g., Rado 1949; Wolpe 1969). This notion finds some support in two surveys. Bieber et al. (1963) noted that 70 of the 106 clients in their survey reported fear of or aversion to female genitalia. In a survey of homosexuals, heterosexuals, and bisexuals, Ramsey and Van Velzen (1968) found that both homosexuals and heterosexuals had strong negative emotional feelings concerning sexual practices with the nonpreferred sex. Freund, Langevin, Cibiri, and Zajac (1973) obtained similar findings in homosexuals and heterosexuals on attitudinal and penile response measures.

Clinically, the best course is to increase heterosexual arousal before decreasing deviant arousal. There are two reasons for this. First, providing alternative patterns of sexual arousal is sometimes sufficient treatment in that deviant arousal then decreases spontaneously (e.g., Herman, Barlow, and Agras 1974). If this does occur, treatment can be terminated at this point and the complications of an aversive procedure are avoided. Second, decreasing deviant arousal before providing the client with alternative arousal leaves the client with no arousal for a time and thus no sexual outlet. Since sexual arousal is a major pleasure or reinforcer, its removal may lead to severe depression.

Among the several procedures to increase heterosexual responsiveness recently tested is a classical conditioning procedure (Herman, Barlow, and Agras 1974). Although this technique successfully increased heterosexual arousal in our client, further testing revealed that the many procedural difficulties with this technique precluded widespread application. An alternative behavior therapy technique that seems more successful was described recently by Barlow and Agras (1973). Derived from the work on errorless discrimination in the laboratories of experimental psychology (Terrace 1966), this procedure concentrates on "fading in" heterosexual stimuli during periods of sexual arousal in an effort to change stimulus control of sexual responsiveness. In this procedure, one male and one female slide were superimposed on one another. Through the use of an adjustable transformer, a decrease in the brightness of the male slide resulted in a simultaneous increase in the brightness of the female slide. During treatment the female stimulus was faded in, contingent on the subject maintaining 75 percent of a full erection as measured by a strain gauge device, through a series of 20 steps ranging from 100 percent male brightness to 100 percent female brightness. The technique was investigated in three controlled, single case experiments with homosexuals. A reversal experimental design was also utilized, which consisted of fading, then a control procedure where fading was reversed or stopped, and then a return to fading.

The first homosexual completed the fading procedure and became sexually aroused to the female slide alone in six sessions. This arousal generalized to female slides in separate measurement sessions and to reports of heterosexual behavior. In the control phase, when fading was reversed, heterosexual arousal and reports of heterosexual behavior dropped considerably. When the female slide was faded in once more, heterosexual arousal increased. Homosexual responsiveness remained high throughout the experiment.

In the second experiment heterosexual arousal rose during the initial fading, continued rising, but then dropped sharply during a control phase in which fading was stopped at the halfway point and the slides shown separately, and rose once again when fading was reintroduced. Again homosexual arousal remained high throughout treatment, but 1- and 3-month followups showed that it dropped sharply after termination, *without* therapeutic attempts to accomplish this goal. This experimental procedure and result was replicated with a third homosexual. Although this technique has been tested on homosexuals, there is no apparent reason why it could not be used with other deviates, such as pedophiliacs.

Decreasing deviant arousal. To return to our client, three components of sexual deviation, that is, gender role deviation, inadequate heterosocial skills, and deficits in heterosexual arousal, responded to treatment. As noted previously, treatment often stops here because deviant arousal sometimes decreases "spontaneously" or because the client does not want to eliminate deviant arousal, as with many homosexuals. In this particular case, homosexual arousal remained strong and the client was quite adamant about eliminating this source of sexual arousal.

At this point, and at this point only, it is appropriate to consider aversion therapy. Due to the early popularity of aversion therapy described in the beginning of the chapter, these procedures have undergone more development and testing in clinical situations than treatments directed at other components of sexual deviation. Evidence cited in the beginning of the chapter and elsewhere (e.g., Barlow 1974) demonstrates that aversive techniques can be effective if the treatment goal is the narrow one of decreasing deviant arousal. While electrical aversion has been the most popular aversion technique, covert sensitization (Cautela 1966, 1967), where the patient imagines both the chain of events comprising the deviant behavior as well as the aversive situation, also is effective (Barlow, Leitenberg, and Agras 1969). In fact, recent evidence indicates that this procedure may be more effective than electrical aversion in some instances (Callahan and Leitenberg 1973). If further research bears it out, this will be a major advance for behavior therapy since the necessary apparatus and the unpleasantness of peripheral electrical shock could be avoided.

In the transsexual case, a combination of electrical aversion and covert sensitization successfully eliminated deviant arousal. Treatment of this fourth and last component marked the end of formal intervention in this case. At this point the client had adequate heterosexual arousal, little or no deviant arousal or gender role deviation, and ample heterosocial skills. Followup visits, consisting mostly of support and advice on new situations, continued sporadically for several months. At a

2-year followup, the client was attending college and dating regularly.

A concluding note

Despite success with this case, we are a long way from the development of a treatment package that can be routinely applied to every client. Increased sophistication in assessment procedures should pinpoint additional aspects of sexual deviation requiring therapeutic intervention. Treatments now in use will most likely become obsolete as future clinical research uncovers more effective procedures. The wide-ranging individual differences among clients previously thought to be similar ensure increased complexity for our research efforts, as we seek to answer major questions concerning human behavior. But the scientific underpinnings of the behavior therapy approach provide the necessary base for a truly cumulative set of principles unencumbered by dogma or blind adherence to unproven assumptions. As these principles and facts emerge through painstaking research, we should begin to realize more fully our goals of relieving human suffering and enhancing human functioning.

Social skills training

Michel Hersen
Department of Psychiatry, Western Psychiatric Institute and Clinic, University of Pittsburgh School of Medicine
Richard M. Eisler
Veterans Administration Center, Jackson, Mississippi
University of Mississippi Medical Center

20

When you say someone has a "good personality," at least part of the description derives from the person's good social skills. The development of appropriate social skills allows a person to engage in enjoyable activities that might otherwise be avoided because of a lack of skills. While most social skills training has been done with the ubiquitous college sophomore and problems such as dating and social interaction, Hersen and Eisler point out that training in social skills is an integral aspect of resocializing the chronic mental patient and increasing the adaptive behaviors of depressed clients.

Experimenters across several theoretical orientations have found a significant relationship between social functioning and behavior disorders; however, the straightforward treatment of social skills has only recently been undertaken. After discussing the relevance of social skills training in the treatment of behavior disorders, the authors proceed to describe how they, and others, train clients in social skills by utilizing role playing, instruction and feedback, and modeling procedures. Generally speaking, these treatment procedures have been successful in the laboratory setting but have not generalized to real-life conditions. Greater generalization has been reported in experimental/clinical settings than in laboratory research. Hopefully such generalization will be maintained as training in social skills becomes a more widely used clinical procedure.

The relationship between impairment of social interpersonal functioning and various behavior disorders has been alluded to in most contemporary theories of psychopathology. While the literature is replete with descriptions of the interpersonal inadequacies exhibited by psychiatric patients of many diagnostic categories, there are few approaches that generate treatment strategies for interpersonal problems involved in many disorders. This deficiency is especially surprising in the behavior modification literature, where the influence of environmental factors in the development of behavior disorders is heavily stressed.

The role of the social environment has been documented in the development and maintenance of maladaptive patterns in children and chronic mental patients. With respect to less severe disorders in adolescents and adults, an individual's ability to interact successfully with others in his natural environments at school, home, and work might bear relevance to the probability of developing a variety of disorders. Interpersonal or social skills variables may be of prime importance in the prevention and treatment of many psychiatric problems.

While many forms of treatment designated for individuals labeled schizophrenic, character disorder, neurotic, and various categories of "social deviance" have acknowledged the existence of poor interpersonal adjustment, most have chosen to focus treatment efforts on "symptom" removal or have been relatively unstructured attempts to improve socialization through a therapeutic milieu (Cumming and Cumming 1962) or group therapy (Sager and Kaplan 1972). More recently, however, behavioral clinicians have focused their efforts on improving the social skills of their clients (Hersen, Eisler, and Miller 1973).[1] Involved in these attempts are treatment techniques designed to improve an individual's ability to communicate with and respond more effectively to others in the natural environment. Differences between these efforts at social rehabilitation and earlier attempts, using therapeutic milieu and group therapy concepts, are that in current social skills training specific social deficits are analyzed in terms of their verbal and nonverbal component behaviors. There is less emphasis on the notion that encounters involving confrontation and comprehension of the reasons for one's inappropriate behavior will lead to change in the absence of specific guidance on *how* to change. Additionally, the social learning approaches insist on precise measures of behavior change rather than relying on self-report indices that correlate poorly with the patient's overt behavior.

Admittedly, social skills training for a variety of behavior disorders associated with interpersonal deficits is in its early developmental stages. The purpose of the present chapter is to place some of the relevant issues in historical perspective, describe early behavioral ap-

[1] Social skills refers to a composite of specific verbal and nonverbal behaviors in interactions with others.

proaches to interpersonal problems, discuss techniques that have been used, and delineate some future directions.

Social skills and behavior disorders

Historical antecedents

The fact that psychiatric patients have deficits in social-interpersonal maturity has been documented by Zigler and Phillips and their colleagues (Levine and Zigler 1973; Phillips and Zigler 1961, 1964; Zigler and Levine 1973; Zigler and Phillips 1959, 1961a, 1961b) in a series of diagnostically oriented studies over the past 16 years. In an initial study, Zigler and Phillips (1959) reported that state hospital patients, when compared with a sample of nonhospitalized individuals in the same geographic region, evidenced greater impoverishment in social achievement. They also noted that, diagnostically, persons labeled schizophrenic and character disorder were more socially inadequate than those labeled manic-depressive and neurotic.

To further assess the relationship between social-interpersonal achievement and psychopathology, Zigler and Phillips (1961a) developed a yardstick of interpersonal functioning termed *Social Competence.* This measure, used to assess premorbid social performance (before the disorder was assessed), was based on variables such as age, educational and occupational level attained, employment history, and marital status. Since data comprising social competence were obtained retrospectively from case history material, it was not possible to determine experimentally which factors had had the most profound influence on level of social development (for example, genetic endowment, previous learning history, or opportunities afforded by socio-economic status).

Phillips and Zigler (1961) found that individuals of varying social competence exhibited different types of disorders. Patients who had relatively high social competence tended to have problems in the sphere of verbalization and ideation (that is, obsessions, phobias, and sexual preoccupations). Less socially competent patients generally expressed their symptomatology in terms of direct action, such as suicide attempts, physical assaults, emotional outbursts, and irresponsible behavior.

In studying the outcome of psychiatric treatment, Zigler and Phillips (1961b) found that premorbid social competence was related to the probability that the patient would make a satisfactory posthospitalization life adjustment. Patients who evidenced relatively good social functioning prior to their hospitalization tended to have shorter periods of institutionalization and a lower rate of rehospitalization following discharge than did patients with more inadequate social skills. Thus, in determining outcome of hospitalization, initial level of social competence was found to be a more significant factor than type of psychiatric treatment received. Unfortunately, the consistent finding that social competence rather than psychiatric diagnosis may be one of the major factors discriminating individuals who are hospitalized in mental institutions from those who are not has had surprisingly little effect on prevention, assessment, and treatment.

Assertive training

One of the first attempts by behavioral clinicians to improve the social skills of clients was related to a broad group of therapeutic procedures generally referred to as assertive training. As described by Wolpe and Lazarus, assertive training was a method for helping people to overcome anxiety elicited by interpersonal encounters. The rationale for assertive training was presented as follows:

> When anxiety inhibits the behavior called for in interpersonal relations there are also undesirable *consequences.* The individual is almost inevitably left at an objective disadvantage *vis-à-vis* others. . . . His unexpressed impulse continues to reverberate within him. . . . In many cases these persistent discharges produce somatic symptoms and even pathological changes in predisposed organs. . . . Although the most common class of assertive responses involved in therapeutic actions is the expression of anger and resentment, the term "assertive behavior" is used quite broadly to cover all socially acceptable expressions of personal rights and feelings. (Wolpe and Lazarus 1966, p. 39)

This view hypothesized that if an individual could be encouraged to express his feelings more adequately in interpersonal situations, anxiety would gradually be inhibited since it was assumed to be incompatible with assertive expression of feelings. The operant aspects in assertive training were also considered. That is, acts of interpersonal assertiveness were programmed to meet with favorable consequences in the client's natural social environment and thus be reinforced.

In the early clinical work on assertive training the expression of socially appropriate irritations and angry feelings was emphasized. More recently, however, assertive training has been broadened to include the expression of positive feelings such as the ability to communicate praise, affection, and approval (Lazarus 1971). Assertive training has been applied to a wide variety of clinical problems. In addition to its use with clients described as passive neurotics, assertive training has been used in the treatment of such disorders as sexual dysfunction, alcoholism, and depression. Weinman, Gellbart, Wallace, and Post (1972) used aspects of assertive training procedures to increase interpersonal interactions in withdrawn, chronic "schizophrenic" mental patients. Similarly, Hersen, Turner, Edelstein, and Pinkston (1975) used a number of therapeutic procedures including social skills training to rehabilitate a withdrawn schizophrenic. At the conclusion of the treatment this client was gainfully employed for the first time in 3 years.

In many respects, the theoretical notions underlying social skills training extend beyond Wolpe's (1958) original formulation that anxiety inhibits interpersonal responsiveness. In a variety of clients exhibiting different behavior disorders, it appears that appropriate social skills have never been learned. Because of these deficits, the individual has great difficulty obtaining the kinds of social reinforcement that are required. In the absence of appropriate social interaction, various forms of deviant behaviors including delusional speech, crying spells, and antisocial conduct became reinforced and maintained by the attention these behaviors invariably elicited from others.

Social skills and treatment of depression

The clinical syndrome of depression has recently received increased attention from behaviorally oriented clinical researchers. The operant conceptualization (discussed at length in Chapter 12 in this volume) views the depressed individual as receiving a low rate of social reinforcement from his environment. Low rate of reinforcement may be due to loss of contact with significant interpersonal partners through death, divorce, or separation. Another possibility is that the depressed person has a weak behavioral repertoire and emits relatively few behaviors that can be reinforced. Finally, lack of social reinforcement may be due, in part, to the fact that the depressed individual emits a relatively high rate of behaviors that are aversive to others.

As noted in Chapter 12, there are many problems associated with the area labeled depression. The first problem concerning us here is the definition of depressive behaviors with respect to observation and measurement. In general, the depressed person evidences a slowing of most motor activities, reports a loss of appetite and ability to sleep, frequently has somatic preoccupations, and has obsessions about feelings of worthlessness and guilt, as well as thoughts about committing suicide. A second problem involves finding suitable treatments for depression. At issue is the controversy over whether the causes are related to internal biochemical factors (the so-called endogenous depressions) or are due primarily to sudden environmental changes (referred to as the reactive depressions). Irrespective of etiology, persons labeled depressed are traditionally treated with a combination of antidepressant medication and some form of supportive psychotherapy. If depression is intimately tied with unhappy life circumstances such as social isolation, an unrewarding job, or lack of adequate leisure-time activities, environmental changes are often indicated.

Recently, Lewinsohn and his colleagues (Lewinsohn, in press; Lewinsohn, Weinstein, and Alper 1970; Libet and Lewinsohn 1973) emphasized lack of social skills as an important antecedent condition for depressive behaviors. Social skill is defined as "the complex ability to both emit behaviors that are positively reinforced and not to emit behaviors that are punished by others" (Libet and Lewinsohn 1973, p. 304). The definition of social skill is made in terms of the consequences (positive, neutral, or negative) of an individual's reactions toward another person. Libet and Lewinsohn (1973) compared the differences in social behaviors of small groups of depressed and nondepressed control subjects. The results indicated that depressed individuals emitted fewer behaviors of an *initiative* type than their nondepressed counterparts. Depressed individuals focused their behavior primarily on one person in the group whereas nondepressed individuals distributed their communications more equally among all group members. In addition to a longer latency of response, depressed individuals emitted fewer positive statements relative to all comments made than did nondepressed individuals. Thus, lack of initiative, failure to distribute responses to a number of individuals in a social group, relative lack of positive statements made toward others, and long latency of response appeared to support the hypothesis that depressed individuals were less skillful in eliciting social reinforcement than nondepressed individuals. Of course, results of this study do not demonstrate that depressed individuals are *innately* less socially skillful than nondepressed individuals, but merely that they did not demonstrate such skills relative to control subjects. It is possible, on the other hand, that individuals predisposed to depression do not possess such skills and must be taught how to elicit social reinforcement from others.

Lewinsohn and other behaviorally oriented clinicians (Lewinsohn, in press; Liberman and Raskin 1971) are now studying the social behavior of depressed individuals in the context of family interaction. These naturally occurring social interactions may provide us with an opportunity to observe more closely which contingent patterns of action and reaction strengthen depressive behaviors and maintain the depressed individual's relatively impoverished social relationships. Treatment might then consist of helping the depressed individual develop patterns of response that are more pleasing to others, thereby eliciting more positive social responses from significant others. In addition to its use in the treatment of depression, it is becoming apparent that social skills training will be of use in treating individuals with a variety of other disorders reflecting interpersonal deficits.

Social skills and treatment of minimal dating

Social skills training has recently been applied to the target problem of "minimal dating" behavior with populations of male college students. Subjects selected for these studies are generally psychiatrically normal young men who admit to feelings of social anxiety in heterosexual situations and who report a low frequency of dating behavior that they would like to change.

Most theoretical views of minimal dating conceptualize the problem in terms of anxiety conditioned to heterosexual situations, negative self-evaluations with respect to social competence, and/or actual behavioral deficits in heterosocial skills. In some of the studies a comparison is made between specific behavioral techniques, including skills training, and the more traditional counseling methods to increase dating behavior.

Using a population of nondating male college students, Martinson and Zerface (1970) compared the effectiveness of "eclectic" counseling with a semistructured program of arranged interactions with female college students. Individuals in the "eclectic" counseling group were seen by a professional counselor once a week for 5 weeks with instructions to discuss their concerns about dating. Clients in the structured interactions group met once a week for 5 weeks with a randomly selected female student who was interested in improving her own social skills. Prior to their arranged meetings, male and female participants were instructed to discuss their personal difficulties in social interaction. Additionally, a delayed treatment control group of males received no treatment during the study.

The structured interactions group had a significantly greater decrease in self-reported fear of dating than did the other two groups. Subjects in the structured interactions group demonstrated an increased frequency of dating girls (other than the experimental participants) when compared with the counseling and control groups. While it is difficult to pinpoint the variables related to greater improvement in the experimental group, it would appear that *in vivo* exposure to the feared social interaction plus feedback from the female participants were more effective in increasing actual dating than discussions with a professional counselor.

A more direct attempt to influence the social skills deficits of minimal daters was evaluated by MacDonald, Lindquist, Kramer, McGrath, and Rhyne (1973). These authors assumed that males presenting a target problem of nondating fail to approach dating situations because they lack the skills necessary to obtain reinforcement for their efforts. In this formulation, reduction in anxiety or attempts to increase self-concept would be ineffective because these conditions result from poor performance or actual failures in dating attempts. Subjects in two experimental (direct social skills training) programs involving behavior rehearsal with and without extra-session assignments were compared with "attention-placebo" and waiting list controls. The primary treatment for the social skills groups consisted of behavior rehearsal with instructions and verbal feedback. More specifically, males were taught to discriminate between approachable and unapproachable females, how to initiate and maintain conversations, how to listen and ask appropriate questions, how to respond to nonverbal cues, and when to terminate conversations appropriately. The group that received social skills training with assignments outside of treatment were asked to practice these behaviors with casual female acquaintances.

While the results were not unequivocal, both social skills groups showed behavioral improvement on role-played interactive sequences with female confederates. There was little relationship between general measures of anxiety and social skill. Anxiety reduction on one measure was achieved only in those individuals who evidenced significant social skills improvement. This result suggests that socially experienced anxiety may change after mastery of a situation, and that treatment measures designed to reduce anxiety prior to social skills training may be unnecessary. Followup of these students, unfortunately, was not long enough to determine whether improvements in social skills carried over into actual dating practices.

Assessment and treatment

Measurement of social skills deficits

The precise measurement of specific social skills deficits is needed from both the research and the clinical frameworks. To evaluate empirically the efficacy of his treatment interventions, the researcher must be able to show relevant increases or decreases in target behaviors. Similarly, the clinician who is data-conscious is interested in obtaining an objective appraisal of his efforts. Thus, when the effects of specific treatment strategies on designated behaviors are under consideration, both the researcher and clinician are intent on answering the question: "Is my specific technique effective in changing the behaviors reflecting social skills deficits?"

In measuring social skills deficits several approaches are possible. When interpersonal behaviors are being assessed, a question arises as to whether measurement should be done in the natural environment (for example, observation of how the depressed patient interacts with family members at the dinner table) or whether role playing or analogue situations will be used. Obviously, the assessment procedure within the natural environment is the preferred mode. However, when such assessment is not feasible for a variety of practical reasons *and* it can be demonstrated that role-playing procedures are related to behavior in the natural environment, then interactions simulating real-life circumstances may be considered as a suitable alternative.

There is a question whether changes should be monitored on specific component behaviors (number of initiations at conversation, length of comments, amount of speech relative to others) or on more "global" dependent variables such as clinical ratings of depression. For example, in a recent study Hersen and Miller (1974) treated a reactively depressed client with assertive training techniques, with attention focused on increasing the following target behaviors: (1) the client's eye contact with his interpersonal partner; (2) the length of his responses to queries; (3) the number of requests made of his interpersonal partner; and (4) the number of independent initiations at conversation. The global effects of treatment were examined by having the client periodically fill out a self-report scale of depression and by having nursing assistants on the ward rate objective measures of depression. In another study (Eisler, Miller, Hersen, and Alford, in press), the effects of assertive training on specific aspects of marital interaction (speech duration, eye contact, references to drinking in conversation, and requests made to the interpersonal partner) were examined in an alcoholic and his wife. In addition, the effects of treatment on the husband's alcoholism were assessed by taking blood/alcohol measures in his natural environment before, during, and after treatment. In this case interactional target variables and the general drinking problem were assessed. Although it is preferable to evaluate both the "clinical syndrome" and specific target behaviors, in the clinical context the necessary recording equipment and availability of observers may, at times, preclude a more formal evaluation of component behaviors.

Related to this is the issue of what particular system (physiological, self-report, motoric) the clinical researcher is interested in using for his dependent variable. Although when speaking of an individual's deficits in social functioning one usually refers to his verbal and nonverbal communications, physiological concomitants (for example, galvanic skin response or heart rate in a situation requiring an assertive response) of social skills behaviors cannot be overlooked. Moreover, the individual's attitudes and verbal reports of how he feels about engaging in a situation requiring specific social skills such as assertiveness are equally important. As noted elsewhere (Hersen 1973; Hersen, Eisler, and Miller 1973), a complete evaluation and comprehensive treatment must involve attention to the three response systems. It is likely that therapeutic attention to one system at the expense of another will lead to only partial success and subsequent evidence of problem behaviors.

For example, if a client evidences appropriate social behavior in a situation requiring assertive responding but still experiences subjective discomfort, it is probable that anxiety will inhibit subsequent performance if not specifically treated. On the other hand, if the client's anxiety is decreased but he is not taught new ways of responding, then his social discomfort in the situation will be increased, resulting in intensified anxiety. Such increases in anxiety may retard the development and performance of new behavioral repertoires.

The development of relevant measures of social skills deficits is not always a straightforward matter. Sometimes clients deficient in social skills present problems which *appear* unrelated to their social skills deficits, such as anxiety, depression, insomnia, tension headaches and other psychosomatic disorders. At first blush the specific deficits may not be apparent to the therapist. Only after a careful behavioral assessment has been completed will the therapist be able to identify specific targets needing improvement. At this juncture in the treatment process the therapist and client must agree as to which of the deficits need remediation.

Although the focus of the behavioral analysis and treatment is on uncovering specific deficits and introducing techniques to improve the client's behavioral repertoire, a particular client may be described more generally as socially unskilled. At times he may be described as unassertive. When such a label is used, what are the component behaviors that lead to the judgment of overall unassertiveness? This issue was examined in a recent study by Eisler, Miller, and Hersen (1973). Thirty randomly selected male psychiatric patients were videotaped while responding to 14 analogue situations requiring assertive responding. To approximate the natural situation, a female research assistant sat next to the patient and prompted his responses. A typical situation used in this study follows.

> *Narrator:* You have just come home from work and as you settle down to read the newspaper you discover that your wife has cut out an important article in order to get a recipe on the back of it.
>
> *Role Model Wife:* I just wanted to cut out a recipe before I forgot about it. (Eisler, Miller, and Hersen 1973, p. 96)

Following the prompt by the role model wife, the patient was expected to answer as if he were actually in the narrated situation.

On an *a priori* basis, a number of nonverbal and verbal behaviors were selected for study: duration of looking, smiles, duration of reply, latency of response, loudness of speech, fluency of speech, compliance content, content requesting new behavior, and affect. Two independent judges viewed the videotapes retrospectively and rated patients on the aforementioned categories. In addition, each patient was given a rating for overall assertiveness. Patients were then dichotomized at the median into two groups with high and low overall assertiveness. Statistical analyses showed that patients perceived as most assertive evidenced longer replies, louder speech, more requests for new behavior from their interpersonal partners, and greater affect when responding. In addition, high assertive patients evidenced shorter latencies of response and fewer instances of compliance content than low assertive patients.

Current treatment procedures

The specific techniques used in social skills training will in part be determined by the client's history. If the client initially developed the requisite social skills and then became inhibited as a function of anxiety and/or punishment for his efforts at social interaction, then a technique directed toward reducing anxiety in social situations would be considered appropriate. For example, one might consider applying standard systematic desensitization (Wolpe 1958), a technique in which the client is asked to imagine his approaching the anxiety-evoking situation (that is, the situation requiring particular social skills such as asking an attractive girl for a date) in gradual steps under conditions of deep muscular relaxation. After successful completion of the hierarchy of steps in imagination, the client would be expected to carry out the approach behavior *in vivo.* An alternative strategy would have the client carry out all steps on an *in vivo* basis from the inception of therapy. A totally different alternative would be to "flood" the patient with the anxiety-provoking situations, as in implosion therapy (Stampfl and Levis 1967). A detailed discussion of whether systematic desensitization or flooding is to be used is well beyond the scope of this chapter. However, the choice of treatment is often dictated by the specifics of the case and the stylistic characteristics of the therapist (see Chapter 11 in this volume).

If the client never acquired the requisite social skills, or through long-standing inhibition had few opportunities to practice his social repertoire, then it behooves the therapist to apply techniques aimed at building or rebuilding the client's social behavior. A number of basic technical operations are used in all forms of social skills training.

In developing a client's repertoire of social responses, treatment is applied within the context of behavior rehearsal. Behavior rehearsal is defined as "a procedure whereby more desirable responses to interpersonal conflict situations are practiced under the supervision of the therapist" (Eisler and Hersen 1973, p. 112). Typically, the client and therapist role-play the particular situations in which the client evidences social skills deficits. For example, if the client experiences difficulties making reasonable requests from significant others in his environment, the therapist, with the help of the client, will construct social situations relevant to the client's difficulties. Initially the therapist will observe the client's responses in the role-played encounters. Such initial observations serve as baseline data. These observations may indicate that the client is deficient in any of a number of definable approach behaviors (verbal and nonverbal). For example, the client may fail to maintain eye contact with his partner and may speak in an inaudible voice. With such deficits it has been shown that simple instructional control in which the therapist merely tells the client to increase his rate of eye contact and to speak in a more audible voice, may lead to sufficient improvements (Eisler, Hersen, and Agras 1973; Hersen et al. 1973).

In many instances instructional control can be bolstered by giving the client feedback on his performance. That is, after the therapist has given a specific instruction ("Look at your partner when you speak.") and the client begins to initiate the behavior in subsequent practice sessions, the therapist will comment on the client's performance. Such commentary should be as precise and specific as possible ("Your introductory comments to Jane were fine. However, even though you looked at her when you asked her for a date, I had difficulty hearing you. Next time speak up."). Although the exact mechanisms accounting for the efficacy of feedback are not fully understood, "the administration of feedback to patients regarding specific aspects of their behavior has proven to effect positive changes in relevant target behaviors" (Eisler and Hersen 1973, p. 112). The use of audio and videotape feedback has also been recommended as adjunctive techniques in helping the client acquire social skills. Serber (1972) has emphasized the use of videotape feedback in shaping the nonverbal components of assertive behavior in unassertive clients.

The individual and combined uses of instructions and feedback are helpful during role-playing sessions when the client has some notion of the kinds of social behaviors that are required. However, in more difficult cases, where behavioral repertoires are extremely limited, additional techniques will be needed to elicit successive approximations of social responses. Modeling, an observational learning technique, has proven effective in helping clients develop new patterns of responses (see Eisler, Hersen, and Miller 1973; Gutride, Goldstein, and Hunter 1973; Hersen et al. 1973). In a recent study, Eisler, Hersen, and Miller (1973) showed that unassertive patients who observed an assertive model on videotape improved their responses on five of eight components of assertiveness after only four short sessions of observation. Improvement in assertive responding was even greater when instructions and modeling were combined (Hersen et al. 1973).

In an actual clinical context the therapist, in role-played situations, will frequently provide the client with a model for the specific behaviors requiring change. Usually the client will evidence deficits in social functioning within several areas such as absence or low rate of eye contact, long latency of response, failure to initiate conversations, and short responses. In modeling new behaviors for the client it is recommended that the therapist deal with one deficit at a time until the client has mastered each component separately. More specifically, the therapist will draw attention in sequence to each component behavior modeled by giving the client instructions and feedback (Eisler 1974).

Although it is convenient from a research standpoint to provide the client with a standardized filmed or videotaped model that he can emulate, exigencies of the clinical situation frequently will not allow for such precision. Kazdin (1974a) recently examined the possibility of using an alternative modeling approach, known as covert modeling (Cautela 1971), in attempts to increase the social skills of unassertive subjects. In covert modeling, Kazdin asked his unassertive subjects to imagine situations in which a model responded in an assertive fashion. In a second group (covert modeling and reinforcement), subjects were asked to imagine a model acting assertively, following which the model self-reinforced for his assertive behavior. The results of this study showed that both the covert modeling and covert modeling plus reinforcement groups performed significantly better in a role playing situation and on self-report inventories than the delayed treatment and no-modeling controls.

While in therapy, the client will have numerous opportunities to practice his developing repertoire of social responses (behavior rehearsal). As the client begins to approximate the target responses required for adequate social functioning, the therapist will offer encouragement and praise (social reinforcement). Such social reinforcement serves both to maintain the client's motivation in treatment and to provide him with additional feedback on his performance at a given point in time.

Generalization and maintenance of therapeutic gains

Techniques for bringing about rapid improvement in social deficit behaviors (depression, unassertiveness, minimal dating, schizophrenic withdrawal) are readily available to practicing clinicians. However, despite the relative ease with which change is accomplished in the therapeutic context, a major problem involves the transfer and maintenance of gains into the client's natural environment. Research findings to date are mixed with respect to generalization. For example, in the case of assertive training, although some transfer is reported, it is generally limited to the types of social interactions modified during experimental treatment (Hersen, Eisler, and Miller 1974; Kazdin 1974a; McFall and Lillesand 1971; McFall and Marston 1970; McFall and Twentyman 1973). Of course, brevity of treatment and lack of followup in these studies may account for the somewhat disappointing results.

As noted previously, Martinson and Zerface (1970) found that nondating college males exposed to arranged interactions with college females subsequently increased their actual dating behavior. Improvements were recorded at the 3- and 8-week followups. In most cases the subjects were dating girls other than those who participated in the original experimental treatment.

Reports in the clinical literature appear to be fairly optimistic with respect to transfer of training into the natural environment (e.g., Eisler 1974; Fensterheim 1972; Hersen et al. 1974; Lazarus 1971; Liberman and Raskin 1971). Probably the major difference in the clinical cases is that the therapist programs the client's social environment to reinforce the newly acquired repertoire of responses.[2] Liberman and Raskin (1971) describe the case of a depressed woman whose family was instructed to pay frequent attention to her coping behaviors but to ignore instances of depressive behavior.

> They were taught to acknowledge her positive actions with interest, encouragement, and approval. Overall, they were not to decrease the amount of attention focused on the patient but rather switch the contingencies of their attention from "sick woman" to "housewife and mother." Within one week her depressed behavior decreased sharply and her "healthy" behavior increased. (p. 521)

To further evaluate the role of social reinforcement in this case, after 2 weeks the family was instructed to once again pay more attention to the patient's sick behavior. Shortly thereafter her depression increased. When the family was reinstructed to pay attention to her coping abilities or social skills, she once again showed considerable improvement. At a 1-year followup the patient's improvement had been maintained.

Such a case is a dramatic example of the importance of having the patient's social environment reinforce her positive initiatives. In this respect, Wolpe (1969) cautions therapists using assertive training procedures to *"never instigate an assertive act that is likely to have seriously punishing consequences for the patient"* (p. 67). To the contrary, the therapist must ensure that the client will experience success when he first prac-

[2] In the clinical situation the therapist also obtains reports from the client on the level of success obtained in the natural environment. Thus, there is further opportunity for shaping of social responses in subsequent therapy sessions.

tices his new responses in his natural environment. Similarly, Eisler (1974) recommends that the client be given homework assignments in his natural environment that are likely to be reinforced. In addition, there is an apparent need for periodic re-evaluations of clients following discharge to ensure that environmental reinforcement is sufficient. If recidivism occurs, booster treatment, aimed at both restructuring social skills and furthering environmental manipulation, is warranted.

A concluding note

The theory, rationale, and treatments discussed in this chapter are based on the notion that many forms of psychiatric disorders represent *major* deficits in social skills rather than mere evidence of discrete symptomatology (that is, anxiety, depression). Although the relationship between social competence and psychiatric disorder has been studied for many years and given empirical confirmation, only recently have clinicians paid attention to the specific social skills deficits underlying many forms of psychopathology.

Inasmuch as many clients have never learned the requisite social repertoires needed to cope with the ordinary and extraordinary interpersonal situations of life, a primary therapeutic task involves a concerned effort to help these clients develop viable social responses. We have described the basic technical operations used during the treatment of social skills deficits related to depression, minimal dating, unassertiveness, and schizophrenic withdrawal. Although the techniques for bringing about rapid improvements in social deficit behaviors are readily available to most practicing clinicians, they are infrequently employed in therapy. Moreover, the strategies for ensuring transfer from the clinical context to the client's natural environment must be examined more carefully. In short, clinical outcome studies in which the long-term effects of social skills training are assessed have yet to be carried out.

If, in the future, such studies should confirm the long-term effects of social skills training for a variety of psychiatric disorders, some of the traditional assumptions regarding psychiatric disorder and treatment will have to undergo major re-evaluation. At that point, instead of viewing most behavior disorders in terms of the quasi-medical model, we are more likely to view clients and patients in light of their *particular deficiencies in the development of appropriate social skills.*

Alcohol and drug abuse

Peter M. Miller and Richard M. Eisler
Veterans Administration Center, Jackson, Mississippi
University of Mississippi Medical Center

21

Alcoholism and drug abuse represent two challenging social problems, and two problems with which almost every person has had direct contact, either in himself, a friend, or a relative. The treatment of these problems is exceptionally difficult because the behavior to be reduced, that is, ingestion of alcohol or certain drugs, usually provides an immediate and powerful reinforcer.

In this chapter Miller and Eisler discuss a number of social, psychological, and physiological factors associated with alcoholism and drug abuse. Although most early behavioral approaches were aversion therapy programs, the emphasis has switched to more comprehensive programs based on three objectives: (1) to decrease the immediate reinforcing properties of drugs; (2) to develop new behaviors incompatible with alcohol and drug abuse; and (3) to modify the client's environment so that he receives maximum reinforcement for activities other than drug and alcohol abuse. Assessment of treatment effectiveness has been enhanced by the use of physiological and behavioral measures in addition to the more traditional self-report measures, which are fairly invalid with clients undergoing treatment for these problems.

The authors maintain that community self-help groups may fit within the behavioral framework in that total environments are often changed and the client is provided with a coping model. In contrast to the objective of total abstinence as encouraged by most community self-help groups, one finding emerging from the behavior modification research with alcoholism is that total abstinence is not essential for successful rehabilitation programs. With adequate and comprehensive programs, clients may learn or relearn controlled drinking skills.

The use of substances that lead to excessive psychological or physical dependence poses both a hazard for the individual and widespread problems for society. In recent times drug abuse (especially narcotics) has occurred most frequently among lower-class urban males living in deteriorated areas of the city. Within this context, addiction was perceived as a function of social and economic deprivations. Addiction among more affluent individuals was considered to be a result of personality maladjustment; that is, the addict was characterized as a sociopath or antisocial personality who had little impulse control (Monroe, Ross, and Berzins 1971). Alcohol, on the other hand, has been an acceptable drug used by the majority in this country. It is interesting to note that society did not appear particularly concerned over the issue of drug addiction until it spread from the ghetto into middle-class suburbia. A similar pattern of public apathy had existed with the abuse of alcohol, since only "Skid Row bums" were considered to be true alcoholics.

Alcohol is by far the most abused drug in our society. Approximately 80 to 90 million individuals in the United States consume alcohol and 9 million of these are considered to be alcoholics. While heroin addiction is also a devastating problem, it affects only about 250,000 individuals. Wald and Hutt (1972) note that approximately 750,000 of the 15 million people who have used marijuana are frequent users. Other drugs such as amphetamines, barbiturates, and LSD are abused on a much smaller scale.

In this country, the most frequently abused drugs include the following: alcohol, opium and its derivatives (morphine, heroin), the hallucinogens (LSD, mescaline, psilocybin), cannabis (hashish, marijuana), stimulants (amphetamines), barbiturates, tranquilizers such as meprobamate (Equanil, Miltown), chlordiazepoxide (Librium), and diazepam (Valium). Some of these substances are physically addicting while others may produce psychological dependence. Physical addiction is usually defined in terms of the presence of physiological withdrawal symptoms subsequent to discontinuation of drug use after a period of excessive intake. This phenomenon is most typically observed with alcohol and heroin. While some substances such as marijuana may not be physically addicting, they can be abused for psychological reasons. An excessively strong desire for the pleasant emotional state produced by a drug in lieu of a more satisfying lifestyle is known as drug dependence.

Definition of abuse

Differentiation between *use* and *abuse* of alcohol or drugs has been a complex issue in the field of addiction. With "hard" drugs such as heroin (where there is no medical indication for its use) any use at all may constitute abuse. Most drugs, including alcohol, have certain prescribed and acceptable medicinal, social, or religious uses in our society. The simplest way to define abuse appears to be in terms of the effects of drug or alcohol intake on the individual's ability to function successfully in his environment. Thus, a problem exists if taking drugs significantly interferes with the individual's social, vocational, marital, emotional, or physical functioning in his or her day-to-day life. It is difficult to define abuse in terms of amount consumed since some individuals are able to tolerate relatively large quantities of alcohol and/or certain drugs over a period of time with few apparent detrimental effects. Others are grossly affected by relatively small amounts of a drug. Motivations for drug intake are sometimes considered in determining abuse. For example, temporary use of tranquilizers to relieve stress induced by a death in the family might be an acceptable reason for drug use while extended use to escape responsibilities or forget about current marital problems would not. However, the loss of functioning that can be attributed to drug use is easier to delineate than the individual's motives and therefore provides a more practical measure of abuse.

Etiology of drug abuse

Sociological factors

Sociologically, the incidence of drug use varies from culture to culture and from subgroup to subgroup within a culture. Three major factors related to incidence include the availability of a drug within a culture, the context within which it is used, and the sanctions imposed on its abuse. Social groups in which alcohol and/or drugs are used within certain prescribed religious or medical contexts tend to experience less substance abuse. For example, Jews have a very low incidence of alcoholism. This is often attributed to the fact that wine drinking occurs in the context of religious traditions, with the norms for consumption narrowly prescribed. Extensive social and religious censure is associated with excessive use of alcohol. Of all countries in the world, Israel has the lowest absolute level of alcohol consumption. For those Jews who depart from their cultural and religious traditions or who are assimilated into a more diverse culture, such as those in the United States, there is a much higher incidence of abuse.

At times alcohol or drug *abuse*, rather than *use* itself, is sanctioned by the societal group. Certain American Indian tribes had the tradition of chewing cactus, which contains the hallucinogenic substance mescaline. In order to reach a higher level of communication with the gods, ceremonies were held in which the participants became high on mescaline to the point of stupor, hallucinations, and time distortion. Such substance abuse, occurring within very narrowly defined circumstances, was encouraged and reinforced by their culture.

In order to combat substance abuse many societies have imposed severe legal penalties. In the long run such punishment methods have not significantly affected the incidence of abuse. One reason is that the sanctions are often difficult to enforce due to the availability and widespread use of alcohol and drugs. In addition, the imposition of a sanction, such as Prohibition, enhances the reinforcement obtained from the abuse of alcohol in that it becomes a "dangerous" or "adventurous" behavior.

Physiological factors

The influence of physiological factors in the etiology of substance abuse is poorly understood. Several physiological theories have been put forth to explain the causes of alcohol abuse. R. J. Williams (1946) postulated that through a genetic defect alcoholics have a marked nutritional deficiency. He hypothesized that an individual's alcohol consumption increases as a function of the lack of certain essential vitamins. However, experimental investigations have not supported this theory.

Another popular theory of alcohol abuse is that it is inherited. Goodwin (1971) recently reviewed the research literature, which shows that alcoholism does run in families. If an individual has a parent or blood relative who is an alcoholic, he or she is more likely to abuse alcohol. This fact, however, does not necessarily implicate genetic factors. Studies on social role modeling (Bandura 1969) suggest that exposure to a model who exhibits inappropriate drinking patterns can teach a child to respond in a similar manner when provided with the opportunity. On the other hand, children who are reared in abstinent families tend to be more likely to abuse alcohol if they drink at all. These children are not provided with adult models who confine their drinking to social occasions. Early in life they do not learn appropriate means of how, when, where, and why to drink.

It may be that rather than direct genetic links there are physiological predispositions which affect abuse of a substance. For example, an individual with low gastrointestinal tolerance for alcohol may be less likely to abuse it. After one or two drinks he may experience slight discomfort or nausea and thus terminate drinking. The person who becomes an alcoholic may be able to tolerate more, and hence obtain less negative physiological feedback. While he may experience a hangover the next day, "punishment" occurs too long after drinking to have any great effect. Similarly, due to biochemical differences, some individuals may experience greater pleasant effects (highs) from a particular drug than others, and thus be more likely to use it repeatedly.

Psychological factors

While a number of psychological theories based upon various formulations of personality development have been postulated to account for drug abuse (McCord and McCord 1960), the present chapter will focus on a social-learning approach, which is the basis of behavior modification treatment strategies.

Within a social-learning framework alcohol and drug abuse are viewed as socially acquired, learned behavior patterns maintained by numerous antecedent cues and consequent reinforcers that may be of a psychological, sociological, or physiological nature. Such factors as reduction in anxiety, increased social recognition and peer approval, enhanced ability to exhibit more varied, spontaneous social behavior, or the avoidance of physiological withdrawal symptoms may maintain substance abuse (Miller 1973b; Miller and Barlow 1973; Cahoon and Crosby 1972). In this regard, it is often necessary to differentiate between *precipitating causes* and *maintaining causes.* Let us suppose that a middle-aged housewife is experiencing marital difficulties and begins to drink excessively in order to relieve tension and worry regarding her marriage. She and her husband eventually obtain a divorce and her drinking increases. She has established a pattern whereby excessive drinking becomes contingent upon any emotionally stressful event. Being intoxicated relieves her anxiety and allows her to escape temporarily from stressful circumstances. Once drinking has increased to a daily frequency she finds that early morning drinking is reinforcing since it relieves agitation and hangover from the previous evening's drinking. She may associate with others who drink to excess through contacts made in bars. At this point the *precipitating factor* (stress of marital problems) is no longer present. Her drinking continues for other *maintaining reasons* such as peer approval, encouragement, recognition, and/or avoidance of withdrawal symptoms. Treatment must be geared toward the most currently potent maintaining factors, since the initial causes may have little relevance to her present drinking pattern. Once drinking is brought under control through treatment, intervention efforts aimed at teaching her how to deal more appropriately with stressful events would certainly decrease the chance of relapse.

The same reasoning may be applied to the abuse of other drugs. Narcotics use, for example, may be precipitated by social modeling, desire for peer approval, or any of a variety of social-psychological factors. Once physical addiction is well established, treatment applied only toward these precipitating causes would hardly be sufficient. Continued drug taking to avoid unpleasant withdrawal symptoms may become the most potent reinforcer for the behavior once it is established. In this regard, Wikler (1968) hypothesizes that physical dependence is further maintained by repeated associations between environmental cues (persons, places, situations) and aversive withdrawal symptoms. The instrumental activity of drug taking in the presence of these cues is reinforced by an escape from or avoidance of physiological withdrawal.

Specific maintaining factors

The factors precipitating and maintaining drug abuse are numerous and vary greatly from individual to individual. Poor or nonexistent models for the appropriate use of addicting substances may be involved. A child may be exposed to a parent who regularly consumes an array of medications at the slightest indication of psychological discomfort. Society also reinforces this behavior through advertising which advocates drugs as the answer to many of life's problems. Many physicians reinforce this pattern by prescribing sleeping medications, tranquilizers, antidepressants, and diet pills without sufficient evaluation of psychological factors underlying the patient's request for drugs.

Families that teach tolerance of frustration and discomfort together with adaptive ways of dealing with life's problems help to ensure that reliance on drugs will not be necessary or desirable. In fact, drug-taking behavior under stressful conditions is often considered aversive by some individuals since their problem-solving skills become less efficient. In a laboratory analogue drinking study, Miller, Hersen, Eisler, Epstein, and Woote (1974) observed that while alcoholics consumed more alcohol under conditions of social stress, social drinkers actually reduced their consumption in these circumstances. In a sense they have learned ways to deal with stress that are incompatible with increased drug intake.

Peer pressure together with recognition and attention from significant others often serve to precipitate and eventually maintain abusive drug taking. Adolescents are particularly susceptible to the effects of peer reinforcement. Status is obtained in youth peer groups on the basis of the variety of drugs ingested or one's tolerance for large quantities of drugs. Certainly the reinforcement obtained from a "new experience" or from the pleasurable physiological effects of some drugs plays an important role.

Friends and relatives often unwittingly provide recognition and attention for drug abuse. For example, in a study of chronic alcoholics and their wives, Hersen, Miller, and Eisler (1973) found that during a videotaped conversation, wives gave their husbands significantly more nonverbal attention (looking, smiling) whenever alcohol-related topics were being discussed. Attention ceased when their interaction was related to other topics.

Drugs and alcohol may also serve to reduce aversive emotional or cognitive states and replace them with more positive ones. In this regard, certain environmental circumstances associated with boredom, depression, anxiety, agitation, or self-depreciating thoughts elicit substance abuse. Teasdale and Hinkson (1971) found that users of amphetamine-barbiturate combinations subjectively report less social anxiety, increased self-esteem, and feelings of euphoria after drug usage. In the absence of drugs, these users reported themselves to be highly anxious and lacking in self-confidence, with a high frequency of negative self-statements, hesitancy to attempt new behavior patterns, and so on. Thus, cognitive changes induced by drugs may serve as a reinforcer for continued use.

A number of studies have investigated anxiety reduction as an etiological factor in alcoholism. A number of years ago, various experiments (Clark and Polish 1960; Masserman and Yum 1946) indicated that animals under stress not only develop a strong preference for alcohol solutions but also apparently learn to escape stress by consuming such solutions. The evidence with humans, however, is equivocal. Nathan and O'Brien (1971) and Nathan, Titler, Lowenstein, Solomon, and Rossi (1970) found that chronic, Skid Row alcoholics actually experienced heightened anxiety and depression subsequent to drinking. In an attempt to further investigate this phenomenon, Miller, Hersen, Eisler, and Hilsman (1974) evaluated the effects of stressful interpersonal encounters on the drinking behavior of alcoholics and social drinkers. As compared to a nonstressful interpersonal condition, social stress, accompanied by increased pulse rate, increased the drinking of alcoholics and tended to decrease consumption in social drinkers. Other investigations (Allman, Taylor, and Nathan 1972; Higgins and Marlatt, in press) suggest a complex relationship between stress and drinking, which appears to involve *subject characteristics, type of stress* (interpersonal versus environmental), and the *context* within which the stress occurs.

In some individuals, substance abuse allows for expression of an enhanced behavioral repertoire. A shy, inhibited person may find that he or she is able to respond more spontaneously, or become more assertive under the influence of drugs. Often, however, the more spontaneous behavior is then exhibited to an extreme so that rather than being assertive the individual becomes hostile or socially inappropriate. Intoxication or being "high" sometimes allows an individual to engage in socially unacceptable behaviors without censure; the individual has an "excuse" for deviant behavior patterns.

Traditional treatment approaches

Traditionally, treatment of substance abuse has been based on a variety of theories and has received little systematic evaluation. Traditional treatment approaches for alcohol abuse include individual and group psychodynamic therapy (Brunner-Orne 1958; Silber 1959), psychodrama (Weiner 1967), milieu therapy (Kendall 1967), medications such as tranquilizers, antidepressants, LSD, and Antabuse (Abramson 1960; Kissin and Charnoff 1967), and community abstinence groups (Alcoholics Anonymous 1955). Drug abuse programs have utilized individual and group psychotherapy, Synanon (self-help group), and methadone maintenance.

A major hindrance to the evaluation of treatment strategies has been the lack of objective measures of the behavior to be changed. Recently, however, new measures have been developed.

Assessment techniques

Self-report measures

In traditional treatment programs, a widely used measure to assess changes is the self-report of the patient. Both alcohol and drug abusers are notoriously poor in accurately describing their behavior. Self-assessment is often influenced by forgetfulness, misperception, and distortion. In addition, to avoid certain negative consequences, such as censure and criticism or being dropped from the program, the client may provide the counselor or therapist with the information that will please him the most (Simkins 1971). While other measures such as reports from relatives and friends, number of "busts" for possession and/or sale, and number of hospitalizations are also used, they have their limitations (Miller 1973b).

Physiological measures

Since it is not practically feasible to observe directly an individual's drug-taking behavior during his day-to-day life, correlative *physiological measures* have been developed for use in the natural environment. Most methadone maintenance programs for heroin abuse have utilized periodic urinanalysis for ongoing assessment of their clients (Edwards 1970; Goldstein and Brown 1970). Miller, Hersen, Eisler, and Watts (in press) and Miller (1974) have utilized breathalyzer analysis (breath tests similar to those used by police officers to detect intoxicated motorists) to assess the blood/alcohol levels of alcoholics in treatment. Usually these are administered at unspecified times with little prior notice to the patient.

Drug abuse researchers are also developing an array of analogue measures necessary to objectively evaluate clinical procedures. A recent case study by Elkin, Williams, Barlow, and Stewart (1974) provides a model of objective evaluation. One of the most interesting features of assessment in this case was the pre- and posttreatment measurement of physiological responses to videotaped scenes of the patient "shooting up." At times, however, more precise information on an individual's alcohol or drug behavior is needed, so behavioral measures have recently been developed.

Behavioral measures

One of the fundamental precepts of the behavior modification approach to treatment is the necessity of precise, quantifiable, and verifiable measures of behavior. To date, behavioral measures of substance abuse behavior have been conducted in laboratory analogue settings. A number of investigators in the area of alcoholism have developed measures of drinking behavior that can easily be *administered within a hospital or laboratory setting*. One such measure (Mello and Mendelson 1965; Miller, Hersen, and Eisler, in press; Nathan et al. 1970; Nathan and O'Brien 1971) involves an operant drinking device whereby a simple motor task such as lever pressing is rewarded with predetermined amounts of alcohol. Records of number and pattern of responses permits a detailed, objective measure of the patient's "motivation" to obtain alcohol under various experimental conditions.

Marlatt, Deming, and Reid (1973) and Miller and Hersen (1972) separately developed a surreptitious task in which patients were asked to rate, on a variety of taste dimensions, various alcoholic and nonalcholic beverages. At the termination of each rating session the exact amount of alcoholic versus nonalcoholic beverages consumed were calculated without the patient's knowledge. Liberman (1968) used a similar choice situation to evaluate the treatment of two chronic morphine addicts.

In an attempt to obtain a more naturalistic measure of drinking behavior, Schaefer, Sobell, and Mills (1971) and Mills, Sobell, and Schaefer (1971) utilized a simulated experimental bar setting in which patients were allowed to order drinks of their choice. Observers then recorded number and kinds of drinks ordered, as well as frequency and magnitude of sips. Simulated living room setups with alcohol available are sometimes used with patients who do not drink in bars so that the laboratory situation more closely approximates the alcoholic's drinking environment in the community. These measures have been found to be very useful in the study of alcoholism. Thus far, they have been used to evaluate treatment strategies (Miller, Hersen, Eisler, and Hemphill 1973; Miller et al., in press), analyze the influence of specific antecedents of alcohol consumption (Miller, Hersen, Eisler, Epstein, and Woote 1974), and to assess behaviorally an individual's motivation for treatment (Miller, Hersen, Eisler, and Elkin 1974).

A model behavioral treatment program

A truly comprehensive behavioral approach to substance abuse has yet to be implemented and systematically evaluated over a significant period of time. Various treatment programs, however, utilize certain aspects of the behavioral approach. The results of efforts to evaluate specific behavior modification treatment strategies will be presented within the context of a model intervention program.

All clinicians do not adhere to the "disease" model of alcohol abuse, which assumes that once an alcoholic always an alcoholic. In fact, recent experimental evidence seriously questions the assumption that alcoholics have lost complete control of their drinking and can never drink, even socially, again (Ewing 1973; Marlatt et al. 1973; Paredes, Hood, Seymour, and Gollob 1973; Sobell and Sobell 1973b). Thus, behaviorists assume that with the appropriate treatment, controlled social drinking may be a legitimate goal for some alcoholics. Sobell and Sobell (1973a) have delineated specific aspects of treatment in this regard. A model behavioral treatment program for alcohol and drug abuse has three major objectives (Miller and Barlow 1973; Miller, Stanford, and Hemphill 1974): (1) to decrease the immediate reinforcing properties of the drug; (2) to teach the individual new behaviors that are incompatable with substance abuse, such as being appropriately assertive; and (3) to rearrange the individual's social and vocational environment so that he receives maximum reinforcement for activities that do not involve the use of drugs. We will review the treatment procedures designed to accomplish each of these objectives.

Decreasing drug-taking behavior

Aversion therapies. A number of methods have been reported to decrease the immediate reinforcing properties of drugs and the antecedent cues associated with their abuse. The most widely used technique in this category is aversion therapy. Essentially, aversion therapy involves the repeated pairing of a noxious stimulus with the sequence of behaviors leading to drug or alcohol intake and with the wide variety of environmental cues (hypodermic syringe, liquor bottles, drinking buddies) that elicit the behavior. There are three basic varieties of aversion therapy: chemical, electrical, and verbal.

During chemical aversion the sight, smell, and/or taste of alcohol or drugs are contingently associated with either nausea induced by an emetic or muscular and respiratory paralysis induced by Anectine. Chemical aversion therapy using nausea-inducing agents (either emetine or apomorphine) has been used extensively in the treatment of alcoholism (Kant 1945; Lemere, Voegtlin, Broz, O'Halleren, and Tupper 1942; Raymond 1964; Thimann 1949). Although success with chemical aversion varies, Lemere and Voegtlin (1950) present the most comprehensive and long-term followup on the treatment. These investigators obtained followup data on over 4,000 patients and reported that 1 year after completion of treatment 60 percent of the group remained totally abstinent from alcohol. Periodic booster treatments given on an outpatient basis were considered essential. However, there are no well-controlled followup studies comparing chemical aversion using emetices with other types of treatment. Reports of chemical aversion treatments with drug addicts are rare, but individual cases of success have been reported (Raymond 1964; Liberman 1968).

Chemical aversion using drugs that induce paralysis have also been used most extensively with alcoholics (Clancy, Vanderhoof, and Campbell 1967; Farrar, Powell, and Martin 1968; Sanderson, Campbell, and Laverty 1963), although its use with heroin addicts has also been reported (Thompson and Rathod 1968). The rationale behind this technique is that very powerful aversive sensations (momentary respiratory paralysis) must be associated with drug intake for conditioning to be successful. However, controlled research on this technique with alcoholics has shown that it is no more effective than less aversive procedures.

The use of aversion procedures with drug addicts is still relatively unexplored. Thompson and Rathod (1968) describe the use of aversion treatment with a group of young heroin addicts. While the addict prepares a "fix," Anectine is injected into his arm. When paralysis is imminent (in about 10 seconds), the patient is instructed to inject the heroin. Brief paralysis then ensues followed by administration of oxygen. On the basis of urine analysis 8 of 10 patients who completed five treatments remained drug-free for varying lengths of time, with the longest followup being 5 months. Many more long-term controlled outcome studies are needed, however, before this technique can be used routinely. Obviously, to consent to this type of treatment patients must be highly motivated to change.

Electrical aversion (shock) has also been used with varying rate of success with alcoholics (Blake 1965, 1967; Hsu 1965; Kantorovich 1928; Miller and Hersen 1972) and drug addicts (Lesser 1967; Wolpe 1965). In this procedure an unpleasant electric shock, typically administered to the forearm, fingers, or leg, is made contingent upon drug-taking behavior. At times a patient may be provided with a small portable shock apparatus and instructed to shock himself at home whenever he feels an urge for drugs (Wolpe 1965). Recent studies have questioned the extent of generalization obtained using this procedure and have demonstrated the importance of extraneous therapeutic factors in determining successful outcome (Hallam, Rachman, and Falkowski 1972; Miller et al. 1973). These other factors include positive therapeutic set, specificity of the procedure, and therapeutic demand characteristics.

Blachly (1971) developed a new use for electrical aversion in dealing with the "needle ritual" observed in many ex-addicts. As a result of strong associations between "shooting up" and the pleasurable sensations induced by heroin, many addicts who no longer use drugs will continue to inject themselves with nondrug solutions (water, saline). In Blachly's procedure, the patient injects himself with saline in front of a group of other addicts and receives an electrical discharge from the special "electric needle" provided, whenever he attempts to depress the syringe. The results suggest that repetitions of this procedure lead to decreases in frequency of injecting behavior.

Finally, verbal aversion, or covert sensitization, was developed by Cautela (1966; see Chapter 8 in this volume). In this procedure, imagined scenes of drug or alcohol intake are repeatedly associated with vivid descriptions of unpleasant scenes. For example, a patient might be instructed to imagine herself in her favorite bar about to order a beer and then asked to imagine that she is feeling nauseous and vomiting. The nature of the aversive scene used depends upon events that are reported by the patient to be unpleasant to her. For example, in treating a 15-year-old gasoline sniffer with covert sensitization, Kolvin (1967) utilized imagined scenes of falling as the aversive stimulus. Patients are often advised to utilize these aversive images in their natural environment in a self-control manner. Successful uses of this treatment with alcoholics (Anant 1967; Ashem and Donner 1968; Cautela 1966; Miller 1959; Miller and Hersen 1972) and with heroin addicts (Wisocki 1973) have been reported.

In general, aversion therapy seems most effective when the patient can utilize it in a self-control manner. Present data indicate that this process may best be facilitated through the combined use of chemical and verbal aversion (Blanchard, Libet, and Young 1973; Bandura 1969).

Medications. Medications are frequently used to decrease the positive value of urges for alcohol or drugs. Methadone, for example, is a synthetic narcotic used in the treatment of heroin addiction. Initially advocated by Dole and Nyswander (1965), methadone, taken daily in oral form, suppresses the "narcotic hunger" or craving for heroin that most addicts experience. Taken orally in standard doses methadone produces no euphoria, nor do patients develop a tolerance so that they need more of the drug. At higher doses, methadone acts as a blocking agent which prevents the euphoric effects of heroin. Methadone is distributed daily to heroin addicts at specified private and governmental drug abuse agencies throughout the country. Continuous monitoring is strict, with urinalysis performed frequently to assess drug levels in the system. Success rates of methadone maintenance programs vary. Most drug addiction specialists agree that abstinence from heroin through methadone is far from a satisfactory treatment (Conner and Kremen 1971; Kleber 1970). Those programs that combine methadone maintenance with intensive efforts to improve the client's social, vocational, emotional, and environmental circumstances are more likely to be effective in the long term.

Disulfiram (Antabuse) is a maintenance medication used in the treatment of alcoholism (Bowman, Simon, Hine, Macklin, Crook, Burbridge, and Hanson 1951; Bourne, Alford, and Bowcock 1966). This drug is taken by alcoholics each day in pill form. Ingestion of alcohol while Antabuse is in the patient's system leads to nausea, dizziness, vomiting, increased heart rate and blood pressure, and chest pains. In most cases Antabuse acts in a preventive sense in that the thought about these severe reactions inhibits drinking. As with methadone maintenance, success rates often depend upon the population involved and other apsects of the treatment process. Bandura (1969) points to the need for a well-controlled outcome study comparing the effects of Antabuse maintenance with various other forms of alcoholism treatment. The major problem with this strategy, of course, is that alcoholics may stop taking Antabuse when they have a strong urge to drink. Frequently, court-imposed requirements (for drunken driving offenders or chronic public drunkenness offenders) help to ensure continued ingestion of the drug. Bigelow, Liebson, and Lawrence (1973) have used the opportunity to work each day as a reinforcer for Antabuse taking. They required clients to ingest Antabuse in the presence of clinic staff as a precondition to employment each day.

Teaching incompatible behaviors

Decreasing responses to alcohol and/or drugs is far from a sufficient treatment. The addict must be taught more adaptive behavior patterns. This is necessary for two reasons: these new responses provide behaviors that are incompatible with addiction, and they provide the addict with a wider variety of ways to derive satisfaction from life.

The majority of alcoholics and individuals who are dependent on drugs tend to receive little reinforcement from their social milieu for activities unrelated to drinking or drug ingestion. Therefore, decreasing their use of these substances by itself is but one step in their rehabilitation. Many of these individuals have problems handling the stress of everyday life, and have little skill in interpersonal relationships.

One strategy for ensuring that individuals stay free of an intoxicant once they are withdrawn is to teach them social behaviors incompatible with drinking which will elicit more positive responses from their environment (see Chapter 20, "Social skills training"). A variety of training techniques have been used to shape prosocial behaviors including assertive training, observing models engage in successful interpersonal interactions, and behavioral contracts whereby appropriate social behaviors are reinforced by various individuals in the natural environment (wife, employer, teacher).

In one case study Eisler, Miller, and Hersen (1974) trained three passive husbands, one of whom was an alcoholic, to respond more assertively to situations involving interactions with their wives. Although the wives were not involved in training, the couples' marital interaction showed significant improvement. In addition, the alcoholic husband evidenced decreases in alcohol consumption following training. In another case study (Eisler, Hersen, and Miller, in press), an alcoholic who had problems being assertive with his boss and with employees in his charge was asked to rehearse interpersonal encounters with someone who roleplayed the behavior of the individual he came into contact with at work. Instructions and feedback were administered to the client to decrease his compliance with their unreasonable requests and to help him improve his style of delivering responses so that he became more "convincing" in his relationship with those at work.

When it is clear that a person has good interpersonal skills in his repertoire but does not use them sufficiently, behavioral contracts between the individual and a person with whom he has frequent interactions may be used. Usually the contract specifies that the partner will reinforce him verbally or materially contingent upon his delivery of prosocial responses. An illustration of behavioral contracting between a husband and wife who used both marijuana and barbiturates in a deteriorating marriage is provided by Polakow and Doctor (1973). Both partners delivered praise and other reinforcement to the other contingent upon specified nondrug activities such as looking for a job or providing satisfactory verbal communications. A 12-month followup revealed that neither partner was any longer taking drugs and both reported a more satisfying marital relationship.

It would appear that part of the reason many individuals initially turn to alcohol and other drugs is to secure satisfaction or a sense of well-being not currently available in their social environment. Often the ability to have satisfying relationships with other people has deteriorated, and this is compounded by drug use. It then becomes necessary, in the course of treatment, to identify the deficiencies in the individual's social repertoire which prevent him from obtaining gratifications in his relationships with others.

Rearranging environmental contingencies

A third aspect of treating the addict is based on principles of operant conditioning, and thus focuses on the consequences of his behavior. It is assumed that the addict receives more reinforcement (either positive or negative) when taking the drug than when he is off the drug. The object of treatment is to provide maximum environmental reinforcement for not being intoxicated and punishment or withdrawal of reinforcement for taking drugs.

In a series of controlled laboratory experiments, Cohen, Leibson, and Faillace (1971b) at Baltimore City Hospital have repeatedly demonstrated the powerful influence of rearranging consequences for alcohol consumption in alcoholics. These authors allowed a 39-year-old chronic alcoholic free access to 24 ounces of 94 proof ethanol each day. During contingent reinforcement weeks the subject was placed in an enriched ward environment (opportunity to work for money, recreation room, television, phone) if he drank less than 5 ounces of alcohol on a particular day. Consumption of more than this limit resulted in placement in an impoverished environment and loss of all privileges for the remainder of the day. This chronic alcoholic was able to maintain this moderate drinking pattern as long as these contingencies were in effect. Other reinforcers used in in-patient settings to decrease consumption have included monetary rewards (Cohen, Liebson, Faillace, and Speers 1971) and visits to a girlfriend (Bigelow, Liebson, and Griffiths 1973).

Operant principles have also been used in in-patient settings in the context of a token economy system. The token economy provides a controlled environment designed to reinforce more adaptive behaviors. In a token economy, patients earn points or credits for highly specified appropriate behaviors and lose points for behaviors not consistent with treatment objectives. Points are spent to purchase hospital privileges and passes. Token economies have been used with alcoholic patients to foster increased vocational behavior (Narrol 1967) and socially adaptive responses considered incompatible with addiction (Cohen, Liebson, and Faillace 1971a; Miller, Hersen, Eisler, and Hilsman 1974; Rozynko, Flint, Hammer, Swift, Kline, and King 1971). Glicksman, Ottomanelli, and Cutler (1971) have also used the token economy for treatment of hospitalized heroin addicts. In this program patients must earn a specified number of points in order to be released from the hospital. Points are also earned for a variety of appropriate, goal-oriented behaviors in social and academic ward activities.

The use of operant treatment strategies for alcohol and drug abuse in outpatient settings has also been reported. While these applications have more clinical relevance than the in-patient studies reported above, they are much more difficult to administer, for the therapist or counselor frequently must rely on community agents (friends, relatives, employers, courts, social service workers) to implement the contingency management strategies. With training and support, however, these individuals have become quite effective.

Miller et al. (in press) used tokens exchangeable for goods in the hospital commissary contingent upon zero blood/alcohol levels in a 49-year-old alcoholic. Blood/alcohol concentrations were assessed via random biweekly breathalyzer tests administered to the patient in his home environment. During the control phase of the study the patient received the tokens regardless of his blood/alcohol level. The results indicated that application of reinforcement contingencies was responsible for marked decreases in alcohol consumption when compared to the control phase.

Miller (1974) demonstrated similar findings with a group of chronic Skid Row alcoholics who had been arrested numerous times for public drunkenness. These individuals were provided with required goods and services, such as meals, clothing, cigarettes, and shelter, through community agencies contingent upon their sobriety. Intoxication resulted in a 5-day suspension of the goods and services. Excessive drinking was assessed by direct observations and by randomly administered breathalyzer tests. As a result of the program the alcoholics significantly decreased their number of public drunkenness arrests and increased number of days employed. No changes were observed in a control group receiving services on a noncontingent basis.

Hunt and Azrin (1973) instituted a more comprehensive operant program with less debilitated alcoholics. In addition to individual social skills training for the alcoholic, relatives and friends were trained to provide pleasurable marital, family, and social activities *only* during periods of sobriety. Intoxication resulted in a loss of these reinforcers. An innovative aspect of the program consisted of establishing a "nonalcoholic" social club for the clients. The club provided social activities in return for a monthly fee. No alcoholic beverages were allowed and anyone arriving at the club in an intoxicated state was refused admittance. Compared to a control group receiving routine hospital care, the community reinforcement group of patients spent significantly fewer days drinking, unemployed, and away from home.

There are few operant programs with individuals addicted to drugs. Those that have been reported are based on behavioral or contingency contracting. This can be accomplished through an agreement between marital partners as discussed previously (Miller 1972; Polakow and Doctor 1973), or through a direct agreement between therapist and client. Boudin (1972), for example, used contingency contracting to treat a young female amphetamine abuser. One of the major aspects of the contract involved a joint bank account between the therapist and client into which the client deposited $500. The therapist held 10 signed checks of $50 each on this account. Drug-taking behavior by the client resulted in a $50 check being sent to the Ku Klux Klan by the therapist. The client was a black graduate student and loss of $50 in this manner was highly aversive. The author reported a 15-month followup in which the client remained drug-free even though the contract was in effect for only 3 months.

Community self-help groups

Bandura (1969) has discussed the similarities between a behavioral approach to drug addiction and certain aspects of self-help groups. The two most well-known groups of this nature are Synanon and Alcoholics Anonymous. Synanon (Deissler 1972) is essentially a therapeutic community administered by ex-drug addicts. The addict is treated as a rational being, rather than a sick one, and emphasis is placed on confrontation regarding present behavior and adjustment. Self-reliance is stressed within a highly structured, family-oriented community. Addicts live in or at least keep very close contact to this community. Alcoholics Anonymous (AA 1955) is a self-help group organized to help alcoholics. Again, group interaction and affiliation within a religious context are essential elements of the program, with total abstinence as the goal.

A behavioral analysis shows that these groups provide a potently reinforcing group atmosphere which does not tolerate drug or alcohol abuse. New, more adaptive patterns of behavior are encouraged and reinforced through group approval and increased status within the group. Drinking buddies and addicted friends are replaced with more appropriate role models exhibiting complete abstinence. The fact that the "helping agents" were once abusers of drugs or alcohol and therefore represent successful coping models may foster imitation of their behavior and enhance their reinforcing value.

Overview

Behavior modification, both as a methodology and a technology, offers a viable approach to the analysis and treatment of alcohol and drug abuse. Basically, the behavioral orientation emphasizes a systematic, experimental approach to a field that has for too long relied on clinical impressions and anecdotal data in the search for applicable knowledge. Treatment strategies based on the behavioral model have, over the past several years, become more realistic. That is, there is a trend away from the use of a single treatment technique such as aversion therapy and toward a comprehensive treatment program as outlined in this chapter. The combined use of self-management and social skills training, to develop more appropriate alternatives to excessive drug use, together with operant strategies to modify reinforcing consequences of behavior, appear to have great promise and to deserve further clinical use and evaluation.

Behavioral management of obesity[1]

D. Balfour Jeffrey
Emory University

22

While millions of dollars and hours are spent in weight reduction programs for cosmetic reasons, obesity is a major health problem, especially as it relates to dysfunctions of the cardiovascular system. Considerable research has been conducted with behavioral approaches to the reduction of obesity. This may be attributed in part to the easy and clear-cut measurement of weight. However, research has shown the most effective programs to be those that focus on changing eating habits rather than focusing on weight reduction per se. In this chapter, Jeffrey reviews the literature on behavioral approaches to the treatment of obesity, summarizes certain methodological problems in obesity research, and outlines a comprehensive behavior modification program. In the absence of some therapist contact or group support (pressure?), it is unlikely that the use of this program or any other will result in a significant weight loss which will be maintained over time. However, it seems possible that a problem-solving approach (e.g., the program of Mahoney and Mahoney, in press) may help to overcome this problem through personalized guidelines.

[1] The author wishes to thank Roger C. Katz for his helpful comments on an earlier draft of this manuscript. Additional information about the behavioral management of obesity may be obtained from D. Balfour Jeffrey, Department of Psychology, Emory University, Atlanta, Georgia, 30322.

Obesity is a major health problem in the United States, and in other countries as well.[2] Currently there are approximately 70 million overweight Americans, 20 million of whom are actively trying to lose weight. Countless hours of effort, along with millions of dollars, are spent annually by people hoping to reduce. However, traditional medical, dietary, and psychotherapeutic approaches to obesity have failed to produce encouraging results (Stunkard 1958). In his review of the literature, Stunkard (1958) concluded, "Most obese persons will not stay in treatment for obesity. Of those who stay in treatment most will not lose weight and of those who do lose weight, most will regain it" (p. 79).

In order to improve upon existing treatment approaches to obesity, and because of the apparent environmental determinants of this condition, some investigators have begun to apply behavior modification techniques in treating overweight clients. One of the first published accounts of this work was presented by Ferster, Nurnberger, and Levitt (1962), who proposed a behavioral model for conceptualizing and treating obesity. This was followed by Stuart's (1967) now classic article, which presented a modified version of the approach of Ferster and his colleagues along with successful results obtained from treating eight overweight women with these methods. Since then there have been numerous reports on the behavioral control of obesity (see reviews by Abramson 1973; Hall and Hall 1974; Stunkard and Mahoney, in press).

Underlying most behavioral treatments of obesity are the following assumptions: (1) obesity results from excess caloric intake in relation to energy expended; (2) behaviors leading to food consumption and physical activity are under environmental control; and (3) decreased caloric intake and increased energy expenditure can be achieved by having the individual modify his environment and himself. While environmental manipulations may be extremely useful in controlling obesity, environmental factors are not necessarily the only set of etiological factors behind this problem. Stunkard and Mahoney (in press) rightfully argue that both biological and environmental factors must be considered.

The present chapter focuses on behavioral approaches to the management of obesity. Specifically, the purposes of this chapter are threefold: (1) to describe the behavior modification principles that have been successfully used in the treatment of obesity; (2) to provide an overview

[2] Obesity will be defined as any weight 10 percent or more over normal body weight according to the U.S. Department of Agriculture statistics. The tables of normal weights take into account the sex, height, and build of an individual. For a more detailed discussion of what constitutes obesity, see Stuart and Davis (1972).

of some research issues in the field; and (3) to propose a comprehensive model for the management of obesity.

Behavior modification principles used

As you know from Chapter 7, two important classes of behavior modification principles derive from the effects of antecedent and consequent stimuli. The behavioral treatment of obesity is presented in terms of these principles.

Consequent control of behavior

Therapist reinforcement. In most treatment programs there is implicit if not explicit social reinforcement from the therapist for successful weight control. Wollersheim (1970) showed that clients who received therapist and group social reinforcement for weight control lost more weight than clients given expectation-social pressure to do well, traditional insight therapy, or no treatment at all. Penick, Filion, Fox, and Stunkard (1971) also used therapist and group social reinforcement to facilitate weight loss in overweight subjects.

A number of studies have used therapist-dispensed tangible reinforcers such as tokens, personal valuables, and money. In a study by Harmatz and Lapuc (1968), overweight psychiatric clients were paid $5 each week they lost weight; paying the subjects contingently produced encouraging weight loss. In another study (Jeffrey, Christensen, and Katz, in press), subjects were asked to deposit some of their own money with the experimenters. These subjects were then paid a portion of the deposit each week they lost weight. Initially there was no contingency for missing the weekly therapy meetings, so unwittingly the experimenters encouraged absence from meetings when the subjects did not lose weight. This problem was corrected by changing contingencies so that subjects lost more money for not attending than if they attended and did not make their weight loss goal. Subjects lost an average of 27 pounds during treatment. Two of the subjects maintained their weight a year after treatment. Unfortunately, however, the other two regained most of the weight they had lost. In another study (Hall 1972), subjects who were paid from a research grant were successful in reducing. Finally, Mann (1972) had subjects deposit money and/or personal valuables which they could earn back only by losing weight according to a predetermined schedule. Employing an ABAB reversal design, Mann demonstrated that weight could be controlled by the contingencies. However, this study was not without its difficulties as (1) patients resorted to diuretics, starvation, and induced vomiting to make their weight loss goals, and (2) there were no followup data to test the maintenance of the treatment effects.

In general, therapist social and tangible reinforcement have been effective in producing weight loss during treatment. However, since the effects of therapist-dispensed reinforcement have not always endured, researchers have started to investigate environmental reinforcement and self-reinforcement as means of facilitating the maintenance of weight loss.

Environmental social reinforcement. We know that a person's behavior is controlled to a large extent by his social environment. Consequently the maintenance of weight loss might be enhanced if important people in the client's environment were actively utilized to reinforce the client's efforts to lose weight. Stuart and Davis (1972) discuss the importance of enlisting the help of the client's loved ones in undertaking a weight loss program. A number of studies have included environmental social reinforcement; however, few have systematically investigated this component. Encouraging results were reported in a study that instructed subjects to ask their family and friends not to criticize them about their weight, and to give them praise for appropriate dietary behavior (Mahoney 1973). Further work is necessary in this area of reprogramming the immediate social environment to reinforce living thin rather than living heavy.

Self-reinforcement. In efforts to facilitate the maintenance of weight loss, some researchers have investigated the application of self-reinforcement. The basic assumption of self-reinforcement is that the client will eventually have to manage his own weight in the absence of therapist support. Training the client in self-management skills should increase the probability that he will be able to maintain his weight successfully after formal treatment has ended. To train subjects in self-reinforcement, Jeffrey and Christensen (1972) had them make a list of positive consequences associated with losing weight, and then instructed them to read this list each day they met their weight improvement goals. The procedure seemed to be effective; however, it was impossible to measure objectively how frequently and appropriately the subjects reinforced themselves. In order to validate experimentally the efficacy of self-control procedures, Mahoney (1974) and Jeffrey (1974a) had subjects deposit money with an experimenter and then had the subjects reward themselves if they made their weight goals. This procedure allowed for objective measurement of both the act and the effects of self-reinforcement. Mahoney found that self-reinforcement for weight loss was more effective than self-monitoring alone and no-treatment. Even more interesting was the finding that self-reinforcement for improvements in eating habits was more effective than self-reinforcement for weight loss. Jeffrey found that self-reinforcement was as effective as external reinforcement (therapist-controlled) during treatment and more effective in promoting maintenance of weight loss after treatment ended.

Aversive control. Studies that have investigated punishment or avoidance conditioning paradigms have usually employed electric shock (Meyer and Crisp 1964), noxious odors (Foreyt and Kennedy 1971), or noxious covert stimuli (Cautela 1972b) to eliminate the consumption of problematic foods. In a review of these procedures, Abramson (1973) wrote, "It appears safe to conclude that despite some early enthusiasm, there is little evidence to indicate that aversive procedures are an effective treatment for obesity" (p. 548).

A major purpose of aversive control procedures is to eliminate a response. However, unlike smoking treatment programs where the goal is abstinence, the goal in obesity treatment programs is not elimination of eating but a reduction in the amount of food consumed. In retrospect, theoretically and empirically, it seems better to employ positive control procedures that shape appropriate eating behavior rather than to employ direct aversive conditioning procedures.

Antecedent stimulus control

Operant conditioning research has clearly demonstrated that conditioned discriminative stimuli are major determinants of animal and human behavior. One would expect that through numerous pairings of antecedent food cues (smell, sight, taste, food ads, food displays) with subsequent food consumption, the antecedent cues themselves would set the stage for the purchase and consumption of food. Schachter and his associates (1971) have conducted numerous studies that show that obese individuals are more responsive to external, environmental food cues, while normal weight individuals are more responsive to internal, physiological food cues. Laboratory and naturalistic studies, which have manipulated perceived time with normal and obese subjects, have shown that the obese subjects will be influenced to eat if environmental cues indicate it is "mealtime" while normal weight subjects tend to be guided by internal cues to eat (Goldman, Jaffa, and Schachter 1968; Schachter and Gross 1968). Studies have also found that obese subjects are more influenced by the sight, smell, and taste of food than normal weight subjects.

The implications of these findings for the treatment of obesity are clear: researchers and therapists need to examine carefully antecedent discriminative stimuli that control food consumption, and to have the client either eliminate them or develop alternative noneating responses to these stimuli. Ferster, Nurnberger, and Levitt (1962) were the first to draw attention to the importance of stimulus control in the treatment of obesity. Some of their stimulus control procedures consisted of keeping food only in the kitchen, eating more slowly, and eating only in the dining area. Since then there has been increasing sophistication in the development of procedures to modify food buying, storing, preparing, serving, and eating—all of which are designed to strengthen appropriate eating habits (e.g., Hagen 1969; McReynolds 1973; Stuart and Davis 1972).

Additional procedures

Consequent and antecedent stimulus control principles have been used extensively in the management of obesity. In addition to these principles, techniques such as self-monitoring and behavioral contracting are also frequently employed.

Self-monitoring. In the treatment of obesity, self-monitoring has been used to collect data on weight, eating habits, and physical activity. It can also serve other useful purposes. For example, self-monitoring may help the client become more aware of eating and exercise habits while simultaneously acting as a reinforcer for progress or as a reminder that improvement has not been occurring. A number of studies have employed self-monitoring of weight, and an increasing number of studies have included self-monitoring of eating habits. A review of these studies indicates that self-monitoring has an initial reactive effect of producing mild weight loss. Over a longer period, however, it is usually not sufficient to sustain therapeutic gains (Stunkard and Mahoney, in press). In short, self-monitoring is a helpful supplementary technique in weight reduction programs.

Goal setting. In goal setting, the experimenter and/or the subject specifies weight or habit improvement goals. Goal setting is almost always a component of weight control programs but it has not received the experimental attention it deserves. Subjects often set unrealistic weight loss goals, which diminish the likelihood that reinforcement will occur immediately, if at all. Research has shown that it is important to make sure that the terminal goal is realistic for the person, and the terminal goal should be broken down into intermediate and weekly goals so that progress can be measured and reinforced on an ongoing basis (Bandura 1969).

Developing alternative competing responses. In addition to providing the necessary nutrients and energy for life, eating food can fill time for a person who is bored, soothe a person who is upset, entertain a person at a party, or ease a person through a stressful situation. Thus, an effective treatment program must not only provide sound nutrition and food management, but must also provide feasible noneating alternatives to meet the many non-nutritive functions eating may serve. Stuart and Davis (1972) present a number of excellent alternatives. For example, they suggest calling a friend when lonely, engaging in hobbies when bored, and taking a walk when upset.

Life situation and readiness to lose weight. Permanent weight loss requires a permanent alteration in eating and exercise habits. Changing habits takes a great deal of effort over a long period of time. If a person is not ready to make this commitment, it may be unwise for him to begin a weight loss program at that point in his life. For example, if a person is under a lot of stress at home or is in a transition stage from school to work, it is usually better to have the person deal with these situations first and then later consider embarking on a weight loss program (Jeffrey, Christensen, and Pappas 1973).

The therapist and client can further assess the appropriateness of a weight management program by seeking answers to the following questions:

1. Is it medically safe for the client to lose weight? (It is best to have the client check with a physician before beginning to lose weight.)
2. Does the client have good, long-term reasons for losing weight?
3. Are important people in the client's life willing to help him lose weight?
4. Is the client's life situation—family, friends, work—sufficiently stable so that he can focus on a long-term effort to modify permanently his eating and exercise habits?

Behavioral contracting. An obesity management contract is usually an agreement between the therapist and the client specifying what the client will do for a stated period of time. The contract is assumed to aid in the process of weight loss because it specifies terminal behaviors and contingencies while also motivating the client to follow the treatment program. In the last few years an increasing number of studies have reported the use of behavioral contracts in weight control intervention (e.g., Harris and Bruner 1971; Mann 1972).

Research issues

Numerous studies demonstrate that behavioral approaches offer great promise for the understanding and treatment of obesity. However, to ensure that we do not begin to believe that behavior modification is a panacea for obesity, this section will briefly discuss some of the limitations of current work. For a more detailed discussion, see the reviews by Abramson (1973), Hall and Hall (1974), Jeffrey (1974c), and Stunkard and Mahoney (in press).

Attrition rate

People leaving treatment prematurely has been a problem for traditional approaches to reducing, and a recent study by Harris and Bruner (1971) indicates that it is no less a problem for learning-based therapies. Since failure to report dropouts can seriously affect the interpretation of research findings, it would seem prudent to report at least the number of clients who do not complete treatment, and to include these individuals in the analysis of treatment results. It would also seem advisable to investigate systematically the factors that cause clients to drop out of treatment.

Standardized improvement criteria

In psychotherapy research, standardized improvement criteria need to be established for each problem area so that studies can be meaningfully compared (Bergin 1971). The advantage of establishing a standardized measure for reporting weight loss is that it would permit comparison of the effectiveness of different weight reduction treatments, regardless of the theoretical model or the specific techniques employed. Since at present there is not a standardized criterion, it would seem prudent to report at least the pre- and posttreatment weights for each subject undergoing treatment so that sufficient data are available for later comparisons.

Intermediate and long-term followups

Much of the initial enthusiasm in drug and psychodynamic therapies for the treatment of obesity has proven to be ill founded when long-term, empirically based followups have been conducted (Stunkard 1958). Much of the recent enthusiasm for behavior modification approaches has been based on dramatic demonstrations of weight loss over short periods of time. However, the history of obesity research indicates that the findings from short-term followup data are still insufficient to permit more than guarded optimism about the efficacy of behavior therapy in the treatment of obesity. There is a clear need to include intermediate (6 months) and long-term (over 1 year) followup data in weight investigations to determine the durability of treatment effects. While empricially derived data of this kind may temper some of the current enthusiasm surrounding behavioral approaches to obesity, they may also provide a better basis for modifying and improving existing treatment procedures.

Research strategies and significance

In general, the research methodology employed in behavioral studies has been a substantial improvement over previous obesity research (Stunkard and Mahoney, in press). For example, Wollersheim (1970) employed a factorial group design; others have utilized objective clinical case studies (e.g., Stuart 1967); and still others have employed intrasubject designs (e.g., Hall 1972; Mann 1972). Although it may be important to establish methodological rigor and statistical significance, by themselves these are insufficient criteria to evaluate the total significance of a study (Jeffrey 1974b; Lykken 1968). The ultimate criterion is whether an investigation contributes to the understanding of obesity and to the development of effective treatment programs. Since numerous experimental studies have included either a no-treatment control or a waiting-list control group and have found a weight change of no more than plus or minus two pounds (Hall and Hall 1974), one may ask whether any useful information can be gained by including any more such standard control groups. The information yield would now seem to be far greater if the control subjects of future studies were given some other type of treatment and thereby provide information on the efficacy of alternative programs.

Reinforce the reporting of individual differences

The initial halo of success surrounding behavioral treatment of obesity has masked the fact that there have been great individual differences, with some clients even gaining weight (e.g., Harris and Bruner 1971; Penick et al. 1971). To shed more light on the individual variations, it would be useful if intersubject (group) designs reported individual subject data as well as group data. It is probable that different clients will respond better to individually designed behavior modification programs. Some studies (Penick et al. 1971; Wollersheim 1970) have already started to deal with this issue but much more work is necessary to develop good behavioral predictors of therapy outcome.

A comprehensive behavioral program

A review of the literature indicates that broad behavior modification principles such as consequent and antecedent stimulus control can be used successfully in the management of obesity. Therapist-controlled social and tangible reinforcements have produced dramatic reductions in weight during the treatment period. Efforts to promote maintenance of weight loss after termination of treatment have recently focused on environmental reinforcement and self-reinforcement. Research has indicated that self-reinforcement is as effective as external reinforcement in producing weight loss and is more effective in promoting maintenance of weight loss. On the other hand, punishment and avoidance conditioning procedures have been relatively ineffective in producing or sustaining weight loss.

The operant conditioning literature on discriminative stimuli and Schachter's research on the responsiveness of overweight people to external stimuli have provided important data on the role of antecedent stimuli in controlling the excessive eating of obese individuals. These findings have resulted in the development of treatment programs that emphasize alteration of relevant antecedent stimuli to eating, such as different ways of buying, storing, preparing, and serving food.

Present research on self-monitoring, goal setting, developing alternative competing responses, life situation analysis, and behavioral contracting seem to indicate that these components also aid in successful weight management, although their exact contributions are presently unknown.

Initially most investigators focused on weight loss, but recently they have begun focusing on modifying the more important eating and exercise habits. Earlier intervention programs emphasized the treatment phase, while current programs have begun to emphasize the initial assessment of the client and the later maintenance of the weight loss in addition to the treatment phase.

Based on the research findings and clinical experiences of the author and others in the field, a $3 \times 3 \times 2$ dimensional model for the behavioral management of obesity is proposed. This conceptual model is designed to provide a comprehensive approach to the management of obesity—one that includes the behavior modification principles previously discussed, and one that takes into account the clinical complexity of this problem. Many of the components of the proposed model have already been tested in the previously cited studies; however, further experimental research is needed to evaluate the entire model.

The first dimension, which was originally suggested by Stuart (1971), consists of three treatment components: learning principles, modification of eating habits, and modification of physical activity habits. This dimension stresses the application of behavior modification principles of consequent and antecedent control to the permanent modification of nutrition and exercise habits (see Figure 22-1). The next dimension consists of three intervention stages: assessment, treatment, and maintenance. As already mentioned, most research to date has focused on the treatment stage; however, the initial assessment of the person's difficulties and the eventual maintenance of weight loss need to receive equal emphasis. The last dimension consists of two human factors—client and therapist variables—which are also important in determining a successful outcome to therapy.

Let's explore the applications of this model to the treatment of an

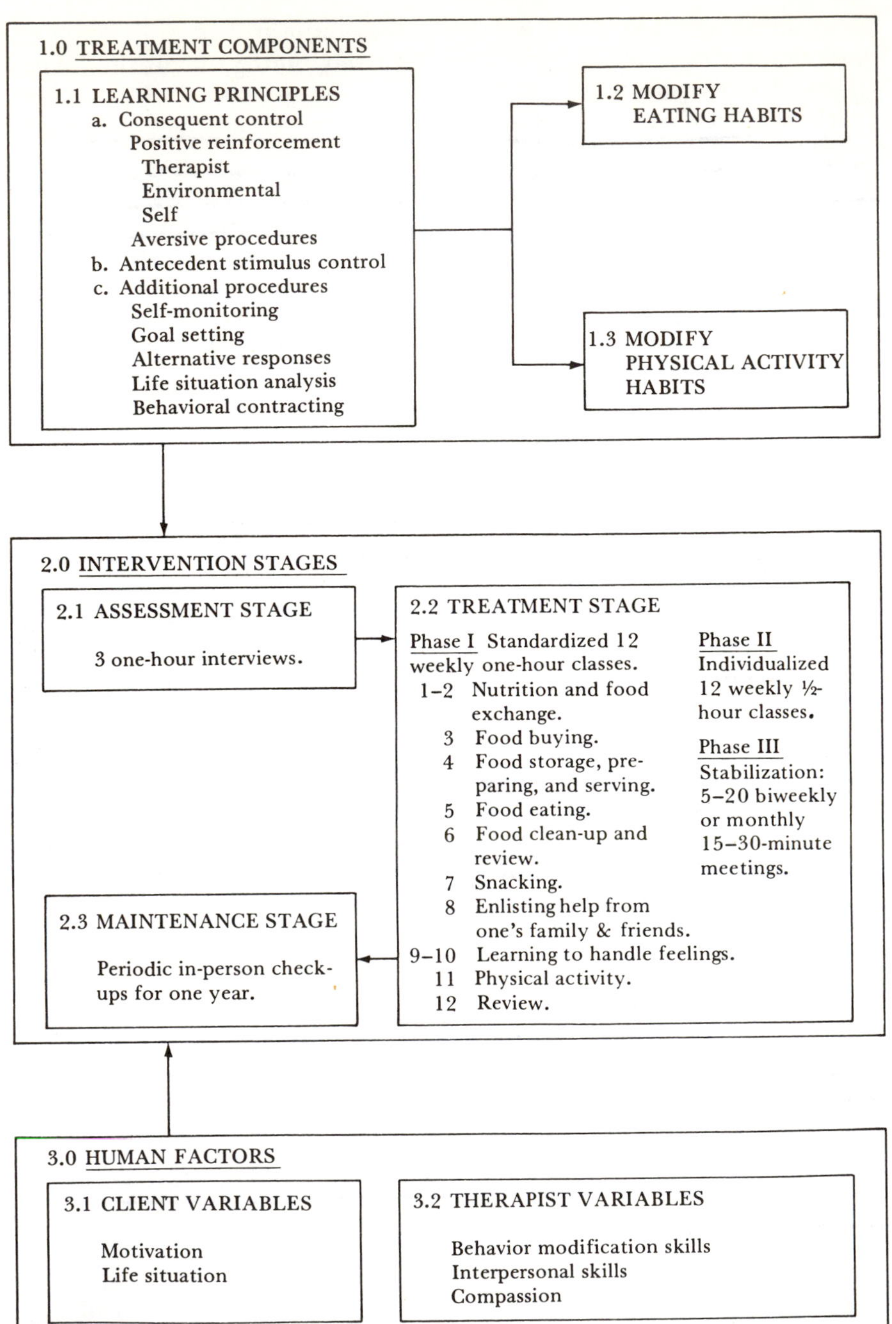

Figure 22-1 A 3 × 3 × 2 dimensional model for the behavioral management of obesity

obese individual. This program can be used with groups as well as with individuals and it can be used in outpatient, day-care, or in-patient facilities. Adjustments in the program for a particular individual are appropriate.

Assessment stage

The assessment stage consists of 3 one-hour interviews, which are broken down as follows.

Interview one. Before the client sees the therapist he completes a weight history inventory. After the inventory is completed the therapist explains to the client that the first three interviews are to describe the program and to conduct an assessment of the client's weight-related behaviors and readiness to engage in a weight loss program. No decision is made until the third interview on whether it is appropriate to begin the treatment. This time allows both client and therapist to decide whether the client should undertake such a program at this point in his life. The client is told that the rationale of the program is to help him reduce his caloric intake and to increase his energy expenditure by modifying specific eating and exercise habits. He is also told that treatment will continue until he reaches his desired weight and that the maintenance stage will continue for 1 year thereafter. Finally, he is asked to have a physical examination to make sure that he can participate in moderate reductions of food intake and in moderate increases in energy expenditure.

With information from the weight inventory as a guide, the therapist conducts a behavioral interview (Kanfer and Saslow 1969; see Chapter 9 in this volume). Information is collected about weight goals, onset of obesity, previous attempts to lose weight, eating habits, physical activity patterns, reasons for wanting to lose weight, and whether important people in the client's life will help or hinder him in losing weight.

From the beginning the therapist stresses the importance of the client's participation in his own treatment. The therapist instructs the client to record daily for 2 weeks his weight, food consumed, and all physical activity. Forms are provided for recording this information (see Figures 22-2, 22-3, and 22-4). The client is also given a small booklet that contains information about nutrition and specific weight control techniques (Mahoney and Jeffrey 1974).

Interview two. The client's self-monitored weight, eating, and exercise records are carefully evaluated. The eating diary is examined for any patterns such as evening snacking, weekend binges, or eating elicited by particular situations or moods. Type, frequency, and duration

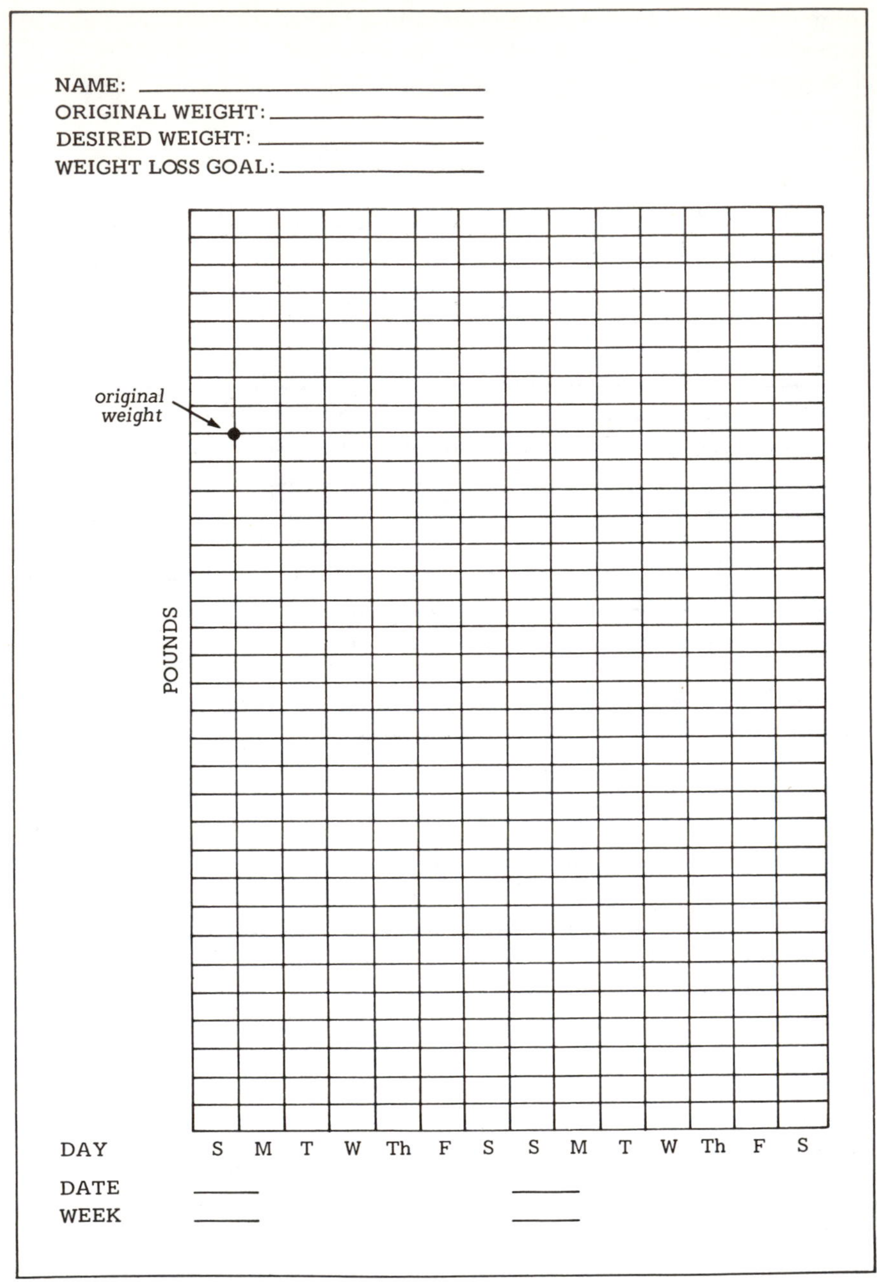

Figure 22-2 Daily weight graph for an obesity control program

NAME: ______					
	ANTECEDENT EVENTS (Time, place, situation, and mood before and while eating)	EATING RESPONSE			CONSEQUENT EVENTS (Mood and activities following eating)
		Food	Amount	Calories	
BREAKFAST					
MORNING					
LUNCH					
AFTERNOON					
DINNER					
EVENING					

Figure 22-3 Food consumption diary for an obesity control program

of the physical activity are noted. The advantages of staying obese versus becoming thin are discussed with the client.

A behavioral contract is prepared which specifies the desired behaviors and the contingencies of the program. The client's terminal and intermediate weight, eating habit improvement, and physical activity improvement goals are then reviewed. The contract also specifies the amount of money or valuables to be deposited by the client and the conditions for earning them back. The client is then asked to deposit a

NAME: ______						
TIME	LOCATION	ALONE OR WITH PARTNER	PHYSICAL ACTIVITY			FEELINGS AFTER ACTIVITY
			Type	How long, far, or number of times	Calories expended	

Figure 22-4 Physical activity diary for an obesity control program

substantial amount which he would miss if he did not earn it back. The usual recommendation for the contingency contract is that the therapist pay the client one-fourth of his deposit when he reaches his terminal weight goal, and one-fourth when he maintains his weight for one year; the *client pays himself* the remaining one-half during the treatment for improvements in his eating and exercise habits. (Note the self-reward is *not* for weight loss.) The client loses his entire deposit if he drops out of the program. In the second interview the contract is filled in but *not* signed. The client is told to think seriously about his commitment as well as the conditions of the contract before his weight management program.

Interview three. The client is weighed and his eating and physical activity diaries are examined. The contract is further reviewed and any questions are answered. If the client and therapist are fully satisfied about the terms of the contract, the client deposits his money or personal valuables with the therapist and the contract is signed by both parties.

Treatment program stage

The treatment stage is divided into three phases. Phase I consists of 12 weekly one-hour classes in food and exercise management. Phase II consists of 12 half-hour weekly classes devoted to specific difficulties the client may encounter in managing his food and exercise assignments. Phase III consists of biweekly or monthly 15- to 30-minute meetings which focus on stabilizing newly acquired eating and exercise habits. Behavior principles such as stimulus fading and reinforcement thinning are systematically included in the sequencing of this treatment phase.

Phase I: Standard classes. The general format in Phase I is first to present information about a particular topic, then to assess the individual's present behavioral assets and deficits in regard to that topic, and finally to plan an assignment for the individual for the coming week. The next meeting is spent evaluating progress and difficulties in implementing the previous week's assignment; then the topic for the coming week is presented.

The client is told that weight management is promoted if the individual learns to reward himself appropriately for successful attainment of weight control goals. He is further told that he should reward himself only if he meets his weekly assignment—he should not reward himself if the weekly assignment is not met. Half of the initial deposit is divided into 12 equal shares; one share can be earned back during each week of Phase I. Any money the client does not reward himself during weekly meetings is refundable on request at the end of Phase I.

Classes 1 and 2: Nutrition and a food exchange diet. Basic information is provided on nutrition and the importance of a well-balanced diet. Since one purpose of the program is to permanently alter eating habits and to avoid temporary crash dieting, no strict diet is recommended. Instead a "food exchange" diet (Stuart and Davis 1972; Turner 1965) is recommended, as it provides guidance on what to eat, but at the same time allows the individual to eat according to his own food preferences. The client's eating patterns, physical activity history, and weight loss goals are again reviewed. With this information an individualized daily food calorie plan is selected which should lead to weekly weight loss of between 1 and 4 pounds. If the client is moderately to severely overweight, an initial weight loss of 2 to 4 pounds per week is recommended. As the client approaches his desired weight, however, the goal is lowered to 1 or 2 pounds weekly.

At the end of the first class the client is instructed to spend the next week implementing his food exchange diet. Class 2 is spent reviewing the client's progress and additional aspects of the diet are explained. Classes 3 through 6 focus on altering food management behaviors.

Class 3: Food buying. If people do not have high-calorie foods in the house, they cannot eat them. Consequently it is important to alter their food buying habits. With the information about nutrition and food exchange diets, the client is told to buy only those foods that meet the food exchange diet requirements. Other foods should not be purchased. The individual is instructed to prepare a food list before shopping, to buy only from that list, to shop when full instead of when hungry, and not to buy extra quantities of food.

Class 4: Food storage, preparing, and serving. Research on stimulus control of overeating indicates that for an obese individual, food out of sight is often out of mind. Clients are thus instructed to assess present food storage practices and whenever possible to store their food so that it cannot be easily seen or reached. An example is to take food out of the living room or off the kitchen table and put it in opaque containers in the cupboards. In preparing food, clients are instructed to plan and follow a menu that includes items from the general food exchange diet as well as one of their favorite foods. Moderate intake of favorite foods is encouraged as a way of maintaining a positive association between eating and reducing. Clients are also instructed to serve smaller portions of food and to place their food on smaller dishes.

Class 5: Food eating. Eating is an enjoyable experience for most normal weight people and should also be an enjoyable experience for the overweight. However, most overweight people eat so much so fast they do not have time to enjoy their food or to realize when they are physiologically full (that is, when their stomachs are full). Clients are told to enjoy their food by eating slowly and thinking about how good each small morsel of food tastes. They are instructed to put smaller quantities of food on the fork, to chew and swallow slowly, and to wait between bites. Finally, clients are told to focus their attention on how full their stomach feels, and when it feels full, to *stop* eating.

Class 6: Food clean-up and review. Overweight individuals often finish their meals and while sitting at the table afterwards begin to nibble away at the leftovers until none remain. This problem can be solved in part by buying, preparing, and serving smaller quantities of food. If there are still leftovers, the individual is instructed to clear the table as soon as he finishes eating and to put away any leftovers to remove further temptation. The rest of this session is spent reviewing classes 1–5.

Class 7: Snacking. Snacking, from nibbling to gluttonous food binges, is often a major problem of the obese. The client's food record is examined to identify any snacking problems, and if necessary a specific plan is developed to decrease snacking. Many of the food management tips already discussed can be used to decrease snacking difficulties. For example, if a person does not buy his favorite snack, he will not have it to eat; if he buys a low-calorie snack (popcorn or celery) he can still snack but will have a smaller caloric intake. Snackers often skip breakfast or lunch and then eat between meals because they say they are hungry. However, an examination of their eating record often reveals that they consume more calories munching than if they eat a nutritious breakfast and lunch. Consequently, snackers are instructed to eat at their regular mealtimes and to skip or substantially reduce their in-between-meal munching.

Class 8: Enlisting the help of one's family and friends. The importance of significant others in helping or hindering the client's attempts to lose weight has already been mentioned. Now is the time to have the obese person actively enlist their help in managing his weight. He should ask his family and friends: (1) not to criticize his fatness but rather to praise him for his weight management progress; (2) to buy, prepare, and serve small, low-calorie foods; (3) not to offer additional portions of food; (4) to talk about things other than food; and (5) to engage in nonfood-related activities.

Classes 9 and 10: Learning to handle feelings and life situations in noneating ways. Most people encounter situations in which they are anxious, depressed, lonely, angry, bored, or exhausted. Obese individuals often handle their feelings by eating excessively, while normal weight people react in noneating ways. To help clients learn new noneating ways of handling feelings, their eating records are re-examined to identify the type and frequency of situations in which they handle feelings by eating. A number of good alternatives can then be suggested and practiced. Some of these alternatives are the following: (1) develop a list of friends to visit or call when upset or lonely; (2) plan a number of activities, such as going to a movie, shopping for clothes, visiting a museum, to engage in when feeling anxious or depressed; (3) develop long-term interests and hobbies to handle boredom; (4) learn appropriate ways to express anger; and (5) exercise when upset.

Class 11: Physical activity and energy expenditure. Classes 1 through 10 have focused on losing weight by decreasing caloric intake; class 11 focuses on losing weight by increasing energy expenditure. This class (1) provides information about the importance of increased energy expenditure as a healthy way to reduce, (2) examines the pretreatment physical activity record, and (3) has the client plan his own program for increased energy expenditure. The following suggestions are offered to the client for planning and implementing his physical activity program:

1. Increased energy expenditure can come from increased physical activity—such as walking to the store rather than driving, or walking up the stairs rather than taking an elevator—as well as from strenuous exercises and sports.
2. Select physical activities that fit into one's lifestyle and situation. Trying to ice skate during the summer or to play 4 hours of golf daily may be very difficult to arrange.
3. Arrange the physical activity so that it becomes part of one's regular or weekly schedule—then there is always time for it.
4. Find a friend to exercise with.
5. Enroll in an adult education physical fitness class, join a YMCA or health club, or participate in a sports league if these help provide the social enjoyment needed to stay interested in physical activity.
6. Keep a simple record of physical activity to measure progress.

Class 12: Review. This class reviews the previous lessons on food and physical activity management.

Phase II. This phase consists of 12 weekly half-hour meetings which focus on food and physical activity management problems that give the individual particular difficulty. Formal tangible self-rewards are discontinued. However, the client is told to continue rewarding himself at home when he meets his weight management goals. The client is encouraged to develop his own covert and overt self-reward system. For example, if he masters a troublesome snacking period, he might covertly congratulate himself and overtly buy a smaller pair of pants.

Phase III. This phase consists of 5 to 20 biweekly or monthly 15- to 30-minute meetings. The purpose of these meetings is to stabilize new eating and physical activity habits. The client is encouraged to continue rewarding himself as he manages his weight. Meetings continue until the person reaches his desired weight, at which time he is refunded one-fourth of his initial deposit.

Maintenance followup stage

When the desired weight is achieved the treatment stage is terminated and the maintenance stage begun. The emphasis is to have the client sustain his eating and exercise habits at a level that will maintain his weight loss. The client continues to meet for 15- to 30-minute biweekly or monthly meetings. The same type of thinning and fading procedures employed during treatment are implemented during maintenance. The meetings become shorter and less frequent. The rate of fading out meetings depends on the client's ability to maintain his eating and physical activity habits. Whatever the rate of fading, some personal contact should be continued for 1 year. Booster programs should be available to the client if any sign of relapse is encountered. If the client maintains his desired weight for a year he is paid the remaining one-fourth of his deposit. Any money not earned at the end of the maintenance stage is given to a nonprofit agency.

Human factors

Numerous studies have attempted to discover psychological correlates of obesity (Hall and Hall 1974; Stunkard 1958). Although current research is inconclusive about personality characteristics of the obese, there appear to be two important client variables that should be considered in implementing an intervention program. One variable is the motivation of the client. If the client does not want treatment or refuses treatment, there seems to be very little that can be done for him. It is important to note that most successful behavior modification studies have involved motivated clients who wanted to lose weight. Obviously this does not mean that motivation alone is a sufficient condition for successful weight loss, but the client's motivation does appear to be a necessary precondition. A second variable is the client's life situation and readiness to lose weight. If his current life situation is not conducive to losing weight, it is probably best that he first resolve problematic aspects of his life before a long-term weight loss program.

In addition to client variables, there are also therapist variables that seem to be important in the success of weight loss programs. Psychotherapy research indicates that these include therapeutic and interpersonal skills (e.g., Fiske, Hunt, Luborsky, Orne, Parloff, Reiser, and Tuma 1970; Paul 1969a). Although there has been little systematic research into therapist variables in behavioral programs for obesity, the literature on psychotherapy does suggest several important considerations. First, the therapist needs to be competent in behavior modification principles and knowledgeable about basic nutrition and exercise principles. Second, the therapist needs to have basic interviewing and interpersonal skills. Third, the therapist needs to care about the client and be sensitive to the client's needs at all times.

Current research indicates that behavior modification offers great promise for the treatment of obesity. Behavior modification can be considered an advancement in the management of obesity. However, it should not be considered a panacea or an easy solution to this complex and difficult health problem.

Quitting smoking

Judith Flaxman
University of North Carolina at Chapel Hill

23

Many people have quit smoking; however, most of them have begun at least once more often than they have quit. This defines the outcome of most therapies (both self-induced and therapist-directed) designed to reduce cigarette smoking. In spite of the demonstrated relationship between cigarette smoking and respiratory and cardiovascular problems, approximately 35 percent of the United States population smokes cigarettes.

Flaxman organizes her evaluative review of behavioral therapies for quitting smoking around four barriers to success: (1) development and maintenance of motivation to quit smoking; (2) withdrawal symptoms; (3) the habit component in smoking; and (4) the needs filled by smoking. Flaxman maintains that a good treatment program should attempt to remove all four barriers. The strategies that seem most likely to effect a reduction or termination of smoking are: the rapid breathing of hot, smoky air, a procedure developed by Lichtenstein and his colleagues; abrupt cessation of smoking at a predetermined date; and providing alternatives to the needs met by cigarette smoking.

Tobacco was introduced to the Western world with the discovery of the Americas and became one of the treasures of the New World (Wagner 1971). Of the many substances people have tried to smoke, tobacco is one of the few that has gained lasting popularity (Domino 1973).

The use of tobacco spawned a controversy almost from the beginning—did smoking cause ills or cure them? In the United States this controversy largely subsided with the report of the Advisory Committee to the Surgeon General, *Smoking and Health* (U.S. Public Health Service 1964). It is now accepted, at least by the medical community in the United States, that smoking is harmful to health.

Notwithstanding the scientific demonstration of the harmfulness of smoking, many people continue to smoke; in 1970, 31 percent of the adult women and 42 percent of the adult men in the United States were smokers (American Cancer Society 1974). These individuals can be placed on a continuum in their attitudes about the dangers of smoking, ranging from the few impervious individuals who neither believe nor care that smoking can harm them, to the person with a laryngectomy who has firsthand knowledge of the harm that smoking can do, but continues to smoke, despite the fact that he must do it through a tube inserted in his windpipe. In view of this range of attitudes, smokers have been classified as the uninformed, the unbelieving, the unmotivated, and the unable (Straits 1965).

It is the last classification, the unable, that best describes the smokers who come to the attention of therapists. These individuals believe that smoking may be harmful to their health and wish to quit but have found it impossible to do so. Given this population, it is not surprising that published reports describing attempts at smoking modification have largely been reports of failure. While recent studies have identified some promising directions for further research, it can fairly be said that at the present time no definitive technique for quitting smoking exists.

During treatment—whatever the type—a fair number of people will quit smoking, only to resume when treatment ends. An exhaustive survey of the smoking studies published in 1973 demonstrates this relapse problem: only 20 to 30 percent of successfully treated subjects were still abstinent when they were contacted for followup information (Hunt and Bespalec 1974). A less extensive study (McFall and Hammen 1971) found that when overall success rates from 10 studies were adjusted to include dropouts, an average of 26 percent of subjects (with a range of 7 to 40 percent) had quit smoking by the end of treatment, and an average of 13 percent (with a range of 9 to 17 percent) were still not smoking at followup. These success rates are similar to those obtained from placebo treatment, which involved taking motivated individuals and giving them attention and a structured, albeit irrelevant, treatment. Such a placebo treatment resulted in a success rate of 28 percent at the end of treatment, which dropped to 5 percent at the 6-month followup (McFall and Hammen 1971).

Perhaps the motivating effects of partial reinforcement are responsible for the smorgasbord of behavior modification treatments currently available for smoking. In order to review the various treatments in a meaningful way, this chapter is organized around four barriers to quitting smoking: (1) development and maintenance of motivation to quit smoking; (2) withdrawal symptoms; (3) the habit component in smoking; and (4) the needs filled by smoking. Discussion of each impediment to quitting smoking is followed by a discussion of the smoking modification techniques most directly aimed at coping with that particular aspect of the problem.

Ideally, the development of effective techniques progresses in a cumulative fashion, so that the more recent treatment approaches take into account earlier, less successful techniques. In such an ideal scheme, the earliest techniques might focus on only one problem in quitting smoking (for example, developing and maintaining motivation to quit smoking), while the most recent techniques would be aimed at several problems (for example, helping the smoker maintain motivation and deal with withdrawal, as well as substituting new behavior for the needs filled by smoking). Since research is rarely done in the way that books on research suggest that it should be done (Bachrach 1965), it is gratifying to find that this ideal scheme is even roughly approximated in real life, and that it leads to increasingly successful treatments.

Development and maintenance of motivation to quit smoking

A father is driving hurriedly through the pouring rain to pick up his children at school. Noticing that he is out of cigarettes, he makes a detour to replenish his supply, and arrives late at his children's school, finding them thoroughly drenched by the rain. He realizes that smoking has made him a bad father, feels terrible, throws away his cigarettes, and never smokes again. In this example, quitting smoking can be viewed as the result of a powerful attitudinal upheaval. Such an attitude change functions as an overriding set, and serves to disrupt old habits, while immediate action preserves the emotional component of the decision, thereby maintaining the new behavior (Premack 1970).

As in the example, the "revelation" must be a powerful one—our ex-smoker really cares about being a good father. In addition, the "revelation" must be acted upon immediately—the moment would have been lost if the negligent father had decided to quit smoking on his next vacation, and made sure he kept a spare carton of cigarettes in his car in the meantime.

Motivational impediment

Each year, possibly through a process similar to the one described above, many individuals quit smoking. The American Cancer Society (1974) reports that 25.4 percent of the women and 38.8 percent of the men who were smoking cigarettes in 1966 had quit smoking by 1970. Information about the health hazards of smoking provided the logical impetus for quitting; health problems were the primary cause for concern about smoking. But, at the present time, more than 10 years after the publication of the Surgeon General's Report, the impact of health information has diminished, since virtually every smoker has been repeatedly confronted with it through the media.

As a defense against the widely disseminated health information, many smokers appear to have created homemade "cancer correlation tables" (Meyer, Friedman, and Lazarsfeld 1973), which may include Grandpa, who is 95 years old and smokes two packs of cigarettes a day, and the clean-living athlete who dropped dead on the playing field at the age of 25. Other smokers apparently tolerate a great deal of dissonance (Bernstein 1970), often being even better informed than nonsmokers about the hazards of smoking (Meyer, Friedman, and Lazarsfeld 1973). Private rationalizations about smoking and the extinction of the impact of health statistics make it difficult to motivate people to quit smoking prior to the time that their own health or the health of someone close to them is in immediate danger.

Behavioral treatments

In an attempt to induce artificially the requisite, powerful realization of the personal implications of smoking, Janis and Mann (1965) had subjects read scripts and improvise in the role of a patient who discovers she has lung cancer. While most smoking studies use volunteers who have expressed a desire to quit smoking, Janis and Mann's subjects did not know that the role-play experience was intended to influence their smoking. Nevertheless, subjects in the group that role-played reduced their smoking rates significantly more than subjects in a control group who were given comparable information about the dangers of smoking. However, a more extensive attempt to induce a large number of volunteers to quit smoking through role playing was unsuccessful (Mausner and Platt 1971).

Less sophisticated "scare tactics" employ films, slides, and actual demonstrations of diseased body parts to make information about smoking-related diseases meaningful. Quit-smoking clinics in many cities are run by the Seventh Day Adventists, who use audiovisual material and demonstrations of the effects of smoking as the backbone of their Five-Day Plan. An evaluation of one such program found that 28 percent of the participants had quit smoking 3 months after the program had ended. By comparison, 17 percent of the untreated controls had also quit smoking at the followup, and the two groups did not differ significantly (Guilford 1972). These success rates are consistent with the 12 to 18 percent range in success rates found in several uncontrolled followup studies of Five-Day Plan clinics (Schwartz 1969). Techniques whose main thrust is scaring people about smoking in order to develop the requisite motivation for successful quitting seem to yield no more success than unaided attempts at quitting.

Withdrawal symptoms

Upon quitting smoking some smokers experience distressing withdrawal symptoms that interfere with their efforts to remain abstinent. Consequently, many techniques have been directed toward helping people cope with the withdrawal period. Brief treatments, like those described above, fail to take this problem into account, as they end almost before the withdrawal period has begun.

Addiction or habituation?

The problem of withdrawal from cigarettes is, of course, related to the question of addiction. While no one doubts that smoking is a strongly ingrained habit, most researchers do not consider smoking an addiction. For example, the 1964 Surgeon General's Report (U.S. Public Health Service 1964), relying on the World Health Organization's definition of addiction, concluded that smoking is not an addiction, but is instead an "habituation." This distinction is based, in part, upon the fact that the detrimental effects of smoking are personal, not societal. The smoker may crave cigarettes ("I'd walk a mile for a Camel"), but he does not become involved in crime, as the deprived heroin addict may, in order to satisfy his need for the drug. However, it is possible that this distinction between nicotine addiction and heroin addiction is one of degree rather than a qualitative difference between the two.

Physical symptoms

Whether smoking is considered an addiction or an habituation, the existence of a withdrawal syndrome, at least in some smokers, has recently gained general acceptance (Jaffe 1974). Among heavy smokers who were paid to stop smoking for a week, heart rate and blood pressure dropped significantly in comparison with a group that continued to smoke (Knapp, Bliss, and Wells 1963). These effects were replicated in lesser degree in subjects who unsuspectingly smoked cigarettes with lower nicotine content than those to which they had been accustomed. The conclusion drawn by the psychiatrists who carried out this research was that the heavy cigarette smoker appears to be a true addict.

Although the physiological withdrawal symptoms caused by smoking cessation are minor compared to the withdrawal sickness experienced when an addict gives up heroin or alcohol, the psychological effects of withdrawal are reputed to be legion. Martha Weinman Lear

(1974), a freelance writer who has attempted to quit smoking numerous times, illustrates the agony of withdrawal with the following dialogue:

> *Taxicab driver:* Jesus, I'm suffering, let me tell you. I'm trying to quit smoking.
> *Passenger:* Ah. How long ago did you quit?
> *Driver:* Twenty minutes ago. (p. 73)

Case studies show that withdrawal from smoking may be distressing. For example, a 29-year-old housewife was reported to develop an incapacitating obsession with a strong odor that came from her vagina when she quit smoking ("Smoker's Psychosis" 1973). Another, somewhat less pathological reaction was columnist Joseph Alsop's (1973) recorded bout with a malady that has stricken many students, the incompetence syndrome: an inability to do tasks requiring mental effort and concentration, such as creative writing.

More commonly, withdrawal from smoking has been demonstrated to be accompanied by hostility, aggressiveness, and irritability in monkeys and in man (Hutchinson and Emley 1973). The desire to have something in the mouth, reported by 59 percent of the subjects in one retrospective study (Wynder, Kaufman, and Lesser 1967), and the increased appetite, reported by 82 percent, are also prominent withdrawal symptoms. Disorientation or inability to concentrate, as described by Joseph Alsop, has been found to be less common, with 20 percent of Wynder, Kaufman, and Lesser's (1967) ex-smokers reporting this problem.

Withdrawal symptoms seem to differ somewhat from person to person, and they may even vary from time to time in the same person. Withdrawal symptoms have been demonstrated to be susceptible to experimental manipulation. A group of student nurses who were asked to refrain from smoking for a day, ostensibly for the sake of a study on heart rate, were persuaded that they were feeling *fewer* withdrawal symptoms when given an inert pill that was said to cause irritability, nervousness, and hunger, than a control group given a pill for which no side effects were specified (Barefoot and Girodo 1972). This study is encouraging in regard to the possibility of manipulating smokers' perceptions of their experiences during withdrawal.

Behavioral treatments

Maintaining self-control despite the aversive consequences (withdrawal symptoms) of not smoking is difficult. There is a delicate balance between the ability to control behavior and the desire to do so (Ferster 1970).

A direct, though not strictly behavioral, approach to the problem of withdrawal involves the use of medication. Drug therapy in smoking cessation has employed lobeline (marketed as Bantron or Nicoban), a drug whose actions mimic some of the effects of nicotine. The results of several drug therapy programs using lobeline have been called "dismal" (Bernstein 1970); only 8 to 17 percent of the subjects who were successful at the end of treatment remained abstinent at the followup (Hunt and Bespalec 1974). Apparently, this pharmacological substitute for nicotine is not an adequate substitute for cigarette smoking.

Indirect approaches to the problem of withdrawal are aimed at maintaining commitment to quitting smoking in spite of withdrawal symptoms. Two such techniques have had moderate success. Janis and Hoffman (1971) used a "buddy system," which involved daily phone calls between partners. They obtained significantly more success with a group of subjects who had daily phone contact with a partner than with control subjects, at the time of the 1-year followup. Abstinence data were not reported, but subjects who were assigned buddies decreased their smoking from an average of 32 cigarettes per day to an average of 8.

Another motivational technique required that subjects bet a sum of money on their ability to quit smoking; this was combined with a public commitment by having their names published in a school newspaper (Elliott and Tighe 1968). This approach is similar to the De Gaulle technique—the General strode into his office one day, announced that he no longer smoked cigarettes, and acted accordingly (Schneider 1968). Elliott and Tighe's technique was successful for approximately 37 percent of the subjects treated. Harris and Bruner (1971) and the present author (unpublished data) have found that the major obstacle to such a program lies in obtaining subjects who are willing to participate in it; a great deal of confidence seems to be needed before people are willing to take the required financial risk.

Habit in smoking

A recent trend in smoking cessation studies has been the attempt to decrease the painful effects of withdrawal and, at the same time, act directly to weaken the smoking habit.

Extent of the habit

When smoking is an hourly event day after day, it obviously must be a deeply ingrained habit; a person who smokes 20 cigarettes a day (one pack) puffs on a cigarette about 60,000 times a year, or 150 times a day (Jarvik 1970). No conscious bodily function (even elimination) comes close to this in sheer numbers, and the number of cigarette puffs per day for a moderate smoker easily rivals the number of bar presses or pecks on a button that experimental psychologists demand of the rats or pigeons they condition in learning laboratories. The strength of this habit is such that when tobacco cigarettes were made unavailable, smokers in one study turned to lettuce cigarettes, which they unanimously disliked (Jarvik 1970).

Because of the frequency of cigarette smoking and the duration of the habit, the event that "calls for a cigarette," becomes almost synonymous with a conditioned stimulus for smoking. Because of its repetitive nature, smoking sometimes becomes a functionally autonomous or self-perpetuating behavior. This situation is expressed by smokers who say, "I don't know why I smoke—I don't enjoy it anymore." The pervasiveness of this kind of complaint led to the facetious proposal that we "take the habit out of our vices and put the pleasure back in" (Hunt and Matarazzo 1970).

Some measures of habit have been found to bear a relationship to ability to quit smoking. Those who have smoked the longest and inhale the most frequently are found to have the most difficulty in quitting smoking (Graham and Gibson 1971). Interestingly, the number of cigarettes smoked per day, another measure of habit, was not found to be related to success in quitting smoking.

Behavioral treatments

A concern with the habit aspects of smoking has generated two learning approaches to quitting smoking: tapering-off techniques, which are intended to weaken the smoking habit gradually, and aversive conditioning techniques, aimed at abruptly suppressing smoking.

Gradual quitting procedures. Numerous gradual quitting procedures have been investigated in an attempt to develop an effective method which would minimize the painful aspects of withdrawal. Gradual procedures generally have been unsuccessful.

Some of the simplest approaches to gradual quitting involve monitoring and restricting cigarette intake either by foregoing certain regularly smoked cigarettes or by increasing the time interval between cigarettes. A smoker may also take fewer puffs per cigarette or employ a cigarette holder to allow the inhalation of increasingly less smoke per puff.

A mechanical device for increasing the time interval between cigarettes is a cigarette case with a time lock that allows it to be opened only after a specified period of time (Azrin and Powell 1968). Results with this device have been poor; apparently, there was no transfer of effects from the treatment period (when the cigarette case was used) to the

Amazing
Health Discovery

New Scientific Filter

If you can't or don't want to quit smoking but are worried about the consequences, there is now a FOOL-PROOF way for ABSOLUTELY SAFE SMOKING. Remarkable invention by European scientist takes the worry out of inhaling FOREVER. Smoke passes out of cigarette, then into special cagelike filter section containing live white laboratory rat. Rat gets the cancer, you get the smoking pleasure. When rat becomes sickly, simply throw out and replace. Average rodent good for a month's smoking. Enjoy smoking again and give your health a break at the same time. Unconditionally approved by famous Columbia University! ORDER NOW! Scientific filter-kit includes filter cage, 4 rats, and 6-month supply of food pellets. Send $19.95, postage included, to: MIK-O-DON PRODUCTS, Box 99, Grand Central Station, N.Y. 10044.

Figure 23-1 SOURCE: *National Lampoon*, March 1973, 64. Reprinted by permission of the *National Lampoon*.

posttreatment period (no cigarette case), as relapse occurred in all instances.

Another mechanical device is a cigarette case that delivers an electric shock if opened before a set time. Use of this device was equally unsuccessful; rather than suppressing smoking the device suppressed attempts to quit smoking, as subjects stopped carrying the cigarette case (Powell and Azrin 1968).

A set of gradual procedures has been devised to narrow the vast array of stimuli to which smoking is probably conditioned. In some of these studies subjects were instructed to carry a portable timer whose buzz signaled a legitimate cigarette break. During the course of treatment, the timer was reset for increasingly longer time intervals so that smoking was eventually scheduled out of existence. Use of this technique produced no improvements over control procedures, however, and success rates ranged from 12 to 40 percent (the latter in a group that was told only to cut down on their smoking) (Bernard and Efran 1972; Levinson, Shapiro, Schwartz, and Tursky 1971; Upper and Meredith 1970). Most discouraging was the Levinson et al. 50 percent dropout rate and the informal interview data collected by Bernard and Efran indicating that the subjects who did the best were those who stopped smoking precipitously rather than following the schedule.

Another approach to minimizing the stimuli for smoking consists of identifying the situational stimuli associated with smoking and then having the person rank these stimuli according to the difficulty he would have in abstaining from smoking in each situation (Gutmann and Marston 1967). The subject is then instructed to give up cigarettes in the situation ranked as easiest, progressing up the hierarchy at a rate of about 3 days per situation. However, neither Gutmann and Marston (1967), Marston and McFall (1971), nor Sachs, Bean, and Morrow (1970), who expanded the hierarchy to include thoughts and feelings that were stimuli for smoking, reported any degree of success with this technique.

Other stimulus control approaches include smoking only in an increasingly inaccessible chair (Nolan 1968) or in the bathroom (L. A. Hall, personal communication, 1974), the latter being reminiscent of preadolescent smoking. There is no reason to believe, however, that these techniques will succeed where other gradual techniques have failed.

It is not surprising that a direct comparison found gradual quitting to be significantly less successful than quitting abruptly on a target date (Flaxman 1974). The failure of gradual quitting is consistent with the finding that individuals who have cut down their cigarette intake are more likely to "relapse" than persons who have quit totally (Upper and

Meredith 1970). The partial reinforcement effects of gradual cessation strategies may work against their own success. Despite the appeal of gradual quitting, the available data suggests that such techniques for smoking cessation are ineffective, and their use should be discouraged. In general, the feasibility of any gradual change strategy where the target behavior is the suppression of a response, as in alcoholism, drug addiction, and smoking, deserves further study.

Aversive conditioning procedures. Three types of aversive stimuli have been used to suppress smoking: electric shock, imaginal stimuli (by means of covert sensitization), and physical stimuli (using warm, smoky air and rapid smoking). Most have been unsuccessful.

One successful aversive conditioning technique, unkindly described as "blowing smoke up people's noses" (Yafa 1973), uses rapid smoking alone or in conjunction with warm, smoky air as the noxious stimulus. Each trial requires the subject to smoke rapidly (inhaling every 6 seconds, in as normal a fashion as possible), while warm, smoky air is blown in his face. This lasts as long as he can tolerate it (generally about 3 minutes), and as many trials as possible are given in each session. Sessions are held for 3 consecutive days, and then less frequently, as needed.

Using warm, smoky air and rapid smoking, Schmahl, Lichtenstein, and Harris (1972) obtained 64 percent abstinence in their subjects 6 months after treatment. Lichtenstein, Harris, Birchler, Wahl, and Schmahl (1973) eliminated the warm, smoky air component with no loss of effectiveness, and rapid smoking alone yielded a 60 percent success rate at the end of 6 months.

The success of rapid smoking as an aversive conditioning technique is consistent with the hypothesis that treatment is more effective when the noxious stimulus employed shares the same sensory mode as the behavior to be suppressed (Wilson and Davison 1969). Furthermore, as recommended in punishment theory (Berecz 1972), every instance of the target behavior (smoking) is punished since subjects are emphatically instructed not to smoke between sessions. If they want a cigarette very badly, they may request an additional session. Besides promoting an aversion to smoking, rapid smoking has the added benefit of providing some relief from withdrawal symptoms, since smoking can occur daily, albeit in an aversive situation. For a few hours after an aversion session the craving for a cigarette is usually reported to be diminished. In addition, the demand to smoke only in the lab, combined with free access to sessions, sets up a strong expectation of success.

Failure to replicate the successes reported by Lichtenstein and his associates has been noted in two recent studies. Lando (1975) achieved 33 percent success with his rapid smoking group at the end of 1 year, and Flaxman (1974) obtained an overall 6-month success rate of 41 percent for warm, smoky air and rapid smoking in combination with other procedures. In the group that followed Lichtenstein's procedures most closely, however, only 25 percent of Flaxman's subjects were abstinent at the end of 6 months. In the four comparisons she made between the rapid smoking groups and their controls, Flaxman found significantly greater effectiveness for rapid smoking only when it was combined with a particularly ineffective gradual quit procedure and was compared to the use of that procedure alone. Thus, rapid smoking salvaged an ineffective gradual quit treatment, but in the other three combination treatments it was no more effective than its control.

Procedural problems, such as the shorter length of the rapid smoking trials in Flaxman's study and the encouragement of at-home aversive conditioning in Lando's, may explain the failure to replicate Lichtenstein's success. Further investigation of the rapid smoking strategy, however, will be required before more confident conclusions can be drawn.

Combination of procedures. Aversive conditioning approaches other than warm, smoky air and rapid smoking have been generally unsuccessful. Combinations of aversive conditioning techniques with self-control procedures or motivational manipulations have, however, yielded some success. Chapman, Smith, and Layden (1971) used electroshock in combination with self-control techniques and obtained a 1-year success rate of 55 percent. The self-control techniques involved rehearsing reasons for not smoking in as convincing a manner as possible, smoking in one place only, switching to a less preferred brand of cigarettes, and developing new activities for structuring time.

Using a somewhat different combination of techniques, Best and Steffy (1971) employed electrical aversion therapy and a unique motivation-building procedure. Three groups of smokers were instructed to quit smoking during the first, second, or third week of a treatment program consisting of group aversive conditioning sessions (electric shock). Six weeks after treatment the most successful group was the one that had smoked for the longest interval during treatment. Four months later, however, there were no differences among the groups and most of the subjects had begun smoking again.

In summary, the bulk of recent behavior modification studies have attempted to help the smoker to deal with withdrawal from smoking and to counter the smoking habit. While gradual quit approaches have been unsuccessful in this regard, one particularly appropriate aversive conditioning technique, rapid smoking, shows a great deal of promise. Evidence indicates that other combinations of techniques aimed at these two barriers to quitting smoking may also be effective.

The needs filled by smoking

The less than perfect success rate in even the best studies available warrants consideration of an issue that has been ignored until now—why, besides for reasons of habit and to avoid withdrawal, do people smoke? What are the characteristics of cigarettes that have made smoking an enduring worldwide habit? A clear understanding of the motivation for smoking may suggest ways to improve smoking cessation treatments.

Reasons for smoking

Smoking generally begins in adolescence as a role-defining activity. Children and adolescents appear to start to smoke out of curiosity, and to impress others (Schwartz 1970). Similarly, college women who smoke report that cigarettes are an important component of their self-image (Mausner and Platt 1971).

For the novice, the pharmacological effects of smoking are at first unknown and then unpleasant; coughing, dizziness, and nausea are usually experienced until tolerance develops. Very shortly after the initiation phase, however, indirect evidence suggests that the pharmacological action of cigarettes, with nicotine as the active element, becomes quite reinforcing (Jarvik 1970). The actual mechanisms involved in the reinforcing effects of nicotine on the brain and the peripheral nervous system have been the subject of a great deal of controversy. Smoking is usually considered to be a stimulant to the peripheral nervous system (U.S. Public Health Service 1964). However, some of its actions, for example, on brain waves, support the paradoxical claim that nicotine or some integral part of the smoking act also exerts a relaxant effect on the central nervous system (Brown 1973).

The reasons people give for smoking support the seemingly contradictory evidence that smoking is both relaxing and stimulating pharmacologically. When asked why they smoke, most adult smokers agree to one or more of the following reasons: (1) cigarettes provide tension reduction, pleasurable relaxation, stimulation, or sensorimotor manipulation; (2) smoking is automatic; or (3) it is very unpleasant to be without a cigarette (Ikard, Green, and Horn 1969). Taken at face value, the first of these reasons suggest that cigarettes serve to change affect by relaxing as well as stimulating smokers.

Eysenck (1973) suggests that the reason for the paradoxical claims regarding the needs filled by cigarettes is that smoking serves to in-

Figure 23-2 SOURCE: United Feature Syndicate, 1973. Reprinted by permission of United Feature Syndicate, Inc.

crease or decrease arousal, depending on the smoker's momentary level of arousal, his usual level of arousal, and the precise dosage of nicotine he ingests, over which he has "fingertip" control. Eysenck suggests that the habitual smoker uses nicotine in a very sensitive way to bring himself to the precise level of arousal he requires at the moment, as reflected when an individual says "smoking calms me down," as well as "a cigarette gets me going in the morning."

Individuals who are more dependent upon the affect-changing properties of cigarettes experience greater difficulty giving them up. In one study, the men who reported that they smoked in order to relieve tension were most likely to fail in their attempts to quit smoking (Schwartz and Dubitzky 1968). A related finding was that those with the lowest levels of personal adjustment also were apt to fail to quit.

Data from the famous Midtown Manhattan study of mental health confirms the greater likelihood of quitting smoking among "the well" or asymptomatic, but only for men (Srole and Fischer 1973). The foregoing suggests that an aspect of the smoking experience neglected by most studies is the necessity for some smokers to learn new ways to regulate arousal level.

It should be noted that evidence regarding motivational factors in smoking does not contradict evidence regarding the habit component in smoking. Individuals may smoke partly out of habit and partly for the various reasons described above. Habit in smoking and reasons for smoking can be viewed as being analogous to primary and secondary reinforcement in phobias, where the phobic behavior is habitual and may have secondary reinforcing properties as well. In continuing smoking, it is likely that the relative contributions of habit and motivation differ from person to person.

Behavioral treatments

A recent study by Flaxman (1974) used an abrupt cessation strategy and an extensive package of self-control techniques to aid people in regulating arousal and restructuring their lives without cigarettes. This abrupt strategy was a target-date quitting procedure in which subjects spent 2 weeks in treatment before they quit smoking. During the target-date period subjects attended twice-weekly individual treatment sessions, practiced the self-control techniques, and recorded each cigarette smoked.

The self-control package used in this study involved several techniques oriented toward substituting new habits for smoking, such as developing a new hobby (Ober 1968), using worry beads for tactile stimulation (Chapman, Smith, and Layden 1971), and practicing muscle relaxation (Cautela 1970). Other techniques aimed at helping the smoker resist the impulse to smoke (especially during the first few weeks without cigarettes) were thought-stopping to interrupt ruminations about smoking (Cautela 1970) and changing or introducing novel stimuli into the person's life in order to alter or lessen the cues for smoking (Goldiamond 1965). In addition, motivation was maintained by means of rehearsal of reasons for quitting smoking (Chapman, Smith, and Layden 1971), self-reinforcement (Mahoney, Moura, and Wade 1973), and public commitment by having the subjects tell friends that they were quitting smoking and sending letters to that effect to five friends or relatives whose names the subjects supplied.[1] Subjects were strongly urged to try all techniques in order to develop an individualized set of activities that they found comfortable and effective.

[1] A modification of Elliot and Tighe's (1968) approach.

In an eight-cell design, subjects were randomly assigned to treatments involving the same combination of self-control techniques and individual attention from an experimenter. Flaxman found that the two treatments in which subjects stopped smoking on a target date were significantly more successful than either quitting cold turkey or tapering off. At a 6-month followup, 50 percent of the subjects who had used a target-date quitting procedure were abstinent. The group that received warm, smoky air and practiced rapid smoking in addition to using a target date had a 62 percent success rate at 6-month followup. It is noteworthy that the two target-date quitting groups did not differ significantly from each other.

Flaxman's study replicates Chapman, Smith, and Layden's (1971) success with self-control techniques and is consistent with the success of self-control packages in other problem areas such as weight loss (see Chapter 22 in this volume). It also demonstrates that gradual quitting and immediate quitting impede the effectiveness of such procedures, while target-date quitting seems to facilitate it.

In a complicated treatment such as the one Flaxman used, it is impossible to tell what the effective elements are until the treatment is dismantled and its component elements are tested. It is possible that one important element of the successful treatment package involved using self-control techniques to develop new habits to substitute for smoking. Apparently, the 2-week period prior to quitting smoking was required for the effectiveness of the self-control package, perhaps because subjects learned the techniques better when they had more time to practice. Elements intended to maintain motivation and to help subjects cope with withdrawal are also likely to have been important.

This approach exemplifies the use of behavioral techniques to cope with three of the major problems engendered by quitting smoking: maintaining motivation, getting through withdrawal, and developing new habits to substitute for smoking. Focus on the last of these issues has been heretofore lacking and perhaps future studies will profitably concentrate on it.

A concluding note

Recent developments seem to warrant a note of cautious optimism regarding the potential of smoking cessation techniques. We now know that smoking cessation must be abrupt, although it need not be immediate, and a number of techniques for accomplishing it seem to be viable. Aversive conditioning by means of rapid smoking is one such technique, and a self-control package that includes long-term substitutes for smoking as well as commitment building elements, perhaps through target-date quitting, is another. Attempts to develop new and incompatible habits comprise an area that has been particularly neglected so far.

Hopefully, additional research will further validate the effectiveness of some of the methods discussed here so that success in smoking cessation will become the rule, not the exception. The model of smoking cessation developed here suggests that smoking modification will eventually entail individualized treatments based on the smoker's anticipated difficulties in the areas of motivation, discomfort during withdrawal, habit, and the needs filled by cigarettes.

In view of the yearly trends in per capita cigarette consumption in the United States (American Cancer Society 1974), it is unlikely that those interested in helping people quit smoking will run out of subjects in the near future. The self-control issues raised in seeking effective techniques for quitting smoking are similar to those in other areas (weight loss, drug and alcohol addiction, studying problems) where immediate gratification must be delayed in order to secure long-term benefits. Thus, while research on effective techniques for quitting smoking is valuable in its own right, it is likely to have useful implications for other behavior problems as well.

Behavioral treatment of marital problems[1]

Hyman Hops
University of Oregon

24

In this chapter Hops provides a description of the behavioral marital therapy developed by him and his colleagues at the University of Oregon. The paper presents a behavioral interpretation of the marital relationship, based primarily on operant and social learning principles.

The treatment program consists of: (1) pinpointing and discriminating specific positive and negative behaviors, with emphasis on the positive; (2) training in communication skills such as improving listening skills, sharing communication equally, and reducing aversive behaviors, especially those that lead to sidetracking of issues; (3) training in problem solving, negotiation, and compromise; and (4) signing contracts regarding specific behaviors to be emitted and specific reinforcers contingent upon those behaviors. This program incorporates training in communication skills similar to that employed by Guerney and his colleagues (1973).[2] The contracting aspect of the therapy is similar to the early behavioral exchange programs of Stuart (1969) and Knox (1971), though the reinforcers are not to be exchanged on a quid pro quo *basis, but rather are independent of the marital relationship itself. Although not discussed here, sexual problems in the marriage may also be included in the treatment program. The*

[1] Most of the ideas presented in this chapter were formulated through the author's interaction with his colleagues Jerry Patterson and Bob Weiss and all the students who participated in the deliberations.

[2] Additional details regarding this program are available from B. Guerney, Ph.D., Beecher House, Pennsylvania State University, University Park, Pennsylvania, 16802.

type of sexual therapy employed may be rehabilitative in nature, similar to that employed by Masters and Johnson, or it may be preventive and "enriching" as demonstrated by the sexual enhancement training conducted by LoPiccolo (1974; cf. Horn 1975).

This chapter demonstrates the relevance of operant and social-learning principles to a conceptualization of marriage and marital distress. In addition, it suggests the utilization of these principles in developing solutions to marital problems. The treatment techniques developed thus far still lack a solid empirical basis; the data used have been largely of the self-report type with none of the strengths of reliable observation data collected outside the laboratory by trained observers. Even so, the technology developed does offer considerable promise.

Much of the work reported here was carried out at the University of Oregon and the Oregon Research Institute (Patterson and Hops 1972; Weiss, Hops, and Patterson 1973; Patterson, Hops, and Weiss 1974). This chapter also relies upon the work of other investigators who have made significant contributions to the field (Azrin, Naster, and Jones 1973; Goldstein and Francis 1969; Liberman 1970; Stuart 1969, 1972). Marital problems which are the result of sexual dysfunctioning in one or both members will not be discussed here (see Masters and Johnson 1970), nor will treatments that provide help to only one member of the marital dyad. For example, systematic desensitization and assertion training have been used with one marital partner for a variety of sexual and marital problems, ranging from frigidity to communication difficulties (Lazarus 1968a). This chapter will view marital distress as the result of a breakdown in the marital social system which prevents the couple from maintaining a satisfactory relationship. The problems treated may be viewed as those that are responsive to operant and social learning principles.

Marital relationships

Marital relationships may be viewed as one example of the many dyadic or two-person associations that adults engage in throughout a lifetime. On the basis of the social learning model, we can assume that most relationships are formed because there is sufficient potential for mutual reinforcement. For example, it is likely that we pick friends who have social, professional, or recreational interests similar to our own, as well as similar attitudes and values, because interacting with these individuals produces positive reinforcement. We are unlikely to pick friends with whom we have little in common or with whom we would constantly argue (unless arguing is reinforcing). Relationships are maintained as long as both members continue to supply enough positive reinforcement to each other. If one member of the dyad changes his or her behavior so that continued interaction becomes nonreinforcing or even punishing to the other, it is likely that the relationship will deteriorate and eventually cease.

Short-term or open-ended relationships are defined as those for which there are no social or legal pressures compelling the members to continue the association under all conditions. If a "friend" becomes nonreinforcing and even aversive, then one simply drops this friend and goes on to find someone with whom interaction is more pleasurable. Partnerships, employee-employer, and doctor-patient relationships are further examples of open-ended social systems.

Marital relationships, on the other hand, are illustrative of a closed social system. Two people marry, presumably, in the expectation that the married condition will increase the availability of positive reinforcers, such as sharing activities, fulfilling sexual needs, raising children. However, when expectations are not met and the relationship fails to become or remain positive, there exist sufficient legal, social, and religious sanctions to prohibit many from divorcing. Divorce itself may be a punishing experience. In fact, many couples continue to live unsatisfactory lives together rather than go through a divorce. Several studies have shown that about one couple in five consider themselves unhappy (Renne 1970). Furthermore, the situation appears to get worse during the first 10 years of the marriage (Rollins and Feldman 1970).

Hill and Aldous (1969) have described the marriage relationship as "a partnership contract without an escape clause." The marital couple is one of the few alliances in our society which traditionally has planned for *permanence*. Strangely enough, it is expected that this pair will survive a multitude of demanding situations, such as illnesses, financial reverses, changes in homes and jobs, the needs of children, the attractiveness of others, and so on. When you consider the amount and the kind of training that individuals have to prepare them for this task, it would seem to be an impossible one. Premarital dating and engagement are obviously insufficient and inadequate practice for learning the variety of behavioral responses required to adjust to the changing conditions. The current high rate of divorce (approximately one out of every two to three marriages) may not reflect a dissatisfaction with marriage as a lifestyle, but instead illustrates the inability of many couples to maintain satisfactory long-term relationships.

Only after a couple has been married do they experience the problems that arise when two people live together and have the opportunity to practice the marital roles in full. One study compared married and engaged couples on the extent to which the partners agreed about various areas of the relationship. The two areas that separated the two groups most were sex and communication. The engaged couples, because of their limited interaction, were not aware of the critical problems that can arise with day-to-day interaction. In a premarital course Knox and Patrick (1971) had students keep diaries and compare the data to earlier estimates of their partner's expected behavior. Some individuals reported large discrepancies between what their partners said they did and their actual behavior. For example, one student found that her fiancé was a "goof-off"; he spent less time studying than he estimated he did. Such discrepancies do not usually become apparent until the couple are married and living together.

A first marriage that ends in divorce may be simply a dress rehearsal for success during later marriages, since many couples do go on to find satisfactory partners. Perhaps the increasingly frequent pattern of nonmarital cohabitation is beneficial because it permits the individuals to practice the behaviors before making a final commitment. On the other hand, it may be necessary not only to live together but to receive training in the resolution of problems as they arise. One high school in Oregon offers a one-semester class called Contemporary Family Life, during which students are paired as "married couples." They spend their time visiting supermarkets to check prices, collecting data on automobile, health, and life insurance, and attempting to work out solutions to problems in the areas of cooking, housing, and the like. They also receive lectures from experts in various fields. If marital discord is assumed to be the result of the couple's inability to deal with the many changes that must inevitably occur during their marital interaction, perhaps premarital training of some sort is required. Otherwise, more difficult retraining may be required later.

Behavioral view of marriage and its problems

Let us examine the marital relationship and some of its problems in behavioral terms. A satisfactory marriage may be assumed to be one in which the reciprocal exchange of reinforcers is satisfactory to both spouses. Because of the interactive nature of the marital relationship, changes in the behavior of one spouse will require adjustments or concomitant changes in the behavior of the other. If the supply of reinforcers being dispensed by one spouse to the other suddenly decreases, due to changing work habits, for example, then the other member must adapt to a new situation which is less reinforcing. If the change is temporary, it is likely to have no significant effect on the marriage. However, if it is more permanent, the deprived spouse may attempt to alter the situation by changing the behavior of the partner in order to bring the supply of reinforcers up to the previously satisfactory level or else to look outside the relationship for the answer. Somehow, a solution is required.

Nonworking wives may be good examples of the spouse who faces consistently low supplies of reinforcement from the partner. Early in the marriage, the husband comes home and discusses his workday with his wife. After some time, the frequency of this behavior decreases. The husband, interacting with people at work all day, is satiated; his wife, deprived of adult company all day, is now anxious to interact and proceeds to ask a multitude of questions. Unfortunately, he is exhausted and would rather sit and watch television, have a drink, eat, read, and refrain from interacting. The likely result of this behavior, which virtually places his wife on extinction, is continued nagging by the wife in order to elicit a positive response from her husband. This is one of the most frequent complaints noted by marital therapists. (While the example used here is rather traditional, there are many marriages in which the roles have been reversed. Unfortunately, the effect is the same: one spouse eventually becomes the nag.)

In any long-term two-person relationship, requests for change in the behavior of one person by the other is a continuing process. As two people learn to live with each other, the independence for which they had been previously reinforced becomes less appropriate. Each must be constantly aware of the needs of the other. Plans have to be worked at together and decisions made jointly. When to eat, when to go out, are now two-person problems and require joint decisions. Changes in the surrounding environment require many of these early decisions to be altered repeatedly. Unfortunately, few couples have had the necessary training to respond to such situations with rational problem-solving behavior.

Requests for change are likely to be reasonable at first. If the other person complies with the request or if the couple is able to work out an arrangement satisfactory to both, then the problem is solved. However, if the requested change in behavior does not occur after repeated requests, discussions, and promises, then the next request is likely to be accompanied by an aversive stimulus—"Damn it! You *never* do what I want you to. Just like *your* whole family."—a statement designed not for productive problem solving, but simply to zap or punish the partner. Unfortunately, there is considerable evidence that these aversive behaviors elicit aversive responses in the partner as well. The end result is a pattern of pain-producing interaction occasionally culminating in physical violence.

Some patterns of negative interaction may be maintained by what

Patterson and his colleagues (Patterson and Cobb 1971; Patterson and Hops 1972; Patterson and Reid 1970) have called the "coercion process." This occurs when one member of the dyad delivers requests for change accompanied by high intensity aversive stimuli which the other cannot ignore (for example, screaming, yelling, shouting, crying, temper tantrums, physical violence). The "coercive" behavior forces the partner to comply with the request, reinforcing the aversive behavior of the complainer and increasing the likelihood of its recurrence. The victim's compliant behavior is also strengthened through the negative reinforcement paradigm, since the change in behavior turns off the aversive requests by the spouse. Thus, the two continue to reinforce each other, strengthening an interaction pattern that produces pain for both.

Following this pattern of negative interaction, it is likely that both members will begin avoiding each other. The result can be seen in classic behavior patterns: long silences at dinner, absence or very low frequency of affectionate responses and intercourse, low rates of joint recreational activities, and boring, lifeless evenings in front of that neutral moderator, the television set.

Intervention procedures

The behavioral treatment of marital problems had modest beginnings. Wives were trained to shape simple behaviors in their husbands (for example, the number of clothes dropped, frequency of "I love you" statements) using both antecedent (graphs posted, similar statements by wives) and consequent (allowing clothes to pile up) events. Negotiations consisted of spouses trading off one behavior change (10 minutes of talk time) for a change in the other (sleeping in the nude). However, the complexities of marital interaction required the development of more comprehensive treatment packages. The more comprehensive approach usually involves teaching the couple a set of skills (rearranging the contingencies that control their behavior), which increases the probability that they will continue to use the procedures after formal treatment has stopped. This section will describe several program components and the problem behaviors they have been designed to ameliorate.

Pinpointing and discrimination training

When couples come in seeking help for marital problems, the behavior therapist notices two problems critical to the success of the treatment. First, their language is nonspecific and vague. Using a term coined by Ogden Lindsley in *Precision Management,* we might say that they are unable to "pinpoint" behaviors they wish to change in each other. "We have a communication problem." "She is not very considerate." Such statements make it difficult to determine precisely what the problems are, and moreover, the couple themselves are not able to agree on precisely what behaviors they are discussing.

The second problem involves their inadequate discrimination skills. They find it difficult to discriminate between spouse positive and negative behavior, thus causing faulty data collection. They no longer recognize or attend to behaviors in each other's repertoires that they find positive and wish to maintain or have accelerated. All behaviors are seen as negative and statements such as "He *always* treats me badly," or "She *never* has a good word to say," are frequently heard. When they are asked to make a list of positive behaviors in the spouse, a long silence ensues.

As a first step, then, it is necessary to teach the couple to pinpoint behaviors. Solving a problem described as "We have a dull life" leaves one uncertain as to where to begin. When it is more precisely defined as "We go to the movies about twice a year," or "We invite people over about once every 4 months," the goals of the intervention program are pinpointed as well. Even affective behaviors such as "He doesn't love me anymore" must be redefined. Restating the difficulty as "He seldom kisses or hugs me" and "We have sexual intercourse about once every 2 months" pinpoints the problem in behavioral terms and allows the individual to record the frequency of such behaviors.

The therapist works with the couple until they are able to specify behaviors precisely. Complaints are written on a chalkboard and each item is worked on until the specific behavior is identified. Home assignments can be given in which they are asked to make lists of specific behaviors in themselves and their spouses.

At Oregon, we developed a P and D or Spouse Observation Checklist to help couples learn pinpointing [3] and also to serve as a data base for evaluating generalization of treatment from laboratory or office to the home. It consists of several hundred pinpointed behaviors of one spouse as experienced by the other. Each behavior is recorded as either a Pleasure (P) or a Displeasure (D). For example, a spouse may record a P for a good meal cooked by the other or a D for having a question ignored by the other spouse.

Initially, we asked our couples to go to the chalkboard and list the precise behaviors they would like to change in their spouses. In many cases, one spouse (usually the wife) would complete a list of 20 items in 5 minutes, while the struggling mate would have 2 or

[3] The present system was established following discussions with Eric Haughton, whose attempts to modify his own interactions led to the initial use of the P and D system.

PLEASES	DATE:									
	AM	PM	AM	PM	AM	PM	AM	PM	AM	PM
kissed me										
answered the phone when I was busy										
asked for my advice										
turned up the heat										
called me on the phone from work										
took her blouse off first when undressing										
PLEASES GRAND TOTAL										

DISPLEASES	DATE:									
	AM	PM	AM	PM	AM	PM	AM	PM	AM	PM
yelled at me for smoking										
turned away from me when asked for a kiss										
dropped clothes on the floor										
missed toilet bowl when urinating.										
punished child										
broke promise to repair something										
DISPLEASES GRAND TOTAL										

Figure 24-1 Example of weekly P and D recording chart

3 poorly defined items such as "I would like her to get off my back." At present, each spouse is handed the check list from which they select those items that describe both the P and D behaviors of their spouses. In addition, the P and D check list is a means of data collection. Record forms (see Figure 24-1) on which the items selected by each spouse are listed, are taken home and twice daily each partner records occurrence and frequency of occurrence. The couples are instructed to add new items to the list as they occur to them during their daily interaction. In this way, training in pinpointing is a continuous process.

As stated earlier, many couples have difficulty in recognizing positive behaviors in their spouses. The marital interaction has deteriorated so that each spouse has become an S^D or discriminative stimulus for aversive events only. In other words, the presence of the spouse signals only displeasure. Videotape has been used very effectively to break down this emphasis on negative events and teach them to recognize positive aspects of each other's behavior. Couples are asked to interact for approximately 3 to 5 minutes while being recorded. The videotape is replayed and each of the partners is asked to count the number of positive events in his or her own behavior. Next, another short interaction is recorded following which partners are asked to count positive behaviors in the spouse. This is done several times until there is an increase in the number of positive behaviors counted. The increased count is due partly to the improved discrimination by the spouses and partly to the fact that each spouse tries to act more positively. Thus, while the procedure is used primarily to teach them how to discriminate better between positive and negative behaviors, it has the additional effect of training them to interact positively as well.

Azrin, Naster, and Jones (1973) have spouses examine the daily rating data each collects on the other to provide feedback and make them aware of how they see each other. On recommendation from Haughton, we found that immediate feedback could be used to train spouses to become aware of how each was reacting to the other's behavior. For example, if the husband recorded a P following a behavioral response by the other, he would say, "That was a P," thus communicating to the spouse the effect of her behavior. If the behavior was displeasing, that too was communicated.

Occasionally, a behavior was perceived as a P or D but had not been delivered with that intent. For example, a husband might say to his wife following dinner, "That was the best dinner I've had in the last month," and she would respond, "That's a D!" In other words, while the husband intended to deliver an approval or praise, the wife indicated that she thought he was being critical of her general cooking skills. By telling each other how the behavior was received and checking upon its intent, the wife realizes that part of the problem is her reaction to her husband's behavior, while he becomes aware of the fact that he may have to state his compliments differently for them to be accepted as such.

Some couples are asked to practice "love days" during which one spouse triples the number of positive behaviors he or she normally dispenses. Since the spouse is aware of the partner's attempts to increase pleasing behavior, he or she would be looking for them and the results would be reflected in the data count for that day. On other days, not more than once or twice a week, the other partner would attempt to do the same.

In summary, couples are trained to pinpoint behaviors, to count them regularly, and to discriminate between positive and negative responses with the emphasis on the former.

Communication skills training

As a result of pinpointing and discrimination training, improvement in communication is likely to take place indirectly. However, emphasis on communication skills may still be required after the pinpointing phase is completed. The specific goals of communication training may vary from couple to couple, but emphasis is given to improving listening skills, sharing communication equally, and reducing aversive behaviors and those that sidetrack issues.

Listening. Many spouses are so intent on verbalizing their own point of view that they simply do not listen to their partner's opinions before going on to make the next response. Unfortunately, few problems are resolved because they are usually on two different tracks either parallel or moving away from each other. To make communication a two-way interaction, it is necessary first to teach the couple listening skills.

Some couples are taught to paraphrase the last statement of the spouse simply to ensure that they heard the other's words. Often, a "Yes" or "Unhuh" is sufficient evidence. In addition, they may be given homework to do during scheduled talk times and tape record their discussions. These would be returned to the therapist at the next session to determine whether any improvement in their behavior had occurred.

Sharing. Many couples have interaction patterns in which one member dominates the dialogue by a ratio of as much as 90 to 10. When the nondominant spouse is questioned, the other is likely to answer. One such couple was asked to plan an ideal day for themselves, that is, a high rate P day. The wife responded immediately with her ideas about what they should do. The submissive, rather withdrawn husband had no opportunity to present his ideas. On another occasion, when it was arranged that he present first, his choice of an ideal was very different from hers, yet previously he had been unable to disagree with her.

Training often takes the form of simply having each spouse speak for a specific period of time, perhaps allowing 1 or 2 minutes for each to make a response. If there is no response by one member during his or her scheduled interval, then the other may proceed. In addition, questions by the therapist may be directed at both members equally so that both points of view are heard.

THE LOCKHORNS

"OF COURSE I ALWAYS SEE LEROY'S SIDE.....
THAT'S HOW I KNOW IT'S WRONG."

Figure 24-2 SOURCE: King Features Syndicate, 1974. Reprinted by permission of King Features Syndicate, Inc.

Reduce aversive and sidetracking behaviors. As a part of communication training, couples are taught to reduce their aversive or negative verbal behaviors, such as sarcasm or ridicule. In addition, they are trained to decrease the frequency of behaviors that sidetrack discussions, such as changing the subject, excusing their own actions.

Some individuals have nonverbal responses that are obvious put-downs but they simply act as if they were unaware that they are behaving like that. A woman we had worked with screwed up her face every time she disagreed with a statement by her husband. Using videotape feedback, we showed her what she was doing and how her husband reacted to her put-down behavior. Then we reinforced her for reducing the frequency of these behaviors and for stating in a nonaversive manner that she disagreed.

One husband could not make a positive response even after being complimented by his wife. We asked each of them to think of something positive the spouse had done during the last week and then publicly state it. The wife started by saying, "I really appreciate your help with the packages at mother's last weekend." The husband's quick response was, "I always help you with those damn packages!" We told him that was an incorrect response since his wife had made a positive statement for which another positive statement was deserved. We emphasized that all statements were to be taken at face value and that he should not read any other meanings into them. After three attempts, he was finally able to say "Thank you."

The "love days" also facilitated positive interaction; the high rate of positive behaviors dispensed by one spouse provided frequent opportunities for the other to react in kind.

Thus, communication training taught couples to listen, to share communication equally, and to decrease put-downs while simultaneously increasing positive reinforcement.

Problem solving and negotiation training

At this stage, couples are taught how to solve problems as a unit. In other words, we are only partially interested in training couples to solve specific current problems; the long-range goal is to provide the couples with a set of skills that will enable them to continue to solve problems as they occur during the rest of their married life.[4]

First, couples are taught to work toward solutions to problems in a progressive, future-oriented manner. Old complaints and problems are not discussed unless they can directly contribute to the solution of a present problem. Using their previously learned communication skills, both partners make contributions to the problem-solving sessions and recognize each other's suggestion with positive verbal reinforcement.

Second, couples are taught a most important concept—that changes in each other's behavior are negotiable. They are taught to think about their own and their spouse's behavior changes in "behavioral economic" terms. For example, a request by the husband for an improvement in housecleaning may be considered by the wife to be equivalent to improvements in her husband's yard and garage cleaning. Such exchanges have to be arranged for each couple, depending upon their own value system. It is conceivable that what may be equal exchanges for one couple (for example, 10 minutes of talk time equals $50 spending money) may be considered irrelevant by another.

Third, they are taught to compromise their demands in order to find solutions. Compromise was found to be an almost nonexistent behavior during baseline problem-solving sessions with our distressed couples. If neither partner is willing to be flexible in requests for behavior change in the other, then negotiation is impossible. The following is an example of a situation in which a compromise by one partner led to solution of a problem. A wife complained that her husband never hung up his clothes when he took them off at night. Since she was working she did not have the time during the day to hang them up for him. Her husband argued that she dominated the closet

[4] After some weeks in therapy, however, one couple decided to break up; an old beau returning to town offered the wife substantially more reinforcement than her husband. She indicated, however, that she would appreciate the skills she had learned in her new relationship.

space with her clothes and therefore it was a hassle for him to get in there at all. The wife suggested that she would remove unseasonable clothes and provide him with a specific designated area. He agreed to hang up his clothes if she were to do this. This amiable solution to a problem that was upsetting to both partners was made possible by the wife's ability to compromise. In the past, they would have continued to argue about the space problem, neither one willing to give, and probably introducing such sidetracks as "Well, what do you want me to do with my clothes. I don't have enough room for myself," "We need a bigger house," or "You got them out, you can put them back."

Contingency contracting

The couple, having negotiated changes in each other's behavior using the problem-solving, communication, and reinforcement skills learned previously, is now ready to be taught how to set up contracts. Contracting is a means of setting forth behavior change agreements. Obviously, agreeing to do something does not necessarily mean that one will follow through with the promised behavior change. Thus, contracts for behavior change agreements are written, and consequences are made contingent upon the behavior changes within them. This process is called *contingency contracting:* consequences are set up to positively reinforce compliance with the contract and to punish failure to comply.

Most contracts that have been used are based on a simple *quid pro quo* arrangement, a simple exchange agreement. One spouse agrees to do something in exchange for a behavior change in the other. For example, the husband may agree to take his wife out to dinner once a week, if she washes his socks and irons his shirts once a week. However, in this simple model, failure by either spouse to comply with the terms returns the couple to their initial position; if she does not wash his socks he will not take her out, and vice versa. What is more, there may be arguments about who is to go first.

At Oregon, we have tried to set up *independent consequences,* that is, consequences that are independent of whether the other person changes. The wife's consequences for washing and ironing would be independent of whether or not the husband took her out to dinner. If she did complete her agreed upon task, she would earn an evening out by herself to bridge or bowl. If she did not, she would not earn the right to go out. However, the husband still had to keep up his end of the bargain and take her out for dinner, for which he would receive, as a positive consequence, $5 extra out of the weekly budget to spend on himself.

It should be clear that consequences established this way help to ensure that at least one spouse will keep to the terms of the contract and do not involve a "you go first" problem, since there is no first. Furthermore, the system automatically reinforces the behavior change of those who do comply.

Contracts should emphasize positive consequences for behavior change. However, in some situations, negative consequences or penalties are required. If a positive reward system by itself seems to be ineffective, then positive and negative consequences may be tried. One husband agreed to spend 10 minutes a day in talk time with his wife. However, he was failing to find the time daily, and began making up excuses. We suggested that they add a negative consequence to the contract; failure to comply would mean he had to miss the Saturday college football game, his favorite sport. He objected strenuously to the recommendation, and said it was not fair and he was not willing to give up the football game. Instead, he suggested giving up something he did not value so greatly, such as going to his mother's on Sunday. It was pointed out to him that he did not have to give up anything as long as he kept to the terms of the contract to which he had agreed. And further, his hesitancy about taking a risk seemed to indicate a definite unwillingness to negotiate on his part. He finally accepted the argument, as well as the penalty, which never had to be used.

Thus, well-designed contingency contracts should have the following characteristics.

1. Behavior changes should be specific.
2. Behavior change of one spouse should be independent of the behavior change agreed to by the other.
3. Consequences should be positive and independent of whether the other spouse complies. Furthermore, positive consequences for one spouse should not come at a high cost to the other.
4. Negative consequences should be set, if necessary. However, they should not involve reward for the other spouse.

Figure 24-3 is an example of one such contract covering several areas of behavior change.

Training in contingency contracting must include a fade out or gradual withdrawal of the therapist's involvement, with more and more reliance placed on the couples' ability to establish their own contracts. After the behaviors necessary for effective contracting have been shaped, therapist reinforcement is faded. To accomplish this, the first contract is set up during a weekly session with direct supervision and suggestions offered by the therapist. After completing this task, the couple works on a second contract during a session with less direct involvement by the therapist. The third contract is begun during a weekly session but is completed at home by the couple. It is then shown

	NAME: Dick	NAME: Jane
CONVERSATION AND SEX		
Accelerate:	10 minutes of talk about Dick's day as it concerns studies and future - every day.	Sleeps in nude every night except during periods.
Reward:	1 bottle of beer per 10 minutes.	30¢ a day to be spent in any way I see fit.
Penalty:	Write two letters, e.g., to friends or relatives.	Heavy housework, e.g., 1) wash windows in 1 room 2) clean oven 3) wax floors 4) shampoo rug
HOME TIME AND CHILD TRAINING		
Accelerate:	Dick will be home four evenings per week, explicitly Monday, Wednesday, Friday, and Saturday. Of these, Jane will have one night out, one at her option, and two will be shared family nights.	Jane will spend involved, meaningful time with children, reading, art projects, excursions, reading readiness, etc., at the rate of 7 half-hour periods per week.
Reward:	One-half hour sense relaxation exercises with Jane.	Late cooking or dinner together with Dick is earned for 3 points (one point per half-hour with kids). One point may also be exchanged for 15 minutes help from Dick.
Penalty:	Complete the whole kitchen shebang alone after dinner.	Complete RCAF exercises at my level for failure to spend time with kids on any day.

Figure 24-3 Sample contingency contract for several areas of behavior change

to the therapist during the following session for her advice and encouragement. In the last step, the couple is asked to begin and complete a contract at home on their own, and return with it in the following session. When the couple is able to complete this last task, there is every good indication that the necessary behaviors have been acquired.

As defined here, contracts are not permanent agreements. Couples are always informed that if a contract is not found to be satisfactory then renegotiation is in order. However, we always asked our couples to maintain every contract for a minimum of 1 week. We may not be aware of the value of the agreed upon behaviors or the consequences until they have been experienced. In addition, there are some individuals who enter into contracts but are not committed to actual compliance with the terms. Instead, they may try to change the terms before the consequences can be delivered. Our 1-week minimum forces the couple to let the contract take effect, thus improving the chances that both individuals will think more seriously about the details built into future contracts.

A concluding note

We have conceptualized marriage and marital distress in behavioral terms. The behavioral intervention procedures for marital distress are: training in pinpointing and discrimination, training in communication skills, problem-solving and negotiation training, and contingency contracting (with independent consequences).

Our preliminary evaluations of the intervention procedures indicate considerable promise. The data collected in the laboratory show that couples trained in problem-solving skills show significant increases over baseline measures. Furthermore, the P and D data suggest some generalization of these effects to the home (Patterson, Hops, and Weiss 1975; Weiss, Hops, and Patterson 1973). Future research is required to evaluate the various components of the intervention package and to replicate the tentative results.

The future of behavior modification[1]

Frederick H. Kanfer and Laurence G. Grimm
University of Illinois at Urbana-Champaign

25

Frederick Kanfer has been one of the major contributors to the advancement of behavior therapy, and he and Grimm provide both suggestions and predictions regarding trends in behavior modification. This chapter ties together much of the material from Parts I and II with the applications presented in Part III.

The authors list the following ten areas as in need of exploration: (1) adoption of the behavioral model for clinical intervention; (2) reinforcement mechanisms; (3) aggression and altruism; (4) group processes and behavior change; (5) taxonomy and diagnosis; (6) social systems analysis; (7) reactance and countercontrol; (8) self-regulation and self-control; (9) control of physiological responses; and (10) language and thinking. Kanfer and Grimm advocate the study of the interactions *between psychological processes and the socio-cultural matrix, as both are viewed as significant components of the "human system." If behavior modification moves in these directions it seems likely that human behavior will be more adequately understood. Such expansion and application of knowledge is the hallmark of behavioral science.*

The social sciences are still in a rudimentary stage, abounding in promises, but meager in unshakable principles. Even though there have been no drastic breakthroughs changing the face of psychology, there has been progress in the last decade. Perhaps the most significant step

[1] The authors wish to express their appreciation to Charles R. Spates for his assistance on an earlier version of this chapter.

in the area of clinical psychology has been the increased acceptance of experimentation as a basis for theorizing and for practical application. A comprehensive theory of human behavior, the mortar in the structure of knowledge about persons, is gradually developing. Most significantly, the direction of the work has changed. Previously, the most widely used theories of personality and pathology were built on clinical observations, intuitions, and common assumptions about human behavior. The result was a proliferation of grand theoretical systems (Hall and Lindzey 1957). There is now a tendency to develop models of more specific behavioral functioning based on the general knowledge in the social sciences and bolstered by laboratory and field research with an eye toward the future integration of these data and models into a more encompassing framework. In the area of behavior modification one major direction has been the detailed examination of the interaction between limited response classes and their environmental determinants. The results have often necessitated the expansion of an oversimplified and narrow conditioning paradigm that has failed to consider the particular context in which events occurred.

This trend can be seen as part of a shift in emphasis from an attempt to understand the nature of man to an emphasis in understanding the nature of man's interaction with his physical and social environment as the key for describing, predicting, and altering human behavior. This change seems consistent with a trend toward a broader orientation in science that views the observed phenomena in the social and cultural context of the scientific enterprise. In the life sciences, as in the physical sciences, there is a growing awareness that the very phenomena that are under study are continuously altered by rapid changes in the composition of our atmosphere, our flora and fauna, our dietary and mating habits, and our medical and technological interventions with so-called natural processes. The impact of manmade changes is even greater in the social sciences. The key role of man's own activities in altering the psychological and social phenomena which interest us must be recognized. As we gain increased control over the potentially destructive natural and manmade forces that threaten man's existence, questions need to be raised concerning the optimal physical, biological, and social conditions that man can create for himself and the possible negative consequences of such "interference" with nature (see Dubos 1968; Feinberg 1969; Ferkiss 1969; Skinner 1971; Taylor 1968; Toffler 1970).

These considerations make it necessary to view recent changes in psychology in a broader context. As in other sciences, research in psychology is no longer perceived as an effort solely to uncover nature's secrets in order to control natural processes for the benefits of mankind. Instead, it has been recognized that one of the most important influences in human development and differentiation is man's own creation of social and physical environments and the establishment of structures and institutions that in turn make specific demands on the individual which he must meet to survive. Eisenberg (1972) has suggested that "man is his own chief product." This awareness has led to increasing interest in studying what man *does* and the effects of his actions on himself and on his social and physical environment, rather than asking what man *is* or should strive to be. This philosophical view of man is becoming increasingly popular in psychology (Bandura 1969; Kanfer and Phillips 1970) and underlies a number of investigations on the reciprocal interaction of the person with his environment (Bowers 1973; Mischel 1971).[2]

At the experimental level, Raush (1965), for example, in analyzing sequential interactions among children, found that hostile children characteristically affected their social environment so that previously nonhostile peers emitted an increased amount of aggressive behavior. This, in turn, further escalated the behavior of the original child toward increased hostility.

This same reciprocal interactional process has been observed in individuals who initiate competing behaviors in a situation where either cooperative or competitive behaviors could earn reinforcement (Kelley and Stahelski 1970). Individuals who habitually assume a competitive style often create the setting events that elicit competitive behaviors from others. The initiator thus creates an environment that serves to maintain his stylistic mode of behavior (Wachtel 1973). In Bowers' (1973) words, "Situations are as much a function of the person as the person's behavior is a function of the situation" (p. 327).

The interactional model represents an alternative to (1) a strict S-R model where man is viewed as a passive organism responding strictly to impinging external stimulation, and (2) models that portray man as an autonomous agent, behaving in his environment mainly on the basis of internal forces and a spirit of free will. The interactionist approach posits that man creates much of his own physical and social environment, which in turn affects his behavior. For example, the construction of the atomic bomb led to widespread modifications in international affairs, one outgrowth of which was the Cold War. But the ever-present danger of total annihilation and the irrationality of escalated armamentation has led to efforts toward strict international control of atomic weapons (Carter 1974).

A second characteristic of the interactional approach is based on a

[2] *Ed. Note.* This is comparable to the assumption of "reciprocal determinism" discussed in Chapter 10.

closed-loop view of human behavior (Kanfer 1971; Kanfer and Karoly 1972). In this view, a person's responses are continually readjusted on the basis of feedback from his preceding behavior and its impact on the environment. This process has been referred to as self-regulation (Bandura 1969; Kanfer 1970).

In all likelihood a shift to interactionism will produce a model of man that is probabilistic rather than categorical, dynamic rather than static. That is, prediction is not absolute but can indicate, much as in weather forecasting, our degree of confidence that an event will occur. Our limited knowledge of factors that may underlie the behavior to be predicted and uncertainty about the intervention of unplanned future events limit predictability. The dynamic nature of the model rests on the temporal continuity of behavior, which suggests the need for a unit of analysis in terms of long time intervals instead of a description of behavior frozen at any moment.

In order to yield meaningful predictions, an interactional model must take into account not only genetic and biological factors and social settings but also cultural parameters. For example, deviant behaviors are not viewed simply as personal characteristics, but are examined in the context of the person's social environment (e.g., Davison and Neale 1974; Ullmann and Krasner 1975). As an example, witness the recent decision by the American Psychiatric Association to "declassify" homosexuality as a psychiatric illness. It recognizes that homosexual behavior may in many instances be a viable lifestyle, not necessarily associated with psychological impairment. In addition to considering the social matrix, however, we must also examine the momentary utility of the behavior for the individual's long-term psychological functioning. Broad and flexible genetic, biological, and (learning-acquired) psychological predispositions have been blanketed previously by the term "personality." Only recently has research begun to provide analyses of the separate complex processes and the social parameters that determine individual behavior.

With this interactional perspective in mind, ten areas will be presented that promise research findings conducive to a better understanding of human behavior.

Behavior modification

The abandonment of a psychological model that likens all behavior problems to infectious diseases has led to more effective modes of behavior change. It is realized by behavioral psychologists that an individual's responses are inextricably interwoven in a total behavior repertoire. Thus, changes in one set of responses can lead to alterations of interconnected behaviors. Nevertheless, deviant behaviors are not regarded as the result of underlying psychic processes. Instead, direct intervention in disturbing behavior patterns is carried out. The shift from a search for underlying causes of behavior pathology to a focus on the person's interactional behavior has resulted in the development of treatment techniques that have radically increased the success of therapy with persons who exhibit phobias, depressive disorders, psychoses, developmental retardation, and a variety of neurotic behaviors (Yates 1970; Chapters 11 through 24 in this volume). In addition, these techniques have contributed to increased success in the treatment of other problems. For example, disturbances in children have been ameliorated by means of parental training and family treatment that focus directly on the problematic behaviors (e.g., Becker 1971).

The view that behavioral disorders do not erupt as symptoms of a disease process and the increased realization that effective behavior modification can be carried out by minimally trained persons has increased the number of people receiving assistance. It has also led to wide use of community resources to restore adequate functioning and prevent behavioral deterioration (Tharp and Wetzel 1969). These recent trends give every indication of becoming more popular in the future. Moreover, the proliferation of various encounter, human potential, and self-help groups, which sometimes operate without professional leadership, further reflects the belief that improved psychological functioning can be obtained without complex analysis of the causes of behavior.

An important contribution of the development of competing personality models and treatment approaches has been an increased emphasis on evaluation of treatment procedures in terms of outcome criteria that can easily be understood and agreed upon not only by various professionals but also by public agencies and institutions and by the paraprofessional staff that carries a major burden in mental health programs. Research on the behavior therapies has been most explicit in identifying treatment procedures and goals (Kiesler 1971). However, behavior therapy has developed by extension from the experimental psychology laboratory to the clinic. Its strength lies in its empirical base and coherent theoretical structure. To date it has offered very little to guide the practitioner in selecting different types of behavioral techniques for the particular contents of a client's problems. The question is whether existing behavioral models are comprehensive enough to allow the clinician to extrapolate specific treatment techniques to a wide array of problems. Presently, all behavior theory can offer are basic principles. Their judicious application to a particular case remains an art that is heavily dependent on the skill of the clinician. Whether this problem will be solved in the future by more sophisticated experimental designs in outcome research is difficult to say. But we fully agree with Paul (1969a) when he states, "The ultimate questions to be answered in behavior modification research appear to be: *What* treatment, by *whom,* is most effective for *this* individual with *what* specific problem, under *which* set of circumstances and *how* does it come about?" (p. 44; italics added).

The methodology proposed by Paul can be directly applied to attack the questions raised by an interactional model. Although people have different learning histories, genetic endowments, and social environments, uniqueness of individual problems may not be an insurmountable obstacle. All persons experience some regularities in the effectiveness of different behavioral styles, even in seemingly diverse situations. As a result, some consistency is developed in their approach to difficult situations. That is, behavior variability is "constrained" by the social milieu, which sanctions only a finite number of interpersonal or stress-reducing behaviors. However, behavioral styles can be utilized over a number of situations. The sanctioning of such behavioral styles is also in part a function of the person's socio-economic status, sex, and skill in specific areas. Thus, these behavior regularities can become "patient-characteristics" that may differentially interact with a given treatment modality. In addition, certain behaviors seem to be more or less vulnerable to situational change (Moos 1969) and perhaps also to therapeutic interventions. Hence the necessity for adopting a research methodology that attempts to discover the many critical variables that affect the individual case.

Another uncharted research area concerns the assessment of long-range and collateral effects of a change upon nonproblematic behaviors. For example, some clinicians have taught their clients decision-making or problem-solving strategies to remedy immediate problems. They also hope to provide a basis for the client to deal effectively with future conflict situations without the aid of the therapist. The success of these methods need further experimental verification.

Reinforcement mechanisms

As the importance of analyzing the details of behavioral interactions is recognized, research focus shifts toward investigation of the consequences of actions rather than on their antecedents alone. Current behavior modification techniques have used the concept of reinforcement around which to organize the data on social learning and behavior change. Recent research has suggested that the ubiquitous use of the concept may not be warranted (Rozin and Kalat 1971). It appears that in each species some response classes can be more easily modified than others. Seligman (1970) has suggested a continuum of preparedness, defined by the amount of environmental input necessary before a response can reliably be considered to have been learned. It is asserted that organisms vary in their preparedness to associate certain behavioral events with certain stimulus events. Qualifications in acquiring responses using an operant paradigm have been demonstrated by Thorndike (1964) and Konorski (1967), indicating that some behaviors are more susceptible to reinforcement than others.

These findings have implications for clinical psychology (Wilson and Davison 1969), suggesting the importance of considering the content or topography of the behavior to be eliminated or acquired in matching various stimuli and responses. Thus, in practice, one might expect inappropriate behaviors such as excessive alcohol consumption or compulsive eating to be more amenable to change through the utilization of gustatory aversive stimulation, as opposed to, say, electric shock (Rachman and Teasdale 1969; Revusky and Gorry 1973).

The results of these studies challenge the belief in the generality of the laws of learning, since laws based on arbitrary associations at one end of the preparedness continuum may not be valid in accounting for behaviors at the other end of the continuum. This intriguing area will, no doubt, receive continued attention as investigators address themselves to such questions as: Do different laws of learning hold along the continuum? Do different cognitive mechanisms covary with it? Do different physiological mechanisms also covary with preparedness? (Seligman 1970).

The more subtle effects of bringing a behavior under control of external reinforcers have also been studied (Davidson and Steiner 1971; Turner, Foa, and Foa 1971). This research suggests that reinforcing operations are often embedded in contextual variables that can have long-term or secondary influences on behavior, and the outcomes of these combinations may not always be desirable. For example, Deci (1972) has found that when a behavior has been maintained by "intrinsic reinforcement," the addition of external reinforcement such as money alters stimulus control so that subsequent removal of the external reinforcer causes the behavior to decline below its original rate. The effects this might have on a person's creativity or self-initiation are as yet unknown. As an illustration, suppose a young fellow enjoyed gardening. Every week he cuts the grass, trims bushes, and weeds the flower bed. On hot days you find him, hose in hand, leisurely watering the lawn. Perhaps he likes the feeling of soil in his hands or the sensation of seeing the grass transformed from parched brown to a healthy dark green. His mother, however, decides that he should get paid for his "hard work." How would this affect the boy's attitudes toward gardening? If payment is later discontinued it is quite possible that his gardening activities will decline below their original rate. Hence, parents, hospital staff, and teachers must be aware of the potential deleterious effects of some reinforcement programs.

Clearly, research is needed on the relationship between response topography and stimulus content to further clarify the interaction between biological predispositions and learning. Furthermore, contextual cues and the immediate and long-term effects of reinforcement on a person's behavior repertoire should receive continued exploration. Such additional information should strengthen the empirical foundation of reinforcement mechanisms and learning theory in general.

Aggression and altruism

For its own protection and survival, society is most urgently concerned with the individual behaviors that inflict damage on other group members (aggression) and those behaviors that seem to have little immediate advantage for the person but are beneficial to the group members (altruism). In traditional concepts, antisocial and prosocial acts have been viewed as part of man's inherent morality. For example, wars and conflicts have been seen as natural outlets for aggressive instincts. In contrast, Bandura (1973) and others have suggested that aggressive behavior is not an inevitable quality of man's social interactions but rather a product of conditions operating within a society that promote or retard the development of such behaviors. Similarly, research on altruism (e.g., Krebs 1970; Rosenhan 1972) has suggested that the disposition to be concerned about or offer assistance to our fellow man is not an instinctive attribute but a function of social learning. Prosocial behavior may have to be carefully nurtured by group practices and alternative modes of conflict resolution offered to decrease instances of aggression. The important features for relating altruistic and aggressive behaviors of individuals to group norms and demands have yet to be studied (Platt 1973). If these behavior patterns are heavily influenced by the social conditions under which a person lives, we will need a detailed analysis of the specific environmental factors that enable persons to acquire skills in handling aggression and expressing altruism.

Group processes and behavior change

In recent years, a variety of group techniques have flourished. Their intended purpose has been the improvement of interpersonal relationships and the encouragement of the development of individual potentials. Of special interest is the utility of these group processes in the prevention of behavior disorders. Sensitivity groups, encounter groups, growth centers, Gestalt therapy groups, and others have found enthusiastic followers across the country (Howard 1971). However, little research has been offered that would support the theoretical rationale of the human potential movements or demonstrate their effectiveness. Serious research on the group as an agent of change (e.g., Jacobs and Spradlin 1974) is only beginning to appear, and the phenomenon requires considerable further attention. Moreover, little information has been gathered on how individual behavior change techniques are affected by group structures that alter the treatment context (Lieberman 1975). For example, what are the effects of the diffusion of control of contingencies that is inevitable in a group? What are the effects on the individual who receives conflicting contingencies from group members? How do social interactional variables such as group cohesion and competition interact with behavior change methods? In addition to understanding the process and outcome of group influence, we also need guideposts for the construction of such rehabilitative institutions as halfway houses or other facilities located in the community. If the prediction of Rogers (1968) and others is correct—that an essential feature in promoting future mental health lies in earlier training in interpersonal communications—then the contributions of group processes to such outcomes will have to be subjected to intensive research.

Taxonomy and diagnosis

The traditional classification of behavior disorders has been under heavy attack for numerous reasons. Not only have there been demonstrations of relatively low reliability for the most widely used classification schemes, but serious questions have been raised concerning the utility of such classifications in predicting responsiveness to different therapeutic interventions (Kanfer and Saslow 1969). The taxonomy of pathological behaviors, consistent with an interactional model, would require not only a description of particular response dimensions but also of the characteristic demands for various behaviors that are made by the person's environment. Without a clear understanding of the behavioral repertoire that is expected and supported by the social environment it is difficult to characterize a group of behaviors as deviant or pathological.

There are numerous examples of unusual behaviors under unusual circumstances that are quite common for these situations and may serve an adaptive purpose (Bettelheim 1943; Cohen 1953; Lifton 1954). For example, a group of South American soccer players recently stranded in the Andes mountains after a plane crash resorted to cannibalism to survive (Read 1974). Closer to our experiences, consider the adaptive behaviors of a timid, withdrawn child who has been continually punished by an alcoholic father for any expressions of spontaneity. Diagnosis must be viewed as a joint assessment of the person's behavior and environmental demands, taking into account not only *how* the individual behaves but *under what circumstances.* This approach to diagnostics represents a logical extension of an interactionist framework that seeks to replace a structural system of classification.

Currently there is an urgent need for research that would eventually lead to categorization of behavior on a limited number of dimensions, reflecting response classes that are particularly unacceptable or absolutely required in a given social setting. For example, at the moment we cannot fully describe the behavioral repertoire expected and supported in a 4-year-old child, much less that of an adult who lives in a particular subculture. Without this information it becomes difficult to judge the insufficiency or deviance of a person's repertoire from what is necessary for his proper functioning.

The technical side of the assessment problem concerns the current lack of adequate assessment instruments. A few attempts have been made to develop assessment procedures for highly specific behavior patterns, such as assertiveness, social confidence, or fear behaviors (Geer 1965; Hersen, Eisler, and Miller 1973; Paul 1966).

In keeping with an interactional model it becomes necessary to develop instruments for assessing man's physical and social environment. Investigators have only recently turned their attention to this area. In fact, of 280 articles and studies cited by Craik in a recent annual review article on environmental psychology (1973), only three were published over 10 years ago.

Traditional assessment has been based on the assumption that enduring qualities of the person account for much of the behavior variance. As models of behavior shift in emphasis toward environmental factors, it becomes necessary to devise instruments to assess important features of the physical and social settings in which they operate. Future research such as that conducted by Moos and others will continue to provide valuable information on the characteristics of man's social and physical environment (Appleyard 1969; Barker 1968; Griffitt and Veitch 1971; Moos 1968; Moos and Insel 1974).

Social systems analysis

The application of behavior modification has been the focus of intense criticism by psychologists, legislators, and others. A consideration of all the criticism raised by adversaries of behavior modification is beyond the scope of this chapter. However, of particular relevance to the interactional perspective presented here are criticisms concerning the supposed "values" of behavior modification. Among the most recent authors taking behavior modification to task are Braginsky and Braginsky (1974), who characterize it as a "scientized" version of the "Protestant, capitalistic morality of our society-at-large . . . where man can be exploited, degraded, and duped in the name of science" (pp. 72–73).

To be sure, the application of any technology, whether it be psychotherapy or electronic hardware, carries certain values (London 1964). However, it is a monumental error to confuse and blur the line between the technology and its application. To blame the abuses of behavior modification on its principles and techniques is as irrational as blaming airplanes for the napalm bombing in Vietnam.

What can a behavior analysis offer to the area of values and objectives? Recent trends in psychology suggest that psychologists will be called upon with increasing frequency to analyze large social systems ranging from schools and institutions to whole communities. An attempt at such an analysis would entail, among other things, assessment of (1) the institutional objectives, (2) the target behaviors implied by the objectives, and (3) the discrepancy between (1) and (2). For illustrative purposes we shall briefly consider the education setting.

In most instances, behavior modifiers have responded to requests by teachers to help them solve classroom management problems (Kanfer 1973). They typically begin by asking the teacher to clarify her objectives. In most cases, the teacher offers a description of classroom changes she would like to see. For example, she may wish to achieve better academic performance and less disruption. Unstated are such ultimate goals as training the child to be a more productive and responsible citizen as he reaches adulthood. The next step usually involves an analysis of the relationship between the teacher's behaviors and those of the students. After adequate observation a behavior modification program is instituted.

The approach in which the behavior analyst accepts the original goals of the teacher (and in many instances pushes for them) has been criticized by Winett and Winkler (1972; see also O'Leary 1972 for a rejoinder). These authors reviewed a number of behavior modification studies conducted in public school classrooms and concluded that behavior modifiers exhibited a preoccupation with such student behaviors as obedience, orderliness, quietness, and docility. These criticisms are well taken. It now seems desirable to apply behavioral principles in a functional analysis of the total school system in assessing *how* the child is taught, *what* he is taught, and the *purpose for which* he is taught (Kanfer 1973).

The establishment of objectives implies a selection of choices based on values. Nevertheless, an analysis of the interrelations among objectives can be achieved without questioning the objectives themselves. It is possible that the results of such an investigation may also shed light on the adequacy of certain teaching techniques in reaching a stated objective, or reveal basic incongruities between various objectives. As an illustration, suppose the principal of a school stated two educational objectives: obedience to classroom demands, and the development of independent, self-reliant children. By gathering data and conducting a functional analysis of behaviors required to reach each objective, one might conclude that the objectives are incompatible and thus suggest a change in either the techniques or the goals.[3]

To summarize, recent trends suggest that in the future psychologists will be called upon more and more to offer analyses of social systems and become involved in their modification. Psychologists will have to address such complex issues as institutional assessment, long-term and societal effects of systems change, and the development of research methodologies appropriate for this domain.

Reactance and countercontrol

Psychological techniques are showing increased promise for achieving systematic influence on behavior. Behavior modification applications have already demonstrated effectiveness in changing the behavior of individuals and groups. These advances make it imperative to examine also the negative reactions that persons might exhibit in response to the imposition of controls. All psychological treatments can be conceptualized as attempts to influence another person, even if only temporarily. A thorough explication of the variables relevant to countercontrol is important for understanding the treatment process, as well as the social organizations in which the client lives. Once broad-scale effective behavior change methods are available, the conditions under which, by whom, and for whom, behavior control will be exercised must be studied and social rules for the limits of application must be provided.

Recent laboratory research has dealt with the problem of perceived threat to freedom (Brehm 1966; Steiner 1973), while social, political, and conceptual issues have focused on the possible application of behavioral controls to individuals and populations through the use of be-

[3] It should be stated that we are not advocating that behavior modifiers remove themselves from important public issues. But rather it should be made clear what personal values underlie a set of recommendations.

havioral, electronic, and biochemical techniques (Delgado 1969; London 1969; Skinner 1971).

The increased relevance of psychology to socio-political questions is a reflection of an increased awareness that behavior is not only internally controlled but that social conditions are critical forces in behavior regulation. And, in turn, individual behavior changes can affect the socio-political structure of a group (Braginsky and Braginsky 1974). Harsh criticisms of behavior modification methods by such diverse political sources as those on the extreme right *and* those on the extreme left indicate the importance of studying these psychological processes and their probable role in implementing behavior change programs.

Self-regulation and self-control

An environmental approach to man's behavior stresses the importance of the person's dependence on external influences. Previous sections have raised some of the issues surrounding external control (Deci 1972; Steiner 1970), such as the role of perceived threat to freedom and diminished "intrinsic motivation" in the effectiveness of externally controlled contingency management programs. The utilization of self-regulation and self-control techniques may offer partial solutions to these problems by allowing the person a greater amount of control over his own behavior. This can be an important asset to clinicians who may not have the means of instituting widespread environmental changes to influence their clients' behaviors. Self-regulatory techniques should enable individuals to maintain some consistency by adherence to self-generated standards, even in the face of changing environmental models and contingencies. Moreover, the self-regulatory model provides for the attainment of increased self-awareness of observable behaviors, thoughts, and feelings by training in self-monitoring (Kazdin 1974b).

Recent research has also clarified the processes by which a person can alter his own behavior, relatively independent of temporary environmental inputs, and the means by which he can alter his environment in order to select among different future controlling influences (see Bandura 1971b; Kanfer and Zich 1974; Mahoney and Thoresen 1974; Thoresen and Mahoney 1974). This relatively new analysis of self-processes expands the Skinnerian model to include the role of cognitive and self-generated behaviors as supplemental determinants of personal actions. However, while some clinical techniques using self-control and self-reinforcement procedures have already shown some success (Kanfer 1975; Mahoney, Moura, and Wade 1973), the theoretical basis for these techniques remains incomplete. From a theoretical point of view, this research may provide a bridge between traditional treatment methods that focus on intrapsychic processes and techniques employing mainly external contingencies of behavior control. Perhaps as researchers continue to deal with the theoretical, methodological, and practical applications of self-regulatory process, it will become clearer what social conditions and individual training programs must be combined to maximize personal satisfactions, while meeting the societal demands necessary to maintain effective social organization.

Control of physiological responses

Emotions have long been conceptualized as central in many behavior problems, indeed, in man's everyday functioning. Current research on biofeedback mechanisms points to the application of learning principles in the control of physiological processes (see Shapiro, Barber, DiCara, Kamiya, Miller, and Stoyva 1973). Although research in this area is quite recent, clinical applications of biofeedback are spreading (Schwartz 1973; see Chapter 15 in this volume). Investigators have already demonstrated the usefulness of electronic feedback displays of autonomic activity in alleviating psychosomatic conditions, including essential hypertension, Raynaud's disease, and tension headaches (Shapiro and Schwartz 1972). In addition, Lang (1969) has developed an on-line computer system that could greatly enhance the effectiveness and administration of systematic desensitization by continuous monitoring of a number of autonomic responses.

Though the initial success of biofeedback techniques in altering internal processes is encouraging, a number of questions basic to this enterprise remain unanswered (Shapiro 1973). What kinds of feedback displays provide maximum effect? What role do thoughts, imagery, beliefs, attitudes, and suggestion play in biofeedback? What autonomic responses are most amenable to operant control? Can voluntary control of visceral functions be integrated with such practices as yoga, autogenic procedures, and meditation? How can patient motivation be sustained over a number of biofeedback sessions? And, how can the beneficial effects be maintained after feedback devices are removed (see Blanchard and Young 1973; Blanchard and Young 1974b; Engel 1974)?

Closely related to the development of biofeedback techniques is a revised conceptualization of psychosomatic disorders. Graham (1971) has cogently stated the need for a revision of the traditional approaches to psychosomatic ailments. He proposes a detailed analysis of the interactions between behavioral, sociological, and physiological variables as a basis for approaching any illness or behavior deviation. New theorizing and research that examines the relative contribution of these variables to clinical problems would appear to be a critical area of inquiry.

Language and thinking

Early attempts to transfer the principles of operant conditioning, formulated from animal laboratory research, to human behavior and clinical psychology focused primarily on verbal conditioning (see Kanfer 1968). In fact, Krasner (1962) conceptualized the clinician in interview therapy as a "social reinforcement machine." More recently, investigators have reported clinically significant behavior changes by modifying clients' self-verbalizations (Meichenbaum 1974). In fact, Ellis has constructed a whole system of psychotherapy based on the modification of "irrational internal sentences" (Ellis 1962).

These advances have been made in spite of the fact that the genesis of language and thought processes is poorly understood. Neither the extreme structural (Chomsky 1965) nor the extreme environmental position (Skinner 1957) has satisfactorily explained the acquisition of language skills, the nature of thinking, imagery, fantasy, and similar cognitive processes. Although it is possible to proceed pragmatically with techniques that utilize existing language systems without fully understanding the basic processes, it is likely that more powerful tools could be developed if the genesis and nature of these behaviors were better known.

Summary and conclusion

With the possible exceptions of self-management models and techniques and the advances in voluntary control of autonomic activity, there have been no recent breakthroughs in the area of behavior modification. Operant conditioning and other behavioral techniques have become more sophisticated, but for the most part, the basic theoretical framework has been the same since the early 1950s (see Skinner 1953).

We are currently witnessing an abandonment of all-encompassing theories and efforts to design "critical" experiments. Instead, investigators have begun addressing subareas highlighted by the problems encountered in the application of behavior modification techniques. There also seems to be a shift from a primary interest in studying the human organism in isolation to an understanding of man in relation to his environment and to himself (see Krasner and Ullmann 1973). The whole range of behaviors from performance on simple laboratory tasks to the complex rearranging of one's life through self-control, the role of motivation and emotions, and the definition of psychological abnormality, have been placed more heavily in the context of the social environment, and have been viewed as the product of complex and changing influences by external and internal environments. In contrast to earlier socially oriented psychological theories, the interactional perspective emphasizes the importance of changes within *both* the person and the social milieu with the hope of achieving greater harmony, be it through better education for facing life's problems or through changing social conditions so that fewer problems need to be faced. As psychology demonstrates the effectiveness of methods for behavioral control, the increased concern of society has resulted in expansion of research to problems that are critical to our understanding of the ways in which social systems operate and the reciprocal interaction between man and his cultural milieu. Closely related to this is the increasing interest in developing a taxonomy of the physical and social settings within which we operate. In addition to expanding our understanding of man's relation to societal factors and group processes, further research is needed into the basic mechanisms of human responding in such areas as autonomic learning and reinforcement mechanisms.

Behavior modification has made great strides in the development of techniques that can be applied to a number of different problems in various settings. Though further technological refinements will most certainly be profitable, they will be inadequate for dealing with many of the problems confronting society today. A more promising future for both psychology and society may be shaped by increasing our knowledge of the interactions between psychological processes and our sociocultural matrix—both equally significant components of the "human condition." Such an approach should help us to better understand not only man, but also the social institutions he has created, and allow us to contribute toward improving both.

References

Abel, G. G.; Blanchard, E. B.; Barlow, D. H.; and Mavissakalian, M. Identifying specific erotic cues in sexual deviations by audio-taped descriptions. *Archives of Sexual Behavior,* in press.

Abel, G. G.; Levis, D.; and Clancy, J. Aversion therapy applied to taped sequences of deviant behavior in exhibitionism and other sexual deviations: A preliminary report. *Journal of Behavior Therapy and Experimental Psychiatry* 1 (1970): 59–66.

Abramson, E. E. A review of behavioral approaches to weight control. *Behaviour Research and Therapy* 11 (1973): 547–556.

Abramson, H. *Use of LSD in psychotherapy.* New York: Josiah Macy, Jr. Foundation, 1960.

Agnew, W. M., and Pyke, S. W. *The science game.* Englewood Cliffs, N.J.: Prentice-Hall, 1969.

Agras, S., and Marshall, C. The application of negative practice to spasmodic torticollis. *American Journal of Psychiatry* 122 (1965): 579–582.

Aiken, L. H. Patient problems are problems in learning. *American Journal of Nursing* 70 (1970): 1916–1918.

Aillon, G. A. Biochemistry of depression: A review of the literature. *Behavioral Neuropsychiatry* 3 (1971): 2–19.

Akiskal, H. S., and McKinney, W. T. Depressive disorders: Toward an unified hypothesis. *Science* 182 (1973): 20–29.

Alcoholics anonymous. New York: Cornwall Press, 1955.

Alexander, A. B.; Chai, H.; Creer, T. L.; Miklich, D. R.; Renne, C. M.; and Cardoso, R. A. The elimination of chronic cough by response suppression shaping. *Journal of Behavior Therapy and Experimental Psychiatry* 4 (1973): 75–80.

Alexander, A. B.; Miklich, D. R.; and Hershkoff, H. The immediate effects of systematic relaxation training on peak expiratory flow rates in asthmatic children. *Psychosomatic Medicine* 34 (1972): 388–394.

Alford, G. S.; Blanchard, E. B.; and Buckley, T. M. Treatment of hysterical vomiting by modification of social contingencies: A case study. *Journal of Behavior Therapy and Experimental Psychiatry* 3 (1972): 209-212.

Alinsky, S. D. *Rules for radicals.* New York: Random House, 1971.

Allen, K. E.; Hart, B. M.; Buell, J. S.; Harris, F. R.; and Wolf, M. M. Effects of training the mother in reinforcement procedures. *Behaviour Research and Therapy* 4 (1966): 79–84.

Allen, J. D.; Phillips, E. L.; Phillips, E. A.; Fixsen, D. L.; and Wolf, M. M. *The achievement place novel.* Lawrence: University of Kansas Printing Service, 1972.

Allen, J. E., and Harris, F. R. Elimination of a child's excessive scratching by training the mother in reinforcement procedures. *Behaviour Research and Therapy* 4 (1966): 79–84.

Allen, K. E.; Hart, B. M.; Buell, J. S.; Harris, F. R.; and Wolf, M. M. Effects of social reinforcement on isolate behavior of a nursery school child. *Child Development* 35 (1964): 511–518.

Allen, K. E.; Henke, L. B.; Harris, F. R.; Baer, D. M.; and Reynolds, N.J. The control of hyperactivity by social reinforcement of attending behavior in a preschool child. *Journal of Educational Psychology* 58 (1967): 231–237.

Allman, L. R.; Taylor, H. A.; and Nathan, P. E. Group drinking during stress: Effects on drinking behavior, affect, and psychopathology. *American Journal of Psychiatry* 129 (1972): 669–678.

Allport, G. W. *Pattern and growth in personality.* New York: Holt, Rinehart & Winston, 1961.

Alsop, J. The incompetence syndrome. *The Washington Post,* 1973.

American Cancer Society. *Cancer facts and figures '74.* New York: American Cancer Society, 1974.

American Psychiatric Association. *Diagnostic and statistical manual of mental disorders.* 2nd ed. Washington, D.C.: American Psychiatric Association, 1968.

Anant, S. S. A note on the treatment of alcoholics by a verbal aversion technique. *Canadian Psychologist* 8 (1967): 19–22.

Annon, J. S. The therapeutic use of masturbation in the treatment of sexual disorders. In R. D. Rubin; J. P. Brady; and J. D. Henderson, eds., *Advances in behavior therapy.* Vol. 4. New York: Academic Press, 1973. Pages 199–215.

Anthony, W. A.; Buell, G. J.; Sharratt, S.; and Althoff, M. E. Efficacy of psychiatric rehabilitation. *Psychological Bulletin* 78 (1972): 447–456.

Appleyard, D. Why buildings are known: A predictive tool for architects and planners. *Environment and Behavior* 1 (1969): 131–156.

Arthur, A. Z. Diagnostic testing and the new alternatives. *Psychological Bulletin* 72 (1969): 183–192.

Ash, P. The reliability of psychiatric diagnoses. *Journal of Abnormal and Social Psychology* 44 (1949): 272–276.

Ashem, B., and Donner, L. Covert sensitization with alcoholics: A controlled replication. *Behaviour Research and Therapy* 6 (1968): 7–12.

Assembly Committee on Criminal Procedure. *Deterrent effects of criminal sanctions.* Sacramento: State of California, 1968.

Atkins, B. M., and Glick, H. R., eds. *Prisons, protests, and politics.* Englewood Cliffs, N.J.: Prentice-Hall, 1972.

Atthowe, J. M., Jr. Behavior innovation and persistence. *American Psychologist* 28 (1973a): 34–41.

Atthowe, J. M., Jr. Token economies come of age. *Behavior Therapy* 4 (1973b): 646–654.

Atthowe, J. M., Jr. Movement and goal direction within token economies. In R. L. Patterson, ed., *Maintaining effective token economies.* New York: Thomas, in press.

Atthowe, J. M., Jr., and Krasner, L. A preliminary report on the application of contingent reinforcement procedures (token economy) on a "chronic" psychiatric ward. *Journal of Abnormal Psychology* 73 (1968): 37–43.

Atthowe, J. M., Jr., and McDonough, J. M. *Operations re-entry.* (Film of Veterans Administration Hospital, Palo Alto, California. Released by Indiana University.) Washington, D.C.: United States Department of Health, Education and Welfare, Social and Rehabilitation Services, 1969.

Ausubel, D. P. Personality disorder is disease. *American Psychologist* 16 (1961): 69–74.

Axelrod, S.; Hall, R. V.; Weis, L.; and Rohrer, S. Use of self-imposed contingencies to reduce the frequency of smoking behavior. In M. J. Mahoney and C. E. Thoresen, eds., *Self-control: Power to the person.* Belmont, Calif.: Brooks/Cole, 1974. Pages 77–85.

Ayllon, T., and Azrin, N. H. The measurement and reinforcement of behavior of psychotics. *Journal of the Experimental Analysis of Behavior* 8 (1965): 357–383.

Ayllon, T., and Azrin, N. *The token economy: A motivational system for therapy and rehabilitation.* New York: Appleton-Century-Crofts, 1968.

Ayllon, T.; Haughton, E.; and Hughes, H. B. Interpretation of symptoms: Fact or fiction? *Behaviour Research and Therapy* 3 (1965): 1–8.

Ayllon, T., and Michael, J. The psychiatric nurse as a behavioral engineer. *Journal of the Experimental Analysis of Behavior* 2 (1959): 323–334.

Ayllon, T., and Roberts, M. D. *Motivation in offender rehabilitating environments project. First year of research and operation: Final report.* Atlanta, Ga.: Department of Offender Rehabilitation, 1973.

Azrin, N. H. *Responses to questions asked of the panel of experts.* In the United States District Court for the Western District of Missouri, Southern Division, 1974. Available from National Prison Project, Washington, D.C.

Azrin, N. H., and Holz, W. C. Punishment. In W. K. Honig, ed., *Operant behavior: Areas of research and application.* New York: Appleton-

Century-Crofts, 1966. Pages 380–447.

Azrin, N. H.; Holz, W.; and Goldiamond, I. Response bias in questionnaire reports. *Journal of Consulting Psychology* 25 (1961): 324–326.

Azrin, N. H.; Hutchinson, R. R.; and Hake, D. F. Extinction induced aggression. *Journal of the Experimental Analysis of Behavior* 9 (1966): 191–204.

Azrin, N. H.; Naster, B. J.; and Jones, R. Reciprocity counseling: A rapid learning-based procedure for marital counseling. *Behaviour Research and Therapy* 11 (1973): 365–382.

Azrin, N. H., and Nunn, R. G. Habit reversal: A method of eliminating nervous habits and tics. *Behaviour Research and Therapy* 11 (1973): 619–628.

Azrin, N. H., and Powell, J. Behavioral engineering: The reduction of smoking behavior by a conditioning apparatus and procedure. *Journal of Applied Behavior Analysis* 1 (1968): 193–200.

Azrin, N. H., and Powell, J. Behavioral engineering: The use of response priming to improve prescribed self-medication. *Journal of Applied Behavior Analysis* 2 (1969): 39–42.

Azrin, N.; Rubin, H.; O'Brien, F.; Ayllon, T.; and Roll, D. Behavioral engineering: Postural control by a portable operant apparatus. *Journal of Applied Behavior Analysis* 1 (1968): 99–108.

Bachrach, A. J. *Psychological research: An introduction.* 2nd ed. New York: Random House, 1965.

Baer, D. M.; Wolf, M. M.; and Risley, T. R. Some current dimensions of applied behavior analysis. *Journal of Applied Behavior Analysis* 1 (1968): 91–97.

Bailey, J. S.; Timbers, G. D.; Phillips, E. L.; and Wolf, M. M. Modification of articulation errors of pre-delinquents by their peers. *Journal of Applied Behavior Analysis* 4 (1971): 265–281.

Bailey, J. S.; Wolf, M. M.; and Phillips, E. L. Home-based reinforcement and the modification of pre-delinquents' classroom behavior. *Journal of Applied Behavior Analysis* 3 (1970): 223–233.

Baker, B. L. Symptom treatment and symptom substitution in enuresis. Paper presented at the annual meeting of the Association for Advancement of the Behavior Therapy, Washington, D.C., September 1967.

Baker, B. L., and Kahn, M. A reply to "Critique of 'Treatment of insomnia by relaxation training': Relaxation training, Rogerian therapy, or demand characteristics." *Journal of Abnormal Psychology* 79 (1972): 94–96.

Bancroft, J.; Jones, H.; and Pullan, B. A simple transducer for measuring penile erection, with comments on its use in the treatment of sexual disorders. *Behaviour Research and Therapy* 4 (1966): 239–241.

Bandura, A. Influence of models' reinforcement contingencies on the acquisition of imitative responses. *Journal of Personality and Social Psychology* 1 (1965): 589–595.

Bandura, A. *Principles of behavior modification.* New York: Holt, Rinehart and Winston, 1969.

Bandura, A. Psychotherapy based upon modeling principles. In A. E. Bergin and S. L. Garfield, eds., *Handbook of psychotherapy and behavior change: An empirical analysis.* New York: Wiley, 1971a. Pages 653–708.

Bandura, A. Vicarious and self-reinforcement processes. In R. Glaser, ed., *The nature of reinforcement.* New York: Academic Press, 1971b. Pages 228–278.

Bandura, A. *Aggression: A social learning analysis.* Englewood Cliffs, N.J.: Prentice-Hall, 1973.

Bandura, A.; Blanchard, E. B.; and Ritter, B. The relative efficacy of desensitization and modeling approaches for inducing behavioral, affective, and attitudinal changes. *Journal of Personality and Social Psychology* 13 (1969): 173–199.

Bandura, A.; Grusec, J. E.; and Menlove, F. L. Vicarious extinction of avoidance behavior. *Journal of Personality and Social Psychology* 5 (1967): 16–23.

Bandura, A.; Jeffery, R. W.; and Gajdos, E. Generalizing change through self-directed performance. *Behavior Research and Therapy* 13 (1975): 141–152.

Bandura, A.; Jeffery, R. W.; and Wright, C. L. Efficacy of participant modeling as a function of response induction aids. *Journal of Abnormal Psychology* 83 (1974): 56–64.

Bandura, A., and Menlove, F. L. Factors determining vicarious extinction of avoidance behavior through symbolic modeling. *Journal of Personality and Social Psychology* 8 (1968): 99–108.

Bandura, A., and Walters, R. H. *Social learning and personality development.* New York: Holt, Rinehart & Winston, 1963.

Bannister, D. Pscychology as an exercise in paradox. *Bulletin of the British Psychological Society* 19 (1966): 21–26.

Bar, L. H. J., and Kuypers, B. R. M. Behaviour therapy in dermatological practice. *British Journal of Dermatology* 88 (1973): 591–598.

Barber, T. Pitfalls in research: Nine investigator and experimenter effects. In R. Travers, ed., *Handbook of research on teaching.* 2nd ed. Chicago: Rand McNally, 1975, in press.

Barber, T. X., and Hahn, K. W. Experimental studies in "hypnotic" behavior: Physiologic and subjective effects of imagined pain. *Journal of Nervous and Mental Disease* 139 (1964): 416–425.

Barefoot, J. C., and Girodo, M. The misattribution of smoking cessation symptoms. *Canadian Journal of Behavioral Science* 4 (1972): 358–363.

Barker, J. Aversion therapy of sexual perversions. *British Journal of Psychiatry* 109 (1963): 696.

Barker, R. G. *Ecological psychology: Concepts and methods for studying the environment of human behavior.* Stanford, Calif.: Stanford University Press, 1968.

Barlow, D. H. Increasing heterosexual responsiveness in the treatment of sexual deviation: A review of the clinical and experimental evidence. *Behavior Therapy* 4 (1973): 655–671.

Barlow, D. H. The treatment of sexual deviation: Towards a comprehensive behavioral approach. In K. S. Calhoun; H. E. Adams; and K. M. Mitchell, eds., *Innovative treatment methods in psychopathology.* New York: Wiley, 1974.

Barlow, D. H., and Agras, W. S. Fading to increase heterosexual responsiveness in homosexuals. *Journal of Applied Behavior Analysis* 6 (1973): 355–366.

Barlow, D. H.; Agras, W. S.; Leitenberg, H.; Callahan, E. J.; and Moore, R. C. The contribution of therapeutic instruction to covert sensitization. *Behaviour Research and Therapy* 10 (1972): 411–415.

Barlow, D. H.; Agras, W. S.; and Reynolds, E. J. Direct and indirect modification of gender specific motor behavior in a transsexual. Paper presented at the meetings of the American Psychological Association, Honolulu, September 1972.

Barlow, D. H.; Becker, R.; Leitenberg, H.; and Agras, W. S. A mechanical strain gauge for recording penile circumference change. *Journal of Applied Behavior Analysis* 3 (1970): 73–76.

Barlow, D. H.; Leitenberg, H.; and Agras, W. S. The experimental control of sexual deviation through manipulation of the noxious scene in covert sensitization. *Journal of Abnormal Psychology* 74 (1969): 596–601.

Barnard, G. W.; Flesher, C. K.; and Steinbook, R. M. The treatment of urinary retention by aversive stimulus cessation and assertive training. *Behaviour Research and Therapy* 4 (1966): 232–236.

Barnes, K. E.; Wootton, M.; and Wood, S. The public health nurse as an effective therapist–behavior modifier of preschool play behavior. *Community Mental Health Journal* 8 (1972): 3–7.

Barrish, H.; Saunders, M.; and Wolf, M. Good behavior game: Effects of individual contingencies for group consequences on disruptive behavior in a classroom. *Journal of Applied Behavior Analysis* 2 (1969): 119–124.

Beck, A. T. *Depression: Causes and treatment.* Philadelphia: University of Pennsylvania Press, 1967.

Beck, A. T.; Feshbach, S.; and Legg, D. The clinical utility of the digit symbol test. *Journal of Consulting Psychology* 26 (1962): 263–268.

Beck, A. T.; Ward, C. H.; Mendelson, M.; Mock, J.; and Erbaugh, J. An inventory for measuring depression. *Archives of General Psychiatry* 4 (1961): 561–571.

Becker, H. S. *Outsiders: Studies in the sociology of deviance.* New York: Free Press, 1963.

Becker, W. C. *Parents are teachers.* Champaign, Ill.: Research Press, 1971.

Becker, W. C.; Madsen, C. H.; Arnold, C. R.; and Thomas, D. R. The contingent use of teacher attention and praise in reducing classroom behavior problems. *Journal of Special Education* 1 (1967): 287–307.

"Behavior Mod" behind the walls. *Time,* March 11, 1974, pp. 74–75.

Bem, S. L. Verbal self-control: The establishment of effective self-instruction. *Journal of Experimental Psychology* 74 (1967): 485–491.

Benjamin, S.; Marks, I. M.; and Huson, J. Active muscular relaxation in desensitization of phobic patients. In I. M. Marks; A. E. Bergin; P. J. Lang; J. D. Mattarazzo; G. R. Patterson; and H. H. Strupp, eds., *Psychotherapy and behavior change.* Chicago, Ill.: Aldine, 1972.

Bennett, P. S., and Maley, R. F. Modification of interactive behaviors in chronic mental patients. *Journal of Applied Behavior Analysis* 6 (1973): 609–620.

Berecz, J. Modification of smoking behavior through self-administered punishment of imagined behavior: A new approach to aversion therapy. *Journal of Consulting and Clinical Psychology* 38 (1972): 244–250.

Bergin, A. E. Some implications of psychotherapy research for therapeutic practice. *Journal of Abnormal Psychology* 71 (1966): 235–246.

Bergin, A. E. The evaluation of therapeutic outcomes. In A. E. Bergin and S. L. Garfield, eds., *Handbook of psychotherapy and behavior change: An empirical analysis.* New York: Wiley, 1971. Pages 217–270.

Bergin, A. E., and Garfield, S. L., eds. *Handbook of psychotherapy and behavior change: An empirical analysis.* New York: Wiley, 1971.

Bergin, A., and Strupp, H. *Changing frontiers in the science of psychotherapy.* Chicago and New York: Aldine-Atherton, 1972.

Bernard, H. S., and Efran, J. S. Eliminating versus reducing smoking using pocket timers. *Behaviour Research and Therapy* 10 (1972): 399–401.

Bernhardt, A. J.; Hersen, M.; and Barlow, D. H. Measurement and modification of spasmodic torticollis: An experimental analysis. *Behavior Therapy* 3 (1972): 294–297.

Berni, R.; Dressler, J.; and Baxter, J. C. Reinforcing behavior. *American Journal of Nursing* 1 (1971): 2180–2183.

Berni, R., and Fordyce, W. E. *Behavior modification and the nursing process.* St. Louis, Mo.: C. V. Mosby, 1973.

Bernstein, D. A. The modification of smoking behavior: An evaluative review. In W. A. Hunt, ed., *Learning mechanisms in smoking.* Chicago: Aldine, 1970. Pages 3–41.

Bernstein, D. A. Behavioral fear assessment: Anxiety or artifact? In H. Adams and P. Unikel, eds., *Issues and trends in behavior therapy.* Springfield, Ill.: Thomas, 1973.

Bernstein, D. A., and Borkovec, T. D. *Progressive relaxation: A manual for therapists.* Champaign, Ill.: Research Press, 1973.

Bernstein, D. A., and Nietzel, M. T. Procedural variation in behavioral avoidance tests. *Journal of Consulting and Clinical Psychology* 41 (1973): 165–174.

Best, J. A., and Steffy, R. A. Smoking modification procedures tailored to subject characteristics. *Behaviour Therapy* 2 (1971): 177–191.

Bettelheim, B. Individual and mass behavior in extreme situations. *Journal of Abnormal and Social Psychology* 38 (1943): 417–452.

Bieber, B.; Bieber, I.; Dain, H. J.; Dince, P. R.; Drellich, M. G.; Grand, H. G.; Grundlach, R. H.; Kremer, M. W.; Wilber, C. B.; and Bieber, T. D. *Homosexuality.* New York: Basic Books, 1963.

Bigelow, G.; Liebson, I.; and Griffiths, R. Experimental analysis of alcoholic drinking. Paper presented at the American Psychological Association, Montreal, 1973.

Bigelow, G.; Liebson, I.; and Lawrence, C. Prevention of alcohol abuse by reinforcement of incompatible behavior. Paper presented at the Association for Advancement of Behavior Therapy, Miami, December 1973.

Bijou, S. W., and Baer, D. M. *Child development: A systematic and empirical theory.* Vol. 1. New York: Appleton-Century-Crofts, 1961.

Bijou, S. W., and Baer, D. M. Some methodological contributions from a functional analysis of child development. In L. P. Lipsett and C. S. Spiker, eds., *Advances in child development and behavior.* Vol. 1. New York: Academic Press, 1963. Pages 197–231.

Bijou, S. W., and Baer, D. M. *Child development: Readings in experimental analysis.* Vol. 3. New York: Appleton-Century-Crofts, 1967.

Bijou, S. W.; Peterson, R. F.; Harris, F. R.; Allen, K. E.; and Johnston, M. S. Methodology for experimental studies of young children in natural settings. *Psychological Record* 19 (1969): 177–210.

Bindrim, P. Nudity as a quick grab for intimacy in group therapy. *Psychology Today* 3 (1969): 24–28.

Birk, L.; Huddleston, W.; Miller, E.; and Cohler, B. Avoidance conditioning for homosexuality. *Archives of General Psychiatry* 25 (1971): 314–323.

Birk, L.; Miller, E.; and Cohler, B. Group psychotherapy for homosexual men by male-female cotherapists. *Acta Psychiatrica Scandinavica,* Supplementum 218 (1970): 9–36.

Birnbrauer, J. S.; Bijou, S. W.; Wolf, M. M.; and Kidder, J. D. Programmed instruction in the classroom. In L. P. Ullmann and L. Krasner, eds., *Case studies in behavior modification.* New York: Holt, Rinehart and Winston, 1965a. Pages 350–363.

Birnbrauer, J. S.; Wolf, M. M.; Kidder, J. D.; and Tague, C. E. Classroom behavior of retarded pupils with token reinforcement. *Journal of Experimental Child Psychology* 2 (1965b): 219–235.

Blachly, P. H. An "electric needle" for aversive conditioning of the needle ritual. *International Journal of the Addictions* 6 (1971): 327–328.

Blake, B. G. The application of behavior therapy to the treatment of alcoholism. *Behaviour Research and Therapy* 3 (1965): 75–85.

Blake, B. G. A follow-up of alcoholics treated by behavior therapy. *Behaviour Research and Therapy* 5 (1967): 89–94.

Blalock, H. M. *Causal inferences in nonexperimental research.* Chapel Hill: University of North Carolina Press, 1964.

Blanchard, E. B. The relative contributions of modeling, informational influences, and physical contact in the extinction of phobic behavior. *Journal of Abnormal Psychology* 76 (1970): 55–61.

Blanchard, E. B.; Libet, J. M.; and Young, L. D. Apneic aversion and covert sensitization in the treatment of a hydrocarbon inhalation addiction: A case study. *Journal of Behavior Therapy and Experimental Psychiatry* 4 (1973): 383–387.

Blanchard, E. B., and Young, L. D. Self-control of cardiac functioning: A promise as yet unfulfilled. *Psychological Bulletin* 79 (1973): 145–163.

Blanchard, E. B., and Young, L. D. Clinical applications of biofeedback. *Archives of General Psychiatry* 30 (1974a): 573–589.

Blanchard, E. B., and Young, L. D. Of promises and evidence: A reply to Engel. *Psychological Bulletin* 81 (1974b): 44–46.

Blinder, M. G. The pragmatic classification of depression. *American Journal of Psychiatry* 123 (1966): 259–269.

Blom, B. E., and Craighead, W. E. The effects of situational and instructional demand on indices of speech anxiety. *Journal of Abnormal Psychology* 83 (1974): 667–674.

Bobey, M. J., and Davidson, P. O. Psychological factors affecting pain tolerance. *Journal of Psychosomatic Research* 14 (1970): 371–376.

Bockoven, J. S. *Moral treatment in American psychiatry.* New York: Springer, 1963.

Bolstad, O. D., and Johnson, S. M. Self-regulation in the modification of disruptive behavior. *Journal of Applied Behavior Analysis* 5 (1972): 443–454.

Bootzin, R. R. Stimulus control treatment for insomnia. *Proceedings of the 80th Annual Convention of the American Psychological Association* 7 (1972): 395–396.

Boring, E. G. Intelligence as the tests test it. *New Republic* 35 (1923): 35–37.

Boring, E. G. When is human behavior predetermined? *Scientific Monthly* 84 (1957): 189–196.

Borkovec, T. D. The comparative effectiveness of systematic desensitization and implosive therapy and the effect of expectancy manipulation on the elimination of fear. Unpublished doctoral dissertation, University of Illinois, 1970.

Borkovec, T. D. Effects of expectancy on the outcome of systematic desensitization and implosive treatments for analogue anxiety. *Behavior Therapy* 3 (1972): 29–40.

Borkovec, T. D., and Fowles, D. C. Controlled investigation of the effects of progressive and hypnotic relaxation on insomnia. *Journal of Abnormal Psychology* 82 (1973): 153–158.

Borkovec, T. D.; Kaloupek, D. G.; and Slama, K. M. The facilitative effect of muscle tension-release in the relaxation treatment of sleep disturbance. *Behavior Therapy,* in press.

Boudin, H. M. Contingency contracting as a therapeutic tool in the deceleration of amphetamine use. *Behavior Therapy* 3 (1972): 604–608.

Bourne, P. G.; Alford, J. A.; and Bowcock, J. Z. Treatment of Skid Row alcoholics with disulfiram. *Quarterly Journal of Studies on Alcohol* 27 (1966): 42–48.

Bowers, K. S. Situationism in psychology: An analysis and a critique. *Psychological Review* 80 (1973): 307–336.

Bowman, K. M.; Simon, A.; Hine, C. H.; Macklin, E. A.; Crook, G. H.; Burbridge, N.; and Hanson, K. A clinical evaluation of tetraethylthiuram disulphide (Antabuse) in the treatment of problem drinkers. *American Journal of Psychiatry* 107 (1951): 832–838.

Boyer, J. L. Coronary heart disease as a pediatric problem. *American Journal of Cardiology* 33 (1974): 784–786.

Brady, J. P. The place of behavior therapy in medical student and psychiatric resident training. *Journal of Nervous and Mental Disease* 157 (1973): 21–26.

Braginsky, B. M., and Braginsky, D. D. *Mainstream psychology: A critique.* New York: Holt, 1974.

Braukmann, C. J.; Maloney, D. M.; Fixsen, D. L.; Phillips, E. L.; and Wolf, M. M. Analysis of a selection interview training package for predelinquents at Achievement Place. *Criminal Justice and Behavior* 1 (1974): 30–42.

Brehm, J. W. *A theory of psychological reactance.* New York: Academic Press, 1966.

Bridger, W. H., and Mandel, I. J. A comparison of GSR fear responses produced by threat and electric shock. *Journal of Psychiatric Research* 2 (1964): 31–40.

Bridger, W. H., and Mandel, I. J. Abolition of the PRE by instructions in GSR conditioning. *Journal of Experimental Psychology* 69 (1965): 476–482.

Brierley, H. The treatment of hysterical spasmodic torticollis by behaviour therapy. *Behaviour Research and Therapy* 5 (1967): 139–142.

Broden, M.; Bruce, C.; Mitchell, M. A.; Carter, V.; and Hall, R. V. Effects of teacher attention on attending behavior of two boys at adjacent desks. *Journal of Applied Behavior Analysis* 3 (1970): 199–203.

Broden, M.; Hall, R.; Dunlop, A.; and Clark, R. Effects of teacher attention and a token reinforcement system in a junior high school special education class. *Exceptional Children* 36 (1970): 341–349.

Broden, M.; Hall, R. V.; and Mitts, B. The effect of self-recording on the classroom behavior of two eighth-grade students. *Journal of Applied Behavior Analysis* 4 (1971): 191–199.

Brown, B. B. Additional characteristic EEG differences between smokers and non-smokers. In W. L. Dunn, Jr., ed., *Smoking behavior: Motives and incentives.* New York: Wiley, 1973. Pages 67–81.

Brown, H. A. Role of expectancy manipulation in systematic desensitization. *Journal of Consulting and Clinical Psychology* 41 (1973): 405–411.

Brown, P., and Elliot, R. The control of aggression in a nursery school class. *Journal of Experimental Child Psychology* 2 (1965): 102–107.

Bruch, H. Perils of behavior modification in treatment of anorexia nervosa. *Journal of the American Medical Association* 230 (1974): 1419–1422.

Brunner-Orne, M. Group therapy of alcoholics. *Quarterly Journal of Studies on Alcohol* 19 (1958): 164–165.

Buehler, R. E.; Patterson, G. R.; and Furniss, J. M. The reinforcement of behaviour in institutional settings. *Behaviour Research and Therapy* 4 (1966): 157–167.

Buell, J.; Stoddard, P.; Harris, F.; and Baer, D. M. Collateral social development accompanying reinforcement of outdoor play in a preschool child. *Journal of Applied Behavior Analysis* 1 (1968): 167–173.

Burchard, J. D. Systematic socialization: A programmed environment for the habilitation of antisocial retardates. *Psychological Record* 17 (1967): 461–476.

Burgess, A. *A clockwork orange.* New York: Norton, 1963.

Burgess, E. P. Elimination of vomiting behavior. *Behaviour Research and Therapy* 7 (1969a): 173–176.

Burgess, E. P. The modification of depressive disorders. In R. D. Rubin and C. M. Franks, eds., *Advances in behavior therapy,* 1968. New York: Academic Press, 1969b. Pages 193–199.

Bushell, D.; Wrobel, P. A.; and Michaelis, M. L. Applying "group" contingencies to the classroom study behavior of preschool children. *Journal of Applied Behavior Analysis* 1 (1968): 55–61.

Buss, A. H. *Psychopathology*. New York: Wiley, 1966.

Byrne, Donn. The repression-sensitization scale: Rationale, reliability and validity. *Journal of Personality* 29 (1961): 334–349.

Cahoon, D. D. Issues and implications of operant conditioning: Balancing procedures against outcomes. *Hospital and Community Psychiatry* 19 (1968): 228–229.

Cahoon, D. D., and Crosby, C. C. A learning approach to chronic drug use: Sources of reinforcement. *Behavior Therapy* 3 (1972): 64–71.

California Assembly Office of Research. *Deterrent effects of criminal sanctions*. Sacramento, Calif.: Assembly Committee on Criminal Procedure, 1968.

Callahan, E. J., and Leitenberg, H. Aversion therapy for sexual deviation: Contingent shock and covert sensitization. *Journal of Abnormal Psychology* 81 (1973): 60–73.

Campbell, D. T., and Stanley, J. C. Experimental and quasi-experimental designs for research and teaching. In N. L. Gage, ed., *Handbook of research on teaching*. Chicago: Rand McNally, 1963. Pages 171–246.

Carlson, N. A. "Behavior modification" and the Federal Center for Correctional Research, Butner, North Carolina. Statement before the House Committee on the Judiciary, Subcommittee on Courts, Civil Liberties, and the Administration of Justice, February 27, 1974. Available from the U.S. Bureau of Prisons, Washington, D.C.

Carter, B. Nuclear strategy and nuclear weapons. *Scientific American* 230 (1974): 20–31.

Cattell, R. B., and Scheier, I. H. *The meaning and measurement of neuroticism and anxiety*. New York: Ronald, 1961.

Cautela, J. R. Treatment of compulsive behavior by covert sensitization. *Psychological Record* 16 (1966): 33–41.

Cautela, J. R. Covert sensitization. *Psychological Reports* 20 (1967): 459–468.

Cautela, J. R. Behavior therapy and self-control: Techniques and implications. In C. M. Franks, ed., *Behavior therapy: Appraisal and status*. New York: McGraw-Hill, 1969. Pages 323–340.

Cautela, J. R. Treatment of smoking by covert sensitization. *Psychological Reports* 26 (1970): 415–420.

Cautela, J. R. Covert modeling. Paper read at the meetings of the Association for Advancement of Behavior Therapy, Washington, D.C., September 1971.

Cautela, J. R. Rationale and procedures for covert conditioning. In R. D. Rubin; H. Fensterheim; J. D. Henderson; and L. P. Ullmann, eds., *Advances in behavior therapy*. New York: Academic Press, 1972a. Pages 85–96.

Cautela, J. R. The treatment of overeating by covert conditioning. *Psychotherapy: Theory, Research and Practice* 9 (1972b): 211–216.

Cautela, J. R., and Wisocki, P. A. The use of male and female therapists in the treatment of homosexual behavior. In R. Rubin and C. Franks, eds., *Advances in Behavior Therapy, 1968*. New York: Academic Press, 1969.

Chambers, G. S., and Hamlin, R. M. The validity of judgments based on "blind" Rorschach records. *Journal of Consulting Psychology* 21 (1957): 105–109.

Chaneles, S. *The open prison*. New York: Dial, 1973.

Chapman, R. F.; Smith, J. W.; and Layden, T. A. Elimination of cigarette smoking by punishment and self-management training. *Behaviour Research and Therapy* 9 (1971): 255–264.

Chesser, E., and Meyer, V. Behavior therapy and psychosomatic illness. In O. W. Hill, ed., *Modern trends in psychosomatic medicine*. New York: Appleton-Century-Crofts, 1970. Pages 262–276.

Chomsky, N. *Aspects of the theory of syntax*. Cambridge, Mass.: M.I.T. Press, 1965.

Clancy, J.; Vanderhoof, E.; and Campbell, P. Evaluation of an aversive technique as a treatment for alcoholism: Controlled trial with succinylcholine-induced apnea. *Quarterly Journal of Studies on Alcohol* 28 (1967): 476–485.

Clark, D. F. The treatment of monosymptomatic phobia by systematic desensitization. *Behaviour Research and Therapy* 1 (1963): 63–68.

Clark, R., and Polish, E. Avoidance conditioning and alcohol consumption in rhesus monkeys. *Science* 132 (1960): 223–224.

Cleeland, C. S. Behavioral technics in the modification of spasmodic torticollis. *Neurology* 23 (1973): 1241–1247.

Clonce v. *Richardson,* 379 Federal Supplement, 338. Federal District Court for Missouri, Western District, 1974.

Cochran, B. Conference report: Behavior modification institute. *Hospital and Community Psychiatry* 20 (1969): 16–18.

Cohen, E. A. *Human behavior in the concentration camp*. New York: The Universal Library, 1953.

Cohen, H. L. *Responses to questions asked of the panel of experts*. In the United States District Court for the Western District of Missouri, Southern Division, 1974. Available from National Prison Project, Washington, D.C.

Cohen, H. L., and Filipczak, J. A. *A new learning environment: A case for learning*. San Francisco, Calif.: Jossey Bass, 1971.

Cohen, H. L.; Filipczak, J. A.; Bis, J. S.; Cohen, J. E.; and Larkin, P. Contingencies applicable to special education—motivationally oriented design for an ecology of learning. Washington, D.C.: U.S. Department of Health, Education, and Welfare, 1968.

Cohen, M.; Liebson, I.; and Faillace, L. A. The modification of drinking in chronic alcoholics. In N. K. Mello and J. H. Mendelson, eds., *Recent advances in studies of alcoholism: An interdisciplinary symposium*. Washington, D.C.: U.S. Government Printing Office, 1971a.

Cohen, M.; Liebson, I.; and Faillace, L. A. The role of reinforcement contingencies in chronic alcoholism: An experimental analysis of one case. *Behaviour Research and Therapy* 9 (1971b): 375–379.

Cohen, M.; Liebson, I.; Faillace, L.; and Speers, W. Alcoholism: Controlled drinking and incentives for abstinence. *Psychological Reports* 28 (1971): 575–580.

Cohen, S. I., and Reed, J. L. The treatment of "nervous diarrhea" and other conditioned automatic disorders by desensitization. *British Journal of Psychiatry* 114 (1968): 1275–1280.

Conner, T., and Kremen, E. Methadone maintenance—is it enough? *International Journal of the Addictions* 6 (1971): 279–298.

Cooke, G. Evaluation of the efficacy of the components of reciprocal inhibition psychotherapy. *Journal of Abnormal Psychology* 73 (1968): 464–467.

Cooper, A. J. A case of bronchial asthma treated by behavior therapy. *Behaviour Research and Therapy* 1 (1964): 351–356.

Copeland, R. E.; Brown, R. E.; and Hall, R. V. The effects of principal-implemented techniques on the behavior of pupils. *Journal of Applied Behavior Analysis* 7 (1974): 77–86.

Costello, C. G. Depression: Loss of reinforcers or loss of reinforcer effectiveness? *Behavior Therapy* 3 (1972): 240–247.

Couch, R. H., and Allen, C. M. Behavior modification in rehabilitation facilities. A review. *Journal of Applied Rehabilitation Counseling* 4 (1973): 88–95.

Coyne, P. H.; Peterson, L. W.; and Peterson, R. F. The development of spoon-feeding behavior in a blind child. *The International Journal for the Education of the Blind* 18 (1968): 108–112.

Craighead, W. E. The role of muscular relaxation in systematic desensitization. In R. D. Rubin, J. P. Brady, and J. D. Henderson, eds., *Advances in behavior therapy.* Vol. 4. New York: Academic Press, 1973. Pages 177–197.

Craighead, W. E., and Mercatoris, M. The use of mentally retarded residents as paraprofessionals: A review. *American Journal of Mental Deficiency* 78 (1973): 339–347.

Craighead, W. E., and Meyers, A. W. Behavior modification with the autistic child in the classroom setting. Paper presented at the meetings of the Association for Advancement of Behavior Therapy, Miami, December 1973.

Craik, K. H. Environmental psychology. In P. H. Mussen and M. R. Rosenzweig, eds., *Annual Review of Psychology* 24 (1973): 403–422.

Crano, W. D., and Brewer, M. B. *Principles of research in social psychology.* New York: McGraw-Hill, 1973.

Cressey, D. R. Adult felons in prison. In L. E. Ohlin, ed., *Prisoners in America.* Englewood Cliffs, N.J.: Prentice-Hall, 1973. Pages 117–150.

Cumming, E., and Cumming, J. *Closed ranks.* Cambridge, Mass.: Harvard University Press, 1957.

Cumming, J., and Cumming, E. *Ego and milieu.* New York: Atherton Press, 1962.

Curran, D., and Parr, D. Homosexuality: An analysis of 100 male cases seen in private practice. *British Medical Journal* 1 (1957): 797–801.

Daniels, L. K. Treatment of urticaria and severe headache by behavior therapy. *Psychosomatics* 14 (1973): 347–351.

Darden, Grey. *Poppe Project.* (Film No. 6701) Berkeley, Calif.: Extension Media Center, University of California, 1965.

Davidson, A. R., and Steiner, I. D. Reinforcement schedules and attributed freedom. *Journal of Personality and Social Psychology* 19 (1971): 357–366.

Davis, M. H.; Saunders, D. R.; Creer, T. L.; and Chai, H. Relaxation training facilitated by biofeedback apparatus as a supplemental treatment in bronchial asthma. *Journal of Psychosomatic Research* 17 (1973): 121–128.

Davison, G. C. Differential relaxation and cognitive restructuring in therapy with a "paranoid schizophrenic" or "paranoid state." *Proceedings of the 74th Annual Convention of the American Psychological Association* 2 (1966): 177–178.

Davison, G. C. Systematic desensitization as a counterconditioning process. *Journal of Abnormal Psychology* 73 (1968): 91–99.

Davison, G. C. Appraisal of behavior modification techniques with adults in institutional settings. In C. M. Franks, ed., *Behavior therapy: Appraisal and status.* New York: McGraw-Hill, 1969. Pages 220–278.

Davison, G. C. Counter-control in behavior modification. In L. A. Hamerlynck; L. C. Handy; and E. J. Mash, eds., *Behavior change: Methodology, concepts and practice.* Champaign, Ill.: Research Press, 1973. Pages 153–167.

Davison, G. C., and Neale, J. M. *Abnormal psychology: An experimental clinical approach.* New York: Wiley, 1974.

Davison, G. C., and Stuart, R. B. Behavior therapy and civil liberties. *American Psychologist* 30 (1975): 755–763.

Davison, G. C., and Valins, S. Maintenance of self-attributed and drug-attributed behavior change. *Journal of Personality and Social Psychology* 11 (1969): 25–33.

Davison, G. C., and Wilson, G. T. Critique of "Desensitization: Social and cognitive factors underlying the effectiveness of Wolpe's procedure." *Psychological Bulletin* 78 (1972): 28–31.

Davison, G. C., and Wilson, G. T. Processes of fear-reduction in systematic desensitization: Cognitive and social reinforcement factors in humans. *Behavior Therapy* 4 (1973): 1–21.

Deci, E. L. Intrinsic motivation, extrinsic reinforcement and inequity. *Journal of Personality and Social Psychology* 22 (1972): 113–120.

Deissler, K. J. Synanon, how it works, why it works. In P. H. Blachly, ed., *Progress in drug abuse.* Springfield, Ill.: Thomas, 1972. Pages 49–61.

Delgado, J. M. R. *Physical control of the mind.* New York: Harper, 1969.

Dement, W. C. *Some must watch while some must sleep.* Stanford, Calif.: Stanford Alumni Association, 1972.

DeRisi, W. J. *Responses to questions asked of the panel of experts.* In the United States District Court for the Western District of Missouri, Southern Division, 1974. Available from National Prison Project, Washington, D.C.

Derogatis, L. R.; Klerman, G. L.; and Lipman, R. S. Anxiety states and depressive neuroses: Issues in anosological discrimination. *Journal of Nervous and Mental Disease* 155 (1972): 392–403.

DiScipo, W. J., and Feldman, M. C. Combined behavior therapy and physical therapy in the treatment of a fear of walking. *Journal of Behavior Therapy and Experimental Psychiatry* 2 (1971): 151–152.

Dole, V., and Nyswander, M. A medical treatment for diacetylmorphine (heroin) addiction: A clinical trial with methadone hydrochloride. *Journal of the American Medical Association* 193 (1965): 646–650.

Domino, E. F. Neuropsychopharmacology of nicotine and tobacco smoking. In W. L. Dunn, Jr., ed., *Smoking behavior: Motives and incentives.* New York: Wiley, 1973. Pages 5–32.

Dorfman, W. Panel discussion: Current concepts of depression. *Psychosomatics* 10 (1969): 51–54.

Drabman, R. S. Child versus teacher administered token programs in a psychiatric hospital school. *Journal of Abnormal Child Psychology* 1 (1973): 66–87.

Drabman, R., and Lahey, B. B. Feedback in classroom behavior modification: Effects on the target child and her classmates. *Journal of Applied Behavior Analysis* 7 (1974): 591–598.

Drabman, R., and Spitalnik, R. Training a retarded child as a behavioral teaching assistant. *Journal of Behavior Therapy and Experimental Psychiatry* 4 (1973a): 269–272.

Drabman, R., and Spitalnik, R. Social isolation as a punishment procedure: A controlled study. *Journal of Experimental Child Psychology* 16 (1973b): 236–249.

Drabman, R.; Spitalnik, R.; and O'Leary, K. D. Teaching self-control to disruptive children. *Journal of Abnormal Psychology* 82 (1973): 10–16.

Drabman, R.; Spitalnik, R.; and Spitalnik, K. Sociometric and disruptive behavior as a function of four types of token economies. *Journal of Applied Behavior Analysis* 7 (1974): 93–101.

Drabman, R. S.; and Tucker, R. Why classroom token economies fail. *Journal of School Psychology* 12 (1974): 178–188.

Dubos, R. *So human an animal.* New York: Scribner, 1968.

Dulany, D. E. Awareness, rules, and propositional control: A confrontation with S-R behavior theory. In T. R. Dixon and D. L. Horton, eds., *Verbal behavior and general behavior theory.* Englewood Cliffs, N.J.: Prentice-Hall, 1968. Pages 340–387.

Dunlop, E. Use of antidepressants and stimulants. *Modern Treatment* 2 (1965): 543–568.

Dunn, L. M. Special education for the mildly retarded—is much of it justifiable? In W. C. Becker, ed., *An empirical basis for change in education.* Chicago: Science Research Associates, 1971. Pages 41–59.

D'Zurilla, T. J., and Goldfried, M. R. Problem solving and behavior modification. *Journal of Abnormal Psychology* 78 (1971): 107–126.

Edmonds, C. Severe somnambulism: A case study. *Journal of Clinical Psychology* 23 (1967): 237–239.

Edwards, C. C. Conditions for investigational use of methadone for maintenance programs for narcotic addicts. *Federal Register* 35 (1972): 9014–9015.

Edwards, N. B. Case conference: Assertive training in a case of homosexual pedophilia. *Journal of Behavior Therapy and Experimental Psychiatry* 3 (1972): 55–63.

Efron, R. The effect of olfactory stimuli in arresting uncinate fits. *Brain* 79 (1956): 267–281.

Efron, R. The conditioned inhibition of uncinate fits. *Brain* 80 (1957): 251–262.

Eisenberg, L. The human nature of human nature. *Science* 176 (1972): 123–128.

Eisenman, R. Critique of "Treatment of insomnia by relaxation training": Relaxation training, Rogerian therapy, or demand characteristics. *Journal of Abnormal Psychology* 75 (1970): 315–316.

Eisler, R. M. Assertive training in the work situation. Unpublished manuscript, 1974.

Eisler, R. M., and Hersen, M. Behavioral techniques in family-oriented crisis intervention. *Archives of General Psychiatry* 28 (1973): 111–116.

Eisler, R. M.; Hersen, M.; and Agras, W. S. Videotape: A method for the controlled observation of nonverbal interpersonal behavior. *Behavior Therapy* 4 (1973): 420–425.

Eisler, R. M.; Hersen, M.; and Miller, P. M. Effects of modeling on components of assertive behavior. *Journal of Behavior Therapy and Experimental Psychiatry* 4 (1973): 1–6.

Eisler, R. M.; Hersen, M.; and Miller, P. M. Shaping components of assertive behavior with instructions and feedback. *American Journal of Psychiatry,* in press.

Eisler, R. M.; Miller, P. M.; and Hersen, M. Components of assertive behavior. *Journal of Clinical Psychology* 29 (1973): 295–299.

Eisler, R. M.; Miller, P. M.; and Hersen, M. Effects of assertive training on marital interaction. *Archives of General Psychiatry* 30 (1974): 643–649.

Eisler, R. M.; Miller, P. M.; Hersen, M.; and Alford, H. Effects of assertive training on marital interaction. *Archives of General Psychiatry,* in press.

Elkin, T. E.; Williams, J. G.; Barlow, D. H.; and Stewart, W. R. Measurement and modification of I.V. drug abuse: A preliminary study using succinylcholine. Unpublished manuscript. University of Mississippi Medical Center, 1974.

Elliott, R., and Tighe, T. Breaking the cigarette habit: Effects of a technique involving threatened loss of money. *Psychological Record* 18 (1968): 503–513.

Ellis, A. Outcome of employing three techniques of psychotherapy. *Journal of Clinical Psychology* 13 (1957): 344–350.

Ellis, A. *Reason and emotion in psychotherapy.* New York: Lyle-Stuart, 1962.

Ellis, A. *The essence of rational psychotherapy: A comprehensive approach to treatment.* New York: Institute for Rational Living, 1970.

Ellis, A. *Growth through reason.* Palo Alto, Calif.: Science and Behavior Books, 1971.

Ellis, A., and Harper, R. A. *A guide to rational living.* Hollywood: Wilshire, 1961.

Ellsworth, J. R. Reinforcement therapy with chronic patients. *Hospital and Community Psychiatry* 20 (1969): 238–240.

Ely, A. L.; Guerney, B. G., Jr.; and Stover, L. Efficacy of the training phase of conjugal therapy. *Psychotherapy: Theory, Research, and Practice* 10 (1973): 201–207.

Engel, B. T. Comment on self-control of cardiac functioning: A promise as yet unfulfilled. *Psychological Bulletin* 81 (1974): 43.

Engel, B. T.; Nikoomanesh, P.; and Shuster, M. M. Operant conditioning of rectosphincteric responses in the treatment of fecal incontinence. *New England Journal of Medicine* 290 (1974): 646–649.

Erickson, M. L. Group violations, socioeconomic status, and official delinquency. *Social Forces* 52 (1973): 41–52.

Evans, D. R., and Bond, I. K. Reciprocal inhibition therapy and classical conditioning in the treatment of insomnia. *Behaviour Research and Therapy* 7 (1969): 323–325.

Evans, G. W., and Oswalt, G. L. Acceleration of academic progress through the manipulation of peer influence. *Behaviour Research and Therapy* 6 (1968): 189–195.

Ewing, J. A. Some recent attempts to inculcate controlled drinking in patients resistant to Alcoholics Anonymous. Paper presented at National Council on Alcoholism Annual Meeting, April 1973.

Eysenck, H. J., ed. *Behavior therapy and the neuroses.* New York: Pergamon Press, 1960.

Eysenck, H. J. *Experiments in behavior therapy.* New York: Pergamon Press, 1964.

Eysenck, H. J. *The effects of psychotherapy.* New York: International Science Press, 1966.

Eysenck, H. J. Personality and the maintenance of the smoking habit. In W. L. Dunn, Jr., ed., *Smoking behavior: Motives and incentives.* New York: Wiley, 1973. Pages 113–146.

Fairweather, G. W.; Sanders, D. H.; Maynard, A.; and Cressler, D. L.. *Community life for the mentally ill: An alternative to institutional care.* Chicago: Aldine, 1969.

Fairweather, G. W., and Simon, R. A further follow-up comparison of psychotherapeutic programs. *Journal of Consulting Psychology* 27 (1963): 186.

Farrar, C. H.; Powell, B. J.; and Martin, L. K. Punishment of alcohol consumption by amneic paralysis. *Behavior Research and Therapy* 6 (1968): 13–16.

Faulkner, C. B., and Saunders, A. J. *Proposed questions of law and proposed facts as agreed by counsel for petitioners and respondents.* Filed in U.S. District Court for the Western District of Missouri, Southern Division, on November 15, 1973.

Fazio, A. F. Use of behavioral techniques in bladder training with a flaccid neurogenic bladder condition: A case study. Paper presented at the 82nd Annual Convention of the American Psychological Association, New Orleans, 1974.

Feallock, R. A., and Miller, L. K. The design and evaluation of a worksharing system for experimental living. Unpublished paper, University of Kansas, 1974.

Federal Bureau of Prisons. *START—revised program.* Washington, D.C.: Federal Bureau of Prisons, 1972.

Feinberg, G. *The Prometheus project.* New York: Doubleday, 1969.

Feinsilver, D., and Gunderson, J. Psychotherapy for schizophrenics—Is it indicated? A review of the relevant literature. *Schizophrenia Bulletin,* no. 6 (1972): 11–23.

Feldman, M. P., and MacCulloch, M. J. The application of anticipatory avoidance learning to the treatment of homosexuality. I. Theory, technique, and preliminary results. *Behaviour Research and Therapy* 2 (1965): 165–183.

Feldman, M. P., and MacCulloch, M. J. *Homosexual behavior: Therapy and assessment.* Oxford: Pergamon Press, 1971.

Feldman, M. P.; MacCulloch, M. J.; Mellor, V.; and Pinschof, J. The application of anticipatory avoidance learning to the treatment of homosexuality: III. The sexual orientation method. *Behaviour Research and Therapy* 4 (1966): 289–299.

Fensterheim, H. Behavior therapy: Assertive training in groups. In C. J. Sager and H. S. Kaplan, eds., *Progress in group and family therapy.* New York: Brunner/Mazel, 1972. Pages 156–169.

Ferkiss, V. C. *Technological man: The myth and the reality.* New York: Braziller, 1969.

Ferster, C. B. Classification of behavioral pathology. In L. Krasner and L. P. Ullmann, eds., *Research in behavior modification.* New York: Holt, Rinehart and Winston, 1965. Pages 6–26.

Ferster, C. B. Animal behavior and mental illness. *Psychological Record* 16 (1966): 345–356.

Ferster, C. B. Comments on paper by Hunt and Matarazzo. In W. A. Hunt, ed., *Learning mechanisms in smoking.* Chicago: Aldine, 1970. Pages 91–102.

Ferster, C. B. A functional analysis of depression. *American Psychologist* 28 (1973): 857–870.

Ferster, C. B.; Nurnberger, J. I.; and Levitt, E. B. The control of eating. *Journal of Mathetics* 1 (1962): 87–109.

Fiske, D. W.; Hunt, H. F.; Luborsky, L.; Orne, M. T.; Parloff, M. B.; Reiser, M. F.; and Tuma, A. H. Planning of research and effectiveness of psychotherapy. *Archives of General Psychiatry* 22 (1970): 22–32.

Fixsen, D. L.; Phillips, E. L.; and Wolf, M. M. Achievement Place: The reliability of self-reporting and peer-reporting and their effects on behavior. *Journal of Applied Behavior Analysis* 5 (1972): 19–30.

Fixsen, D. L.; Phillips, E. L.; and Wolf, M. M. Achievement Place: Experiments in self-government with pre-delinquents. *Journal of Applied Behavior Analysis* 6 (1973): 31–47.

Flanders, J. A review of research on imitative behavior. *Psychological Bulletin* 69 (1968): 316–337.

Flaxman, J. Smoking cessation: Gradual vs. abrupt quitting. Paper presented at the meeting of the Association for Advancement of Behavior Therapy, Chicago, November 1974.

Flippo, J. R., and Lewinsohn, P. M. Effects of failure on the self-esteem of depressed and non-depressed subjects. *Journal of Consulting and Clinical Psychology* 36 (1971): 151.

Fordyce, W. E. Automated training system for wheelchair pushups. *Public Health Reports* 83 (1968): 527–528.

Fordyce, W. E. Operant conditioning as a treatment method in management of selected chronic pain problems. *Northwest Medicine* 69 (1970): 580–581.

Fordyce, W. E. An operant conditioning method for managing chronic pain. *Postgraduate Medicine* 53 (1973): 123–128.

Fordyce, W. E.; Fowler, R. S.; and DeLateur, B. An application of behavior modification technique to a problem of chronic pain. *Behaviour Research and Therapy* 6 (1968): 105–107.

Fordyce, W. E.; Fowler, R. S.; Lehman, J. F.; and DeLateur, B. J. Some implications of learning in problems of chronic pain. *Journal of Chronic Diseases* 21 (1968): 179–190.

Fordyce, W. E.; Fowler, R. S.; Lehman, J. F.; DeLateur, B. J.; Sand, P. L.; and Trieschman, R. B. Operant conditioning in the treatment of chronic pain. *Archives of Physical Medicine and Rehabilitation* 54 (1973): 399–408.

Fordyce, W. E.; Sand, P. L.; Trieschman, R. B.; and Fowler, R. S. Behavioral systems analyzed. *Journal of Rehabilitation* 37 (1971): 29–33.

Foreyt, J. P., and Kennedy, W. A. Treatment of overweight by aversion therapy. *Behaviour Research and Therapy* 9 (1971): 29–34.

Fowler, R. S.; Fordyce, W. E.; and Berni, R. Operant conditioning in chronic illness. *American Journal of Nursing* 69 (1969): 1226–1228.

Frank, J. D. *Persuasion and healing.* 2nd ed. Baltimore: Johns Hopkins, 1973.

Freeman, B. J.; Roy, R. R.; and Hemmick, S. Extinction of a phobia of physical examinations in a 7-year-old mentally retarded boy. Paper presented at the 82nd Annual Meeting of the American Psychological Association, New Orleans, 1974.

Freeman, H. E., and Simmons, O. G. *The mental patient comes home.* New York: Wiley, 1963.

Freire, P. *Pedagogy of the oppressed.* New York: Herder & Herder, 1971.

Freud, S. *The problem of anxiety.* New York: Norton, 1936.

Freudenberg, R. K., and Robertson, J. P. S. Symptoms in relation to psychiatric diagnosis and treatment. *Archives of Neurological Psychiatry* 76 (1956): 14–22.

Freund, K. Some problems in the treatment of homosexuality. In H. J. Eysenck, ed., *Behavior therapy and the neuroses.* New York: Pergamon Press, 1960.

Freund, K. A laboratory method for diagnosing predominance of homo- or hetero-erotic interest in the male. *Behaviour Research and Therapy* 1 (1963): 85–93.

Freund, K. Diagnosing heterosexual pedophilia by means of a test for sexual interest. *Behaviour Research and Therapy* 3 (1965): 229–234.

Freund, K. Diagnosing homo- or heterosexuality and erotic age preference by means of a psychophysiological test. *Behaviour Research and Therapy* 5 (1967): 209–228.

Freund, K.; Sedlarcek, F.; and Knob, K. Simple transducer for mechanical plethysmography of the male genital. *Journal of the Experimental Analysis of Behavior* 8 (1965): 169–170.

Freund, K.; Langevin, R.; Cibiri, S.; and Zajac, Y. Heterosexual aversion in homosexual males. *British Journal of Psychiatry* 122 (1973): 163–169.

Freund, K.; McKnight, C. K.; Langevin, R.; and Cibiri, S. The female child as a surrogate object. *Archives of Sexual Behavior* 2 (1972): 119–133.

Freund, K.; Nagler, E.; Langevin, R.; Zajac, A.; and Steiner, B. Measuring feminine gender identity in homosexual males. *Archives of Sexual Behavior* 3 (1974): 249–261.

Friedman, A. S. Minimal effects of severe depression on cognitive functioning. *Journal of Abnormal and Social Psychology* 69 (1964): 237–243.

Friedman, M. *Pathogenesis of coronary artery disease.* New York: McGraw-Hill, 1969.

Friedman, M., and Rosenman, R. H. *Type A behavior and your heart.* New York: Knopf, 1974.

Friedman, P. Legal regulation of applied behavior analysis in mental institutions and prisons. *Arizona Law Review* 17 (1975): 39–104.

Furman, S. Intestinal biofeedback in functional diarrhea: A preliminary report. *Journal of Behavior Therapy and Experimental Psychiatry* 4 (1973): 317–321.

Galbraith, D. A.; Byrick, R. J.; and Rutledge, J. T. An aversive conditioning approach to the inhibition of chronic vomiting. *Canadian Psychiatric Association Journal* 15 (1970): 311–313.

Gannon, L., and Sternbach, R. A. Alpha enhancement as a treatment for pain: A case study. *Journal of Behavior Therapy and Experimental Psychiatry* 2 (1971): 209–213.

Garber, N. B. Operant procedures to eliminate drooling behavior in a cerebral palsied adolescent. *Developmental Medicine and Child Neurology* 13 (1971): 641–644.

Gardner, H. The carnival of communal styles. *Harpers* 246 (March 1973): 10.

Gardner, J. E. Behavior therapy treatment approach to a psychogenic seizure case. *Journal of Consulting Psychology* 31 (1967): 209–212.

Garfield, Z. H.; Darwin, P. L.; Singer, B. A.; and McBrearty, J. F. Effect of "in vivo" training on experimental desensitization of a phobia. *Psychological Reports* 20 (1967): 515–519.

Geer, J. H. The development of a scale to measure fear. *Behaviour Research and Therapy* 3 (1965): 45–53.

Geer, J. H., and Katkin, E. S. Treatment of insomnia using a variant of systematic desensitization: A case report. *Journal of Abnormal Psychology* 71 (1966): 161–164.

Geer, J. H., and Turtletaub, A. Fear reduction following observation of a model. *Journal of Personality and Social Psychology* 6 (1967): 327–331.

Geis, H. J. Rational emotive therapy with a culturally deprived teenager. In A. Ellis, ed., *Growth through reason.* Palo Alto, Calif.: Science and Behavior Books, 1971. Pages 46–107.

Gerst, M. D. Symbolic coding processes in observational learning. *Journal of Personality and Social Psychology* 19 (1971): 7–17.

Glaser, D. *The effectiveness of a prison and parole system.* Indianapolis: Bobbs-Merrill, 1964.

Glass, G. V.; Willson, V. L.; and Gottman, J. M. *Design and analysis of time-series experiments.* Boulder, Col.: Colorado Associated University Press, 1973.

Glasscote, R. M. *Halfway houses for the mentally ill: A study of programs and problems.* Washington, D.C.: Joint Information Service, APA and NIMH, 1971.

Glicksman, M.; Ottomanelli, G.; and Cutler, R. The earn-your-way credit system: Use of a token economy in narcotic rehabilitation. *International Journal of the Addictions* 6 (1971): 525–531.

Glidewell, J. C., and Swallow, C. S. *The prevalence of maladjustment in elementary schools.* Chicago: University of Chicago Press, 1968.

Glynn, E. L. Classroom applications of self-determined reinforcement. *Journal of Applied Behavior Analysis* 3 (1970): 123–132.

Glynn, E. L., and Thomas, J. D. Effect of cueing on self-control of classroom behavior. *Journal of Applied Behavior Analysis* 7 (1974): 299–306.

Glynn, E. L.; Thomas, J. D.; and Shee, S. M. Behavioral self-control of on-task behavior in an elementary classroom. *Journal of Applied Behavior Analysis* 6 (1973): 105–113.

Goffman, E. *Asylums: Essays on the social situation of mental patients and other inmates.* Chicago: Aldine, 1962.

Goldberg, M. J. Patuxent. *Mental Health* 57, no. 4 (1973): 24–25.

Goldfarb, R. L. American prisons: Self-defeating concrete. *Psychology Today* 7, no. 8 (1974): 20–24, 85–89.

Goldfarb, R. L., and Singer, L. R. Maryland's defective delinquency law and the Patuxent Institution. *Bulletin of the Menninger Clinic* 34 (1970): 223–234.

Goldfarb, R. L., and Singer, L. R. *After conviction.* New York: Simon and Schuster, 1973.

Goldfried, M. R. Systematic desensitization as training in self-control. *Journal of Consulting and Clinical Psychology* 37 (1971): 228–234.

Goldfried, M. R., and Pomeranz, D. M. Role of assessment in behavior modification. *Psychological Reports* 23 (1968): 75–87.

Goldfried, M. R., and Sprafkin, J. N. *Behavioral personality assessment.* Morristown, N.J.: General Learning Press, 1974.

Goldiamond, I. Self-control procedures in behavior problems. *Psychological Reports* 17 (1965): 851–868.

Goldiamond, I. A diary of self-modification. *Psychology Today* 7 (1973): 95–102.

Goldiamond, I. Toward a constructional approach to social problems: Ethical and constitutional issues raised by applied behavior analysis. *Behaviorism* 2 (1974): 1–84.

Goldiamond, I. Singling out behavior modification for legal regulation: Some effects on patient care, psychotherapy and research in general. *Arizona Law Review* 17 (1975): 105–126.

Goldman, R.; Jaffa, M.; and Schachter, S. Yom Kippur, Air France, dormitory food, and the eating behavior of obese and normal persons. *Journal of Personality and Social Psychology* 10 (1968): 117–123.

Goldstein, A. J. Separate effects of extinction, counter-conditioning and progressive approach in overcoming fear. *Behaviour Research and Therapy* 7 (1969): 47–56.

Goldstein, A., and Brown, B. W. Urine testing schedules in methadone maintenance treatment of heroin addiction. *Journal of the American Medical Association* 214 (1969): 311, 315.

Goldstein, A. P.; Heller, K.; and Sechrest, L. B. *Psychotherapy and the psychology of behavior change.* New York: Wiley, 1966.

Goldstein, M. K., and Francis, B. Behavior modification of husbands by wives. Paper presented at the meeting of the National Councils on Family Relations, Washington, D.C., 1969.

Goldstein, M. K.; Stein, G.; and Smolen, D. M. Remote medical behavioral monitoring: Some rudiments of ambulatory health assessment and care delivery. Unpublished manuscript, Veteran's Administration Hospital and University of Florida, Gainesville, Florida, 1974.

Goodell, C. E. *Political prisoners in America.* New York: Random House, 1973.

Goodkin, R. Case studies in behavioral research in rehabilitation. *Perceptual and Motor Skills* 23 (1966): 171–182.

Goodwin, D. W. Is alcoholism hereditary? A review and critique. *Archives of General Psychiatry* 25 (1971): 545–549.

Gotestam, K. G., and Melin, L. Covert extinction of amphetamine addiction. *Behavior Therapy* 5 (1974): 90–92.

Gottman, J. M., and Leiblum, S. R. *How to do psychotherapy and how to evaluate it.* New York: Holt, 1974.

Graham, D. T. Psychosomatic medicine. In N. S. Greenfield and R. A. Sternback, eds., *Handbook of psychophysiology.* New York: Holt, Rinehart & Winston, 1972. Pages 839–924.

Graham, S., and Gibson, R. W. Cessation of patterned behavior: Withdrawal from smoking. *Social Science and Medicine* 5 (1971): 319–337.

Granick, S. Comparative analysis of psychotic depressives with matched normals on some untimed verbal intelligence tests. *Journal of Consulting Psychology* 27 (1963): 439–443.

Green, R., and Money, J., eds. *Transsexualism and sex reassignment.* Baltimore: Johns Hopkins, 1969.

Greenwood, C.; Hops, H.; Delquadri, J.; and Guild, J. Group contingencies for group consequences in classroom management: A further analysis. *Journal of Applied Behavior Analysis* 7 (1974): 413–425.

Griffitt, W., and Veitch, R. Hot and crowded: Influences of population density and temperature on interpersonal affective behavior. *Journal of Personality and Social Psychology* 17 (1971): 92–98.

Grings, W., and Lockhart, R. Effects of "anxiety-lessening" instructions and differential set development on the extinction of GSR. *Journal of Experimental Psychology* 66 (1963): 292–299.

Grinker, R. R.; Miller, J.; Sabshin, M.; Nunn, R.; and Nunally, J. *The phenomena of depressions.* New York: Hoeber, 1961.

Grunbaum, A. Causality and the science of human behavior. *American Scientist* 40 (1952): 665–676.

Guilford, J. S. Group treatment vs. individual initiative in the cessation of smoking. *Journal of Applied Psychology* 56 (1972): 162–167.

Gurin, G.; Veroff, J.; and Feld, S. *Americans view their mental health: A nationwide survey.* New York: Basic Books, 1960.

Gurman, A. S. Treatment of a case of public-speaking anxiety by *in vivo* desensitization and cue-controlled relaxation. *Journal of Behavior Therapy and Experimental Psychiatry* 4 (1973): 51–54.

Gutmann, M., and Marston, A. Problems of subject's motivation in a behavioral program for the reduction of cigarette smoking. *Psychological Reports* 20 (1967): 1107–1114.

Gutride, M. E.; Goldstein, A. P.; and Hunter, G. F. The use of modeling and role playing to increase social interaction among asocial psychiatric patients. *Journal of Consulting and Clinical Psychology* 40 (1973): 408–415.

Haas, H.; Fink, H.; and Hartfelder, G. The placebo problem. *Psychopharmocology Service Center Bulletin* 2 (1963): 1–65.

Hagen, R. L. Group therapy versus bibliotherapy in weight reduction. Unpublished doctoral dissertation, University of Illinois, 1969.

Hall, C. S., and Lindzey, G. *Theories of personality.* New York: Wiley, 1957, 1970.

Hall, R. V., and Broden, M. Behavior changes in brain injured children through social reinforcement. *Journal of Experimental Child Psychology* 5 (1967): 463–479.

Hall, R. V.; Lund, D.; and Jackson, D. Effects of teacher attention on study behavior. *Journal of Applied Behavior Analysis* 1 (1968): 1–12.

Hall, S. M. Self-control and therapist control in the behavioral treatment of overweight women. *Behaviour Research and Therapy* 10 (1972): 59–68.

Hall, S. M., and Hall, R. G. Outcome and methodological considerations in behavioral treatment of obesity. *Behavior Therapy* 5 (1974): 352–364.

Hallam, R.; Rachman, S.; and Falkowski, W. Subjective attitudinal and physiological effects of electrical aversion therapy. *Behaviour Research and Therapy* 10 (1972): 1–13.

Halpern, D., and Kottke, F. Training of control of head posture in children with cerebral palsy. *Development Medicine and Child Neurology* 10 (1968): 249.

Hamilton, M. A rating scale for depression. *Journal of Neurology, Neurosurgery, and Psychiatry* 23 (1960): 56–61.

Hamilton, M., and Schroeder, H. E. A comparison of systematic desensitization and reinforced practice procedures in fear reduction. *Behaviour Research and Therapy* 11 (1973): 649–652.

Hannum, J. W.; Thoresen, C. E.; and Hubbard, D. R. A behavioral study of self-esteem with elementary teachers. In M. J. Mahoney and C. E. Thoresen, eds., *Self-control: Power to the person.* Belmont, Calif.: Brooks/Cole, 1974. Pages 144–155.

Harmatz, M. G., and Lapuc, P. Behavior modification of overeating in a psychiatric population. *Journal of Consulting and Clinical Psychology* 32 (1968): 583–587.

Harris, F. R.; Johnston, M. K.; Kelley, C. S.; and Wolf, M. M. Effects of positive social reinforcement on regressed crawling of a nursery school child. *Journal of Educational Psychology* 55 (1964): 35–41.

Harris, F. R.; Wolf, M. M.; and Baer, D. M. Effects of social reinforcement of child behavior. *Young Children* 20 (1964): 8–17.

Harris, M. B. Self-directed program for weight control: A pilot study. *Journal of Abnormal Psychology* 74 (1969): 263–270.

Harris, M. B., and Bruner, C. G. A comparison of a self-control and a contract procedure for weight control. *Behaviour Research and Therapy* 9 (1971): 347–354.

Hart, B. M.; Allen, K. E.; Buell, J. S.; Harris, F. R.; and Wolf, M. M. Effects of social reinforcement on operant crying. *Journal of Experimental Child Psychology* 1 (1964): 145–153.

Hart, B. M.; Reynolds, N. J.; Baer, D. M.; Brawley, E. R.; and Harris, F. R. Effect of contingent and non-contingent social reinforcement on the cooperative play of a preschool child. *Journal of Applied Behavior Analysis* 1 (1968): 73–76.

Hartig, M., and Kanfer, F. H. The role of verbal self-instructions in children's resistance to temptation. *Journal of Personality and Social Psychology* 25 (1973): 259–267.

Hastorf, A. H.; Schneider, D. J.; and Polefka, J. *Person perception.* Reading: Mass.: Addison-Wesley, 1970.

Hathaway, S. R., and McKinley, J. C. A multiphasic personality schedule: The measurement of symptomatic depression. *Journal of Psychology* 14 (1942): 73–84.

Hauck, P. A RET theory of depression. *Rational Living* 6 (1971): 32–35.

Haughey, J. C. The commune-child of the 1970's. *America* 124 (1971): 254–256.

Haughton, E., and Ayllon, T. Production and elimination of symptomatic behavior. In L. P. Ullmann and L. Krasner, eds., *Case studies in behavior modification.* New York: Holt, 1965. Pages 268–284.

Hauserman, N.; Walen, S. R.; and Behling, M. Reinforced racial integration in the first grade: A study in generalization. *Journal of Applied Behavior Analysis* 6 (1973): 193–200.

Hawkins, R. P.; McArthur, M.; Rinaldi, P. C.; Gray, D.; and Schaftenaur, L. Results of operant conditioning techniques in modifying the behavior of emotionally disturbed children. Paper presented at the 45th Annual International Council for Exceptional Children Convention in St. Louis, 1967.

Haynes, S. N.; Follingstad, D. R.; and McGowan, W. T. Insomnia: Sleep patterns, anxiety level, and behavior therapy. *Journal of Psychosomatic Research* 18 (1974): 69–74.

Haynes, S. N.; Woodward, S.; Moran, R.; and Alexander, D. Relaxation treatment of insomnia. *Behavior Therapy* 5 (1974): 555–558.

Hays, W. L. *Statistics for psychologists.* New York: Holt, 1963.

Heap, F. R.; Boblitt, W. E.; Moore, C. H.; and Hord, J. E. Behavior-milieu therapy with chronic neuropsychiatric patients. *Journal of Abnormal Psychology* 76 (1970): 349–354.

Heckel, R. B.; Wiggins, S. L.; and Salzberg, H. C. Conditioning against silences in group therapy. *Journal of Clinical Psychology* 18 (1962): 216–217.

Hedberg, A. G. The treatment of chronic diarrhea by systematic desensitization: A case report. *Journal of Behavior Therapy and Experimental Psychiatry* 4 (1973): 67–68.

Hedgepeth, W. The commune way keeps spreading because maybe it'll be different here. *Look* 35, no. 6 (1971): 63–70.

Herman, S. H.; Barlow, D. H.; and Agras, W. S. An experimental analysis of classical conditioning as a method of increasing heterosexual arousal in homosexuals. *Behavior Therapy* 5 (1974): 33–47.

Herman, S. H.; Barlow, D. H.; and Agras, W. S. An experimental analysis of exposure to "explicit" heterosexual stimuli as an effective variable in changing arousal patterns of homosexuals. *Behaviour Research and Therapy* 12 (1974): 335–345.

Herman, S., and Tramontana, J. Instructions and group versus individual reinforcement in modifying disruptive group behavior. *Journal of Applied Behavior Analysis* 4 (1971): 113–119.

Hersen, M. Self-assessment of fear. *Behavior Therapy* 4 (1973): 241–257.

Hersen, M., and Barlow, D. H. *Strategies for studying behavior change.* New York: Pergamon, 1976.

Hersen, M., and Eisler, R. M. Behavioral approaches to study and treatment of psychogenic tics. *Genetic Psychology Monographs* 87 (1973): 289–312.

Hersen, M.; Eisler, R. M.; Alford, G. S.; and Agras, W. S. Effects of token economy on neurotic depression: An experimental analysis. *Behavior Therapy* 4 (1973a): 392–397.

Hersen, M.; Eisler, R.; and Miller, P. M. Development of assertive responses: Clinical measurement and research considerations. *Behaviour Research and Therapy* 11 (1973): 505–521.

Hersen, M.; Eisler, R. M.; and Miller, P. M. An experimental analysis of generalization in assertive training. Unpublished manuscript, 1974.

Hersen, M.; Eisler, R. M.; Miller, P. M.; Johnson, M. B.; and Pinkston, S. G. Effects of practice, instructions, and modeling on components of assertive behavior. *Behaviour Research and Therapy* 11 (1973b): 443–451.

Hersen, M., and Miller, P. M. Social skills training for neurotically depressed clients. Unpublished manuscript, 1974.

Hersen, M.; Miller, P. M.; and Eisler, R. M. Interactions between alcoholics and their wives: A descriptive analysis of verbal and nonverbal behavior. *Quarterly Journal of Studies on Alcohol* 34 (1973): 516–520.

Hersen, M.; Turner, S. M.; Edelstein, B. A.; and Pinkston, S. G. Effects of phenothiazines, token economy, social skills training, and job retraining in a withdrawn schizophrenic. Unpublished manuscript, 1975.

Hewett, F. M.; Taylor, F. D.; and Artuso, A. A. The Santa Monica Project: Evaluation of an engineered classroom design with emotionally disturbed children. *Exceptional Children* 35 (1969): 523–529.

Higgins, R. L., and Marlatt, G. A. The effects of anxiety arousal upon the consumption of alcohol by alcoholics and social drinkers. *Journal of Consulting and Clinical Psychology,* in press.

Hilgard, E. G., and Bower, G. H. *Theories of learning.* New York: Appleton-Century-Crofts, 1966.

Hill, O. W., ed. *Modern trends in psychosomatic medicine.* New York: Appleton-Century-Crofts, 1970.

Hill, R., and Aldous, J. Socialization for marriage and parenthood. In D. A. Goslin, ed., *Handbook of socialization theory and research.* Chicago: Rand McNally, 1969. Pages 885–950.

Hilts, P. J. *Behavior mod.* New York: Harper's Magazine Press, 1974.

Hinkle, J. E., and Lutker, E. R. Insomnia: A new approach. *Psychotherapy: Theory, Research and Practice* 9 (1972): 236–237.

Hoch, P. Schizophrenia. In P. Hoch and J. Zubin, eds., *Psychopathology of schizophrenia.* New York: Grune & Stratton, 1966.

Hodges, E. F. Crime prevention by the indeterminate sentence law. *American Journal of Psychiatry* 128 (1971): 291–295.

Holland, J. G., and Skinner, B. F. *The analysis of behavior.* New York: McGraw-Hill, 1961.

Homme, L. E. Perspectives in psychology, XXIV: Control of coverants, the operants of the mind. *Psychological Record* 15 (1965): 501–511.

Homme, L. E. Contiguity theory and contingency management. *Psychological Record* 16 (1966): 233–241.

Homme, L. E.; deBaca, P. C.; Devine, J. V.; Steinhorst, R.; and Rickert, E. J. Use of the Premack Principle in controlling the behavior of nursery school children. *Journal of the Experimental Analysis of Behavior* 6 (1963): 544.

Houten, R. V.; Morrison, E.; Jarvis, R.; and McDonald, M. The effects of explicit timing and feedback on compositional response rate in elementary school children. *Journal of Applied Behavior Analysis* 7 (1974): 547–555.

Houts, P. S., and Scott, R. A. *Goal planning in mental health rehabilitation.* Hershey, Penna.: The Milton S. Hershey Medical Center, 1972.

Howard, J. *Please touch.* New York: Dell, 1971.

Hsu, J. J. Electroconditioning therapy of alcoholics: A preliminary report. *Quarterly Journal of Studies on Alcohol* 26 (1965): 449–459.

Hull, C. L. *Principles of behavior.* New York: Appleton-Century-Crofts, 1943.

Hunt, G. M., and Azrin, N. H. A community reinforcement approach to alcoholism. *Behaviour Research and Therapy* 11 (1973): 91–104.

Hunt, J. McV. *Intelligence and experience.* New York: Ronald, 1961.

Hunt, M. L., and Gibby, R. G. *Patterns of abnormal behavior.* Boston: Allyn and Bacon, 1957.

Hunt, W. A., and Bespalec, D. A. An evaluation of current methods of modifying smoking behavior. *Journal of Clinical Psychology* 30 (1974): 431–438.

Hunt, W. A., and Matarazzo, J. D. Habit mechanisms in smoking. In W. A. Hunt, ed., *Learning mechanisms in smoking.* Chicago: Aldine, 1970. Pages 65–90.

Hunt, W. A.; Wittson, C. L.; and Hunt, E. B. A theoretical and practical analysis of the diagnostic process. In P. H. Hoch and J. Zubin, eds., *Current problems in psychiatric diagnosis.* New York: Grune & Stratton, 1953. Pages 53–65.

Hutchinson, R. R., and Emley, G. S. Effects of nicotine on avoidance, conditioned suppression and aggression response measures in animals and man. In W. L. Dunn, Jr., ed., *Smoking behavior: Motives and incentives.* New York: Wiley, 1973. Pages 171–196.

Ikard, F. F.; Green, D. E.; and Horn, D. A scale to differentiate between types of smoking as related to the management of affect. *The International Journal of Addictions* 4 (1969): 649–659.

Irwin, J. *The felon.* Englewood Cliffs, N.J.: Prentice-Hall, 1970.

Israel, M. *Journal of Behavioral Technology,* 1971.

Iwata, B., and Bailey, J. Reward versus cost token systems: An analysis of the effects on students and teacher. *Journal of Applied Behavior Analysis* 7 (1974): 567–576.

Jackson, B. Treatment of depression by self-reinforcement. *Behavior Therapy* 3 (1972): 298–307.

Jackson, G. *Soledad brother.* New York: Bantam, 1971.

Jacobs, A., and Spradlin, W., eds. *The group as an agent of change.* New York: Behavioral Publications, 1974.

Jacobson, E. The electrophysiology of mental activities. *American Journal of Psychology* 44 (1932): 677–694.

Jacobson, E. *Progressive relaxation.* Chicago: University of Chicago Press, 1938.

Jaffe, J. H. Tobacco addiction. *Science* 185 (1974): 1039–1040.

Janis, I. L., and Hoffman, D. Facilitating effects of daily contact between partners who make a decision to cut down on smoking. *Journal of Personality and Social Psychology* 17 (1971): 25–35.

Janis, I. L., and Mann, L. Effectiveness of emotional role-playing in modifying smoking habits and attitudes. *Journal of Experimental Research in Personality* 1 (1965): 84–90.

Jarvik, M. E. The role of nicotine in the smoking habit. In W. A. Hunt, ed., *Learning mechanisms in smoking.* Chicago: Aldine, 1970. Pages 155–190.

Jeffrey, D. B. A comparison of the effects of external control and self-control on the modification of weight. *Journal of Abnormal Psychology* 83 (1974a): 404–410.

Jeffrey, D. B. Self-control: Methodological issues and research trends. In M. J. Mahoney and C. E. Thoresen, eds., *Self-control: Power to the person.* Belmont, Calif.: Brooks/Cole, 1974b. Pages 166–199.

Jeffrey, D. B. Some methodological issues in obesity research. *Psychological Reports* 35 (1974c): 623–626.

Jeffrey, D. B., and Christensen, E. R. The relative efficacy of behavior therapy, will power, and no-treatment control procedures on the modification of obesity. Paper presented at the annual meeting of the Association for Advancement of Behavior Therapy, New York, October 1972.

Jeffrey, D. B.; Christensen, E. R.; and Katz, R. C. Behavior therapy weight reduction programs: Some preliminary findings on the need for follow-ups. *Psychotherapy: Therapy, Research and Practice,* in press.

Jeffrey, D. B.; Christensen, E. R.; and Pappas, J. P. Developing a behavioral program and therapist manual for the treatment of obesity. *Journal of the American College Health Association* 21 (1973): 455–459.

Jenkins, W. O.; Witherspoon, A. D.; DeVine, M. D.; deValera, E. K.; Muller, J. B.; Barton, M. C.; and McKee, J. M. *The post-prison analysis of criminal behavior and longitudinal follow-up evaluation of institutional treatment.* Elmore, Ala.: Rehabilitation Research Foundation, 1974.

Johnson, M., and Bailey, J. S. Cross-age tutoring: Fifth graders as arithmetic tutors for kindergarten children. *Journal of Applied Behavior Analysis* 7 (1974): 223–232.

Johnson, W. G. Some applications of Homme's coverant control therapy: Two case reports. *Behavior Therapy* 2 (1971): 240–248.

Johnson, W. G., and Pollack, I. W. Efficiency and the delivery of mental health care. Unpublished paper, Rutgers Medical School, 1973.

Johnston, M. K.; Kelley, C. S.; Harris, F. R.; and Wolf, M. M. An application of reinforcement principles to development of motor skills of a young child. *Child Development* 37 (1966): 379–387.

Jones, H. G. The application of conditioning and learning techniques to the treatment of a psychiatric patient. *Journal of Abnormal and Social Psychology* 52 (1956): 414–420.

Jones, M. C. The elimination of children's fears. *Journal of Experimental Psychology* 7 (1924): 382–390.

Jones, W. P. Communes and Christian intentional community. *Christian Century* 90 (July 17, 1973): 73–75.

Kahn, M.; Baker, B.; and Weiss, J. M. Treatment of insomnia by relaxation training. *Journal of Abnormal Psychology* 73 (1968): 556–558.

Kanfer, F. H. Vicarious human reinforcements: A glimpse into the black box. In L. Krasner and L. P. Ullmann, eds., *Research in behavior modification.* New York: Holt, 1965. Pages 244–267.

Kanfer, F. H. Verbal conditioning: A review of its current status. In T. R. Dixon and D. L. Horton, eds., *Verbal behavior and general behavior theory.* Englewood Cliffs, N.J.: Prentice-Hall, 1968. Pages 254–290.

Kanfer, F. H. Self-regulation: Research, issues, and speculations. In C. Neuringer and J. L. Michael, eds., *Behavior modification in clinical psychology.* New York: Appleton, 1970. Pages 178–220.

Kanfer, F. H. The maintenance of behaviors by self-generated stimuli and reinforcement. In A. Jacobs and L. B. Sachs, eds., *The psychology of private events: Perspectives on covert response systems.* New York: Academic Press, 1971. Pages 39–59.

Kanfer, F. H. Behavior modification. A few opinions on critical issues. Paper presented at the meetings of the American Psychological Association, Montreal, September 1973.

Kanfer, F. H. Self-management techniques. In F. H. Kanfer and A. P. Goldstein, eds., *Helping people change.* New York: Pergamon, 1975.

Kanfer, F. H., and Karoly, P. Self-control: A behavioristic excursion into the lion's den. *Behavior Therapy* 3 (1972): 398–416.

Kanfer, F. H., and Phillips, J. S. A survey of current behavior therapies and a proposal for classification. In C. M. Franks, ed., *Behavior therapy: Appraisal and status.* New York: McGraw-Hill, 1969. Pages 445–475.

Kanfer, F. H., and Phillips, J. S. *Learning foundations of behavior therapy.* New York: Wiley, 1970.

Kanfer, F. H., and Saslow, G. Behavioral diagnosis. In C. M. Franks, ed., *Behavior therapy: Appraisal and status.* New York: McGraw-Hill, 1969. Pages 417–444.

Kanfer, F. H., and Zich, J. Self-control training: The effects of external control on children's resistance to temptation. *Developmental Psychology* 10 (1974): 108–115.

Kanno, C. K. *Eleven indices: An aid in reviewing state and local mental health and hospital programs.* Washington, D.C.: Joint Information Service, APA and NIMH, 1971.

Kant, F. The use of conditioned reflex in the treatment of alcohol addicts. *Wis-*

consin Medical Journal 44 (1945): 217–221.

Kanter, R. M. *Commitment and Community.* Cambridge, Mass.: Harvard, 1972.

Kantorovich, N. V. An attempt of curing alcoholism by associated reflexes. *Novoye Refleksologii Nervnoy i Fiziologii Sistemy* 3 (1928): 436–445. Cited by G. H. S. Razran. Conditioned withdrawal responses with shock as the conditioning stimulus in adult human subjects. *Psychological Bulletin* 31 (1934): 111–143.

Kaplan, H. S. *The new sex therapy: Active treatment of sexual dysfunctions.* New York: Brunner/Mazel, 1974.

Karlins, M., and Andrews, L. M. *Biofeedback: Turning on the power of your mind.* New York: Warner Books, 1973.

Katz, R. C. Single session recovery from a hemodialysis phobia: A case study. *Journal of Behavior Therapy and Experimental Psychiatry* 5 (1974): 205–206.

Katz, R. C., and Zlutnick, S. *Behavioral therapy and health care; principles and applications.* New York: Pergamon, 1974.

Kaufman, A.; Baron, A.; and Kopp, R. E. Some effects of instructions on human operant behavior. *Psychonomic Monograph Supplements* 1 (1966): 243–250.

Kaufman, K. F., and O'Leary, K. D. Reward, cost, and self-evaluation procedures for disruptive adolescents in a psychiatric hospital school. *Journal of Applied Behavior Analysis* 5 (1972): 293–309.

Kaufman, M. E. The effects of institutionalization on development of stereotyped and social behaviors in mental defectives. *American Journal of Mental Deficiency* 71 (1967): 581–585.

Kazdin, A. E. The failure of some patients to respond to token programs. *Behavior Therapy and Experimental Psychiatry* 4 (1973a): 7–14.

Kazdin, A. E. Methodological and assessment considerations in evaluating reinforcement programs in applied settings. *Journal of Applied Behavior Analysis* 6 (1973b): 517–531.

Kazdin, A. E. The effect of vicarious reinforcement on attentive behavior in the classroom. *Journal of Applied Behavior Analysis* 6 (1973c): 71–78.

Kazdin, A. E. Role of instructions and reinforcement in behavior changes in token reinforcement programs. *Journal of Educational Psychology* 64 (1973d): 63–71.

Kazdin, A. E. Effects of covert modeling and model reinforcement on assertive behavior. *Journal of Abnormal Psychology* 83 (1974a): 240–252.

Kazdin, A. E. Self-monitoring and behavior change. In M. J. Mahoney and C. E. Thoresen, eds., *Self-control: Power to the person.* Belmont, Calif.: Brooks/Cole, 1974b. Pages 218–246.

Kazdin, A. E. *Behavior modification in applied settings.* Homewood, Ill.: Dorsey, 1975a.

Kazdin, A. E. Recent advances in token economy research. In M. Hersen, R. M. Eisler, and P. M. Miller, eds., *Progress in behavior modification.* New York: Academic Press, 1975b.

Kazdin, A. E. Statistical analysis for single-case experimental designs. In

M. Hersen and D. Barlow, eds., *Strategies for studying behavior change.* New York: Pergamon Press, 1976.

Kazdin, A. E., and Bootzin, R. R. The token economy: An evaluative review. *Journal of Applied Behavior Analysis* 5 (1972): 343–372.

Kazdin, A. E., and Moyer, W. Training teachers to use behavior modification. In S. Yen and R. McIntire, eds., *Teaching behavior modification.* Kalamazoo, Mich.: Behaviordelia, in press.

Keller, F. S. Goodbye teacher. . . . *Journal of Applied Behavior Analysis* 1 (1968): 79–89.

Kelley, H. H., and Stahelski, A. J. Social interaction basis of cooperators' and competitors' beliefs about others. *Journal of Personality and Social Psychology* 16 (1970): 66–91.

Kelly, J. F., and Hake, D. F. An extinction induced increase in an aggressive response with humans. *Journal of the Experimental Analysis of Behavior* 14 (1970): 153–164.

Kendell, L. The role of the nurse in the treatment of the alcoholic patient. In R. Fox, ed., *Alcoholism: Behavioral research, therapeutic approaches.* New York: Springer, 1967. Pages 285–292.

Kent, R. N.; O'Leary, K. D.; Diament, C.; and Dietz, A. Expectation biases in observational evaluation of therapeutic change. *Journal of Consulting and Clinical Psychology* 42 (1974): 774–780.

Khan, A. U.; Staerk, M.; and Bonk, C. Role of counter-conditioning in the treatment of asthma. *Journal of Asthma Research* 11 (December 1973): 57–62.

Kiesler, D. J. Experimental designs in psychotherapy research. In A. E. Bergin and S. L. Garfield, eds., *Handbook of psychotherapy and behavior change.* New York: Wiley, 1971. Pages 36–74.

Kimble, G. A. *Hilgard and Marquis' conditioning and learning.* New York: Appleton-Century-Crofts, 1961.

Kimmel, H. D. Instrumental conditioning of autonomically mediated behavior. *Psychological Bulletin* 67 (1967): 337–345.

Kimmel, H. D. Instrumental conditioning of autonomically medicated responses in human beings. *American Psychologist* 29 (1974): 325–335.

Kincaid, K. *A Walden Two Experiment.* New York: Morrow, 1973.

Kinsman, R. A. Project Summary: Relaxation control in the treatment of asthma. *Progress Report,* NIMH Grant MH-20080, March 1972.

Kirigin, K. A.; Phillips, E. L.; Fixsen, D. L.; and Wolf, M. M. Modification of the homework behavior and academic performance of pre-delinquents with home-based reinforcement. Symposium on Behavior Analysis in Education, Lawrence, Kansas, 1971.

Kirkpatrick, R. A. Learning theory in the treatment of chronic disease. *Northwest Medicine* 71 (1972): 899–902.

Kissin, B., and Charnoff, M. Clinical evaluation of tranquilizers and antidepressant drugs in the long term treatment of chronic alcoholism. In R. Fox, ed., *Alcoholism: Behavioral research, therapeutic approaches.* New York: Springer, 1967. Pages 234–241.

Kleber, H. The New Haven methadone program. *International Journal of the Addictions* 5 (1970): 457–458.

Knapp, P. H.; Bliss, C. M.; and Wells, H. Addictive aspects in heavy cigarette smoking. *American Journal of Psychiatry* 119 (1963): 966–972.

Knecht v. *Gillman,* 488 F. 2d 1136 (8th Cir. 1973).

Knox, D., and Patrick, J. A. You are what you do: A new approach in preparation for marriage. *The Family Coordinator* 20 (1971): 109–114.

Koch, S. Psychology and emerging conceptions of knowledge as unitary. In T. W. Wann, ed., *Behaviorism and phenomenology.* Chicago: University of Chicago Press, 1964. Pages 1–41.

Kohlenberg, R. J. The punishment of persistent vomiting: A case study. *Journal of Applied Behavior Analysis* 3 (1970): 241–245.

Kohlenberg, R. J. Operant conditioning of human anal sphincter pressure. *Journal of Applied Behavior Analysis* 6 (1973): 201–208.

Kohlenberg, R. J. Treatment of a homosexual pedophiliac using *in vivo* desensitization: A case study. *Journal of Abnormal Psychology* 83 (1974): 192–195.

Kolvin, I. "Aversive imagery" treatment in adolescents. *Behaviour Research and Therapy* 5 (1967): 245–248.

Kondas, O. and Scetnicka, B. Systematic desensitization as a method of preparation for childbirth. *Journal of Behavior Therapy and Experimental Psychiatry* 3 (1972): 51–54.

Konorski, J. *Integrative activity of the brain.* Chicago: University of Chicago Press, 1967.

Kora, T. Morita therapy. *International Journal of Psychiatry* 1 (1965): 611–640.

Krasner, L. The therapist as a social reinforcement machine. In H. H. Strupp and L. Luborsky, eds., *Research in psychotherapy.* Vol. 2. Washington, D.C.: American Psychological Association, 1962.

Krasner, L. and Ullmann, L. P. *Behavior influence and personality: The social matrix of human action.* New York: Holt, 1973.

Krebs, D. L. Altruism—an examination of the concept and a review of the literature. *Psychological Bulletin* 73 (1970): 258–302.

Kubany, E. S.; Weiss, L. E.; and Sloggett, B. B. The good behavior clock: A reinforcement/time out procedure for reducing disruptive classroom behavior. *Journal of Behavior Therapy and Experimental Psychiatry* 2 (1971): 173–179.

Kuhn, T. S. *The structure of scientific revolutions.* Chicago: University of Chicago Press, 1962.

Kushner, M. The operant control of intractable sneezing. In C. D. Spielberger, R. Fox, and B. Masterton, eds., *Contributions to general psychology.* New York: Ronald Press, 1968. Pages 361–365.

Lacey, J. I. Psychophysiological approaches to the evaluation of psychotherapeutic process and outcome. In E. Rubinstein and M. B. Parloff, eds., *Research in psychotherapy.* Vol. 1. Washington, D.C.: National Pub. Co., 1959. Pages 160–208.

Lacey, J. I. Somatic response patterning and stress: Some revisions of activation theory. In M. H. Appley and R. Trumbull, eds., *Psychological stress: Issues in research.* New York: Appleton-Century-Crofts, 1967. Pages 14–42.

Lacey, J. I., and Lacey, B. B. Verification and extension of the principle of autonomic response stereotypy. *American Journal of Psychology* 71 (1968): 50–73.

Lader, M. H., and Mathews, A. M. A physiological model of phobic anxiety and desensitization. *Behaviour Research and Therapy* 6 (1968): 411–421.

Lal, H., and Lindsley, O. Therapy of chronic constipation in young child by rearranging social contingencies. *Behaviour Research and Therapy* 6 (1968): 484–485.

Lamontagne, Y., and Marks, I. M. Psychogenic urinary retention: Treatment by prolonged exposure. *Behavior Therapy* 4 (1973): 581–585.

Lando, H. A comparison of excessive and rapid smoking in the modification of chronic smoking behavior. *Journal of Consulting and Clinical Psychology* 43 (1975): 350–355.

Lanes, S. G. Communes: A firsthand report on a controversial life-style. *Parents Magazine* 46 (1971): 61–118.

Lang, P. J. Fear reduction and fear behavior: Problems in treating a construct. In J. M. Shlien, ed., *Research in psychotherapy.* Vol. 3. Washington, D.C.: American Psychological Association, 1968. Pages 90–102.

Lang, P. J. The mechanics of desensitization and the laboratory study of human fear. In C. M. Franks, ed., *Behavior therapy: Appraisal and status.* New York: McGraw-Hill, 1969a. Pages 160–191.

Lang, P. J. The on-line computer in behavior therapy research. *American Psychologist* 24 (1969b): 236–239.

Lang, P. J., and Melamed, B. C. Case report: Avoidance conditioning therapy of an infant with chronic ruminative vomiting. *Journal of Abnormal Psychology* 74 (1969): 1–8.

Lanyon, R. I., and Goodstein, L. D. *Personality assessment.* New York: Wiley, 1971.

Layton, M. M. Behavior therapy and implications for psychiatric nursing. *Perspective Psychiatric Care* 4 (1966): 38–52.

Lazarus, A. A. Behavior therapy and marriage counseling. *Journal of the American Society of Psychosomatic Dentistry and Medicine* 15 (1968a): 49–56.

Lazarus, A. A. Learning theory and the treatment of depression. *Behaviour Research and Therapy* 6 (1968b): 83–89.

Lazarus, A. A. *Behavior therapy and beyond.* New York: McGraw-Hill, 1971.

Lazarus, A. A. *Clinical behavior therapy.* New York: Brunner/Mazel, 1972.

Lazarus, A. A. Multimodal behavioral treatment of depression. *Behavior Therapy* 5 (1974): 549–554.

Lear, M. W. All the warnings gone up in smoke. *The New York Times Magazine* (March 1, 1974): 18–19, 21, 90–91.

LeBow, M. D. *Behavior modification: A significant method in nursing practice.* Englewood Cliffs, N.J.: Prentice-Hall, 1973.

Lefcourt, H. M. The function of the illusions of control and freedom. *American Psychologist* 28 (1973): 417–425.

Lemere, F., and Voegtlin, W. L. An evaluation of the aversion treatment of alcoholism. *Quarterly Journal of Studies on Alcohol* 11 (1950): 199–204.

Lemere, F.; Voegtlin, W. L.; Broz, W. R.; O'Halleren, P ; and Tupper, W. E. Conditioned reflex treatment of chronic alcoholism: II. Technic. *Diseases of the Nervous System* 3 (1942): 243–247.

Lesser, R. Behavior therapy with a narcotics user: A case study. *Behaviour Research and Therapy* 5 (1967): 251–252.

Levine, J., and Zigler, E. The essential-reactive distinction in alcoholism: A developmental approach. *Journal of Abnormal Psychology* 81 (1973): 242–249.

Levinson, B. L.; Shapiro, D.; Schwartz, G. E.; and Tursky, B. Smoking elimination by gradual reduction. *Behavior Therapy* 2 (1971): 477–487.

Levis, D. J. Implosive therapy: A critical analysis of Morganstern's review. *Psychological Bulletin* 81 (1974): 155–158.

Levitt, E. E. The results of psychotherapy with children: An evaluation. *Journal of Consulting Psychology* 21 (1957): 189–196.

Levitt, E. E. *The psychology of anxiety.* New York: Bobbs-Merrill, 1967.

Levitt, E. E. Research on psychotherapy with children. In A. E. Bergin and S. L. Garfield, eds., *Handbook of psychotherapy and behavior change: An empirical analysis.* New York: Wiley, 1971. Pages 474–494.

Lewinsohn, P. M. The behavioral study and treatment of depression. In M. Hersen; R. M. Eisler; and P. M. Miller, eds., *Progress in behavior modification.* Volume I. New York: Academic Press, 1974.

Lewinsohn, P. M. Clinical and theoretical aspects of depression. In K. S. Calhoun; H. E. Adams; and K. M. Mitchell, eds., *Innovative treatment methods in psychopathology.* New York: Wiley, 1974.

Lewinsohn, P. M., and Atwood, G. E. Depression: A clinical-research approach, the case of Mrs. G. *Psychotherapy: Theory, Research, and Practice* 6 (1969): 166–171.

Lewinsohn, P. M., and Graf, M. Pleasant activities and depression. *Journal of Consulting and Clinical Psychology* 41 (1973): 261–268.

Lewinsohn, P. M., and Libet, J. Pleasant events, activity schedules, and depressions. *Journal of Abnormal Psychology* 79 (1972): 291–295.

Lewinsohn, P. M., and Shaffer, M. Use of home observations as an integral part of the treatment of depression: Preliminary report and case studies. *Journal of Consulting and Clinical Psychology* 37 (1971): 87–94.

Lewinsohn, P. M., and Shaw, D. A. Feedback about interpersonal behavior as an agent of behavior change: A case study in the treatment of depression. *Psychotherapy and Psychosomatics* 17 (1969): 82–88.

Lewinsohn, P. M.; Weinstein, M. S.; and Alper, T. A behavioral approach to the group treatment of depressed persons: A methodological contribution. *Journal of Clinical Psychology* 26 (1970): 525–532.

Lewinsohn, P. M.; Weinstein, M. S.; and Shaw, D. A. Depression: A clinical-research approach. In R. D. Rubin and C. M. Franks, eds., *Advances in behavior therapy, 1968*. New York: Academic Press, 1969. Pages 231–240.

Liberman, R. Aversive conditioning of drug addicts: A pilot study. *Behaviour Research and Therapy* 6 (1968): 229–231.

Liberman, R. Behavioral approaches to family and couple therapy. *American Journal of Orthopsychiatry* 40 (1970): 106–118.

Liberman, R. P. Behavioral modification of schizophrenia: A review. *Schizophrenia Bulletin* No. 6. Rockville, Maryland: NIMH, 1972. Pages 37–48.

Liberman, R. P., and Raskin, D. E. Depression: A behavioral formulation. *Archives of General Psychiatry* 24 (1971): 515–523.

Libet, J. M., and Lewinsohn, P. M. Concept of social skill with special reference to the behavior of depressed persons. *Journal of Consulting and Clinical Psychology* 40 (1973): 304–312.

Lichtenstein, E.; Harris, D. E.; Birchler, G. R.; Wahl, J. M.; and Schmahl, D. P. Comparison of rapid smoking, warm, smoky air, and attention placebo in the modification of smoking behavior. *Journal of Consulting and Clinical Psychology* 40 (1973): 92–98.

Lieberman, M. A. Group methods. In F. H. Kanfer and A. P. Goldstein, eds., *Helping people change.* New York: Pergamon, 1975.

Lifton, R. J. Home by ship: Reaction patterns of American prisoners of war repatriated from North Korea. *American Journal of Psychiatry* 110 (1954): 732–739.

Lipe, D., and Jung, S. M. Manipulating incentives to enhance school learning. *Review of Educational Research* 41 (1971): 249–280.

Loeb, A.; Beck, A. T.; Diggory, J. C.; and Tuthill, R. Expectancy, level of aspiration, performance, and self-evaluation in depression. *Proceedings, 75th Annual Convention of the American Psychological Association.* (1967): 193–194.

Loeb, A.; Feshback, S.; Beck, A. T.; and Wolf, A. Some effects of reward upon the social perception and motivation of psychiatric patients varying in depression. *Journal of Abnormal and Social Psychology* 68 (1964): 609–616.

Logan, F. A. *Fundamentals of learning and motivation.* Dubuque, Iowa: William C. Brown, 1969.

Lomont, J. F., and Brock, L. Cognitive factors in systematic desensitization. *Behaviour Research and Therapy* 9 (1971): 187–195.

London, P. *The modes and morals of psychotherapy.* New York: Holt, 1964.

London, P. *Behavior control.* New York: Harper & Row, 1969.

LoPiccolo, J. A behavioral approach to sexuality: I. Sexual dysfunction; II. Promoting sexual growth in non-dysfunctional couples. Workshop presented at the meetings of the Association for Advancement of Behavior Therapy, Chicago, November 1974.

Lovaas, O. I.; Schaeffer, B.; and Simmons, J. Q. Building social behavior in autistic children by use of electric shock. *Journal of Experimental Research in Personality* 1 (1965): 99–109.

Lovitt, T. C., and Curtiss, K. A. Academic response rate as a function of teacher- and self-imposed contingencies. *Journal of Applied Behavior Analysis* 2 (1969): 49–53.

Lubin, B. Adjective checklists for the measurement of depression. *Archives of General Psychiatry* 12 (1965): 57–62.

Luborsky, L. The latest work on comparative studies. Paper read at the Society for Psychotherapy Research Meeting, Denver, 1974.

Luckey, R. E.; Watson, C. M.; and Mussick, J. K. Aversive conditioning as a means of inhibiting vomiting and rumination. *American Journal of Mental Deficiency* 73 (1968): 139–142.

Lutker, E. R. Treatment of migraine headache by conditioned relaxation: A case study. *Behavior Therapy* 2 (1971): 592–593.

Lykken, D. Statistical significance in psychological research. *Psychological Bulletin* 70 (1968): 151–159.

Lynch, J. J.; Thomas, S. A.; Mills, M. E.; Malinow, K.; and Katcher, A. H. The effects of human contact on cardiac arrhythmia in coronary care patients. *Journal of Nervous and Mental Disease* 158 (1974): 88–99.

MacCorquodale, K., and Meehl, P. E. On a distinction between hypothetical constructs and intervening variables. *Psychological Review* 55 (1948): 95–107.

MacDonald, M. L.; Lindquist, C. U.; Kramer, J. A.; McGrath, R. A.; and Rhyne, L. L. Social skills training: The effects of behavior rehearsal in groups on dating skills. Unpublished manuscript, 1973.

Mackey v. *Procunier,* 477 F. 2d 877 (9th Cir. 1973).

MacPherson, E. L. R. Control of involuntary movement. *Behaviour Research and Therapy* 5 (1967): 143–145.

MacPherson, E. L. R. Selective operant conditioning and deconditioning of assertive modes of behaviour. *Journal of Behavior Therapy and Experimental Psychiatry* 3 (1972): 99–102.

Madsen, C. H.; Becker, W. C.; and Thomas, D. R. Rules, praise, and ignoring: Elements of elementary classroom control. *Journal of Applied Behavior Analysis* 1 (1968): 139–150.

Madsen, C. H.; Becker, W. C.; Thomas, D. R.; Koser, L.; and Plager, E. An analysis of the reinforcing function of "sit down" commands. In R. K. Parker, ed., *Readings in educational psychology.* Boston: Allyn and Bacon, 1970. Pages 265–278.

Madsen, C. H., Jr., and Madsen, C. K. *Teaching/discipline: A positive approach for educational development.* Boston: Allyn and Bacon, 1974.

Mahoney, M. J. Toward an experimental analysis of coverant control. *Behavior Therapy* 1 (1970): 510–521.

Mahoney, M. J. The self-management of covert behavior: A case study. *Behavior Therapy* 2 (1971): 575–578.

Mahoney, M. J. Research issues in self-management. *Behavior Therapy* 3 (1972): 45–63.

Mahoney, M. J. Clinical issues in self-control training. Paper presented at the American Psychological Association, Montreal, August 1973.

Mahoney, M. J. *Cognition and behavior modification.* Cambridge, Mass.: Ballinger, 1974a.

Mahoney, M. J. Self-reward and self-monitoring techniques for weight control. *Behavior Therapy* 5 (1974b): 48–57.

Mahoney, M. J. The sensitive scientist in empirical humanism. *American Psychologist,* in press.

Mahoney, M. J., and Jeffrey, D. A manual of behavioral self-control procedures for the overweight. *Journal of Selected Documents in Psychology,* 1974.

Mahoney, M. J.; Kazdin, A. E.; and Lesswing, W. J. Behavior modification: Delusion or deliverance? In C. M. Franks and G. T. Wilson, eds., *Annual review of behavior therapy: Theory and practice.* Vol. 2. New York: Brunner/Mazel, 1974. Pages 11–40.

Mahoney, M. J., and Mahoney, B. K. *Permanent weight control.* New York: Norton, 1976.

Mahoney, M. J.; Moura, N. G.; and Wade, T. C. Relative efficacy of self-reward, self-punishment, and self-monitoring techniques for weight loss. *Journal of Consulting and Clinical Psychology* 40 (1973): 404–407.

Mahoney, M. J., and Thoresen, C. E. *Self-control: Power to the person.* Belmont, Calif.: Brooks/Cole, 1974.

Malament, I. B.; Dunn, M. E.; and Davis, R. Pressure sores: An operant conditioning approach to prevention. *Archives of Physical Medicine and Rehabilitation,* in press.

Mann, R. A. The behavior-therapeutic use of contingency contracting to control an adult behavior problem: weight control. *Journal of Applied Behavior Analysis* 5 (1972): 99–109.

Marlatt, G. A.; Demming, B.; and Reid, J. B. Loss of control drinking in alcoholics: An experimental analogue. *Journal of Abnormal Psychology* 81 (1973): 233–241.

Marston, A. Personality variables related to self-reinforcement. *Journal of Psychology* 58 (1964): 169–175.

Marston, A. R., and McFall, R. M. Comparison of behavior modification approaches to smoking reduction. *Journal of Consulting and Clinical Psychology* 36 (1971): 153–162.

Martin, G.; England, G.; Kaprowy, E.; Kilgour, K; and Pilek, V. Operant conditioning of kindergarten-class behavior in autistic children. *Behaviour Research and Therapy* 6 (1968a): 281–294.

Martin, M.; Burkholder, R.; Rosenthal, T.; Tharp, R.; and Thorne, G. Programming behavior change and reintegration into school milieux of extreme adolescent deviates. *Behaviour Research and Therapy* 6 (1968b): 371–383.

Martin, M. L.; Weinstein, M.; and Lewinsohn, P. M. The use of home observations as an integral part of the treatment of depression. The case of Mrs. B. Unpublished manuscript, University of Oregon, 1968.

Martinson, W. D., and Zerface, J. P. Comparison of individual counseling and a social program with nondaters. *Journal of Counseling Psychology* 17 (1970): 36–40.

Marx, M., ed., *Psychological theory.* New York: Macmillan, 1951.

Maslow, A. H. *The psychology of science: A reconnaissance.* Chicago: Henry Regnery, 1966.

Masserman, J. H. *Behavior and neurosis.* Chicago: University of Chicago Press, 1943.

Masserman, J. H., and Yum, K. S. An analysis of the influence of alcohol on experimental neurosis in cats. *Psychosomatic Medicine* 8 (1946): 36–52.

Massie, H. N., and Beels, C. C. The outcome of family treatment of schizophrenia. *Schizophrenia Bulletin,* No. 6. Rockville, Md.: NIMH, 1972. Pages 24–36.

Masters, W. H., and Johnson, V. E. *Human sexual response.* Boston: Little, Brown, 1966.

Masters, W. H., and Johnson, V. E. *Human sexual inadequacy.* Boston: Little, Brown, 1970.

Matson, F. W. Matson replies to Skinner. *Humanist* 31 (1971): 2.

Mattocks, A. L., and Jew, C. C. Assessment of an aversion treatment program with extreme acting-out patients in a psychiatric facility for criminal offenders. Unpublished report, California Medical Facility, Vacaville, undated. On file with the University of Southern California Law Library, Los Angeles, California.

Mausner, B., and Platt, E. S. *Smoking: A behavioral analysis.* New York: Pergamon, 1971.

Max, L. W. Breaking up a homosexual fixation by the conditioned reaction technique: A case study. *Psychological Bulletin* 32 (1935a): 734 (abstract).

Max, L. W. An experimental study of the motor theory of consciousness: II. Action-current responses in deaf mutes during sleep, sensory stimulation and dreams. *Journal of Comparative Psychology* 19 (1935b): 469–486.

Max, L. W. Experimental study of the motor theory of consciousness: IV. Action-current responses in the deaf during awakening, kinaesthetic imagery, and abstract thinking. *Journal of Comparative Psychology* 24 (1937): 301–344.

McConnell, J. V. Criminals can be brainwashed—now. *Psychology Today* 3, no. 11 (1970): 14–18, 74.

McConnell, J. V. Letter-to-the-editor. *APA Monitor* 5, no. 8 (1974a): 2–3.

McConnell, J. V. *Understanding human behavior.* New York: Holt, 1974b.

McCord, W., and McCord, J. *Origins of alcoholism.* Stanford, Calif.: Stanford, 1960.

McCray v. *Maryland,* Misc. Pet. No. 4363, Montgomery City, Maryland District Court, 1971 (excerpted in 40 U.S. L.W. 2307).

McDonald, L., and Miles, D. G. *Evaluation of work as therapy for psychiatric patients.* Denver, Col.: Fort Logan Mental Health Center, 1969.

McFall, R. M., and Hammen, C. L. Motivation, structure, and self-monitoring: Role of nonspecific factors in smoking reduction. *Journal of Consulting and Clinical Psychology* 37 (1971): 80–86.

McFall, R. M., and Lillesand, D. B. Behavior rehearsal with modeling and coaching in assertion training. *Journal of Abnormal Psychology* 77 (1971): 313–323.

McFall, R. M., and Marston, A. R. An experimental investigation of behavior rehearsal in assertive training. *Journal of Abnormal Psychology* 76 (1970): 295–303.

McFall, R. M., and Twentyman, C. T. Four experiments on the relative contributions of rehearsal, modeling, and coaching to assertion training. *Journal of Abnormal Psychology* 81 (1973): 199–218.

McGlynn, F. D.; Mealiea, W. L.; and Nawas, M. M. Systematic desensitization of snake-avoidance under two conditions of suggestion. *Psychological Reports* 25 (1969): 220–222.

McKee, J. M. The use of programmed instruction in correctional institutions. *Journal of Correctional Education* 22, no. 4 (1970): 8–12, 28–30.

McKee, J. M. Contingency management in a correctional institution. *Educational Technology* 11, no. 4 (1971): 51–54.

McKee, J. M.; Smith, R. R.; Wood, L. F.; and Milan, M. Selecting and implementing an intervention approach that employs correctional officers as behavior change agents. In M. A. Bernal, ed., *Training in behavior modification.* Belmont, Calif.: Brooks/Cole, in press.

McLaughlin, T., and Malaby, J. Reducing and measuring inappropriate verbalizations in a token classroom. *Journal of Applied Behavior Analysis* 5 (1972): 329–333.

McLean, P. D.; Ogston, K.; and Grauer, L. A behavioral approach to the treatment of depression. *Journal of Behavior Therapy and Experimental Psychiatry* 4 (1973): 323–330.

McMichael, J. S., and Corey, J. R. Contingency management in an introductory psychology course produces better learning. *Journal of Applied Behavior Analysis* 2 (1969): 79–83.

McReynolds, W. T. A comparison of stimulus control and behavior control treatments of obesity. Unpublished report, University of Missouri, 1973.

Meares, R. A. Behavior therapy and spasmodic torticollis. *Archives of General Psychiatry* 28 (1973): 104–107.

Meichenbaum, D. Cognitive factors in behavior modification: Modifying what people say to themselves. Paper presented at the Fifth Annual Meeting of the Association for the Advancement of Behavior Therapy, Washington, D.C., 1971a.

Meichenbaum, D. H. Examination of model characteristics in reducing avoidance behavior. *Journal of Personality and Social Psychology* 17 (1971b): 298–307.

Meichenbaum, D. Cognitive modification of test anxious college students. *Journal of Consulting and Clinical Psychology* 39 (1972): 370–380.

Meichenbaum, D. Cognitive factors in behavior modification: Modifying what clients say to themselves. In C. M. Franks and G. T. Wilson, eds., *Annual review of behavior therapy, theory and practice.* Vol. 1. New York: Brunner/Mazel, 1973. Pages 416–431.

Meichenbaum, D. *Cognitive behavior modification.* Morristown, N.J.: General Learning Press, 1974.

Meichenbaum, D. H.; Bowers, K.; and Ross, R. Modification of classroom behavior of institutionalized female adolescent offenders. *Behaviour Research and Therapy* 6 (1968): 343–353.

Meichenbaum, D. H., and Cameron, R. Training schizophrenics to talk to themselves: A means of developing attentional controls. *Behavior Therapy* 4 (1973): 515–534.

Meichenbaum, D. H., and Goodman, J. Training impulsive children to talk to themselves: A means of developing self-control. *Journal of Abnormal Psychology* 77 (1971): 115–126.

Mello, N. K., and Mendelson, J. H. Operant analysis of drinking patterns of chronic alcoholics. *Nature* 206 (1965): 43–46.

Mellville, K. *Communes in the counter-culture.* New York: Morrow, 1972.

Melton, L. H. The effects of sensitivity and assertive training upon the performance of nursing students. Unpublished master's thesis, University of North Carolina, 1973.

Meltzoff, J., and Kornreich, M. *Research in psychotherapy.* New York: Atherton, 1970.

Mendels, J. *Concepts of depression.* New York: Wiley, 1970.

Merbaum, M., and Lukens, H. C., Jr. Effects of instructions, elicitations, and reinforcements in the manipulation of affective verbal behavior. *Journal of Abnormal Psychology* 73 (1968): 376–380.

Meyer, A. S.; Friedman, L. N.; and Lazarsfeld, P. F. Motivational conflicts engendered by the on-going discussion of cigarette smoking. In W. L. Dunn, Jr., ed., *Smoking behavior: Motives and incentives.* New York: Wiley, 1973. Pages 243–254.

Meyer, V., and Crisp, A. H. Aversion therapy in two cases of obesity. *Behaviour Research and Therapy* 2 (1964): 143–147.

Meyers, A. W.; Craighead, W. E.; and Meyers, H. H. A behavioral approach to community mental health. *American Journal of Community Mental Health* 2 (1974): 275–285.

Meyers, A. W.; Farr, J. H.; and Craighead, W. E. Eliminating female orgasmic dysfunction with sexual reeducation. In J. D. Krumboltz and C. E. Thoresen, eds., *Behavioral counseling methods.* New York: Holt, in press.

Meyerson, L.; Kerr, N.; and Michael, J. L. Behavior modification in rehabilitation. In S. W. Bijou and D. M. Baer, eds., *Child development: Readings in experimental analysis.* New York: Appleton-Century-Crofts, 1967. Pages 214–239.

Michael, J. L. Rehabilitation. In C. Neuringer and J. L. Michael, eds., *Behavior modification in clinical psychology.* New York: Appleton-Century-Crofts, 1970. Pages 52–85.

Michael, J. Statistical inference for individual organism research: Mixed blessing or curse? *Journal of Applied Behavior Analysis* 7 (1974): 647–653.

Mikulic, M. A. Reinforcement of independent and dependent patient behaviors by nursing personnel: An exploratory study. *Nursing Research* 20 (1971): 162–165.

Milan, M. A. *An ecological experiment in corrections: A programmed environment for behavior modification.* Elmore, Ala.: Rehabilitation Research Foundation, 1971.

Milan, M. A., and McKee, J. M. Behavior modification: Principles and applications in corrections. In D. Glaser, ed., *Handbook of criminology.* Chicago: Rand McNally, 1974. Pages 745–776.

Milan, M. A.; Wood, L. F.; Williams, R. L.; Rogers, J. G.; Hampton, L. R.; and McKee, J. M. *Applied behavior analysis and the Important Adult Felon Project I: The cellblock token economy.* Elmore, Ala.: Rehabilitation Research Foundation, 1974.

Miller, L. K. *Principles of everyday behavior analysis.* Belmont, Calif.: Brooks/Cole, 1974.

Miller, L. K., and Feallock, F. A behavioral system for group living. In E. Ramp and G. Semb, eds., *Behavior analysis and education—1973.* Englewood Cliffs, N.J.: Prentice-Hall, in press.

Miller, L. K., and Lies, A. A. Everyday behavior analysis: A new direction for applied behavior analysis. *Behavior Voice* 2, no. 1 (1974): 5–13.

Miller, L. K.; Lies, A. A.; Paterson, D. L.; and Feallock, R. The positive community: A strategy for applying behavioral engineering to the redesign of family and community. In L. A. Hamerlynck; L. C. Handy; and E. J. Marsh, eds., *Parenting: The change, maintenance, and directions for healthy family behaviors,* in press.

Miller, L. K., and Weaver, F. G. The use of "concept programming" to teach behavioral concepts to university students. In J. Johnston, ed., *Behavior research and technology in higher education.* Springfield, Ill.: Charles C Thomas, 1974.

Miller, M. M. Treatment of chronic alcoholism by hypnotic aversion. *Journal of the American Medical Association* 171 (1959): 1492–1495.

Miller, N. Biofeedback: Evaluation of a new technique. *New England Journal of Medicine* 290 (1974): 684–685.

Miller, P. M. The use of behavioral contracting in the treatment of alcoholism: A case study. *Behavior Therapy* 3 (1972): 593–596.

Miller, P. M. Behavioral assessment in alcoholism research and treatment: Current techniques. *International Journal of the Addictions* 8 (1973a): 831–837.

Miller, P. M. Behavioral treatment of drug addiction: A review. *International Journal of the Addictions* 8 (1973b): 511–519.

Miller, P. M. A behavioral intervention program for the chronic public drunkenness offender. Paper presented at the meetings of the Association for Advancement of Behavior Therapy, Chicago, November 1974.

Miller, P. M., and Barlow, D. H. Behavioral approaches to the treatment of alcoholism. *Journal of Nervous and Mental Disease* 157 (1973): 10–20.

Miller, P. M., and Hersen, M. Quantitative changes in alcohol consumption as a function of electrical aversive conditioning. *Journal of Clinical Psychology* 28 (1972): 590–593.

Miller, P. M.; Hersen, M.; and Eisler, R. M. Relative effectiveness of instructions, agreements, and reinforcement in behavioral contracts with alcoholics. *Journal of Abnormal Psychology,* in press.

Miller, P. M.; Hersen, M.; Eisler, R. M.; and Elkin, T. E. A retrospective analysis of alcohol consumption on laboratory tasks as related to therapeutic outcome. *Behaviour Research and Therapy* 12 (1974): 73–76.

Miller, P. M.; Hersen, M.; Eisler, R. M.; Epstein, L. H.; and Woote, L. S. Relationship of alcohol cues to the drinking behavior of alcoholics and social drinkers: An analogue study. *Psychological Record* 24 (1974): 61–66.

Miller, P. M.; Hersen, M.; Eisler, R. M.; and Hemphill, D. P. Electrical aversion therapy with alcoholics: An analogue study. *Behaviour Research and Therapy* 11 (1973): 491–497.

Miller, P. M.; Hersen, M.; Eisler, R. M.; and Hilsman, G. Effects of social stress on operant drinking of alcoholics and social drinkers. *Behaviour Research and Therapy* 12 (1974): 67–72.

Miller, P. M.; Hersen, M.; Eisler, R. M.; and Watts, J. G. Contingent reinforcement of lowered blood/alcohol levels in an outpatient chronic alcoholic. *Behaviour Research and Therapy,* in press.

Miller, P. M.; Stanford, A. G.; and Hemphill, D. P. A social-learning approach to alcoholism treatment. *Social Casework* 55 (1974): 279–284.

Miller, S. B. The contribution of therapeutic instructions to systematic desensitization. *Behaviour Research and Therapy* 10 (1972): 159–169.

Miller, W. R., and Seligman, M. E. P. Depression and the perception of reinforcement. *Journal of Abnormal Psychology* 82 (1973): 62–73.

Mills, K. C.; Sobell, M. B.; and Schaefer, H. H. Training social drinking as an alternative to abstinence for alcoholics. *Behavior Therapy* 2 (1971): 18–27.

Mischel, W. *Personality and assessment.* New York: Wiley, 1968.

Mischel, W. *Introduction to personality.* New York: Holt, 1971.

Mitchell, K. R. The treatment of migraine: An exploratory application of time limited behavior therapy. *Technology* 14 (1969): 50.

Mitchell, K. R., and Mitchell, D. M. Migraine: An exploratory treatment application of programmed behavior therapy techniques. *Journal of Psychosomatic Research* 15 (1971): 137–157.

Mitford, J. *Kind and usual punishment.* New York: Random House, 1973.

Monahan, J., and O'Leary, K. D. Effects of self-instruction on rule-breaking behavior. *Psychological Reports* 29 (1971): 1059–1066.

Monroe, J. J.; Ross, W. F.; and Berzins, J. I. The decline of the addict as "psychopath": Implications for community care. *International Journal of the Addictions* 6 (1971): 601–608.

Moore, N. Behavior therapy in bronchial asthma: A controlled study. *Journal of Psychosomatic Research* 9 (1965): 257–276.

Moorefield, C. W. The use of hypnosis and behavior therapy in asthma. *American Journal of Clinical Hypnosis* 13 (1971): 162–168.

Moos, R. H. The assessment of the social climates of correctional institutions. *Journal of Research in Crime and Delinquency* 5 (1968): 174–188.

Moos, R. H. Sources of variance in response to questionnaires and in behavior. *Journal of Abnormal Psychology* 74 (1969): 405–412.

Moos, R. H. Assessment of the psychosocial environments of community-oriented psychiatric treatment programs. *Journal of Abnormal Psychology* 79 (1972): 9–18.

Moos, R. H. Conceptualization of human environments. *American Psychologist* 28 (1973): 652–665.

Moos, R. H., and Insel, P. M. *Issues in social ecology: Human milieus.* Palo Alto: National Press Books, 1974.

Morgan, A. E. *The community of the future.* Ann Arbor: Braun-Brumfield, 1957.

Morgan, J., and O'Brien, J. S. The counterconditioning of a vomiting habit by sips of gingerale. *Journal of Behavior Therapy and Experimental Psychiatry* 3 (1972): 135–137.

Morgan, W. G. Nonnecessary conditions or useful procedures in desensitization: A reply to Wilkins. *Psychological Bulletin* 79 (1973): 373–375.

Morganstern, K. P. Implosive therapy and flooding procedures: A critical review. *Psychological Bulletin* 79 (1973): 318–334.

Morganstern, K. P. Cigarette smoke as a noxious stimulus in self-managed aversion therapy for compulsive eating: Technique and case illustration. *Behavior Therapy* 5 (1974): 255–260.

Morris, N., and Hawkins, G. *The honest politician's guide to crime control.* Chicago: University of Chicago Press, 1970.

Morrison, J. B., and Beck, A. T. The efficacy of anti-depressant drugs: A review of research (1958–1972). *Archives of General Psychiatry* 30 (1974): 667–674.

Mosher, L. R., and Feinsilver, D. *Special report: Schizophrenia.* Rockville, Md.: NIMH Center for Studies of Schizophrenia, 1971.

Mowrer, O. H. A stimulus-response analysis of anxiety and its role as a reinforcing agent. *Psychological Review* 46 (1939): 553–565.

Mowrer, O. H. *Learning theory and the symbolic processes.* New York: Wiley, 1960.

Mullen, F. G. The treatment of a case of dysmenorrhea by behavior therapy techniques. *Journal of Nervous and Mental Disease* 147 (1968): 371–376.

Mullen, F. G. Treatment of dysmenorrhea by professional and student behavior therapists. Paper presented at Fifth Annual Meeting of the Association for the Advancement of Behavior Therapy, Washington, D.C., 1971.

Munford, P. R.; Reardon, D.; Liberman, R. P.; and Allen, L. Contingency management of chronic coughing and aphonia. Paper presented at the 82nd Annual Convention of the American Psychological Association, New Orleans, 1974.

Murphy, C. V., and Mikulas, W. L. Behavioral features and deficiencies of the Masters and Johnson program. *Psychological Record* 24 (1974): 221–227.

Murten, T. Too good for Arkansas. In B. M. Atkins and H. R. Glick, eds., *Prisons, protests, and politics.* Englewood Cliffs, N.J.: Prentice-Hall, 1972. Pages 168–180.

Narrol, H. G. Experimental application of reinforcement principles to the analysis and treatment of hospitalized alcoholics. *Quarterly Journal of Studies on Alcohol* 28 (1967): 105–115.

Nash, J. L. Behavior therapy in an army mental hygiene clinic: Deconditioning of a phobia: A case report. *Military Medicine* 136 (1971): 639.

Nathan, P. E., and O'Brien, J. S. An experimental analysis of the behavior of alcoholics and non-alcoholics during prolonged experimental drinking. *Behavior Therapy* 2 (1971): 455–476.

Nathan, P. E.; Titler, N. A.; Lowenstein, L. M.; Soloman, P.; and Rossi, A. M. Behavioral analysis of chronic alcoholism. *Archives of General Psychiatry* 22 (1970): 419–430.

National Advisory Commission on Criminal Justice Standards and Goals. *Corrections.* Washington, D.C.: U.S. Government Printing Office, 1973.

National Institute of Mental Health, *Mental Health Information Publication No. 5027,* Rockville, Md., 1970.

National Institute of Mental Health, Mental Health Statistics. *Residential treatment centers for emotionally disturbed children 1969–1970.* Rockville, Md.: Series A, No. 6, 1971.

Neher, A. Probability pyramiding, research error and the need for independent replication. *Psychological Record* 17 (1967): 257–262.

Neisworth, J. T., and Moore, F. Operant treatment of asthmatic responding with the parent as therapist. *Behavior Therapy* 3 (1972): 95–99.

Nicassio, P., and Bootzin, R. A comparison of progressive relaxation and autogenic training as treatments for insomnia. *Journal of Abnormal Psychology* 83 (1974): 253–260.

Nimmer, W. H., and Kapp, R. A. A multiple impact program for the treatment of injection phobias. *Journal of Behavior Therapy and Experimental Psychiatry* 5 (1974): 257–258.

Nisbett, R. E., and Schachter, S. Cognitive manipulation of pain. *Journal of Experimental Social Psychology* 2 (1966): 227–236.

Nolan, J. D. Self-control procedures in the modification of smoking behavior. *Journal of Consulting and Clinical Psychology* 32 (1968): 92–93.

Nolan, J. D.; Mattis, P. R.; and Holliday, W. C. Long-term effects of behavior therapy: A 12-month follow-up. *Journal of Abnormal Psychology* 76 (1970): 88–92.

Nolen, P. A.; Kunzelmann, H. P.; and Haring, N. G. Behavioral modification in a junior high learning disabilities classroom. *Exceptional Children* 34 (1967): 163–168.

Notterman, J. M.; Schoenfeld, W. N.; and Bersh, P. J. A comparison of three extinction procedures following heart rate conditioning. *Journal of Abnormal and Social Psychology* 47 (1962): 674–677.

Nunnally, J. C., Jr. *Popular conceptions of mental health.* New York: Holt, 1961.

Nutter, R. W.; Gruise, D. G.; Spreng, L. F.; Weckowicz, T. E.; and Yonge, K. A. Effect of monetary incentive on concept attainment in depressed subjects. *Canadian Psychiatric Association Journal* 18 (1973): 13–20.

Ober, D. C. Modification of smoking behavior. *Journal of Consulting and Clinical Psychology* 32 (1968): 543–549.

O'Brien, F., and Azrin, N. H. Behavioral engineering: Control of posture by informational feedback. *Journal of Applied Behavior Analysis* 3 (1970): 235–240.

O'Leary, K. D. The effects of self-instruction on immoral behavior. *Journal of Experimental Child Psychology* 6 (1968): 297–301.

O'Leary, K. D. Behavior modification in the classroom: A rejoinder to Winett and Winkler. *Journal of Applied Behavior Analysis* 5 (1972): 505–511.

O'Leary, K. D., and Becker, W. C. Behavior modification of an adjustment class: A token reinforcement program. *Exceptional Children* 33 (1967): 637–642.

O'Leary, K. D., and Becker, W. C. The effects of intensity of a teacher's reprimands on children's behavior. *Journal of School Psychology* 7 (1968): 8–11.

O'Leary, K. D.; Becker, W. C.; Evans, M. B.; and Saudargas, R. A. A token reinforcement program in a public school: A replication and systematic analysis. *Journal of Applied Behavior Analysis* 2 (1969): 3–13.

O'Leary, K. D., and Drabman, R. S. Token reinforcement programs in the classroom: A review. *Psychological Bulletin* 75 (1971): 379–398.

O'Leary, K. D.; Drabman, R. S.; and Kass, R. Maintenance of appropriate behavior in a token program. *Journal of Abnormal Child Psychology* 1 (1973): 127–138.

O'Leary, K. D.; Kaufman, K. F.; Kass, R. E.; and Drabman, R. S. The effects of loud and soft reprimands on the behavior of disruptive students. *Exceptional Children* 37 (1970): 145–155.

O'Neil, S. The application and methodological implications of behavior modification in nursing research. In M. Batey, ed., *Communicating nursing research: The many sources of nursing knowledge.* Boulder, Col.: WICHE, 1972.

O'Neil, S. Rationale for the use of behavior management in health care intervention. Paper presented at Behavior Management in Health Care Intervention Workshop at The Pennsylvania State University, April 29–May 1, 1974a.

O'Neil, S. The search for reinforcers. *Nursing* 4 (1974b): 38–46.

Orne, M. T. On the social psychology of the psychological experiment: With particular reference to demand characteristics and their implications. *American Psychologist* 17 (1962): 776–783.

Orne, M. T., and Scheibe, K. E. The contribution of non-deprivation factors in the production of sensory deprivation effects: The psychology of the "panic button." *Journal of Abnormal and Social Psychology* 68 (1964): 3–12.

Osborne, J. G. Free time as a reinforcer in the management of classroom behavior. *Journal of Applied Behavior Analysis* 2 (1969): 113–118.

Otto, H. A. Communes: The alternative life style. *Saturday Review* 54, no. 17 (1971): 16–21.

Ovesey, L; Gaylin, W.; and Hendin, H. Psychotherapy of male homosexuality. *Archives of General Psychiatry* 9 (1963): 19–31.

Packard, R. G. The control of "classroom attention": A group contingency for complex behavior. *Journal of Applied Behavior Analysis* 3 (1970): 13–28.

Palkes, H.; Stewart, M.; and Kahana, B. Porteus maze performance of hyperactive boys after training in self-directed verbal commands. *Child Development* 39 (1968): 817–826.

Paredes, A.; Hood, W. R.; Seymour, H.; and Gollob, M. Loss of control in alcoholism: An investigation of the hypothesis, with experimental findings. *Quarterly Journal of Studies on Alcohol* 34 (1973): 1146–1161.

Parrino, J. J. Reduction of seizures by desensitization. *Journal of Behavior Therapy and Experimental Psychiatry* 2 (1971): 215–218.

Parrino, J. J.; George, L.; and Daniels, A. C. Token control of pill-taking behavior in a psychiatric ward. *Journal of Behavior Therapy and Experimental Psychiatry* 2 (1971): 181–185.

Patterson, G. R. An application of conditioning techniques to the control of a hyperactive child. In L. P. Ullmann and L. Krasner, eds., *Case studies in behavior modification.* New York: Holt, Rinehart & Winston, 1965. Pages 370–375.

Patterson, G. R. Responsiveness to social stimuli. In L. Krasner and L. P. Ullmann, eds., *Research in behavior modification.* New York: Holt, Rinehart & Winston, 1965. Pages 157–178.

Patterson, G. R. Behavioral intervention procedures in the classroom and in the home. In A. E. Bergin and S. L. Garfield, eds., *Handbook of psychotherapy and behavior change: An empirical analysis.* New York: Wiley, 1971. Pages 751–775.

Patterson, G. R., and Cobb, J. A. A dyadic analysis of "aggressive" behaviors. In J. P. Hill, ed., *Minnesota symposia on child psychology.* Vol. 5. Minneapolis: University of Minnesota Press, 1971. Pages 72–129.

Patterson, G. R., and Hops, H. The prediction of change: An outline of a six second personality theory. Unpublished manuscript, Oregon Research Institute, 1969.

Patterson, G. R., and Hops, H. Coercion, a game for two: Intervention techniques for marital conflict. In R. E. Ulrich and P. Mountjoy, eds., *The experimental analysis of social behavior.* New York: Appleton-Century-Crofts, 1972. Pages 424–440.

Patterson, G. R.; Hops, H.; and Weiss, R. L. Interpersonal skills training for couples in early stages of conflict. *Journal of Marriage and the Family* 37 (1975): 295–303.

Patterson, G. R., and Reid, J. B. Reciprocity and coercion: Two facets of social systems. In C. Neuringer and J. L. Michael, eds., *Behavior modification in clinical psychology.* New York: Appleton-Century-Crofts, 1970. Pages 133–177.

Patterson, G. R., and Rosenberry, C. A social learning formulation of depression. Paper presented at the meeting of the International Conference on Behavior Modification, Banff, Alberta, 1969.

Patuxent Institution. *Maryland's defective delinquency statute: A progress report.* Maryland Department of Public Safety and Corrections, 1973.

Paul, G. L. *Insight vs. desensitization in psychotherapy: An experiment in anxiety reduction.* Stanford: Stanford University Press, 1966.

Paul, G. L. The strategy of outcome research in psychotherapy. *Journal of Consulting Psychology* 31 (1967): 109–118.

Paul, G. L. Behavior modification research: Design and tactics. In C. M. Franks, ed., *Behavior therapy: Appraisal and status.* New York: McGraw-Hill, 1969a. Pages 29–62.

Paul, G. L. Chronic mental patient: Current status—future directions. *Psychological Bulletin* 71 (1969b): 81–94.

Paul, G. L. Outcome of systematic desensitization I: Background, procedures, and uncontrolled reports of individual treatment. In C. M. Franks, ed., *Behavior therapy: Appraisal and status.* New York: McGraw-Hill, 1969c. Pages 63–104.

Paul, G. L. Outcome of systematic desensitization II: Controlled investigations of individual treatment, technique variations, and current status. In C. M. Franks, ed., *Behavior therapy: Appraisal and status.* New York: McGraw-Hill, 1969d. Pages 105–159.

Paul, G. L., and Bernstein, D. A. *Anxiety and behavior: Treatment by systematic desensitization and related techniques.* New York: General Learning Press, 1973.

Paul, G. L.; Tobias, L. L; and Holly, B. L. Maintenance psychotropic drugs in the presence of active treatment programs: A "triple blind" withdrawal study with long-term mental patients. *Archives of General Psychiatry* 27 (1972): 106–115.

Paykel, E. S.; Meyers, J. K.; Dienelt, M. N.; Klerman, G. L.; Lindenthal, J. J.; and Pepper, M. P. Life events and depression: A controlled study. *Archives of General Psychiatry* 21 (1969): 753–760.

Penick, S. B.; Filion, R.; Fox, S.; and Stunkard, A. J. Behavior modification in the treatment of obesity. *Psychosomatic Medicine* 33 (1971): 49–55.

Perzan, R. S.; Boulanger, F.; and Fischer, D. G. Complex factors in inhibition of defecation: Review and case study. *Journal of Behavior Therapy and Experimental Psychiatry* 3 (1972): 129–133.

Peterson, D. R. *The clinical study of social behavior.* New York: Appleton-Century-Crofts, 1968.

Peterson, L. R. Operant approach to observation and recording. *Nursing Outlook* 15 (1967): 28–32.

Phares, E. J. *Locus of control: A personality determinant of behavior.* Morristown, N.J.: General Learning Press, 1973.

Phillips, E. L. Achievement place: Token reinforcement procedures in a home-style rehabilitation setting for "pre-delinquent" boys. *Journal of Applied Behavior Analysis* 1 (1968): 213–223.

Phillips, E. L.; Phillips, E. A.; Fixsen, D. L.; and Wolf, M. M. Behavior shaping works for delinquents. *Psychology Today* 7, no. 1 (1973): 75–79.

Phillips, E. L.; Phillips, E. A.; Fixsen, D. L.; and Wolf, M. M. *The teaching-family handbook.* University of Kansas Printing Service, 1975.

Phillips, E. L.; Wolf, M. M.; and Fixsen, D. L. Achievement place: Development of the elected manager system. *Journal of Applied Behavior Analysis* 6 (1973): 541–561.

Phillips, L., and Draguns, J. G. Classification of the behavior disorders 171. *Annual Review of Psychology* 22 (1971): 447–482.

Phillips, L., and Rabinovitch, M. S. Social role and patterns of symptomatic behaviors. *Journal of Abnormal and Social Psychology* 57 (1958): 181–186.

Phillips, L., and Zigler, E. Social competence: The action-thought parameter and vicariousness in normal and pathological behaviors. *Journal of Abnormal and Social Psychology* 63 (1961): 137–146.

Phillips, L., and Zigler, E. Role orientation, the action-thought dimension and outcome in psychiatric disorder. *Journal of Abnormal and Social Psychology* 68 (1964): 381–389.

Platt, J. Social traps. *American Psychologist* 28 (1973): 641–651.

Polakow, R. L., and Doctor, R. M. Treatment of marijuana and barbiturate dependency by contingency contracting. *Journal of Behavior Therapy and Experimental Psychiatry* 4 (1973): 375–377.

Poole, A. D., and Yates, A. J. The modification of excessive frequency of urination: A case study. *Behavior Therapy* 6 (1975): 78–86.

Powell, J., and Azrin, N. The effects of shock as a punisher for cigarette smoking. *Journal of Applied Behavior Analysis* 1 (1968): 63–71.

Premack, D. Toward empirical behavior laws: I. Positive reinforcement. *Psychological Review* 66 (1959): 219–233.

Premack, D. Reversibility of the reinforcement relation. *Science* 136 (1962): 255–257.

Premack, D. Reinforcement theory. In D. Levin, ed., *Nebraska symposium on motivation: 1965.* Lincoln, Neb.: University of Nebraska, 1965. Pages 123–180.

Premack, D. Mechanisms of self-control. In W. A. Hunt, ed., *Learning mechanisms in smoking.* Chicago: Aldine, 1970. Pages 107–123.

Premack, D. Catching up with common sense or two sides of a generalization: Reinforcement and punishment. In R. Glaser, ed., *The nature of reinforcement.* New York: Academic Press, 1971. Pages 121–150.

President's Commission on Law Enforcement and Administration of Justice. *The challenge of crime in a free society.* Washington, D.C.: U.S. Government Printing Office, 1967.

Price, G.; Simmons, J. B.; and Haynes, S. M. Stimulus control treatment of insomnia: A replication design. Paper presented at the meetings of the Southeastern Psychological Association, Hollywood, Fla., May 1974.

Price, K. P. The application of behavior therapy to the treatment of psychosomatic disorders: Retrospect and prospect. *Psychotherapy: Theory, Research, and Practice* 11 (1974): 138–155.

Quarti, C., and Renaud, J. A new treatment of constipation by conditioning: A preliminary report. In C. M. Franks, ed., *Conditioning techniques in clinical practice and research.* New York: Springer, 1964. Pages 219–227.

Quay, H. C.; Sprague, R. L.; Werry, J. S.; and McQueen, M. M. Conditioning visual orientation of conduct problem children in the classroom. *Journal of Experimental Child Psychology* 5 (1967): 512–517.

Rachlin, H. *Introduction to modern behaviorism.* San Francisco: Freeman, 1970.

Rachman, S. Treatment of anxiety and phobic reactions by systematic desensitization psychotherapy. *Journal of Abnormal and Social Psychology* 58 (1959): 259–263.

Rachman, S. Systematic desensitization. *Psychological Bulletin* 67 (1967): 93–103.

Rachman, S. Clinical applications of observational learning, imitation, and modeling. *Behavior Therapy* 3 (1972): 379–397.

Rachman, S., and Teasdale, J. *Aversion therapy and behaviour disorders: An analysis.* Coral Gables, Fla.: University of Miami, 1969.

Rado, S. An adaptational view of sexual behavior. In P. Hoch and J. Zubin, eds., *Psychosexual development in health and disease.* New York: Grune & Stratton, 1949.

Ramsey, R. W., and Van Velzen, V. Behavior therapy for sexual perversions. *Behaviour Research and Therapy* 6 (1968): 17–19.

Raskin, A. The NIMH collaborative depression studies: A progress report. *Psychopharmacology Bulletin* 8 (1972): 55–59.

Rathus, S. A. Motoric, autonomic and cognitive reciprocal inhibition of a case of hysterical bronchial asthma. *Adolescence* 8 (1973): 29–32.

Ratliff, R. C., and Stein, N. H. Treatment of neurodermatitis by behavior therapy: A case study. *Behaviour Research and Therapy* 6 (1968): 397–399.

Raush, H. L. Interaction sequences. *Journal of Personality and Social Psychology* 2 (1965): 487–499.

Raymond, M. J. The treatment of addiction by aversion conditioning with apomorphine. *Behaviour Research and Therapy* 1 (1964): 287–291.

Read, P. P. *Alive: The story of the Andes survivors.* New York: Lippincott, 1974.

Recidivism leveling off at 33% in federal jails. Newark *Star Ledger,* April 12, 1974, p. 2.

Reisinger, J. J. The treatment of "anxiety-depression" via positive reinforcement and response cost. *Journal of Applied Behavior Analysis* 5 (1972): 125–130.

Renne, K. S. Correlates of dissatisfaction in marriage. *Journal of Marriage and the Family* 32 (1970): 54–67.

Revusky, S., and Gorry, T. Flavor aversions produced by contingent drug injection: Relative effectiveness of apomorphine, emetine, and lithium. *Behaviour Research and Therapy* 11 (1973): 403–409.

Reynolds, G. S. *A primer of operant conditioning.* Glenview, Ill.: Scott, Foresman, 1968.

Rimm, D. C., and Masters, J. C. *Behavior therapy: Techniques and empirical findings.* New York: Academic Press, 1974.

Ringer, V. M. J. The use of a "token helper" in the management of classroom behavior problems and in teacher training. *Journal of Applied Behavior Analysis* 6 (1973): 671–677.

Risley, T. R. Behavior modification: An experimental-therapeutic endeavor. In L. A. Hammerlynck, P. O. Davidson, and L. E. Acker, eds., *Behavior modification and ideal mental health services.* Calgary, Canada: University of Calgary Press, 1970. Pages 103–127.

Ritter, B. The use of contact desensitization, demonstration-plus-participation, and demonstration alone in the treatment of acrophobia. *Behaviour Research and Therapy* 7 (1969): 157–164.

Roberts, M. D. *Implementation and analysis of rehabilitation and resocialization procedures in a correctional setting.* Unpublished doctoral dissertation, Georgia State University, 1974.

Roberts, R. E. *The new communes.* Englewood Cliffs, N.J.: Prentice-Hall, 1971.

Robertson, S.; DeReus, D.; and Drabman, R. Peer and college student tutoring as reinforcement in a token economy. Unpublished manuscript, Florida Technological University, 1975.

Robinson, J. C., and Lewinsohn, P. M. Behavior modification of the speech characteristics in a chronically depressed man. *Behavior Therapy* 4 (1973): 150–152.

Rogers, C. R. A theory of therapy, personality, and interpersonal relationships, as developed in the client-centered framework. In S. Koch, ed., *Psychology: A study of a science.* Vol. 3. New York: McGraw-Hill, 1959. Pages 184–256.

Rogers, C. R. Interpersonal relationships: U.S.A. 2000. *Journal of Applied Behavioral Science* 4 (1968): 265–280.

Rogers, C. R., and Skinner, B. F. Some issues concerning the control of human behavior: A symposium. *Science* 124 (1956): 1057–1066.

Rollins, B. C., and Feldman, H. Marital satisfaction over the family life cycle. *Journal of Marriage and the Family* 22 (1970): 20–28.

Rollins, H.; McCandless, B.; Thompson, M.; and Brassell, W. Project success environment: An extended application of contingency management to inner city schools. *Journal of Educational Psychology* 66 (1974): 167–178.

Rosenberry, C.; Weiss, R. L.; and Lewinsohn, P. M. Frequency and skill of emitted social reinforcement in depressed and nondepressed subjects. Unpublished manuscript, University of Oregon, 1968.

Rosenhan, D. L. Learning theory and prosocial behavior. *Journal of Social Issues* 28 (1972): 151–163.

Rothman, D. J. Decarcerating prisoners and patients. *Civil Liberties Review* 1 (1973): 8–30.

Rotter, J. B. *Social learning and clinical psychology.* Englewood Cliffs, N.J.: Prentice-Hall, 1954.

Rozin, P., and Kalat, J. W. Specific hungers and poison avoidance as adaptive specializations of learning. *Psychological Review* 78 (1971): 459–486.

Rozynko, V. V.; Flint, G. A.; Hammer, C. E.; Swift, K. D.; Kline, J. A.; and King, R. M. An operant behavior modification program for alcoholics. Paper presented at the Western Psychological Association, April 1971.

Rubin, B. Prediction of dangerousness in mentally ill criminals. *Archives of Psychiatry* 27 (1972): 397–407.

Ryle, G. *The concept of mind.* New York: Barnes and Noble, 1949.

Sachs, D. A., and Mayhall, B. Behavioral control of spasms using aversive conditioning with a cerebral palsied adult. *Journal of Nervous and Mental Disorders* 152 (1971): 362–363.

Sachs, L. B.; Bean, H.; and Morrow, J. E. Comparison of smoking treatments. *Behavior Therapy* 1 (1970): 465–472.

Sager, C. J., and Kaplan, H. S., eds., *Progress in group and family therapy.* New York: Brunner/Mazel, 1972.

Sammons, Robert A. Systematic Resensitization in the Treatment of Depression. Paper presented at the meetings of the Association for Advancement of Behavior Therapy, Chicago, November 1974.

Sand, P. L.; Fordyce, W. E.; and Fowler, R. S. Fluid intake behavior in patients with spinal-cord injury: Prediction and modification. *Archives of Physical Medicine Rehabilitation* 54 (1973): 254–262.

Sand, P. L.; Trieschman, R. B.; Fordyce, W. E.; and Fowler, R. S. Behavior modification in the medical rehabilitation setting: Rationale and some applications. *Rehabilitation Research and Practice Review* 1 (1970): 11–24.

Sanders, R.; Smith, R. S.; and Weinman, B. S. *Chronic psychosis and recovery.* San Francisco: Jossey-Bass, 1967.

Sanderson, R. E.; Campbell, D.; and Laverty, S. G. An investigation of a new aversive conditioning treatment for alcoholism. *Quarterly Journal of Studies on Alcoholism* 24 (1963): 261–275.

Sandifer, M. G.; Hordern, A.; Timbury, G. C.; and Green, L. M. Similarities and differences in patient evaluation by U.S. and U.K. psychiatrists. *American Journal of Psychiatry* 126 (1969): 206–212.

Sank, L. I., and Biglan, A. Operant treatment of a case of recurrent abdominal pain in a 10-year-old boy. *Behavior Therapy* 5 (1974): 677–681.

Sarason, I. G. *Personality: An objective approach.* 2nd ed. New York: Wiley, 1972.

Sarbin, T. R. Anxiety: Reification of a metaphor. *Archives of General Psychiatry* 10 (1964): 630–638.

Sarbin, T. R. On the futility of the proposition that some people be labeled "mentally ill." *Journal of Consulting Psychology* 31 (1967): 447–453.

Sarbin, T. R., and Mancuso, J. C. Failure of a moral enterprise: Attitudes of the public toward mental illness. *Journal of Consulting and Clinical Psychology* 35 (1970): 159–173.

Sargent, J. S.; Walters, E. D.; and Green, E. E. Psychosomatic self-regulation of migraine headaches. *Seminars in Psychiatry* 5 (1973): 415–428.

Saunders, A. G. Behavior therapy in prisons: Walden II or Clockwork Orange? Paper presented at the meetings of the Association for Advancement of Behavior Therapy, Chicago, November 1974.

Saunders, A. G.; Milstein, B. M.; and Roseman, R. Motion for partial summary judgment. Filed in U.S. District Court for the Western District of Missouri, Southern Division, January 7, 1974. Available from National Prison Project, Washington, D.C.

Schachter, S. The interaction of cognitive and physiological determinants of emotional state. In L. Berkowitz, ed., *Advances in experimental social psychology.* Vol. 1. New York: Academic Press, 1964. Pages 49–80.

Schachter, S. *Emotion, obesity and crime.* New York: Academic Press, 1971.

Schachter, S., and Gross, L. P. Manipulated time and eating behavior. *Journal of Personality and Social Psychology* 10 (1968): 98–106.

Schachter, S., and Singer, J. E. Cognitive, social, and physiological determinants of emotional state. *Psychological Review* 69 (1962): 379–399.

Schaefer, H. H.; Sobell, M. B.; and Mills, K. C. Baseline drinking behaviors in alcoholics and social drinkers: Kinds of sips and sip magnitude. *Behaviour Research and Therapy* 9 (1971): 23–27.

Scheff, T. J. The role of the mentally ill and the dynamics of mental disorder: A research framework. *Sociometry* 26 (1963): 436–453.

Scheff, T. J. *Being mentally ill: A sociological theory.* Chicago: Aldine, 1966.

Schlanger, B. B. Environmental influences on the verbal output of mentally retarded children. *Journal of Speech and Hearing Disorders* 19 (1954): 339–343.

Schmahl, D. P.; Lichtenstein, E.; and Harris, D. E. Successful treatment of habitual smokers with warm, smoky air and rapid smoking. *Journal of Consulting and Clinical Psychology* 38 (1972): 105–111.

Schmidt, H. O., and Fonda, C. P. The reliability of psychiatric diagnosis: A new look. *Journal of Abnormal and Social Psychology* 52 (1956): 262–267.

Schmidt, J. R.; Nessel, J. J.; and Malamud, T. J. *An evaluation of rehabilitation services and the role of industry in the community: Adjustment of psychiatric patients following hospitalization.* New York: Fountain House Foundation, 1969.

Schneider, P. Pick a pack of trouble. *The Reader's Digest,* June 1968, pp. 71–74.

Schnelle, J. F. A brief report on invalidity of parent evaluations of behavior change. *Journal of Applied Behavior Analysis* 7 (1974): 341–343.

Schwab, J. J.; Brown, J. M.; Holzer, C. E.; and Sokolof, M. Current concepts of depression: The sociocultural. *International Journal of Social Psychiatry* 14 (1968): 226–234.

Schwartz, G. E. Biofeedback as therapy: Some theoretical and practical issues. *American Psychologist* 28 (1973): 666–673.

Schwartz, G. E., and Shapiro, D. Biofeedback and essential hypertension: Current findings and theoretical concerns. *Seminars in Psychiatry* 5 (1973): 493–503.

Schwartz, J. L. A critical review and evaluation of smoking control methods. *Public Health Reports* 84 (1969): 483–506.

Schwartz, J. L. Adolescent smoking behavior: Curiosity, conformity and rebellion. In C. E. Bruess and J. T. Fisher, eds., *Selected Readings in Health.* New York: Macmillan, 1970. Pages 109–120.

Schwartz, J. L., and Dubitzky, M. Requisites for success in smoking withdrawal. In E. F. Borgatta and R. R. Evans, eds., *Smoking, health, and behavior.* Chicago: Aldine, 1968. Pages 231–247.

Schwitzgebel, R. K. *Development and legal regulation of coercive behavior modification techniques with offenders.* Public Health Service Publication 2067. Washington, D.C.: U.S. Government Printing Office, 1971.

Sechrest, L. Incremental validity: A recommendation. *Education and Psychological Measurement* 23 (1963): 153–158.

Seligman, M. E. P. On the generality of the laws of learning. *Psychological Review* 77 (1970): 406–418.

Seligman, M. E. P. Learned helplessness. *Annual Review of Medicine* 23 (1972): 407–412.

Seligman, M. E. P. Fall into helplessness. *Psychology Today* 7 (1973): 43–48.

Seligman, M. E. P. *Helplessness.* San Francisco: W. H. Freeman, 1975.

Seligman, M. E. P., and Groves, D. Nontransient learned helplessness. *Psychonomic Science* 19 (1970): 191–192.

Seligman, M. E. P., and Maier, S. F. Failure to escape traumatic shock. *Journal of Experimental Psychology* 74 (1967): 1–9.

Selltiz, C.; Jahoda, M.; Deutsch, M.; and Cook, S. W. *Research methods in social relations.* New York: Holt-Dryden, 1959.

Selye, H. *The stress of life.* New York: McGraw-Hill, 1956.

Selye, H. Stress: It's a G.A.S. *Psychology Today,* September 3, 1969, 25–56.

Serber, M. Teaching the nonverbal components of assertive training. *Journal of Behavior Therapy and Experimental Psychiatry* 3 (1972): 179–183.

Sergeant, H. G. S., and Yorkston, N. J. Verbal desensitization in the treatment of bronchial asthma. *Lancet* 2 (1969): 1321–1323.

Shapiro, A. K. A contribution to a history of the placebo effect. *Behavioral Science* 5 (1960): 109–135.

Shapiro, A. K. Placebo effects in medicine, psychotherapy, and psychoanalysis. In A. E. Bergin and S. L. Garfield, eds., *Handbook of psychotherapy and behavior change.* New York: Wiley, 1971. Pages 439–473.

Shapiro, D. Preface. In D. Shapiro; T. X. Barber; L. V. DiCara; J. Kamiya; N. E. Miller; and J. Stoyva, eds., *Biofeedback and self-control, 1972: An Aldine annual on the regulation of bodily processes and consciousness.* Chicago: Aldine, 1973.

Shapiro, D.; Barber, T. X.; DiCara, L. V.; Kamiya, J.; Miller, N. E.; and Stoyva, J., eds. *Biofeedback and self-control, 1972: An Aldine annual on the regulation of bodily processes and consciousness.* Chicago: Aldine, 1973.

Shapiro, D., and Schwartz, G. E. Biofeedback and visceral learning: Clinical applications. *Seminars in Psychiatry* 4 (1972): 171–184.

Shaw, W. A. The relation of muscular action potentials to imaginal weight lifting. *Archives of Psychology,* no. 247 (1940): 50.

Sherman, A. R. Real-life exposure as a primary thearapeutic factor in the desensitization treatment of fear. *Journal of Abnormal Psychology* 79 (1972): 19–28.

Sherman, T. M., and Cormeir, W. H. An investigation of the influence of student behavior on teacher behavior. *Journal of Applied Behavior Analysis* 7 (1974): 11–21.

Shipley, C. R., and Fazio, A. F. Pilot study of a treatment for psychological depression. *Journal of Abnormal Psychology* 82 (1973): 372–376.

Shorkey, C., and Taylor, J. Management of maladaptive behavior of a severely burned child. *Child Welfare* 52 (1973): 543–547.

Sibley, S.; Abbott, M.; and Cooper, B. Modification of the classroom behavior of a "disadvantaged" kindergarten boy by social reinforcement and isolation. *Journal of Experimental Child Psychology* 7 (1969): 203–219.

Sidman, M. *Tactics of scientific research.* New York: Basic Books, 1960.

Silber, A. Psychotherapy with alcoholics. *Journal of Nervous and Mental Disease* 129 (1959): 477–485.

Simkins, L. J. The reliability of self recorded behavior. *Behavior Therapy* 2 (1971): 83–87.

Sirota, A. D., and Mahoney, M. J. Relaxing on cue: The self-regulation of asthma. *Journal of Behavior Therapy and Experimental Psychiatry* 5 (1974): 65–66.

Skinner, B. F. *Walden II.* New York: Macmillan, 1948.

Skinner, B. F. *Science and human behavior.* New York: Macmillan, 1953.

Skinner, B. F. *Verbal behavior.* New York: Appleton-Century-Crofts, 1957.

Skinner, B. F. Behaviorism at fifty. *Science* 140 (1963): 951–958.

Skinner, B. F. *Beyond freedom and dignity.* New York: Knopf, 1971.

Smeets, P. M. Withdrawal of social reinforcers as a means of controlling rumination and regurgitation in a profoundly retarded person. *Training School Bulletin* 67 (1970): 158–163.

Smith, R. E.; Diener, E.; and Beaman, A. L. Demand characteristics and the behavioral avoidance measure of fear in behavior therapy analogue research. *Behavior Therapy* 5 (1974): 172–182.

Smith, R. L. *A quiet revolution: Probation subsidy.* Washington, D.C.: U.S. Department of Health, Education, and Welfare, 1972.

Smith, R. R.; Hart, L. A.; and Milan, M. A. *Correctional officer training in behavior modification: Final report.* Elmore, Ala.: Rehabilitation Research Foundation, 1973.

Smith, R. R., and Milan, M. A. *A survey of home furlough policies of American correctional agencies.* Elmore, Ala.: Rehabilitation Research Foundation, 1971.

Smoker's Psychosis. *Human Behavior,* October, 1973, p. 28.

Sobell, M. B., and Sobell, L. C. Individual behavior therapy for alcoholics. *Behavior Therapy* 4 (1973a): 49–72.

Sobell, M. B., and Sobell, L. C. The need for realism, relevance and operational assumptions in the study of substance dependence. Paper presented at International Symposium on Alcohol and Drug Research, Toronto, October 1973b.

Solomon, R. L.; Kamin, L. J.; and Wynne, L. C. Traumatic avoidance learning: The outcomes of several extinction procedures with dogs. *Journal of Abnormal and Social Psychology* 48 (1953): 291–302.

Solomon, R. L., and Wynne, L. C. Traumatic avoidance learning: The principles of anxiety conservation and partial irreversibility. *Psychological Review* 61 (1954): 353–385.

Speck, R. V. *The new families.* New York: Basic Books, 1972.

Spielberger, C. D. *Anxiety: Current trends in theory and research.* Vol. 1. New York: Academic Press, 1972.

Spivack, G., and Shure, M. B. *Social adjustment of young children: A cognitive approach to solving real life problems.* San Francisco: Jossey-Bass, 1974.

Srole, L., and Fischer, A. K. Smoking behavior 1953 and 1970: The midtown Manhattan study. In W. L. Dunn, Jr., ed., *Smoking behavior: Motives and incentives.* New York: Wiley, 1973. Pages 255–266.

Stampfl, T. G., and Levis, D. J. Essentials of implosive therapy: A learning-theory–based psychodynamic behavioral therapy. *Journal of Abnormal Psychology* 72 (1967): 496–503.

Stanford, P. A model, clockwork orange prison. *The New York Times Magazine,* September 17, 1972, pp. 71–75, 78–84.

Starlin, C. Peers and precision. *Teaching Exceptional Children,* Spring 1971, 129–140.

Steadman, H. J., and Cocozza, J. J. We can't predict who is dangerous. *Psychology Today* 8, no. 8 (1975): 32–35, 84.

Steiner, I. D. Perceived freedom. In L. Berkowitz, ed., *Advances in experimental social psychology.* Vol. 5. New York: Academic Press, 1970. Pages 187–248.

Steinman, C. The case of the frightened convict. *The Nation* 217 (1973): 590–593.

Sterman, M. B., and Friar, L. Suppression of seizures in an epileptic following sensorimotor EEG feedback training. *Electroencephology and Clinical Neurophysiology* 33 (1972): 89–95.

Sternbach, R. A. *Pain patients: Traits and treatment.* New York: Academic Press, 1974.

Stevenson, I., and Wolpe, J. Recovery from sexual deviations through overcoming nonsexual neurotic responses. *American Journal of Psychiatry* 116 (1960): 737–742.

Strain, P. S., and Timm, M. A. An experimental analysis of social interaction between a behaviorally disordered preschool child and her classroom peers. *Journal of Applied Behavior Analysis* 7 (1974): 583–590.

Straits, B. C. Sociological and psychological correlates of adoption and discontinuation of cigarette smoking. Mimeographed. University of Chicago, 1965.

Strange, J. R. *Abnormal Psychology: Understanding Behavior Disorders.* New York: McGraw-Hill, 1965.

Stuart, R. B. Behavioral control of overeating. *Behaviour Research and Therapy* 5 (1967): 357–365.

Stuart, R. B. Operant interpersonal treatment for marital discord. *Journal of Consulting and Clinical Psychology* 33 (1969): 675–682.

Stuart, R. B. *Trick or treatment: How and when psychotherapy fails.* Champaign, Ill.: Research Press, 1970.

Stuart, R. B. A three-dimensional program for the treatment of obesity. *Behaviour Research and Therapy* 9 (1971): 177–186.

Stuart, R. B. Behavioral remedies for marital ills: A guide to the use of operant-interpersonal techniques. Paper presented at the International Symposium on Behavior Modification, Minneapolis, Minn., October 1972.

Stuart, R. B., and Davis, B. *Slim chance in a fat world: Behavioral control of obesity.* Champaign, Ill.: Research Press, 1972.

Stunkard, A. J. The management of obesity. *New York State Journal of Medicine* 58 (1958): 79–87.

Stunkard, A. J. New therapies for the eatory disorders: Behavior modification of obesity and anorexia nervosa. *Archives of General Psychiatry* 26 (1972): 391–398.

Stunkard, A. J., and Mahoney, M. J. Behavioral treatment of the eating disorders. In H. Leitenberg, ed., *Handbook of behavior modification.* New York: Appleton-Century-Crofts, in press.

Suinn, R. M. Behavior modification for prevention of cardiovascular disease. Paper presented at the 82nd Annual Convention of the American Psychological Association, New Orleans, 1974a.

Suinn, R. M. Behavior therapy for cardiac patients. *Behavior Therapy* 5 (1974b): 569–571.

Sulzbacher, I. S., and Houser, J. E. A tactic to eliminate disruptive behaviors in the classroom: Group contingent consequences. *American Journal of Mental Deficiency* 73 (1968): 88–90.

Sundberg, N. D., and Tyler, L. E. *Clinical Psychology.* New York: Appleton-Century-Crofts, 1962.

Surratt, P. R.; Ulrich, R. E.; and Hawkins, R. P. An elementary student as a behavioral engineer. *Journal of Applied Behavior Analysis* 2 (1969): 85–92.

Surwit, R. S. Biofeedback: A possible treatment for Raynaud's disease. *Seminars in Psychiatry* 5 (1973): 483–490.

Szasz, T. S. The myth of mental illness. *American Psychologist* 15 (1960): 113–118.

Szasz, T. S. The psychiatric classification of behavior: A strategy of personal constraint. In L. D. Eron, ed., *The classification of behavior disorders.* Chicago: Aldine, 1966. Pages 125–170.

Tasto, D. L., and Chesney, M. A. Muscle relaxation treatment for primary dysmenorrhea. *Behavior Therapy* 5 (1974): 668–672.

Taulbee, E., and Wright, A. A psychosocial-behavioral model for therapeutic intervention. In C. D. Spielberger, ed., *Current topics in clinical and community psychology.* New York: Academic Press, 1971.

Taylor, D. W. Treatment of excessive frequency of urination by desensitization. *Journal of Behavior Therapy and Experimental Psychiatry* 3 (1972): 311–313.

Taylor, G. R. *The biological time bomb.* New York: World Pub. Co., 1968.

Teasdale, J. D., and Hinkson, J. Stimulant drugs: Perceived effect on the interpersonal behavior of dependent patients. *International Journal of the Addictions* 6 (1971): 407–417.

Terrace, H. S. Stimulus control. In W. K. Honig, ed., *Operant behavior: Areas of research and application.* New York: Appleton-Century-Crofts, 1966. Pages 271–344.

Tharp, R. G.; Watson, D.; and Kaya, J. Self-modification of depression. *Journal of Consulting and Clinical Psychology* 42 (1974): 624.

Tharp, R. G., and Wetzel, F. J. *Behavior modification in the natural environment.* New York: Academic Press, 1969.

Thimann, J. Conditioned-reflex treatment of alcoholism. II. The risks of its application, its indications, contraindications, and psychotherapeutic aspects. *New England Journal of Medicine* 241 (1949): 406–410.

Thomas, D. R.; Becker, W. C.; and Armstrong, M. Production and elimination of disruptive classroom behavior by systematically varying teacher's behavior. *Journal of Applied Behavior Analysis* 1 (1968): 35–45.

Thomas, S. A.; Lynch, J. J.; and Mills, M. E. Psychosocial influence on heart rhythm in the coronary care unit. *Heart and Lung,* 1975.

Thompson, I. G., and Rathod, N. H. Aversion therapy for heroin dependence. *Lancet* 2 (1968): 382–384.

Thoresen, C. E., and Mahoney, M. J. *Behavioral self-control.* New York: Holt, 1974.

Thorndike, E. L. *Animal intelligence.* New York: Hafner, 1964 (Macmillan, 1911).

Timbers, G. D.; Phillips, E. L.; Fixsen, D. L.; and Wolf, M. M. Modification of the verbal interaction behavior of a pre-delinquent youth. Presented at the meetings of the American Psychological Association, Washington, D.C., September 1970.

Tobias, L. L., and MacDonald, M. L. Withdrawal of maintenance drugs with long-term hospitalized mental patients: A critical review. *Psychological Bulletin* 81 (1974): 107–125.

Todd, F. J. Coverant control of self-evaluation responses in the treatment of depression: A new use for an old principle. *Behavior Therapy* 3 (1972): 91–94.

Toffler, A. *Future shock.* New York: Random House, 1970.

Tokarz, T. P., and Lawrence, P. S. An analysis of temporal and stimulus factors in the treatment of insomnia. Paper presented at the meetings of the Association for Advancement of Behavior Therapy, Chicago, November 1974.

Tomlinson, J. R. The treatment of bowel retention by operant procedures: A case study. *Journal of Behavior Therapy and Experimental Psychiatry* 1 (1970): 83–85.

Toomey, T. C. Behavioral treatment of the autonomic components of chronic, non-organic and oral-facial pain. Paper presented at the 82nd Annual Convention of the American Psychological Association, New Orleans, 1974.

Trexler, L. Further thoughts on depression. *Rational Living* 7 (1972): 32–34.

Trotter, S. Proposed violence center "swirling in controversy." *APA Monitor* 5, no. 4 (1974): 5.

Trotter, S., and Warren, J. Behavior modification under fire. *APA Monitor* 5, no. 4 (1974): 1, 4.

Turnage, J. R., and Logan, D. L. Treatment of a hypodermic needle phobia by *in vivo* systematic desensitization. *Journal of Behavior Therapy and Experimental Psychiatry* 5 (1974): 67–69.

Turnbull, J. W. Asthma conceived as a learned response. *Journal of Psychosomatic Research* 6 (1972): 59–70.

Turner, D. *Handbook of diet therapy.* Chicago: University of Chicago Press, 1965.

Turner, J. L.; Foa, E. B.; and Foa, U. G. Interpersonal reinforcers: Classification, interpersonal relationship and some differential properties. *Journal of Personality and Social Psychology* 19 (1971): 168–180.

Turner, M. B. *Philosophy and the science of behavior.* New York: Appleton-Century-Crofts, 1967.

Turner, S. M.; Hersen, M.; and Alford, H. Effects of massed practice and meprobamate on spasmodic torticollis: An experimental analysis. *Behaviour Research and Therapy* 12 (1974): 259–260.

Ullmann, L. P. Abnormal psychology without anxiety. Paper presented at Western Psychological Association Symposium: "The Concept of Anxiety: A Reexamination," San Francisco, May 1967.

Ullmann, L. P., and Krasner, L., eds., *Case studies in behavior modification.* New York: Holt, 1965.

Ullmann, L. P., and Krasner, L. *A psychological approach to abnormal behavior.* Englewood Cliffs, N.J.: Prentice-Hall, 1969, 1975.

Ulrich, R.; Wolfe, M.; and Bluhm, M. Operant conditioning in the public schools. *Educational Technology Monographs* 1, no. 1 (1968).

Underwood, B. J. *Psychological research.* New York: Appleton-Century-Crofts, 1957.

Upper, D., and Meredith, L. A timed-interval procedure for modifying cigarette-smoking behavior. Paper presented at the meetings of the American Psychological Association, Washington, D.C., September 1970.

U.S. modifies its own behavior, ends jail study. *New York Times,* News of the Week in Review, February 10, 1974, p. 3.

U.S. News & World Report. "Group living" catches on and goes middle class. *U.S. News and World Report,* February 25, 1974, pp. 38–40.

U.S. Public Health Service. *Smoking and Health.* Report of the Advisory Committee to the Surgeon General of the Public Health Service. Washington, D.C.: U.S. Department of Health, Education, and Welfare, 1964, Public Health Service Publication 1103.

Valett, R. E. A social reinforcement technique for classroom management and behavior disorders. *Exceptional Children* 33 (1966): 185–189.

Valins, S. Cognitive effects of false heart-rate feedback. *Journal of Personality and Social Psychology* 4 (1966): 400–408.

Velie, L. The intimate life of a commune. *Reader's Digest,* March 1973, pp. 94–99.

Veysey, L. *The communal experience.* New York: Harper & Row, 1973.

Wachtel, P. Psychodynamics, behavior therapy, and the implacable experimenter: An inquiry into the consistency of personality. *Journal of Abnormal Psychology* 82 (1973): 324–334.

Wagner, S. *Cigarette Country: Tobacco in American History and Politics.* New York: Praeger, 1971.

Wahler, R. G.; Sperling, K. A.; Thomas, M. R.; Teeter, N. C.; and Luper, H. L. The modification of childhood stuttering: Some response-response relationships. *Journal of Experimental Child Psychology* 9 (1970): 411–428.

Walker, H.; Mattson, R.; and Buckley, N. Special class placement as a treatment alternative for deviant behavior in children. In F. Benson, ed., *Modifying deviant social behaviors in various classroom settings.* Eugene, Oregon: University of Oregon, 1968.

Walton, D. The application of learning theory to the treatment of a case of bronchial asthma. In H. J. Eysenck, ed., *Behavior therapy and the neuroses.* New York: Pergamon Press, 1960a. Pages 188–189.

Walton, D. The application of learning theory to the treatment of a case of neurodermatitis. In H. J. Eysenck, ed., *Behavior therapy and the neuroses.* New York: Pergamon Press, 1960b. Pages 272–274.

Walton, D. Application of learning theory to the treatment of a case of somnambulism. *Journal of Clinical Psychology* 17 (1961): 96–99.

Wanderer, Z. W. The validity of diagnostic judgments based on "blind" Machover figure drawings. *Dissertation Abstracts* 26 (1966): 67–68.

Wanderer, Z. Existential depression treated by desensitization of phobias: Strategy and transcript. *Journal of Behavior Therapy and Experimental Psychiatry* 3 (1972): 111–116.

Warren, J. Pot-pourri. *APA Monitor* 5, no. 4 (1974): 3.

Wasik, B. The application of Premack's generalization on reinforcement to the management of classroom behavior. *Journal of Experimental Child Psychology* 10 (1970): 33–43.

Wasik, B.; Senn, K.; Welch, R.; and Cooper, B. Behavior modification with culturally deprived school children: Two case studies. *Journal of Applied Behavior Analysis* 2 (1969): 181–194.

Watson, D. L.; Tharp, R. G.; and Krisberg, J. Case study in self-modification: Suppression of inflammatory scratching while awake and asleep. *Journal of Behavior Therapy and Experimental Psychiatry* 3 (1972): 213–215.

Watson, J. B. *Behaviorism.* Chicago: University of Chicago Press, 1924.

Watson, J. B., and Rayner, R. Conditioned emotional reactions. *Journal of Experimental Psychology* 3 (1920): 1–14.

Weber, S. J., and Cook, T. D. Subject effects in laboratory research: An examination of subject roles, demand characteristics, and valid inference. *Psychological Bulletin* 77 (1972): 273–295.

Weidner, F. *In vivo* desensitization of a paranoid schizophrenic. *Journal of Behavior Therapy and Experimental Psychiatry* 1 (1970): 79–81.

Weil, G., and Goldfried, M. R. Treatment of insomnia in an eleven-year-old child through self-relaxation. *Behavior Therapy* 4 (1973): 282–284.

Weimer, W. B. *Psychology and the conceptual foundations of science.* Hillsdale, N.J.: Erlebaum, in press.

Weiner, B. The clockwork cure. *The Nation* 215 (1972): 433–436.

Weiner, H. B. Psychodramatic treatment for the alcoholic. In R. Fox, ed., *Alcoholism: Behavioral research, therapeutic approaches.* New York: Springer, 1967. Pages 218–233.

Weinman, B.; Gellbart, P.; Wallace, M.; and Post, M. Inducing assertive behavior in chronic schizophrenics: A comparison of socioenvironmental, desensitization, and relaxation therapies. *Journal of Consulting and Clinical Psychology* 39 (1972): 246–252.

Weiss, R. L.; Hops, H.; and Patterson, G. R. A framework for conceptualizing material conflict, a technology for altering it, some data for evaluating it. In L. A. Hamerlynck; L. C. Handy; and E. J. Mash, eds., *Behavior change: Methodology, concepts and practice.* Champaign, Ill.: Research Press, 1973. Pages 309–342.

Weiss, R. M. The relative efficacy of deep-muscle relaxation and autogenic feedback training in the modification of cold-pressor pain and headaches. Paper presented at the 82nd Annual Convention of the American Psychological Association, New Orleans, 1974.

Wener, A. E., and Rehm, L. P. Depressive affect: A test of behavioral hypotheses. *Journal of Abnormal Psychology* 84 (1975): 221–227.

Wenrich, W. W. *A primer of behavior modification.* Belmont, Calif.: Brooks Cole, 1970.

Wexler, D. B. Reflections on the legal regulation of behavior modification in institutional settings. *Arizona Law Review* 17 (1975): 132–141.

Whalen, C. K., and Henker, B. A. Creating therapeutic pyramids using mentally retarded patients. *American Journal of Mental Deficiency* 74 (1969): 331–337.

Whelan, R. J., and Haring, N. G. Modification and maintenance of behavior through systematic application of consequences. *Exceptional Children* 32 (1966): 281–289.

White, J. C., and Taylor, D. J. Noxious conditioning as a treatment for rumination. *Mental Retardation* 5 (1967): 30–33.

Whitney, L. R. Behavioral approaches to the nursing of the mentally retarded. *Nursing Clinics of North America* 1 (1966a): 641–650.

Whitney, L. R. Operant learning theory: A framework deserving nursing investigation. *Nursing Research* 15 (1966b): 229–235.

Whitney, L. R., and Barnard, K. E. Implications of operant learning theory for nursing care of the retarded child. *Mental Retardation* 4 (1966): 26–29.

Wiggins, J. S. *Personality and prediction: Principles of personality assessment.* Reading, Mass.: Addison-Wesley, 1973.

Wikler, A. Interaction of physical dependence and classical and operant conditioning in the genesis of relapse. In A. Wikler, ed., *The addictive states.* Baltimore: Williams and Wilkins, 1968.

Wilkins, W. Desensitization: Social and cognitive factors underlying the effectiveness of Wolpe's procedure. *Psychological Bulletin* 76 (1971): 311–317.

Wilkins, W. Desensitization: Getting it together with Davison and Wilson. *Psychological Bulletin* 78 (1972): 32–36.

Wilkins, W. Desensitization: A rejoinder to Morgan. *Psychological Bulletin* 79 (1973): 376–377.

Williams, J. G.; Barlow, D. H.; and Agras, W. S. Behavioral measurement of severe depression. *Archives of General Psychiatry* 27 (1972): 330–333.

Williams, J. L. *Operant learning: Procedures for changing behavior.* Belmont, Calif.: Brooks/Cole, 1973.

Williams, R. J. The etiology of alcoholism: A working hypothesis involving the interplay of hereditary and environmental factors. *Quarterly Journal of Studies on Alcohol* 7 (1946): 567–587.

Wilson, G. T., and Davison, G. C. Aversion techniques in behavior therapy: Some theoretical and metatheoretical considerations. *Journal of Consulting and Clinical Psychology* 33 (1969): 327–329.

Wilson, G. T., and Davison, G. C. Process of fear reduction in systematic desensitization: Animal studies. *Psychological Bulletin* 76 (1971): 1–14.

Winett, R. A., and Winkler, R. C. Current behavior modification in the classroom: Be still, be quiet, be docile. *Journal of Applied Behavior Analysis* 5 (1972): 499–504.

Wisocki, P. A. The successful treatment of a heroin addict by covert conditioning techniques. *Journal of Behavior Therapy and Experimental Psychiatry* 4 (1973): 55–61.

Wittenborn, J. R.; Holzberg, J.; and Simon, B. Symptom correlates for descriptive diagnosis. *Genetic Psychology Monographs* 47 (1953): 237–301.

Wohl, T. H. Behavior modification: Its application to the study and treatment of childhood asthma. *Journal of Asthma Research* 9 (1971): 41–45.

Wolf, M.; Birnbrauer, J.; Lawler, J.; and Williams, T. The operant extinction, re-instatement and re-extinction of vomiting behavior in a retarded child. In R. Ulrich; T. Stachnik; and J. Mabry, eds., *Control of human behavior: From cure to prevention.* Glenview, Ill.: Scott, Foresman, 1970. Pages 146–149.

Wolf, M. M.; Giles, D. K.; and Hall, R. V. Experiments with token reinforcement in a remedial classroom. *Behaviour Research and Therapy* 6 (1968): 51–64.

Wolf, M. M.; Phillips, E. L.; and Fixsen, D. L. The teaching-family: A new model for the treatment of deviant child behavior in the community. In S. W. Bijou and E. Ribes-Inesta, eds., *Behavior modification.* New York: Academic Press, 1972. Pages 51–62.

Wolf, M., and Risley, T. Analysis and modification of deviant child behavior. Paper presented at the meetings of the American Psychological Association, Washington, D.C., September 1967.

Wollersheim, P. Effectiveness of group therapy based upon learning principles in the treatment of overweight women. *Journal of Abnormal Psychology* 76 (1970): 462–474.

Wolpe, J. *Psychotherapy by reciprocal inhibition.* Stanford: Stanford University Press, 1958.

Wolpe, J. Conditioned inhibition of craving in drug addiction: A pilot experiment. *Behaviour Research and Therapy* 2 (1965): 285–288.

Wolpe, J. *The practice of behavior therapy.* New York: Pergamon, 1969.

Wolpe, J. Transcript of initial interview in a case of depression. *Journal of Behavior Therapy and Experimental Psychiatry* 1 (1970): 71–78.

Wolpe, J., and Lazarus, A. A. *Behavior therapy techniques.* New York: Pergamon, 1966.

Woodward, M. The diagnosis and treatment of homosexual offenders. *British Journal of Delinquency* 9 (1958): 44–59.

Wright, L.; Nunnery, A.; Eichel, B.; and Scott, R. Behavioral tactics for reinstating natural breathing in infants with tracheostomy. *Pediatrics Research* 3 (1969): 275–278.

Wynder, E. L.; Kaufman, P. L.; and Lesser, R. L. A short-term follow-up study of ex-cigarette smokers. *American Review of Respiratory Diseases* 96 (1967): 645–655.

Yafa, S. H. Zap! You're normal. *Playboy Magazine,* July 1973, 87, 90, 184, 186–188.

Yates, A. J. Symptoms and symptom substitution. *Psychological Review* 65 (1958): 371–374.

Yates, A. J. *Behavior therapy.* New York: Wiley, 1970.

Yates, A. J., and Poole, A. D. Behavioral analysis in a case of excessive frequency of micturition. *Behavior Therapy* 3 (1972): 449–453.

Yorkston, N. J.; McHugh, R. B.; Brady, R.; Serber, M.; and Sergeant, H. G. S. Verbal desensitization in bronchial asthma. *Journal of Psychosomatic Research* 18 (1974): 371–376.

Zborowski, M. *People in pain.* San Francisco: Jossey-Bass, 1969.

Zigler, E., and Levine, J. Premorbid adjustment and paranoid-nonparanoid status in schizophrenia: A further investigation. *Journal of Abnormal Psychology* 82 (1973): 189–199.

Zigler, E., and Phillips, L. Case history data and psychiatric diagnosis. Unpublished manuscript, Worcester State Hospital, 1959.

Zigler, E., and Phillips, L. Psychiatric diagnosis and symptomatology. *Journal of Abnormal and Social Psychology* 63 (1961a): 69–75.

Zigler, E., and Phillips, L. Social competence and the process-reactive distinction in psychopathology. *Journal of Abnormal and Social Psychology* 65 (1961b): 215–222.

Zigler, E., and Phillips, L. Social competence and outcome in psychiatric disorder. *Journal of Abnormal and Social Psychology* 63 (1961c): 264–271.

Zimmerman, E.; Zimmerman, J.; and Russell, C. Differential effects of token reinforcement on instruction-following behavior in retarded students instructed as a group. *Journal of Applied Behavior Analysis* 2 (1969): 101–112.

Zuckerman, M. Physiological measures of sexual arousal in the human. *Psychological Bulletin* 75 (1971): 297–329.

Zuckerman, M., and Lubin, B. *Manual for the Multiple Affective Adjective Check List.* San Diego: Educational and Industrial Testing Service, 1965.

Zung, W. K. A self-rating depression scale. *Archives of General Psychiatry* 12 (1965): 63–70.

Author index

Subject index

There are many terms used in this book that will be new to a reader unfamiliar with behavior modification. We felt, however, that a glossary would not be of great use, since it would offer definitions completely out of the context of the theories of which they are part. Instead, we have included "definition" subentries for all important terms in the subject index.

CDEFGHIJ–VB–79876